The Bible

The Bible

*A Historical and
Literary Introduction*

Bart D. Ehrman

University of North Carolina
at Chapel Hill

New York   Oxford
OXFORD UNIVERSITY PRESS

Oxford University Press is a department of the University of Oxford.
It furthers the University's objective of excellence in research,
scholarship, and education by publishing worldwide.

Oxford New York
Auckland   Cape Town   Dar es Salaam   Hong Kong   Karachi
Kuala Lumpur   Madrid   Melbourne   Mexico City   Nairobi
New Delhi   Shanghai   Taipei   Toronto

With offices in
Argentina   Austria   Brazil   Chile   Czech Republic   France   Greece
Guatemala   Hungary   Italy   Japan   Poland   Portugal   Singapore
South Korea   Switzerland   Thailand   Turkey   Ukraine   Vietnam

For titles covered by Section 112 of the US Higher Education Opportunity Act,
please visit www.oup.com/us/he for the latest information about pricing and
alternate formats.

Published by Oxford University Press
198 Madison Avenue, New York, New York 10016
http://www.oup.com

Library of Congress Cataloging-in-Publication Data
Ehrman, Bart D.
The Bible : a historical and literary introduction / Bart D. Ehrman.
pages cm
Includes index.
ISBN 978-0-19-530816-7
1. Bible—Introductions. I. Title.
BS475.3.E37   2013
220.6'1—dc23

2013016320

Printing number: 9 8 7 6 5 4 3
Printed in Canada on acid-free paper

To Mom

Brief Contents

Contents

List of Boxes

List of Maps

Preface

Surely the single most difficult course to teach in the curriculum of biblical studies is the one-semester Introduction to the Bible that covers the entire corpus, from Genesis to Revelation. In some ways it is an impossible task. There is so much to consider—the content of all (or most of?) the books, the scholarship on them, the evidence that makes the scholarship necessary and its conclusions sensible. But the course can also be exciting, stimulating, and extraordinarily important. For many undergraduate students it is their one chance to learn about the Bible in an institution of higher learning and to see what scholars are saying about it. In many instances these students will have heard about the Bible, and possibly even participated in studies of the Bible, in faith contexts; rarely will any of these students have seen how the Bible is more typically approached in academic contexts. In many other instances, students will be completely unfamiliar with the Bible, its stories, its themes, its teachings. In some instances the one-semester Introduction to the Bible will be a gateway to more in-depth, upper-level courses; but often the course will be the one opportunity the student has to learn biblical studies in a formal academic setting. Having a textbook that presents the Bible and biblical scholarship in a way that is not only adequate but also interesting and compelling is obviously a *sine qua non* for such a course.

I took on the task of writing this textbook with fear and trembling, but it proved to be an unusually exhilarating experience. By far the most difficult task—once I decided on my historical and literary approach—was knowing what to leave out. A book that competently covers the field at the very beginning level would probably be 1500 pages. That's obviously not possible. But a more succinct treatment has an obvious downside: given the constraints of time and space, one has to make decisions and, to some extent, an instructor's choice of which textbook to use hinges on a basic compatibility with the decisions of the book's author. I hope I have made mine well; I have certainly made them deliberately and conscientiously.

I think there are several major desiderata for introductory-level textbooks (although it is surprising how few textbooks pass muster on even the majority of these). They should:

- be well written and engaging for the undergraduate student, rather than dry and boring;
- be highly informative in a lively way;
- provide coverage of all the truly major issues of both content and scholarship without getting bogged down in less than truly major ones;
- engage the mind of the student and allow the student to see the force of the arguments that have led scholarship to the various conclusions that it has reached, rather than simply present what scholars say as established fact; and
- not be idiosyncratic in their views but represent the best of consensus scholarship.

In the field of biblical studies, a textbook should:

- encourage students to read the Bible itself and yet provide adequate overviews of the most important matters raised in that reading;
- not assume that students already have a fair grasp, let alone mastery, of the primary materials;
- stress both the historical and literary nature of the material (especially since many students will have only approached these texts from a devotional/confessional/theological point of view previously, if they have approached them at all);
- represent the current state of biblical scholarship without burdening students with information (which they will find to be of very little use indeed) concerning which scholar says what about this, that, or the other thing, except where a truly exceptional contribution has been made by a scholar in a field with which he or she is particularly associated (think Wellhausen).

Above all, a textbook should be engaging, informative, accurate, clear, and interesting. I hope mine approaches these ideals; whether it does or not, I have written it with them in mind.

APPROACH

Various instructors obviously have different ways of approaching the introductory course. For instructors who wish that the textbook would give more thorough coverage of the *content* of each biblical book (mine discusses each and every one of the books of the Tanakh, the Apocrypha/Deuterocanonical writings, and the New Testament, but it does not provide, say, outlines or full summaries of them all), then I would suggest adopting in-class or homework exercises to achieve that end; conversely, for those instructors who are more particularly worried that students might settle for the textbook and not read the primary texts, I would suggest course incentives (quizzes, short summary papers, and so on) that ensure that familiarity with the Bible itself is a constituent component of the learning process. My view is that if a textbook is engaging and interesting, it can be molded to the particular emphases and agendas of individual instructors.

As is obvious from the title of this book and the content of its chapters, I have approached the writings of the Bible from historical and literary perspectives rather than confessional or theological. Anyone who wants to add theological reflections to what is covered in the book should find that it is completely amenable to that kind of use; anyone who does not want to do so will find it quite simple to expand on the historical and literary discussions already in the book.

FEATURES

I have included a number of pedagogical features with both the student and the teacher in mind. Each chapter begins with a section called "What To Expect," which gives a brief summary of what is about to happen in the chapter; at the end of each major discussion is a section called "At a Glance," which provides a brief but detailed summation of what has been covered. Within the chapters there are plentiful figures (maps, charts, relevant photos) and, most important, a number of boxes that deal with intriguing, relevant, and important side issues. I see these boxes as among the most interesting parts of the book, and students should be encouraged to read and engage with them.

Throughout each chapter, key terms are placed in bold at their first occurrence, and the bold-faced terms of that chapter are given in a list at the end. All these terms are then defined more thoroughly in the glossary at the back of the book. Each chapter also includes an annotated bibliography as Suggestions for Further Reading. I have worked to keep the annotations very brief but also informative (and evaluative). To help students not only to review the content of each chapter but also to engage with it personally, I have included at the end of each chapter three or four questions in which I ask them to "Take a Stand." These are meant to allow students to think through some of the key issues of the chapter for themselves and to express their perspectives and understandings of these matters in their own words.

ANCILLARIES

Oxford University Press offers instructors and students a comprehensive ancillary package for *The Bible: A Historical and Literary Introduction*.

An Instructor's Manual with Computerized Test Bank on CD includes:

- A randomizable test bank of multiple-choice questions
- Essay/discussion questions for each chapter
- Chapter summaries
- Pedagogical suggestions, Web links, and media resources for each chapter
- Sample syllabi
- PowerPoint lecture outlines for each chapter

A companion website for both instructors and students is available at **www.oup.com/us/ehrman**.

- For instructors, this site includes the Instructor's Manual, available for download. The Instructor's Resources section of the site is password-protected; contact your OUP sales representative for access.
- For students, the site includes a number of study tools including reading guides for each chapter, interactive flash cards with key terms and definitions, relevant Web links and media resources, and multiple-choice self-quizzes for practice.

Learning Management System (LMS) cartridges are available in formats compatible with any LMS in use at your college or university and include the following:

- The Instructor's Manual and Computerized Test Bank
- Student resources from the companion website

ACKNOWLEDGMENTS

I am very pleased to acknowledge fellow scholars who have selflessly read through the manuscript and made extraordinarily useful suggestions. First, I have had the assistance of two graduate students who have helped me with various aspects of the project: Jason Combs, PhD candidate in early Christian studies at UNC-Chapel Hill (currently dissertating, bless his soul); and Maria Doerfler, PhD candidate in early Christian studies at Duke (also dissertating, at this moment, and as of Fall 2013 an assistant professor at Duke Divinity School). I asked three friends and colleagues in the Hebrew Bible to go over the chapters involving the Tanakh with serious attention to both the big picture and the details: Michael Coogan, Professor of Hebrew Bible at Stonehill College, a premier scholar in the field and an exceptional textbook writer himself; David Lambert, assistant professor of Hebrew Bible at UNC-Chapel Hill—a terrifically bright colleague, abreast of current scholarship, who reads with a very keen eye; and Julia O'Brien, Professor of Hebrew Bible at Lancaster Theological Seminary, one of my oldest friends in the field and an inordinately generous but challenging reader of my work for years, based on her own years of superb research and teaching. These three have saved me from many egregious errors and directed me along paths that I did not intend to take—all to the good. Residual mistakes and problems, are, alas, my own, many of them due to my occasional refusal to attend to these colleagues' sage advice.

Oxford University Press, in addition, solicited a veritable army of readers for both the Hebrew Bible chapters and for the entire manuscript. Included in this group were the following who agreed to be identified: Lisa Marie Belz, Ursuline College; Ralph J. Brabban, Chowan University; Rangar Cline, University of Oklahoma; Michael D. Coogan, Harvard Divinity School; Beth Glazier-McDonald, Centre College; C. David Grant, Texas Christian University; David Halleen, Richland College; Wayne Kannaday, Newberry College; Micah D. Kiel, St. Ambrose University; David Lambert, University of North Carolina at Chapel Hill; Paul Mirecki, University of Kansas; Vivian-Lee Nyitray, University of California Riverside; Julia M. O'Brien, Lancaster Theological Seminary; Austin D. Ritterspach, Indiana University-Purdue University Indianapolis; Laura Schmidt Roberts, Fresno Pacific University; Susan Setta, Northeastern University; and Peter Zaaz, Siena College.

Once again I cannot thank these colleagues enough for the selfless assistance, keen insights, and stellar advice. The book is much stronger because of them. Again, any residual faults are not because of them but because of me.

Finally, my deepest thanks and appreciation go to the editorial staff at Oxford University Press who made this book both a possibility and a reality: my longtime friend and stalwart editor at Oxford University Press, Robert Miller, the executive editor who was inordinately generous in waiting for the book, long overdue; Lauren Mine, development editor, who worked tirelessly in helping imagine and shape the book and to bring it home; and Emily Krupin, assistant editor par excellence who tended to countless details throughout the entire process.

For quotations of the Hebrew Bible and Deutero-canonical books, I have mainly relied on the NRSV but on some occasions the translations are my own; translations of the New Testament are mine.

I have dedicated this book to my mother, who at 86 still takes me trout fishing. She was my first and best Bible teacher.

1

What Is the Bible? And Why Is It So Hard to Understand?

WHAT TO EXPECT

In this chapter we will cover a number of highly important introductory matters. We will first consider reasons for studying the Bible—not only religious reasons for those who have a personal commitment to the text, but also historical and literary reasons relevant to everyone, whether a believer or not. We will take a broad look at what the Bible is: how it is divided into the Hebrew Bible (the Christian Old Testament) and the New Testament, which books are in each of these testaments, and how they are organized and structured.

We will next consider the entire sweep of biblical history as it is laid out in the two testaments—from the creation of the world in Genesis, through the history of Israel, to the history of Jesus and early Christianity, and on up to the culmination of history with the destruction of the world in the book of Revelation.

A large portion of the chapter will consider the challenges that the Bible poses for anyone who wants to understand it from a historical perspective. It is a very large collection of books, all written at different times by different authors to different audiences for different reasons and with different points of view; in many places it is difficult to corroborate through archaeology or other ancient sources; and we do not have the original copies of any of the Bible's writings.

The chapter will end with an excursus that talks about the value and challenges of using a literary and historical approach to the Bible.

The Bible is the most commonly purchased, widely read, and deeply cherished book in the history of Western civilization. It is also the most widely misunderstood, misinterpreted, and misused. These reasons alone make it worth our time to study it. We can begin by considering the importance of the Bible in greater depth.

WHY STUDY THE BIBLE?

People study the Bible, and should study the Bible, for lots of reasons—religious, historical, and literary.

Religious Reasons

Most people who study the Bible do so, of course, for religious reasons. Many people revere the Bible as the word of God and want to know what it can teach them about what to believe and how to live. In this book, our study of the Bible will not promote any particular religion or theology—Baptist, Catholic, Jewish, Lutheran, agnostic, or anything else. We will instead be approaching the Bible from a historical and literary point of view. But even in this approach, there are religious reasons for studying the Bible—even for people who are not themselves religious or interested in becoming religious. That is because to understand our world, we need to have a firm grasp on the book that stands at the heart of the Jewish and Christian religions.

Historical Reasons

Arguably the most important reason for studying the Bible from a historical point of view is its importance in the history of Western civilization. The dominant religion of Europe and the New World for many centuries has been Christianity; and Christianity, as we will see, grew out of and alongside Judaism. The Bible is essential to both religions, and both continue to assert an enormous influence on Western culture. This is true not only on the individual level, as these religions guide people in their thoughts, beliefs, and actions, but it is also true on the broadest imaginable historical scale. Christianity has had the single greatest impact on Western civilization of any religion, ideology, or worldview, whether looked at culturally, socially, politically, or economically. No institution can even come close to the organized Christian church for its wide-ranging impact on the West. Without understanding the Bible, one cannot fully understand its historical effects on the world we inhabit.

More than that, the Bible has influenced and continues to influence millions and millions of people's lives. It is widely known that the Bible is the best-selling book of all time, without any serious competitor. What is not always appreciated is that the Bible is the best-selling book every year, year in and year out. So many copies of the Bible are sold every year that no one has been able to add them all up. One estimate from 2005 indicated that just in the United States, some twenty-five million copies of the Bible were sold. But what is most astounding is that the vast majority of those Bibles were sold to people who already *had* Bibles: over nine out of ten American households own at least one copy of the Bible, and the average household has four. As an article in the *New Yorker* magazine put it, this "means that Bible publishers manage to sell twenty-five million copies a year of a book that almost everybody already has."[1]

Americans not only like owning and buying Bibles. They also like reading them. A Gallup poll taken in 2000 indicated that 16 percent of Americans claimed to read the Bible every day, 21 percent at least once a week, and 12 percent at least once a month.[2] That means that fully half the population of the United States reads the Bible every month. Of how many other books can *that* be said?

What is even more impressive is the number of people who believe the Bible. Another, more recent, Gallup poll shows that three out of ten Americans believe that the Bible is the absolute word of God and is to be interpreted literally. Another five out of ten do not think that it is to be interpreted literally, but that it is nonetheless the word of God. This means that eight out of ten Americans—fully 80 percent—believe that the Bible is the inspired word of God.

The Bible's vast influence is a strong reason to study it, whether or not we are believers. Sincere believers who follow what they understand to be

---

1 Daniel Radosh, "Why Publishers Love the Bible," *New Yorker* December 18, 2006; see http://www.newyorker.com/archive/2006/12/18/061218fa_fact1#ixzz1nstdNqma

2 http://www.gallup.com/poll/2416/Six-Ten-Americans-Read-Bible-Least-Occasionally.aspx

the Bible's key teachings have frequently done a world of good throughout history, sometimes through enormous sacrifice. The Bible teaches to "love your neighbor as yourself," to "do unto others as you would have them do unto you," and many other selfless ethical principles. Anyone who follows such teachings can do real service to the human race and work to make society better.

But the Bible has also been used for extremely harmful and malicious purposes over the years—for example, in helping justify war, murder, and torture during the Crusades and Inquisitions of the Middle Ages. In the American South, the Bible was used to justify slavery and white supremacy. The Bible continues to be used to justify war, the slaughter of innocent lives, the oppression of women and of gays, and of just about everyone else that someone does not like. In part this may be because the Bible itself is, in places, a very violent book—not just in the Old Testament (for example, with the slaughter of the Canaanites by the Israelites, as mandated by God, in the book of Joshua) but also in the New Testament (as in the destruction of the human race by God in the Book of Revelation). And so, in the opinion of many, people not only use the Bible but also misuse it. This gives us all the more reason to study it.

Literary Reasons

In addition to religious and historical reasons for studying the Bible, there are literary reasons. For anyone interested in great literature, it is essential to have a grasp on the writings found in the Old and New Testaments. This is for two reasons. For one thing, the Bible contains some of the great literary gems of the world's literature. Just as some examples:

- The Book of Genesis: here is a book that contains some of the most familiar stories of the Bible, as it describes in powerful and moving

FIGURE 1.1. A page from Codex Leningradensis, the oldest surviving complete manuscript of the Hebrew Bible, produced around 1000 C.E.

terms the creation of the world, the first humans, the beginning of civilization, and the lives of the great ancestors of the Jewish people.

- Psalms: some of the great poetry of antiquity can be found among the 150 Psalms, traditionally attributed to the great King of Israel, David.
- Job: there is no work from the ancient world that grapples more strenuously with the question of why there is suffering than the book of Job.
- Isaiah: one of the great prophets of ancient Israel, Isaiah sends forth warnings of the danger of breaking God's law and extends much-needed comfort to those who have suffered for their sins.
- The Gospel of John: long a favorite among Christian readers, this account of Jesus' life portrays him as a divine being come to earth for the salvation of all who believe in him.
- The Letter to the Romans: the most prominent author of the New Testament, the apostle Paul, describes in this letter how a person can be made right with God through the death and resurrection of Jesus.
- The Revelation of John: this, the final book of the New Testament, indicates how all of human history will come to a climactic end with the destruction of the world as we know it.

A second literary reason for studying the Bible is that it is impossible to understand a good deal of Western literature without it, as many of its stories and themes and phrases are cited, alluded to, paraphrased, reworked, and explored in many of the greatest authors of the West: Chaucer, Milton, Shakespeare, T. S. Eliot, and hundreds of others.

WHAT IS THE BIBLE?

What exactly *is* this book that has made such an enormous religious, cultural, historical, and literary impact on our civilization? In the briefest terms, the Bible is the Jewish and Christian scriptures, consisting of sixty-six separate books that deal with ancient Israel and early Christianity, starting at the very beginning with the creation of the world in the book of Genesis and going to the very end with the destruction of the world and its recreation in the book of Revelation. These sixty-six books are divided into two "**canons**" (that is, "collections of books"—we will discuss the term "canon" at greater length in a moment, Box 1.1). The first is the thirty-nine-book Hebrew Bible (called this because it was written in Hebrew), also known as the Jewish Scriptures; Christians call this canon the "Old Testament" (some Christian churches have more than thirty-nine books in their canon, as we will see later). Second is the distinctively Christian canon of twenty-seven books called the "New Testament." Taken together, the entire collection of sixty-six books (or more, in some churches) constitutes the Christian Bible.

The Layout of the Hebrew Bible (The Christian Old Testament)

We will soon discuss the different names given to the Jewish Scriptures/Hebrew Bible/Old Testament. For now we can consider how it is structured and organized. As it turns out, there are different ways of numbering the books found in this canon, and different ways of organizing their sequence.

THE ENGLISH BIBLE In the English Bible—the one you will be using for this course—the Jewish Scriptures are presented in three parts: historical books (seventeen books altogether); poetic books (five books); and prophetic books (seventeen books). (See Box 1.2.)

Historical books. The historical books are the first seventeen books of the Bible and are subdivided into two groups. First are the five books of the **Pentateuch** (a word that literally means "the five scrolls"). These are the books that describe the creation of the world, the founding of the nation of Israel, the exodus of the people of Israel from slavery in Egypt, and the giving of the Law of Israel to Moses. Since most of these books deal specifically with this Law, they are sometimes called the "Law of Moses." The Hebrew word for "law" is **Torah**, and so sometimes these books are simply called the Torah.

After the Pentateuch come the other twelve historical books, which describe the history of the nation of Israel from the time they were given the Promised Land (roughly, the land where modern Israel is located), through the days in which they were ruled by kings, with two different kingdoms, Israel in the north and Judah in the south, until

BOX 1.1 THE CANON OF SCRIPTURE

The English term "canon" comes from a Greek word that originally meant "ruler" or "measuring rod." A canon was used to make straight lines or to measure distances. When applied to a group of books, it refers to a recognized body of literature. Thus, for example, the canon of Shakespeare refers to all of Shakespeare's authentic writings.

With reference to the Bible, the term "canon" denotes the collection of books that are accepted as authoritative by a religious body. Thus, for example, we can speak of the canon of the Jewish Scriptures or the canon of the New Testament.

both kingdoms were conquered and destroyed—first the north by the nation of Assyria and then the south by the nation of Babylon. The historical books end by describing the events that transpired when the people held in captivity in Babylon were allowed to return to Judah, to restore the Temple where God was to be worshiped and rebuild the city walls.

Poetic books. There are five books of poetry in the Jewish Scriptures, which are not concerned with the history of Israel but with setting forth some of the great literary masterpieces of ancient Hebrew writing, including such books as Psalms and the book of Job.

Prophetic books. Just as the seventeen historical books were divided into two subcategories (five books of Torah; twelve of other historical narratives), so too with the prophetic books. These are writings of ancient Israelite **prophets**—persons called by God to deliver a message to his people Israel. The message, in most cases, is not good: the people have strayed from God and, unless they repent and return to him, they will be punished.

Five of these books are considered **Major Prophets**, and twelve are **Minor Prophets**. The difference between the two groups is not one of importance but of length: the major prophets are much longer, the minor prophets much shorter.

And so it is relatively easy to remember the structure of the Jewish Scriptures in the English Bible. *Five* books of Torah; *twelve* other historical books. *Five* poetic books. *Five* major prophets; *twelve* minor prophets.

THE HEBREW BIBLE Anyone who was to read the Bible in the original Hebrew language would find the same books as in the English Bible, but they are numbered differently—the same thirty-nine books are now only twenty-four in number—and arranged in a different order, according to Hebrew names.

The Torah. As already mentioned, there are five books in the Torah, the Law of Moses. This is the first and most important section of the Hebrew Bible.

BOX 1.2 CHARTS OF HEBREW AND ENGLISH BIBLES

The Bible in Hebrew and in English have the same books, but they are numbered differently (for example, the twelve minor prophets in the English Bible are counted as just one book in Hebrew). They are also organized differently. As we will see in Box 1.3, different Christian denominations have different books included in their "Old Testament," as Roman Catholic

and Eastern Orthodox churches include books that Protestants consider to be the "Apocrypha." These books are excluded not only from the Protestant Bible but from the Hebrew Bible as well. (See Box 1.3.) The following charts show the organization and books of the Hebrew Bible and the Protestant Old Testament.

(continued)

BOX 1.2 CHARTS OF HEBREW AND ENGLISH BIBLES *(continued)*

THE HEBREW BIBLE		
The Torah (5 books)	**Nevi'im (= The Prophets) (8 books)**	**Kethuvim (= The Writings) (11 books)**

Genesis
Exodus
Leviticus
Numbers
Deuteronomy
	Former Prophets (4 books)
	  Joshua
	  Judges
	  Samuel (count as one book)
	  Kings (count as one book)
	Latter Prophets (4 books)
	  Isaiah
	  Jeremiah
	  Ezekiel
	  The Twelve (count as one book)
	    Hosea
	    Joel
	    Amos
	    Obadiah
	    Jonah
	    Micah
	    Nahum
	    Habakkuk
	    Zephaniah
	    Haggai
	    Zechariah
	    Malachi
		Job
		Psalms
		Proverbs
		Ruth
		Song of Songs
		Ecclesiastes
		Lamentations
		Esther
		Daniel
		Ezra-Nehemiah (1 book)
		Chronicles (1 book)

THE ENGLISH BIBLE		
The Historical Books (17 books)	**Poetic Books (5 Books)**	**Prophets (17 books)**

Pentateuch (5 books)
  Genesis
  Exodus
  Leviticus
  Numbers
  Deuteronomy
 	
Other Historical Books
(12 books)
  Joshua
  Judges
  Ruth
  1 and 2 Samuel
  1 and 2 Kings
  Ezra
  Nehemiah
  Esther
  1 and 2 Chronicles
	Job
	Psalms
	Proverbs
	Ecclesiastes
	Song of Songs
		Major Prophets (5 books)
		  Isaiah
		  Jeremiah
		  Lamentations
		  Ezekiel
		  Daniel
		
		Minor Prophets (12 books)
		  Hosea
		  Joel
		  Amos
		  Obadiah
		  Jonah
		  Micah
		  Nahum
		  Habakkuk
		  Zephaniah
		  Haggai
		  Zechariah
		  Malachi

BOX 1.3 CHARTS OF PROTESTANT, ROMAN CATHOLIC, AND ORTHODOX OLD TESTAMENTS

As mentioned in Box 1.2, some Christian denominations have additional books in the Old Testament that are not included in the Hebrew Bible or in the Protestant Old Testament. Protestants consider these books to be the "Apocrypha"; the churches that include them consider them "deuterocanonical." There are three categories of these other books. Ten of them are included in all Bibles of the Roman Catholic Church and the Eastern Orthodox Churches. But the Greek Orthodox Bible and the Slavonic Orthodox Bible have several additional books as well (not in the Roman Catholic canon). All of these books are not included at the end in an appendix, but are interspersed in appropriate places among the books found in the Hebrew Bible. We will be discussing most of these books in chapter 9.

Additional Books in Roman Catholic and Orthodox Old Testaments
Tobit
Judith
Additions to Esther
Wisdom of Solomon
    Ecclesiasticus (also called the Wisdom of Jesus Son of Sirach)

Baruch
Letter of Jeremiah
Additions to Daniel (three additional stories: Prayer of Azariah and the Song of the Three Jews, Susanna, Bel and the Dragon)
1 Maccabees
2 Maccabees

Still Other Books in Greek Orthodox Old Testament
Prayer of Manasseh
Psalm 151
1 Esdras
3 Maccabees
4 Maccabees (in an appendix)

Other Books in Slavonic Orthodox Old Testament
Prayer of Manasseh
Psalm 151
2 Esdras
3 Esdras
3 Maccabees

The Nevi'im. The Hebrew word "**Nevi'im**" means "prophets," but the word does not refer only to spokespersons of God who predict what is going to happen in the future. It also refers to anyone who speaks forth the word of God. In the Hebrew Bible, there are two groups of Nevi'im: the "Former Prophets" and the "Latter Prophets."

The **Former Prophets** make up four books that are considered the "historical books" in the English Bible (See Box 1.2): Joshua, Judges, 1 and 2 Samuel (counted as just one book), and 1 and 2 Kings (counted as one book). The **Latter Prophets** are more or less the books that are considered Prophets in the English Bible, and also are now four in number: Isaiah, Jeremiah, Ezekiel, and "the twelve" (this is the twelve Minor Prophets, considered now to be just one book).

The Kethuvim. The Hebrew word "**Kethuvim**" means "writings." This consists of the remaining eleven books of the Jewish Scriptures.

Since the three parts of the Hebrew Bible are Torah, Nevi'im, and Kethuvim, this canon is sometimes called the **Tanakh** (taking the first letter from each division, T-N-K, and adding vowels). And so Tanakh is simply another designation for the Jewish Scriptures, as found in the original Hebrew.

The Layout of the New Testament
There is just one way to number the twenty-seven books of the New Testament, and they are given in the same order and sequence no matter what language you are reading them in. Unlike the Hebrew Bible, the New Testament was originally written in Greek. There are four sections to the New Testament.

THE GOSPELS The New Testament begins with four Gospels: books that describe the life, ministry, death, and resurrection of Jesus. As such,

BOX 1.4 LAYOUT OF THE NEW TESTAMENT

Gospels: The Beginnings of Christianity (4 books)
- Matthew
- Mark
- Luke
- John

Acts: The Spread of Christianity (I book)
- Acts of the Apostles

Epistles: The Beliefs, Practices, and Ethics of Christianity (21 books)

Pauline Epistles
- Romans
- 1 and 2 Corinthians
- Galatians
- Ephesians
- Philippians
- Colossians
- 1 and 2 Thessalonians
- 1 and 2 Timothy
- Titus
- Philemon

General Epistles
- Hebrews
- James
- 1 and 2 Peter
- 1, 2, and 3 John
- Jude

Apocalypse: The Culmination of Christianity (I book)
- The Revelation of John

This schematic arrangement is somewhat simplified. All of the New Testament books, for example (not just the epistles), are concerned with Christian beliefs, practices, and ethics; and Paul's epistles are in some ways more reflective of Christian beginnings than the Gospels. Nonetheless, this basic orientation to the New Testament writings can at least provide a basic overview of the early Christian literature.

they can be considered to be books that describe the *beginnings* of Christianity.

ACTS   The second section of the New Testament contains just a single book, the Acts of the Apostles, which describes the activities of Jesus' followers after his death and resurrection as they converted others to the Christian religion throughout the Roman empire. As such, it describes the *spread* of Christianity.

THE EPISTLES   Altogether there are twenty-one epistles—that is, personal letters written by Christian leaders to various churches or individuals, giving them instructions about what to believe and how to live. Thirteen of these letters claim to be written by the most important figure in early Christianity outside of Jesus, the apostle Paul; the other eight are written by yet other apostolic figures. These books, then, describe the *beliefs* and *ethics* of Christianity.

REVELATION   The final category again contains just a single book, the Revelation, or Apocalypse, of John. This is a book that describes what will happen at the very end, when God destroys this world in an act of cataclysmic judgment and brings in a new heavens and earth. As such, it describes the *culmination* of Christianity.

PUTTING THE BIBLE ON THE MAP

To understand what the various authors of the Bible had to say, we have to put them in their own historical context rather than pretend they were writing in our context. Theirs was a very different world from ours, and we need to understand that world if we are to make sense of what they were saying to their readers living at the time. And so, here at the outset, I will begin to contextualize the Bible in a very basic and broad way by putting it on the map—geographically, historically, and culturally.

Geographically

In terms of geography, most of what happens in the Bible takes place in what is today Israel and Palestine, on the eastern side of the Mediterranean Sea, with some events involving other nations of what is called the **ancient Near East;** that is, the region and the countries of antiquity that roughly correspond to what today we call the Middle East, including Egypt and the lands of Mesopotamia in the region of the Tigris and Euphrates rivers (especially Assyria and Babylonia) and—from farther West—Greece and Rome. Figures 1.2, 1.3, and 1.4 should help familiarize you with the geography of the region.

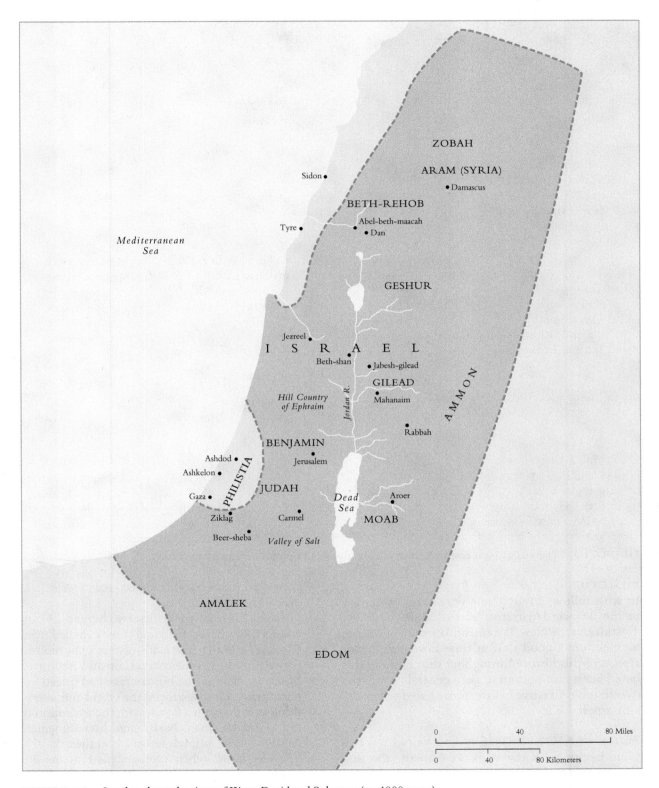

FIGURE 1.2. Israel at about the time of Kings David and Solomon (ca. 1000 B.C.E.).

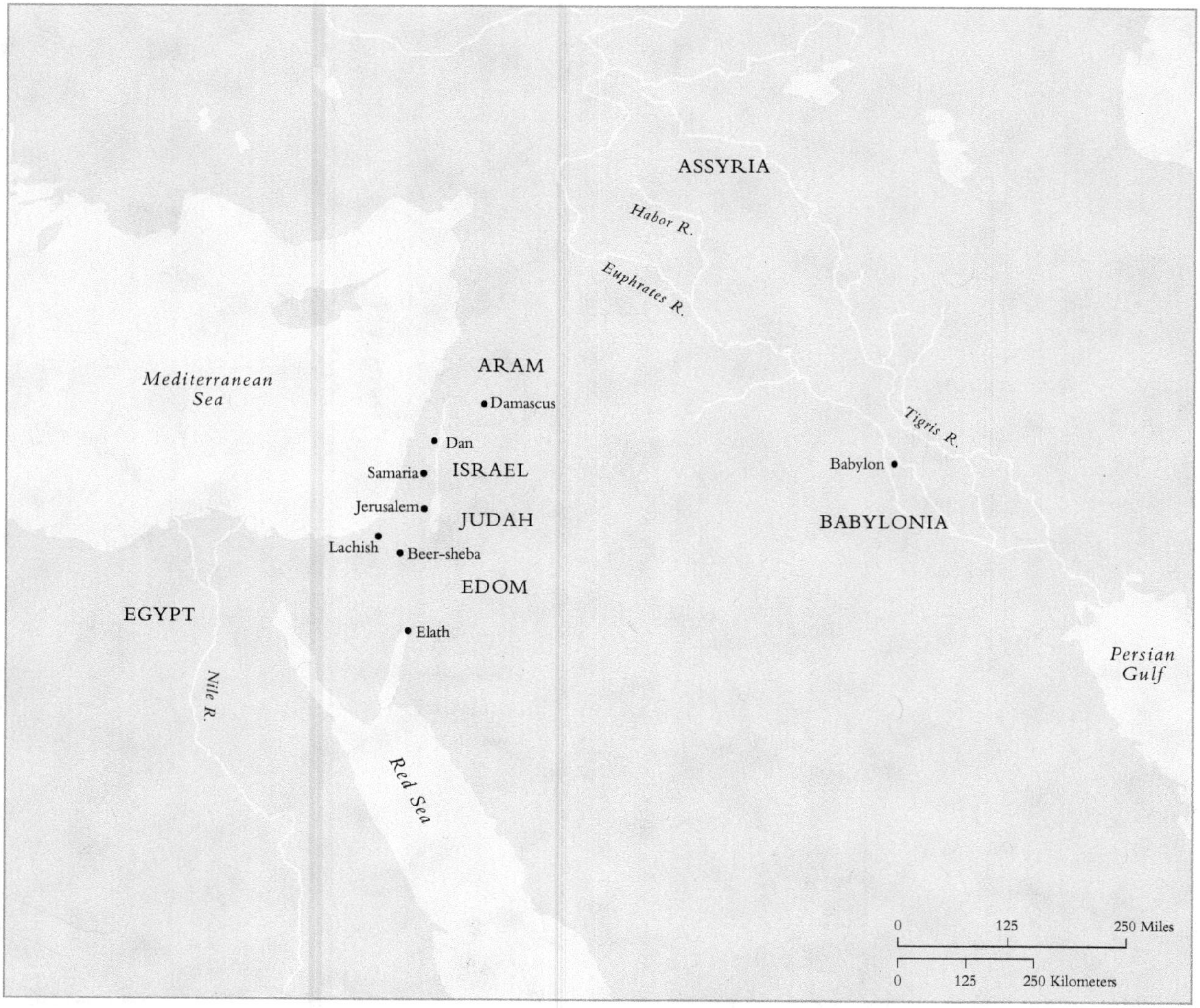

FIGURE 1.3. The ancient Near East at the time of the early Hebrew prophets (8th century B.C.E.).

Historically

In what follows I will give a very rough summary of the historical narrative of the Bible, both the Tanakh and the New Testament. We will, of course, be spending a good deal of time discussing major aspects of this history throughout the course of this book, but it is important to get a general flow of the overarching narrative before starting to discuss specific aspects of it.

FOUR MAJOR PRIMEVAL EVENTS The Bible begins with the book of Genesis, the first eleven chapters of which are principally concerned with four events that took place prior to what we might think of as recorded history:

- *Creation:* when God created the world and everything in it.
- *Garden of Eden:* when the first two humans, Adam and Eve, disobeyed God and were expelled from Paradise, and the aftermath of that expulsion in the relationship of their sons Cain and Abel.
- *Flood:* when, after the human race had spread exponentially, God destroyed the world and everything in it through a flood, with the exception of the righteous man Noah and his immediate family and the animals he saved on the ark.
- *Tower of Babel:* when humans tried to build a gigantic tower only to be frustrated by God, who made them speak different languages, leading to the different cultures and civilizations of the earth.

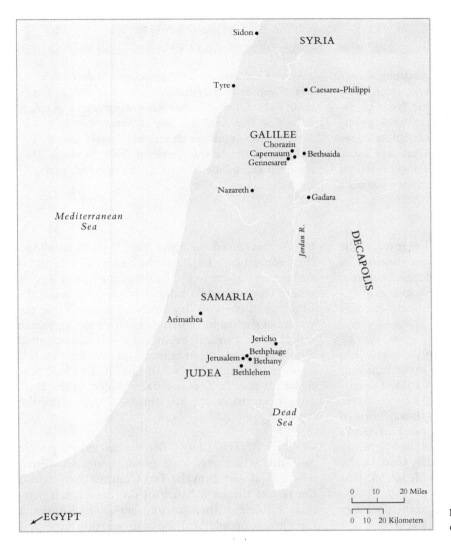

FIGURE 1.4. Palestine in the Days of Jesus.

BOX 1.5 CITING CHAPTERS AND VERSES

Ancient manuscripts of the Bible, whether the Hebrew Scriptures or the Greek New Testament, did not use punctuation, paragraph divisions, or even spaces to separate words. And so it should be no surprise to learn that the chapter and verse divisions found in modern translations of the Bible are not original (as if Isaiah, writing his prophecies, or Paul, writing his letter to the Romans, would have thought to number his sentences and call them verses!).

Chapter divisions started appearing in Bibles in the high Middle Ages, and verse divisions a couple of centuries later, after the invention of printing. These divisions are meant to indicate longer (chapter) and shorter (verse) sense units, although almost everyone agrees that in some places the divisions have not been made very sensibly.

Today, the standard way of indicating a Bible reference is to cite the name of the book, followed by the chapter number, then a colon (or a period), and then the verse number. And so, Joshua 1:8 means the book of Joshua, chapter 1, verse 8.

BOX 1.6 THE COMMON ERA AND BEFORE THE COMMON ERA

Many students will be accustomed to dating ancient events as either A.D. (which does not stand for "After Death" but for *anno domini*, Latin for "year of our Lord") or B.C. ("Before Christ"). This terminology may make sense for Christians, for whom A.D. 2012 is indeed "the year of our Lord 2012." It makes less sense, though, for Jews, Muslims, and others for whom Jesus is not the "Lord" or the "Christ." Scholars have therefore devised a different set of abbreviations as more inclusive of others outside the Christian tradition. In this book I will follow the alternative designations of C.E. ("the Common Era," meaning common to people of all faiths who utilize the traditional Western calendar) and B.C.E. ("Before the Common Era"). In terms of the older abbreviations, then, C.E. corresponds to A.D. and B.C.E. to B.C.

FOUR MAJOR PATRIARCHS   The rest of the book of Genesis deals mainly with four ancestors of the people of Israel, their wives, and their children. In terms of a historical timeline, these events allegedly occurred sometime in the eighteenth century B.C.E. (See Box 1.6.)

- *Abraham*. Out of all the peoples of the earth God called Abraham and promised to make him into a great nation and to give him the land of promise (what became Israel).
- *Isaac*. Even though Abraham's son Isaac (born of his wife Sarah) came as a fulfillment of God's promise to Abraham of a descendant, he was nearly sacrificed by Abraham when tested by God; but he lived on to have children with his wife Rebekah in fulfillment of God's promises.
- *Jacob*. One of twins, Jacob inherited the promises and was renamed "Israel." With his several wives he had twelve sons who were to become the original heads of the twelve tribes that made up Israel.
- *Joseph*. Among the twelve, Joseph was the favored son who, because of jealousy, was sold by his brothers into slavery in Egypt. But God showered his favor on Joseph and he rose to a position of power in Egypt in time for him to save the rest of his family from starvation as they migrated from the land of Canaan to join him.

ENSLAVEMENT AND EXODUS   After the death of Joseph and his brothers, the descendants of Jacob multiplied in Egypt and became a large nation. Many years later the Egyptians feared their numbers and enslaved them. God heard the cries of his people and raised up for them a savior, Moses, who performed miracles through the power of God and finally convinced the Egyptian Pharaoh to release the people. Once he did so, he had second thoughts and pursued them to the banks of the Sea of Reeds, where God worked a mighty miracle allowing the Israelites to cross on dry land and then causing the waters of the sea to return and drown the Egyptian army. This "exodus" event became a foundational moment for the nation of Israel and was later looked back upon as the time when God had called them to be his people. It is normally placed in the thirteenth century B.C.E. (so, some 400 years after the death of Joseph).

GIVING OF THE LAW   Moses then led the people into the wilderness to a great mountain, Sinai, where God gave him the Ten Commandments and the rest of the Law. Much of the Pentateuch contains a listing of these various laws, which instruct the chosen people both how to worship God and how to behave in community with one another.

WANDERING IN THE WILDERNESS   The people of Israel proved to be disobedient to God, however, and so were forced to wander in the wilderness for forty years while the generation that experienced the Exodus died off and their children then were brought to the brink of the Promised Land, which they were to inherit from God. The wandering in the wilderness is narrated in the book of Numbers; in the book of Deuteronomy, before he himself dies, Moses instructs those now about to enter the Promised Land about the Law he had received from God forty years earlier.

CONQUEST OF THE LAND   The land was already occupied by other peoples living in walled cities, however. And so, to inherit the land, the

Israelites had to conquer it. Led by Moses' successor Joshua, the Israelites destroyed the cities and towns of the land and occupied them, themselves. The conquest and distribution of the land is described in the book of Joshua.

JUDGES For some two centuries the Israelites did not have a national government but were ruled by charismatic leaders known as "judges." These were military persons who helped different tribes of Israel fend off their enemies in the land, enemies who attacked them whenever the Israelites proved disobedient to the law of God.

KINGS Eventually the people of Israel realized that they would have greater peace and prosperity if they were unified under a single government headed by a king. Three great kings ruled over all of Israel: Saul, David, and Solomon. Their rules and adventures are narrated in 1 and 2 Samuel and 1 Kings. They would have reigned in roughly the tenth century B.C.E. A civil war erupted after Solomon's death, leading to the secession of the ten northern tribes. This northern kingdom took on the name Israel; the southern two tribes became known as Judah. The books of 1 and 2 Kings narrate the political events of these two nations, the north ruled by a variety of dynasties and the south by kings always descended from David. The northern kingdom of Israel was eventually destroyed in 722 B.C.E. by the armies of Assyria; the southern kingdom of Judah survived for another century and a half until it was destroyed—along with the capital city and the central sanctuary, the Temple in Jerusalem—by the Babylonians in 586 B.C.E. The leaders and many of the people of Judah were taken into **exile** into Babylon.

EXILE AND RETURN In less than fifty years the Babylonians were overtaken by the Persians, who allowed the leaders and people to return to Judah to rebuild Jerusalem, its Temple, and its walls. Two of the leaders of the return were Ezra and Nehemiah, and the events associated with their leadership of the people are found in the books that go under their names. The history of the Hebrew Bible ends with the city of Jerusalem and the Temple functioning anew, although in less splendor and glory than before, under a much weaker local government still subject to Persian rule.

THE LIFE, DEATH, AND RESURRECTION OF THE MESSIAH The New Testament begins some four centuries later with the birth of Jesus, who is understood by the Gospel writers to be a descendant of David and who comes in order to fulfill the promises to Israel. According to the Gospels, however, Jesus' significance was not as a political or military leader like his ancestors, the Davidic kings. His salvation was spiritual. His teachings represented a new and true interpretation of what God wants from his people (as originally indicated in the Law of Moses); his many miraculous deeds demonstrated that he was uniquely the Son of God, and his death and resurrection occurred in order to restore people into a right standing before God. Jesus' death is usually dated to 30 C.E. or so.

THE SPREAD OF THE CHRISTIAN CHURCH After Jesus' death and resurrection, the good news of his salvation was spread throughout the Roman empire by his apostles, chief of whom was the apostle Paul, originally a persecutor of the church who converted to faith in Christ after having a vision of him. The book of Acts discusses the spread of the Christian gospel, first among Jews in Jerusalem and then among **gentiles** (that is, non-Jews who previously had worshiped other gods than the God of Israel). One of the major issues confronting the early Christian church was whether gentiles had to adopt the practices of the Law of Moses—in effect, by becoming Jews—in order to have the salvation offered by Christ's death and resurrection. Guided by the strong opinions of the apostle Paul, the early church leaders decided that Christ's salvation was for all people, both Jew and gentile, so that the Law of Moses no longer had any binding force on those born outside the nation of Israel. The book of Acts ends with Paul imprisoned for preaching his gospel, in about 60 C.E.

THE END OF TIME The New Testament concludes with the Revelation, or Apocalypse, of John, which describes the events at the end of time, when God destroys this wicked world in a series of cataclysmic disasters and sends all those opposed to him into eternal torment before bringing in a utopian kingdom for the chosen people, a "new heavens and earth," where there will be no more pain, misery, evil, or suffering.

A CRITICAL ASSESSMENT Later in this chapter we will begin to see that a number of archaeologists and historians have claimed that there are problems

FIGURE 1.5.   A page from Codex Vaticanus, one of the oldest and best manuscripts of the New Testament (4th century). This page contains the beginning of the book of Hebrews.

in the historical narratives of both the Hebrew Bible and the New Testament. In this widespread scholarly view, it is not clear that the history narrated in the Bible really happened in every instance exactly as it is described. This is obviously a serious and fundamental issue. You yourself will need to decide where you stand on it, as even the scholars are divided: some conservative Jewish and Christian scholars insist that everything the Bible says is true and historically correct, whereas most other scholars maintain that the problems are real and will not go away. Throughout this book we will not be focusing just on the negative claims of critical scholars—"this didn't really happen," or "that must be a myth"—but it will be important to recognize what those claims are and why they are so persuasive to so many scholars who devote themselves to this kind of research. At the same time, the Bible is about a lot more than just historical events. It is a treasure trove of amazing and powerful literature, which needs to be appreciated in all its rich fullness. Whatever else one might say about the Bible, no one can deny that it contains some of the most compelling and beautiful literature to have come down to us from the ancient world. And so we will not simply be criticizing the historical narratives of the Bible; we will also strive to understand its overarching message and learn the various and sundry lessons that its different authors were trying to convey.

To understand these lessons, though, we need to continue situating the Bible in its broader context. We have already discussed its geographical and historical context; we can finally consider some aspects of its cultural context.

Culturally

For the cultural context of biblical times, we need to consider both the political and the religious worlds of antiquity.

THE POLITICAL CONTEXT   A good bit of the Bible, both Old and New Testaments, is deeply connected with political realities. In comparison with other nation-states throughout its history, Israel was relatively weak and readily overthrown by the greater powers that dominated the ancient Near East

at different periods. Several other political powers play a highly significant role in the life of Israel:

- *Egypt.* As we have seen, the ancient stories concerning the Exodus—arguably the formative experience of the Israelite people—are intimately tied to the dominance of Egypt, one of the perennial powerhouses of ancient times.
- *Assyria.* On the other side of the Fertile Crescent was Assyria, whose rise to world dominance in the eighth century B.C.E. led to conflict with the northern nation of Israel. In 722 B.C.E. the Assyrian armies destroyed the capital city Samaria and devastated the land. Many of the people of Israel were deported to other parts of the Assyrian empire, and those who remained intermarried with foreigners brought into the land. In effect, that brought an end to the descendants of the northern ten tribes of Israel for all time.
- *Babylonia.* A century and a half later the other Mesopotamian power, Babylonia, had conquered the Assyrians and, like their predecessors, were asserting their influence over other parts of the Fertile Crescent to the west. Eventually the powerful king Nebuchadnezzar attacked the southern nation of Judah, laid siege to the capital city of Jerusalem, and destroyed it and its Temple in 586 B.C.E. Many of the prominent people of Judah were taken into exile back to the capital city of Babylon.
- *Persia.* The nation of Persia soon conquered the Babylonians and then allowed the people of

---

BOX 1.7 TIMELINE FOR THE HEBREW BIBLE

The following timeline gives either the presumed dates (for the most ancient figures and events) or the actual dates that scholars are relatively certain about (for example, for the fall of the northern kingdom of Israel and the southern kingdom of Judah):

The Primeval History: year 1!
Call of Abraham: ca. 1750 B.C.E.
Joseph to Egypt: ca. 1690 B.C.E.
Moses and the Exodus: ca. 1250 B.C.E.
Joshua and the Conquest of the Promised Land: ca. 1210 B.C.E.
Period of the Judges: ca. 1210–1025 B.C.E.

The Beginning of the United Monarchy (Saul, David, Solomon): ca. 1025 B.C.E.
The Divided Monarchy (Israel and Judah): 928 B.C.E.
Assyrian Destruction of Israel (the north): 722 B.C.E.
Babylonian Destruction of Judah (the south) and exile: 586 B.C.E.
The Return to the Land under Persia: 538 B.C.E.
Rebuilding of Jerusalem and the Temple: 520–430 B.C.E.
Conquests of Alexander the Great: 332 B.C.E.
Judea ruled by Egypt: 300–198 B.C.E.
Judea ruled by Syria: 198–142 B.C.E.
The Maccabean Revolt: 167–142 B.C.E.
The Maccabean Rule: 142–63 B.C.E.
Conquest of Palestine by Romans: 63 B.C.E.

Judah to return to the land (in 538 B.C.E.), where they rebuilt Jerusalem and the Temple. They were ruled by a local governor (not a king) but were subject to Persian rule.

- *Greece and the Hellenistic Kingdoms.* The Persians were eventually conquered by the Greeks under the great warrior-king Alexander the Great. Alexander's empire was divided up after his untimely death in 323 B.C.E., and Judah was ruled first by the Egyptians and then the Syrians.
- *Rome.* After a rebellion in which Judah achieved self-rule for about eighty years, the rising power of Rome came in and conquered the land for itself (63 B.C.E.). By the time of the New Testament, the land of Judea, as it was now called, as well as the northern part of the land, now called Galilee, were again under foreign domination. It is in that context that Jesus was born during the reign of the first Roman emperor, Caesar Augustus. He was to die some thirty years later at the hands of the Roman governor of Judea, Pontius Pilate.

THE RELIGIOUS CONTEXT   As difficult as it is to summarize the political world of the Bible in a few paragraphs, it is even harder to synthesize the religious world. There were many, many religions—hundreds of religions—scattered throughout the world of the Bible, in Egypt, Canaan (where Israel came to be), Assyria, Babylon, Persia, Greece, and Rome. And yet there were several features that almost all of these different religions, over all the centuries covered by the Bible, had in common. Before detailing these features it is important to stress that there are two reasons—seemingly contradictory reasons—that these religions are important for understanding ancient Israelite and early Christian religion. On one hand, many Israelites, and then **Jews** (originally, "Jews" were people who lived in Judea; eventually they came to be identified with their descendants who kept aspects of the Law of Moses, even if they lived elsewhere), and then Christians flat-out rejected all the other religions and held to a completely different set of religious beliefs and practices. On the other hand, ironically, these other religions influenced biblical religions in significant ways. Both of these seemingly contradictory strands of rejection and assimilation are important for a complete understanding of the Bible, its authors, and their times.

If we were to try to summarize the major aspects of ancient religion outside of ancient Israel and outside of early Christianity, we might focus on the following features shared by just about all other lands and peoples:

1. *Polytheism.* All ancient religions were polytheistic, meaning that they worshiped many gods, not just one. Most ancient religions believed that there were lots of gods with lots of different functions: gods of war, gods of weather, gods of health, gods of agriculture, gods of various places—forests, rivers, homes, the hearth—and on and on. Even if there were thought to be several chief gods, or even just one, there was no sense that a person should have to restrict his or her worship only to them or only to him. There were lots of gods, they all deserved to be worshiped, and none of them insisted that you worship him or her alone. All people who worshiped many gods—in other words, everyone except for Jews—are sometimes called "pagans" by modern scholars. The term **pagan**, in this historical context, does not have negative connotations; it simply refers to someone who followed any of the polytheistic religions of antiquity.

2. *Emphasis on the present life.* The vast majority of ancient religions believed in worshiping the gods because life was very difficult and lived near the edge, and the gods could provide for people what they could not provide for themselves. People cannot make sure that it rains, or that the crops grow, or that a child recovers from an illness, or that a mother survives childbirth, or that the enemies don't conquer your village. But the gods can.

3. *Divine power.* That, then, was why, in great part, the gods were worshiped: they were mighty and deserved to be worshiped, and they could use their might to make life possible and even happy. The proper worship of the gods is what provided humans with access to divine power, necessary to survive this life and to live well.

4. *Cultic acts.* The gods were worshiped through cultic acts. The word "**cult**" in this context does not refer to some kind of weird, sectarian group that engages in bizarre and secretive practices. It refers to the "care" of the gods (it is based on a Latin word). Humans show their care of the gods by performing sacrifices (of animals, for example, or by throwing a bit of food on a fire) and by saying prayers. These

were the two chief ways gods were worshipped, and they are what the gods asked for and even demanded from their people.

5. *Sacred places.* Almost all ancient religions had sacred locations, spaces that were thought to be "holy" or "set apart" from all other places because they were connected with a god or with gods. And so there were sanctuaries and temples where sacrifices could be made and where prayers, especially, could be said.

These, in very simple and rough outline, are what ancient religions were all about. As you can tell, these religions were very different from what people today—at least people in the twenty-first-century Western World—tend to think of as religion. Largely *missing* from ancient religions were a number of features of what we today might think of as having central importance:

1. *Doctrines and beliefs.* For many people today, religion is principally about what you believe, the doctrines you hold (e.g., about God, about Christ, about salvation). Ancient religions did not stress doctrines and, odd as this might seem, ancient religious leaders (among the pagans) did not think that it much mattered what you believed. What mattered is what you did, as you participated in the ancient cults devoted to the gods.

2. *Ethics.* Modern religion is largely about how you live your life, avoiding "sins" of various kinds and doing good works. Ancient religions did not stress ethics; to participate in these religions, for the most part, it did not matter *how* you lived your life (with some major exceptions: you shouldn't murder your parents, for example). Ancient people were, of course, ethical—at least as ethical as most people today are. But ethics were not part of religion; they were a matter of communal life or, sometimes, in later periods, of philosophy.

3. *Afterlife.* Many people today are religious out of a concern for the afterlife. They want to experience ecstasy in heaven rather than torment forever in hell, if given the choice. Again this may seem strange, but most ancient people did not think that your religion had any bearing on what would happen to you after you died. It appears that the majority of people in antiquity did not believe there would even be an afterlife. Those who did rarely thought that being highly

religious would make a difference to what kind of life it would be.

4. *Sacred books.* In most of the religions we know intimately today, books play a central role: the Torah, the New Testament, the Qur'an. Not in ancient religions. Books were almost never a part of a religion, and there was almost no sense that a book contained the inspired word of God that could direct people in knowing what to believe and how to act (in part because doctrines and ethics were not part of what it meant to be religious).

5. *Separation of church and state.* In the United States, at least, we think that church and state need to be kept separate so the government cannot tell us how we ought to worship. That was not the case in the ancient world (or in much of any world before the American Revolution). Ancient cities and nations understood that the gods were on their side, and so they worshiped their city or national gods out of duty and respect—and to make sure that things continued to go well. There was no separation of politics and religion in antiquity. The gods supported the state, and the state urged and even required the worship of the gods.

6. *Exclusivity.* Most of the religions we are familiar with today are exclusivistic—by which I mean that if you are a member of one religion, you cannot be a member of another. If you are a Jew you are not, as a rule, also a Hindu; Baptists are not Shintoists; Muslims are not Mormons. You have to choose, one or the other. Not so in ancient religions. Since these religions were polytheistic, you could adhere to just about any number of them. The ancient religions tended to be tolerant of one another, as were the gods they worshiped. There was no sense that you had to stop worshiping your old gods if you started worshiping new gods. These religions were both polytheistic and tolerant.

I stated already that the religions of ancient Israel and early Christianity were both resistant to and influenced by the other religions of their environment. Both aspects are highly significant for understanding the Bible. First, the religion of ancient Israel—including the later religion of Judaism, as accepted and followed by Jesus and his original disciples—was distinctive from other religions in many ways.

1. *The One God*. Most ancient Israelites, and then Jews at the time of the New Testament, did not worship many gods but the one God that they believed was the only true God. It had not always been that way in Israel. In the very remote past, and on and off throughout their checkered history, many Israelites probably did worship other gods. That is why the Law of Moses insists that they worship only the One—since the people of Israel (some of them) were inclined to worship others as well. And even in the Hebrew Bible there are indications that Israelites accepted the *existence* of other gods, even while they insisted that these others were not to be worshiped. That is why one of the Ten Commandments says "You shall have no other gods before me." This commandment presupposes that the other gods exist. But they definitely are not to be worshiped. Only the God of Israel is to be. As we will see, by the time we get to the later portions of the Hebrew Bible there are prophets who insist that the God of Israel in fact is the one and only God. No others exist. This appears to have been the view of Jesus and his earliest followers as well, and is a feature of ancient Judaism that makes it totally unlike the other religions of its environment.

2. *The Covenant*. Ancient Israelites, and then Jews, maintained that this one God had made a special **covenant** with them, the people of Israel. A covenant is a political pact or a peace treaty. The idea was that God had called Israel to be his unique chosen people, as was evident in the fact of the exodus, when he saved them from their slavery in Egypt. Unlike all other peoples, who worshiped other gods, Israelites were distinctively the possession of the one true God, who created the world.

3. *The Law*. The Law of Moses was an important feature of ancient Israelite religion, as it was eventually for all Jews and then for Jesus. Many Christians today misunderstand the significance of the Law in Jewish religion. The Law was never meant to be a list of undoable do's and don'ts that God had commanded his people, and that he then used to condemn them once they failed to keep it. The Law was almost never seen as an enormous religious burden. On the contrary, the Law presented God's directives to his people, showing them how to worship him

and how to live in community together. What could be better than that? The God of the universe had told his people how they could best relate to him and to each other. This was the greatest gift God had given his people, and most religious Jews considered it a joy to keep. No one, so far as we know, thought that they had to keep the Law in order to earn God's favor. Quite the contrary, God had already chosen Israel to be his people; keeping the Law simply meant doing what he asked, as one of his chosen people. The covenant, then, involved the "election" (or choosing) of the people of Israel by God and the obedience to God by the people (by keeping the Law).

4. *Sacred places*. Other religions had numerous religious sanctuaries and temples. At one time in the history of early Israel, it was also thought that God could be worshiped with sacrifices in various sacred spots. Eventually, as we will see, many Israelites came to think that there was only one place on earth that God could be properly worshiped: in the Temple in the city of God, Jerusalem. It came to be thought that God himself actually dwelt in the Temple, in the holiest portion of it, the **Holy of Holies**, a sacred room where God was physically present on earth. After the Temple was destroyed by the Babylonians in 586 B.C.E. and Jews were scattered to different places around the Mediterranean (Egypt, Babylonia, and other lands), they started worshiping together in groups, saying prayers and recalling the ancient traditions of their people. These gatherings were called "**synagogues**." Eventually, by the time of Jesus, synagogues were actual buildings where Jews gathered together for worship. Sacrifices were not made in the synagogues, however, as Jews continued to think that it was only in the Temple in Jerusalem that sacrifices could be performed. That Temple was rebuilt about fifty years after it was destroyed, and this second Temple functioned for over 500 years until it too was destroyed by the Romans in 70 C.E., about forty years after the death of Jesus.

And so, ancient Israelites generally rejected the other polytheistic religions of their environment in favor of their own religion, which stressed the worship of the one God of Israel who had created heaven and earth and called Israel to be his people.

FIGURE 1.6. The famous scroll of the prophet Isaiah, discovered among the Dead Sea Scrolls: our oldest surviving copy of the book.

The Torah told people how they could worship God and how they were to relate to one another. At a later time this was the religion of Jesus and his followers, as well. It became the foundation of Christianity, which transformed the religion in significant ways, although the ideas that there was only one God and that he had saved his chosen people lived on in the new religion.

I have pointed out already that ancient Israel, and then early Christianity, not only rejected much of the religion found in the world around them but also assimilated a good deal from other religions. This does seem highly paradoxical, but it is one of the assured findings of modern times. In no small measure this finding has literally been made on the basis of discoveries—as ancient pagan texts have been uncovered that were written at times *earlier* than the biblical accounts we have, but are so similar in many ways to what we find in the Bible that it is clear the biblical authors were retelling stories widely known throughout the world of their times.

We will see instances of these kinds of cultural "borrowings" throughout our study. In the next chapter, for example, we will discuss an ancient writing called *Enuma Elish*, which is a Mesopotamian account of the creation of the world. It has a large number of similarities to what can be found in Genesis—even though it was written centuries before Genesis. We will also consider one of the great epics of antiquity, known as *Gilgamesh* (named after its main character), which presents an account of the universal flood that is similar in a number of astounding ways to the story of Noah and the ark,

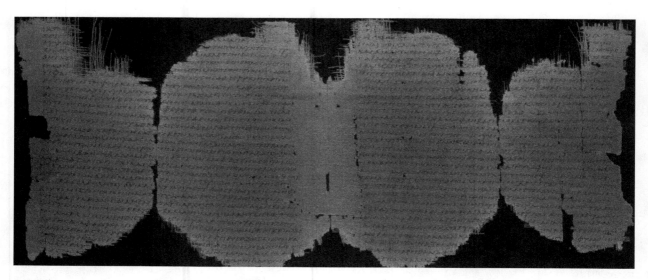

FIGURE 1.7.   Several pages of P⁴⁵, the oldest surviving (though fragmentary) copy of the Gospel of Luke, from the early third century.

even though it too dates from many centuries before Genesis. When we get to the New Testament we will see that Jesus was not the only person thought in his time to be a miracle-working son of God, but that there are Greek and Roman stories too of supernatural men who were miraculously born, who allegedly could heal the sick, and cast out demons, and raise the dead, and who at the end of their lives went up to heaven to live in the divine realm.

Israelites, Jews, and Christians certainly did have distinctive religious traditions that made them stand out among their pagan neighbors. At the same time, they were not completely unique. They too took stories, traditions, beliefs, and practices from their world; they too were in many ways very much like others in their environment.

CHALLENGES OF STUDYING THE BIBLE

Even though the Bible is so obviously valuable as great literature, and important to the religious lives of literally billions of people throughout history, it is also obviously difficult to understand. If it were *easy* then everyone would understand it, and no one would disagree about its meaning. But the reality is that there are hundreds and hundreds of different interpretations of the Bible—all by people who claim to know what it means.

There are many factors that make it difficult to interpret the Bible. The following are some of the more obvious ones.

The Size and Extent of the Corpus

As we have already begun to see, the Bible is a very big book. The Old Testament is much larger than the New Testament: its thirty-nine books are about three and a half times as extensive. And taken together, all sixty-six books cover a lot of ground. These books were written at different times, in different places, by different authors addressing different concerns for different audiences and often expressing different points of view. No wonder it is hard to get a handle on it all.

I have repeatedly said that there are sixty-six books in the Bible, but that depends on which books one includes and, as we have seen, how one counts. Some Christian denominations have additional books. The Roman Catholic church and the Eastern Orthodox churches, for example, have additional writings in the Old Testament known as the deuterocanonical writings. These are not found in the Jewish Bible and are called the "**Apocrypha**" by Protestant Christians. (See Box 1.3.) Most of our study will focus on the thirty-nine books that everyone agrees are part of the Jewish Scriptures and the twenty-seven books of the New Testament, although we will look at most of the deuterocanonical books as well, in due course (see chapter 9).

Languages

As already mentioned, the Bible was not originally written in English but in ancient languages that very few people—outside of biblical scholars and others with advanced training—actually can read any longer. The Jewish Scriptures were written in Hebrew (with a few small sections in a related language: Aramaic) and the New Testament in Greek. This means that whenever you read a passage of the Bible you are reading it in translation and, as anyone knows who has worked extensively in another language, something is always lost in translation. That is why there are so many different translations of the Bible available today.

There are different philosophies of how to translate ancient texts into modern languages, but the reality is that it is never possible to come up with a perfect translation that will convey exactly the original meaning of the text, no matter how hard you try. That is one of the reasons that different people will have different interpretations of the same passage, depending on which translation they are using. But even scholars who read the texts in the original languages have wide-ranging differences among themselves over what the texts actually mean. That, in no small part, is because of some of the other problems that the Bible presents to its readers and interpreters.

Dates

The books of the Bible were not all written at one time and in one place. They were written over a long period of time in different places, and that causes problems because language changes over time. Just as you may have difficulty reading the Elizabethan English of Shakespeare, and quite serious difficulty reading the Middle English of Chaucer, and find it completely impossible to read the Old English of Beowulf, so too readers of Hebrew and Greek can have difficulty understanding the language as it evolved in different times and places.

Even apart from this problem of language, it is simply very hard to understand literature written over such a wide range of dates. With respect to the Hebrew Bible, it was traditionally believed that the

Torah was written by Moses in, say, the thirteenth century B.C.E. The last book of the Jewish Scriptures to be written—it was believed—was from the fourth century B.C.E. That is a time range of 900 years.

As it turns out, many scholars have come to believe that both of those dates are probably wrong. In this view it is unlikely—for reasons we will see in the next chapter—that Moses wrote the Torah. The oldest books of the Bible are some of the prophets, such as Amos and Isaiah, whose work originated in the eighth century B.C.E. And the last book of the Hebrew Scriptures is more recent than traditionally thought, dating from the second century B.C.E. Still, that is a 600-year gap from the oldest to the most recent book. Moreover, this is the entire corpus of surviving Hebrew literature (from this period). Imagine trying to master all of English literature written from the year 1400 to now.

The New Testament covers a much briefer span of time: the earliest books were the writings of Paul in the 50s C.E.; the last book was probably 2 Peter, written around 120 C.E. But even here we have a 70-year span of time. And here too we have nearly all of the early Christian writings, almost (not quite) all written within a century of the death of Jesus around the year 30 C.E.

Authors

Numerous authors produced the books that eventually came to be included in the Bible. It is very difficult, as we will see, to know just how many and who they were.

The traditional view of the Jewish Scriptures was that Moses wrote the Torah; Joshua wrote the book of Joshua; king David wrote the Psalms; his son, King Solomon, wrote the poetic books Proverbs, Ecclesiastes, and the Song of Songs; and that the various prophets (e.g., Amos, Isaiah) all wrote in their own names. As we will see, modern scholars have found reasons to dispute many of these claims. A number of these books—even the five books of the Torah—are, in fact, anonymous. No one claims to be their author. The same is true of the other historical books. What is even more problematic, a number of the books claim to be written by authors who, it is now recognized, almost certainly could not have written them, for reasons we will see in later chapters.

We have a similar situation when it comes to the New Testament. Some of its books were written by known authors (for example, some of the letters of the apostle Paul). But other books were anonymous, including the Gospels. We *call* them Matthew, Mark, Luke, and John, but their real authors never reveal their names to us. It was only about a hundred years after they were written that Christians started claiming that these particular people wrote them; and we will see why scholars have called these claims into question. Even more troubling, scholars widely hold that a number of the authors of the New Testament claimed to be someone other than who they really were. Some of the letters that claim to be written by Paul, for example, appear not to have been written by him but by a different author (or authors) claiming to be him. We will see what evidence these scholars have adduced for these views, and you will need to make up your own mind.

It is frankly impossible to know how many authors produced the books that are now in the Jewish Scriptures (over twenty—but how many?). For the New Testament, it appears that there were something like sixteen different authors (some of them who they claimed to be, others writing anonymously, others falsely claiming to be a famous apostle). All of this creates enormous problems for interpreting these books. Different authors naturally have different points of view, perspectives, ideas, and beliefs. The Bible does not have a single point of view, but many. Studying the Bible means being sensitive to all these differences at every point.

Genres

The Bible not only contains sixty-six books written by dozens of different authors; these books, and portions within these books, represent many different genres of literature. A **genre** is a "kind" of writing, a literary form. In English, for example, we have novels, short stories, lyrical poems, and newspaper editorials. Each of these kinds of writing has certain characteristics that we as readers understand and take for granted, characteristics that help us make sense of how an author is trying to communicate. Within poetry broadly we have certain kinds, each of which has its own rules for how it is to be written and how it is, then, to be understood (e.g., sonnets, epics, limericks). In order to understand any given poem we have to understand its form or genre. So too we have different expectations of a fictional short story and a report in a science journal, of a novel and a biography, of a lyrical poem and an editorial. Since we are accustomed to these various genres, we usually don't think much about them. But the Bible also contains numerous genres, and some of them are not all that familiar to us. They include the following:

- Historical narratives
- Biographies
- Novellas
- Myths
- Legends
- Annals
- Poetry
- Proverbs
- Wisdom sayings
- Prophecies
- Apocalypses
- Gospels
- Epistles
- Sermons
- Treatises

In order to understand what an author is trying to communicate, we have to understand what genre of writing he or she has used. One problem many modern interpreters of the Bible have is that they are not familiar with the various genres and fail, then, to interpret the writing in light of the genre the author has used. This happens, for example, when someone interprets a myth as if it were a scientific report, or a legend as if it were a biographical narrative, or an apocalypse as if it were a literal description of events that are yet to transpire. We will look at various genres throughout our study, in an attempt to see what the different biblical authors were trying to communicate.

Internal Tensions

Another significant challenge in interpreting the Bible is one that I alluded to earlier. Numerous scholars have maintained that the Bible has within its pages numerous discrepancies, inconsistencies, and contradictions. As I have stressed, this is an issue that you will need to resolve for yourself once you have looked at the evidence. Whether you end up agreeing with these scholars or not, the apparent (or real) discrepancies cause numerous headaches for interpreters trying to make sense of the books of the Bible. At the same time, for reasons I will stress more fully in the excursus at the end of this chapter, these discrepancies have a very positive value as well, in that they show us that each book of the Bible has its *own* message that it is trying to convey. By seeing the differences among the books, we are

FIGURE 1.8. A famous medieval manuscript of the Gospels in Latin, called the Lindisfarne Gospels, renowned for its intricate artwork; this is the first page of the Gospel of John.

better able to see what the message of each is, in a way that is impossible so long as you assume that every book, and every author, is trying to say pretty much the same thing.

Problems with Archaeology and External Verification

In addition to the apparent, or real, internal discrepancies, inconsistencies, and contradictions of the Bible, there is the problem that in a number of very important instances, what the Bible says appears to contradict what archaeologists and scholars of other ancient sources from the time have found. In chapters 3 and 4 we will be considering several key examples. These difficulties raise the

question of whether we are to interpret some of the stories of the Bible as historical accounts of what actually happened in the past—or as something else.

Historical Contexts and Worldviews

One of the fundamental lessons we will be learning throughout the course of our study is that if we want to understand something, we have to put it in its proper context. Any time you take something out of context, you misunderstand it. Nowhere is that more obvious or important than with the Bible. This can easily be illustrated.

In the book of Isaiah, written in the eighth century B.C.E., there is a prophecy that has historically been very important to Christians thinking about the birth of Jesus. In some English translations of the passage, we read: "The Lord himself will give you a sign. A virgin shall conceive and bear a son, and you shall call his name Immanuel" (Isaiah 7:14). Because this same verse gets quoted in the Gospel of Matthew 1:21, it is typically understood by Christians to be a prophecy about the coming messiah: his mother will be a virgin. According to this reading, Isaiah was looking forward to the coming of the savior of the people—the **messiah** (which literally means "anointed one," referring to the one favored by God whom God sends in order to save his people)—who will come into the world not in a normal way, but by a virgin birth.

That is indeed how the author of Matthew understood what Isaiah was trying to say. But anyone who interprets Isaiah itself in light of Matthew's understanding may not be reading Isaiah in its own context, but in the later context of the Gospel writer living 800 years later. To understand what Isaiah himself was trying to say, it is important to understand his words in his own context. Among other things, that means reading all of Isaiah chapters 7 and 8 to see what the prophet was referring to. When you read those chapters (go ahead and read them) it is clear that the prophet is not predicting the coming of a future messiah, even if later interpreters read him in this way.

For one thing—this may not be clear in English translations—the author does not appear to be speaking about a child who is to be born of a virgin. This is obviously a significant matter! Most modern translators of Isaiah recognize that the Hebrew word sometimes translated "virgin" (for example, in the King James Bible) is actually *mistranslated*. The Hebrew word in question does not mean "virgin" in the sense of a woman who has never had sex, but "young woman"—independently of whether this young woman has had sex or not. And so, in modern versions the verse is given a more accurate translation: "The Lord himself will give you a sign. A *young woman* has conceived and will bear a son. . . ." The problem is that when the author of Matthew, 800 years later, quoted the verse, he was not quoting it from the original Hebrew but from the Greek translation of the Hebrew Bible (called the **Septuagint**), which used a Greek word that sometimes meant "woman who has never had sex." And so Matthew cites the passage as if it were talking about a virgin. But that is not what the original Hebrew word meant.

Even more than that, Isaiah chapter 7 is quite clear as to its own meaning. Here is the context: The king of the nation of Judah, Ahaz, is upset because a war is brewing. Two of the neighboring countries—Israel and Syria to the north—have ganged up and are in the process of attacking Judah, and Ahaz does not know what to do. Isaiah comes to him and delivers him a prophecy. A young woman will soon give birth to a child. And what is significant about that? Why is that a "sign" from the Lord? Because of what Isaiah says next: before this child is old enough to know the difference between good and evil, the two kings will relent and return home and Judah will be saved (Isaiah 7:16). In other words, in a couple of years the crisis will be resolved.

Read Isaiah in its own context, and this is what the passage means. Matthew interpreted in a very different context and read Isaiah 7:14 in reference to the coming of Jesus into the world. In other words, he took the words of Isaiah and applied them to a different context. For anyone who wants to know what Isaiah himself was talking about, it is important to read him in his *own* context. At the same time, if anyone wants to understand how Matthew interpreted the verse, she or he has to read Matthew in *his* own context, in which he was trying to prove that Jesus "fulfilled prophecy"—in this case, a prophecy that the future savior would be born of a virgin (even if that is not what Isaiah himself meant).

Knowing the historical context of a writing is of paramount importance if you want to interpret the writing correctly. Not only that, but it is important to understand what individual words and phrases meant in their own context—since words mean different things in different contexts. If you change the context of a word, or a phrase, you can completely change what the word or phrase means. Just to pick a single example. What would it mean if you called someone "the son of God"? In our modern context, if you were to say that Jesus is "the son of God," you almost certainly would mean that he is himself God, a member of the Trinity, closely related to God the Father from eternity past. But as it turns out, that is not what the phrase "son of God" meant to most people in the ancient world.

In ancient Judaism, for example, the "son of God" could be anyone—for example a human, or an angel—who was used by God in order to do his will on earth. In a passage that I mentioned earlier in this chapter, 2 Samuel 7, King David is told that he will always have a descendant ruling as king over the nation of Judah. Specifically, he is told that he will have a son (this is referring to his child Solomon, the next king after David); and God tells David, "I will be a father to him and he will be a son to me" (2 Samuel 7:14). Solomon, then, was the son of God. As were the other kings in Israel—as seen, for example, in Psalm 2, "I will tell of the decree of the Lord, He said to me 'You are my son, today I have begotten you.'" This is referring to the coronation ceremony of the king: on the day he became king, he then became the son of God. He was God's son because even though he was fully human, he mediated God's will to his people on earth.

This is a far cry from the Christian notion that the "Son of God" was a member of the Trinity from eternity past. It is the same phrase, but it means different things in different contexts.

In pagan contexts (remember: "pagans" were non-Jews, non-Christians who were polytheists—that is, worshipping many gods) the "son of God" had yet a different meaning, at least by the time of the New Testament. In Greek and Roman mythology a son of God was literally someone who was born to the sexual union of a divine being and a human being. In other words, a god like the Greek Zeus would have sex with a woman he desired (usually because she was gorgeous), and the child that was born would be half human, half divine—a **demi-god**. This is not at all what Christians later said about Jesus, both because his mother did not have sex with *anyone*, let alone God, and because he was not half human and half divine (according to later theologians) but fully human and fully divine. Still, if you were speaking to a Roman pagan and you said that someone was the "son of God," they would think you were referring to a demi-god, not to a member of the Trinity (they, of course, did not believe in the Trinity). Again: if you change the context of a word or phrase—or of a sentence, a paragraph, or a book—you change what it means.

And this makes understanding the Bible very difficult. It was not written in our context, in the twenty-first-century English-speaking world. It was written in an ancient context. Or rather, even more confusing, it was written in a large number of ancient contexts. Remember, the Bible contains books that were produced over an 800-year time span, written by different authors, to different audiences, for different reasons, and on different occasions. We have to know something about these different contexts, for each of the ancient writings, if we are to have any hope of understanding them.

The Texts of the Bible

As a final complication in the interpretation of the Bible, we need to consider the fact that we don't actually have the original writings of any of the books that were later considered Scripture. What I mean by this is that whoever wrote the book of Genesis—or the book of Proverbs, or the Gospel of Mark, or the letter of 1 John—produced his writing, and then someone copied it by hand. (There was no other way to get a copy in the years before desktop publishing, word processors, copy machines, or even carbon paper.) Then someone else copied it by hand. And someone else copied one of the copies. And someone else copied the copy of the copy. And someone else copied the copy of the copy of the copy. . . . We don't have the original writing, or the first copies, or the copies of the first copies. We have only later copies. And most of these later copies are much later than the originals; in fact, they are *centuries* after the originals.

The reason this matters is that everyone who copies a long text makes mistakes. And anyone who copies a copy with mistakes copies the mistakes. And makes his own mistakes. And whoever copies that mistaken copy of a mistaken copy copies the mistakes, and makes his own mistakes. And so on. For centuries. Most of the time these mistakes will be in small, picayune, insignificant details. But sometimes, on relatively rare occasions, they involve major changes of the text.

We will be examining this problem at greater length in chapter 15, for both the Hebrew Bible and the New Testament. For now we can consider just some of the basic issues.

THE HEBREW BIBLE   The Hebrew Bible that is available today—on which all English translations are based—is derived, for the most part, from a single **manuscript** (that is, a "handwritten copy") that dates to 1000 C.E. If parts of the Hebrew Bible were first written in the eighth century B.C.E. (e.g., Amos, Isaiah), then this copy is over 1700 years after the originals. We are fortunate that in the twentieth century a discovery of much older manuscripts was made, among the **Dead Sea Scrolls**—a collection of writings of various kinds, dating to about the time of before Jesus and a century before, discovered by accident by a Bedouin boy in a cave in the wilderness just west of the Dead Sea in what is now Israel. Among the Dead Sea Scrolls were copies of nearly all the books of the Bible; some of these copies were nearly complete (for example, the book of Isaiah); others of them were just in fragments. But all of them date to a time nearly a thousand years earlier than our otherwise oldest manuscript. This was a hugely significant find. It allows us to determine how accurately the Hebrew Bible was copied over the course of a thousand years after the beginning of Christianity.

In some instances it was copied very accurately indeed. In other instances it was not copied nearly as accurately. But the bigger problem still remains: we have no certain way of knowing how well the manuscripts were copied in the hundreds of years of copying *before* the time of the Dead Sea Scrolls. This means that we cannot know with complete certainty just what the original words of the ancient Israelite authors were. That obviously makes interpretation a rather tenuous matter. It is hard to know what an author meant by his words if you aren't sure which words he actually used.

THE NEW TESTAMENT Things are very different when it comes to the New Testament. In this case, we have no shortage of materials to work with. As opposed to the very few manuscripts of the Hebrew Bible from the Middle Ages, we have hundreds—thousands—of copies of the New Testament. Altogether we have over 5600 copies—either complete copies or fragmentary copies—of parts of the New Testament in the original Greek

language. That's the good news. The bad news is that many of these copies are very different from one another, as this or that scribe changed a word here or there, a phrase, an entire story. Words got added to the text. Words got taken out of the text. Words got changed in the text. And so scholars have to do their best to reconstruct what the authors originally wrote, given the fact that we do not have their original writings—or the first copies of their writings, or copies of the copies, or copies of the copies of the copies. It is a long and arduous task, and obviously extremely important, especially for those who think that the words matter. And that should include everyone who takes the Bible seriously, whether they are believers or not, since this, the most important book of Western civilization, means something very different depending on what words you find in the text.

CONCLUSION

To summarize our discussion to this point: there are all sorts of reasons to study the Bible. But there are also enormous complications that make this study difficult. These complications are especially acute for those who want to read the Bible not only for the religious lessons that it may convey, but also from a literary and a historical perspective—which are the perspectives we will be adopting for this book. I will say a few words to explain the difference between these various perspectives in the brief excursus that follows.

EXCURSUS THE BIBLE AND THE BELIEVER

Most of the people who are deeply interested in the Bible in modern American culture are committed Jews or Christians who have been taught that this is a book of sacred texts unlike other books. For many—especially many Christian believers—the Bible is the inspired word of God. In communities of faith that hold such views, the Biblical books are usually studied not from a literary perspective that takes seriously their genres, literary features, and the possible presence of discrepancies and inconsistencies, and even less from a historical perspective that asks whether they may contain historical difficulties and mistakes. You yourself

may find these literary and historical approaches to stand at odds with how you have been taught to approach the Bible. If so, then it is for you in particular that I want to provide these brief additional reflections in this excursus.

OUR LITERARY APPROACH

There are a great number of ways that one can approach any text—including the texts of the Bible—as literary works. In our approach we will be taking the Biblical writings seriously as pieces of ancient literature. We will look for such matters as the structure of the texts and their overarching literary themes, trying to determine how each writing can be understood through a careful reading that takes into account the flow of the narrative, the recurrence of important motifs, and the possibility that earlier sources have been used by an author in producing his account. In particular we will be keen to situate the various parts of the Bible in relationship to their appropriate literary genre, on the assumption that without knowing how a particular genre "works," it is impossible to know how a particular writing *in* that genre can be interpreted. We will need to learn, for example, about such things as Hebrew poetry, and proverbs, legends, myths, Gospels, and apocalypses.

Such literary approaches may strike readers as novel—as when we discuss some of the narratives of Genesis as "legends," or try to interpret the book of Revelation as a clear instance of an ancient "apocalypse." But we will see that such approaches can significantly illuminate the writings in question.

On a literary level we will also be stressing that each book (or part of a book) needs to be read for what it, itself, is saying. One of the key things we will notice is that there are many, many differences among the different parts of the Bible—and indeed, sometimes there are key differences even within a single book of the Bible. In some instances these differences represent tensions, discrepancies, and even contradictions. The reason to point out the contradictions between one author and another, or one book and another, or even one passage and another is not simply so the student can come away from the course saying, "See! The Bible is full of contradictions!" Quite the contrary, the discrepancies and contradictions in such a big book as the Bible alert us to the fact that the Bible is not a single book but is lots and lots of books, written by many different authors, at different times, in different places, for different purposes, to different audiences, in different contexts, even in different languages.

This kind of literary approach stresses that each writing needs to be read on its own terms, to be allowed to say what it has to say, without assuming that what one author, one book, or one part of a book is saying is exactly (or even approximately) the same as what some other is saying. As we will see, rather than hindering our study of these various writings that eventually became the Bible, these literary conclusions open up the possibility of new and exciting interpretations that would otherwise be impossible if we were to assume that every author and every book of the Bible were basically saying the same thing.

OUR HISTORICAL APPROACH

In addition to a literary approach to the Bible, we will be taking a historical approach. On one hand we will want to establish the historical setting of the writings of the Bible, to the best of our ability, determining when each writing was produced and within what social, cultural, and political context. These historical judgments will affect how we read and understand these texts, since if we take a text out if its own historical context we change its meaning (just as someone does when they take *your* words out of context). Without knowing that the book of Jeremiah was written in the sixth century B.C.E. during a time of national crisis, or that the Gospel of John was probably written in the last decade of the first century C.E., some sixty years after the events it narrates, we simply cannot understand them as the historical documents they are.

Our historical approach to the Bible will also involve asking how we can use literary works of the Bible to determine what really happened in the past—for example, in the history of ancient Israel, or in the life of Jesus, or in the experiences of the early church. This kind of historical question is made necessary, in part at least, by the literary fact I have just mentioned, that we have so many accounts that appear to have discrepancies among themselves. To determine which, if any, of the biblical sources is historically accurate in what it says, we will look to see if there are other, external sources that can verify or call into question the accounts of the Bible—for example, as they describe the exodus of the children of Israel from Egypt or the events surrounding the life and death of Jesus. And we will certainly want to consider what the findings of archaeology can tell us.

This kind of historical approach to the Bible is very different from a confessional approach (taken by *some* kinds of believers, but not all) that accepts everything the Bible says at face value and maintains that all of the historical events that it narrates actually happened in the way they are described. To expand a bit on the important difference between a historical and a confessional approach, I need to talk about what historians do and how they use sources—such as the books of the Bible—in their work.

(continued)

EXCURSUS THE BIBLE AND THE BELIEVER *(continued)*

Historians deal with past events that are matters of the public record. The public record consists of human actions and world events—things that anyone can see or experience. Historians try to reconstruct what probably happened in the past on the basis of data that can be examined and evaluated by every interested observer of every persuasion. Access to these data does not depend on presuppositions or beliefs about God. This means that historians, as historians, have no privileged access to what happens in the supernatural realm; they have access only to what happens in this, our natural world. The historian's conclusions should, in theory, be accessible and acceptable to everyone, whether the person is a Hindu, a Buddhist, a Muslim, a Jew, a Christian, an atheist, a pagan, or anything else. Unlike the kind of confessional approach that simply accepts the biblical accounts as describing what God did among the Israelites or in the lives of the early Christians, the historical approach asks what we can establish as probably happening without appealing to particular beliefs in God.

I can illustrate the point by considering some specific instances, first from outside the Bible. Historians can tell you the similarities and differences between the worldviews of Mohandas Gandhi and Martin Luther King Jr., but they cannot use their historical knowledge to tell you that Gandhi's belief in God was wrong or that Martin Luther King's was right. This judgment is not part of the public record and depends on theological assumptions and personal beliefs that are not shared by everyone conducting the investigation. Historians can describe to you what happened during the conflicts between Catholics and Lutherans in sixteenth-century Germany, but they cannot use their historical knowledge to tell you which side God was on. Likewise—moving to stories within the Bible—historians can tell you what may well have happened when the people of Israel entered into the Promised Land, but they cannot tell you that God empowered them to destroy their enemies. So too, historians can explain what probably happened at Jesus' crucifixion, but they cannot use their historical knowledge to tell you that he was crucified for the sins of the world.

Does that mean historians cannot be believers? No, it means that if historians tell you that Martin Luther King Jr. had a better theology than Gandhi, or that God was on the side of the Protestants instead of the Catholics, or that God destroyed the walls of Jericho, or that Jesus was crucified for the sins of the world, they are telling you this not in their capacity as historians but in their capacity as believers. Believers are interested in knowing about God, about how to behave, about what to believe, about the ultimate meaning of life. The historical disciplines cannot supply them with this kind of information. Historians who work within the constraints of their discipline are limited to describing, to the best of their abilities, what probably happened in the past.

Many such historians, including a large number of those mentioned in the bibliographies scattered throughout this book, find historical research to be completely compatible with—even crucial for—traditional theological belief; others find it to be incompatible. This is an issue that you yourself may want to deal with as you grapple intelligently with how the historical approach to the Bible affects your faith commitments positively, negatively, or not at all. I should be clear at the outset, though, that this book will neither tell you how to resolve this issue nor urge you to adopt any particular set of religious convictions. Our approach instead will be literary and historical, trying to understand the Bible as a set of literary texts that can be studied like all great literature and, from the perspective of history, using whatever evidence happens to survive in order to reconstruct what probably happened in the past.

That is to say, this book will not try to convince you either to believe or to disbelieve the faith claims of the Bible; it will describe what these claims are and how they came into existence. The book is not going to persuade you that Isaiah really did or did not have a vision of God, or that Jesus really was or was not the Son of God. It will try to establish what they both said, based on the historical data that are available. The book is not going to discuss whether the Bible is or is not the inspired word of God. It will show how we got this collection of books and indicate what these books say and reflect on how scholars have interpreted them. This kind of information may well be of some use for the reader who happens to be a believer; but it will certainly be useful to one—believer or not—who is interested in literature and history, and especially the literature and history of ancient Israel and of early Christianity.

At a Glance: What Is The Bible?

- There are not only religious reasons for wanting to study the Bible, but also historical and literary reasons.
- The Bible consists of **66** books: **39** in the Hebrew Bible and **27** in the New Testament (with Roman Catholic and Orthodox churches having a larger Old Testament canon).
- It is important to understand the broad sweep of the history of ancient Israel and the history of the early Christian church if we are to place the books of the Bible in their proper contexts.
- There are numerous problems connected with the study of the Bible: it is a very large book, written over

an 800-year period of time, in languages—Hebrew and Greek—largely unfamiliar to modern readers. Its books were produced by numerous different authors writing to different audiences for different reasons and with different perspectives. The Bible may contain internal discrepancies and cannot be verified, in places, through archaeology. Nonetheless, it is a terrifically important, powerful, and moving collection of writings.
- Our study of the Bible in this book will be from a historical and literary, not a confessional, point of view.

Take a Stand

1. You are talking to your roommate, who does not understand why you need to take a course on the Bible. In her opinion, the Bible is a very simple book to understand: all you have to do is read it and you can know what it means. Explain why you're interested in taking a course like this, and what—from what you've read so far—you expect you might be able to learn.

2. You tell the teacher of your Sunday School class that you are taking a course that studies the Bible from a historical and literary perspective, rather than from the perspective of faith. Your teacher thinks that this is a waste of time, since only someone with a religious commitment to the Bible can understand it. Do you agree or disagree? State your reasons why.

3. Your brother tells you that in his opinion all religions are, and always have been, basically the same. Based on what you've learned so far, do you buy it? Give him an alternative point of view that he needs to think about.

Key Terms

Ancient Near East, 8
Apocrypha, 20
Babylonian exile, 13
Canon, 4 .
Cult, 16
Dead Sea Scrolls, 25

Gentile, 13
Genre, 22
Gospels, 7
Holy of Holies, 18
Jew, 16
Kethuvim, 7

Major Prophets, 5
Messiah, 24
Manuscript, 25
Minor Prophets, 5
Nevi'im, 7
Pagan, 16

Pentateuch, 4
Prophet, 5
Septuagint, 24
Synagogue, 18
Tanakh, 7
Torah, 4

Suggestions for Further Reading

Coogan, Michael and Bruce Metzger, eds. *Oxford Companion to the Bible*. New York: Oxford University Press, 1993. A superb dictionary of all things biblical, ideal for both beginning and advanced students.

Freedman, David Noel, ed. *The Anchor Bible Dictionary*. New York: Doubleday, 1992. This is a six-volume dictionary with articles covering every major aspect of biblical studies. A highly valuable research tool for all serious students.

May, James L., ed. *HarperCollins Bible Commentary*. San Francisco: HarperSanFrancisco, 2000. A one-volume commentary on every book of the Bible; a great reference work for anyone wanting help with difficult passages.

Powell, Mark Allan, ed. *HarperCollins Bible Dictionary*. New York: HarperOne, 2011. An excellent one-volume dictionary covering all the important topics of relevance to the study of the Bible.

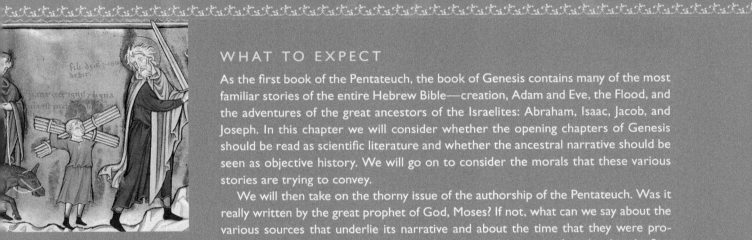

2

The Book of Genesis

WHAT TO EXPECT

As the first book of the Pentateuch, the book of Genesis contains many of the most familiar stories of the entire Hebrew Bible—creation, Adam and Eve, the Flood, and the adventures of the great ancestors of the Israelites: Abraham, Isaac, Jacob, and Joseph. In this chapter we will consider whether the opening chapters of Genesis should be read as scientific literature and whether the ancestral narrative should be seen as objective history. We will go on to consider the morals that these various stories are trying to convey.

We will then take on the thorny issue of the authorship of the Pentateuch. Was it really written by the great prophet of God, Moses? If not, what can we say about the various sources that underlie its narrative and about the time that they were produced? And what can we say about the relationship of the stories found in this, the first book of the Bible, with narratives found in other cultures of the ancient Near East?

The book of Genesis is one of the most widely read and influential books in history. Here is where we find some of the great stories known throughout our culture: the story of creation, of Adam and Eve, Cain and Abel, Noah and the Flood, stories of the great Israelite ancestors Abraham and Sarah, Isaac and Rebekah, Jacob and Rachel, Joseph and his brothers. Readers have long enjoyed these tales and have taken them with the utmost seriousness. In some parts of America today, the book continues to be read as a scientific textbook explaining how our world and life itself came into existence, and as a historically accurate description of the lives of the fathers and mothers of the faith. In this chapter we will discuss whether these are the best ways to understand this great work of ancient Hebrew literature.

We have already seen that Genesis is the first book of the Torah, which is also known as the Pentateuch; that is, "the five scrolls," referring to the books of Genesis, Exodus, Leviticus, Numbers, and Deuteronomy. The term *"torah"* is sometimes translated as "law," and these five books go under that designation because a very large portion of them contain the Law that was given to Moses on Mount Sinai, a Law that became the very basis for Jewish worship and communal life together. But the word *"torah"* more properly means something like "direction" or "instruction." The instruction given by these books is provided not only in the Ten Commandments and the other laws given to Moses, but also in the stories they tell and the lessons these stories convey. The book of Genesis is almost all about stories, and great stories they are.

The English title of the book is highly appropriate. The term "genesis" refers to the "origin" or "coming into being" of something. It is conceptually related to the Hebrew title for the book, "In the Beginning." These are the opening words of the book in Hebrew, and in fact the entire book is about beginnings and origins: the beginnings of the material world, of humans, of civilization, and of the nation of Israel.

Not only has this book exerted an enormous influence on Western culture, but its literary narratives and the historical problems they present can give us insights into the entire Pentateuch: its accuracy, historical value, sources, and authorship. The traditional view of Genesis is that it, like the rest of the Pentateuch, was written by Moses in the thirteenth century B.C.E. This view is many centuries old: it was the view of most, possibly all, Jews by the time of Jesus, as attested in a number of different writings from the time. As we will see, modern scholarship has challenged this view. Scholars now generally think that the book was not written by a single individual but that it, like the rest of the Pentateuch, is made up of a number of earlier sources, each composed at different times in the history of ancient Israel and edited together into a single narrative sometime in the sixth century B.C.E.—some 700 years after Moses was dead and gone.

THE CONTENTS OF GENESIS AND THE CHALLENGES THEY POSE

We have already seen that the book of Genesis can be roughly divided into two parts:

1. Chapters 1–11 contain what is called the **Primeval History**—the events that transpire at the beginning of time; and
2. Chapters 12–50 present the **Ancestral History**—the stories of the great patriarchs (i.e., forefathers) and matriarchs of ancient Israel.

Especially when talking about the Primeval History, we are using the term "history" in a very loose sense, simply to refer to events that an author thought had happened in the past. In this case it is the remote past, at the beginning of time. Later we will ask whether it makes sense to try to understand the stories of Genesis as historical in the more commonly accepted sense of the term—as things that really happened as described—or whether there are better ways to make sense of them.

The Primeval History

I will not provide a full and exhaustive summary of all that happens in the Primeval History—or for any of the other portions of the Bible we examine. I will instead assume that you have read the material yourself, carefully, several times, in order to familiarize yourself with it. Here I will simply mention some of the highlights by way of refreshing your memory and making sure we are all on the same page.

BRIEF SUMMARY OF THE HIGHLIGHTS

- *The Creation of the World.* Genesis 1 gives the famous account of God's creation of the world and all that is in it. There are actually ten stages of creation, starting with the famous words "And God said, 'Let there be light,' and there was light" (1:3). The ten stages of creation are (1) light; (2) firmament; (3) dry land; (4) plants; (5) sun, moon, and stars; (6) water animals; (7) birds; (8) land animals; (9) humans; and (10) a day of rest. What is striking is that these ten events are organized according to seven days; on most days God creates one thing; on two days he creates two things; on the final day he creates nothing, but takes it as a day of rest.
- *Adam and Eve* (chapters 2–3). The first man (Hebrew word: "adam") is formed by the LORD God out of the soil of the earth ("adamah"); the LORD God then creates animals to be his companions but since none is suitable for him, the LORD God takes a rib from Adam and forms it into a woman. The two are in the Garden of Eden until they eat the forbidden fruit (at the instigation of the serpent) and are cast out of Eden as a result.
- *Cain and Abel* (chapter 4). The first two sons of Adam and Eve are born and, as adults, Cain out of jealousy murders his brother Abel and is forced outside of his land.
- *The Flood of Noah* (chapters 6–9). The earth becomes populated and wicked, so God decides to destroy it by a worldwide flood. He chooses Noah to save as a righteous man and instructs

him to build an enormous ark, on which he is to bring pairs of every living species, along with his own family. All other living things are destroyed, and after the flood the human race starts over again.

- *The Tower of Babel* (chapter 11). The human race decides to build a large city with a tall tower so as to reach up to heaven (where God dwells); but God confounds the project by confusing their languages, so that now rather than being able to talk with one another they all sound as if they are "babbling." This is the beginning of different languages and different forms of human civilization over the earth.

A literary and historical study of Genesis has to ask: what kind of literature is this Primeval History? On the surface, for example, Genesis 1–2 seems to be an attempt to explain how the world, and humans, really came into existence. That is, it appears, at least, to be something like an ancient scientific treatise. But can we take it to be some kind of science? The rest of the Primeval History seems to present a historical account of very ancient events and people. And is that the best way to understand it—as some kind of history? For many years, biblical scholars have argued that there are insurmountable problems with thinking of these chapters as either science or history—at least as those terms are now used.

THE PRIMEVAL HISTORY: THE CHALLENGES OF SCIENCE Throughout parts of America today, the Primeval History of Genesis is taken literally, as a factual description of what happened at the creation of the world and the appearance

FIGURE 2.1. First day of Creation (separation of light from darkness); second day (separation of waters from firmament); third day (plants); fourth day (sun, moon and stars) (Genesis, 1:3–19).

of life and of humans on earth. Sometimes this view even seeps into science curricula in schools, so that students learn that the world and all life was literally created in six 24-hour days, that Adam and Eve were real people and the first two humans—no Big Bang, no billions of years to form the planets, no evolution of life forms. More scientifically inclined readers of Genesis sometimes try to reconcile the accounts of the Primeval History with the claims of science—for example, by saying that the six "days" of creation were actually geological periods of billions of years, or that Adam and Eve were the first *Homo sapiens*, not the first humanoids.

For most biblical scholars, though, the reality is that Genesis is not a science book and the author(s) of Genesis had no more knowledge of the modern scientific account of how the universe, and human life, came into being than of rocket science, quantum physics, or the latest iPad technology. This is an ancient book with an ancient point of view, not a modern book with a modern point of view. You yourself can see whether the accounts of the Primeval History gel with the claims of science by considering the following points:

- In Genesis, the entire universe and all life forms on earth are created in six literal days. These do not appear to be geological periods. Notice how they are marked: "there was evening and morning, the first day." These seem to be 24-hour days that have evenings and mornings; they begin at night (as in traditional Jewish reckoning) and end during the day.

- These evenings and mornings happen before there was a sun, moon, or stars. It is hard to imagine where the light was supposed to come from without any of these celestial phenomena (it cannot be from the Big Bang, as those who want to reconcile the account with science claim; the Big Bang did not create evenings and mornings!). The point is that this author does not appear to be giving us a scientific description.

- Plant life, in this account, is created on earth before there was a sun. But according to modern science, plant life requires the sun.

- The various species are created as fully developed; they do not evolve, in contrast to the views of modern science.

- So too, each creature is a separate creation, not a related species.

- Humans ("adam" in chapter 2) are formed from dirt, rather than evolved from lower life forms; and "woman" is formed in a separate act of creation, from Adam's rib.

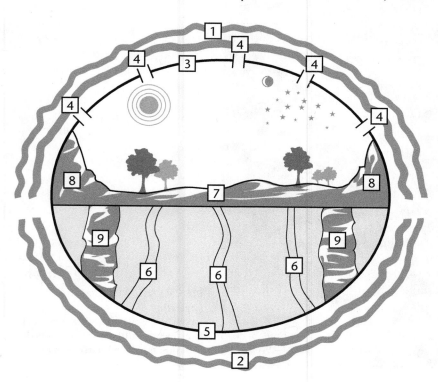

FIGURE 2.2. This is a diagram of how ancient Israelites understood the world, as it is described in the creation account of Genesis 1. Around the world is water, both above (1) and below (2) where the earth itself is. The water is kept out of the world by the firmament, both above the earth (3) and beneath it (5); but the water comes down, in the form of rain, when holes open in the firmament (4), and it comes up, in the form of rivers, lakes, and oceans from below (6). The dry land, or earth (7), is between the waters; according to other parts of the Bible, the mountains on earth (8) support the upper firmament, and the earth itself is supported from below by pillars (9).

BOX 2.1 CREATION IN 4004 B.C.E.?

In 1650 C.E., an Irish archbishop and scholar, James Ussher, engaged in a detailed study of when the world began. Ussher based his calculations on the genealogies of the Bible, starting with those in the book of Genesis (which state not only who begat whom but also indicate, in many instances, how long each of the people thus begotten lived) and a detailed study of other ancient sources, such as Babylonian and Roman history. On these grounds, he argued that the world was created in 4004 B.C.E.—in fact, humans were created on the sixth day at noon on October 23. This chronology became dominant throughout Western Christendom. It was printed widely in King James Bibles and continues to be believed by non-evolutionarily minded Christians today.

This has been a useful dating for many Christians since that time. For many centuries—going back in fact to the early second century C.E.—there have been Christians who thought that the world would last for 6000 years. The reason is a bit complicated. According to a passage in the New Testament, "with the Lord, one day is like a thousand years, and a thousand years are like one day" (2 Peter 3:8; based on Psalms 90:4). Now, if the creation took God six days to complete, and each day is a thousand years, then the creation must be destined to last a thousand years. Right? That would mean it would all end about 2000 years after Jesus was born.

Why, though, did Archbishop Ussher not simply round things off a bit and opt for the year 4000 B.C.E., say,

sometime in late afternoon? It was because he realized full well that there was a problem or two with our modern calendars. The calendar we use was invented in the sixth century C.E. by a Christian monk named Dionysius Exiguus (whose name translates into English as "Dennis the Short"). Dionysius began the new era (C.E. or A.D.) with the year 1. He had no alternative option to that, since the concept of zero was not mathematically worked out yet in the sixth century, and so the first year could not have been 0. But even more than that, Dionysius Exiguus miscalculated the date of Jesus' birth, from which the era had its beginning. For if Jesus was in fact an infant during the reign of King Herod—as related by both Matthew and Luke in the New Testament—then he must have been born no later than 4 B.C.E., the year of Herod's death. This creates a problem, of course, for those who continue to work with the abbreviations A.D. (anno domini: Latin for The Year of our Lord) and B.C. (Before Christ)—since, as sometimes noted, according to the calendar we use, Jesus was actually born four years Before Christ!

The larger problem, though, for literalistic Christians who believe that the universe came into being not some thirteen billion years ago, as modern astronomers maintain, but in 4004 B.C.E., as Ussher claimed, and who think that the world is supposed to exist for exactly six thousand years based on the six days of creation in Genesis, is that it should have ended already, by noon on October 23, 1997.

• The account of the flood presupposes a flood over the entire earth, which is physically impossible (no matter *how* much it rains) and in contradiction to the geological record.

Whether Genesis 1–2 was meant by its author to be an *ancient* account of science is an interesting question to entertain. But for most readers it is clear that if it is meant as science, it is ancient and not modern science, which, with its Big Bang and theory of evolution, has a very different account of how the universe and humans arrived on the scene.

THE PRIMEVAL HISTORY: THE CHALLENGES OF "HISTORY" Not only do some readers of Genesis take the Primeval History as presenting

scientific fact, some also take it as historically reliable: there really were an Adam and Eve and a Cain and Abel; there really was a Noah's ark; there really was a Tower of Babel. As I have already indicated, biblical scholars call the first eleven chapters of Genesis a Primeval "History" in only the loosest sense. These chapters describe events in primitive, prehistoric times. But many modern readers find them hard to accept as real history or as real science. To explain why this is so, I need to say something about the nature of historical research and about how historians reconstruct what happened in the past.

"History" is the reconstruction of the past based on surviving evidence. In order to reconstruct what happened in earlier periods of history, historians need evidence. This evidence normally involves human observers who have reported what they have experienced, or material evidence that gives a good indication of what has taken place. Unfortunately, we do not have either kind of access to the events narrated in the Primeval History. And the accounts, looked at from a strictly historical point of view, appear to be riddled with other kinds of problems. Consider the following points:

- For parts of Genesis—for example, the creation story of Genesis 1—there were not and could not be any human observers.
- For the other parts, we have no record from anyone allegedly living at the time (if these books were written by Moses, it was many thousands of years after the events; or, if we trust the findings of science, billions of years).
- We have no material record of any of the alleged events: no evidence of a Garden of Eden (with

a flaming sword at its entrance to keep out potential visitors); no geological record of a worldwide flood.

- The account makes claims that seem to many readers implausible. As just one example: these ancestors of the human race live inordinately long lives, far longer than humanly possible. Adam lived 930 years; Seth, 912 years; Kenan, 910 years; and the world's all-time oldest man, Methuselah, 969 years. These accounts also include an episode of snakes that talk (in the Garden of Eden) and, apparently, walk (since God later deprives the snake of its legs).
- Many readers believe that the accounts lack concern for plausibility:
  - At the beginning the only people are Adam, Eve, Cain, and Abel. Cain kills Abel, and God exiles Cain from the land. Cain is afraid that whoever finds him in his wanderings will kill

BOX 2.2 THE THREE-STORIED UNIVERSE

The mythical thought world of ancient writers—including the writers of the Bible—was entirely different from the one we inhabit today. Nowhere does that become more clear and obvious than in considering their "**cosmology**"—their understanding of the world we live in. Modern cosmologists tell us that our little planet is part of a solar system circling a rather average star in a galaxy with something like 200 billion stars; that there are some 100 billion other galaxies; and that this is just within our own universe. There may, in fact, be many, many universes (the so-called multiverse). The ancients literally had no idea at all that things were like that. The authors of Genesis were no exception. They lived (they thought) in what we might call a simple three-storied universe.

For them, of course, the earth was not part of a solar system of planets circling around the sun. The earth was the center of the universe. When God created the universe, he first formed a "firmament"—that is, a solid boundary—to separate the "waters above from the waters below" (Genesis 1:6-7). This firmament is the sky (Genesis 1:8). Above the sky is water. That's why it rains, when there are holes in the sky. And below the dry ground (which God made to appear the next day) there is also water. That's why there are rivers and oceans and lakes—it is the water from

underneath seeping up. And that's our world. Note: God did not create the water. It was there already, but was a huge chaotic mess. His creation involved separating it to make room for "earth." (See Figure 2.2).

When Noah's flood came, it was not simply that it rained a lot. God was reverting the world back to the chaos that existed before the creation when the whole thing was water. And so water came down, and water came up (see Genesis 7:11). It was a very dangerous situation.

In ancient three-storied cosmologies, God lives up above the sky, we live down here on the dry land, and the dead live somewhere underneath us. Up, down, and the middle. That may be why it was a problem when the people of earth wanted to build a tall tower in Genesis 11. They were getting up close to where God was; a bit further and they would have been there. And so God had to confuse their languages so they could no longer communicate with each other and complete the task. God didn't want any mortal company up there.

We will find a similar cosmology in the New Testament. When Jesus dies, he goes down to the realm of the dead. And then he is raised up back to the land of the living. And then he ascends further up to the realm of God. Why does Jesus physically go "up"? Because that's where God is, up there, above the sky.

him (4:14). But who will find him? There are only three humans on earth at this point.

- Cain then goes out and marries a wife (4:17). But where did she come from?
- Cain's first son builds a city (4:17). A city? There are only five people on the planet (Adam, Eve, Cain, and Cain's wife and son).

- There appear to be numerous internal contradictions among the stories, which have made many readers question their historical plausibility. Chief among these are the tensions between the two accounts of creation in Genesis 1 and 2, as we will discuss later, and apparent internal discrepancies in the story of the Flood.

- Much of the narrative involves activities of the divinity (or divinities. Notice 1:26, "Let us make humankind." Us? There appears to be more than one divine being involved. See also 6:2, "the sons of God"—who appear to be supernatural divine beings). The problem is that historians—as we saw in the excursus in chapter 1—cannot establish what happens in the supernatural, divine realm, but only in the human realm.

THE PRIMEVAL HISTORY AS LITERARY MYTH

From a literary perspective it should be clear that it is a real challenge to consider the Primeval History either as science or as history in the normally accepted meanings of the terms. But that is not to denigrate the narrative. Not in the least! These are terrific, moving, and powerful stories. But they are probably best understood to be stories, not scientific explanations or historical accounts. More specifically, these stories can be best appreciated when they are recognized as myths.

The term "myth" should not be taken in a negative sense. It can be used in a very positive sense. A brief working definition of **myth** would be "a story about God or the gods and their activities, which tries to make sense of the world and our place in it." Myths are common to nearly all religions and all peoples. Unlike scientific and historical claims, myths by their very nature are not susceptible of proof or demonstration. You can't show that they really happened. What matters for myths are the *truth claims* that they make. These truth claims are not subject to verification or disproof; they are rooted in beliefs about the world, and they attempt to convey these beliefs in imaginative stories. And the Primeval History of Genesis is nothing if not imaginative stories. These are stories that no doubt were told and retold over the years by word of mouth, in what we might call the **oral tradition**. As they were passed down over the centuries from one storyteller to another, they were changed, shaped, formed, improved, lengthened—all in an attempt to make them convey important points that the various storytellers wanted to make. One should not say that these stories are "just" myths. They should be celebrated as myths because myths can convey very powerful lessons.

When read as myths instead of as science or history, these stories can convey some of the following lessons (and many more, if you dig deeper):

- The **Sabbath** day is rooted in the very fabric of creation. Ancient and modern Jews observe the Sabbath. For them, the seventh day of the week is to be a day of rest, when no work is to be done. It is a holiday, once a week, every week. Among (many) other things, the account of creation in Genesis 1 is designed to show that the idea of a Sabbath day was present at the very beginning of things and written into the fabric of existence. I pointed out that there were ten acts of creation in Genesis 1. You might wonder why, then, the creation did not take ten days, since most of the acts of creation took an entire day. It appears that the author of this account took an earlier description of creation and condensed it, so that rather than taking place in ten discrete time periods, it took place in seven. And why have nine events of creation occur in six days instead of nine? It is so the Creator could have the seventh day as a day of rest. This means that the idea of a day of rest is written into the creation itself; it is not simply some kind of human rule invented by someone who thought taking a day off every week would be a good idea. God himself rested on the seventh day, on the first seventh day in the history of the universe, and from then on every seventh day was to be a day of rest.
- Humans are superior to all other kinds of life. Whether you agree with this view or not, Genesis 1:26 is clear in stating that the humans, both male and female, were created as the pinnacle of creation and were given "dominion" over all other forms of life. Nothing else living is as important to God as humans—who are created in the "image" of God, meaning, apparently, that they, unlike other creatures, are made to be very

BOX 2.3 SONS OF GOD AND THE DAUGHTERS OF MEN

One of the most mysterious and even bizarre stories in Genesis happens right at the beginning of the Flood narrative (chapter 6), where we are told that the "sons of God" looked down among the human "daughters," saw that they were beautiful, and came down and had sex with them leading to the Nephilim. The word "nephilim" means "fallen ones." According to Numbers 13:33, the Nephilim were giants. Apparently, for the story in Genesis 6, there were angelic beings (the "sons of God") who lusted after human women, and their offspring were giants. It is at that point that God decides to destroy the world.

This brief episode has parallels in other ancient mythologies. It is common in Greek myths, for example, for one of the gods to find a particular woman irresistibly attractive, to come down in human guise, have sex with her, and then to have an offspring that is something more than mortal. One of the most famous stories about such a liaison involves the king of the gods, Zeus, who sees a gorgeous woman, Alcmene, and decides he has to have her. Her husband, Amphitryon, is a general in the Greek army who is away at war. Not able to control himself, Zeus comes to Alcmene in the spitting image of Amphitryon himself. Alcmene assumes that her husband has returned from battle, welcomes him with open arms, and takes him to bed. Zeus enjoys the festivities so much that he orders the constellations to stop in their paths, so as to prolong the night.

When Zeus finally has his fill, and the constellations begin again to move, he returns to heaven. As it turns out, that is exactly when Amphitryon returns home—dismayed and distraught that Alcmene is not overjoyed at seeing him after his long absence, not understanding of course that she thinks she has just spent a wild and very long night frolicking in his arms.

In any event Alcmene has been made pregnant by Zeus. And who is her child? None other than the demi-god Heracles (in Latin: Hercules). (See Box 11.3.)

---

much like God. And as God exercises authority over all creation, humans are to exercise authority over all other forms of life.

- Unlike other living creatures, humans have come to know the difference between good and evil (having eaten the forbidden fruit). But unlike God, humans are inclined to do the wrong rather than the right. That is the clear message of the Garden of Eden, where the wily snake (who is not identified as Satan in the story) convinces an easily convinced Eve to eat the forbidden fruit (which is not called an apple); and it is even clearer in the aftermath, in the story of Cain and Abel, where jealousy drives Cain to murder his own brother. There are only four people on earth at this point: two of them directly disobey the one thing God commanded them not to do, and one of them commits fratricide. Things do not look good for the human race.

- Disobedience to God brings severe punishment. For their disobedience, Adam and Eve get expelled from paradise. For murdering his brother, Cain is cast out from his land to be a sojourner on the earth. And later, for the widespread wickedness of the human race, God decides to destroy the entire lot of them by bringing a flood to annihilate all life except what Noah can save on the ark. For the author of these accounts, sin is serious business—a matter of life and death.

There is much, much more that we could say about the literary lessons of the Primeval History. It would be easy to write an entire textbook on these eleven chapters alone. But as you familiarize yourself with the stories by reading and rereading them, seeing them not as science and not as history but as literary myth, you will yourself see more and more what the ultimate objectives and points of the stories are. They are brilliant accounts about the beginning of life and are meant to teach their readers serious theological lessons about what life in this world is all about.

The Ancestral History

As we move into the Ancestral History of Genesis 12–50, we shift gears from writings about the very beginnings of human life and civilization to writings about the ancestors of Israel. Here are stories that can presumably be situated in the history of the ancient Near East, with its migrations of populations, settlements in the land that was to become Israel, kings and pharaohs, and interactions among tribes of people competing for limited resources. Before discussing the historical character of these stories—did they really happen?—I will again provide a brief summary of some of the highlights. Once more I am assuming that you have read and reread these fascinating chapters, so that what I provide here is simply a reminder of some of the key moments (not mentioning each and every episode).

BRIEF SUMMARY OF THE HIGHLIGHTS

- The Call of Abraham, chapter 12. Abraham, who at this point of the story is named Abram, is told by God to leave his country (he started out in Ur, in the land that later was to become Babylonia) and go to the land of Canaan, where God would make of him a great nation; that is, by giving him innumerable descendants whom God would bless. We are not told why God chose Abram in particular but he was, as a result of this calling, to become the father of the nation of Israel.
- The Covenant with Abraham, chapter 15. Abram, now in the land of Canaan, is concerned that despite God's earlier promise, he has no son. God speaks with him and reassures him that his descendants will be as numerous as the stars, and he makes a **covenant** with Abram that these descendants will inherit the land of Canaan as their own.
- The Birth of Ishmael, chapter 16. Abram and his wife Sarah (named Sarai at this point of the narrative) are concerned that no child is forthcoming, and so she gives him her maidservant, Hagar, to have sex with so he can have his progeny. The result of their union is Ishmael; but after Ishmael is born, God informs Abram that in fact the promise would be fulfilled by a child born of Sarah.
- Abraham Gets Older, chapter 17. In fact, he gets really old. Abram is 99 years old, Sarah is 90, and still there is no child. God makes a covenant with Abram that he will have numerous descendants, changes his name to Abraham, which was widely taken to mean "father of a multitude," and gives him the sign of the covenant: all of his male descendants are to be circumcised to show they belong to the covenant God has made.
- Sodom and Gomorrah, chapter 19. Among the interesting intervening stories scattered throughout these chapters is the account of Sodom and Gomorrah, two cities that God destroys for their exceeding wickedness. He saves from them only Abraham's nephew Lot, Lot's wife, and their two daughters. But Lot's wife disobeys instructions for escape given to them by angels, looks back upon the cities while in flight, and is turned into a pillar of salt.
- Birth of Isaac, chapter 21. Finally, in fulfillment of his promise God allows Sarah to become pregnant and she bears Abraham a son, Isaac.
- The Sacrifice of Isaac, chapter 22. In one of the most moving stories of the entire Bible, Abraham is instructed to offer up his son Isaac as a human sacrifice to God—the very son that God had for so long promised to give him as the start of innumerable descendants. Abraham is obedient to God's demand and prepares to slaughter his son, only to be stopped at the last second by an angel who informs him that God is satisfied that he will obey him no matter what the consequences.
- Isaac and Rebekah, chapter 24. Abraham arranges for his son Isaac to marry a woman from his own relatives back in his original home city, rather than one of the local Canaanite women. The arranged marriage with Rebekah takes place.
- Jacob and Esau, chapters 25–27. Rebekah bears Isaac twins, Esau (the first born, and so the one who is to inherit his father's property) and Jacob. Jacob manages to swindle the birthright away from Esau and to receive his father's ultimate blessing. His name will later be changed to "Israel," which means "one who wrestled with God."
- Jacob and His Family, chapters 29–35. Over the course of a number of years, Jacob marries two sisters, the plain Leah and the beautiful Rachel, and with the two of them, along with two of their maidservants, he has twelve sons. These twelve (more or less) will become the heads of what will be the twelve tribes of Israel.
- The Joseph Stories, chapters 37–50. One of the younger sons, Joseph, is the favorite of Jacob, and out of jealousy his brothers sell him into slavery to Egypt. But God is with Joseph and through a series of intriguing and providential events, Joseph becomes second in command to the Pharaoh, king of Egypt. Meanwhile, the rest of the family back in Canaan begins to suffer from a persistent drought and famine, so they go to Egypt to beg for food. Joseph is in position to supply it but keeps his identity secret from his brothers, who have no clue that they are dealing with the sibling they had so abused. Finally Joseph reveals his identity, the family is restored together, and the entire clan settles in Egypt under Joseph's protection.

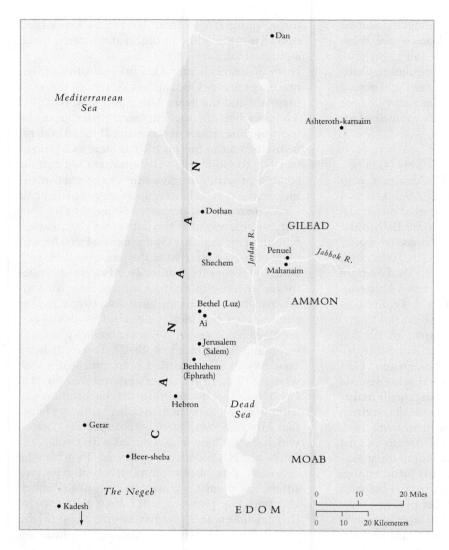

FIGURE 2.3. The land of Canaan and the places mentioned in Genesis in connection with the ancestors of Israel.

THE PATRIARCHAL HISTORY: THE CHALLENGES OF "HISTORY" Over the centuries, Jewish and Christian readers of Genesis 12–50 have taken its stories as historical descriptions of what really happened to the patriarchs and matriarchs of ancient Israel. Many modern scholars, however, have pointed out problems with taking the accounts as descriptions of things that really happened the way they are described. There are three kinds of problems that are commonly noted:

- *Anachronisms*: An **anachronism** is an event, institution, phenomenon, item, or anything else mentioned in a story that does not fit into the time period that the story presupposes. As a modern example, if a letter supposedly written by a seventeenth-century settler in Colonial America mentioned "the United States," you would know you have problems. According to any sensible time frame for the stories of the Patriarchal History, Abraham must have been living—if he indeed lived—sometime in the eighteenth century B.C.E. Scholars arrive at this date by counting backward from dates that are relatively secure (e.g., if David was King around the year 1000, and the conquest of Canaan had taken place 250 years or so before that, and the exodus 40 years before that . . .). But there are features of the stories that can't be fit into that framework—or even into the framework of the thirteenth century B.C.E., when Moses allegedly wrote these accounts. For example:

- The nation of the Philistines, mentioned in chapters 21 and 26, does not appear on the scene of history until the twelfth century B.C.E.
- So too the city of Beersheba, mentioned in the Isaac stories, was not settled until the twelfth century B.C.E.
- The Arameans, mentioned in the stories about Jacob, are not attested until the eleventh century B.C.E.
- Camels, who figure in several of these stories, were not actually domesticated in this part of the world until the eleventh century B.C.E.

These are just a few examples. If historians are right about these claims, then it is difficult to see how these stories could be accepted as historically accurate in their details.

- *Internal inconsistencies*: The stories of the Patriarchal History appear to contain numerous internal discrepancies. Some of these are indeed hard to reconcile: you can see this for yourself by looking up passages (see below). Scholars have observed that inconsistences like these typically occur when stories that had been passed down as oral tradition over long periods of time come to be written down by someone who does not recognize that the details in one part of the account do not gel with those of another part. As some examples (read these for yourself in context):
  - The patriarch Jacob is renamed "Israel" in 32:28, and told that he will no longer be called Jacob; but then he *is* called Jacob in 33:1 and, yet more oddly, in 35:10 is name is changed from Jacob to Israel (as if it hadn't already been changed).
  - Jacob's son Benjamin is said in one place to have been born in the town of Bethlehem

FIGURE 2.4. A relief from Egypt showing young men being circumcised (from around 2200 B.C.E.); ancient Israelites were not the only society to practice circumcision.

(35:16) and in another place in Paddan-aram (35:26).

- Joseph is said to have been "the" son of Jacob's old age (37:3) even though the narrative indicates that in fact Benjamin was the last son to be born.
- When Joseph has a dream of grandeur in which the sun, moon, and eleven stars bow down to him, Jacob asks, incredulously, whether he really thinks that his father, mother, and brothers would all reverence him (37:10). But according to the narrative, his mother was already dead.
- When Joseph's brothers sell him to a caravan of traders heading toward Egypt, is it made up of Midianites (descended from Abraham's son Midian, 25:2; see 37:28, 36) or of Ishmaelites (descended from his other son Ishmael, chapter 26; 37:25-27)?
- Who then sells Joseph to Egypt? The Midianites (37:36) or the Ishmaelites (39:1)?

- *Doublets:* A doublet occurs when the same story, with only some details changed, is told on two occasions in a narrative. This typically happens with oral traditions that are written down, as several versions of the same incident are told over the years. As just two examples from the Patriarchal History:
  - The Covenant with Abraham. In 17:2 the LORD tells Abraham that he "will" make a covenant with him, that he will have multiple descendants. This statement may strike careful readers as strange, since in 15:18 God had *already* "made a covenant with Abraham" and had already promised to give him innumerable descendants.
  - The Wife Who Is Just a Sister. In chapter 12 Abraham and Sarah go to a foreign land (Egypt) and he instructs her to say that she is his sister, rather than his wife, for fear that the authorities might kill him for her. She is taken into Pharaoh's household, apparently as part of his harem, but God informs Pharaoh of the real situation. Pharaoh confronts Abraham, and then lets him go. In chapter 20 virtually the same thing happens with Abraham and Sarah but this time it is in Gerar, ruled by the king Abimelech. And in chapter 26 it happens yet a third time, again in Gerar with Abimelech, but this time it is with Isaac and Rebekah. Here is not simply a doublet but a triplet: the

same basic story told on three different occasions with this or that detail changed.

All of these problems—the anachronisms, internal inconsistencies, and doublets—are taken by many readers to show that in the stories of the Patriarchal History we are not dealing with an objective account of what really transpired in the eighteenth century B.C.E. But possibly the stories are not meant to be read as purely historical narratives. In fact, a good case can be made that with these stories we are not dealing with history but with legends.

THE PATRIARCHAL HISTORY AS LEGEND

Whereas "myths" involve activities of God or the gods, "legends" have to do with people who could, in theory, be actual historical persons. The following may serve as a brief working definition of **legend**: "Fictional narratives about real or alleged historical figures told in order to entertain, to teach a moral, and/or to explain why things are as they are."

No one can doubt that the patriarchal narratives are entertaining. Abraham's (near) sacrifice of Isaac, Jacob's stealing of Esau's birthright, Joseph's adventures in Egypt—these are among the great stories of Western civilization. They also are designed to teach a moral, in case after case (I will give a few examples in a moment). And many of them are designed to explain why things are as they are: why do we Israelites practice circumcision? (It was the covenant that God made with our forefather, Abraham.) Where did the Midianites come from? (They are our distant relatives, descendants from Abraham's son Midian.) What is that pillar of salt doing here in the wilderness? (It was Lot's wife, who was punished for looking back at the destruction of Sodom and Gomorrah.) What is this shrine? (It was placed here by our ancestor Jacob, after he wrestled with an angel.) And so on.

From a literary point of view, the legends of the Patriarchal History function on two levels: as part of the bigger story of Israel on one hand, and as individual stories with individual "moral lessons" on the other. In terms of the bigger story these legends, passed down over the years in the oral traditions among storytellers of ancient times, fulfilled several overarching functions. Here I might mention two:

In part, the entire narrative is designed to explain where the people of Israel came from. When these stories were written down in later centuries, as we will see, there was a group of people living in the land identified as Israel who understood themselves to be related to one another by blood and to have had a common history with one another. These stories indicate what that common history was and where this group of people originally came from. From a literary point of view, whether this accounting of the origins of the people of Israel is historically accurate or not is more or less beside the point. What matters—and what mattered for the storytellers—is that these accounts provided a plausible explanation of how they came into existence as a people.

The very beginning of this story in Gen 12:1–3 is absolutely fundamental to this explanation:

> Now the LORD said to Abram, "Go from your country and your kindred and your father's house to the land that I will show you. I will make of you a great nation, and I will bless you, and make your name great, so that you will be a blessing. I will bless those who bless you, and the one who curses you I will curse; and in you all the families of the earth shall be blessed."

For this legend, the beginnings of the people of Israel was not a matter of historical happenstance or accident. It was part of the plan of the Lord God himself. Out of all the nations of the earth, God chose one man and promised that his descendants would be great. And numerous. And blessed. They would be the unique people of God. Anyone who opposed them would be opposed by God. And it would be through this group of descendants, this clan that sprang from the loins of Abraham, that the entire world would be blessed. They would be the Chosen Ones of God. That is quite a legend to tell about one's own people. Those telling these stories were indicating that they, the people of Israel at the time, were divinely ordained as the special ones chosen by God through whom God would mediate his will on earth.

The stories of Genesis from this point on are all, in one way or another, about the fulfillment of this initial call of Abraham and the promise given to him. For the promise to be fulfilled, Abraham obviously needs an heir. But he is childless. As the stories proceed, and Abraham begins to age, the tension builds. How will God fulfill his promise to Abraham of a multitude of descendants if Abraham

has no heir? How can his descendants become a mighty nation if he can't even have children? Out of frustration, Abraham and Sarah attempt a futile solution on their own: Sarah gives her husband sexual access to her servant, Hagar, thinking that in this way the promise can be fulfilled. But this is a human solution to a divine promise, and it is doomed to failure. This is not what God had in mind.

Finally, as an exceedingly old couple, Sarah and Abraham conceive a child. And so, the solution to the problem of the promise is realized: the heir is born (chapter 21). But in the very next chapter (22), God orders Abraham to kill the heir! He is to sacrifice his son to God, sacrifice everything he has lived for to the one who demands all things—even if it means, apparently, revoking his own promise. Unbeknownst to Abraham, however, it is all a test to see if he will be faithful to God no matter what, even if it makes no sense, even if it means murdering his own child. Abraham proves that his devotion to God exceeds everything else, and he carries out God's unreasonable demand. But God is then satisfied that Abraham is willing to be faithful to the fullest degree imaginable and stays his knife-wielding hand before he can strike the boy dead. And so the tension in the story is resolved: Abraham has an heir, he is faithful to the God who called him, and the promise now can be fulfilled.

Isaac grows up and has two sons, one through whom the promise will be fulfilled—Jacob, renamed Israel. Israel has twelve sons. But the entire family is threatened by death from famine. They are to be saved miraculously, however, as God mysteriously works behind the scenes of human deprivation to fulfill his purposes. The brothers of Joseph sell him off as a slave to Egypt, but God manages to make their unrighteous act an act of mercy. Through miraculous events in Egypt, Joseph is put in a position to save his entire family from extermination and so be able to fulfill the promise that God had given their ancestor Abraham. The entire family moves to Egypt, and they begin to multiply there. And so begins the history of the people of Israel, at least as it is told in these powerful and moving legends.

Another, larger function of all these stories will not be obvious from simply reading them to the end of Genesis and stopping there. For the story goes on in the next book of the Pentateuch. The ancient Israelites who told and retold the stories of the Patriarchs knew that the next major figure in

FIGURE 2.5. Abraham's sacrifice of Isaac, from a thirteenth-century manuscript.

the history of the people would be Moses, and that the greatest event that consolidated the people into a great nation was their deliverance from slavery in Egypt. God worked mighty miracles, especially at the exodus event itself, showing in definitive and irrefutable terms that he was the Almighty whose purposes could not be thwarted even by the most powerful nation on earth (Egypt) and its most powerful leader (the Pharaoh). In the back of the mind of both storytellers and story-hearers of the legends of Genesis was the truly enormous event, the salvation from Egypt that bound the people together into a mighty nation.

But if the people of God came from the land of Israel, what were they doing in Egypt? Seen from a literary perspective, the legends of Genesis—especially the Joseph stories of chapters 37–50—are designed to get Abraham's descendants into the land of Egypt so that they can grow into a mighty nation there, come to be enslaved, and thus *require* a powerful act of salvation. God would bring them forth from slavery and destroy their enemies, prior to bringing them back to the land that had been promised to their forebear Abraham. In many ways, the final third of the book of Genesis is a set-up for what is going to happen in the book of Exodus.

BOX 2.4 CIRCUMCISION

In Genesis 17, Abraham is told that circumcision will be the "sign of the covenant." All of his male descendants are to be circumcised; this will show that they belong to the covenant that God made with Abraham that he would make his descendants numerous, that he would give them the land, and, by implication, that they would be his chosen people.

Circumcision involved the removal of the foreskin of the penis. Eventually it became a rite performed on boys eight days after birth. But it appears that originally (before the stories of Genesis) it was practiced as a puberty rite, as a boy moved into manhood and was ready and able to be married. (Although one might suspect that this would not be the most opportune time to have this kind of surgical operation done. Maybe that is why they moved it back into infancy.) (See Figure 2.4)

It was not a rite practiced only among ancient Israelites, however, but also among other peoples in the ancient Near East. Jeremiah 9:25–26, for example, indicates that Egyptians, Edomites, Moabites, and Ammonites also circumcised. Although it was popular in some cultures, those that did not practice it often found it to be a very odd procedure indeed. You do *what* to your infants?

The original function of circumcision has been much debated among historians and anthropologists. If it was a puberty rite originally, then it may have literally "marked" a male for manhood. Some trace of this function can be found in Genesis 34:14–17, one of the powerfully moving stories of the Pentateuch. A woman named Dinah, one of the sisters of the twelve sons of Jacob, was raped by a neighboring prince named Shechem. Shechem, afterwards, wanted to marry her but the twelve sons of Jacob would not allow it since he was uncircumcised. On only one condition could the marriage take place—and other intermarriages afterward: if all the men of Shechem received circumcision. For some reason the men of Shechem agreed. And three days after the operation, while all the men were still deep in pain and basically immobile, two of Jacob's sons, Simeon and Levi, went into the city with swords drawn and slaughtered all the men in the city in an act of vengeance for what Shechem had done to their sister.

The legends of Genesis function not only in terms of the larger story of the Pentateuch but also individually, as each one has a lesson that it is trying to teach its readers and listeners. Some of these lessons are of importance to the later nation of Israel as a group. Chief among these lessons is one that continues to play a role in the politics of the Middle East today. Who has the right to the land of Israel? This is not only an issue with rather enormous consequences in our own day and age. It was an issue very much alive in the ancient world as well. The problem then was comparable, in many ways, to the problem now. There were other people living in the land at the time. Did they have any right to live there? And what about the people of Israel? Do they have the right to live there? Should they all live there? Or should the land be only the land of Israel, so those who were (are) not descendants of Abraham through Isaac and through Jacob have no business being there and should be either exterminated or expelled from their homes?

We will see that the biblical authors had a clear answer to this question. The land belongs to the descendants of Israel. And it belongs to them not because they were there first, because, in fact, they were *not* there first. It belongs to them because God promised it to them. This is the Promised Land. At the very beginning, with Abraham himself—before there ever was an heir to the promise, let alone a family of descendants, let alone an entire nation of descendants, way back at the beginning—God himself, the maker of heaven and earth, promised this land to Abraham as part of the covenant that he made with him. This land belongs to Israel and no one else. This is a powerful legend, with an understanding of the land that has enormous consequences. We will see the consequences for the dwellers of Canaan in the books of Joshua and Judges. The consequences, obviously, still live on.

The morals taught by the legends of Genesis apply not only to Israel as a nation, they apply to individuals within that nation as well, as story after story of Genesis attempts to make a point about what it means for the descendants to live in faithful relationship to the God who called them. Nowhere can this be seen more clearly than in the stories about Joseph.

At different times in the history of Israel, as we saw in the previous chapter, individuals were exiled from the land and forced (or chose) to live in other places around the Mediterranean. In almost every other instance that we know about, displaced peoples who moved to new localities tended to adopt the religious practices, customs, and beliefs of their new location. Jews, on the other hand, have long been known to hold on to the religion of their ancestors no matter where they lived. The stories about Joseph show not only how that is possible, but how faithfulness to the God of Israel will be rewarded even if that faithfulness is manifest among a foreign people with alien religions and customs. This lesson must have resonated strongly with Jews of later times, who lived outside the land but still adhered to the religion that began in the land.

Joseph is sold into slavery in Egypt, and the stories told about his adventures there are all driven by a concern to show that the God of Israel blesses him even though he is no longer in Israel. First he becomes the slave of a wealthy aristocrat, Potiphar. Because God is with him, Joseph rises through the ranks of the servants until he becomes the steward of the entire household. But, as with most of the stories of Genesis, this one will not be told without a crisis in which something miraculous needs to happen in order to allow the hero of the legend to thrive despite difficulties. In this case, Potiphar's wife tries to seduce the handsome Joseph, and when he repels her advances she cries rape. Joseph is sent off to prison.

But since God is with him, he rises through the ranks of the prisoners until he achieves a position of status there. And what is more, because God gives him the supernatural power to interpret dreams, he is put in a situation where, when summoned, he can inform the Pharaoh about the dire meaning of his nightmares, leading the Pharaoh to release him from bondage, put him in his service, and elevate him to be his right-hand man. Joseph may be stranded in a foreign land with alien customs, but since he remains faithful to his God he not only survives but thrives. Here is a lesson for all those forced from their homes into exile. They need to remain faithful to their God, and he will reward them.

Another individual moral of the story is equally evident, especially when we get to the end of the book. After the brothers of Joseph come to Egypt begging for food, and after a long series of intriguing episodes, Joseph reveals his identity to them and

they all rejoice together in their incredible good fortune. The entire clan, including the patriarch, Jacob, moves to Egypt to be provided for by Joseph. But then Jacob dies, and the brothers become extremely fearful: has Joseph treated them well simply for the sake of their father? Will he turn on them, now that Jacob is dead? They beg Joseph to forgive them for their crime of selling him into slavery, and Joseph replies to them with one of the most impressive statements of the entire Pentateuch: "Do not be afraid! Am I in the place of God? Even though you intended to harm me, God intended it for good, in order to preserve a numerous people, as he is doing today. So have no fear; I myself will provide for you and your little ones" (Genesis 50:19-21).

"You intended to harm me, but God intended it for good." This is a powerful lesson, meant to be taken from this legend of the sons of Jacob. God works behind the scenes to bring about what is best for his people. Not only can he overcome adversity

FIGURE 2.6. Joseph being sold by his brothers, from a thirteenth-century manuscript of the Bible.

and hardship, drought and famine, slavery and imprisonment. He can turn the brutal, harsh, and malignant actions of spiteful people into good, effecting his salvation precisely through mean and sinful acts meant to destroy others. Nothing can stop God from achieving his purposes. What someone may interpret as horrific catastrophe can, in the long run, be used by God to bring about peace, harmony, deliverance, and even prosperity.

AUTHORSHIP: WHO WROTE THE PENTATEUCH?

To this point of our study we have learned two crucial features of the book of Genesis that can contribute to our understanding of how this book came into existence in the first place: it is part of a larger collection of narratives (and laws) that make up the five books of the Pentateuch; and its myths and legends were originally passed down in the oral tradition, by word of mouth, from one generation to the next. Given the origins of these stories among the storytellers of ancient Israel, what can we say about the author of this book—or, rather, of all five books? Who wrote the Pentateuch?

The Traditional View

Since well before the days of Jesus it was believed that the author of the Pentateuch was none other than its leading character, Moses. In the next chapter we will see that Moses appears on the scene at the very beginning of the book of Exodus, as an infant wonderfully protected from destruction, who became a spokesperson of God, a great prophet used by God to perform the miracles that led to the exodus of the people of Israel from their slavery in Egypt. After the exodus Moses became the leader of the people as they journeyed to Mount Sinai on the Sinai Peninsula, where he was given the Ten Commandments and the rest of the Law. He then led the people in the wilderness for forty years, before giving them the Law a second time in the book of Deuteronomy as they stood on the brink of the Promised Land, poised to conquer the land that God had promised to give them as the descendants of Abraham.

In the ancient world, down to relatively modern times, it was believed not only that the laws were given to Moses on Mount Sinai (and written by him) but also that Moses himself wrote the entire Torah—all five books. This included, of course, the book of Genesis. Who could know better not just what happened at the Exodus, on Mount Sinai, and in the wilderness, but also what had happened before, from the time of creation? It was Moses in particular who was known to have talked with God. God revealed the Torah to him.

Challenges to the Traditional View

Periodically over the course of history, during the Middle Ages, there were readers, students, and scholars of the Torah who raised significant questions about whether Moses did write, or could have written, these five books. The questions increased among European scholars during the seventeenth century; the questions came to be raised systematically in the eighteenth century; and they came to a head in the nineteenth century, when an entirely different view of authorship came be expressed and popularized, so much so that it now dominates scholarship. This is the view that no one person was responsible for the Pentateuch—and certainly not Moses—but that as a whole these books were assembled from previously existing written accounts (all of them based on oral traditions) that were edited into the five-book whole, many centuries after the events they describe would have taken place.

THE EARLY CRITICISMS   Early in the history of Pentateuchal criticism, those who questioned whether Moses could be seen as the author of the Torah pointed out that nowhere in any of the five books is he ever named as their author. That is to say, these books are all anonymous. And there is nothing in the books themselves that would make a reader suspect that the main character discussed in them was the one who wrote these things down. In all the accounts of Exodus through Deuteronomy, where Moses is by far the leading character, he is talked about in the third person. Never does the author indicate what "I" was doing or what "we" were doing. These books appear to be written *about* Moses, not *by* him.

Moreover, there are passages that are very difficult indeed to ascribe to Moses, the most famous of which is Numbers 12:3, which indicates: "Now the man Moses was very humble, more so than anyone else on the face of the earth." This does not sound very much like what an author would say about himself, even if it were true—especially if he was, in fact, the most humble person on the face of the earth!

Other passages almost certainly could not have been written by Moses. For example, as is commonly noted, Deuteronomy 34:5–12 describes in detail Moses' death. How could Moses, as an author writing the Pentateuch, describe his own death as a past event? Or consider another commonly cited text, from Genesis 36:31, which states: "These are the kings who reigned in the land of Edom, before any king reigned over the Israelites." This is a verse that presupposes that the author knows of a time when kings were to rule over Israel. But that would not happen for over two centuries *after* the death of Moses (after the Israelites conquered the land in the book of Joshua and were then ruled over by tribal leaders for at least two hundred years, as described in the book of Judges). Genesis must, then, have been written at least during the monarchy—or even later.

NINETEENTH- AND TWENTIETH-CENTURY OBSERVATIONS

As already mentioned, the critical scrutiny of the traditional view of the Mosaic authorship of the Pentateuch deepened and became more rigorous as scholarship advanced. In addition to the problems just mentioned, other troubling features of the narratives came to the fore. I have already mentioned the fact that there are numerous anachronisms in the stories of Genesis: camels were not domesticated in Canaan in Abraham's time (despite what is said in the stories), for instance—or in the time of Moses. So too the Philistines did not exist as a nation yet. Nor did the city of Beersheba. The stories that contain such references could not have been written in Moses' day in the thirteenth century B.C.E.; they must be dated to a time no earlier than the eleventh century B.C.E. or so, and possibly much later.

What is more, there are clear indications that these books were not written by one author at all, especially in the internal tensions that can be found among the stories and the various doublets that they present.

The internal tensions came to be seen as particularly significant. Nowhere were these tensions more evident than in the opening accounts of the very first book of the Pentateuch, in the creation stories of Genesis chapters 1 and 2. Scholars came to recognize that what is said in Genesis 1 cannot be easily (or at all) reconciled with what is said in Genesis 2. These do not appear to be two complementary accounts of how the creation took place; they appear to be two accounts that are at odds with each other in fundamental and striking ways. Read them carefully yourself. Make a list of what happens in chapter 1, then a list of what happens in chapter 2, and compare your lists. Among other things you will notice the following:

- According to Genesis 1, plants were created on the third day; only later, on the sixth day, were humans created. But not according to Genesis 2. There we are told that "the LORD God formed man from the dust of the ground" *before* there were any plants or herbs on the earth (2:4, 7).
- According to Genesis 1, all the animals, of all kinds, were created before humans, on the fifth and sixth days. But according to Genesis 2, "man" was created first (2:7), and then the animals—who were made in order to provide companionship for the man (2:19). Note: it was only after man was made that "the LORD God formed *every* animal of the field and every bird of the air." None of the animals existed, according to this account in chapter 2, before the man was made.
- According to Genesis 1, humans, both male and female, were created at the same time, as the pinnacle of all creation (1:26–27). But in Genesis 2 the LORD God first creates "man" (adam); he then creates all the animals in order to provide a companion for "man." And when none of them is deemed suitable, then and only then does the LORD God make a woman out of a rib that he has taken from the man.
- It was also noted by careful scholars that the deity is called different things in the two accounts. In Genesis 1 the deity is called, in Hebrew, *Elohim*—the word that is normally simply translated in English as "God" (even though it is plural); but in Genesis 2 the deity is suddenly called *Yahweh Elohim*, which comes into English usually as "LORD God." The word **Yahweh** was believed in ancient Israel to be the personal name for God, and eventually it was regarded as being so holy that faithful Jews were not allowed even to pronounce it without committing a blasphemy. (See Box 2.5.) God is called by this personal name thousands of times

BOX 2.5 THE PERSONAL NAME OF GOD

God is called by many names in the Bible, including Lord, God, Lord God, God Almighty, God the King, and Lord God of Hosts. But there is one term used for God that appears to have been thought of by ancient Israelites as his actual, personal name. In English this is often given as *Yahweh*, based on the Hebrew word YHWH. Ancient Hebrew did not have vowels, only consonants, and so we do not actually know how the word was pronounced, although "Yahweh" is a good guess. Since this special name of God consists of four letters, it is sometimes referred to as the **tetragrammaton** (literally, "the four letters").

Because God himself was thought to be so holy, it eventually came to be considered improper, or even blasphemous, to call him by his personal name. And so, when ancient Jews read the Scriptures out loud, and came to the tetragrammaton, instead of pronouncing it they would say, instead, the word *Adonai*, the Hebrew word for "Lord." That is why, even today, English translations as a rule do not give the personal name of God

as *Yahweh* when it occurs—as it does thousands of times in the Hebrew Bible—but instead translate it as LORD (with capital letters, to differentiate it from the translation of *Adonai* as "Lord").

By the seventh or eighth century C.E., Jewish scribes added vowels to the text of the Hebrew Bible, in part to make it easier to read. But in order to make sure that ancient readers of the biblical texts did not inadvertently say the name *Yahweh* when they came to it, they provided it with the vowels that went instead with the word *Adonai*. This combination of consonants and vowels was very difficult to pronounce, and so readers would be alerted to the divine name, and would simply speak it as "*Adonai*."

It was this strange conglomeration of consonants and vowels—keeping the consonants of the tetragrammaton but using the vowels of the word "Adonai"—that led to the invention of a new word in English: "Jehovah" (since JHVH is the English equivalent of YHWH).

---

in the Hebrew Bible. But he is called a number of other things as well, such as Lord, God Almighty, and God the King. It is striking that only one of these terms is used in Genesis 1, and the other term occurs only in Genesis 2. That would make sense if the two stories came from different sources, each with its own view of what happened at the creation and each with its own favored term for the deity.

- In that connection, it was noticed that the two accounts seem to have different conceptions of the deity (not just different terms for him). In Genesis 1, God is the Powerful, Almighty, Creator of all things; he is distant and remote and above all things. But not in Genesis 2 and its companion story about Adam and Eve in the Garden of Eden in Genesis 3. There God is portrayed in **anthropomorphic** terms—that is, he appears virtually in human guise. He is here on earth; he works with the dirt; he performs an operation on Adam; he walks through the garden of Eden in the cool of the evening (3:8); he doesn't know where Adam and Eve are hiding (3:9); and he talks with

them and wants to know—as if he doesn't know—if they've done something he told them not to do (3:11).

- Finally, the interests of the two stories are different in key ways. We have already seen that the first creation account, among other things, wants to stress that the Sabbath observance is rooted in the fabric of existence. The second account has nothing like that concern. Here there seems to be an interest in explaining some of the ultimate questions that people have asked over the centuries: Why do women experience such pain in childbirth? Why is it so difficult to provide enough food to eat? Why are men dominant over women? It is also interested in explaining less pressing curiosities, such as why snakes crawl on their bellies instead of walk around like other creatures.

These kinds of differences suggested to scholars of the eighteenth and nineteenth centuries that Genesis 1–3 was not providing one account composed by one author at one time, but two different accounts composed by two different authors at two different times—with different interests, understandings of the deity, and views about what happened when humans were created.

Moreover, and just as important, the literary inconsistencies of Genesis are not unique to these two chapters. On the contrary, there are such problems scattered throughout the book. You can see this for yourself simply by reading the text very carefully. Read, for example, the story of the Flood in Genesis 6–9, and you will find comparable differences. One of the most glaring is this: according to Genesis 6:19, God told Noah to take two animals "of every kind" with him into the ark; but according to Genesis 7:2, God told him to take *seven pairs* of all "clean animals" and two of every other kind of animal. Well, which is it? And how can it be both?

You can find similar differences in other parts of the Pentateuch. In the next chapter, for example, we will be looking at the ten plagues that Moses miraculously performed against the Egyptians in order to convince the reluctant Pharaoh to let the children of Israel go free from slavery. These are terrific stories, as good as the accounts of the Patriarchs in Genesis. But scholars have long detected similar discrepancies. It has been noted, for example, that in the fifth plague, the LORD killed "all of the livestock" of the Egyptians (9:6). So, based on this account one would think that "all" of the livestock were, indeed, dead. But then, just a few verses later, Moses performs the seventh plague, in which a terrible hailstorm killed not just humans but also all the "livestock" of the Egyptians that had been left in the fields (see 9:19-20; 25). It has been widely concluded that this story was patched up from at least two earlier accounts, which, when spliced together, created an inconsistency.

Such differences occur not only within this or that book of the Pentateuch; similar problems are found to occur between one book and the next, making it appear that the same author is not responsible for the entire work. And so, for example, in Exodus, in one of Moses' early encounters with the deity, God tells him "I am the LORD (*Yahweh*). I appeared to Abraham, Isaac, and Jacob as God Almighty (Hebrew: *El Shaddai*), but by my name 'The LORD' (*Yahweh*) I did not make myself known to them" (Exodus 6:3). Here God is saying that the patriarchs of Genesis did not know the personal name of God, Yahweh; they only knew him as God Almighty, El Shaddai. But that will come as

a very big surprise to a careful reader of Genesis. For it is quite clear in Genesis not only that God appeared to the patriarchs as The LORD (*Yahweh*), but that they called him by that name. Consider Genesis 4:26: "At that time people began to invoke the name of the LORD (*Yahweh*)." Or even more telling, Genesis 15:6–8:

> And he [Abraham] believed the LORD (*Yahweh*), and the LORD reckoned it to him as righteousness. Then he said to him, "I am the LORD (*Yahweh*) who brought you from Ur of the Chaldeans, to give you this land to possess." But he said, O Lord GOD (*Adonai Yahweh*), how am I to know that I shall possess it?"

According to Exodus, God never appeared to or revealed himself to Abraham as Yahweh; according to Genesis, he did. There are clearly different sources that have been incorporated into these stories. That is made all the more evident by the doublets (and the triplet) that we observed earlier in the Patriarchal narratives.

THE DOCUMENTARY HYPOTHESIS   The most popular solution to the problem of the authorship of the Pentateuch is known as the **Documentary Hypothesis**. In its most widespread form, this is the view that behind the Pentateuch there are actually four different written sources (all of them based on oral traditions), written by different authors, living at different times in the history of ancient Israel, with different points of view and emphases, that have been edited together into one long five-volume work.

The scholar whose name is most widely associated with this hypothesis was a German Professor of Hebrew Bible named Julius Wellhausen, who lived from 1844 to 1918. Wellhausen did not invent the documentary hypothesis, but he did work out its details in a more compelling way than any of his predecessors. And he managed to convince an entire host of fellow scholars of its persuasiveness, starting with his major 1878 publication (in German), *History of Ancient Israel*. Among other things, Wellhausen claimed that the four sources of the Pentateuch were written centuries after the events they narrate, and by authors living centuries removed from one another. As a result, the accounts do not represent eyewitness reports (for example, by Moses) and are not historically reliable. We do not know who the actual authors of these sources were, but Wellhausen called them by four initials, the J source, the E source, the D source, and the P source. In his view, they were written in this order. Sometimes, as a result, this is known as the **JEDP** hypothesis.

To understand the hypothesis, it will help to bear in mind the broad historical sketch of ancient Israel that I gave in chapter 1, since different ones of these sources were written in different periods of Israel's history. In one of the commonly adopted forms of this hypothesis, it works like this:

- The **J** source was the first source to be written. From it comes a number of the stories in Genesis and Exodus, including, for example, the second creation account and the story of Adam and Eve in Genesis 2–3. The source is called J because its preferred name for the deity is *Yahweh*—which in German is spelled *Jahweh* (and so, it is named after the first initial of the deity's name). It is widely thought that this source was written in, and based on oral traditions in, the southern part of the land, that is, in Judah (which is a second reason it could be called J). The reason for this location: many of the traditions of the patriarchs found in Genesis 12–50 take place in southern locations. Among its distinctive features, J had a particularly anthropomorphic understanding of the deity (as in both the Garden of Eden and Flood stories). Many scholars have thought that the J source was written during the United Monarchy, possibly in the tenth century B.C.E. during the reign of Solomon.
- The **E** source was the second to be written. E also contained a number of the narratives of the Pentateuch, but nothing in what we have called the Primeval History. Its stories appear to begin with Genesis 15. It is called E because it prefers the name *Elohim* (= "God") for the deity. Unlike J, it appears to have been written in, and to have been based on oral traditions from, the northern part of the land, Israel—which sometimes was called, instead, Ephraim (after its most important tribe; hence another reason to call it E). In this source, God communicates with people through his prophets and by sending dreams. E may have been written a century or so

after J, possibly in the middle of the ninth century B.C.E. At some point, possibly a century after that (after the fall of the northern Kingdom to Assyria), an editor appears to have taken the J source and the E source and combined them into a longer narrative. In so doing, the editor cut out a good bit of E, so that E is represented more fragmentarily in the Pentateuch than the other sources.

- The **D** source stands out in a particularly distinctive way, in that it is the source that lies behind the entire book of Deuteronomy and only (or almost only) there. Hence the name D. Moreover, the date of D is usually thought of as more certain than the other sources. In the book of 2 Kings we read a story about how a "book of the law" was discovered in the Temple during the reign of the good king Josiah (2 Kings 22:8). This would have been around 621 B.C.E. Many scholars think that this "book" was in fact the D source, or at least a large portion of it (possibly chapters 12–26), so that the book was composed some time earlier, possibly in the mid-seventh century B.C.E. The D source narrates the giving of the Law by Moses, but this version of the Law differs in significant ways from that found in the rest of the Pentateuch (Exodus, Leviticus, and Numbers). Whoever put J, E, D, and P together at a later date solved this problem by making Deuteronomy its own book and indicating that it represented the *second* giving of the Law by Moses. It is often thought that the D traditions, like E, originated in the northern part of Israel. But since one of its most important themes is that sacrifices to God are to be performed only in the central sanctuary (the Temple in Jerusalem), not wherever Israelites choose to make them, this source may have been edited and expanded by an author living in the south.
- Finally, the **P** source is so named because it is chiefly concerned with matters of interest to priests—for example, laws given by Moses about sacrifices, rituals, the observance of festivals, kosher foods, circumcision, genealogies (such as in Genesis 5 and 10), and so on. This priestly source, like E, prefers the name *Elohim* for the deity but uses a number of other names (such as *El Shaddai*, as we saw in Exodus 6:2–3). As we have seen, P's view of the deity is as one who is remote and above it all; he does not communicate

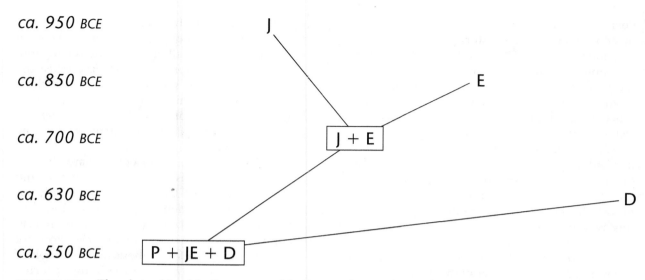

ca. 950 BCE

ca. 850 BCE

ca. 700 BCE

ca. 630 BCE

ca. 550 BCE

FIGURE 2.7.   The relationship of the four sources of the Pentateuch, according to the Documentary Hypothesis.

with people directly, or through angels or dreams. The traditions of P are scattered throughout the Pentateuch, but mainly in the laws found in Exodus, Leviticus, and Numbers, which we will be examining in the next chapter. P's interest is not only in law per se, however. The very first chapter of the Pentateuch—the creation account, with its emphasis on the Sabbath day—is from P, and so is the very final chapter of the Pentateuch, Deuteronomy 34. The reason the Pentateuch begins and ends with P is that P was not only a written source of material for the Pentateuch; its author, living perhaps in the middle of the sixth century B.C.E., possibly soon after the Babylonian exile had begun, may have been the one who edited all the other sources together and created out of them one long narrative, the Pentateuch as we have it today.

The final edition of JEDP, possibly created by the P editor, represents then an amalgamation of the four sources. In some places of the Pentateuch it is relatively simple to see how the editor did his work. For example, we have seen that there are two stories of the creation. The P account is in Genesis 1:1–2:4; the J account is in Genesis 2:5–3:24. In other places the final editor performed a more complicated exercise in which he wove one account into another so that a few verses come from, say, J and another few from P, and so on, back and forth.

And so, for example, in the Flood story, Genesis 6:5–8 is J; 6:9–22 is P; 7:1–5 J; 7:6–16 P; 7:16–23 J; 7:24–8:5 P.

In yet other places, especially involving the materials of J and E, the interweaving is so complicated that it is almost impossible to discern where one source ends and the other begins—so much so that some scholars prefer to speak of "the JE source" rather than J and E as separate sources.

THE SCHOLARLY VIEW TODAY   It is impossible to speak about a single scholarly opinion about the Documentary Hypothesis today. Some scholars reject the idea that J and E were separate sources; some think that there were far more sources than the four; some propose radically different dates for the various sources (for example, one increasingly popular proposal is that the earliest sources were written in the seventh century; other scholars maintain that none of the sources was produced before the Babylonian exile in the sixth century). A number of scholars have produced mind-numbingly complicated proposals that try to take better into account all of the nuances of the data.

But it is possible to speak about a scholarly consensus on some of the truly critical points, including the following:

• However we account for the final product of the Pentateuch, it was not written in whole or even in part by Moses, or by any one person—certainly no one living as early as the thirteenth century B.C.E.

- The Pentateuch as we now have it is composed of a variety of written sources that have been woven together, all of which are themselves based on earlier oral traditions that had been in circulation for a long period of time as storytellers told and retold the stories about much earlier times.
- These various sources were written at different periods of time in the history of ancient Israel.
- Each of these sources embodies a distinctive set of concerns and a variety of views—about God, about Israel, about what is religiously important.
- The sources may not be, and indeed probably are not, reliable for the history that they narrate—that is, they may not and probably do not give historically accurate information about the Primeval History, the Ancestral History, or the Exodus and the life of Moses. This makes it very difficult indeed to know what happened in any of the periods discussed in the Pentateuch, from the beginning of time to the point at which Israel was (allegedly) poised to enter into the Promised Land immediately after the death of Moses.
- Each source may, on the other hand, provide useful information concerning the period of time when it was composed.
- Unfortunately, since we don't know for certain (with the possible exception of the D source) when that was, even this information is not definitively useful for writing an authoritative account of the history of Israel.

ORAL TRADITIONS AND CULTURAL PARALLELS

Given the circumstance that the Pentateuch is based on written sources that themselves are rooted in oral traditions, what can we say about these oral traditions? The short answer is that there is not much to say, apart from the few points I have already made: stories about primeval times, about the ancestors, about Moses and the Exodus and the giving of the Law, were in circulation in different parts of the land that became Israel, for a very long time. Storytellers in different places emphasized different things: different understandings of God,

different religious practices, different important figures from within the history of the people. Some of these stories (such as those embedded in the J source) were in circulation in the southern part of Israel; others (such as those of D) were from the north.

There is one surprising fact about the early stories that were in circulation, however—at least it was surprising to the nineteenth-century scholars who discovered it (in hindsight, it should not be surprising at all). This is that the stories in oral circulation in ancient Israel were sometimes modeled on and often influenced by the stories told by other, non-Israelite, people in the ancient Near East. This came as a surprise simply because European and American Bible scholars (who were, frankly, just about the only Bible scholars there were at that time) had assumed that the stories of the Pentateuch were *sui generis*, one of a kind, distinct to the Bible. Archaeological discoveries convincingly demonstrated that this was not so. Ancient Israel was not as distinct from its surroundings as had once been thought.

Enuma Elish

Between 1848 and 1876 seven clay tablets were discovered in excavations of the ancient city of Nineveh. They came to be published in 1876 by George Smith of the British Museum. These tablets were written in cuneiform script and altogether contained about 1100 lines of poetry, which bore remarkable similarities to the account of creation in Genesis 1. There were, to be sure, very significant differences. The author(s) of the poem were Babylonian, not Israelite, and so they did not worship one God but acknowledged a multiplicity of gods. The text was principally concerned with narrating the story that showed how one of the gods, Marduk, had become the head God after a cosmic and divine battle with his divine enemies. The overriding interest of the story was to show that this Babylonian deity was indeed the one most worthy of worship. The text ends, in fact, with an account of how all the other gods came to acknowledge and celebrate Marduk, the patron God of Babylon, as the king.

But in the course of the narrative there is an account of the creation of the world with striking parallels to the Priestly account. The poem begins with the words: "When above the skies had not been named, nor earth below pronounced by name. . . ." The words "when above" are, in the original of the poem, "*enuma elish.*" And so that is the title given to the work by scholars today. Sometimes it is called The Babylonian Epic of Creation—although that is a bit of misnomer, since the creation account in the story plays only a small role in the overall narrative. But it is striking that the opening sounds a good bit like the opening of Genesis. Although Genesis 1:1 is often translated, "In the beginning, God created the heavens and the earth. And the earth was formless and void . . . ," an alternative, possibly superior translation is, "When God began to create the heavens and the earth, the earth was formless and void." This is similar to the line that begins Enuma Elish. More striking, there are similarities in both concept and in vocabulary between the two accounts of creation. So much so that one scholar, Alexander Heidel, called his edition of the text "The Babylonian Genesis."

The similarities between the two accounts are generally judged to be too significant to be accidental. But the Babylonian version could not have borrowed its images and metaphors and vocabulary from Genesis. It appears that Enuma Elish was originally composed in the twelfth century B.C.E. and, at one point, was publicly performed in Babylon.

The Priestly source of the Pentateuch was produced centuries later—strikingly, soon after the destruction of Judah by Babylon, when the leadership and many of the elite of Judah had been taken in captivity back to Babylon. It is not implausible that the author of the P source was drawing on the traditions found now in Enuma Elish, modifying them in light of his own view that it was the God of Israel who was the creator of this world, not Marduk of Babylon.

The Gilgamesh Epic

In 1853 several fragments of a different ancient text were discovered in the ruined palace of ancient Nineveh. The texts, also written in cuneiform script, were deciphered by George Smith. Since then they have been recognized as containing one of the great epics of ancient literature, named after its lead character **Gilgamesh,** a king of the city of Uruk in southern Mesopotamia. Numerous other fragments of the epic have since been discovered and pieced together. They tell the story of this great hero, Gilgamesh, especially in his relationship with a one-time wild and uncivilized but now tamed companion, Enkidu.

The epic is highly episodic, going from one adventure to the next, but there are many striking parallels to what can be found in the Primeval History of Genesis; for example, in the tale of the Garden of Eden. One portion of the epic was immediately found to be particularly significant: a story of the flood with unmistakable similarities to the account in Genesis. At one point of the narrative Gilgamesh is said to meet with a man who had become immortalized, named Utnapishtim. Utnapishtim tells Gilgamesh how he had survived a flood sent from the gods in order to destroy all the living things on earth. He was instructed by the gods to "Put aboard the seed of all living things, into the boat, the boat that you are to build."[1] He is instructed on how to build the boat and what dimensions to make it. He is told to take his relatives onboard as well. The rains descended, the massive flood occurred, all the peoples of the earth were destroyed. The boat comes to rest on a

FIGURE 2.8. One of the clay tablets discovered in 1853 containing the Gilgamesh epic, in which the Babylonian story of the universal flood is told, in many ways similar to the account of Noah and the ark in Genesis.

---

1   Taken from Stephanie Dalley, *Myths from Mesopotamia: Creation, The Flood, Gilgamesh, and Others* (New York: Oxford University Press, 1989), p. 110.

BOX 2.6   THE STORY OF ATRAHASIS

There are a number of ancient tales from around the world about a flood that destroyed the human race; these stories are not limited to Genesis and Gilgamesh. Another ancient Near Eastern text that tells the tale is called "Atrahasis," after the name of the main character. An old version of the story comes from Babylon, written on clay tablets that date to the beginning of the seventeenth century B.C.E., many centuries before the J and P sources of Genesis.

In this account, the gods are upset that the earth has grown so overpopulated (all the noise is causing a disturbance) and so decide to destroy it with a flood. Atrahasis is instructed to build a boat; it is to have both upper decks and lower decks, and is to be covered with bitumen (presumably for waterproofing). He does as he is told and then gathers all the animals onboard, along with his family, before sealing the door. And then it happens:

> The Flood roared like a bull,
> Like a wild ass screaming the winds howled
> The darkness was total, there was no sun.[2]

In this version of the story, the flood lasts just seven days and nights, but it has its intended effect of, well, controlling the population. Afterward, Atrahasis makes a sacrifice to the gods.

Some modern readers have suggested that the reason there are so many flood stories in ancient texts is because there really was a worldwide flood that destroyed the entire human race except one man (Noah? Utnapishtim? Atrahasis?) and his family, and the animals he saved. Since, however, that is physically impossible (for a flood to cover the earth), and since there is no geological evidence for any such thing—in fact, just the opposite: there is undeniable evidence that nothing like this actually happened—it is more logical to think that these various texts arose in cultures that were rooted in areas susceptible to occasional floods, some of which were so severe that they became the stuff of myth.

_____

2   Dalley, *Myths from Mesopotamia*, p. 31.

mountain. As the waters dry up, Utnapishtim sends out a dove, which returns when there is no dry place to perch; then a swallow with the same result; and then a raven, which does not return. After leaving the boat, Utnapishtim makes a sacrifice to the gods.

All of these points have clear parallels to the Genesis story of the Flood and again, this cannot be accidental. Nor could Genesis have influenced this Mesopotamian myth. The earliest accounts of Gilgamesh date from before 2000 B.C.E., many centuries before the J and P sources of the story of Noah.

CONCLUSION

The Priestly account of creation, the J source's version of the Garden of Eden, and the account of the Flood in both P and J—all of these have clear parallels in Mesopotamian myths that had been in circulation for centuries before the sources of the Pentateuch were produced. These nineteenth-century discoveries caused quite a stir among scholars and then among the reading public as they became more widely known. They continue to cause a stir among readers today, especially among those who do not realize that the stories of Genesis were not and are not unique, and that they were not and are not the first of their kind to be told in the ancient world. They appear to have been influenced by similar stories told in other contexts, by storytellers who accepted other religions. And so scholars have widely concluded that the stories of Genesis are best seen not as historical narratives of things that really happened, but as myths about God and legends about the ancestors that helped the Israelites better understand who they were, how they came to be, and how, in fact, the world as we know it came into existence.

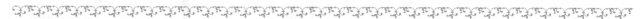

At a Glance: The Book Of Genesis

Because the accounts of the Primeval History stand at odds with the findings of modern science, they are best read not as scientific explanations of how things really came to be, but as ancient myths that are trying to teach deeper truths about the world. So too the narratives of the Ancestral History are best understood not as disinterested histories of the lives of the Israelites' patriarchs and matriarchs, but as legends that attempt to convey lessons to their readers.

Genesis, along with the rest of the Pentateuch, was almost certainly not written by Moses. Because these tales contain such striking anachronisms, discrepancies, and doublets, they appear to represent a number of earlier written sources, themselves based on oral traditions told over the course of a long history. According to the Documentary Hypothesis popularized by Wellhausen, the four sources were J, E, D, and P, each written at a different time by a different author with a different purpose. The four were probably combined together into our Pentateuch sometime after the Babylonian exile.

The oral traditions lying behind these sources were influenced in important ways by other tales told throughout the ancient Near East, including Enuma Elish and the Gilgamesh Epic.

Take a Stand

1. Your roommate tells you that in his opinion, it is possible to reconcile all the apparent conflicts between the creation story of Genesis 1–2 with the findings of modern science. Try it and see: do you agree or not?

2. You're talking to your best friend about the Bible, and she tells you that in her opinion it contains no historical problems or contradictions but is historically accurate in all its details. You yourself are not yet sure what you think. But for the sake of conversation, you tell her your current view based on what you know so far. What is your view?

3. You are attending a Sunday School class that happens to be discussing the book of Genesis. Your teacher says that it was written by Moses. You feel like showing off your newfound knowledge by explaining the reasons some scholars think otherwise. What do you say?

4. Your roommate says that if the world was not created in six days, then there is nothing to learn from the Bible. What do you say?

Key Terms

Anachronism, 40	**Documentary**	**JEDP**, 51	**Primeval History**, 32
Ancestral History, 32	**Hypothesis**, 50	**Legend**, 42	**Sabbath**, 37
Anthropomorphic, 49	*Enuma Elish*, 54	**Myth**, 37	**Tetragrammaton**, 45
Cosmology, 36	**Gilgamesh**, 54	**Oral tradition**, 37	*Yahweh*, 48

Suggestions for Further Reading

NB: For this and all chapters, see the relevant articles (e.g., "Genesis") in the works cited in the Suggestions for Further Reading in chapter 1.

Alter, Robert. *Genesis: Translation and Commentary.* New York: W. W. Norton & Co., 1997. A vibrant translation and discussion of Genesis by one of the world's leading literary critics.

Bloom, Harold. *The Book of J.* New York: Grove Weidenfeld, 1990. A popular account of the J source by one of America's premier literary scholars.

Dalley, Stephanie. *Myths from Mesopotamia.* Oxford: Oxford University Press, 1989. A nice, readable collection of myths in readable English translations, including *Enuma Elish* and *Gilgamesh*.

Finkelstein, Israel and Neil Asher Silberman. *The Bible Unearthed: Archaeology's New Vision of Ancient Israel and the Origin of its Sacred Texts.* New York: Simon and Schuster, 2001. A fascinating discussion of the findings of modern archaeology that shows why the narratives of Genesis are problematic historically.

Friedman, Richard Elliott. *Who Wrote the Bible?* New York: HarperCollins, 1987. A revetting explanation and defense of the Documentary Hypothesis, ideal for beginning students.

Trible, Phyllis. *Texts of Terror: Literary-Feminist Readings of Biblical Narratives.* Philadelphia: Fortress, 1984. A now-classic feminist study of biblical texts, for more advanced students.

3

From Egypt to the Promised Land:
Exodus to Deuteronomy

WHAT TO EXPECT

The final four books of the Torah—Exodus, Leviticus, Numbers, and Deuteronomy—can be seen as containing the heart and soul of the Hebrew Scriptures. Exodus describes the cataclysmic event that led to the formation of the people of Israel as the people of God, the mighty act of deliverance that God performed on their behalf by miraculously saving them from their slavery in Egypt through his prophet Moses. After the crossing of the Sea of Reeds, Moses leads the people to Mount Sinai, where he is given the Ten Commandments and the rest of the Law. The majority of these four books is devoted to setting forth this Law, which involved rules for how the people are to worship Yahweh, how they are to live in community together, and how they are to maintain their distinctiveness from all other people.

After leaving Mount Sinai, the people sin against God and show their lack of faith; he punishes them by forcing them to wander in the wilderness for forty years. At the end of that time, when the generation of those who had escaped Egypt has all but died out, Moses delivers the Law a second time as the people prepare to enter the Promised Land.

In the previous chapter we explored Genesis, the first book of the Pentateuch. In this chapter we will examine the four remaining books: Exodus, Leviticus, Numbers, and Deuteronomy. From a literary perspective, the narrative of the Ancestral History of Genesis was driven by the promises given by God to Abraham at its beginning: he was to have innumerable descendants, and God would give to them the Promised Land. By the end of Genesis, neither promise had been fulfilled. The descendants of Abraham represented just a small clan, and they were residing in Egypt to avoid a famine in Canaan. But, as we have seen, the narrative to that point is designed to set up what is to follow here in Exodus. In Egypt the clan of Jacob

will multiply exponentially into a great nation; and God will perform his greatest act of salvation for his people by delivering them from their slavery to their Egyptian overlord, showing that he indeed is their God and they are his people. He will then give them his Law, in preparation for their coming to the Promised Land.

THE BOOK OF EXODUS

The title of Exodus derives from the most important event that the book narrates—arguably the most significant event in the history of the nation of Israel. It is a miraculous escape from Egypt under the leadership of Moses. As was the case with Genesis, the narrative of Exodus was woven together out of earlier sources, J, E, and P. In a number of passages it is difficult to tell which source is being used; most of the material after chapter 20, however, clearly comes from P, as it is almost entirely concerned with the laws that Moses was given on Mount Sinai. Before he, and the people, can get to Sinai to receive the Law, however, a number of important, even cataclysmic, events have to transpire; these earlier narratives are chiefly from J and E.

A Literary Overview

Once again I will not provide an exhaustive synopsis of the contents of the book but will trust that you have read it carefully, a couple of times. The following summary of some of the highlights is designed to refresh your memory about the most significant episodes:

- *The Enslavement of the Children of Israel* (chapter 1). The clan of Jacob that arrived in Egypt in the time of Joseph numbered 70 persons. But over time they grow at a fantastic rate, so much so that the Egyptians begin to fear them and so, in order to control them, put them into slavery.

- *The Birth and Early Life of Moses* (chapter 2). Even though the Pharaoh orders all male Hebrew children to be killed, Moses is wonderfully saved. By a providential coincidence, he is raised as the son of the Pharaoh's daughter. But as a young man he murders an Egyptian for mistreating a fellow Hebrew, and Moses has to flee to escape the wrath of Pharaoh.

- *The Revelation at the Burning Bush* (chapter 3). While shepherding his flocks in Midian (east of the Gulf of Aqaba), Moses has an encounter with Yahweh at a bush that is burning but not consumed by the fire. Here God reveals his name to Moses ("I Am," or possibly it should be translated, "I Will Cause To Be"—related to the name YHWH) and instructs Moses to return to Egypt to demand freedom for his people.

- *Moses Returns and Confronts Pharaoh.* Moses asks Pharaoh to allow the people to go into the wilderness for three days to hold a celebration in worship of YHWH (chapter 3). Pharaoh's "heart" is "hardened" by God, however. He will

---

BOX 3.1 GOD'S ACTUAL NAME

We earlier saw that the tetragrammaton YHWH was probably understood by ancient Israelites to be the personal name of God. But where did the name come from? It is not only modern readers who are interested in this question. Ancient speakers of Hebrew wanted to know as well. This is evident in the one passage that is widely thought to be an attempt to answer the question but which appears to answer it in three different ways, possibly indicating the confusion over the matter even in antiquity.

When God first reveals himself to Moses at the burning bush in Exodus 3, he instructs him to go to the Israelites in Egypt and on their behalf demand that Pharaoh set them free. Moses is hesitant, though, thinking that the Israelites will not believe that God has sent him. And so he asks God what name he should call him. Then come the three answers (Exodus 3:13–15).

First is this: "God said to Moses, I AM WHO I AM." The Hebrew here is a little difficult to translate, and it may be better rendered "I WILL BE WHO I WILL BE." As you might imagine, this statement has led to numerous interpretations over the years: Is God the "Self-Existent" One (the only One who exists in and of himself: this is what later, more philosophically oriented Jews thought)? Is God saying that who he is will become manifest in what he is about to do? Is God telling Moses to mind his own business, that he will be whoever he chooses to be?

But next he goes on and indicates that "I AM" (or "I WILL BE" or "I WILL CAUSE TO BE") is his actual name: "I AM has sent me to you." This is significant because the word "I AM" in Hebrew is linguistically similar to the name YHWH. Is this an attempt by an ancient Hebrew writer to explain the origins of the sacred name?

In the third instance God gives his name as the tetragrammaton: "YHWH, the God of your ancestors . . . has sent you."

It appears clear, at least, that to this author God's sacred name was somehow related to the word "to be." But how it was related must remain a puzzle to us, just as it apparently was for the author of Exodus.

not let the people go and determines to make the lives of the Hebrew slaves even more miserable (chapters 3–6).

- *The Ten Plagues against Egypt* (chapters 7–12). Moses is empowered by God to perform ten miraculous acts against the Egyptians in an effort to convince Pharaoh to let the people go (he turns all the water in Egypt into blood; there is an infestation of frogs; and gnats; and flies; and locusts; all the livestock are killed; etc.). Pharaoh remains recalcitrant.
- *The Passover* (chapters 11–13). The tenth plague is the worst. Every firstborn human and animal of the Egyptians is killed; but all the Israelites are saved (as the angel of the LORD "passes over" their houses to attack those of the Egyptians).

They are instructed to celebrate the event annually with a special Passover meal.

- *The Exodus* (chapter 14). This final plague is too much for Pharaoh, who sends the people of Israel out. But he then has a change of heart and rouses his entire army to pursue them. Trapped between the charging army and the Sea of Reeds, the Israelites experience the greatest of all miracles: God makes the sea part, they cross on dry land, and as Pharaoh's army comes in pursuit the waters return and all of them are drowned. (Important Note: the Hebrew text does not say this happened at the Red Sea—an enormous body of water further to the south; it was at something called the "Sea of Reeds," which could have been any one of a number of bodies of water between Egypt and

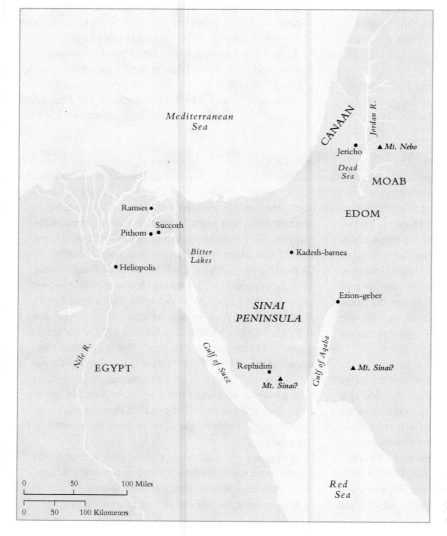

FIGURE 3.1. Places mentioned in the account of the Exodus.

Sinai, north of the coast of Suez. Calling it the "Red Sea" is a mistranslation of the Hebrew.)

- *In the Wilderness* (chapters 15–19). The large nation of Israel (over 600,000 men, not counting women and children) travel in the wilderness, supernaturally fed with special bread sent daily by God ("manna") and otherwise protected and guided by him until they arrive at Mount Sinai, the spot where Moses had originally been confronted by God at the burning bush.

- *The Giving of the Law* (chapters 20–31). Moses goes up on Mount Sinai and receives from God the Ten Commandments and a large number of other laws.

- *The Golden Calf* (chapter 32). In Moses' lengthy absence the people become restless and urge Aaron to make an idol out of gold, in the shape of a calf. They worship it as the god who has delivered them. God tells Moses to go down to his people, and when he sees what they have done—created an idol, expressly forbidden by God—he smashes the two stone tablets on which were written the Ten Commandments and then destroys the calf.

- *The Giving of the Law, Part 2* (chapters 33–40). God gives Moses a second set of tablets with the Ten Commandments and gives him other laws for the people to follow, including instructions on how to construct the "tabernacle," a portable tent that will be used as the central place of worship and sacrifice to God.

Exodus from a Historical Perspective

It has proved difficult for biblical scholars to establish when these events are to have taken place. The most common dating of the exodus event places it around 1250 B.C.E., both because the text indicates that the Israelites had been in Egypt for 430 years (which would coincide roughly with the narrative of Genesis, when Joseph would have gone to Egypt at the beginning of the seventeenth century B.C.E., according to the chronology we adopted there) and because of two other considerations.

BOX 3.2 THE NUMBERING OF THE TEN COMMANDMENTS

The term "the Decalogue" literally means "the ten words." But what are the ten words? You would think that everyone would agree on what they were. But, as it turns out, they don't. There are in fact three major ways of numbering the ten words, and depending on your own religious tradition (if you have one) you are probably accustomed to one or the other and may be surprised to find out that not everyone agrees with you. There is a traditional Jewish numbering, a different numbering accepted by most Protestant churches and the Eastern Orthodox churches, and yet another numbering accepted by the Roman Catholic and Lutheran churches. They work like this:

	Jewish	Protestant and Orthodox	Catholic and Lutheran
I am the LORD your God who brought you out of Egypt	1	(prologue)	1
You shall have no other gods before me	2	1	1
You shall not make idols	2	2	1
You shall not make wrongful use of the Lord's name	3	3	2
Keep the Sabbath day holy	4	4	3
Honor your father and mother	5	5	4
Do not murder	6	6	5
Do not commit adultery	7	7	6
Do not steal	8	8	7
Do not bear false witness	9	9	8
Do not covet your neighbor's (various) things	10	10	9 and 10

The first is a hint provided in Exodus 1:11, that the Hebrew slaves were forced to build the cities of Pi-Ramses and Pithon; both cities actually were rebuilt or reoccupied in the mid-thirteenth century B.C.E. The second is an archaeological discovery of a stele (a stone pillar) erected at the end of the thirteenth century by the Egyptian Pharaoh Merneptah (who ruled 1213–1203 B.C.E.). On this stele is an inscription in which the Pharaoh boasts that he has conquered various other nations, including the land of Israel: "Israel is laid waste, its seed is not."[1] This is the earliest reference from outside the Bible to anything having to do with Israel or the Bible itself, and so is very valuable. What it shows beyond reasonable dispute is that Israel existed in the land, as a recognizable people, sometime in the late thirteenth century. If the events celebrated in the book of Exodus happened sometime soon before this, then they are probably to be dated to the mid-thirteenth century. If that is the case, then it was Merneptah's grandfather, Pharaoh Seti I (1294–1279), who would have first enslaved the Israelites, and Seti's son, Ramses II (1279–1213), who would have been the Pharaoh at the time of the exodus.

But you may well be wondering: if according to the book of Exodus Pharaoh and his "entire army" (see 14:6, 9, 23) were destroyed in the Sea of Reeds, how is it that Egypt was still such a major military power afterward, and that Pharaoh Merneptah could have conquered so many lands as attested on the Merneptah stele?

That is in fact a problem with this narrative. And it is not the only one. Biblical scholars have long identified a number of difficulties that the Exodus account presents—making it hard to think that everything happened as it is described in the book. As was the case with the ancestral narratives of Genesis we may be dealing with legends, not with objective historical facts. Consider the following issues:

IMPLAUSIBILITIES   According to Exodus 12:37, there were about 600,000 "men" among the Israelites who escaped from Egypt. Numbers 1:46–47 gives a more precise count: 603,550 men who were 20 years or older and able to serve as soldiers, not counting the 23,000 Levites. But on the most basic level, how could this be? For one thing, a large army in antiquity could field 20,000 soldiers. Are we to believe that Israel had over 600,000?

Second: how do we explain this kind of population growth? If one counts all the women (surely as many as the men) and all the children (who would presumably be at least as many as the men and women combined), there must have been two and a half or three million people in Israel at this point. Now, according to Exodus 1:5 the clan of Jacob that started in Egypt consisted of 70 persons; and according to Exodus 6:16–20, Moses was in the fourth generation of the clan. His father was Amram, his grandfather was Kohath, and his great grandfather was Levi, one of the sons of Jacob—how could the great-grandchildren of the twelve sons of Jacob number well over two million? In addition, even though demographic statistics for any place in antiquity are notoriously difficult to obtain, the best guesses indicate that the entire population of Egypt at the time was somewhere between two and four million people. Obviously they could not all have been Israelites who left.

CONTRADICTIONS WITH THE KNOWN FACTS OF HISTORY   If two or three million slaves escaped from Egypt and the entire Egyptian army was destroyed while in pursuit, this would obviously be a highly significant event and we surely would find some mention of it, at least in one ancient writing or another. Possibly no Egyptian would have wanted to record the event. But some of the other nations of the region would have been ecstatic to learn that Egypt could no longer field an army; surely they would make note of it for the public record and then swoop down to the south to take over that fertile land for themselves. But we have no such record of the event, and no other nation came in to take advantage of the situation. The reason is obvious. Pharaoh and his entire army were not destroyed at the Sea of Reeds.

Moreover, we still have the mummy of Ramses II, and we know a good deal about his reign from other sources. He certainly never lost two million of his slaves and his entire army. His thirteenth son and successor, Merneptah, also had a successful reign and, as we have seen, had a powerful army that overwhelmed other nations in the region. Egypt continued to be a dominant world force after the mid-thirteenth century B.C.E.

---

1   Translation of J. A. Wilson, in J. B. Pritchard, ed. *Ancient Near Eastern Texts Relation to the Old Testament* (Princeton: Princeton University Press, 1969), p. 378.

FIGURE 3.2. The Merneptah stele (see p. 62), erected by the Pharaoh of Egypt, Merneptah (1213–1203 B.C.E.); this inscription provides the first mention of "Israel" outside the Bible.

I might add that there is no archaeological evidence for anything like the exodus having occurred. Hundreds of chariots cannot be found at the bottom of any of the bodies of water that would be candidates for the Sea of Reeds; there are no Egyptian remains to indicate a massive exodus of two million or more people; and there are no archaeological traces in the wilderness area in any of the possible routes into and out of the Sinai.

As was the case with the stories of Genesis, then, here too we appear to be dealing with legend. The Exodus tradition was hugely important, as it became a kind of "founding legend" for the nation of Israel. It does not appear to be actual history. But did anything happen at all?

A PLAUSIBLE HISTORICAL RECONSTRUCTION

Scholars have long debated what, if anything, actually happened that might have led to the Exodus narratives of the miraculous deliverance of the people of Israel from their slavery in Egypt. Some scholars (who are often labeled "minimalists") think that almost nothing, historically, can be salvaged from this set of stories. Other, more conservative, scholars (often labeled "maximalists") continue to insist that something very much like what is narrated in Exodus took place, despite the fact that apart from the narrative itself we have no evidence of it. Where should we stand on this issue if we approach it strictly from a historical perspective, apart from our religious beliefs?

There are some things to suggest that there may be *some* kind of historical kernel behind these highly imaginative and triumphalistic stories. For example, the name "Moses" is actually Egyptian, not Hebrew. And we do have the fact that later people living in Israel told many, many stories about having originally come as a group from Egypt. At the same time, as we have seen, nothing at all like the scale of events described in Exodus appears to be possible. But it is possible, at least, that some of the people who ended up living in the land of Canaan did come from Egypt and possibly escaped somehow as slaves. If there are historical traces in any of the accounts, they would point to this possibility. If one of the groups remembered that there were two midwives among the escapees, that would be sufficient, possibly, for several hundred people. And so one possibility is that a small group like this—with the leader of someone named Moses?—may well have escaped from their slavery, traveled around for a time, and ended up putting down their roots in Canaan. Later, as they looked back on it all, they thought it was a miraculous event. And as they told stories about it, the miraculous element of the account got bigger and bigger and bigger—as did the peoples' own numbers—until, centuries later, we arrive at the stories told of 600,000 men, not counting the women and children, escaping on foot, led by the great man of God Moses, who plagued the Egyptians horribly and was used by God to part the Sea of Reeds, leading to the destruction of the entire Egyptian army.

This great miracle—as it was devised and developed in the tales told by storytellers over the generations—then came to be seen as the defining moment in making Israel a people and confirming that they were, in fact, the people of God.

The Literary Function of the Legends

This takes us then to the literary function of these legends as they were told and retold, until they were written down by J, E, and P, and then combined together into the one long narrative that makes up the book of Exodus. In their final form as we have them today, these legends are not simply trying to teach historical events that had happened long ago. As with most legends, they are trying to teach their readers and hearers important lessons. In this case, the lessons are about what it means to be Israel and how Israel stands in relationship to the one God who created all things.

- *The Election of Israel.* Within the framework of the Pentateuch, of course, these stories are tied closely to the events of Genesis with the promise to Abraham that he would become a great nation. In Exodus the promise is fulfilled: Israel has become an enormous nation. And it is a nation that has the God of Abraham—the God who created the universe—as its sovereign and protector. This is not just any group of people. This is the people of God, whose prayers God hears, who are protected and sustained by God. For many later Israelites there was no clearer indication of their unique standing before God than the events of the Exodus, where God decisively acted on behalf of his people by saving them from slavery and then delivering to them his Law to guide their worship of him and their communal lives together. Later Israelites drew clear theological lessons from this exodus event: they may be weak but their God, who had shown them special favor, is powerful. He could protect them, and they in turn were to obey what this God asks.

- *God's Sovereignty over All Things.* Key to these theological reflections was the view that this was not simply any God who had chosen Israel. This was the God who had created the universe and all the people of earth. Out of all these people, Israel had been chosen—but God was not simply their own local God. He was the God over all.

FIGURE 3.3. Two of the plagues that Moses brought against Egypt (top: locusts; bottom: darkness) from a Hebrew manuscript.

He was sovereign over and more powerful than any nation, even the greatest force on earth at the time, the nation of Egypt and its mighty ruler Pharaoh. Egypt and Pharaoh were mere pawns in God's almighty plan for his people. Moreover, God is sovereign over all the forces of earth. As the creator of all, he is the Lord of all and can command the elements to do his bidding (as in the plagues, as in the Sea of Reeds).

- *The God Who Saves is the God Who Instructs.* The Law of God was not given to just anyone, but to Israel—the nation God had saved. And that sequence is quite important: first God works his act of salvation for his elect, and then he gives his instructions to those he has chosen. We will explore this relationship of election and Law in the next section of this chapter.

- *The Passover is Rooted in a Historical Event.* A good portion of the plague narrative is taken up with the instructions for the observance of the annual Passover feast (see chapters 12–13). For some

BOX 3.3 THE PASSOVER MEAL

The Torah requires adult males to attend three separate religious festivals every year: Passover, the Feast of Pentecost, and the Feast of Tabernacles. All three were probably agricultural in origin—Passover to celebrate the flock, Pentecost the spring harvest, and Tabernacles the autumn harvest. Eventually they took on other significance. The Passover, for example, came to be identified as a commemoration of the exodus from Egypt.

Originally, presumably, Israelites would simply go to their closest shrine to celebrate these feasts. But when worship was localized in the Temple in Jerusalem, men were required, or at least encouraged, to travel there for the celebrations.

Eventually Passover was combined with the Feast of Unleavened Bread, which lasted seven days and became a major festival of the Jewish calendar. It is still celebrated today in the Passover seder. As is true now, the Passover in ancient Judaism involved a special meal of symbolic foods. Because the Israelites were saved from the plague of the death of the firstborn by killing a lamb

and spreading some of its blood on the doors of their houses, the main course of the meal was in every case a lamb that was sacrificed. The blood was commemorated by the cups of wine drunk at different stages of the meal. The fact that the Israelites were to be prepared to leave Egypt suddenly, as soon as Pharaoh sent the word, was commemorated by the kind of bread eaten—it had to be unleavened, since the Israelites had no time to allow the yeast to work. Bitter herbs were eaten to commemorate the bitterness of slavery in Egypt. And so on.

As we will see, the Passover festival continued to be celebrated in Jerusalem in New Testament times as well. In fact, it will be highly significant for our study of the Gospels and the historical Jesus, since it was during the Passover festival in Jerusalem that Jesus was arrested, tried, and crucified, an event that Christians commemorate in their own Passover-like celebration of the Eucharist. Still, among Jews to this day, the Passover seder is the most frequently performed annual ritual.

---

ancient Israelites (such as the Priestly source of the Pentateuch), just as weekly Sabbath observance is rooted in God's act of the creation of the world (Genesis 1), so too is the annual Passover observance rooted in God's act of salvation of his people, Israel. (See Box 3.3.) In fact, so much alike are these two moments (creation and exodus) that some Israelite thinkers came to consider the exodus to be a new creation, of the people of Israel.

- *God and Killing.* Not all the lessons that could be drawn from the Exodus account may seem equally palatable to modern readers. After the exodus event itself, God will give Moses the Ten Commandments, which will include the injunction "You shall not kill." But, as should be obvious from the entire context of the Bible, what this commandment means is that "you shall not murder a fellow Israelite." God himself is said to have killed the firstborn of every Egyptian family (this is not an easy story to read: imagine every firstborn in all the families in your own town dying overnight), not to mention all the soldiers in Pharaoh's army. And he will later give quite explicit instructions to the Israelites to slaughter

men, women, and children as they start to take over the Promised Land. Many readers today have a triumphalistic sense of satisfaction in reading the stories about how God's enemies are subject to his wrath, but it is important to realize that the God of the Bible (the New Testament as well as the Old) is not a tame God bound by modern views of what is right, just, and fair for all people.

THE LAW OF MOSES (EXODUS, LEVITICUS, NUMBERS)

The Law that God is said to have given to Moses on Mount Sinai is completely central to the Pentateuch, in every way. The various laws are set out, as delivered directly to Moses, in almost the entirety of Exodus 20 through Numbers 10, including the entire book of Leviticus (a book that is misnamed, in that the **Levites**—descendants of Levi who played a significant role in Israelite worship practices—are mentioned only in Leviticus 25:32–33). It is largely because the Law takes up such a large portion of these five books, and occurs in the middle, that the entire collection is traditionally known as the Torah. One could also make the case that the Law is central because it is the overarching point of these books: God chose his people, saved them, and then—as the climax—gave them his "direction" or "instruction" for how to worship him and to live in community together. It should be remembered that virtually the entirety of Deuteronomy also concerns the Law (the term "Deuteronomy" literally means "second law"; in the Pentateuch it is the occasion on which Moses gives the people the Law a second time). But the Law as found in the three books we are considering at this stage comes principally from the P source. P did not originate these laws, however; as we will see, it has drawn on earlier legal codes and put them together into a longer narrative.

The Overall Conception of the Law (and Occasional Misconceptions)

There are widespread misunderstandings of the nature and function of the Law of Moses among modern readers—especially within some elements of the Christian tradition. Many conservative Christians think that the Law of Moses is hopelessly detailed and impossible to keep, even though Jews *have* to keep it for salvation. In this view, it is the Christian gospel that can save people from the condemnation that comes from breaking the Law (which, by its very nature, *has* to be broken, since no one can keep it). Whether or not this view is right theologically, it certainly is not the view of the Law that has been traditional within Judaism. The Law was traditionally seen as the greatest gift God had ever given his people. Here are instructions from the creator of the universe about how to worship him and how to relate to one another. Nothing could be better.

The Law of Moses may seem extraordinarily detailed to outsiders and in places to be arbitrary and pointless. But *every* legal code seems extraordinarily detailed and arbitrary to outsiders. Just think of laws that we have in America. Our laws are far, far more complicated than anything in the Hebrew Bible. Just the laws about how to drive cars and about what one can and cannot do with sexual partners could fill volumes, and would seem bizarre indeed to someone living in different contexts. Or

think of all the laws about what one can or cannot personally consume in terms of, say, liquids, pills, and inhalants. Talk about detailed and seemingly arbitrary!

The Law within ancient Israelite religion, and then later within Judaism, was never meant to be "the way of salvation." It was never thought that a Jew had to earn God's favor by doing the Law, and that when she or he failed (as always happened) it meant being condemned to an eternity in hell. This view very much puts the cart before the horse. In traditional Jewish thinking, salvation has *already* come to Jews by virtue of their election as the people of God. Keeping the Law was the reverential response to the salvation that God had already provided. People did what God wanted precisely out of gratitude for the favor already showered on them, in loving response to his kind and glorious act of salvation.

This overall conception of the Law is presented in the Law itself, in fact, at the very beginning of the legal section of Exodus—after Israel has reached Mount Sinai, and God begins to speak to Moses—in highly significant and meaningful words:

> Thus you shall say to the house of Jacob, and tell the Israelites: You have seen what I did to the Egyptians, and how I bore you on eagles' wings and brought you to myself. Now therefore, if you shall obey my voice and keep my covenant, you shall be my treasured possession out of all the peoples. Indeed, the whole earth is mine, but you shall be for me a priestly kingdom and a holy nation. (Exodus 19:3–6)

Notice the sequence here: first God saved Israel from their slavery in Egypt and "brought" them to himself "on eagles' wings." In response they are to obey his voice and keep the covenant (which he had already made with them). When they do so, they will become a special people before God, "a priestly kingdom and a holy nation." Failing to do what God demanded, of course, had very serious consequences. But there is nothing in the Law that was outrageously difficult to do—any more than is the case with American laws. It really is not that difficult to refrain from idolatry, murder, and sorcery, or to slaughter your ox if it gores your neighbor to death.

Understanding the Law in Its Historical Context: The Suzerainty Treaty

Before looking at specific aspects of the Law, it may be helpful to put it in its broader historical context. Scholars have long realized that the "covenant" that God is said to have made with Israel is like other "covenants" or "peace treaties" known from the ancient Near Eastern environment. One set of such political treaties was called a **Suzerainty Treaty** and is often identified with a people known as the Hittites, who were a dominant force in Asia Minor (modern Turkey) at about the time that the exodus under Moses allegedly took place (say, 1500–1200 B.C.E.). These are called "suzerainty" treaties because they were between an overlord, known as a *suzerain* (in this case the Hittites), and an underling, or a vassal (in this case some other nation that the Hittites had subdued). These treaties were decidedly not between two equal partners. One party was superior to and dominant over the other.

A number of these suzerainty treaties have been uncovered by archaeologists. They typically include six components:

1. Identification of the two parties.
2. A statement of the history of their relationship.
3. Stipulations that the suzerain is placing on the vassal.
4. Provisions for depositing the treaty in a safe or sacred place.
5. The invocation of divine witnesses to the treaty and the intent to observe it.
6. A delineation of the blessings that will come upon the vassal for keeping the required stipulations and of the curses or dire consequences that will befall him for failing to keep them.

It is possible to see the Torah given to Moses as framed in a similar way, both on the large scale (thus Exodus 19:3–6, quoted above, as setting up the giving of the whole Law) and in individual parts. The first set of laws that God gives Moses on the Mount are the Ten Commandments, technically known as the **Decalogue** (which means "the ten words"). Notice how the Decalogue begins: "I am the LORD your God, who brought you out of the land of Egypt, out of the house of slavery" (Exodus 20:2). This statement corresponds to the

first two components of the suzerainty treaty: the two parties are identified and their relevant history is detailed. Then God provides the "stipulations"— the Ten Commandments themselves. Within the Decalogue there is no provision for depositing the two tablets that God gives Moses, but elsewhere we learn that they are to be placed in the sacred "ark of the covenant" (See Box 3.5), the holy box that served as their repository and that was carried with the Israelites in the wilderness and placed, when they camped, in the tabernacle as the place where God was particularly thought to reside.

It would not be possible for God to invoke any "divine witnesses" (the fifth component of the suzerainty treaties), since in Israelite religion he alone is the supreme God. But throughout the Torah there are innumerable references to the blessings that will come to the people for keeping the Law and the curses that will occur should they break it. These occur within the Decalogue as well, for example where God commands that no one is to make an idol to worship, else they and their children will be severely punished, whereas if the commandment is obeyed, God will continue to show his steadfast love to them (Exodus 20:5).

And so the Decalogue—indeed, the entire Torah—can be understood as fitting into its own historical context. It is set up like a peace treaty in which God, the ultimate suzerain, gives stipulations to his vassal, the nation of Israel, which he is justified in requiring because of his past beneficent acts toward them. Keeping these stipulations will allow the vassal to stay in the good graces of its Lord; breaking them will incur his wrath.

Overview of the Laws

There are two major types of laws found in the Torah of Moses. Some of the laws are **apodictic**: this is when a straightforward and absolute command is made, such as "You shall not murder," "You shall not commit adultery," "You shall not steal." Apodictic laws are usually prohibitions of what not to do, but not always. Even in the Decalogue, for example, we have "Remember the Sabbath day and keep it holy" and "Honor your father and mother."

Other laws are **casuistic**: this is when a condition is set forth ("if this happens") and then the consequence ("then this must be done"). Examples

FIGURE 3.4. This mountain, in the southern part of the Sinai Peninsula, is called Jebel Musa; traditionally it has been identified as Mount Sinai, where Moses received the Law.

of this kind of law are abundant in Exodus: "When a slave owner strikes a male or female slave with a rod and the slave dies immediately, the owner shall be punished" (21:20); "When people who are fighting injure a pregnant woman so that there is a miscarriage, and yet no further harm follows, the one responsible shall be fined what the woman's husband demands" (21:22); "If someone's ox hurts the ox of another, so that it dies, then they shall sell the live ox and divide the price of it; and the dead animal they shall also divide" (21:35).

Almost all of the laws found in the Torah serve one of three functions.

- Some laws are instructions about religious practices, principally about how to worship Yahweh, and how not to worship. And so, for example, no physical representations of Yahweh may be made, and no other gods (or idols) are to be worshiped; the Sabbath day is to be kept; certain sacred festivals, such as the Passover, are to be observed.

- Other laws are directions about how the community is to live its life together. And so, for example, we have the casuistic laws just quoted, about slave owners beating slaves, fighters causing miscarriages, and oxen killing one another.

- Yet other laws appear to be designed principally to make the people of Israel "pure"; that is, set apart from all other people in how they live. This final category may explain the practice of circumcision (although see Box 2.5) and the various dietary laws that later Jews would call **kosher food laws** detailing which kinds of food can be eaten (sheep and cows, for example) and which kind cannot (swine and shrimp, for example). Some people have argued over the years that the forbidden foods are made off-limits because they could make people sick; but if you read the restrictions carefully it is clear that some of these foods are not of that sort, and some of the permitted foods can be a very real health problem. It is just as bad to eat raw chicken as to eat raw pork.

BOX 3.4 THE CODE OF HAMMURAPI

The various corpora of legal materials in the Hebrew Bible—the Covenant Code, the Priestly Code, the Holiness Code—were not unique in the ancient world. Far from it. Many peoples had their own legal systems, and in some ways those of other peoples were remarkably similar to those of the ancient Israelites. None is more famous than the **Code of Hammurapi**, which long predated the corpora found in the Hebrew Bible. Hammurapi was a king of Babylonia in the early part of the eighteenth century B.C.E. His law code was inscribed on an eight-foot-high stele made of basalt, discovered in 1901. It contains 282 laws, some of which will sound familiar to those who have read their Hebrew Bibles (with striking differences as well). Here are some samples:[2]

- ¶130: If a man pins down another man's virgin wife who is still residing in her father's house, and they seize him lying with her, that man shall be killed; that woman shall be released.

_____
2   Taken from Martha T. Roth, *Law Collections from Mesopotamia and Asia Minor*, 2nd ed. (Atlanta, GA: Scholars Press, 1997).

- ¶131: If her husband accuses his own wife (of adultery), although she has not been seized lying with another male, she shall swear (to her innocence by) an oath by the god, and return to her house.
- ¶195: If a child should strike his father, they shall cut off his hand.
- ¶196: If an *awilu* (= freeperson) should blind the eye of another *awilu*, they shall blind his eye.
- ¶197: If he should break the bone of another *awilu*, they shall break his bone.
- ¶198: If he should blind the eye of a commoner or break the bone of a commoner, he shall weigh and deliver 60 shekels of silver.
- ¶199: If he should blind the eye of an *awilu*'s slave or break the bone of an *awilu*'s slave, he shall weigh and deliver one-half of his value (in silver).
- ¶209: If an *awilu* strikes a woman of the *awilu*-class and thereby causes her to miscarry her fetus, he shall weigh and deliver 10 shekels of silver for her fetus.
- ¶210: If that woman should die, they shall kill his daughter.

The Various Corpora within the Torah

A large portion of Exodus 20–Numbers 10 (including Leviticus) comes from the Priestly source, but, as mentioned, its unknown author utilized earlier law codes that had been in circulation before his day. Apart from the Decalogue, scholars have identified three such codes that appear to form units within the larger corpus. These three corpora are the following.

THE COVENANT CODE

The **Covenant Code** can be found in Exodus 20:22–23:33. It is the one preexisting unit thought by most scholars to come from E rather than P. Its name comes from 24:7: "Then he took the book of the covenant, and read it in the hearing of the people." The laws given here, right after the Decalogue, are almost entirely casuistic, and they presuppose a time when the people of Israel were already permanently settled on the land and were living among one another with their families, their slaves, and their animals. These are laws that pertain in particular to agricultural communities. The general sense among scholars, then, is that the Covenant Code did not originate back in the time of Moses at all, but from a later period of Israel's history. Some of the many issues dealt with in this corpus are the following:

- *Slaves.* It is assumed that free men will own slaves, and they are treated as property (chapter 21). But there are rules about how to treat them. For example, any male Hebrew slave is to be set free after being enslaved for six years (21:2); a man may sell his own daughter as a sex slave, but if she does not satisfy her master then she can be set free for a price (21:7–8).
- *Violence* (chapter 21). There are numerous laws about violent activity. For example, anyone who hits one of his parents is to be executed; so is anyone who even curses his parents (meaning, apparently, invokes a curse against them). And so is anyone who kidnaps.
- *Property rights* (chapter 21). If someone's ox misbehaves, something is to be done about it. For

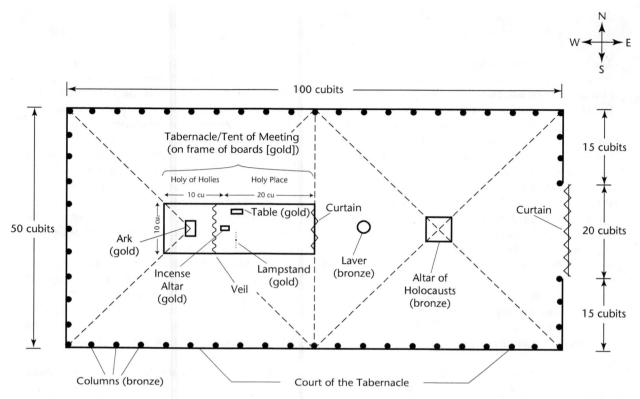

FIGURE 3.5. The tabernacle—the place of worship for the Israelites in the wilderness (and later, until King Solomon built the Temple)—as it is described in the book of Exodus.

example, if an ox gores someone to death, the ox is to be stoned to death and cannot then be eaten; and if that happens with an ox that has been prone to gore people before (not to death), then the owner of the ox is also to be executed.

- *Restitutions* (chapter 22). If someone harms another, or is the indirect cause of harm, some kind of restitution has to be made. For example, anyone who steals a sheep and then slaughters or sells it has to pay the original owner five times its worth; if a neighbor's bonfire causes someone else's crops to be burned, then he must pay to make up for the loss.

- *Women.* It should be obvious by some of these examples that these are laws directed toward adult males. Women and children were considered their property. That is already intimated in the Decalogue, where the final commandment indicates that no one is to covet (that is, want so badly that he is willing to steal) his neighbor's house, wife, slave, ox, or donkey. Here a man's wife is valued right alongside his donkey.

The Priestly Code

The so-called **Priestly Code** is found in Leviticus 1–16. This is a set of laws that, as the name implies, are chiefly concerned with priests, their activities (such as performing sacrifices), and their concerns (such as maintaining ritual purity). The corpus comes, of course, from the P source. Some of the major issues addressed in these laws are as follows:

SACRIFICES (CHAPTERS 1–7) A **sacrifice** is simply some kind of offering made to a deity. All ancient religions, including that of ancient Israel, included the idea that sacrifices could and should be offered to God or to the gods. Historians and anthropologists have long wrestled with the question of how the idea of making a sacrifice originated or what, even, the sacrifice was supposed to do. It may be that there were a variety of answers. Some scholars have thought that since sacrifices typically consist of foodstuffs—animals and vegetables—they originally were thought to provide food and nourishment to the gods, which made them quite happy, needless to say, since no one wants a hungry god on their hands. Sacrifices may, as well, have been seen as simple gifts to the gods of that which is most necessary and important to humans (I give you this gift so that you can reciprocate). It may be that in some instances it was thought that an animal that was sacrificed was somehow a "substitute" for a human who owed his life to a god (take this beast, not me). In some instances sacrifices performed the comparable function of "**atonement**"; that is, the restoration of a right relationship with a god when some kind of breach or transgression had occurred that made the god angry or distant. In a number of the sacrifices mentioned in the Torah, the function was clearly to return a person to a state of ritual purity before God—an issue I will be explaining more fully in a moment. There were several clear side benefits to the entire sacrificial system: in some of the offerings, as we will see, the carcass was kept and eaten, giving worshipers a rare opportunity to eat meat, which was a bit exotic otherwise. Moreover, the priests who performed the sacrifices could themselves benefit from, and thus be paid by, the leftovers.

There are a number of different kinds of sacrifice described and prescribed in Leviticus 1–7, and trying to sort out all the differences among them has created major headaches for scholars of the Hebrew Bible over the years—especially with respect to the question of what each sacrifice was supposed to accomplish. The following are some of the most important ones:

- *Burnt offerings.* In a burnt offering an animal is slaughtered, its blood is spread on the altar (the sacred table on which the sacrifice was made), and it is burned, completely, with nothing left over. The text of Leviticus does not indicate what the purpose of this sacrifice was, exactly.
- *Grain offerings.* Rather than an animal, this is an offering of flour with oil and incense poured over it. It is burned and its smell is said to be pleasing to God. To what end, we are not told.
- *Sacrifice of well-being.* This is another animal sacrifice, where the animal is killed and its blood is sprinkled on the altar. But in this case the whole animal is not burned, only its fatty parts. The rest of the animal gets eaten by the person who brings the sacrifice and by the priests who slaughter it.

- *Sin and guilt offerings.* In these offerings the animal is killed, its blood sprinkled on the altar, and its fatty portions are burned. The rest of the carcass is either taken outside the sanctuary (the holy place) to be burned or simply thrown away. We do know the purpose of these sacrifices: they were offered to "purify" the person who brought them, who had sinned against God and needed to be restored into a right standing with him.

CLEAN AND UNCLEAN FOODS (CHAPTER 11)

The Priestly Code is where we find the clearest expression of the ancient dietary laws—that is, the laws concerning what could and could not be eaten. It should not be thought that ancient Israelites were very peculiar in insisting that certain foods (pork and shellfish, for example) were not to be eaten. A large number of ancient cultures had similar rules and taboos. The question of *why* some foods were permitted in some cultures but forbidden in others is a thorny one; the various food regulations may well have been based on ancient debates that are no longer available to us. Still, in many instances—probably including the laws of Israel—these proscriptions of certain foods were probably less for reasons of health (this is good for you to eat; this is bad) than to make the group distinctive among its neighbors. Swine were sacrificed in religious cults of Israel's neighbors (the hated Philistines, at least); Israelites refused to eat pork. That's probably not an accident.

But it wasn't just pork that was forbidden. In Leviticus 10 it is any land animal that did not have a divided hoof and that chewed the cud. That would include rock badgers and hares, for example. Fish had to have both fins and scales. No birds of prey (vultures, hawks, and buzzards) were allowed. And so on.

RITUAL IMPURITY (CHAPTERS 12–15)

It is difficult for most people in the modern world to get their minds around what ritual impurity is, since in our culture, by and large, we have nothing quite analogous. For the Priestly Code, a person could become ritually impure and needed to perform a ritual act to be restored to a state of purity but it had nothing to do with "sin" or with any kind of disobedience to God. There were simply some things that put a person in a state of impurity where they were not allowed to enter the sanctuary and worship God until the impurity had been removed. Touching a corpse would make a person ritually impure; but so too would childbearing for a woman, and even having a menstruation period. Leprosy and various skin diseases brought impurity, but so too did numerous bodily discharges (e.g., semen). This portion of the Priestly Code explicates the various kinds of ritual impurity and prescribes the steps that need to be taken in order to move from being impure to being pure.

THE DAY OF ATONEMENT (CHAPTER 16)

Of particular importance to the book of Leviticus is an annual day on which the sins of the people could be atoned for (i.e., ceremonially removed). On this day the high priest would offer up a bull as a sin offering for himself. Then he would offer a goat as the sin offering to purify the holy place from the sins of the people over the past year. He would then take another goat, lay his hands on it, confess the sins that the people of Israel had committed, and set the goat loose into the wilderness. The idea was that the goat (a "scapegoat") would carry the sins away so that they would no longer be present among the people.

The Holiness Code

The **Holiness Code** is found in Leviticus 17–26; it too may come from the Priestly source, although in this case there is some debate among scholars whether it was a self-contained preexistent source taken over by P or was instead P's own creation (other scholars think that it was actually written *after* the P source in order to expand upon the laws of P). It is called the "Holiness Code" because the word "holy" is found extensively throughout these various laws, which can be summed up nicely by the compact statement of Leviticus 19:2: "You shall be holy, for I the LORD your God am holy."

Holiness in this context does not mean officious piety ("holier than thou"); the basic idea is that the people of Israel are to be distinct, set apart from everyone else. Just as Yahweh is completely separated from his creation in being above it all, so too his people are to be separate from everyone else as a distinctive people in the midst of those who are not set apart for God. They are separate from all others not only because they behave differently from outsiders—although that is part of it—but also

because, relatedly, they act in ways that make them conform to the will of God. In the ethical realm, among other things this means that "You shall love your neighbor as yourself" (Leviticus 19:18). Your "neighbor" in this case, of course, is someone living in your own community. You are certainly not to love those outside of Israel very much. The Israelites are later instructed to slaughter the Canaanites. But within the community you are to treat others as you yourself want to be treated.

The Holiness Code is filled with both apodictic and casuistic laws, some of them involving religious rituals to be performed and others of them ethical injunctions for behaving in a proper way in the community. These laws include more requirements for sacrifices. They include food laws (Israelites are not to consume the blood of animals, 19:26). They outlaw certain religious practices (augury and witchcraft, 19:26). They prescribe dress codes (Israelite men are not to cut the edges off their hair or beard, 19:27). They include lots of ethical codes, some of which involve family life (a man is not supposed to sell his daughter into prostitution, 19:26; people should defer to the elderly, 19:32). A number of the striking laws have to do with sexual ethics: the Israelite man is not to have sex with his father, mother, stepmother, sister, half-sister, stepsister, aunt, daughter-in-law, or, strikingly, any woman who is having her period. And men were not to have sex with men. There is no law against women having sex with women but, as I have pointed out, these laws are principally aimed at adult males. There are also laws here concerning festivals and feast days. The Holiness Code covers a lot of territory.

But so, naturally, does the entire Law of Moses. This was to be the law of the land for ancient Israel. It is nowhere near as complicated as modern legal codes of, say, modern Western countries. But its function was not simply to regulate life so that society could be a better, happier, and more prosperous place. It was also to guide the Israelite in relationship with God. So in addition to criminal law and civil law there were laws about purity and impurity, laws about sacrifices, laws forbidding certain religious practices, and laws requiring other practices. All in all, these laws were meant to guide the Israelites in their lives with one another and their life with God, the one who had saved them from their slavery in Egypt and chosen them to be his special people. He had delivered them and given them his covenant; they were to respond by following the directions, the instruction, the Torah that he had given.

THE BOOK OF NUMBERS

The book of Numbers, the fourth book in the Pentateuch, receives its name from the fact that at the very beginning in chapter 1, and then again—forty years but only twenty-six chapters later—Moses is told to conduct a census of the people of Israel, of "every male, individually; from twenty years old and upward, everyone in Israel able to go to war" (1:3–4). The reason for these censuses, obviously, is to size up the strength of the army about to go into battle. In Numbers, after ten chapters that take place still at Mount Sinai, the children of Israel set out for the Promised Land, which they are to conquer by destroying the other peoples currently living in it. But something very bad happens en route, and God punishes the people for their lack of faith. They must wait forty years in the wilderness—until the generation of Israelites who experienced the Exodus has died off (in the Bible a generation is forty years)—so that their children, then, can go into the Promised Land. And so the first census is taken in expectation of imminent battles; but by the time—forty years later—the battles are set to commence, another census is necessary. We learn from the first census that the Israelites had 603,550 males twenty years and older able to fight, not counting the 23,000 adult male descendants of Levi who, having sacred duties, were not required to participate in battle (1:46–47). After that generation died off (with only a couple of exceptions) the count was taken up again. The numbers had remained relatively constant: now there are 602,730 male adults "able to go to war" (26:51). After the second census, the fighting begins.

In rough outline, the book of Numbers is structured then as follows:

- *Israel Still at Mount Sinai* (chapters 1–10). This is largely P material, and in addition to the census of the fighting men and a census of the various clans of the Levites we find a number of additional laws given to Moses, a number of offerings made to Yahweh, and then the celebration of the first Passover at Sinai—to commemorate the one-year anniversary of the Exodus.
- *The Wanderings in the Wilderness and Israel's Various Missteps* (chapters 10–20). The children of Israel leave Mount Sinai and are led by a divine cloud out into the wilderness: "the cloud lifted from over the tabernacle of the covenant. Then the Israelites set out by stages from the wilderness of Sinai, and the cloud settled down in the wilderness of Paran" (10:11–12). In the next section we will consider a number of the episodes that happen here in the wilderness; the short story is that the people of Israel are portrayed as perennially discontent and grumbling, and at one point they demonstrate a total lack of faith in Yahweh that he punishes by forcing them to remain in the wilderness for an entire generation before they are led into battle to claim the Promised Land.
- *The Beginnings of the Conquest.* After the forty years are over the people of Israel, led still by Moses, head north following a path to the east of the Dead Sea, in the area known as the Transjordan. There they encounter opposition and begin the battles to overtake the land, defeating their enemies and slaughtering the opposition in a violent act of annihilation. This land is distributed among two and a half of the twelve tribes. The book ends with the people (all two or three million of them) poised on the east bank of the Jordan, ready to cross over to do battle with the peoples of Canaan.

And so, in terms of chronology there is an imbalance in the action that takes place in the final four books of the Pentateuch. From the time the people arrive at Mount Sinai in Exodus 19 until they leave in Numbers 10 (a total of 54 chapters—including all of the book of Leviticus), a total of eleven months passes; but from Numbers 10 to 20 (just 11 chapters) there is a passage of 40 years. Even though not a lot of space is devoted to those years in the narrative, a lot happens—most of it not good from the point of view of Moses and of God himself.

Some Literary Themes of the Narrative

Some of the main themes of the narrative can be summed up under the following headings.

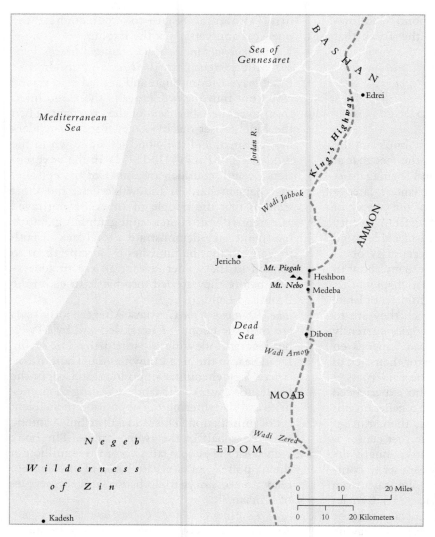

FIGURE 3.6. Areas mentioned in Numbers, at the end of the "wandering in the wilderness" and the beginning of the conquest of the land, in the Transjordan (east of Jordan) area.

THE FRAUGHT RELATIONSHIP WITH GOD

Throughout the account of Israel in the wilderness there runs a constant refrain of human complaint and divine punishment. The Israelites think it is miserable to be off in a barren wilderness, away from the safety and comforts of civilization, and they have no qualms about complaining and moaning about it. God becomes fed up with their complaints and makes them pay in big ways. This happens time and again. The following are some of the key incidents.

THE FOOD SHORTAGE

With two or three million mouths to feed, it is no surprise that there were serious problems with the food supply. Soon after leaving Mount Sinai, the people complain about it:

> The rabble among them had a strong craving; and the Israelites also wept again and said, "If only we had meat to eat! We remember the fish we used to eat in Egypt for nothing, the cucumbers, the melons, the leeks, the onions, and the garlic; but now our strength is dried up, and there is nothing at all but this manna to look at." (Numbers 10:4–6)

The manna was God's daily supply of food for the Israelites from the time they left Egypt. At night the dew would settle on the ground, and in the morning a white, flaky substance would be left behind, which the Israelites would gather and cook in loaves like bread or small cakes. For the most part that is what they subsisted on, day in and day out. And they were tired of it. It may seem like a sensible complaint to the Almighty but God does not see it this way: "Then the LORD became very angry and Moses was displeased" (11:11). God decides to give his ungrateful people what they want by providing them with some serious meat. He tells them that they will have way too much of a good thing:

> You shall eat not only one day, or two days, or five days, or ten days, or twenty days, but for a whole month—until it comes out of your nostrils and becomes loathsome to you—because you have rejected the LORD who is among you and have wailed before him, saying "Why did we ever leave Egypt?" (11:19).

God then sends in enormous numbers of quails who land, and conveniently fall exhausted, outside the presumably very large camp of the Israelites. The quail were three feet deep all around. The people gathered them together and ate them, but God poisoned them with the meat and inflicted them "with a very great plague" (11:33).

THE AUTHORITY OF MOSES In addition to complaining about the food, people complained about the leadership of Moses. Most striking, it was his brother Aaron (the head of all the priests) and his sister Miriam who found reason to object to his high-handed ways: "Has the LORD spoken only through Moses? Has he not spoken through us also?" (12:2). God once again is not pleased. He sends a cloud over their tent and when it lifts, Miriam is covered with leprosy. Moses prays for her, and God makes her remain leprous for seven days before restoring her to health.

Later, three other wannabe leaders, Korah, Dathan, and Abiram, complain that Moses is too self-assertive in his leadership and insist, along with 250 companions, that they too be exalted to positions of authority (chapter 16). This time God is not so kind to the three ringleaders; in the end, "the earth opened up and swallowed them up, along with their households . . . so that they and all that belonged to them went down alive into **Sheol**" (16:32–33); then fire comes from heaven and consumes their 250 cohorts.

Later still, the people of Israel are still found to be complaining:

> The people spoke against God and against Moses, Why have you brought us up out of Egypt to die in the wilderness? For there is no food and no water, and we detest this miserable food." (Numbers 21:5)

This time God responds by sending poisonous snakes among the people, who die when bitten. Moses prays for a solution and God tells him to make a snake out of bronze and to place it on top of a pole. Anyone who looks at the snake will survive the snakebite.

DISOBEDIENCE TO THE LAW In other instances, members of the community violate the Law that Moses had just received some time before on Sinai. One man is found gathering firewood on the Sabbath—the day of rest (Numbers 15:32–36). It is reported to Moses who is told by the LORD that they are to show no mercy. "The whole congregation" takes the man outside the camp and stones him to death.

THE ULTIMATE BETRAYAL: THE REFUSAL TO TRUST YAHWEH The most serious breach with Yahweh happens relatively early in the narrative. This is what causes the children of Israel to remain in the wilderness for forty years. After leaving Mount Sinai, the people have journeyed north so that they are to the south of the Promised Land of Canaan. Moses sends in twelve spies to observe the land, presumably to help him develop a strategy of attack (13:1). The men cross through the land and they are absolutely amazed at what they see. The land is so rich and fertile that it is nothing like what they are experiencing in the wilderness with their daily rations of manna. They cut down a cluster of grapes. It is so enormous they have to carry it on a pole between two of them.

That is the good news. The bad news is very bad indeed. They have found that the land is heavily populated and fortified. The towns are large and walled. And the inhabitants of the land are enormous. By comparison: "to ourselves we seemed like grasshoppers, and so we seemed to them" (13:33). Of the twelve spies only two, Joshua and a man named Caleb, are in favor of pressing the attack. The others are dead set against it and cause a rebellion among the people, who decide to choose another leader to take them back to Egypt (14:4). They want to stone Moses and Aaron. God, of course, is angered. This is what brings about the downfall of that generation. Moses prays for God to forgive their lack of trust, and God indicates that he will forgive the people. But:

> None of the people who have seen my glory and the signs that I did in Egypt and in the wilderness, and yet have tested me these ten times and have not obeyed my voice, shall see the land that I swore to give to their ancestors (14:22–23).

The only exceptions will be Joshua and Caleb. All the others will die off in the wilderness; it will be their children who will enter into the land "flowing with milk and honey."

THE DISOBEDIENCE OF MOSES Even Moses is not destined to enter the Promised Land. In a later incident we find the people complaining once more about their lack of supplies—this time of water (chapter 20). The LORD tells Moses to supply them with water by going up to a certain large boulder and commanding that it bring forth water. Instead of speaking to the boulder, Moses strikes it twice with his staff. The waters gush out, but God is displeased. It may seem like a slight infringement, but it is very significant to God. Because Moses did not do exactly as he was instructed, "therefore you shall not bring this assembly into the land that I have given them" (20:12).

THE CONQUEST OF THE TRANSJORDAN Now that forty years have passed, Israel is ready and able to conquer the Promised Land. As indicated earlier, this time instead of coming into the land from the south (the original plan when the twelve spies had been sent out), they approach from the east, on the other side of the Jordan River. This land is also occupied, and Israel fights the armies of two of the local kings, Sihon of the Amorites and Og of Bashan, fiercely with the sword (it is not clear where the Israelites' weapons came from) and soundly defeat them (chapter 21). After a number of other episodes—which, among other things, include a lengthy account of an unwilling prophet Balaam and his talking donkey (Numbers 22–24)—the second census is taken, more ritual laws are laid

down, and the people, still led by Moses, continue their attack on the people occupying the land in the Transjordan.

Their next victim is the people of Midian, and this account illustrates the policies of war that Yahweh insists his people follow. There is to be a massive slaughter of the opposition. God orders the Israelite army to kill every male, and they do so (31:7); they then burn all their towns. Moses becomes angry, though, when he learns that the women and children were spared. He orders that every male boy and infant be killed, along with every woman who is not a virgin. The young virgins, however, the men can keep for themselves (31:15–18). This, needless to say, will be a brutal conquest—to be continued in the book of Joshua.

Some Historical and Literary Perspectives

Given our earlier discussions about the historical problems with the narratives of the Pentateuch in general, there is no reason to spend considerable time with those found here in the book of Numbers. Here too there are internal inconsistencies, implausibilities, and sundry other issues. Biblical scholars have long thought that it is hard to imagine that two and a half or three million people could be sustained in the wilderness, no matter how much manna was falling on the ground at night. The armies of Israel slaughter the opposition—but with what weapons, exactly? Moreover, how could these massive encampments, not to mention the enormous battles, have occurred and there be no trace of it, at all, in the archaeological record? Furthermore, the numbers of people involved appear internally inconsistent. We have seen that the first census indicated that there were over 600,000 men over the age of 20 in the Israelite camp. But in a separate counting, we are told that all of the firstborn males among the Israelites (from one month old upwards) numbered 22,273 (Numbers 3:43). You can do the math yourself. This would have to mean that every single family among the Israelites had twenty-seven males who were *not* the firstborn.

And so, once again, we appear to be dealing not with historical realities here but with legendary tales which, like the other legends of the Pentateuch, are trying to convey lessons. Here the lessons are relatively clear and straightforward. God is all-powerful and is able to protect and defend his people and make them not only survive but thrive. But disobedience has very dire consequences indeed. All God asks for is trusting acceptance and faithfulness to what he demands. Anything less than that will be severely punished. But in the end, God will act on behalf of his people. For Israel is distinctly his, and the Israelites are the only people he is concerned with. The other peoples—the ones occupying the land that God has promised to give to the descendants of Abraham—not only have no right to live where they do, they have no right to live. Israel is instructed not just to uproot these people from their homes; they are to slaughter them, to the last person (except, in some cases, for the young virgins, whom the men can take for themselves). These are lessons that we will see repeated throughout the historical books of the Hebrew Bible.

THE BOOK OF DEUTERONOMY

The final book of the Pentateuch receives its name, as we have seen, from the circumstance that in it Moses delivers the Law to the Israelites a second time. Deuteronomy literally means "second law," although in principle it is actually the same law, only given on a different occasion. This is the one place in the Pentateuch where we encounter D material, and here we get it in abundance as it is virtually the entire book with the exception of the final chapter, which largely comes from P, as the Priestly editor wraps up his long five-book conglomeration of texts.

This editor was faced with a difficult problem: he had his own account of the giving of the Law, in what is now the legal portions of Exodus, Leviticus, and Numbers; but he had available to him as well this other source, which also told of the giving of the Law but did so in different terms, sometimes very different terms. How was he to solve that problem? He did so by making this the *second* time Moses delivered the Law to the Israelites. Now it is given to the children of those who received it the first time, since the first generation had perished in the wilderness as a punishment for their refusal to trust that Yahweh would fulfill his promises to them by giving them the land. On the verge of crossing the Jordan River to attack the cities of Canaan and so "inherit" the land, the children of Israel once more hear the Law, in preparation for their conquest.

The book of Deuteronomy is set up, then, as Moses' final address to his people. He will not be able to enter the land himself because of his own (somewhat minor) infraction. The book of Deuteronomy will end with his death and burial. But the rest of the book more or less consists of Moses speaking. Among other things he will stress in his farewell address, even more than in the earlier parts of the Pentateuch, the blessings that will accrue to the children of Israel if they are faithful to God and, yet even more, the curses that will plague them if they are not. The curses are particularly dire and take up about four times as much space as the blessings.

The following is a rough literary structure of the main portions of the book:

- *Moses' Opening Speeches* (chapters 1–11). The opening of the book sets up all that will follow: "These are the words that Moses spoke to all Israel beyond the Jordan. . . . Moses undertook to expound this law as follows" (Deuteronomy 1:1, 5). After instructing the Israelites to appoint tribal leaders for themselves, Moses provides a brief review of the history of their wandering in the wilderness and their conquest of the Transjordan. He then launches into an opening restatement of the Law, beginning with the Decalogue (chapter 5). He spends considerable time urging the people to obey the Law and not to rebel again, and concludes this opening set of addresses with a nice summary of his overarching point:

> See I am setting before you today a blessing and a curse: the blessing, if you obey the commandments of the LORD your God that I am commanding you today; and the curse if you do not obey the commandments of the LORD your God, but turn from the way that I am commanding you today, to follow other gods that you have not known. (11:26–28)

The book of Deuteronomy will not only stress the blessings and curses, but also the importance of worshiping God and only God—no others.
- *The Regiving of the Law* (chapters 12–26). These chapters are sometimes called the "**Deuteronomic Code.**" Like the Covenant Code, the

BOX 3.5 THE TABERNACLE AND THE ARK OF THE COVENANT

Nearly all religions have sacred places that are set aside for the worship of the deity. But how can you have a sacred place if you are not settled down in a single location, but are on the move? You can have one if the sacred place is a tent that you move with you.

According to the books of the Pentateuch, Israel was on the move after leaving Egypt and before conquering the Holy Land. According to the Priestly source, P, their sanctuary was in fact a large tent called the **tabernacle**. It was believed in some circles that the tabernacle was a kind of mirror image of the place where God dwelt in heaven. In other words, God lived in a tent. But his tent on earth was very special (and the one in heaven, needless to say, would have been very, very special). In it was housed the **ark of the covenant**, on which God himself was thought to be enthroned in his manifestation here on earth.

The tabernacle was made up of woven curtains on a wooden frame. It could be assembled and disassembled as the people were on the move. It enclosed a large area of 75 x 150 feet—so roughly half the size of a football field. The inside was divided in half: the first half was where any of the Israelites could go; the other half was closed off and was only for the priests. This inner part contained a table where offerings were made, an altar, and a seven-branched lampstand. Deeper inside was a special room called the "holy of holies"—that is, the most holy, or sacred place. This was a curtained-off room that no one could enter except the high priest, on one day of the year, the **Day of Atonement**, when he would make atonement for the people's sins. Inside this holy of holies was the ark itself. (See Figure 3.5).

The ark was an elaborate wooden box, about 4 × 2.5 feet—the size of a modern cedar chest. It was overlaid with gold and had rings on each corner through which poles could be inserted so it could be carried. But more significant, on top of it was a covering that boasted two winged angelic-like beings called "cherubim." In ancient Israel it was believed that God himself sat between these cherubim, so that the ark was his throne. That is why the room that housed the ark was so very holy, and why not just anyone could come in to get a glimpse. It was set apart from all else.

Inside the ark were stored the two tablets that God gave Moses on Mount Sinai, containing the Decalogue. This was a sacred depository, then, for the most sacred of texts: the covenant that God had made with his people Israel.

Holiness Code, and the Priestly Code that we considered earlier, this collection of laws may have once been a self-standing composition; or it may be that the author of the D source simply gathered together a range of earlier laws into this longer collection. The collection is not clearly organized into distinct groupings of laws, but many of the same kinds of laws that we have already considered can be found here as well.

- There are laws about religious ceremonies and regulations—in particular the insistence, distinctive of Deuteronomy, that the only valid worship of Yahweh is to take place in the central sanctuary of the people. We have seen earlier that D was produced during the time of the Israelite monarchy (some 600 years after the days of Moses himself). At that time, the central sanctuary was no longer the tabernacle—the tent the Israelites carried with them around the wilderness—but the Temple in Jerusalem constructed by Solomon. For the author of this book, that is the one and only place where sacrifices are to be made to God. This is a major emphasis of his book.

- There are laws concerning clean and unclean foods, civil laws, and criminal laws—much as in others of the legal corpora. And sometimes (as with the Decalogue) the laws in fact are the very same laws as in the P materials. But there are different laws as well, and some laws that govern people and situations not envisioned in the other legal codes.

- Some Distinctive Laws. Among the instructions that are distinctive to Deuteronomy are those that pertain to kings, prophets, and Levites.

  - The kings of Israel are not to acquire many horses, many wives, or too much gold and silver (17:14–18). These requirements are almost certainly directed against what were known to be abuses of the later kings of Israel; one naturally thinks of King Solomon

FIGURE 3.7. This stele, discovered in 1901, contains the famous Code of Hammurapi of Babylon. The code contains 282 laws (written out underneath the portrayal of Hammurapi receiving them from Shamash, the sun god), many of which are similar to those found in the Torah of Scripture.

(who reigned more than 200 years after this speech was allegedly given), who was not only unbelievably rich but who also had a very bad reputation indeed for having so many wives and concubines—700 princesses and 300 concubines, according to 1 Kings 11:3–4. As we will see, these excesses brought about some rather negative feelings against Solomon by some of the biblical authors, who thought these other wives turned him away from Yahweh. Many of the other kings fared no better; indeed, much worse in the eyes of the later biblical historians. In any event, for many scholars this kind of legislation is a clear and certain indication that Deuteronomy does not present a speech that actually came from the lips of Moses, but that was composed at a much later time in light of problems that had arisen in a different context.

- Prophets. There are two passages (chapters 13 and 18) that deal with false "prophets." As we will see in chapter 5, prophets—that is, religious figures who claimed to be delivering revelations directly from God—arose during the Israelite monarchy. The difficulty with a prophet is that it is not always possible to determine whether his revelation comes from God or is simply something he has made up himself for his own purposes. Deuteronomy provides some guidelines for making those decisions. Once again, this legislation is presupposing a much later historical context long after the days of Moses.

- Levites. The Levites were the descendants of Jacob's son Levi; from their ranks came Aaron, whose descendants were the **priests** who were the ones who officiated at the religious ceremonies in the central sanctuary (in monarchical times, the sacrifices in the Jerusalem Temple). In Deuteronomy the Levites are given greater authority than in other legal codes in that they are equated in places with the priests themselves (all priests were Levites, but not all Levites were priests). This greater prominence may also reflect the interests of later times. Before the Temple became the one and only place where sacrifices could be made, Levites apparently ran religious services in other cultic shrines, especially in the northern part of Israel. Once these practices were disallowed, the Levites were more or less put out of a job. The emphasis on their significance may have been an attempt to give them higher standing in the community with their loss of income and occupation. For this author, "The levitical priests, the whole tribe of Levi . . . may eat the sacrifices that are the LORD's portion." They too are to be treated like priests.

BOX 3.6 THE SHEMA

Historically, one of the most important passages of the entire Torah for Jewish worship, and eventually for Christian understandings of the Old Testament, is found in Deuteronomy 6:4–5:

> Hear, O Israel: The LORD is our God, the LORD alone. You shall love the LORD your God with all your heart, and with all your soul, and with all your might.

These words are traditionally known as the **Shema**—since in Hebrew that is the first word, translated "hear." There have been various translations of the Hebrew of these verses over the years, some of them seeming to emphasize that Judaism is strictly monotheistic: "Hear O Israel, the Lord our God, the Lord is One." But probably the first translation is to be preferred. This foundational statement of what it means to be a follower of the God of Israel is stressing not that other gods do not exist, but that these other gods are not to be accepted or worshiped as gods by the Israelites. Yahweh alone "is our God." And the sacred religious duty of the Israelite is to love Yahweh with his or her whole being.

As we will see, Jesus of Nazareth maintained that this was "the first and great commandment." It is not the first commandment to be given in Scripture—far from it—but for Jesus, and then his followers, it is the one of first importance. Many Jewish readers to this day continue to see it as the cornerstone of their faith.

• *The Covenant Renewal* (chapters 27–28). After Moses gives the Law for the second time, he and the community elders urge the people in stark and vivid language to keep it. Particularly striking are the blessings and curses enunciated in chapter 28. If the people keep the law they will be blessed by Yahweh:

Blessed shall you be in the city, and blessed shall you be in the field. Blessed shall be the fruit of your womb, the fruit of your ground, and the fruit of your livestock . . . Blessed shall you be when you come in and blessed shall you be when you go out. (28:3–6)

Their enemies will melt away before them; they will have abundant crops; they will "abound in prosperity"; and "all the peoples of the earth . . . shall be afraid of you." If, however, they choose not to be obedient, they can expect just the opposite: curses at every turn. Then,

The LORD will send upon you disaster, panic, and frustration in everything you attempt to do until you are destroyed. . . . The LORD will make the pestilence cling to you. . . . The LORD will afflict you with consumption, fever, inflammation, with fiery heat and drought. . . .

The LORD will cause you to be defeated before your enemies. . . . Your corpses shall be food for every bird of the air and animal of the earth. . . . The LORD will afflict you with the boils of Egypt, with ulcers, scurvy, and itch, of which you cannot be healed. . . . You shall become an object of horror, a proverb, a byword among all the peoples where the LORD will lead you. (28:20–37)

• *Moses' Final Speech and Death* (chapters 29–34). Moses then delivers his final address to the people, appoints Joshua to be his successor, and delivers his final blessing on the people. He goes up from the plains of Moab to Mount Nebo, where he is shown the entire Promised Land by God, and then he dies and is buried. But, we are told, no one knows where his grave is. And then the book ends with a final encomium on this great man of God.

Never since has there arisen a prophet in Israel like Moses, whom the LORD knew face to face. He was unequaled for all the signs and wonders that the LORD sent him to perform in the land of Egypt. . . . And for all the mighty deeds and all the terrifying displays of power that Moses performed in the sight of all Israel. (Deut. 34:10–12)

The Historical Context for the D Source

I have already pointed out that some of the laws of Deuteronomy presuppose a later situation, during the monarchy. In the previous chapter I indicated briefly when, more precisely, scholars think we can date the source: to the mid-seventh century B.C.E. (some 600 years after the days of Moses). There are a number of indications that these laws were written down by priests, or Levites, living in the northern part of Israel. If you have read the Pentateuch carefully, you will have noticed that sometimes Mount Sinai is called Mount Horeb. This is the name of the holy mountain preferred in sources such as E and D that are thought to have originated from the north. Other northern concerns are, as we have seen, the Levites and the emphasis on prophecy. At the same time, as I pointed out earlier, the source appears to have been later edited and expanded by an author living in the south, given its emphasis on the need to worship only in the Temple in Jerusalem.

The laws of Deuteronomy, like those of P that we saw earlier, were placed in a conceptual frame that appears to have been informed by political peace treaties known at the time. Since the middle of the twentieth century scholars have been impressed by the similarities between Deuteronomy and a set of treaties discovered in 1956, connected with the Assyrian king Esarhaddon, who ruled in 681–669 B.C.E.—just a few years before the D source would have been written. These treaties are in many ways similar to the Hittite suzerainty treaties we have already examined. In them the suzerain is named, divine witnesses are invoked, the vassals are to swear loyalty to the king alone, and, in particular, there are numerous curses laid upon the vassal if he fails to comply with his commitment to keep the stipulations that have been spelled out. Once again, apart from the invocation of divine witnesses, this sounds very much like what we find in Deuteronomy. Yahweh himself is the Sovereign Lord, the suzerain; Israel is his vassal; the people of Israel are to be loyal to Yahweh and to give allegiance to no other; should they fail to keep their covenantal obligations, numerous severe and even dire curses will descend upon them. The D source appears to be formulated as a kind of political alliance with Yahweh, as formulated by Levites living in the northern part of the kingdom.

But the source became particularly important not in the northern part of Israel, but in the south, in the nation of Judah, during the reign of the good king Josiah.

According to 2 Kings 22–23, in about 612 B.C.E. Josiah sponsored a number of repairs and renovations in the Temple of Jerusalem which, since the days of Solomon over 300 years earlier, had fallen on hard times. In the course of these repairs, Hilkiah, the high priest, is said to have discovered "the book of the law in the house of the LORD" (2 Kings 22:8). Josiah had the book read to him and he shrank in horror. This book indicated that disaster would come upon the people if they did not adhere to its laws. Josiah reacted swiftly and decisively. He called for a special ceremony and had the book read aloud to all the people of Judah, and pledged before them all to keep the commandments found in it.

Then he went on a religious mission. He ordered that all of the vessels dedicated to other gods (especially the god **Baal** and the goddess **Asherah**—Canaanite deities) be removed from the Temple and be destroyed. (One can sense how far the religion had come, if other gods were actually being worshiped in the Jerusalem Temple.) He deposed all the priests in Judah who were dedicated to serving other gods (another indication). He brought out the image of Asherah that was in the Temple and had it destroyed. He destroyed the "houses of the male prostitutes that were in the house of the Lord." He destroyed the shrines and holy places committed to the worship of other gods. He pulled down the altars dedicated to these gods. And generally he cleaned house, rather seriously, in religious terms.

This reform by Josiah emphasized the importance of worshiping Yahweh alone, no other gods, and doing so in the central sanctuary of Jerusalem. In other words, Josiah implemented the strict demands that are now found in the book of Deuteronomy. It is for this reason that scholars have long held that the "book of the Law" that the high priest Hilkiah found in the Temple was none other than the D source, the heart and soul of what was to become the book of Deuteronomy.

This, then, would have been a book that was produced in the northern part of the land of Israel but that came, by some means, to be revered and possibly edited and expanded in the south and then deposited (with a lot of other things, apparently) in the Temple in Jerusalem. It became centrally important for the reforms of Josiah, who was seen by the author of 2 Kings as one of the greatest monarchs in the history of Judah precisely because of his religious reforms. The stature of the book was then assured when, about a century later, it came into the hands of the priestly redactor of the Pentateuch, who incorporated it more or less wholesale into the five-volume work that was then passed down through history as the Torah.

At a Glance: Exodus to Deuteronomy

The book of Exodus describes the birth and life of Moses as he is called by God to deliver the people of Israel from their lives of slavery in Egypt. Working numerous miraculous plagues against the Egyptians, Moses convinces the Pharaoh to let the people go; but they are then chased by the Egyptian army, only to be saved by the intervention of God by the miracle at the Sea of Reeds, where the entire Egyptian army is drowned. Moses then leads the people to Mount Sinai, where he is given the Decalogue and the rest of the Law.

Exodus 20–Numbers 10 (including all of Leviticus) is devoted to detailing this Law. Some of the laws are apodictic (straight commands and prohibitions); others are casuistic (conditional statements: if this, then that). The laws govern how the people of Israel are to engage in proper worship of Yahweh, how they are to behave in relation to one another, and how they are to keep themselves distinct from other peoples.

After Israel leaves Mount Sinai, they repeatedly grumble, complain, and sin against God; God forces them to remain in the wilderness for forty years until the generation that experienced the Exodus dies off. Then, in the book of Deuteronomy, Moses gives their descendants the Law as well, in a second recounting.

There are historical problems throughout these four books, showing that here we are dealing with legends and ancient legal traditions that were only later compiled into a five-book corpus. But the traditions gathered here lie at the heart and soul of ancient Israelite life and religion.

Take a Stand

1. Your parents have learned that your class on the Bible has called into question whether there really was an exodus event under Moses, and they want to know whether you think it matters one way or the other. What do you think?

2. You are in a discussion about religion with your roommates, and one of them tells you that she has learned that Judaism is, and always has been, a highly legalistic religion. It is all about trying to please God by following a detailed and impossible list of do's and don'ts. In her view, no one can possibly do all these things. Do you agree or not? State your reasons, in as much detail as you can.

3. Your professor has given you a writing assignment: you are to discuss three lessons from the books of Exodus and Numbers that you think are particularly helpful, and three others that you think are highly problematic. You have free rein to come up with any lessons you want. Sketch your paper.

Key Terms

Apodictic laws, 67	**Code of Hammurapi**, 69	**Kosher food laws**, 68	**Sheol**, 75
Ark of the Covenant, 78	**Covenant Code**, 69	**Levites**, 65	**Suzerainty Treaty**, 67
Asherah, 81	**Day of Atonement**, 78	**Priests**, 79	**Tabernacle**, 78
Atonement, 71	**Decalogue**, 67	**Priestly Code**, 70	
Baal, 81	**Deuteronomic Code**, 77	**Sacrifice**, 70	
Casuistic laws, 67	**Holiness Code**, 72	**Shema**, 80	

Suggestions for Further Reading

NB: For this and all chapters, see the relevant articles (e.g., "Exodus," "Deuteronomy") in the works cited in the Suggestions for Further Reading in chapter 1.

Blekinsopp, Joseph. *The Pentateuch: An Introduction to the First Five Books of the Bible.* New Haven: Yale University Press, 2000. A comprehensive study of what scholars are saying about the Pentateuch, for advanced students.

Dever, William. *Who Were the Early Israelites and Where Did They Come From?* Grand Rapids: Eerdmans, 2003. One of America's premier archaeologists looks at the archaeological record of ancient Israel to discuss whether the events described in the Pentateuch are historically accurate.

Douglas, Mary. *Purity and Danger: An Analysis of Concepts of Pollution and Taboo.* New York: Routledge, 1966. A now famous classic by a premier anthropologist, this study analyzes the purity laws of the Torah from an anthropological perspective.

Finkelstein, Israel and Neil Asher Silberman. *The Bible Unearthed: Archaeology's New Vision of Ancient Israel and the Origin of its Sacred Texts.* New York: Simon and Schuster, 2001. A fascinating discussion of the findings of modern archaeology that shows why the narratives of the Pentateuch are problematic historically.

Friedman, Richard Elliott. *Who Wrote the Bible?* New York: HarperCollins, 1987. A revetting explanation and defense of the Pentateuch in light of the Documentary Hypothesis, ideal for beginning students.

Roth, Martha. *Law Collections from Mesopotamia and Asia Minor*, 2nd ed. Atlanta: Scholars Press, 1997. A useful collection of laws from ancient lands outside of Israel, including the Code of Hammurapi.

4

The Deuteronomistic History:
Joshua to 2 Kings

WHAT TO EXPECT

When we move beyond the Pentateuch we come to the Deuteronomistic History, an account of the history of Israel from the time of the Conquest, when Israel took over the Promised Land, to the time of the Babylonian Exile when they were expelled from it. The Deuteronomistic History receives its name from the fact that it was written by an author who was heavily influenced by the book of Deuteronomy, with its insistence that if the people of Israel remain faithful to Yahweh they will succeed; if they do not, they will be condemned.

The book of Joshua shows how Israel conquered the Promised Land under the leadership of Joshua. Judges discusses their life in the land when various charismatic leaders both judged and led in battle the different tribes of Israel. The books of Samuel show the transition from the time of tribal organization to a united monarchy when Israel was governed by kings Saul and David. And the books of Kings show how a division of the kingdom followed the rule of the final king over all of Israel, Solomon. During this division, separate kings ruled the north (Israel) and the south (Judah), until the north was destroyed by the Assyrians and the south by the Babylonians.

As we move now beyond the Pentateuch, we come to another collection of historical writings in the Hebrew Bible. Joshua, Judges, 1 and 2 Samuel, and 1 and 2 Kings are usually thought of and treated as a group of books probably all written by the same author (or group of authors). These books narrate the life of Israel once it comes to the Promised Land, as it conquers the peoples already dwelling there, divides up the land, lives in the land as a group of tribes, comes to be ruled by kings, and eventually is defeated by other foreign powers and removed from the land. In the Tanakh these books are considered the "Former Prophets"; modern scholars have preferred calling them the "Deuteronomistic

History," as they record the history of ancient Israel between the entry to the land and the exile in terms highly reminiscent of, and probably dependent on, the religious views set forth in the older D source that makes up the books of Deuteronomy.

THE DEUTERONOMISTIC HISTORY

The six books of the Deuteronomistic History (just four books in the Hebrew Bible, since 1 and 2 Samuel are counted as one book as are 1 and 2

Kings) cover a large span of time, nearly 600 years. These six centuries can be divided up into four more or less discrete time periods:

- *The Period of the Conquest.* The book of Joshua records the conquest of the Promised Land by the invading Israelite army, and then the distribution of the conquered land among the twelve tribes of Israel, each tribe receiving a portion.
- *The Time of the Judges.* The book of Judges tells stories of political and military events in the two centuries or so between the conquest and the time of the monarchy, the time Israel is ruled by kings; the stories focus on certain "judges," military leaders who rule different tribes and lead their battles against enemies in the land.
- *The United Monarchy.* 1 and 2 Samuel and 1 Kings tell of the golden age of ancient Israel as it moves from being a loose confederation of tribes to becoming a united nation ruled by a king—first the troubled Saul, then the glorious David, and then his wise and wealthy but somewhat profligate son Solomon.
- *The Divided Monarchy.* The second portion of 1 Kings and all of 2 Kings covers the time when the nation is split in half with the northern part, Israel, ruled by a series of kings from different families and the southern part, Judah, by a different series of kings—all of them (in the south) descendants of David. The history takes us up to the point where Israel is destroyed by the Assyrians in 722 B.C.E., and then Judah by the Babylonians in 586 B.C.E.

Since the mid-twentieth century scholars have recognized that these books were originally a unit, written by an author or group of authors (or editors) who depended on the book of Deuteronomy (or the D source itself) for its overarching themes and perspectives:

- All history is guided by Yahweh.
- Yahweh requires exclusive worship; no other gods may be worshiped alongside of him.
- The sacrificial cult is to be localized in the Temple in Jerusalem; other cultic sites are strictly forbidden.
- Obedience to these requirements will bring blessings and rewards; disobedience will bring curses and punishment.
- The very bad things that happen throughout the history of Israel are therefore not because of political or military realities (for example, the aggressive foreign policies of much more powerful nations), but because of Israel's disobedience to the demands of Yahweh their God.

The Deuteronomistic Historian (for the sake of convenience I will speak of him as a single author) was, of course, relying on oral traditions (and some no-longer surviving written sources). These spoke of the past history of the nation, from the time of the conquest up to his own day, which was possibly in the late seventh century, soon after Josiah's reform that we have already discussed (see pp. 81–82). He had inherited stories that had been told and retold over the vast stretches of time that separated him from the earliest events that he narrated— 600 years of oral traditions about the early years of the people in the land. We can probably assume, therefore, that there will be some historically accurate information in his accounts but large legendary elements as well.

The author appears to have lived in the southern nation of Judah, which he finds to be less problematic than the northern land of Israel which was in constant violation of God's demands. Unlike the north, during the divided monarchy the south had several "good" kings (especially King Josiah). A good king, for this author, is not one who was militarily successful or politically savvy, but one who followed the dictates of the Torah, especially

---

BOX 4.1 TIMELINE OF THE DEUTERONOMISTIC HISTORY

Joshua and the Conquest of the Promised Land: ca. 1210 B.C.E.

Period of the Judges: ca. 1210–1025 B.C.E.

The Beginning of the United Monarchy (Saul, David, Solomon): ca. 1025 B.C.E.

The Divided Monarchy (Israel and Judah): 922 B.C.E.

Assyrian Destruction of Israel (the north): 722 B.C.E.

Babylonian Destruction of Judah (the south) and exile: 586 B.C.E.

as found in the book of Deuteronomy. The final edition of the multivolume book appears to have been produced and published sometime after the Babylonian exile, and in its final form it is particularly harsh toward the kings of Israel (the north), who are regularly condemned for not adhering to the requirements that Yahweh had set forth for his people.

THE BOOK OF JOSHUA

The book of Joshua is devoted to the conquest of the Promised Land under the leadership of the successor of Moses, Joshua, and the distribution of the conquered territories among the twelve tribes of Israel. If the exodus is thought to have occurred around 1250 B.C.E., the events of this book should be conceived of as happening forty years later, so at the end of the thirteenth century.

Literary Overview

The book contains a number of interesting, powerful, and even disturbing stories, which well repay a careful reading and rereading. Once again, I will not give a blow-by-blow summary of all that takes place, but can indicate some of the highlights to refresh your memory:

- Joshua, as Moses' successor, is given instructions from God—not about how to conquer the land but about the need to remain faithful to the Torah that Moses received. It is that—not military strategy or prowess—which will bring victory:

  > My servant Moses is dead. Now proceed to cross the Jordan, you and all this people, into the land that I am giving to them, the Israelites. . . . Only be strong and very courageous, being careful to act in accordance with all the law that my servant Moses commanded you; do not turn from it to the right hand or to the left, so that you may be successful wherever you go. This book of the law shall not depart out of your mouth; you shall meditate on it day and night, so that you may be careful to act in accordance with all that is written in it. For then you shall make your way prosperous, and then you shall be successful (1:2, 7–8).

- *Preparations for the Attack* (chapters 1–5).
  - Joshua sends spies to scout out the land; they stay with a prostitute named Rahab in the city of Jericho (chapter 2).
  - The people of Israel cross the Jordan, led by the ark, which causes the waters to part to allow them to pass by on dry land (compare the exodus) (chapter 3).
  - The people are prepared to do battle against the various peoples of Canaan: the Canaanites, Hittites, Hivites, Perizzites, Girgashites, Amorites, and Jebusites. We are told that Israel has 40,000 men armed for war (4:13; contrast that with the 600,000 referred to in Numbers).
  - The men all undergo circumcision since, for unexplained reasons, they had not been circumcised as babies (chapter 5).
- *The Conquest of Canaan* (chapters 6–12). The Israelites attack the cities and towns of Canaan, starting with the famous battle of Jericho where the walls came a-tumblin' down.
  - Central Canaan (chapters 6–8). Joshua appears to deploy a "divide and conquer" strategy; he first takes the cities in the central portion of the land and then, once the north and south are split off from one another, attacks each separately.
  - Southern Canaan (chapter 10).
  - Northern Canaan (chapter 11).
- *Division of the Land* (chapters 13–22). The twelve tribes each receive a portion of land. Two of the tribes, Reuben and Gad, and half the tribe of Manasseh had already been given land in the Transjordan. The remaining tribes (including the other half of Manasseh) are given territories in what is today, roughly, Israel and Palestine. These twelve tribes are named after the twelve sons of Jacob, with two exceptions. The descendants of Levi are involved with priestly functions and so do not receive a portion of land; that leaves only eleven tribes. But, instead of Joseph, two tribes named after his sons Ephraim and Manasseh are given allotments, bringing the total number back up to twelve.
- *Renewal of the Covenant* (chapters 23–24). Joshua calls the people together and exhorts them to commit themselves to following the covenant God made with Moses, so that things will go well with them in the land:

  > Now therefore revere the LORD, and serve him in sincerity and in faithfulness; put away

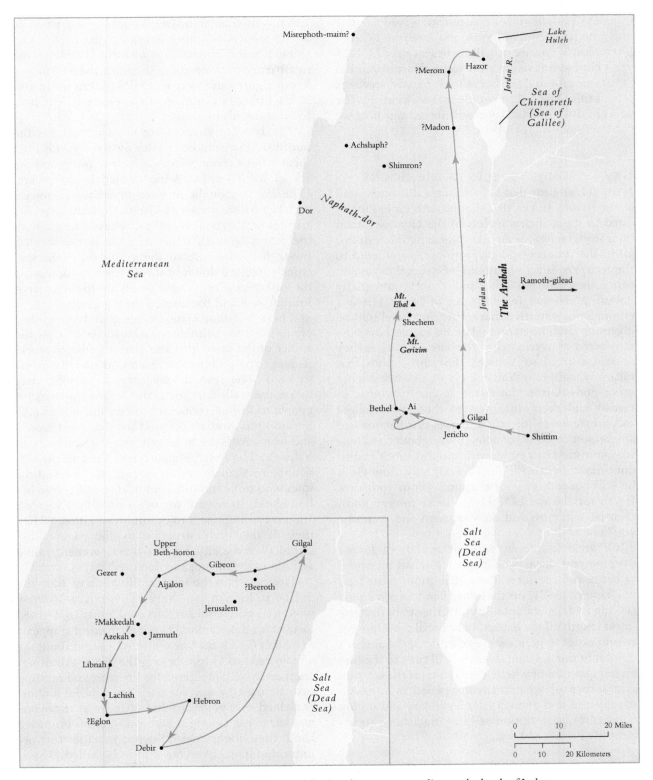

FIGURE 4.1. The route of conquest taken by Joshua and the Israelite army, according to the book of Joshua.

the gods that your ancestors served beyond the River and in Egypt, and serve the LORD. Now if you are unwilling to serve the LORD, choose this day whom you will serve . . . but as for me and my household, we will serve the LORD. . . . The people said to Joshua, "The LORD our God we will serve, and him we will obey." (24:14–15, 24).

Key Literary Aspects of the Books

It should be clear that even though this book is all about assaults and battles, the author is far less interested in the military aspects of the Conquest than he is in the religious aspects. Nor is he interested at all in the innocent people who are slaughtered in the course of Israel's triumphs—he sees them as evil (since they worship other gods) and a potentially polluting element in the midst of Israel. His is a triumphalist narrative that insists that Israel will be given the land, no matter what, no matter how outnumbered or overmatched they are, so long as they remain faithful to Yahweh. For this author that means worshipping Yahweh alone, not worshiping other gods. Given the fact that victory comes so readily and even amazingly to those who follow this simple guideline, it is a marvel that anyone had any reason to do otherwise. Throughout the Deuteronomistic History we will see this motif played out time and again: "[The LORD] is a jealous God; he will not forgive your transgression or your sins. If you forsake the LORD and serve foreign gods, then he will turn and do you harm and consume you" (24:19–20).

Of greatest interest to most readers of Joshua over the years have been its truly captivating stories of battle and conquest (the distribution of the land in chapters 13–21, on the other hand, is somewhat lacking in dramatic intensity). Rather than discussing at length all the battles, here I will focus on just two in order to give a sense of some of the author's dominant themes, and then we will turn to the historical question of whether we can trust the account as a record of what really happened or, instead, should read it as a much later legendary and highly fictionalized description of how Israel came to inherit the Promised Land.

THE BATTLE OF JERICHO

None of the stories of Joshua is better known, more compelling, or more disturbing than the famous battle of Jericho, in chapter 6. Jericho is the first point of attack for the invading Israelite armies. It is said to be a well-fortified city, with thick walls as the first barrier of protection. To attack the city Joshua has to figure out a way to deal with the walls. But he has little strategizing to do, as God tells him how to go about his business.

The Israelite warriors are to march around the outside of the walls once a day for six days. Leading them will be seven priests with rams' horns and the ark of the covenant being carried behind them. (The ark is thought to have supernatural powers that can assure victory.) On the seventh day the army is to march around the city seven times, with the priests blowing their horns; after the seventh time, the people are to shout and the walls will come tumbling down of their own accord, leaving the city defenseless. The warriors are to then march into the city and commence the slaughter.

These are God's instructions, and since they come from the Almighty you can be sure, as the reader of the story, that the plan is going to work. It does. The soldiers march around the city as instructed. The seventh day they do as told, they shout, the walls fall down, and Joshua instructs his people to kill everyone in the city but not to take any booty as spoil; all the gold and silver and bronze and iron vessels are to be put into the sanctuary of Yahweh. The only people to be spared in the onslaught are Rahab—the prostitute who assisted the spies who came into the land in chapter 2—and her household, in reward for what she did. Everyone and everything else is to be, and was, killed: "Then they devoted to destruction by the edge of the sword all in the city, both men and women, young and old, oxen, sheep, and donkeys" (6:21).

This policy of the total annihilation of all living things is known as **"herem"**—from a Hebrew word that simply means "devoted"; that is, devoted to God for destruction. The logic behind it appears to be that God is the one who has brought about the victory, and so to him belong the spoils. All things are then to be slaughtered for his sake, and nothing is to be used by anyone else. The biblical authors explained this policy by indicating that if anyone was left living among the enemies in the Promised Land, they might later influence Israelites to worship other gods. Everyone had to be killed. This is stated explicitly in the earlier expression of the policy of *herem* in the book of Deuteronomy, on the lips of Moses:

BOX 4.2 THE WALLS OF JERICHO

There is no story in the Conquest narrative more impressive than the battle of the invading Israelites against the mighty fortified city of Jericho, with its large population and massive protecting walls. And there is no greater disappointment for avid supporters of the complete accuracy of biblical narratives than the findings of archaeologists who have excavated the site of Jericho and discovered that the description of the great battle cannot be brought into harmony with the realities of history.

In the story, the city of Jericho is so massive and powerful that the 40,000 Israelite warriors cannot simply attack it head-on. God gives them a miraculous victory by devising a plan to cause the walls to fall, ruining the powerful fortifications and giving the invaders direct access to the large city and its many inhabitants.

Modern excavations have shown that the story is almost certainly a legend without historical basis. The first truly scientific archaeological examination of the site was undertaken by Kathleen Kenyon in the 1950s, and her findings have been corroborated since. Archaeologists now know that there was indeed an inhabited site at ancient Jericho from prehistoric times (going back to the Neolithic period). The site was inhabited on and off periodically throughout history—until today. But there was no walled city there—let alone a very large and heavily fortified city—at the end of the thirteenth century, when the so-called Battle of Jericho allegedly took place. At the time, Jericho was a sparsely populated little place, and there were no walls around the city at all.

Judging from the archaeological record, the biblical stories of Rahab the prostitute, the spies who scouted out the land, the attack of the Israelites, the miraculous fall of the walls, the slaughter of all the inhabitants—all of it appears to be the stuff of legend, not an account of real history as it actually happened.

As for the towns of these peoples that the LORD your God is giving you as an inheritance, you must not let anything that breathes remain alive. You shall annihilate them—the Hittites and the Amorites, the Canaanites and the Perizzites, the Hivites and the Jebusites—just as the LORD your God has commanded, so that they may not teach to you to do all the abhorrent things that they do for their gods, and you thus sin against the LORD your God. (Deuteronomy 20: 16–18).

THE BATTLE OF AI The total commitment of God, and Joshua, to the policy of *herem* explains the next intriguing story, the Battle of Ai. Joshua's spies tell him that the next city is not a major concern and that the entire army will not be needed to attack it, just two or three thousand soldiers. Joshua sends them out on what seems to be a routine mission, but instead of taking the city they are beaten back and defeated. Joshua cannot understand why. Once again, though, it is not because of military strategy or power that these battles are won or lost; for this narrative, it is because of faithfulness to God's demands.

As it turns out, the *herem* of Jericho was not complete. Unbeknownst to anyone—including the reader—a soldier named Achan simply could not resist taking some of the spoils for himself from Jericho, a beautiful mantle and some silver and gold. Rather than giving them over to the Lord's sanctuary, he hid them in his tent, and God was displeased. That is why the city of Ai could successfully defend itself—God had allowed this to happen because his directions were not followed to the finest detail.

And what was to happen to Achan as a result, once his sin was discovered? He himself was to be devoted to *herem*. The Israelites take him, his sons, his daughters, his oxen, donkeys, and sheep, his tent, and all of his possessions outside the camp; they stone him to death, destroy everything else with fire, and cast stones over the lot of them. God takes *herem* very seriously, and if Israel wants to be successful in its military exploits it needs to do so as well.

Then follows one of the more intriguing battle scenes in the book. Joshua takes his army to Ai, stations a portion of it behind the city out of sight, for an ambush. The rest of the army attacks the city from the front; the people of Ai come out to meet them in battle and the Israelites, feigning defeat, flee from before them as the people from the city pursue. The ambush then is sprung, the troops behind the city rush into it, set it on fire, and now the people of Ai are trapped between two arms of the advancing forces. They are slaughtered to a person: man, woman, and child.

Joshua proceeds to annihilate one city and town after the other (with only the citizens of Gibeon saving themselves by a clever ruse, narrated in chapter 10). After establishing control of the central area of the land, he turns his attention to the south, where he is fantastically successful: "So Joshua defeated the whole land . . . and all their kinds; he left no one remaining, but utterly destroyed all that breathed, as the LORD God of Israel commanded" (10:40). He then moves into the north where he decisively destroys a coalition of forces drawn up against him, so that, in the end, he "destroyed them with their towns" and "took the whole land, according to all that the LORD had spoken to Moses" (11:21, 23).

These are powerful and moving narratives with a theological point that can scarcely be missed by a careful reader. Moses was given the Law—God's directions/instructions—in the Pentateuch. Joshua is told to keep them; this particularly applies to God's instructions about war—everything is to be destroyed so that Israel can take over the land and live there without foreign influence tempting them to worship other gods. If Joshua and his people, the children of Israel, do what God commands, all will be well and they will succeed fantastically. If they do not, they will pay the consequences.

Modern readers are interested, however, not only in the lessons that these stories convey but also in their historical value. Does the book of Joshua give a reliable account of what actually happened when the children of Israel entered into the Promised Land? Are these stories historically accurate?

The Historical Value of the Narrative

When considering the historicity of the narratives of Joshua, the first thing to reemphasize is that these are not accounts written by eyewitnesses or by anyone who knew an eyewitness. They were written some 600 years later and were based on oral traditions that had been in circulation among people in Israel during all those intervening centuries. Moreover, they are clearly molded according to theological assumptions and perspectives. Biblical scholars have long noted that there is almost nothing in the accounts that suggests the author is trying to be purely descriptive of things that really

happened. He is writing an account that appears to be guided by his religious agenda, not by purely historical interests. That is why, when read closely, one finds so many problems with the narratives.

- *Internal Discrepancies.* As we have seen, parts of Joshua stress that Joshua was fantastically successful in conquering the land: "Joshua defeated the whole land" (10:40); "Joshua took all that land" (11:16); "Joshua took the whole land" (11:23). If it were true that Joshua took "all" the "whole" land—why are there so many parts of the land that the text admits were *not* taken? The Deuteronomistic Historian later has to acknowledge that when "Joshua was old . . . the LORD said to him 'very much of the land still remains to be possessed'" (13:1). And so we are told that Jerusalem had not yet been taken (15:63), or parts of Ephraim (16:10), or parts of Manasseh (17:12–13). At the end of the book Joshua has to persuade the people to drive out the natives living in the land (23:5–13).

- *Tensions with Other Accounts.* A similar problem arises between Joshua and other books of the Deuteronomistic History. In chapter 11, for example, the Israelite forces completely annihilate the city of Hazor: "they put to the sword all who were in it, utterly destroying them; there was no one left who breathed, and he burned Hazor with fire." If that were true, why is it that in the next book, Judges, the Canaanites still very much live in and control Hazor, under their king Jabin, whose powerful army afflicted and oppressed the Israelites (Judges 4)?

- *General Implausibilities.* A number of the stories in Joshua are so chock-full of the miraculous that historians simply cannot deal with them as historical narratives (see the excursus in chapter 1). None of the miracles is more striking than the account in chapter 10, where the Israelite armies are having such a huge success routing the coalition of kings aligned against them that Joshua cries out to the sun to stop its movement in the sky. And the sun stands still at high noon for twenty-four hours before moving on again, giving the Israelites ample time to complete the slaughter. As readers have long noted, it would be a miracle indeed if the earth suddenly stopped rotating on its axis for a day and then started up again, with no disturbance to the oceans, land masses, and life itself!

- *External Verification and Archaeology*. For biblical scholars, just as significant is the surviving physical evidence (or rather lack of it) for the conquest. Archaeologists have long noted that there is scant support for that kind of violent destruction of the cities of Canaan—especially the ones mentioned in Joshua. Think for a second: if one were to look for archaeological evidence or other external verification to support the historical narratives of Joshua, what would one look for?
  - References to the invasion and conquest in other written sources outside the Bible.
  - Evidence that there were indeed walled cities and towns in Canaan at the time.
  - Archaeological evidence that the cities and towns mentioned actually were destroyed at the time (Jericho, Ai, Heshbon, etc.).
  - Shift in cultural patterns: that is, evidence of new people taking over from other peoples of a different culture (as you get in the Americas when Europeans came over, bringing with them their own culture different from that of the native Americans).

And what kind of verification do we actually get for the narratives of Joshua? The answer appears to be: none of the above. There are no references in any other ancient source to a massive destruction of the cities of Canaan. Archaeologists have discovered that few of the places mentioned were walled towns at the time. Many of the specific cities cited as places of conquest apparently did not even exist as cities at the time. This includes, most notably, Jericho, which was not inhabited in the late thirteenth century B.C.E., as archaeologists have decisively shown. (See Box 4.2.) The same thing applies to Ai and Heshbon. These cities were neither occupied, nor conquered, nor re-inhabited in the days of Joshua. Moreover, there is no evidence of major shifts in cultural patterns taking place at the end of the thirteenth century in Canaan. There are, to be sure, some indications that *some* towns in Canaan were destroyed at about that time (two of the twenty places mentioned as being destroyed by Joshua were wiped out at about the right time: Hazor and Bethel). But that is true of virtually every time in antiquity: occasionally towns were destroyed by other towns or burned or otherwise abandoned.

We are left, then, with a very big problem. The accounts in Joshua appear to be non-historical in many respects. This creates a dilemma for historians, since two things are perfectly clear: (a) eventually there was a nation Israel living in the land of Canaan; but (b) there is no evidence that it got there by entering in from the east and destroying all the major cities in a series of violent military campaigns. Where then did Israel come from?

Explanations for the Beginnings of Israel in the Land

Modern scholars have come up with a number of explanations for how the nation of Israel emerged within the land known as Canaan. The following are the four most popular.

1. **The Conquest Theory**. Popularized especially by American archaeologist William Albright in the mid-twentieth century, this view more or less accepts the accounts of Joshua as factually accurate. There really was a conquest of the land by the Israelites. Because of more recent archaeological discoveries, few except the most theologically conservative scholars accept this view today.

2. **The Immigration Theory**. Put forth most compellingly by German scholar Albrecht Alt, this theory indicates that a group of people entered into Canaan from the outside and settled in the sparsely inhabited highlands, only later to infiltrate down into the cities over which they eventually took control. Later, when they retold the stories of how it happened, they described a military conquest that never actually occurred. One problem with this view is that there is nothing in the archaeological record to suggest that the people later known as Israelites owed their existence entirely to *outsiders* coming into the land. Another problem is that there is no evidence that most of the towns and cities were taken over at any point.

3. **A Peasant Revolt**. Popularized by American scholar George Mendenhall, this view maintains that there was a group of Israelites who escaped Egypt, who then joined forces with the economically and politically oppressed peoples in the land of Canaan and eventually overthrew the ruling authorities in a grassroots revolt. Today this view is generally regarded as being built more on modern socio-politico-economic models rather than on archaeological or literary evidence.

At a Glance: The Book of Joshua

The book of Joshua records the conquest of the Promised Land by the invading Israelite armies under the direction of Moses' great successor Joshua. As the first book of the Deuteronomistic History, Joshua stresses that the people of Israel are successful whenever they remain faithful to the Torah that God has given. In conquering the major cities of Canaan, Israel follows the practice of *herem*, in which all the enemies (and their wives and children, and even animals) are to be destroyed.

After the land is subdued, it is divided among the twelve tribes of Israel.

There are serious historical problems with the narratives of Joshua. On one hand, there appear to be numerous internal inconsistencies; on the other hand, archaeological discoveries do not confirm a massive destruction of the walled cities of Canaan. The stories of the book are best understood, then, as legendary accounts of how Israel came into the land.

4. **Gradual Emergence**. Yale Professor John Collins is one of the many scholars today who prefer to talk about the gradual emergence of Israel from within the indigenous population of Canaan. Possibly some groups that later were identified as Israel came from the outside—maybe a group of slaves that escaped from Egypt. But within Canaan a cult of Yahweh emerged, then spread, and eventually a sizeable number of people adhered to it. Later they told stories about how they came to be a separate people from their neighbors.

This final theory is the one that appears to be dominant among scholars today. If it is the one to be accepted, then the book of Joshua is not a historical record of what really happened. There may indeed have been a local hero named Joshua, about whom stories were told—and exaggerated, amplified, and blown out of proportion; and the stories of conquest may recall instances here and there where one town or another was taken over by the worshipers of Yahweh. But on the whole, the book of Joshua would be a legendary account of the conquest, not a historical narrative that can be accepted as accurate in its details.

THE BOOK OF JUDGES

The next book of the Deuteronomistic History is Judges, an account of life in the Promised Land in the time between the conquest and the monarchy. In some ways the theme of the book can be summed up in its final line: "In those days there was no king in Israel; all the people did what was right in their own eyes" (21:25). The problem was that what was "right" in their eyes was not right in God's, and it led to considerable trouble that, the author suggests, would be rectified when the entire land came under the rule of a king. Lacking a king, the various tribes are governed by individuals known as "judges" (hence the title of the book). These are principally military leaders of individual tribes who drive back the forces aligned against the tribe—the Canaanites, Moabites, Midianites, Philistines, and so on—and then rule over the people (of that region) with charismatic authority.

Obviously one of the chief problems confronted by these leaders, one that the author deeply laments, is that contrary to the clear impression given by the book of Joshua, the Promised Land was not—was decidedly not—cleared out of its former residents. They lived on and continued to wreak havoc among the Israelites who settled down after the conquest. Other nations coexisted with the Israelites, nations that worshiped other gods, tempting the Israelites to join with them in their worship. Moreover, throughout the checkered history of the Israelites in this period they not only committed apostasy in worshiping the Baals and Asherahs (the local divinities), they experienced military setback and defeat repeatedly at the hands of precisely those nations that Joshua allegedly had destroyed.

The narrative of the book is highly episodic, one military disaster after the other calling forth a military leader to save the people. The stories cannot be seen as a chronologically sequential account. We are told how long each judge ruled, and when added up they total more than 400 years. But the period between the conquest and the monarchy could be only about half that long. And so it is best to imagine these episodes as overlapping, in different parts of the tribal territories. The judge Ehud, for example, rose up to address the threat of the Moabites in the Transjordan; Deborah (a female judge) and Barak (her male co-leader) were dealing with problems around Mount Tabor, in north Canaan; Gideon dealt with the Midianite crisis in the south, Samson with the Philistines on the Mediterranean coast.

And so the book consists of a variety of stories—terrifically interesting and often moving stories—of various local leaders of different Israelite tribes in the years before there was a centralized government and a king who ruled over the entire nation. The overarching literary themes of the narrative are that the people of Israel, scattered throughout the land, were faced with both external and internal threats. Externally they were oppressed by other peoples, who had not in fact been driven out by the invading armies under Joshua but continued to reside in Canaan and frequently overthrew the Israelites living in the region, forcing them to live under foreign rule. Internally there were frequent rebellions against the will of God, especially as the people committed apostasy. It will come as no surprise to the reader to see that the Deuteronomistic Historian understands this as the real problem. For him, failure to keep the covenant is what leads to military defeat from the other nations residing in the land. But when the people repent and turn back to God, he raises up for them a savior figure, a judge, who delivers them from their oppressors and then rules over them as one empowered by God to do good.

Literary Considerations: The Pattern of Oppression and Restoration

These themes get played out time and again in the narrative in a more or less fixed pattern, spelled out at the outset in 2:11–19, which can be schematized as follows:

- *Apostasy.* The people of Israel depart from their devotion to Yahweh; in the words of the Deuteronomistic Historian, they "did what was evil in the sight of the LORD and worshiped the Baals [that is, the gods of Canaan]; and they abandoned the LORD . . . ." (2:11–13)

- *Oppression.* As a result, God delivers them to other military powers: "So the anger of the LORD was kindled against Israel, and he gave them over to plunderers who plundered them, and he sold them into the power of their enemies." (2:14)
- *Cry for Help.* The children of Israel call out to God in repentance, asking for deliverance.
- *Rise of a Deliverer.* God provides help in the person of a judge: "Then the LORD raised up judges, who delivered them out of the power of those who plundered them." (2:16)
- *Period of Tranquility.* The land then rests in peace and prosperity while the judge governs the people according to the will of God.
- *Return to Apostasy.* After a while, though, the pattern would start again: "Whenever the judge died, they would relapse and behave worse than their ancestors, following other gods, worshiping them and bowing down to them." (2:19)

A Paradigmatic Case: Othniel

If you read carefully the account of the first judge, Othniel, in the sparse and straightforward narrative of 3:7–11, you will see how this pattern plays itself out. It will be repeated in case after case, with the much longer narratives told of such judge-heroes as Ehud, Deborah, Gideon, and the strong-man Samson.

- The Israelites forsake Yahweh and worship other gods. (verse 7)
- He is angry and sells them into the hand of the king of the nation Aram-Naharaim. They serve him for eight years. (verse 8)
- They then cry out to the LORD for help. (verse 9)
- The LORD raises up for them the nephew of Caleb (whom we met in the book of Joshua), a man named Othniel, who defeats the enemy in battle. (verses 9–11)
- The land was then at rest for 40 years (verse 11). Then Othniel dies.
- And the Israelites again committed apostasy. (verse 12)

Some of the More Famous Judges

The stories told of the various judges are entertaining and well worth the time it takes to read and reread them. In several instances we are dealing with some of the more famous incidents of biblical

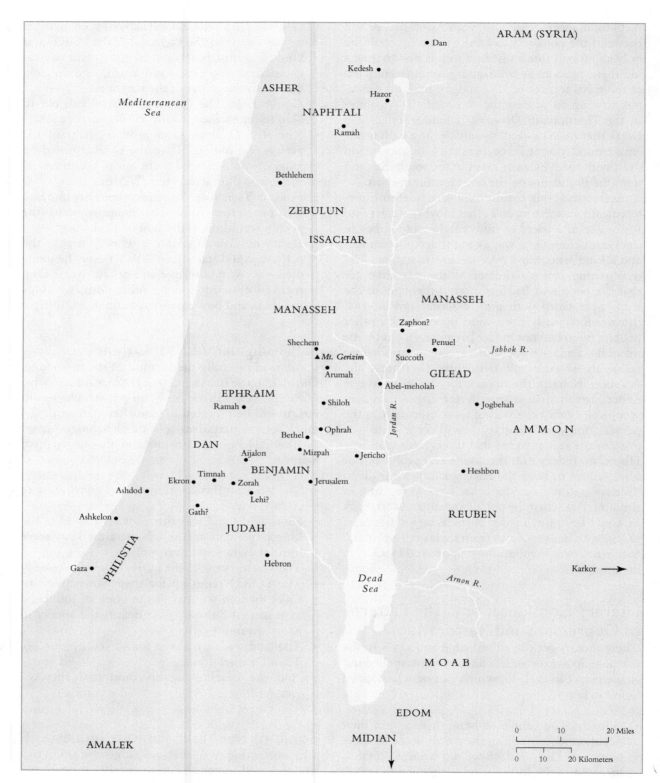

FIGURE 4.2. Key places mentioned in the book of Judges.

history—Jephthah's daughter, for example, and the he-man Samson. I will not summarize all the stories, or give any complete sketches, but will simply point to some of the more interesting episodes in the books.

EHUD   Ehud is the source of a good bit of biblical trivia: he was the one judge we know of who was left-handed. (He was from the tribe of Benjamin, and there was a tradition that all Benjaminites were left-handed; moreover, the story itself indicates that he preferred his left hand.) When Israel is dominated by King Eglon of Moab, God raises up Ehud to deliver them.

The episode is graphic. Eglon is enormously fat; Ehud manages to get a private audience with him; Ehud straps a short sword on his right thigh (so he could access it with his left hand), speaks to him in private, pulls out the sword, thrusts it into his belly, and "the hilt also went in after the blade . . . and the fat closed over the blade. . . and the dirt came out" (3:21). And that is the end of Eglon. Ehud puts him in his private toilet room and flees the palace. No one wants to disturb Eglon while he is doing business; only too late do they realize what has happened. The Israelites attack under Ehud's lead, and the people are delivered.

DEBORAH   Deborah is the first female leader of Israel that we learn about in the Bible (chapters 4–5). Other women have been featured in the stories of the Pentateuch, including Eve, Sarah, Rebekah, Rachel, Miriam (the sister of Moses). But Deborah is actually a judge. And a prophetess. In her time the Israelites are oppressed by the Canaanites, whose armies are commanded by a general named Sisera. Deborah instructs the Israelite leaders how to prepare to engage in battle with the Canaanite troops, but informs her co-leader Barak that Sisera will be killed by "the hand of a woman" (4:9). There is a major battle, the Canaanites are defeated, and Sisera flees on foot. He arrives at the tent of a woman named Jael, who comes out of her tent, greets Sisera, tells him to have no fear, hides him under a rug, and gives him a drink of milk. Then, while he is lying down, asleep under the rug, she takes a tent peg and a hammer and drives the peg through his temple into the ground. With a bit of understatement, the narrator indicates: "and he died."

This is a story then of two women powerfully used by God to deliver his people. There follows a moving song sung by Deborah and Barak, ending in praise of Jael and in a gripping and astonishingly vindictive reflection on what it must have been like for Sisera's mother, waiting for him to return victorious in battle.

GIDEON   The stories of Gideon (chapters 6–7) are meant to show that it is God, not human strength or resolve, that can bring victory to the Israelites. God sees to it that Gideon fights the mighty Midianites, with their 120,000-strong army, with only 300 soldiers. And he delivers a powerful victory. True, there is strategy involved—clever strategy indeed (see 7:15–25). But it is all directed by God in order to demonstrate that he can work miracles on the battlefield for anyone who is completely committed to doing what he commands.

JEPHTHAH   The story of the judge Jephthah is one of the most moving of the book (chapter 11). He is raised up to fight the Ammonites, and on the battlefield he vows to God that if he is victorious he will sacrifice to God whomever it is that first greets him when he returns home. God gives the Ammonites into his hands, and the Israelites inflict a massive defeat. And then the story gets gripping and terribly sad. When Jephthah returns home, it is his own daughter who comes out of his house whom he first sees, his only child and most beloved. But he must be true to his vow and sacrifice her. She asks for two months' time to "bewail my virginity" (11:37)—in other words, to lament the fact that she must die a virgin. She returns and he does as he promised, sacrificing his daughter in fulfillment of the oath he swore to God.

SAMSON   Probably the most famous of the judges was Samson, an ongoing opponent of the hated Philistines, a wild and unbelievably strong man with violent passions, and a lover who could not keep a secret. The key to understanding the stories about Samson (chapters 13–16) is to recognize that from birth he was a **Nazirite.** According to the Torah, a Nazirite was one who took a vow to be specially dedicated to God (Numbers 6:1–21). The vow entailed not ever touching a dead body, not consuming wine or strong drink or any grape products, and never cutting one's hair. Normally

BOX 4.3 JEPHTHAH'S DAUGHTER AND HUMAN SACRIFICE

The story of Jephthah and the sacrifice of his unnamed daughter is reminiscent of other biblical stories and of accounts known from Greek mythology. Most readers will think back on the "sacrifice of Isaac" in Genesis 22, where God orders Abraham to kill his own son. There is a key difference, of course, in that Abraham's hand is stayed at the last minute so that he does not accomplish the act. Not so Jephthah. But there is a reason for that difference: Abraham did not volunteer his child up to God, but was instructed to kill him; Jephthah himself had to sacrifice his daughter because of the vow he made. For the biblical authors, one should not make extravagant promises to God.

There are other instances in the Hebrew Bible of human sacrifices but they are always condemned, either explicitly or implicitly. Deuteronomy 18:9–10 urges the Israelites not to follow the practices of the Canaanites once they enter the land by having their sons of daughters "pass through fire." This is a reference to child sacrifice, in which a child is offered up to the god of fire (in Canaanite religion, a god named Molech). One might think that the only reason to prohibit a practice is because people have indulged in it: there is no reason for

a law that forbids an action that no one engages in. And so child sacrifice probably was practiced to some extent in ancient Israel. There are, in fact, a couple of instances in which Kings of Judah—Ahaz and Manasseh—are explicitly said to make their sons "pass through the fire" as part of their devotion to Molech (2 Kings 16:3; 21:6).

This practice was not confined to ancient Israel and the other peoples of Canaan. It is referred to in the mythology of the ancient Greeks as well, nowhere more famously than in the stories of Iphigenia, daughter of the Greek king Agamemnon. The Greeks are about to set forth in force to fight the Trojan war, but the gods are preventing their departure. Agamemnon learns that for the Greeks to have success, he must first sacrifice his own daughter to the goddess Artemis. Like his Hebrew counterparts, Agamemnon heeds the demands that come from on high and fulfills the demand, sacrificing his beloved Iphigenia. This is a war that does not start off well for the Greeks.

In all these instances the slaughter of one's own child is seen as the ultimate sacrifice and a sign of complete devotion to the deity. How good it is that times have changed.

---

the Nazirite vow was temporary. Samson, however, was a lifelong Nazirite (although he did occasionally violate the rules: he does touch the dead body of a lion, for example, after ripping it apart with his bare hands). In this narrative it is his long hair, never cut because of the vow, that enables him to be massively strong and a mighty opponent of the Philistines, with whom he is in constant conflict and among whom he makes continuous, and violent, mischief. When on one occasion he gets really angry, he kills a thousand of them at one time with just the jawbone of a donkey.

In their determination to discover the source of his strength, his Philistine opponents eventually persuade his lover, Delilah, to discover his secret. She does. It is due to his vow. If his hair were to be cut, he would be a mere mortal again. She betrays him, has his hair cut while he sleeps on her lap, and it leads to his demise and death.

The Violent Rape of an Innocent Woman

The book of Judges ends with one of the most horrific accounts in all of the Hebrew Scripture, of the violent all-night gang rape of an unnamed woman who was the concubine of an unnamed Levite that occurred while they were travelling in foreign lands in the territory of Benjamin (chapter 19). The woman dies of her abuse, and in a grisly act the Levite cuts her limb from limb and sends her twelve body parts throughout the territories of Israel as a call to war. The other tribes answer the call and attack the tribe of Benjamin, almost annihilating it. The author of the narrative suggests rather strongly that this is the kind of violent mayhem that can ensue when the people are not organized into a single political unit governed centrally. There was no king in that day, and so no way to control the outrageous violence that ran amok in the land (19:1; 21:25).

FIGURE 4.3. Samson smiting his enemies with the jawbone of a donkey. From the Catacomb of via Latina in Rome.

The Historical Character of the Narrative

The book of Judges is obviously filled with powerful, moving, and memorable stories. At the same time it seems to present itself—as have the other books we have examined so far—as a historical narrative. But is it? Does it give an account of people and events of real history or, like the other books of the Hebrew Bible, is it largely made up of legendary tales?

INTERNAL TENSIONS As with other parts of the Deuteronomistic History there are a number of internal tensions in the book of Judges that seem to suggest the author is utilizing earlier sources that stood at odds with one another on key issues, making it appear that the author or final editor was not overly concerned with establishing purely historical facts for the record. As just one example:

in 1:8 we are told that the people from the tribe of Judah "fought against Jerusalem and took it. They put it to the sword and set the city on fire." That is pretty straightforward: Jerusalem was destroyed and the local inhabitants killed. But then we read—just some verses later—that Jerusalem was still standing and that the local inhabitants were indeed living there. In this case, it is the tribe of Benjamin that has to deal with them: "But the Benjaminites did not drive out the Jebusites who lived in Jerusalem; so the Jebusites have lived in Jerusalem among the Benjaminites to this day" (1:21). One might argue there is not a contradiction here, since verse 8 is talking about the people of Judah and verse 21 the people of Benjamin; but if verse 8 is right, and there was no one left in Jerusalem and Jerusalem itself had been consumed by fire, then it is difficult to understand how verse 21 can be right also.

EXTERNAL TENSIONS I have already pointed out that the narratives of Judges do not gel well with those of Joshua. According to passages in Joshua, the entire land was taken over from the indigenous peoples; but here the entire problem is that it was not. And there are discrepancies in specific cases as well. According to Joshua 10:33, Joshua's troops encountered King Horam of the city of Gezer and "struck him and his people, leaving him no survivors." If it were true that there were no survivors from the city of Gezer, then it is hard to explain Judges 1:29: "Ephraim did not drive out the Canaanites who lived in Gezer; but the Canaanites lived among them in Gezer."

Or an even starker contrast, this time with an account found in Numbers, an incident that would have happened possibly a generation or two at most before the accounts in Judges. According to Numbers 31, Moses commanded all of Midian to be destroyed. At first his army killed all the men but left the women and children. Moses did not think that was good enough, and ordered them to kill all the boys (infants included) and all the women who had ever had sex. The virgin girls were spoils for the Israelite soldiers (Numbers 31:10–18). But if all that really happened it would be very difficult to explain Judges 6 and 8, where the Israelites are dominated precisely by the Midianites, whose army (of adult men, obviously) numbered 135,000.

The Historical Situation

It should be obvious that with the highly imaginative and entertaining stories of the book of Judges we are again dealing not with historically accurate accounts of things that really happened, but with imaginative tales of the great heroes of the Israelite past. These are probably to be seen legends, not disinterested histories.

What can we say about the historical situation between the time Israel appeared in the land as a group of people who confessed devotion to one God, Yahweh, in different tribes scattered throughout the territories, and the time that these tribes coalesced into a nation ruled by a king?

One possibility is as follows. As we have seen, what later became Israel may have comprised some groups that came into the land from the outside—possibly a group of former slaves in Egypt—but also, and probably in the main, they were indigenous people who came to believe in Yahweh as the only God to be worshiped. These people came to see themselves as distinct from all others, and formed themselves into tribal units. By the end of the thirteenth century B.C.E. these tribes were located in different territories, but they saw themselves as somehow unified and as distinct from other groups in Canaan who worshiped other gods. This "new thing" in Canaan, the Yahweh groups, grew and developed over time, and as the numbers of people committed to Yahweh grew, they told more and more stories about their tribal leaders (later known as judges), about how they came into the land (the conquest narratives), about where they came from (their slavery in Egypt), and about how they came into existence in the first place (the ancestral narratives of Genesis).

Such stories were circulated by word of mouth year after year, century after century, until they came to be written down. That probably did not happen until much later, when these various tribes that swore devotion to Yahweh (even though many of their members may have worshiped other gods as well, or occasionally lapsed and preferred Baal, for example, to Yahweh) coalesced and chose to form a united front under a king. By moving to the status of nationhood, these tribes were able to overcome

At a Glance: The Book of Judges

The book of Judges narrates episodes that allegedly transpired among the various tribes of Israel before there was a king who ruled over all the people as a unified nation. The Deuteronomistic Historian portrays this as a troubled time in the history of Israel, when the people were frequently unfaithful to God, and he delivered them over to their enemies (Moabites, Canaanites, Philistines . . .) as a result. Once they called out for help, however, God intervened and sent a charismatic military leader to save them from their oppressors. Among the well known figures who play a role in the book are the judges Ehud, Samson, and the woman judge Deborah.

some of the pressing political, economic, and military problems they faced when they were simply a fragmented and loosely connected group of tribes. The legends of the formation of the nation of Israel under a king will be told in the next books of the Deuteronomistic History, 1 and 2 Samuel.

1 AND 2 SAMUEL

We have seen that the books of 1 and 2 Samuel are counted as a single book among the Former Prophets in the Tanakh. Their division into two books in English Bibles is sensible: 1 Samuel begins with the last great (arguably the greatest) judge in the history of Israel, Samuel, and the transition to a united monarchy under the charismatic but troubled first king of Israel, Saul; it includes a number of stories of Saul's strained relationship with his eventual successor David. The book ends with the death of Saul and the second volume, then, is almost entirely about the life and reign of David. Together the two books are filled with memorable accounts of these three key figures. These stories derive from a variety of written sources and oral traditions that sometimes appear to be at odds with one another in outlook and perspective. Among other things, at least one of the written sources considers the establishment of the monarchy a good and necessary thing, brought about by Yahweh as a help to his people (recall the last verse of the book of Judges, that when there was no king in Israel everyone "did what was right in their own eyes"). In another source, which in many places provides the dominant voice, the opposite opinion is stated—that the desire for a king among the tribes of Israel was nothing less than a wholesale rejection of God himself, since it was to be he who was the ruler over Israel, not a human monarch. This second opinion may well have come about later in the history of the tradition, when storytellers looked around and saw how truly awful things had become under the kings of Israel and Judah, and when they looked back fondly, if perhaps a bit unrealistically, to the days when there was no king.

Literary Highlights of the Narrative

Here again I will not provide a full and complete synopsis of everything that happens in these books.

The stories are easy to follow and, once again, make for very fine reading. In my discussion I will assume that you have already come to know them firsthand by reading them several times.

Unlike the book of Judges, the books of Samuel do follow a more or less straight chronological structure. Among its many narratives the following are especially to be noted:

- The birth of Samuel, the final great judge, and his call by God. (1 Samuel 1–3)
- The request by the Israelites for a king. (chapter 8)
- The selection of Saul. (chapter 10)
- Saul's early successes as king. (e.g., chapter 12)
- Saul's abject failures as king. (e.g., chapters 13, 15, 28)
- The selection of David to be king. (chapter 16)
- Saul's relationship with David, and David's early adventures. (chapters 16–30)
- The death of Saul. (chapter 31)
- David as king of Judah, in the south. (2 Samuel 2–4)
- David as king over all Israel, north and south. (2 Samuel 5)
- David's acts as king. (2 Samuel 6–24)

Some of the more important literary aspects of these narratives can be discussed briefly in light of the three main characters of the action.

Samuel

As I have pointed out, Samuel is a key transitional figure in the Deuteronomistic History. Before Samuel, there was no nation of Israel. There were the descendants of Jacob, who were loosely organized into twelve tribes living throughout the Promised Land, each of them ruled by charismatic tribal leaders. According to the Deuteronomistic History, this was a chaotic arrangement that led to repeated military and political disaster. Samuel was the last of the great charismatic leaders and is portrayed as superior to all the others (his sons were judges for a time as well, but they are portrayed as losers). He is a powerful figure, righteous, and devoted to Yahweh from his youth. As judge he urges the Israelites to "put away the foreign gods and the **Astartes** [these were female Canaanite deities] from among you. Direct your heart to the LORD and serve him only, and he will deliver you out of the hand of the Philistines" (7:3–4). The Israelites

BOX 4.4 THE PHILISTINES

Once Israel is ensconced in the Promised Land it has numerous foreigners to contend with, such as the Canaanites, Hittites, Hivites, Perizzites, Girgashites, Amorites, and Jebusites. But no opposing nation in the immediate locale proved to be as problematic for Israel as the Philistines, as seen, for example in the narratives connected with Samson, Saul, and David. Who were the Philistines?

There were several organized groups that various Egyptian sources called the "Sea Peoples." These peoples appear to have originated in the area of the Aegean Sea. They attacked Egypt in the early twelfth century B.C.E., but were blocked in their efforts to overthrow the ruling Pharaohs. Eventually some of these Sea People settled in a territory on the western border of Israel along the Mediterranean Coast, due west of the Dead Sea. These were the Philistines.

They inhabited five major cities on or near the coast: Gath, Gaza, Ashkeon, Ashdod, and Ekron. As a

group, they occasionally wanted more land, and that was the difficulty they posed for ancient Israel, which understood itself to be entitled to that part of the eastern Mediterranean since God had given his people the land, originally in the promise to Abraham.

Culturally the Philistines were very different from the Israelites (and the Canaanites). They did not practice circumcision; they had—before the Israelites—superior metal weaponry (see 1 Samuel 13:19–22); and their meat of choice was pork. According to the Deuteronomistic Historian, the Philistines were at times dominant over Israel (see Judges 14); but more than likely that simply means that they were in control of one or more of the tribal regions. With the coming of the monarchy the "Philistine threat" was brought under control, so that after the time of David they more or less pass from the scene.

do so, and God responds by saving them from the Philistines.

As the one clearly recognized by all hands as the representative of Yahweh's will on earth, it is to Samuel that the people of Israel make an appeal: they want to have a king appointed over them to govern them as a nation. The request was not pleasing to either Samuel or God. The LORD tells Samuel that "they have not rejected you, but they have rejected me from being king over them" (8:7). Samuel tries to dissuade them: a king will, in effect, enslave his people; he will steal their land and crops and property; and "in that day you will cry out because of your king, whom you have chosen for yourselves; but the LORD will not answer you in that day" (8:18).

The people refuse to listen, and insist on a king. And God gives them Saul. There are two accounts of how Samuel met and then appointed Saul to be king (see 9:1–10:16 and then 10:17–27). In the first account, significantly, he "anoints" Saul with a vial of oil (pouring it over his head), announcing that "The LORD has anointed you ruler over his people Israel" (10:1). From then on, the king of Israel will be called God's "anointed one," and it was evidently the practice from then on to pour oil on the head of the new king at the time of his inauguration. (See

Box 4.5.) In a special way, the king was God's chosen one. Some of these stories portray the kingship as a good thing, given by God to his people.

Saul

The Deuteronomistic Historian portrays Saul as a powerful military man, but as a troubled figure who has difficulty doing the right thing. In the end he is rejected by God, even though God was the one who chose him in the first place. Still, Saul begins his reign on a high note, defeating and routing the Ammonites who were oppressing the Israelites in the Transjordan territories of Gad and Reuben (chapter 11). But much of the narrative of 1 Samuel is about his failures, which seem very much to be rooted in serious personality disorders. Many of his problems, as we will see in a moment, are related to his terrifically uneasy relationship with the man who was to be his successor, and the greatest king in the history of ancient Israel, David. But others arose simply from mistakes he made, including, notably, the following.

A PREMATURE SACRIFICE   Saul goes out to do battle with the Philistines (chapter 13), who will be his nemesis for most of his reign; Samuel has told him not to start the fighting right away, but to wait until he himself arrives and performs a sacrifice to God to earn divine favors for the war. Saul waits as long as he is told, but Samuel doesn't come. So Saul makes the burnt offering himself. And just then, of course, Samuel arrives. And he is angry. Because Saul refused to wait, "now your kingdom will not continue; the LORD has sought out a man after his own heart; and the LORD has appointed him to be ruler over his people, because you have not kept what the LORD commanded you" (13:14). The new man will be David, secretly anointed, still a youth, by Samuel three chapters later.

A FAILURE OF *HEREM*   Saul is in battle with the Amalekites and is told by God to destroy every last one of them, man, woman, child, infant, and animal (15:3). This is the policy of *herem* we have already seen. Saul does kill all the men, women, children, and infants, but he spares the King Agag and the best of the animals (why waste good meat?). Samuel, and the LORD, are displeased. God states: "I regret that I made Saul King." Samuel tells Saul that "The LORD has torn the kingdom of Israel from you this very day, and has given it to a neighbor of yours, who is better than you." He then himself finishes off the job Saul was to have done himself, hacking "Agag in pieces before the LORD" (15:33).

THE WITCH OF ENDOR   Near the end of his life, after Samuel himself has died, Saul is in battle once again with the Philistines and he is terrified of their overwhelming force. Not knowing how to deal with them he consults a medium who is able to call up the dead for a consultation. He requests to see Samuel; she conjures him up from the realms of the dead, and Samuel is not amused at having his rest disturbed. Saul explains the situation to him, but the spirit of Samuel is unsympathetic. Saul will lose in battle and will himself be killed (chapter 28). And it comes to pass. Three chapters later, Saul falls in battle and the book ends.

David

David is arguably the most important figure in the Hebrew Bible after Abraham and Moses. He is generally regarded as the greatest king in Israel's history, but his personality is much bigger than just that. The Deuteronomistic Historian portrays him as a hero; a giant-slayer; a bandit leader; a mercenary;

a crafty politician; a man of great lusts, appetites, and loves; an adulterer; and the father of the one great dynasty in Israelite history. Among other things, more than Saul before him, David formed the loose confederation of Israelite tribes into a great nation. Had it not been for him, what we think of as the nation of Israel may well never have come into existence.

David first appears on the scene when Saul has started to commit his many errors that lead God to reject him as the legitimate ruler. Like Saul, David is said to be anointed by Samuel in a story designed to show that God chose him not because he was the biggest or best the land had to offer but because he was a man after God's own heart (chapter 16). Once he is anointed—this is while Saul is still the official king—we are told that "the spirit of the LORD came mightily upon David from that day forward" (1 Samuel 16:13).

DAVID AND SAUL   David first meets King Saul when still a young man. An "evil spirit" comes upon Saul and afflicts him. This may be an ancient way of saying that he was clinically depressed. To ease his spirit, he wants someone to play him music and young David is brought in to play the lyre. It worked wonders, and "Saul loved him greatly" and David "became his armor bearer" (1 Samuel 16:21).

Next comes the famous story—possibly the most famous story about David in the Bible—of his confrontation with that giant of a Philistine man, Goliath, whom he defeats in single battle, unthreatening youth that he is, through the crafty use of a sling (chapter 17). This leads to a rout of the Philistines, and when they return from battle the crowds celebrate David more than Saul as the conquering hero. This creates a bad feeling, and things go from bad to worse. Saul becomes afflicted with his evil spirit once more and begins to try to kill David. Things would go on-again and off-again—usually off-again—for the rest of their lives together. David has to flee from Saul's presence, and twice has an opportunity to kill him—as Saul was definitely trying to kill *him*—but refrains, out of respect for the fact that Saul was still "God's anointed one."

Saul's children protect David from the wrath of their father. Michal, Saul's daughter, marries David and intervenes on his behalf; Jonathan, Saul's son, has a lifelong, deeply loving relationship with David and also protects him. Some readers have been particularly struck by the love between David and

Jonathan. We are told that "Jonathan made David swear again his love for him; for he loved him as he loved his own life" (20:17). They are shown weeping and kissing one another (20:41). Later David admits that his love of Jonathan had surpassed even his love for women (2 Samuel 1:26).

It is hard to know historically what to make of the relationship of David and Saul (let alone the relationship of David and Jonathan). As we will see, there are historical difficulties with these various stories. Still, Saul and David were probably real, historical figures, even if most of the stories told about them are filled with legendary accretions. But why do the stories show them in such close relationship and at the same time at such odds? One solution is to say that these stories do not represent historical realities but are designed to deal with a completely different set of problems.

Kingship in ancient Israel was, as a rule, hereditary. Saul was known to be Israel's first king, and David the second, but they were not related by blood. How were storytellers to deal with that fact? It may be that there were two separate sets of stories about two different early kings: Saul, a king over the region in the north of Israel, and David a king over the south. These stories were told and retold until they started to overlap, and the idea that David succeeded Saul, who was ultimately rejected by God, may have arisen to explain why it was that David, not a son of Saul, would come to rule in his place.

David as King

Even though David is anointed by Samuel already in 1 Samuel 16, he is not accepted as king until much later, after the death of Saul. In 2 Samuel 2:11 he becomes acknowledged the king of Judah, the southern part of the kingdom, while Saul's own son Ishbaal rules the north. But then, seven and a half years later, Ishbaal is assassinated and David becomes king over all of Israel, both north and south (5:3–4). He will rule Israel for another thirty-three years, making for a total reign of forty years. 2 Samuel is filled with the stories of those years. Among the most important are the following.

DAVID AND BATHSHEBA   One of the most moving and disturbing stories of these two books is about David and his next door neighbor, Bathsheba, wife of Uriah, a soldier in David's army (chapters 11–12). David sees her bathing (presumably in the nude),

is infatuated with her beauty, takes her into the palace, has sex with her, and she becomes pregnant. But to cover over the misdeed, David calls Uriah back from the front lines expecting him to take his wife to bed (and so appear to be the one who got her pregnant); but Uriah refuses to enjoy the pleasures of conjugal love while his comrades in arms are still experiencing hardship, fighting the king's battles. Feeling he has no other recourse, David arranges for Uriah to be killed in battle. He then takes Bathsheba to be his wife. God punishes David by killing the child after it is born (even though, looked at from another angle, it was not exactly the child's fault). But things turn out well in the (immediate) end. Bathsheba has another child, Solomon. He will eventually become the next king.

DAVID AND ABSALOM   David has a number of sons. One of them in particular proved to be a major personal and political nightmare. After a number of intrigues in the royal palace, which include rape and a vengeance murder, David's son Absalom turns on his father and performs a coup. David has to flee Jerusalem for his life. Eventually their respective armies meet and, in a rather grisly scene, Absalom meets his death. One might expect David to have seriously mixed emotions, but his thoughts are as pure as the driven snow as he mourns his traitorous but beloved son: "O my son Absalom my son, my son Absalom! Would I had died instead of you, O Absalom my son, my, son" (18:33).

DAVID AND GOD   David obviously has his problems and is not a perfect man. He is anything but that. But in his heart of hearts he is devoted to Yahweh, and for the Deuteronomistic Historian that is what counts. Early on in his reign over all Israel, David decides that he wants to build a permanent dwelling place for the ark of the covenant. The central sanctuary is still, all these years after the wandering in the wilderness, the tabernacle (See Box 3.5). David wants to construct a proper residence for God. But in a moving and powerful scene, God delivers his message to David (chapter 7). David will not be allowed to build a house for God. But God will raise up an offspring from David's body, and that one will "build a house for my name and I will establish the throne of his kingdom forever" (2 Samuel 7:13). More than that, this son of David will stand in a unique relationship before God: "I will be a father to him, and he shall

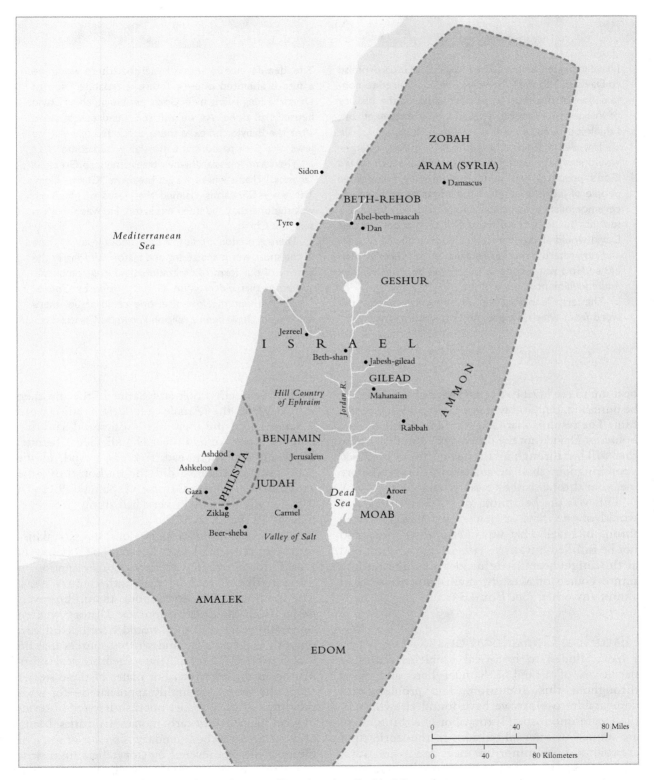

FIGURE 4.4. The Kingdom of Israel in the time of David, as described in 2 Samuel.

BOX 4.5 THE PROMISE TO DAVID AND THE DAVIDIC MESSIAH

I have indicated on pp. 102 and 104 that God's promise to David in 2 Samuel 7 may well be considered to contain one of the most important ideas in the history of Western civilization. That is a bold statement, but I think it can be justified.

The idea that an "anointed one"—that is, a king—would *always* be sitting on the throne of Judah (that's God's promise) was taken seriously by many later people of Judah, even after the kingship had been unceremoniously brought to a complete end by the Babylonians. But how could that be? If God promised that David would always have a descendant on the throne, and now there is no descendant on the throne, then either God was wrong or there will be some kind of *future* fulfillment of his promise.

The term "anointed one" in Hebrew is *mashiah*, the word from which we get the English term "messiah."

The idea developed within Israel that there would be a future anointed one—a future messiah, a "son of David," a king ruling over God's people much as David himself had done. As we will see, hundreds of years after the Babylonian exile there continued to be some Jews who anticipated that a messiah would come.

The term "messiah," when translated into Greek, is "*christos*." That is where we get the name "Christ" from. The early Christians claimed that Jesus of Nazareth was the one that had been expected. He was the messiah, the Christ.

There is no doubt that this claim about Jesus was one of the most world-shattering and history-altering in the history of our form of civilization. And it is completely rooted in that old promise allegedly made by God to David. Without that promise, one could argue, there never would have been a religion known as Christianity.

be a son to me" (7:14). Even if that one sins, he may be punished, but God will not remove his love from him. The result is that God will, in a sense, build a house for David (not the other way around), a house that will last through all the ages: "Your house and your kingdom shall be made sure forever before me, your throne shall be established forever" (7:16).

This was the beginning of the idea that David would always have a descendant sitting on the throne of Israel. That was one promise that could not be fulfilled, given the facts of history. But, odd as this might seem, it is an idea that affected the future course of Western civilization more than almost any other. (See Box 4.5.)

Historical Considerations

I have alluded to historical problems with the narratives of 1 and 2 Samuel here and there throughout this discussion. The problems are comparable to what we have found elsewhere in the Deuteronomistic History. For one thing, there are numerous internal tensions in the stories that are told, in both minor instances and major ways. Check these out for yourself: Who killed Goliath? (Read 1 Samuel 17, but then look at 2 Samuel 21:19.) Were the Philistines a threat during the

days of Samuel? (Look at 1 Samuel 7:13 and then 9:16.) Were the Amalekites destroyed? (Read 1 Samuel 15:8 and then 30:1.) When did Saul first come to know of and meet David? (See 1 Samuel 16:19–21, and then read 17:15–56.) And, as we have noticed already: did the author think the kingship was a good thing (1 Samuel 9:15–17; 2 Samuel 7:14–16) or a very bad thing (1 Samuel 8:5–18; 10:19; 12:12, 17)?

There were almost certainly local kings, real historical figures, Saul and David. The "house of David" for example is found on an inscription in Aramaic that dates from the ninth century B.C.E. The traditions we have about them, however, derive from the Deuteronomistic History written some 400 years after they would have lived, based on both oral traditions and written sources that no longer survive. There may be some historical information in the accounts, but many of these stories should be seen—and highly appreciated—for what they are: stories. They are not disinterested histories of what happened in early monarchial times. Many of them appear to be legendary accounts of some of the great figures revered by storytellers in ancient Israel, who passed along their traditions for several centuries before they were written down and eventually incorporated in the books of Samuel.

At a Glance: The Books of Samuel

1 and 2 Samuel, originally composed as a single book, describe the transition in ancient Israel from the time that each tribe had its own rulers, to the United Monarchy when all the tribes were unified as a single nation ruled by a king. The books derive their name from the first main character, Samuel, the last great judge and the one who would be used by God to anoint the two first kings, Saul and David. These two have a difficult relationship and God eventually withdraws his favor from Saul, who at the end of 1 Samuel is killed in battle against the Philistines. David becomes the greatest king in Israel's history and despite the real problems—both national and personal—his reign is portrayed as something of a golden age in the life of Israel.

1 AND 2 KINGS

As was true with the books of Samuel, 1 and 2 Kings were originally written as a single book, and they still are numbered that way in the Tanakh. In this case there is not an obvious and clear break between the two books; one of them ends and the other simply picks up where the other broke off. Together the books cover nearly 400 years in the history of Israel, from roughly 970 B.C.E. with the death of King David to roughly 560 B.C.E. in the early years of the Babylonian exile. The opening chapters of the book deal with the reign of King Solomon, when Israel continues to be a solid and thriving unity. But then there is a rupture and the nation is split in half, Israel in the north and Judah in the South. The major events of the books can be expressed in the following summary way:

- The death of David. (1 Kings 1)
- The reign of Solomon. (1 Kings 2–11)
- The division of the kingdoms into north and south. (1 Kings 12)
- The interconnected history of the two kingdoms, narrated simultaneously. (1 Kings 12–2 Kings 17)
- The destruction of Israel (the north) by Assyria in 722 B.C.E. (2 Kings 17)
- The ongoing history of Judah (the south). (2 Kings 18–25)
- The overthrow of Judah by Babylon in 586 B.C.E., followed by exile. (2 Kings 24–25)

The Reign of Solomon

As we have seen, Solomon is remembered as one of the three great kings of the United Monarchy. He is not, however, the natural choice to succeed his father David, as his half-brother Adonijah is in fact the eldest of David's surviving sons. But when David is on his death bed, his wife Bathsheba, Solomon's mother, convinces the king to appoint her own son instead. On David's instructions, Solomon is anointed by the high priest Zadok (chapter 1). David gives Solomon some final instructions—including whom to murder as political enemies once he ascends to the throne—and then dies (chapter 2).

POSITIVE ASPECTS OF SOLOMON'S REIGN There were many long-remembered positive aspects of Solomon's reign. The book of 1 Kings portrays Solomon as the wisest man ever to have lived, a view of him established at the outset. Soon after Solomon ascends to the throne, Yahweh appears to him in a dream and asks what he most desires. Instead of asking for a long life (something not always available to kings in turbulent times) or wealth or victory over his enemies, Solomon prays for "an understanding mind to govern your people, able to discern between good and evil." God is said to have been very pleased indeed with this unselfish request, and so grants him a "wise and discerning mind" so that, in Yahweh's words "no one like you has been before you and no one like you shall arise after you" (3:12). In addition, since Solomon does not ask for it, God gives the other things to him as well: abundant wealth, honor, and longevity on the throne.

Later we are told that Solomon's "breadth of understanding was as vast as the sand on the seashore" and that it "surpassed the wisdom of all the people of the east, and all the wisdom of Egypt. He was wiser than anyone" (4:29–30). The wisdom of Solomon became proverbial. In fact, as we will see, the entire book of Proverbs is often thought (wrongly) to have been written by him, in no small part because 1 Kings indicates that he "composed three thousand proverbs" (4:32).

Several stories are told in order to demonstrate Solomon's wisdom. Early on in his reign two women appear before him, each claiming that a certain infant is theirs. Who should get him? Solomon solves the problem by ordering the child to be cut in half, so that each woman will receive her share. When the real mother cries out in horror, Solomon knows whose child it is and the problem is solved. And we're told that "all Israel . . . stood in awe of the king, because they perceived the wisdom of God was in him" (3:28).

Equally famous is the story of the Queen of Sheba (an unknown location: in the area of modern Yemen?), who comes to Jerusalem to see if the stories told about Solomon could be true. She poses difficult questions to him, which he explains at ease, to her immense astonishment. She responds by praising his insights and giving him an enormous quantity of gold, spices, and precious stones. In response we are told that Solomon "gave to the queen of Sheba every desire that she expressed" (10:13). Yes indeed! Later Ethiopian tradition indicated that when she returned home, the Queen delivered Solomon's baby.

As suggested in this story, Solomon was also known for his great wealth. The Deuteronomistic Historian indicates that he was the richest king on earth (10:23), and there are lavish descriptions of his expenditures (10:16-22); the abundant supply of exotic foodstuffs for his daily table (4:22–23); and the massive sacrificial offerings that he made to God (8:63—22,000 oxen and 120,000 sheep in one ceremony). In part, his wealth came from the massive extent of his rule, which far exceeded that of the first king, Saul: "Solomon was sovereign over all the kingdoms from the Euphrates to the land of the Philistines, even to the border of Egypt; they brought tribute and served Solomon all the days of his life" (4:21). No wonder he could eat so well.

The most notable accomplishment of Solomon's reign is that he built the Temple for Yahweh. Solomon's Temple was to become one of the great monuments of the ancient Near East. As we saw previously, the Deuteronomistic Historian indicates that his father, David, had wanted to build a permanent dwelling for the ark of the covenant but was not allowed by God. (This tradition may stem from a later attempt to explain why Israel's greatest king had not himself built Israel's greatest monument: God had other plans.) In 1 Kings 6 we have a description of the Temple as originally constructed by Solomon: 90 feet long, 30 feet wide, and 45 feet high. It is elaborately constructed, of the finest building materials, overlaid on the inside with pure gold and then on the outside as well (6:21–22). Like the tabernacle before it (See Box 3.5), it is divided into sections and includes an inner sanctuary (the holy of holies) that is 30 feet long, wide, and high. That becomes the permanent resting spot for the ark of the covenant. The Temple is also elaborately furnished, with two cherubim in the inner sanctuary that far outstrip those on the ark: these new ones are fifteen feet high and overlaid with gold.

This was a major project in design and construction. We are told that it took seven years to complete (6:38). The very next verse is that Solomon's own palace took *thirteen* years to complete, which has raised for some readers the question of Solomon's ultimate allegiances.

NEGATIVE ASPECTS OF SOLOMON'S REIGN Solomon's reign was not without its problems, however. In fact, there were very serious problems indeed. For one thing, the various construction projects that Solomon undertook—notably the Temple and his own palace, but there were others as well—obviously required a good deal of labor. And, as a good Near Eastern despot—possibly an enlightened one, but a despot nonetheless—Solomon opted not to hire out the jobs to the lowest bidder. The buildings were constructed with forced labor. In other words, Solomon enslaved his own people. On a massive scale: "King Solomon conscripted forced labor out of all Israel; the levy numbered thirty thousand men" (5:13). And that was not all: "Solomon also had seventy thousand laborers and eighty thousand stone cutters in the hill country" (5:51). Later we are told that for these laborers Solomon conscripted Amorites, Hittites, Perizzites, Hivites and Jebusites who had not been destroyed in the conquest and subsequently, but no Israelites (9:20–22). The assumption here appears to be that it is all right to enslave *other* people so long as you don't enslave your own. But these verses evidently come from a separate tradition, since 5:13 indicates that indeed the conscripted

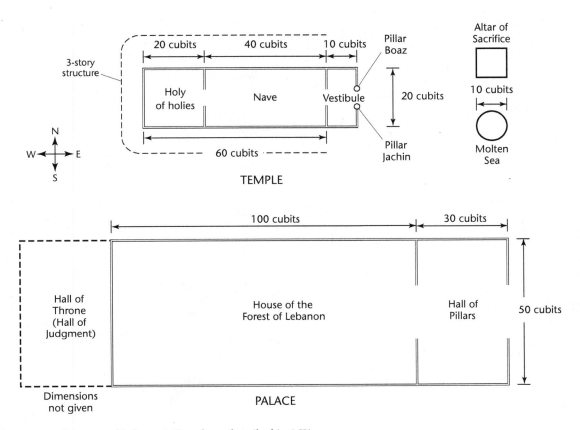

FIGURE 4.5. Diagram of Solomon's Temple, as described in 1 Kings.

laborers were Israelites, and that is the clear statement of 12:4 as well.

In the long run the Deuteronomistic Historian objects to Solomon not because of his dubious labor practices, however, but because of his passion for women: "King Solomon loved many foreign women along with the daughter of Pharaoh: Moabite, Ammonite, Edomite, Sidonian, and Hittite women" (11:1), even though God had forbidden intermarriage with women from other nations outside of Israel (see Deuteronomy 7:1-6). Solomon obviously had a big heart, with a lot of love to give: he is said to have had 700 wives and 300 concubines (11:3). The problem for the author of this text is not polygamy per se: you will have noticed that polygamy was the standard practice up to this point in ancient Israel. It was because these women "turned away his heart after other gods." As the D source feared, marrying pagan spouses is bound to make someone worship pagan gods. And Solomon did so. He built altars for other gods out of respect for his wives, and

God was displeased. Because of this serious infraction, God vowed to take the kingdom away from his successor (11:1–13).

The Divided Monarchy

This is why the kingdom was divided after Solomon's death, according to the Deuteronomistic Historian. The real reasons, historically, may have been somewhat different, as the historian himself suggests. After Solomon dies (11:41–43) his son Rehoboam becomes king. But there is a rebellion among the northern territories, headed by a person named Jeroboam. Jeroboam complains that Rehoboam's father had made life difficult for those in the north, and he (and they) want to know if Rehoboam plans to follow his father's oppressive policies. Rehoboam, in a famous reply, indicates that he in fact will be a harder taskmaster than even Solomon (12:10–15). In response, Jeroboam leads the northern region (consisting of what originally were ten of the

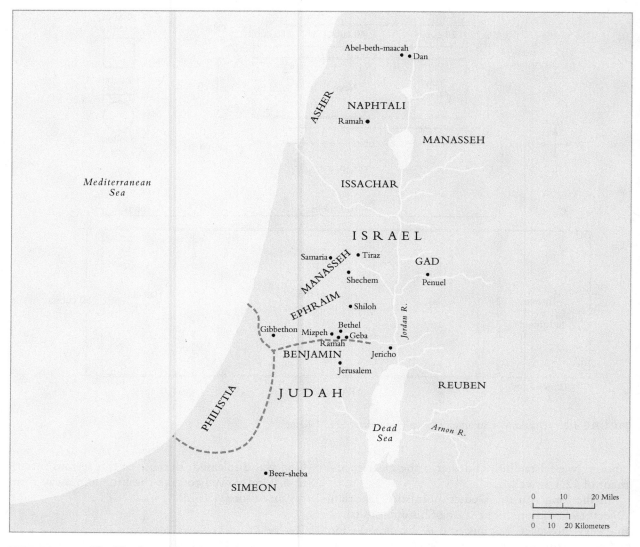

FIGURE 4.6. The Kingdoms of Judah and Israel, after they divided, according to 1 Kings.

tribes—all but Judah and Benjamin) in revolt. And the kingdom from then on is split. There are now two different countries, Judah and Israel, with two different capitals (Jerusalem in the south, Samaria in the north) and two different kings (originally, Rehoboam of Judah and Jeroboam of Israel).

The remaining section of the Deuteronomistic History, from 1 Kings 12 to the end of 2 Kings 25, traces the political histories of the two kingdoms, alternating between the rulers (and sundry episodes) in the north and in the south. A fairly standard formula is followed in these chapters, as the author:

- Indicates the name of the king (either of Judah or of Israel)
- Specifies the date of his accession in relation to the king of the other kingdom (so, for example, "In the second year of King Joash son of Joahaz of Israel, King Amaziah son of Josash of Judah began to reign," 2 Kings 14:1)
- States the length of his reign
- Provides an evaluation of his rule—indicating whether it was good or bad (most of them are bad); the criteria for this judgment are not political, economic, or military, and have little to do with whether the king was "good" in any

BOX 4.6 THE KINGS OF ISRAEL AND JUDAH

The following chart gives the 20 kings of Judah and the 19 kings of Israel (after Solomon), and the dates of their rule:

Judah		Israel	
Rehoboam	922–915 B.C.E.	Jeroboam	922–901 B.C.E.
Abijah	915–913	Nadab	901–900
Asa	913–873	Baasha	900–877
Jehoshaphat	873–849	Elah	877–876
Jehoram	849–843	Omri	876–869
Ahaziah	843–842	Ahab	869–850
Athaliah	842–837	Ahaziah	850–849
Joash	837–800	Jehoram	849–843
Amaziah	800–783	Jehu	843–815
Uzziah	783–742	Jehoahaz	815–802
Jotham	742–735	Jehoash	802–786
Ahaz	735–715	Jeroboam II	786–746
Hezekiah	715–687	Zechariah	746–745
Manasseh	687–642	Shallum	745
Amon	642–640	Menahem	745–737
Josiah	640–609	Pekahiah	737–736
Jehoahaz	609	Pekah	736–732
Jehoiakim	609–598	Hoshea	732–722
Jehoiachin	598–597		
Zedekiah	597–586		

normal sense; the author's concerns are entirely religious. Good kings worship only Yahweh and follow the dictates of Deuteronomy by sponsoring the worship of Yahweh only in the central sanctuary; bad kings do not.
• Gives a report of his death
• Indicates the name of his successor
• And the pattern then repeats itself.

In a number of instances there are stories scattered throughout the discussion of a king's reign, particularly about the activities of "prophets," as we will see in the next chapter.

THE NORTHERN KINGDOM: ISRAEL
Altogether the Deuteronomistic History traces the rule of nineteen kings over Israel, starting with Jeroboam. None of these is related to David; a few of them stand in a dynastic relation (a son succeeding a father), but many of the kings assume the throne through a coup or an assassination, so that no dynasty lasts for very long. All of the kings are judged for doing what was evil before God, since they sponsor the worship of other gods and/or allow for the worship of God outside the central sanctuary in Jerusalem. From a political point of view these alternative sites for worship make sense, since Jerusalem was in Judah and these two nations were often at war with one another. The inhabitants of the north could scarcely go on friendly terms into the territory of the south in order to practice their religion (see 1 Kings 12:27).

The tenor of the author's evaluation of all the kings of the north is set with his description of the reign of Jeroboam himself. Upon assuming the throne he makes "two calves of gold" (recall the incident of the golden calf in Exodus), setting up one in the southern part of his territory, in Bethel (just north of Jerusalem, across the border), and the other in the far north, in what was Dan. This makes it convenient for people in both parts of the country to worship, but obviously the Deuteronomistic Historian considers this to be false religion (outside of the Temple) and idolatrous. Because Jeroboam does this, a prophet of God tells him, in the name of God: "Therefore I will bring evil upon the house of Jeroboam" (14:10). And God means to do so in a rather graphic way: "Anyone belonging to Jeroboam who dies in the city, the dogs shall eat; and anyone who dies in the open country, the birds of the air shall eat; for the LORD has spoken" (14:11).

A list of the kings of Israel can be found in Box 4.6. One succeeds the other, and all of them are condemned for failing to support the worship of Yahweh as directed in the book of Deuteronomy. The kingdom of the north lasts for 200 years, from the split of the Kingdoms in 922 until their over-throw by the Assyrians in 722 B.C.E. The story of the demise of the north occurs in 2 Kings 17. The account begins like most of the others, according to the pattern I mentioned above: "In the twelfth year of King Ahaz of Judah, Hoshea son of Elah began to reign in Samaria over Israel; he reigned nine years. He did what was evil in the sight of the LORD." It is during Hoshea's reign that Assyria, on the far side of the Fertile Crescent, flexes its military muscles and expands to the west. First, under the Assyrian King Shalmanezer, Hoshea is forced to pay tribute; then Shalmanezer attacks Israel, lays siege to the capital city Samaria for three years, and finally, in the ninth year of Hoshea's rule, destroys the city. Many of the people are taken captive to other places. And the north is no more.

The Deuteronomistic Historian has no doubts why this happened: "This occurred because the people of Israel had sinned against the LORD their God" (17:7); in particular, they made shrines to other gods, offered sacrifices to them, and thus served idols, rejecting the commandments of God. In the end, though, God had his way and destroyed the kingdom.

THE SOUTHERN KINGDOM: JUDAH

The southern kingdom of Judah lasted for an

FIGURE 4.7. An officer conducts two Judeans to the king. Detail of the Assyrian conquest of the Jewish fortified town of Lachish (701 B.C.E.).

additional century and a half. 1 and 2 Kings describe a total of twenty kings of the south, cited in Box 4.6. All of these kings were descendants of David (except Athaliah, the one queen to rule), in fulfillment of God's promise that there would always be a son of David on the throne. Most of these kings are also judged negatively by the Deuteronomistic Historian because, like their northern counterparts, they allow or even sponsor the worship of other gods in addition to Yahweh.

There are exceptions, however; most notably the good King Hezekiah, who begins to rule just when Israel starts having its problems with Assyria. According to the Deuteronomistic Historian, here finally is a good king: "He did what was right in the sight of the LORD just as his ancestor David had done. He removed the high places [these were shrines to other gods placed on tall hills and mountains— close to the gods], broke down the pillars, and cut down the sacred pole [i.e., the Asherah]" (2 Kings 18:3–4). As a result of his faithfulness to Yahweh,

BOX 4.7 THE MOABITE STONE

According to the book of Genesis, the people known as the Moabites were distant relatives of the Israelites. The "father of the Moabites" was Moab, who was born of the incestuous relationship of Abraham's nephew Lot with his own (Lot's) daughter, at her initiation, when she made him drunk one night (Genesis 19:37). The Moabites figure in later stories of Israel as the enemy (e.g., during the days of judge Ehud and the Moabite king Eglon; Judges 3:12–30). But there are other close ties between the two peoples: King David's great-grandmother on his father's side was Ruth, a Moabite woman (see the book of Ruth; esp. Ruth 4:17).

Moab was located to the east of the southern part of the Dead Sea, roughly where Jordan is today. We know about the Moabites from other historical records. In 1868 a Christian missionary in Jordan inadvertently discovered an impressive stele now commonly known at the "Moabite Stone," originally erected by a king of Moab named Mesha (See Figure 4.8). It is sometimes, therefore, called the Mesha Stele. (Taken from Martha T. Roth, *Law Collections from Mesopotamia and Asia Minor*, 2nd ed. Atlanta, GA: Scholars Press, 1997). On the thirty-five lines of text on this stone, Mesha records his victory over Israel in the ninth century B.C.E. He reports that his god Chemosh had been displeased with the people of Moab for not being faithful to him but then acted on their behalf, allowing them to destroy their oppressors. One of the cities they conquered was placed under the *herem*, and its inhabitants, therefore, were ritually slaughtered. The Israelites were not the only ones to engage in this disturbing practice. And they were not the only ones who thought that they would be successful in their military endeavors so long as they were faithful to their national deity.

FIGURE 4.8. The famous Moabite stone on which Mesha, king of Moab, records his victory over Israel in the ninth century B.C.E.

Hezekiah is rewarded: "The LORD was with him; wherever he went he prospered."

As we will see in the next chapter, after Samaria fell, Hezekiah too had his troubles with Assyria. But they eventually disappeared, and his son Manasseh began to reign. He, however, was the wicked counterpart to his father in the eyes of the Deuteronomistic Historian. He undid all the reforms his father had made, rebuilt the high places, made altars for Baal, built an Asherah, and sponsored the worship of other gods in the Jerusalem Temple itself (2 Kings 21:2–6). Because of that, God vowed to destroy Jerusalem (21:11–13).

But there was first a bright spot on the horizon. Over twenty years later, when Manasseh's grandson Josiah began to reign, things turned around, as we have seen in our earlier discussions (see pp. 81–82). Josiah undertook massive reforms, cleared out the Temple, made it the special sanctuary for Yahweh once more, destroyed all the shrines to other gods, and tried to compel the Judeans once more to be monotheistic with Yahweh alone as their God. This was in the year 622 B.C.E. But the nation would have just thirty-five more years to survive.

The Babylonians in the meantime conquered the Assyrians in the east. Like their predecessors they had expansionistic ideals and marched through the Fertile Crescent on to Judah. According to 2 Kings 24:10–16, it was during the reign of King Jehoiachin that King Nebuchadnezzar of Babylon came up to Jerusalem and laid siege to the city. Jehoiachin gave himself up. Nebuchadnezzar raided the Temple of all its treasures and took ten thousand Judean captives back with him to Jerusalem, along with the king. Nebuchadnezzar appointed Zedekiah to be king in Jehoiachin's place, and he was to be the last king of Judah, the last of David's descendants ever to sit on the throne.

Zedekiah rebelled against Babylon, and in the ninth year of his reign Nebuchadnezzar returned, not in a good mood. Jerusalem was again laid under siege. After a year a half, the population was starved. The Babylonians then broke through the walls. Zedekiah escaped on foot but was captured. Nebuchadnezzar had Zedekiah's sons slaughtered before his eyes, then gouged his eyes out and took him in chains back to Babylon. The Babylonian army burned the Temple, the palace, and all the houses of Jerusalem, and demolished the walls.

The book of 2 Kings, and with it the Deuteronomistic History, ends with a man named Gedaliah being appointed as the local governor of Judah. He was a local Judean aristocrat, but was under the thumb of the Babylonians. Back in Babylon, King Jehoiachin was released from prison and given a daily allowance and, on that very, very faint hopeful note, the history of Judah comes to a close.

At a Glance: The Books of Kings

1 and 2 Kings were originally written as a single book. The narrative picks up where 2 Samuel ends, at the tail end of the reign of King David, who appoints his son Solomon to be king and then dies. Solomon is a vastly wise and wealthy, if highly despotic, monarch. In the end, it is his many wives that turn him away from strict adherence to the worship of Yahweh. After his death the kingdom is split in half, the southern part, Judah, ruled by his son Rehoboam, and the north, Israel, by Jeroboam. The books of Kings narrate the histories of the kingdoms, with nineteen kings of various dynasties ruling the north, and twenty kings, all descendants of David, ruling the south. In the end, the north is destroyed by the armies of Assyria in 722 B.C.E., and years later the south is destroyed by the armies of Babylonia in 586 B.C.E. In the judgment of the Deuteronomistic Historian, both national catastrophes occurred because the people had turned from Yahweh to worship other gods.

Take a Stand

1. This chapter outlines some of the historical problems in Joshua and Judges. In your opinion, does that lessen their importance as great pieces of literature? Why or why not?

2. Your roommate has not taken the class, but he is interested in the history of ancient Israel. He knows something (a little bit) about the time of the United Monarchy and asks which king you think was better, David or Solomon. What is your view, and how do you back it up? Give him way more information than he wants to know.

3. Some people have seen the principle of divine retribution as one of the themes of the Deuteronomistic History: people get what they deserve, the good are rewarded, and the wicked are punished. Discuss this view. Do you think the Deuteronomistic History stresses this principle? If so, how? And on a personal level, does this principle ring true to your experience?

Key Terms

Astarte, 99

Conquest Theory, 91

Deuteronomistic History, 84

Gradual Emergence Theory, 92

Herem, 88

Immigration Theory, 91

Nazirite, 95

Peasant Revolt Theory, 91

Suggestions for Further Reading

NB: For this and all chapters, see the relevant articles (e.g., "Deuteronomistic History" "1 Samuel," "David") in the works cited in the Suggestions for Further Reading in chapter 1.

Campbell, Anthony and Mark O'Brien. *Unfolding the Deuteronomistic History: Origins, Upgrades, and Present Text.* Minneapolis: Fortress, 2000. A hard-hitting study of modern scholarly views of the Deuteronomistic History, for well advanced students.

Dever, William. *Who Were the Early Israelites and Where Did They Come From?* Grand Rapids: Eerdmans, 2003. One of America's premier archaeologists looks at the archaeological record of ancient Israel to discuss whether the events described in the conquest narrative are historically accurate.

Finkelstein, Israel and Neil Asher Silberman. *The Bible Unearthed: Archaeology's New Vision of Ancient Israel and the Origin of its Sacred Texts.* New York: Simon and Schuster, 2001. A fascinating discussion of the findings of modern archaeology that shows why the narratives of the Conquest through the Divided Monarchy are problematic historically.

McDermott, John J. *What Are They Saying About the Formation of Israel?* Mahwah, NJ: Paulist Press, 1998. Discusses the various scholarly views about how Israel came into existence in the land.

McKenzie, Steven L. *King David: A Biography.* New York: Oxford University Press, 2000. An intriguing and accessible discussion of what we can know about the man, and king, David.

5

The Early Israelite Prophets

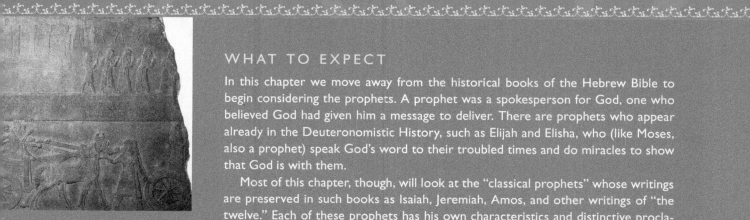

WHAT TO EXPECT

In this chapter we move away from the historical books of the Hebrew Bible to begin considering the prophets. A prophet was a spokesperson for God, one who believed God had given him a message to deliver. There are prophets who appear already in the Deuteronomistic History, such as Elijah and Elisha, who (like Moses, also a prophet) speak God's word to their troubled times and do miracles to show that God is with them.

Most of this chapter, though, will look at the "classical prophets" whose writings are preserved in such books as Isaiah, Jeremiah, Amos, and other writings of "the twelve." Each of these prophets has his own characteristics and distinctive proclamation. But taken together their messages share a number of key points: for all of them, the people of Israel and/or Judah have strayed from the ways of God; God is planning to punish them—normally by being destroyed by their enemies—in part as an attempt to have them repent and return to him. When they do so the punishment will stop and the people will once again be protected by the God who controls all human affairs.

In our sketch of the history of Israel, from the Pentateuch through the Deuteronomistic History, we have seen narratives that focus time and again on the leaders of the people: Moses, Joshua, various judges and kings. That is, of course, how a good deal of history tends to get written, with an emphasis on the power players, their actions, and their personal qualities. But during the time of the monarchy in Israel, another type of figure arose—not one who was a political leader of the people but one who was a critic, looking at the nation's government and leadership from the outside. That figure was known as a prophet.

THE RISE OF THE PROPHETS

We have seen that there are some references to "prophets" already in the Pentateuch. Moses is a prophet, and there is a concern in Deuteronomy that false prophets will arise (Deuteronomy 13, 18). But it is not until we get deep into the Deuteronomistic History—starting with the books of Samuel—that stories about prophets start to appear with any frequency. They come to the fore in particular during the divided monarchy, as related in 1 and 2 Kings.

The English term "prophet" means something like "spokesperson." A prophet is someone who "speaks forth" a message from God, either to an individual, a group, to the entire nation, or to other nations. In Hebrew the term translated as prophet is *nabi*, which probably means something like "one called" by God. Prophets considered themselves especially called or chosen by God to be his spokespersons. In the Hebrew Bible such people are sometimes also called "**seers**," because to them had been revealed a divine vision that they could then articulate to the people.

The reason the prophets begin to appear during the monarchy is that they served as divine critics of the course of political affairs. We have seen that the Deuteronomistic Historian himself evaluates kings not on the basis of their foreign and domestic policies, the success of their military campaigns, or the adequacy of their economies, but on the basis of their religious affiliations. If a king follows in the footsteps of David in worshiping and promoting the worship of Yahweh alone, he is a good king; if he follows in the footsteps of, say, Jeroboam in allowing or enabling the worship of other gods, he is bad. Prophets took a similar task upon themselves, casting judgment on kings—and on the people as a whole—for their religious activities. For the prophets, as for the Deuteronomistic Historian, these activities were not separate from political realities. In the book of 2 Kings, both Israel and Judah are destroyed not because of bad foreign policy or weak armies, but because the kings have disobeyed Yahweh. So too with the prophets of the Hebrew Bible: illicit religious activities lead to disastrous political (and personal) results.

After Moses, the first major prophet to appear on the scene (there are others earlier, who get bit parts) is none other than Samuel, who is not only a judge and an anointer of kings; he is especially portrayed as a prophet. In some ways, the account of his call to be a prophet while still a youth, as narrated in 1 Samuel 3, establishes the pattern for what it means to be a prophet in Israel.

The high priest at the time is Eli, and young Samuel is in the temple serving as his assistant. God personally calls to Samuel at night, and after a bit of confusion—Samuel can't figure out at first who is calling his name—he realizes that it is God himself who is speaking. He then tells God he is willing to listen, and God gives him some bad news. Because Eli's sons have behaved wickedly, God will punish the entire family. Samuel relays the message to Eli and, of course, it all comes true at a later point in the narrative. The Philistines attack Israel, they capture the ark of the covenant (which, as we have seen, was thought to have awesome, divine power connected to it; now it is not available to protect the Israelites), Eli's sons are killed, and then he dies. Samuel was warned in advance, he delivered his message, and it came true. That is what happens with prophets. And in the story, everyone knows it: "And all Israel . . . knew that Samuel was a trustworthy prophet of the LORD" (1 Samuel 3:20).

The emphasis here is that he was a *trustworthy* prophet. The problem with prophecy is that just anyone can claim to be a spokesperson of God. But only some people really are.

Here I should stress an important point about ancient prophets of Israel. It is true that there is an element of prediction in what they proclaim. Usually, as we will see, they proclaim that Israel (or the leaders of Israel) have sinned against Yahweh and he will be punishing them as a result, as in the case of Eli's family. But the prophets' predictions are tied closely and intimately with the *current situation* they find themselves in. Prophets in ancient Israel were not crystal ball gazers, anticipating what was going to happen hundreds or thousands of years in the future, as they are sometimes mischaracterized by religious authors today. Prophets were people who were called by God to speak his word to specific situations in which they themselves lived. This means that to understand the prophets of Jewish Scripture, we have to understand—in every instance—what their particular context was, the situation that they were addressing.

The Narrative Prophets: Elijah and Elisha

There are several prophets who show up in the narratives of the Deuteronomistic History who were not known to have left anything in writing (in contrast to the "classical prophets" of the Hebrew Bible; that is, the "Latter Prophets" that we will be discussing in a moment). These are individuals called by God to speak words of judgment against the nation, its rulers, and/or its religious leadership—including "false prophets." These "narrative prophets" are empowered to deliver a message from God, and proof of their power comes in the fact that they can do miracles. The two best known are Elijah and his successor Elisha. Their stories can be found in 1 Kings 17–2 Kings 13.

Elijah first appears during the rule of the wicked king Ahab of Israel, who sponsored and participated in the worship of the Canaanite deity Baal. According to the Deuteronomistic Historian, Ahab "did more to provoke the anger of the LORD, the God of Israel, than had all the kings of Israel before him" (1 Kings 16:33). Elijah comes on the scene out of the blue and announces that there will now be a drought. And there is a drought. It soon becomes clear why this has happened. As Elijah later tells Ahab, it is "because you have forsaken the commandments of the LORD and followed the Baals" (1 Kings 17:18). Here we have a prophet confronting a leader of the people over an issue of religious allegiance. It is a story that will get played out time and again in the Hebrew Bible.

Just as Yahweh has his prophets, so too does the Canaanite god, Baal, whom the apostates of Israel often choose to worship. Elijah challenges the prophets of Baal to a kind of prophetic duel to see who represents the true, or at least the more powerful, god. Calling all the Israelites together, Elijah upbraids them: "How long will you go limping with two different opinions? If the LORD is God, follow him; but if Baal follow him" (1 Kings 17:21). To help them choose, Elijah challenges the 450 prophets of Baal to a contest: whoever can make the wood on an altar, arranged under a sacrificed bull, ignite to consume the carcass (without using matches!) will be seen as the true prophet. The 450 prophets of Baal have a go at it but to no avail. Elijah then makes his own altar, prepares the wood and the bull, pours four jars of water over the lot (in order to increase the astonishment when this thing ignites), calls on God, and fire falls from heaven and consumes the whole sacrifice—bull, wood, altar, water, and all. The people seize the prophets of Baal and Elijah kill them all.

This sets the tone for the adventures of the narrative prophets, about whom some very good stories are told in these books. Elisha becomes Elijah's disciple (1 Kings 19:19–21), and throughout these narratives the two of them do terrific miracles—miraculously multiplying food, making iron axe heads float on the water, healing the sick, raising the dead. (See Box 5.1.) And all of it is in the context of political critique: the leaders of Israel have led the people into religious apostasy, and God is not pleased. The people need to reject the worship of Baal and worship Yahweh alone. Or very bad things will happen. Those who take the side of Yahweh, on the other hand, can expect miracles. At the end of his life, Elijah is said to be taken up into heaven in a fiery chariot (so he never dies; 2 Kings 2) and Elisha picks up where his master left off, pronouncing judgment and working miracles.

BOX 5.1 THE MIRACLE-WORKING PROPHETS

Many readers of the New Testament Gospels today believe that if Jesus did all the miracles attributed to him, then surely he must be God. Who *else* would be able to make nature obey him, and or the sick with just a word or a touch, or raise someone from the dead? The one who does such things could be none other than God in the flesh. Right?

Anyone who has read their Old Testament carefully knows the answer to this question. Throughout the Jewish Bible prophets of God such as Moses, Elijah, and Elisha can do spectacular miracles—in fact, very similar kinds of miracles to those reported of Jesus. This is not because any of them was God himself come to earth, but because the power of God was at work through them. And so, in the narratives of 1 and 2 Kings we find both Elijah and Elisha

multiplying the food to feed those in need miraculously (1 Kings 17:8–16; 2 Kings 4:42– 44; compare Jesus' feeding the multitudes); making nature obey their commands (1 Kings 17:1–6; 18:41–45; 2 Kings 6:1–7; compare Jesus' calming the storm); healing the sick (2 Kings 5:1–14; as does Jesus) and even raising the dead (1 Kings 17:17–24; 2 Kings 4:8–37; as does Jesus). At the end of his life Elijah ascends to heaven without dying (2 Kings 2:1–12).

When Jesus does his miracles in Matthew, Mark, and Luke, it is not because he is God Almighty. It is because he is God's prophet. This is recognized even by those he helps, as in Luke 7:11–17, where Jesus raises a boy back to life, and the crowd responds not by declaring that Jesus must be God, but by exclaiming, "A great prophet has risen among us!"

FIGURE 5.1. This is an impression of a seal (about an inch high) from the time of Jeroboam II, the king of Israel (the northern kingdom) in the middle of the eighth century B.C.E.; the seal's inscription reads: "Belonging to Shema, the servant of Jeroboam".

The Classical Prophets

Even better known than the narrative prophets Elijah and Elisha are a group of prophets whose writings became part of Scripture—prophets like Amos, Isaiah, Jeremiah, and Ezekiel. In many instances it cannot be determined if these prophets actually wrote their own proclamations or if their followers wrote down what they had heard the prophets proclaim. In either event, these are sometimes known as the "classical" prophets.

As we have seen, the prophets in the English Bible are divided into the five major prophets (Isaiah, Jeremiah, Lamentations, Ezekiel, and Daniel) and the twelve minor prophets (Hosea, Joel, Amos, Obadiah, Jonah, Micah, Nahum, Habakkuk, Zephaniah, Haggai, Zechariah, and Malachi). The difference between the two groups is simply one of length, not importance: major prophets are longer. In the Hebrew Bible the entire (same) group is known as the Latter Prophets and are only four in number: Lamentations and Daniel are not included in the group, and the twelve minor prophets count as one book, "the Twelve."

The classical prophets appear on the scene in the middle of the eighth century B.C.E. (thus, e.g., Isaiah, Amos); the final prophets come from a time after the Babylonian exile, when the people held in captivity were allowed to return to their land of Judah in the middle of the fifth century B.C.E. (e.g., Malachi). And so the classical prophets cover about a 300-year period, and an extremely intense period it was.

Prophets start to appear right before the Assyrians came in to destroy the land of Israel, and they prophecy the coming destruction; other prophets predict the coming of the Babylonians and the destruction of Judah in the south; yet other prophets make their proclamation after these disasters, telling the people of Judah what they need to do in the current situation.

In all cases these prophets were speaking to real political and religious experiences of their own day. They were very much bound to their own contexts. They were not predicting what will happen in the twenty-first century. They were delivering God's word to their own century. And most of the time this word is not good news. The people of God have strayed from his ways, and they need to repent or he will enter into judgment with them. If and when he does that, it will not be pretty.

In our discussions of the classical prophets we will not be able to go into all of them in equal depth. In the present chapter we will look at the "pre-exilic" prophets (those writing before the Babylonian exile), considering at some length two of the most intriguing and compelling eighth-century prophets, Amos and Isaiah, and one of the best known sixth-century prophets, Jeremiah. We will conclude by looking at five other minor prophets who were making their proclamations at about the same time, when the nations of Assyria and Babylon were real and menacing threats for the comparatively tiny nations of Israel and Judah. We will discuss the other prophets—from the time of the exile and after the exile—in chapter 6.

AMOS OF TEKOA

One of the most gripping and compelling prophetic proclamations of the entire Bible comes in a book that is also probably the earliest of all the classical prophets, the book of Amos.

Amos and His Historical Situation

As typically happens in the books of the prophets, the book of Amos begins by situating his proclamation in a firm historical context (it is generally thought that these introductory statements in the prophetic books were added later by editors):

The words of Amos, who was among the shepherds of Tekoa, which he saw concerning

Israel in the days of King Uzziah of Judah and in the days of King Jeroboam son of Joash of Israel, two years before the earthquake. (1:1)

Amos's prophetic activity is dated according to the two kings ruling at the time in Israel and Judah (this was before there were calendars; as a result you could not just say what year you are talking about). Uzziah ruled the south in 785–733 B.C.E. and Jeroboam II the north from 785-745 B.C.E. So the prophecies of Amos are firmly set in the middle of the eighth century. We do not know to which earthquake he is referring. What we do know, from reading the Deuteronomistic History, is that this was a time of turmoil for these two nations—not only in relation to each other, but also in view of the looming menace from Assyria to the Northeast.

Amos indicates that he comes from Tekoa, a town in Judah; and yet his proclamation is not made to this southern kingdom, but to the north. As we will see, some of those who heard this proclamation were not pleased that it was being made by an interloper who was interfering with the affairs of another country.

We learn a bit more about Amo's biography from a revealing passage later in his book. By the time we get to chapter 7, Amos has been pronouncing doom upon the northern land of Israel for its many transgressions. His is not a welcome voice, either with the ruling king or among the religious establishment. One of the chief priests of the cultic shrine at Bethel, a man named Amaziah, complains to Jeroboam about Amo's preaching activities: "Amos has conspired against you in the very center of the house of Israel; the land is not able to bear all his words" (7:10). And what was Amos saying? He was predicting (verse 11) that Jeroboam would soon be killed and the nation of Israel would go into exile from the land.

Amaziah responds to this proclamation by telling Amos to go back home to the land of Judah and to leave Israel and its sacred shrine at Bethel in peace. Amos replies with some of his best known words:

I am no prophet, nor a prophet's son; but I am a herdsman and a dresser of sycamore trees, and the LORD took me from following the flock, and the LORD said to me, "Go prophesy to my people Israel." (Amos 7:14–15)

When Amos claims not to be a prophet he means that he is not one who belongs to a "guild" of prophets—a professional organization of people who claimed to deliver God's word and were paid for it. He is a prophet, instead, because God called him. By profession he is a farmer/shepherd, or possibly one who owns an estate, in the south. But he has to make his proclamation to Israel because God has called him to do so. Amos goes on to make a proclamation about his enemy, the priest Amaziah, telling him that because of his opposition his wife will turn to prostitution, his sons and daughters will all be murdered, his land will be taken from him, and he will die, along with Israel, in exile. Prophets like Amos meant business, and their message was rarely happy.

The Message of Amos

The book of Amos begins by addressing nations outside of Israel, indicating that because of their multiple sins, God would enter into judgment with them (chapters 1–2). This is an important beginning: it shows that God is not simply the God of Judah and Israel, he is the God of all nations and holds all people accountable for their actions. And it shows that national suffering comes not only when one nation mistreats another but also when God intervenes and rains his judgment down upon them. And so Amos starts by attacking the capital of Syria, Damascus:

Thus says the LORD: For three transgressions of Damascus, and for four, I will not revoke the punishment; because they have threshed Gilead with threshing sledges of iron. So I will send a fire on the house of Hazael . . . I will break the gate bars of Damascus and cut off the inhabitants from the Valley of Aven. (1:3–5)

In other words, for three or four sins (meaning: a whole lot of them) committed by the people of Damascus, in Syria, God will judge them. They destroyed the city of Gilead, and so God will reciprocate by destroying them by fire and military invasion.

Amos makes a similar proclamation six more times in chapters 1–2 against Gaza, Tyre, Edom, Ammon, Moab, and even Judah. One gets the sense, reading these harsh castigations of others, that the Israelite hearing these things must be cheering

Amos on from the sidelines, since all of these other nations were thorns in Israel's side at one time or another. But then the prophet turns on those cheering: they are not in a *better* position than these others but in one that is much worse. Now there is a proclamation against Israel:

Thus says the LORD: For three transgressions of Israel, and for four, I will not revoke the punishment; because they sell the righteous for silver and the needy for a pair of sandals— they who trample the head of the poor into the dust of the earth and push the afflicted out of the way. . . . (2:6–7)

In many respects Israel is even more guilty than all the other nations. Israel was the one chosen by God at the Exodus, the one led by God through the wilderness. Even though God had delivered them and called them to be his people, they had turned on him. This was most evident in their failure to care for the needy and oppressed, whom they sold into slavery and on whose heads they trampled. And now God will respond in kind and turn on them:

So, I will press you down in your place just as a cart presses down when it is full of sheaves. Flight shall perish from the swift, and the strong shall not retain their strength, nor shall the mighty save their lives . . . and those who are stout of heart among the mighty shall flee away naked in that day. (2:13–15)

The proclamations against Israel are delivered in rhetorically vibrant and powerful language: "You only have I known of all the families of the earth; therefore I will punish you for all your iniquities" (3:2). Amos wants to insist that it is precisely *because* Israel is the chosen people that their sins are so heinous before God. Being members of the covenant not only brings privileges; it also brings ethical responsibilities for the poor, the hungry, and the oppressed. If these covenantal obligations are shirked, punishment will follow and Israel has only itself to blame.

Amos stresses that the coming suffering for the nation will derive not from the accidents of history, the misfortune of living near a mighty world empire, the bad luck of being a relatively weak and minor nation in the path of an aggressive foreign power. The suffering will come because God is punishing the people for their sin. It is all his doing. Nowhere is this stressed more than in the rhetorical questions of 3:3–6. Each of these questions is to be answered "no," until the logic of the sequence forces one to answer even the final question "no." Do people walk together if they haven't agreed to do so? (Answer: no.) Do lions roar if they don't have any prey? (No.) Does a bird fall into a snare if there isn't a trap set for it? Does a snare spring up if nothing falls into it? Does the trumpet that indicates a military attack sound in the city without making people afraid? And then the climax: "Does disaster befall a city, unless the LORD has done it?" (3:6). Again, the answer must be no. The disaster that is about to fall is not the doing of some foreign, hostile power. It is the act of God.

And why is God so set on punishing Israel? For Amos it is principally because of ethical violations involving issues of social injustice. It is because you "oppress the poor . . . crush the needy"; it is "because you trample on the poor and take from them levies of grain. . . . You . . . afflict the righteous . . . and push the afflicted out of the way" (3:6–7). Amos portrays Israel as rotten to the core: "They do not know how to do right, says the LORD, those who store up violence and robbery in their strongholds" (3:10).

And what will God do in response? There will be military attack, and the nation will fall. "Therefore thus says the LORD God: An adversary shall surround the land, and strip you of your defense; and your strongholds shall be plundered" (3:11); "they shall now be the first to go into exile, and the revelry of the loungers shall pass away" (6:7). And so, in Amos's famous lament: "Fallen, no more to rise, is maiden Israel; forsake on her land, with no one to raise her up" (5:1).

The people of Israel cannot complain that they have not been given fair warning. Not only have the prophets made proclamation, God himself has brought suffering on the people in order to get them to turn back to him. This is stated in a series of divine laments in 4:6–12. God indicates that he brought famine to try to get the people to repent, "yet you did not return to me"; he brought a serious drought, "yet you did not return to me"; he destroyed their crops with blight and mildew and locusts, "yet you did not return to me"; he brought an epidemic and military defeat, "yet you did not return to me." And since they have failed to return to him, despite everything that he has tried to do in order to get them to sit up and take notice, the outcome will be dire: "Therefore thus I will do to you, O Israel; because I will do this to you, prepare to meet your God, O Israel!" (6:12). In this context, "meeting your God" is not a happy occasion.

Amos goes on to stress that what God wants is social justice and ethical behavior. What he does not want is the attempt to thwart his purposes by performing seemingly highly religious activities instead of caring for the poor and hungry. Some people in Israel—probably like many other people in many other times and places—appear to have thought that what God wants is proper worship: performing the sacrifices to God in the proper way, remembering to celebrate religious festivals, conducting proper worship services. But for Amos this is not at all what God really wants. He wants a just society. And so, Yahweh himself is portrayed as saying in no uncertain terms:

> I hate, I despise your festivals, and I take no delight in your solemn assemblies. Even though you offer me your burnt offerings and grain offerings, I will not accept them, and the offerings of well-being of your fatted animals I will not look upon. Take away from me the noise of your songs; I will not listen to the melody of your harps. But let justice roll down like waters, and righteousness like an ever-flowing stream. (5:21–24)

Like other prophets, Amos often spoke using metaphors and parables. In Chapters 7–9 he is said to have seen five visions, each of which were images of judgment—for example, an attack of locusts, a wild fire, and a "plumb line," which is used to see if a wall is straight; if not, you have to tear it down and start again. This is not a hopeful metaphor for the people of God if they do not "line up" well.

The Judean Redaction of Amos

It is impossible, at the end of the day, to know whether Amos himself wrote down these prophecies that bear his name or if they were penned by someone else in his name. What is clear is that he not only made these proclamations orally, probably over a period of years, but that someone—either himself or another scribe—wrote them down and put them in circulation as a written text. Obviously

the predictions are dire, and they do not make for cheerful reading.

But after they had been in circulation for a long while, a later editor made some additions to them so that they would end on a happier note. In biblical scholarship an editor is known as a "**redactor**," and the editorial work done by a redactor is called a "redaction." Scholars have long recognized that the book of Amos as we have it has been redacted.

Near the end of the book we find predictions of the coming destruction of the northern kingdom of Israel in still dire terms: "All the sinners of my people shall die by the sword" (9:10). But then all of a sudden the prophet begins to prophecy that things are going to get better. The house of David (that is, the southern dynasty) will be restored; the walls of the city will be repaired; the city will be rebuilt; there will be abundant harvests; and the wine production will defy imagination (9:11–13).

This part of the book seems to presuppose that the Davidic king has been taken off his throne and that Jerusalem has been destroyed. In that context, the prophet is predicting that now that God has punished his people, he will restore them and things will be good once more. In other words, this ending passage appears to have been written after the destruction of Jerusalem in 586 B.C.E., and to be written from a southern, Judean perspective. How does one explain that, if Amos was living 150 years earlier, prophesying to the north?

It is usually thought that when the book was in circulation a scribe from Judah, living a century and a half later, added the ending of the book (and the other positive messages to Judah throughout the book). Now the book does not end with a dire prediction of an imminent disaster—as Amos' own book appears to have ended, some years before the Assyrian decimation of the northern kingdom in 722 B.C.E. It now ends on a note of promise: the Davidic kingdom will be restored and God will now create a utopia on earth for his people, in which they will experience no more suffering:

> I will restore the fortunes of my people Israel, and they shall rebuild the ruined cites and inhabit them; they shall plant vineyards and drink their wine, and they shall make gardens and eat their fruit. I will plant them upon their land, and they shall never again be plucked up out of the land that I have given them, says the LORD your God. (9:14–15)

Amos as a Representative Prophet

In some ways Amos can be taken as typical of all the prophets of the Hebrew Bible. The following points about the prophets, based on this reading of Amos, are worth noting:

- The prophets are presented as spokespersons of God, who were intervening in the affairs of the nation of Israel (or Judah) when things were not going well.
- The prophets are particularly concerned about social and religious transgressions of the people (Amos is more concerned about social issues; other prophets will be focused more on religious issues—the proper worship of Yahweh).
- The prophets do make predictions, but they are not predicting events that will transpire hundreds or thousands of years after their day. They are speaking to their own situations and must be rooted in their own historical contexts. Their predictions are about what God will do to the people if they do not return to him and behave as he requires.
- The suffering of the nation rests in the hands of God. Yes, people can and do act in ways harmful to others (that's a big part of the problem). But the demise of the nation itself will come because of the act of God. He is the one who brings drought, famine, epidemic, economic hardship, and military disaster. If the nation is faithful to God, it will be rewarded. But if not, it will be harshly punished.
- God is not simply the God of his people. He is the sovereign Lord of the entire earth, and all the other nations do his bidding. He is the creator of all, and he uses all nations to perform his will.

ISAIAH OF JERUSALEM

Overlapping somewhat with the prophetic activities of Amos in the north were those of the prophet Isaiah in the south. The book of Isaiah begins, in typical prophetic fashion, by setting forth the rough dates of the prophet's proclamation: "The vision of Isaiah son of Amoz, which he saw concerning Judah and Jerusalem in the days of Uzziah, Jotham, Ahaz, and Hezekiah, kings of Judah." If, as most scholars think, the account of Isaiah's call to be a prophet in

chapter 6 (which we will explore soon) marks the beginning of his ministry, then it started in the "year that King Uzziah died" (6:1). That would have been 738 B.C.E. The last king mentioned, Hezekiah, ruled 727–698 B.C.E. Isaiah prophesied at least up to the year 701, when the Assyrian king Sennacherib invaded Judah; this means that Isaiah's ministry was a long one, possibly around forty years.

These were indeed eventful years in the life of the southern kingdom of Judah. For one thing, the inhabitants of that land must have looked on in terror as they saw events unfolding to the north, in Israel and its antagonistic and eventually disastrous relationship with the mighty Assyria. During the early part of Isaiah's ministry the Assyrian king, with one of the great names of all time, Tiglath-Pileser (ruled 745–727 B.C.E.), decided to expand his empire and moved against the countries and city-states of the **Levant** (a term used to describe all the countries bordering on the eastern Mediterranean). Several of the countries under threat came together to provide a unified front against an Assyrian assault. But Judah, under King Ahaz, refused to join in, possibly thinking that it was a futile venture. The two countries of Syria and Israel banded together to attack Judah in order to make it join the coalition, and marched down to Jerusalem in full force. Eventually, as things turned out, Judah escaped unscathed. The Syrian and Israelite armies withdrew and the people of the south could breathe better—for a while. Israel was made a vassal state to Assyria, but rebelled in the year 727. That turned out to be a bad idea, as it eventually led to its destruction when the Assyrian king Shalmaneser attacked from the north and in 722—while Isaiah was still active in the south—destroyed the nation of Israel.

Some twenty years later, when Hezekiah was king of Judah, Assyria was once more in an expansionistic mode and proceeded to invade Judah under the rule of the Assyrian king Sennacherib. We know of this assault from several sources. It is discussed in 2 Kings 18:13–19:37, where two different accounts of the invasion have been spliced together; and we have a record of it from Sennacherib himself, as found on a monument called the Taylor Prism that is now housed in the British Museum in London. According to Sennacherib, he had overrun the entire territory of Judea and laid Jerusalem

FIGURE 5.2. A relief showing the Assyrian king Tiglath-Pileser. The upper part shows people and cattle being taken from a captured city; the lower part shows the king on his chariot.

under siege, with King Hezekiah holed up inside. Hezekiah was forced then to surrender and pay a large tribute. Isaiah of Jerusalem was thus engaged in his prophetic activities at an incredibly tense and dangerous time.

Divisions of the Book of Isaiah

We saw at the end of our discussion of the book of Amos that an editor had, at some point, added a few verses at the conclusion in light of the new situation in which he was living. That is not at all unusual among the prophetic books. In the case of Isaiah, however, we are dealing with a situation that is far, far more extreme. For well over a century scholars have recognized that major portions of the book do not actually derive from Isaiah of Jerusalem. The evidence is similar to what we found in Amos: passages that do not fit into Isaiah's own historical context. But in this instance it is even more compelling.

BOX 5.2 SENNACHERIB IN HIS OWN WORDS

In one of those rare places that we have clear external confirmation of a biblical story, the attack on Jerusalem by the Assyrian king Sennacherib is narrated in an inscription on what is known as the Taylor Prism, now in the possession of the British Museum in London. In it, Sennacherib himself boasts in gloating terms of his triumph over King Hezekiah. The following is a partial translation of the inscription. If Sennacherib is even close to telling the truth, this was a thorough and resounding defeat of the king of Judah and must have devastated the inhabitants of Jerusalem (in contrast to the accounts in Isaiah and 2 Kings):[1]

As for Hezekiah, the Judean, who had not submitted to my yoke, I besieged forty-six of his fortified walled cities and surrounding small towns, which were without number. Using packed down ramps and by applying battering rams, infantry attacks by mines, breeches, and siege machines, I conquered them. I took out 200,150 people, young and old,

male and female, horses, mules, donkeys, camels, cattle, and sheep, without number, and counted them as spoil. Himself I locked him up with Jerusalem, his royal city, like a bird in a cage. I surrounded him with earthworks, and made it unthinkable for him to exit by the city gate. . . . I imposed upon him in addition to the former tribute, yearly payment of dues and gifts for my lordship.

He, Hezekiah, was overwhelmed by the awesome splendor of my lordship, and he sent me after my departure to Nineveh, my royal city, his elite troops and his best soldiers which he had brought into Jerusalem as reinforcements, with 340 talents of gold, 800 talents of silver, . . . beds (inlaid) with ivory, armchairs inlaid with ivory, elephant hides, ivory, ebony wood, boxwood, garments with multicolored trim, garments of linen, wool dyed red-purple and blue-purple, vessels of copper, iron, bronze, and tin, chariots, siege shields, lances, armor, daggers for the belt, bows and arrows, countless trappings and instruments of war, together with his daughters, his palace women, his male and female singers. He also dispatched his personal messenger to deliver the tribute and to do obeisance.

1 Taken from M. Cogan and H. Tadmor, *II Kings* (New York: Doubleday, 1988), pp. 338–39, as modified slightly by Michael Coogan, in *The Old Testament: A Historical and Literary Introduction to the Hebrew Scriptures* (New York: Oxford, 2006), pp. 338–39.

Evidence of Multiple Authors

Most of the first 39 chapters of Isaiah clearly date to the ministry of Isaiah of Jerusalem in the eighth century B.C.E. This is obviously true of the very end of the section, written when Hezekiah was king of Judah and was feeling threatened by envoys who had been sent to him from the surging power of Babylon. Isaiah tells Hezekiah that it is true that in the future, the Babylonians will indeed wreak havoc in Judah—but it will not be in Hezekiah's own time (39:5–8). Immediately after this, rather than continuing with a proclamation of eventual doom, the text shifts drastically in an effort to comfort the people of Judah who have now already suffered for the sins they have committed. This portion of the book appears to have been written a century and a half later:

Comfort, O comfort my people says your God. Speak tenderly to Jerusalem and cry to

her that she has served her term, that her penalty is paid, that she has received from the LORD's hand double for her sins. (40:1–2)

Now, according to these later portions of the book God has taken his wrath out on his people, Judah, but will restore them. And what is more, he will now turn on the Babylonians whom he earlier used in order to afflict Judah. (Chaldea, in this quotation, is another name for Babylonia):

Sit in silence, and go in darkness, daughter Chaldea! For you shall no more be called the mistress of kingdoms. I was angry with my people, I profaned my heritage; I gave them into your hand, you showed them no mercy. . . . But evil shall come upon you, which you cannot charm away; disaster will fall upon you, which you will not be able to ward off. (47:5–6, 11)

Judah, on the other hand, will be brought back from exile, through the wilderness, just as Israel once before passed through the wilderness on the way to the Promised Land after its exile in Egypt. Only now there will not be suffering en route; instead, God will make the Judeans' path easy and joyful:

A voice cries out, "In the wilderness prepare the way of the LORD, make straight in the desert a highway for our God. Every valley shall be lifted up, and every mountain and hill be made low; the uneven ground shall become level, and the rough places a plain. Then the glory of the LORD shall be revealed, and all people shall see it together." (40:3–5)

What is more, we are told that Jerusalem "will be rebuilt" (indicating, of course, that it has been destroyed), that the Temple will be as well (so that it too has disappeared), and that this will be done by none other than Cyrus (44:28). Cyrus was the king of Persia who overthrew the Babylonians in 539 B.C.E. and allowed the Judean exiles to return home, to build the walls of Jerusalem.

Clearly this part of Isaiah is not presupposing a time in the eighth century B.C.E. but in the sixth century, after the Babylonians had destroyed Judea and its Temple and taken the people back into exile in Babylonia.

What is more, the final chapters of Isaiah seem to presuppose an even *later* time—after the exiles had

FIGURE 5.3. A relief showing the king of Assyria, Sennacherib, reviewing the spoils taken from the city of Lachish in Judah; the relief was discovered in the king's palace in Nineveh. On the upper left side is an inscription that speaks of Sennacherib as the "king of the world".

returned from captivity and were functioning once again, on a more limited basis, in the land.

How do we explain these anomalies in the book of Isaiah?

The Three Isaiahs

Scholars have long thought that there are three sections of the book of Isaiah, each attributable to a different prophet, living at a different time, facing a different situation. Roughly speaking, the book divides as follows:

First Isaiah. Chapters 1–39 (with some exceptions) go back to Isaiah of Jerusalem, prophesying in the eighth century B.C.E. He is predicting a coming judgment on the nation of Judah.

Second Isaiah. Chapters 40–55 were written by a later prophet who shared many of the perspectives of Isaiah of Jerusalem, but who was living about 150 years later in the middle of the sixth century after the Babylonian captivity had begun. He is preaching consolation for those Judeans who had suffered because of this military defeat.

Third Isaiah. Chapters 56–66 were written by a yet later prophet who appears to have been writing after the exiles had returned from Babylon. He is exhorting the returnees to live in ways pleasing to Yahweh.

At some later time a redactor took these three texts of prophecies and combined them on a single scroll, so that all of them appear to derive from Isaiah of Jerusalem; but in reality, only a portion—though a sizeable portion—of them do. In the following discussion I will be speaking only of First Isaiah; in the next chapter I will discuss the other portions of the book.

The Message of First Isaiah

The message of Isaiah, in essence, is not that different from that which his contemporary Amos preached in the north. Isaiah maintains that the people have strayed from God; this is most evident in the social injustice that pervades society, but it is the leaders of the people who are principally at fault. These problems cannot be fixed simply by attending to proper religious rituals. The nation will be punished by God at the hands of the Assyrians.

Right off the bat Isaiah laments how the people of Israel (meaning, in this case, Judah) have fallen away from God. God had raised them as his own children, but they have rebelled. This is for Isaiah (and God) an astonishing thing:

> The ox knows its owner, and the donkey its master's crib; but Israel does not know, my people do not understand. Ah, sinful nation, people laden with iniquity, offspring who do evil, children who deal corruptly, who have forsaken the LORD, who have despised the Holy One of Israel, who are utterly estranged. (1:3–4)

The sins of the people are largely social and political in nature. They have done evil; their "hands are full of blood" (1:15); they were once righteous and now they are murderers (1:21); their leaders are "rebels and companions of thieves" who love to take a bribe and refuse to defend the weak and powerless (1:21–23). As in Amos, God has already punished the people in order to get them to repent, apparently by an invasion that left the country "desolate" and the cities "burned with fire" (1:7). But they have not heeded. The prophet urges the people to repair their ways: "cease to do evil, learn to do good; seek justice, rescue the oppressed, defend the orphan, plead for the widow" (1:16–17).

In particular, Isaiah stresses that following prescribed religious practices is of no use before God. He, instead, wants people to live in the proper way: "Trample my courts no more; bringing offerings is futile; incense is an abomination to me. New moon and Sabbath . . . I cannot endure solemn assemblies with iniquities . . ." (1:12–13).

In a moving and powerful passage, Isaiah likens the land of Judah to a vineyard that God had planted as his beloved possession. He dug around it, planted it with the best vines (the people), made a watchtower and vat, and expected it to yield grapes. Yet it did not yield grapes, but only wild (sour) grapes. God did all he could for his vineyard, the people of Israel, but they have not borne the proper fruit. So what will God do to his vineyard?

> I will remove its hedge and it shall be devoured; I will break down its wall, and it shall be trampled down. I will make it a waste; it shall not be pruned or hoed, and it shall be overgrown with briars and thorns. . . . For the vineyard of the LORD of hosts is the house of Israel, and the people of Judah are his pleasant planting;

he expected justice [in Hebrew: *mishpat*] but saw bloodshed [Hebrew: *mispah*]; righteousness [Hebrew *sedaqa*], but heard a cry [Hebrew *se'aqa*]. (5:5–7)

Some Key Passages

Among the many intriguing and important passages in this prophet, we might consider in particular the following.

THE CALL OF ISAIAH (CHAPTER 6)

It was in the year of the death of King Uzziah (738 B.C.E.) that Isaiah experienced a call to his prophetic ministry. It is a striking passage: Isaiah indicates that he has had a vision of God himself on his throne, seated high above the Temple (here Isaiah is relying on the image that God is enthroned on the ark in the Holy of Holies); so gigantic is God that just the hem of his robe fills the entire Temple. There are angelic beings called seraphs ("burning ones") attending God and praising him for his holiness. Isaiah is abashed because he is not worthy to have seen this sight, as one who has "unclean lips." But one of the seraphs takes a hot coal from the altar and touches it to Isaiah's lips, cleansing him of his guilt and sin; that is, purifying his words so that he can now speak for God. Then Isaiah hears God ask who he can send on his mission. And Isaiah replies, "Here I am; send me!" (6:8)

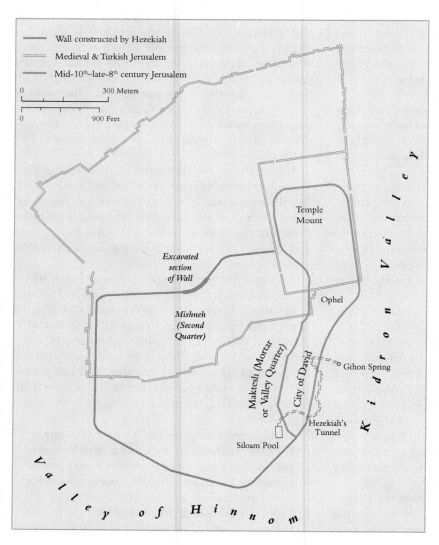

FIGURE 5.4. A plan of the city of Jerusalem as it was built in the time of the pre-exilic prophets, expanded after the exile, and then again in the Middle Ages.

God is sending Isaiah forth to preach to his people but, odd as it may seem, his ministry is supposed to dull the mind, stop the ears, and shut the eyes of those to whom he makes proclamation (6:10). He is abashed and asks how long it will be before anyone can hear his words, and the Lord tells him, "Until cities lie waste without inhabitant, and houses without people, until the LORD sends everyone far away. . . ." Isaiah is bound to preach God's message; no one will listen; and in the end, the land will be destroyed and people taken into exile. Isaiah's ministry did not begin on a high note.

THE SYRO-EPHRAIMITIC WAR (CHAPTERS 7–9)

I have already mentioned the coalition between Syria and Israel (also called "Ephraim," as that was the largest of the original tribes that made up the north), in which they attacked Jerusalem when Ahaz was king to force him to join with them to resist Assyria. In chapter 1, I discussed this passage in order to show that you need to read it in context to make sense of the prediction that "a young woman [not a "virgin"] has conceived and will bear a child, and you will call his name Immanuel" (7:14; see pp. 23–24). The point, as I indicated, is given by the author himself. Before this yet-to-be-born child knows the difference between right and wrong, the two nations at war with Judah will return and leave it unharmed (verse 16). (Eventually, though, the real threat will appear: Assyria.)

This is not the only symbolic child born in the context of this episode. Isaiah goes to give Ahaz advice from the Lord, at the outset, with one of his own sons, named Shear-jashub, a name that means "a remnant will return"—a sign of hope that the people will not be completely destroyed but that some will survive the coming onslaught. Then in chapter 8 Isaiah has sex with a prophetess and she bears him a son, upon whom they bestow the longest name in the Bible: Maher-shalal-hash-baz (8:1). The name means: "the spoil speeds, the prey hurries." We are told that before the child learns to speak its first words, Assyria will devastate both Syria and Israel.

LATER ORACLES

There are a number of gripping passages scattered throughout the book of First Isaiah. Many of them are prophecies of the coming judgment, especially in chapters 1–4. Some indicate that after this judgment takes place a remnant of the people will be saved, as in a passage such as 10:20-27, difficult to interpret, where God states that he will indeed judge his people harshly with a destruction that "is decreed" but a "remnant will return" and then God will punish those he used to harm his people.

This idea of hope after judgment is stronger in Isaiah than it had been in Amos. In particular, Isaiah contains several messianic predictions—that is, predictions of future "anointed ones" who will rule the people righteously, as God demands. In particular, 11:1–9 predicts that out of the stump that was left after the "tree of David" was cut down, a branch would grow. This would be a Davidic king who would delight in the Lord and who would judge with righteousness and might. A utopian kingdom would ensue in which "the wolf shall live with the lamb, the leopard shall lie down with the kid, the calf and the lion and the fatling together, and a little child shall lead them" (11:6).

Finally, a large portion of First Isaiah (chs. 13–23; these chapters were probably added by a different writer) is directed against nations other than Judah—such as Babylon, Assyria, Moab, and Syria—who too would be judged by God for their iniquities. God, for Isaiah, was not simply the national God of Israel. He was the God over the entire earth, and all peoples needed to do what was right in his eyes or they would pay a very severe penalty. But Judah, in the end, would be restored and allowed to start anew when the remnant returned.

JEREMIAH

To look at a third **pre-exilic prophet** we can turn to Jeremiah, who, like Isaiah before him, was a prophet in the southern kingdom and whose ministry lasted some forty years. The book of Jeremiah begins by indicating that Jeremiah was a priest from the town of Anathoth, just a few miles northeast of Jerusalem, "to whom the word of the LORD came in the days of King Josiah, son of Amon of Judah, in the thirteenth year of his reign" (1:2). It goes on to say that he delivered his message during the reign of Jehoiakim and until the eleventh year of the last king of Judah, Zedekiah: "until the captivity of Jerusalem in the fifth month." In other words, Jeremiah's prophecies are to be located in the decades immediately before the destruction of Jerusalem by the Babylonian armies in 586 B.C.E. and, in fact, go somewhat beyond that date.

According to the Deuteronomistic Historian, these were times of serious ups and downs for Judah. There are debates about whether Jeremiah actually began his proclamation in 627 B.C.E. (the thirteenth year of Josiah's reign), or if that was the year he was born. According to 1:4–5, he was "appointed" to be a prophet already while in his mother's womb. However one takes the dating, it was an auspicious time. It was only a few years later that Josiah began to implement his reforms in the religious life of Judah that so enthralled the Deuteronomistic Historian, and that earned him such praise as a king greater than any since the time of David (see pp. 81–82). From reading 2 Kings, one would think that God would especially be on Josiah's side, given his deep commitment and devotion to the cause of destroying all other shrines and altars and urging the worship of Yahweh alone. But history itself did not allow for a happy outcome to Josiah's life. As fate would

have it, in 609 B.C.E. Josiah went out to meet the Pharaoh of Egypt, who was marching north with his army, to a very bad result. In the ensuing clash, at the battle of Megiddo, Josiah met his untimely death. Judah had just thirty-three years left to survive. Babylon was on the rise and posed a clear and certain threat.

The year that Jeremiah dates the beginning of his ministry (627 B.C.E.) was also the year that the Assyrian king Ashurbanipal died. Things went downhill for the Assyrians and fifteen years later, in 612 B.C.E., the capital city of Nineveh fell to the Babylonians. Seven years after that there was a major battle at Carchemish in which the Babylonians defeated the remnants of the Assyrian armies and the Egyptians to gain control over the Fertile Crescent. From then on things looked very bad indeed for the Judeans. As we have seen, there was a first major encounter in 597. The king of Judah, Jehoiakim, decided to stop paying tribute to the Babylonians; he died before a reprisal could occur but his successor Jehoiachin was attacked and taken captive back to Babylon. A second

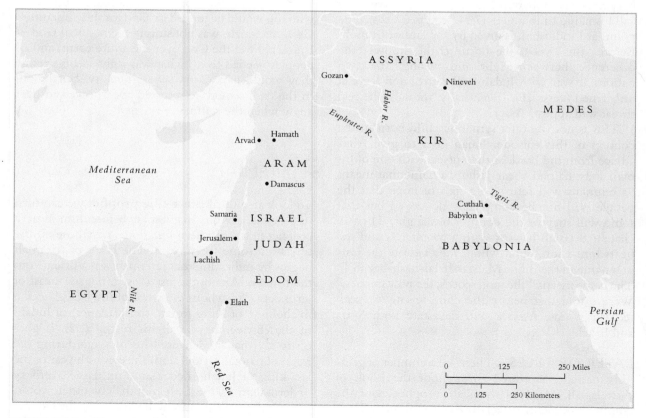

FIGURE 5.5. The ancient Near East at the time of the Divided Kingdom.

revolt occurred under his successor Zedekiah, and that is when King Nebuchadnezzar of Babylon attacked with full force, destroying the walls of Jerusalem, burning the Temple, and taking the people (at least the leaders and aristocrats, and probably a host of others) back into captivity in Babylon.

Jeremiah is presented as issuing his prophecies during all these fearful and tragic times. As might be expected, his prophecies are also fearful and tragic. He tells the Judeans that they have no chance; that God will now enter into judgment with them because of their faithlessness; that they should, in fact, surrender to the Babylonians or else they will be killed; but that eventually God would restore the people. This was not a popular message, and Jeremiah had more than his share of Judean enemies who persecuted him for being the bearer of bad tidings. Even more than any of the prophets, Jeremiah was personally torn by his message and delivered it with considerable angst. Sometimes he is called the "weeping prophet." He had a good deal to weep about.

The Prophecies of Jeremiah

Unlike the other prophetic writings we have considered so far, the book of Jeremiah is clearly divided into discrete sections. The main portions of the book are as follows:

- Oracles delivered against Judah and Jerusalem (chs. 1–26);
- Prose narratives about Jeremiah himself (chs. 26–29; 32, 34–45; note, as with most of the prophets, the proclamations of Jeremiah are normally given as poetry);
- Oracles against other nations (chs. 46–51);
- Final chapter: taken from the Deuteronomistic History (ch. 52; see 2 Kings 24–25).

Chapter One as Programmatic

Many of the themes of Jeremiah's prophetic proclamation are captured in a nutshell at the very outset, in the message delivered in the opening chapter of the book.

- *God's call of the prophet* (1:4–5). Jeremiah is told that the LORD had appointed him to be "a prophet to the nations" even before he was born: "Before I formed you in the womb." This gives not only the sense of predestination, but of

inevitability. Jeremiah could not refuse to deliver his prophetic message. He had no control over it. It was for this reason that he came into the world.

- *Jeremiah's reluctance* (1:6). Jeremiah nonetheless tries to get off the divine hook, showing his reluctance to deliver the message God has given to him. As happens with other great prophets—for example, Moses—Jeremiah claims that he cannot properly speak, since he is still "only a boy."
- *God's command, assurance, and commission* (1:7–10). God in the Bible, however, is not one to take no for an answer: "Do not say 'I am only a boy'; for you shall go to all whom I send you and you shall speak whatever I command you." But God assures him not to be afraid of those who oppose him: "for I am with you to deliver you." Then, in an incident reminiscent of Isaiah 6 (where the seraph touches the prophet's mouth with a burning coal), God touches Jeremiah's lips and tells him that he has now put his message into his mouth.
- *The disastrous message* (1:11–16). Jeremiah sees a "boiling pot, tilted away from the north" (the direction, of course, of Babylonia in relation to Judah) and God tells him, "Out of the north disaster shall break out on all the inhabitants of the land." The city of Jerusalem will be attacked, along with all the cities of Judah. "And I will utter my judgments against them, for all their wickedness in forsaking me." The people of Judah have worshiped other gods and now they must pay the price.
- *The antagonistic reception* (1:17–19). Jeremiah must make a proclamation against all of Judah: its kings, princes, priests, and people. And his hearers will not be pleased: "They will fight against you; but they shall not prevail against you, for I am with you, says the LORD."

Some of the Key Themes

The following are among the key themes found among Jeremiah's prophecies.

1. The people of Judah are faithless. The people of Judah were chosen by God, but they have deserted him. He brought them into the Promised Land, but they defiled it. Through Jeremiah, God pronounces his shock. The Judeans have

done what no people on earth has ever done, rejected the one who saved them:

> Has a nation changed its gods, even though they are not gods? But my people have changed their glory for something that does not profit. Be appalled, O heavens, at this, be shocked be utterly desolate, says the LORD. (2:11–13)
>
> For my people are foolish, they do not know me; . . . They are skilled in doing evil, but do not know how to do good. (4:22)

2. As a result, they will be destroyed by an invading nation.

> I am going to bring upon you a nation from far away, O house of Israel, says the LORD. It is an enduring nation, it is an ancient nation, a nation whose language you do not know, nor can you understand what they say. Their quiver is like an open tomb; all of them are mighty warriors. They shall eat up your harvest and your food; they shall eat up your sons and your daughters; they shall eat up your flocks and your herds; they shall eat up your vines and your fig trees; they shall destroy with the sword your fortified cities in which you trust. (5:15–17; see also, e.g., 29:16–19)

3. Because the coming destruction by the Babylonians is certain, the only hope for survival is to surrender to the Babylonians—not to fight. Any who resist will be destroyed by the sword, by hunger, or by disease. Those who give up will at least preserve their lives (21:9–10; 27:17). So too, those already taken into exile to Babylon (in the first deportation in 597 B.C.E.) should settle in to their lives there, build houses, have families, and "seek the welfare of the city where I have sent you into exile, and pray to the LORD on its behalf" (29:4–7).

4. The sacredness of the Jerusalem Temple will not be enough to avert the disaster (ch. 7). There were those in ancient Judah who believed that since the Temple was the place where God dwelt on earth (enthroned on the ark of the covenant in the Holy of Holies), the Temple and Jerusalem itself were ultimately inviolable.

God would never allow it to be captured. Jeremiah proclaims a contrary message: "Do not trust in these deceptive words: 'This is the temple of the LORD, the temple of the LORD, the temple of the LORD.'" And why not? Because if the people of Judah do what is right and take care of the poor and oppressed, and worship no God but Yahweh, then he will indeed "dwell with you in this place." But if they break God's commandments and worship other gods, "and then come and stand before me in this house, which is called by my name and say, 'we are safe!'"—it will be to no avail. God then asks, in words quoted by another famous prophet living six centuries later (Jesus of Nazareth): "Has this house, which is called by my name, become a den of thieves in your sight?" (7:11). God points out that his sacred sanctuaries have been destroyed in the past when the people were disobedient. The Temple itself will provide no safety for them. If they fail to mend their ways, it, and they, will be destroyed.

5. But eventually God will relent and restore his people. Scholars have questioned whether these passages derive from Jeremiah, or were added only at a later time (like the comforting words at the end of Amos). But in them is expressed a clear hope for the future:

> For the days are surely coming, says the LORD, when I will restore the fortunes of my people, Israel, and Judah, says the LORD, and I will bring them back to the land that I gave to their ancestors and they shall take possession of it. (30:3)
>
> Again I will build you, and you shall be built, O virgin Israel! Again you shall take your tambourines and go forth in the dance of the merrymakers. (31:4)

6. In particular—in one of the most significant passages of the book—God will not simply restore the old covenant with his people; he will make a "new covenant" with them, one that is better even than the old one made with Moses. The previous one required the people of Israel to obey the commandments that Moses delivered. The new covenant will be so thoroughly engrained in the people that they will *naturally* follow it, doing what God demands:

But this is the covenant that I will make with the house of Israel after those days, says the LORD: I will put my law within them, and I will write it on their hearts; and I will be their God, and they shall be my people. No longer shall they teach one another, or say to each other, "Know the LORD," for they shall all know me . . . for I will forgive their iniquity and remember their sin no more." (31:33)

Despite the overwhelming sense of coming doom and destruction, then, there was still a glimmer of hope for the long term.

Jeremiah's Prophetic Object Lessons

Jeremiah proclaimed his message not just through uttering his various dire (and occasionally hopeful) predictions, but also by engaging in prophetic *actions*, which were meant to symbolize the import of his message. And so, in chapter 18, he is sent to observe a potter making a clay vessel; when it did not come out as the potter planned, he destroyed what he was doing and started over. God tells Jeremiah that he, God, is the potter, and the people of Judah are the clay. Since they have not come out as he wanted, they must be destroyed and he will start over again.

In chapter 19 Jeremiah is told to take an earthenware jar and smash it in public; this is to show that Jerusalem will be smashed because it has forsaken God. As Jeremiah puts it, in graphic words:

I [God] will make this city a horror, a thing to be hissed at; everyone who passes by it will be horrified and will hiss because of all its disasters. And I will make them eat the flesh of their sons and the flesh of their daughters, and all shall eat the flesh of their neighbors in the siege. . . . (vv. 8–9)

In chapter 27 Jeremiah is instructed to put a yoke on his neck and to proclaim that everyone and every nation that refuses to accept the yoke of the king of Babylon will be devastated by the sword, famine, and epidemic. The peoples of the east must yield to the superior force of Babylon, because their subservience is assured.

The Person of Jeremiah

More than any other prophet of record, Jeremiah took his message to heart and felt deep and heart-rending anguish at what he was compelled by God to proclaim. He was not a willing predictor of coming doom. He hated his message, but he had no

BOX 5.3 PROPHETIC ATTACKS ON ISRAEL AND ITS LEADERS

As we have repeatedly seen in the classical prophets we have examined—and as we will see even more in the ones yet to be considered—these "spokespersons for God" were not at all reluctant to deliver very harsh messages of condemnation against the people of Israel and Judah, their leaders, and their capital cities, especially Jerusalem. In the opinion of the prophets, the leaders had led the people astray from the true worship of God; the people had all too willingly followed them; and God was soon to act in response by destroying the holy cities and all who opposed him, including the kings, prophets, and priests who were thought to be guardians of the truth.

This point cannot be emphasized enough, in no small measure because of what we will find as we move later

to the history of Judea and into New Testament times. Many readers have read the critiques of the scribes and Pharisees by Jesus (for example, in Matthew 23) as unnecessarily harsh. Others have thought that no Jew faithful to the ancestral traditions of his people could say such things and that Jesus, therefore, must be seen as virulently "anti-Jewish."

But nothing could be farther from the truth. The religion of Israel had a very long (and noble) tradition of inner critique, with prophets declaring that the people and their leaders had gone astray and that God was therefore going to judge them harshly. Jesus thought so, too. He was standing very clearly in a tradition of prophets that extended back nearly 800 years prior to his own day, and he was no more "anti-Jewish" than Amos, Isaiah, or Jeremiah.

FIGURE 5.6.   The prophets condemned the inhabitants of Judah for worshipping other gods. These are some of the many figurines of fertility goddesses that have been discovered in archaeological digs in towns throughout Judah, dating roughly from the time of the prophets. These figurines are about five and a half inches tall.

choice but to deliver it. In the heart-rending words early in his book:

> My anguish, my anguish! I writhe in pain! Oh the walls of my heart! My heart is beating wildly; I cannot keep silent; for I hear the sound of the trumpet, the alarm of war. Disaster overtake disaster, the whole land is laid waste. (4:19–20)

What is more, the prophet suggests that this is actually the anguish that God himself feels at what is to come. He, the prophet, shares God's despair. But, unlike God, Jeremiah is physically abused by those who do not want to hear what he has to say. In chapter 20, one of the prose narratives about Jeremiah, we learn that one of his enemies, the priest Pashur, an official in the Jerusalem Temple, beat Jeremiah and put him in stocks. In chapter 38 his enemies can no longer stand his preaching: he is thrown into an empty cistern, where he sinks into the mud.

Both the anguish Jeremiah felt and the mistreatment he experienced were very real, and Jeremiah complained about it repeatedly to God, in chapters 11–20. This involves a series of passages that are known as the six "confessions" or the "laments" of Jeremiah. In each of them he calls on God, reports what his enemies are saying about him, declares his own innocence at having done anything to deserve his suffering, and prays to God for vengeance (11:18–23; 12:1–6; 15:10–21; 17:14–18; 18:18–23; 20:7–18). His anger can best be seen in his cries for vengeance, as in 18:23 "You O LORD, know all their plotting to kill me. Do not forgive their iniquity, do not blot out their sin from your sight. Let them be tripped up before you; deal with them while you are angry."

But his complaints are directed not only against his human persecutors; they are also directed against God himself for making him deliver the message in the first place, as seen nowhere more graphically than in the final lament:

O LORD, you have enticed [perhaps better: "seduced"] me, and I was enticed; you have overpowered me, and you have prevailed. I have become a laughingstock all day long; everyone mocks me. For whenever I speak, I must cry out, I must shout, "Violence and destruction!" for the word of the LORD has become for me a reproach and derision all day long. If I say "I will not mention him, or speak any more in his name," then within me there is something like a burning fire, shut up in my bones; I am weary with holding it in, and I cannot. (20:7–9)

The lament ends, in a fashion reminiscent of the book of Job (which we will discuss in chapter 8), with Jeremiah cursing the day he was born, expressing his anguished wish that he had never seen the light of day.

Jeremiah's is a powerful message filled with despair, angst, anger, and gloom. And he felt he had no choice but to deliver it. There would, in the end, be redemption for God's people. But before that happened there would be horrible, unspeakable suffering, and Jeremiah would rather die—or never to have lived—than deliver the message.

Now that we have considered at relative length three of the important pre-exilic prophets, we can move on, in shorter order, to consider the remaining six, all of them numbered among "the Twelve" in the Tanakh and among the Minor Prophets in the English Bible.

HOSEA

No prophet of scripture emphasizes the deep and profound love of God for his people, and his bitter sense of betrayal for their unfaithfulness, more than the eighth-century Hosea. Here God is portrayed as the lover of Israel, which has rejected his adoration and become a whore.

Hosea was a contemporary of Amos and was prophesying in the north during almost the same time as Isaiah in the south during the reigns of kings Uzziah, Jotham, Ahaz, and Hezekiah of Judah, and of Jeroboam II in Israel. He shows no knowledge of the destruction of Assyria in 722 B.C.E., and so appears to have stopped his prophetic ministry sometime possibly soon before that.

Like the other prophets we have considered, Hosea maintains that the people of Israel have sinned against God and that as a result, he will harshly judge them. In this case the problem is not principally that they have behaved in unethical ways and perpetrated social injustice and oppression. It is rather that they have rejected the worship of God and indulged, instead, in the worship of other gods. "My people consult a piece of wood and their divining rod gives them oracles. . . . They sacrifice on the tops of the mountains and make offerings upon the hills" (4:12–13). They have, in a sense, prostituted themselves, wantonly going after lovers other than Yahweh: "for a spirit of whoredom has led them astray, and they have played the whore, forsaking their God" (4:12).

In a powerful and gripping set of images, Hosea speaks of the nation of Israel as the onetime spouse of God and mother of God's people, who has, however, rejected her husband. The result will be a horrible punishment for both the nation and its people:

Plead with your mother, plead—for she is not my wife, and I am not her husband—that she put away her whoring from her face, and her adultery from between her breasts, or I will strip her naked and expose her as in the day she was born, and make her like a wilderness and turn her into a parched land, and kill her with thirst. Upon her children also I will have no pity, because they are children of whoredom. For their mother has played the whore. (2:2–5)

Hosea as well uses the image of a legal indictment that God levels against his people. He had made a covenant with them, and they violated it: "the LORD has an indictment against the inhabitants of the land. There is no faithfulness or loyalty. . . . Therefore the land mourns and all who live in it languish" (4:1–3). As a result of this indictment, God "will punish Jacob according to his ways." In places the imagery Hosea uses to describe God's incensed reaction is harsh and violent, seen nowhere more clearly than in 13:4–9. God brought the people out of Egypt and fed them in the wilderness. But they then forgot him. And so,

I will become like a lion to them, like a leopard I will lurk beside the way. I will fall upon them like a bear robbed of her cubs, and will tear open the covering of their heart; there I will devour them like a lion, as a wild animal would mangle them. I will destroy you, O Israel; who can help you? . . . They will fall by the sword, their little ones shall be dashed in pieces, and their pregnant women ripped open.

We saw in the case of Jeremiah that the prophet carried out certain actions in order to convey his prophetic message. Such prophetic acts also occur in Hosea, in graphic and heart-rending terms. At the beginning of the book, in order to illustrate his message, God instructs Hosea to marry a woman who would not be faithful but would become highly promiscuous, to show how Israel has treated God: The LORD said to Hosea, "Go take for yourself a wife of whoredom and have children of whoredom, for the land commits great whoredom by forsaking the LORD" (1:2). And so Hosea does what he is told, marrying an unfaithful woman named Gomer who bears him three children, each of them given a symbolic name. The first is a son and is named Jezreel, in remembrance of a bloody incident carried out by the king Jehu about a century earlier at a place called Jezreel. Gomer conceives a second time and gives birth to a daughter who is named Lo-ruhamah, which means "not pitied." God would no longer have pity on his people. She then bears another son named named Lo-ammi, which means "not my people." No longer would Israel be the people of God.

As with the other prophets we have seen, there are faint—very faint—glimmers of hope even in this graphic description of the prostitution of Israel after other gods. The Lord indicates that he will remove his estranged spouse into the wilderness, and there he will "speak tenderly to her" and rehabilitate her (2:14–23). In illustration of this message Hosea is instructed to go after his wife, who has become so promiscuous, and lure her back into their relationship. That too will be what happens when Israel returns to God, who originally called her his own: "Afterwards the Israelites shall return and seek the Lord their God . . . they shall come in awe to the LORD and to his goodness in these latter days" (3:5). But before that, there are some ugly and bad times ahead: acts of prostitution, as Israel continues to adore and worship other gods more than Yahweh, and misery, as God exposes Israel for the prostitute she is and gives her in full measure the punishment that is her due.

MICAH

Along with Amos, Isaiah, and Hosea, Micah is the fourth of the eighth-century prophets. The introduction to the book indicates that Micah made his proclamation during the reigns of Jotham, Ahaz, and Hezekiah—all southern kings. It also states that Micah came from Moresheth, a Judean village. But it then says that his proclamation was directed against Samaria, the capital of Israel, as well as Jerusalem. Scholars have long expressed doubts that the whole of this seven-chapter book derives from Micah himself. Micah 4:10 refers to the Babylonian captivity, 7:8–10 appear to allude to it, and 7:11 mentions the need for the walls of Jerusalem to be rebuilt. These portions—and possibly others—were thus probably written in the sixth century. While there are debates over various passages (as to when they were written, and by whom), there is a strong scholarly consensus that chapters 1–3 and 6:1–7:6, at least, go back to the proclamation of Micah himself.

In an opening frightful image, Micah refers to God as a kind of divine warrior coming in power to destroy his people:

For lo, the LORD is coming out of his place, and will come down and tread upon the high places of the earth. Then the mountains will melt under him and valleys will burst open, like wax near the fire. . . . All this is for the transgression of Jacob and for the sins of the house of Israel. (1:3–5)

The sin of the people is that they have worshipped other gods. And so God himself will beat into pieces all the idols that have been worshiped and burn them with fire. As was the case with Jeremiah, Micah finds this message to be personally devastating: "for this I will lament and wail" (1:8). Further on, Micah indicates that in addition to idolatry the people have engaged in the economic exploitation of the poor: "They covet fields and seize them; houses, and take them away; they oppress household and house, people and their inheritance" (2:1–3). Moreover, it is especially the leaders of the people who are to blame, the "heads of Jacob and rulers of the house of Israel" (3:1). They in particular should know to do what is good and right. But instead, they "hate the good and love the evil" and, in more graphic terms of exploitation, they "tear the skin of my people and the flesh off their bones . . . break their bones in pieces, and chop them up like meat in a kettle" (3:3).

One passage in particular encapsulates Micah's message, an instance of a **"covenantal lawsuit"**—where God issues a kind of legal indictment of his people for breaking their obligations under the covenant that he made with them (6:1–8). The passage contains these elements:

- *Call for judgment* (vv. 1–2). The LORD has a (legal) controversy with his people, and the mountains, hills, and foundation of the earth are called upon to hear the case.
- *History of salvation* (vv. 3–5). God brought the people out of slavery in Egypt and redeemed them. The clear implication is that they should then keep his covenant and do what he demands, as their part of the covenant.
- *Inefficacy of the cult* (vv. 6–7). No one should think that religious rituals such as burnt offerings—even as severe as human sacrifices of one's own

children—will be sufficient to ward off God's anger.
- *The LORD's demands* (v. 8). God wants people to do what is right among one another and to be devoted completely to God.

Here at the conclusion of this passage is one of the great verses from the writings of the prophets: "He has told you, O mortal, what is good: and what does the LORD require of you, but to do justice, and to love kindness, and to walk humbly with your God" (6:8).

The book ends with a lament of how totally corrupt the faithless people of Israel have become (7:1–6; this part almost certainly goes back to the eighth-century Micah), a statement of the penalty that has been paid for their sins (7:7–10; this may be a later addition), and an indication that in the end God's compassion will triumph over sin and judgment: "Who is a God like you, pardoning iniquity and passing over the transgression of the remnant of your possession? He does not retain his anger forever because he delights in showing clemency" (7:18).

BOX 5.4 THE COMING MESSIAH OF MICAH 5

Readers of the New Testament are very familiar with the story of Jesus' birth. Even though his parents come from Nazareth, where he himself spent his young life until he was baptized, he was actually born—according to the Gospels of Matthew and Luke—in Bethlehem of Judea. And why there? The Gospel of Matthew tells us. It was because the prophet Micah had predicted: "And you, Bethehem, in the land of Judah, are by no means least among the rulers of Judah; for from you shall come a ruler who is to shepherd my people Israel" (Matthew 2:6).

This is a quotation of Micah 5:2, a passage that does indeed appear to be predicting the coming of a messianic figure (see Box 6.6) who will deliver his people. In a later chapter we will consider the birth stories of Matthew and Luke to see if they are consistent with one another. Here it is worth considering what Micah was speaking of in his own historical context. For he does not appear to be predicting the birth of the Son of God in hundreds of years (he was writing 800 years before Matthew).

He does speak of this future "great" one as a ruler of Israel, one who would restore all the faithful again to be part of Israel, who would "feed his flock in the strength

of the Lord." But it is clear what this author has in mind: he is thinking of a future Davidic king—an actual king (Jesus never was that)—who would overthrow the enemy and return Israel to its God-given glorified state. And who is the enemy? There is no real ambiguity in the passage: it is the Assyrians. The Assyrians will be dominated by Israel (Micah 5:5); the leaders of Israel "will rule the land of Assyria with the sword"; and he, the messiah, will "rescue us from the Assyrians."

As is true of all the prophets, Micah was speaking to the people of his own day, addressing problems that had arisen in his own times, and indicating how God was to deal with those problems. At a much later date, Matthew believed Micah was referring to the coming of the spiritual savior who would deliver his people "from their sins." But in his own context Micah was referring to a future son of David who, like the great king himself, would establish Israel as a great nation and protect it from its political enemies. This is not a problem for some interpreters, who maintain that Micah had one point of reference in mind but that Matthew saw a deeper meaning in the prophet's words, relating to events that came to pass in the life of the future messiah.

NAHUM

This short three-chapter book is unusual among the prophets of the Hebrew Bible in not addressing Israel or Judah per se (see also, Obadiah). The book is all about the glee the prophet enjoys over the fact that the capital city of Assyria—Nineveh, the nemesis of both Israel and Judah for so many years—has itself been destroyed. This destruction, needless to say, is interpreted as an act of God upon his enemies in retribution for their sins. The author does not indicate when he was writing, but it must have been sometime—possibly soon—after the fall of Nineveh in 612 B.C.E. He indicates he is from Elkosh, a town that is otherwise unknown but that has been suspected to be in southern Judah.

Like other prophets, Nahum understands the God of Israel to be a God of wrath: "A jealous and avenging God is the LORD, the LORD is avenging and wrathful; the LORD takes vengeance on his adversaries and rages against his enemies" (1:2). No one can stand before his wrathful indignation (1:6). And now he has destroyed the one who created such problems for Judah, which now can celebrate its festivals in peace, since "never again shall the wicked invade you" (1:15).

We are told in no uncertain terms who that wicked one is: Nineveh (2:8). It has experienced a horrible annihilation: "Devastation, desolation, and destruction! Hearts faint and knees tremble, all loins quake, all faces grow pale" (2:10). There are "piles of dead, heaps of corpses, dead bodies without end" (3:3). This has been done by Yahweh himself (2:13) and because of the heinous behavior of the wicked city: "because of the countless debaucheries of the prostitute . . . who enslaves nations through her debaucheries and peoples through her sorcery" (3:4).

The pure joy that the prophet finds in proclaiming the demise of the much-hated capital of Assyria comes to final expression in the book's concluding verse: "There is no assuaging your hurt, your wound is mortal. All who hear the news about you clap their hands over you. For who has ever escaped your endless cruelty?" (3:19). What goes around comes around, and the evil done by Nineveh has now been revisited upon it in full measure. And the prophet could not be happier about it.

Like the prophets before him, Nahum is one who believes that Yahweh is not simply the national God of Israel. He is God over all the earth, and even a power as mighty as great Assyria must ultimately bow before the overwhelming force of the Lord of all.

ZEPHANIAH

The small book of Zephaniah in many ways encapsulates the themes we have seen already in the writings of the other prophets. Judah has sinned horribly against God, and their punishment will be equally horrible; but here God is concerned not only to destroy Jerusalem and its inhabitants; he is the judge of the whole earth and all nations must face his wrath.

The introduction to the book indicates that Zephaniah is the great-great-grandson of Hezekiah. If this is a reference to King Hezekiah (there is no certainty that it is), then the prophet comes from the royal Davidic line. As with most of the other prophets, nothing further is known about him except his dates—he prophesied during the reign of Josiah (so sometime between 640–609 B.C.E.).

The prophet begins on a harsh note indicating that God will sweep away all living creatures from the earth (1:3), and in particular Judah, Jerusalem, and their inhabitants (1:4). The reason for God's anger: the people have worshiped Baal and other pagan gods.

And so Zephaniah speaks of the coming "day of the LORD." This day, when God arrives, will not be a happy time: "That day will be a day of wrath, a day of distress and anguish, a day of ruin and devastation, a day of darkness and doom, a day of clouds and thick darkness, a day of trumpet blast and battle cry against the fortified cities and against the lofty battlements" (1:15). There will be nothing to save people in that day, when God pours out people's blood like dust (1:18).

Jerusalem in particular is singled out as sinful before Yahweh; it is a "soiled, defiled, oppressing city!" (3:1); its officials are corrupt, its prophets are faithless, its priests have profaned what is holy (3:3–4). God has tried to bring it back to himself by punishing it, but to no avail (3:6–7). So the end is near. And not just for Jerusalem, but for other nations as well, including the mighty Nineveh, which will be made into a desolation (1:13–15).

The prophet ends with a strong note of hope that all will be restored once punishment has happened, when Jerusalem has come through its judgment and need "fear disaster no more" (3:15). Then God will be in its midst not as one who destroys but as one who saves, heals, and brings prosperity (3:18–20).

HABAKKUK

The book of Habakkuk is a small gem among the writings of Hebrew prophecy, set up as a kind of dialogue between the prophet and God in which we hear both sides of the conversation. In an unusual fashion (for the prophets), the prophet complains about the injustice that is being done on the earth; God indicates what he is about to do to resolve the problem, and the prophet answers back that the solution is worse than the problem.

We are not told who Habakkuk is (just his name is mentioned in 1:1), or when he is prophesying. He is normally placed in the late seventh or early sixth century—some years, but not too many, before the Babylonian exile. He would, then, have been a contemporary of Jeremiah and, like his more famous fellow-countryman, he had no doubts what was about to happen to Judah for its sins. It was to be wiped out by the Babylonians.

The prophet begins by complaining to God about all the injustice taking place in Jerusalem: "O LORD, how long shall I cry for help, and you not listen . . . Destruction and violence are before me; strife and contention arise. So the law becomes slack, and justice never prevails" (1:2–4).

In reply, God indicates what he is soon to do about the sins of his people. He will bring in the Babylonians to destroy them: "Be astonished! Be astounded! For a work is being done in your days that you would not believe if you were told. For I am rousing the Chaldeans, that fierce and impetuous nation" (1:5–6). God goes on to describe how horrible and powerful the Babylonians are, how

---

BOX 5.5 PROPHETIC THEODICY

Throughout the prophets there is a deep concern to explain the sufferings of the people of Israel and Judah. This is true of Amos, Isaiah, Jeremiah—in fact, nearly all of them. Why have the people sometimes experienced famine, drought, crop failure, epidemics, slaughter, war? Amos is quite clear: God was punishing the people, trying to get them to return to himself (Amos 4:6–11). Why were the Assyrians about to destroy the kingdom of Israel? All of the eighth-century prophets agreed: it was because of the sin of the people. Why was Babylon certain to destroy the nation of Judah? Jeremiah and the other prophets of his day were equally certain: it was God's judgment upon disobedience.

In the modern world, philosophers, theologians, and all thinking people often wonder about why there is such intense suffering in the world. Since the Enlightenment these questions have been pursued, agonized over, answered, and disputed with great intensity. One of the big questions is how there can be so much pain, misery, and agony in the world if God loves people, wants the best for them, and is all-powerful—so that he could prevent suffering if he chose to do so. This issue is called, today,

"**theodicy**"—from the Greek words for "God's righteousness." How can God be truly righteous if he is able to prevent suffering but does not do so? Doesn't that call into question either his power or his love? There are lots and lots of answers to the question of theodicy today, with lots of books written about it every year.

The prophets of the Hebrew Bible did not question suffering in the ways modern people do. They lived in their own worlds and had their own religious perspectives and their own contexts. But in those contexts, their "answers" were reasonably clear and were driven home in page after page of the prophets' writings. Yes, God can make the suffering stop. And yes, he will do so, as soon as the people repent and return to his ways. Because, in fact, much of the suffering is coming from God himself. He is causing it. Why? Because people have sinned and he is punishing them for it, making them want to change how they live. And so in one sense, the national disasters that Israel and Judah experience have occurred because God has wanted to penalize his people. In another sense, of course, for the prophets, it is completely the people's own fault.

prone to violence, how scornful of other kings and rulers of every fortified city, over which they sweep like the wind (1:7–11).

For the prophet, however, this solution to the problem of rampant sin and injustice is worse than the crime. He asks God "why . . . are you silent when the wicked swallow those more righteous than they?" (2:13). The Judeans may be bad, but the Babylonians are much *worse*. Does it make sense to punish the wicked by those who are even more wicked? Is God to allow the Babylonians to wreak havoc among the nations and pay no price?

In further reply, God settles the matter once and for all: the Babylonians too will face judgment for all the evil they themselves have done: "Because you have plundered many nations, all that survive of the peoples shall plunder you" (2:8).

This further solution appears to satisfy the prophet, who complains no more. Instead, he launches into a prayer (all of chapter 3), which describes with awe God's amazing works and concludes by expressing the author's full and complete trust in God, even when life is hard, in one of the most beautiful passages of the minor prophets:

Though the fig tree does not blossom, and no fruit is on the vines; though the produce of the olive fails, and the fields yield no food; though the flock is cut off from the fold, and there is not herd in the stalls, yet I will rejoice in the LORD; I will exult in the God of my salvation. GOD, the Lord, is my strength; he makes my feet like the feet of a deer, and makes me tread upon the heights. (3:17–19)

At a Glance: The Early Prophets of Israel and Judah

A number of the "classical prophets" can be dated from the eighth to the sixth centuries B.C.E.: Amos, Isaiah, Hosea, and Micah (all in the eighth century); Jeremiah, Nahum, Habakkuk, and Zephaniah (from the sixth century). It is not clear if these "spokespersons for God" actually wrote their own works, or if, instead, their followers recorded their words for posterity. Each prophet addressed a particular historical situation; their words were not meant to predict what was to happen hundreds or thousands of years after their own day, but very soon, in their own time, as God responded to his people in judgment for their failure to observe his Torah. For some of the prophets (e.g., Amos) the sins of the people were principally ethical, as the leaders and powerful oppressed and exploited the poor and defenseless; for others (e.g., Hosea),

the sins were more connected with the worship of Yahweh—or rather, the failure to worship Yahweh, and him alone, instead of other gods.

Although the message of each prophet is distinctive—directed, as it is, to his own historical circumstances—together the prophets deliver a resounding denunciation of the people of Israel and Judah. Because the people have strayed from following the ways of God, he will punish them severely. The northern nation of Israel is to be destroyed by the Assyrians, the southern nation of Judah by the Babylonians. Observing proper religious ritual will not, in itself, avert the coming disaster. The people must return to the ways of God and when they do, the punishment will end. God will then restore his people and renew his relationship with them.

Take a Stand

1. One day after class, one of your fellow students tells you that he doesn't understand why your instructor is spending so much time talking about the historical context of prophets like Amos and Isaiah. In his opinion, their writings have a timeless quality and are not tied to any particular historical moment or events. You, on the other hand, want to stand up for your instructor (poor fellow) and decide to defend his approach. Pick three instances in which knowing the historical context of the proclamations of these prophets can assist you in understanding their message.

2. Your roommate has never had a college-level course on the Bible but reads it avidly in her spare time. She tells you that as she reads prophets like Isaiah, Jeremiah, and Micah, their main message is that God is planning to send Jesus into the world in order to save people from their sins. Do you agree, disagree, or both agree *and* disagree (thinking that she is partially, but not completely, right)? Support your case.

3. Outline a paper on "Why Is There Suffering?" from the perspective of one of the classical prophets. Include some reflections, from your own point of view, on whether you find this "solution" to the question of suffering fully satisfying or not.

Key Terms

Covenantal lawsuit, 135   **Redactor**, 120   **Seer**, 115   **Theodicy**, 137
Pre-exilic prophet, 127

Suggestions for Further Reading

NB: For this and all chapters, see the relevant articles (e.g., "Prophets," "1 Isaiah") in the works cited in the Suggestions for Further Reading in chapter 1.

Blenkinsopp, Joseph. *A History of Prophecy in Israel*, 2nd ed. Louisville: Westminster John Knox, 1996. Solid and readable introduction to each of the persons and writings of the Hebrew Bible prophets.

Miller, John. *Meet the Prophets: A Beginner's Guide to the Books of the Biblical Prophets*. New York: Paulist Press, 1987. The subtitle sums it up: this is a discussion of seven of the prophetic books written at an elementary level.

Petersen, David L. *The Prophetic Literature: An Introduction*. Louisville: Westminster John Knox, 2002. A clear and scholarly introduction to the prophets of the Hebrew Bible, focusing on a literary perspective.

Sweeney, Marvin and David Cotter, eds. *The Twelve Prophets*, 2 vols. Collegeville, Minn: Liturgical Press, 2000. Careful and scholarly introduction to and interpretation of the twelve "minor" prophets, for advanced students.

Ward, James. *Thus Says the Lord: The Message of the Prophets*. Nashville: Abingdon, 1991. A solid guide to each of the prophetic books, from a historical perspective.

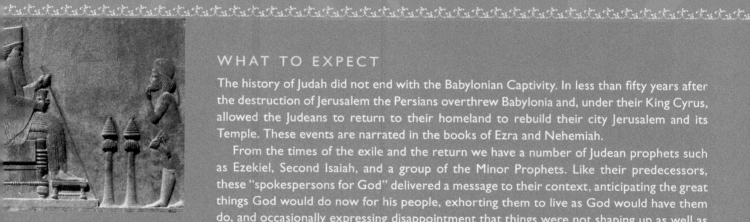

6

The Historians and Prophets
of Exile and Return

WHAT TO EXPECT

The history of Judah did not end with the Babylonian Captivity. In less than fifty years after the destruction of Jerusalem the Persians overthrew Babylonia and, under their King Cyrus, allowed the Judeans to return to their homeland to rebuild their city Jerusalem and its Temple. These events are narrated in the books of Ezra and Nehemiah.

From the times of the exile and the return we have a number of Judean prophets such as Ezekiel, Second Isaiah, and a group of the Minor Prophets. Like their predecessors, these "spokespersons for God" delivered a message to their context, anticipating the great things God would do now for his people, exhorting them to live as God would have them do, and occasionally expressing disappointment that things were not shaping up as well as they had hoped.

After the prophets the history of Judea obviously continued. This chapter ends with a historical sketch that brings that history up nearly to New Testament times.

In continuing our discussion of the prophets of the Hebrew Bible, it is important first to return to the ongoing history of Judah. When we reached the end of the Deuteronomistic History, things looked very bleak indeed. The northern kingdom of Israel had been destroyed by the Assyrians in 722 B.C.E.; this marked the end of the north. Following their military policies the Assyrians transported a large number of people out of Israel, exiled them to other cities around their empire, and imported other conquered peoples into the northern territories. These other peoples intermarried with the Israelites, so that bloodlines within Israel were lost. The ten northern tribes, quite simply, no longer existed.

Things were different with respect to the southern kingdom of Judah, destroyed a century and a half later in 586 B.C.E. by the Babylonians. In this case there was indeed a large deportation of the people, at least of the upper classes; but the people of Judah in exile stayed together in Babylon, established communities there, and by and large married one another and sustained their blood lines. The people who were left in the land lived on much as they did before. As we will see, when less than fifty years later the exiled Judeans—who at about this time (or somewhat thereafter) were first being called "Jews" (or Judeans; i.e., people from Judah)—were allowed to return home, things there were pretty much as they had left them. What was left of the country was an enormous mess following its disastrous last days. But it was a mess that could be cleaned up, at least in part. The returned exiles did clean it up, and the nation survived. And it still survives, as Jews today—not only in the state of Israel but around the world—trace their lineage back to the restoration of Judea (as it was now called) after the exile.

The beginnings of this story are told in two of the important historical books of the Hebrew Bible, Ezra and Nehemiah.

EZRA AND NEHEMIAH

Ezra and Nehemiah come from the third division of the Hebrew Bible, the "writings" (Hebrew: Kethuvim). In English Bibles they are grouped among the historical books, since they deal with the ongoing history of Judea and the events that surrounded the return of the people from exile in Babylon to rebuild the Temple and the city of Jerusalem and to begin again—not as a sovereign nation but as a country under foreign domination, subject to the empire of Persia.

Basic Overview

You will recall that there were two major exiles of captives from Judah to Babylon, one in 597 B.C.E. and then, the ultimately significant one, in 586 B.C.E. This latter deportation occurred after the troops of King Nebuchadnezzar of Babylon finally attacked the city of Jerusalem, destroyed its walls, and burned the Temple. The city was left in ruins and its leaders were removed. According to Jeremiah—who evidently was there himself to see these things happen—the Babylonians took 4600 people into captivity. The Deuteronomistic History ends with a person named Gedaliah appointed to be the governor of Judah, under Babylonian control, with King Jehoiachin released from prison in Babylon and given a living allowance—possibly a sign of hope for things to come.

Soon after that, something significant was to happen that changed everything for both Babylon and the Judeans in exile. The nation of Persia had been on the rise for some time and began to assert itself militarily, not long after the destruction of Judah. In 539 B.C.E., the Persians defeated the Babylonians in battle and in effect destroyed the Babylonian empire. This they did under the Persian king Cyrus, who ruled Persia from 559–530 B.C.E.

Cyrus had a different attitude toward exiled peoples than the Babylonians had. His policy was to allow the people to return to their lands, but to be ruled by him as client nations. In keeping with this policy he issued a decree allowing the Judeans to return. They were led back by a man named Sheshbazzar, and they included in their numbers two future leaders of the people in the land, the high priest Jeshua and the future governor Zerubbabel. Once the Judeans returned they started to rebuild the Temple; some years later they rebuilt the walls of Jerusalem, and they rededicated themselves to the Torah given by Moses. These are the events narrated in the books of Ezra and Nehemiah.

These writings are given as just one book in the Hebrew Bible. Still today, scholars consider them to have been written by a single author using a variety of sources including, significantly, two personal memoirs actually written by the two main characters after whom the books are named. If this view is correct, these will be the first books we have in the history of ancient Israel that incorporate first-person narratives of the leading figures. The contents of the two books can be summarized as follows (as will be seen, some of their contents appear not to be given in chronological order):

- The Return from Exile (Ezra 1–2; this is in 538 B.C.E.)
- The Rebuilding of the Temple (Ezra 3–6; finished around 515 B.C.E.)
- The Recommitment to the Torah (Ezra 7–10; Nehemiah 8–9; around 458 B.C.E.)
- The Reconstruction of the Walls (Nehemiah 1–7; 10–13; around 445 B.C.E.)

The Return from Exile

The book of Ezra begins by indicating that in the first year of the reign of King Cyrus of Persia (this would be 538 B.C.E.) he issued a decree allowing the people in exile to return to Jerusalem to rebuild its Temple. Even though he claims that he has been given this authority by Yahweh—which may seem to be an unlikely statement for a pagan to make—scholars sometimes consider this decree, actually cited in Ezra 1:2–4, to be authentic, something that Cyrus really issued, even if it has been slightly altered by the author of Ezra. (See Box 6.1, The Cyrus Cylinder.) And so the captives were allowed to return home with their families. This was just

BOX 6.1 THE CYRUS CYLINDER

One of the reasons for considering the decree of Cyrus given in Ezra 1:2–4 as basically authentic (even if edited a bit by the author of the book) is that we have a writing from Cyrus himself that seems to confirm its basic sentiment. In 1879 a small barrel-shaped clay document was found in Babylon. It is about nine inches in length and is called the Cyrus Cylinder (Figure 6.2). On it is inscribed, in cuneiform script, a narrative written (rather, dictated to a scribe) by King Cyrus himself. On this cylinder Cyrus indicates that when he conquered Babylon, he worshiped the Babylonian god Marduk and restored the worship of Marduk to its proper state. This, he claims, is what he did as well for other countries that he conquered—making the decree of Ezra 1:2–4

appear to conform with Cyrus's favored policies. As he states on the cylinder (See figure 6.2):

> I returned to these sacred cities on the other side of the Tigris the sanctuaries of which have been ruins for a long time, the images which used to live therein and established for them permanent sanctuaries. I also gathered all their former inhabitants and returned to them their habitations.[1]

---

1 Taken from James B. Pritchard, *The Ancient Near East: An Anthology of Texts and Pictures,* Vol. I (Princeton: Princeton University Press, 1958), p. 208.

---

over 60 years from the first deportation in 597, and just under 50 years from that in 586 B.C.E. The implications are clear: the people returning home are, for the most part, the children and grandchildren of those who had been exiled.

The leader of the returnees is a man named Sheshbazzar, who is called "the prince of Judah" (Ezra 1:9). By calling him a "prince" the author seems to imply that he is from the royal line of David; it is widely thought that he may, in fact, be the man otherwise known as Shenazzar (see 1 Chronicles 3:18), a son of King Jehoiachin himself. Cyrus is said to have restored to Sheshbazzar the treasures that Nebuchadnezzar had purloined from the Temple during his invasion, although a good deal of this treasure had no doubt found a home elsewhere.

Ezra 2:64 indicates that 42,360 people returned to the land from Babylon, along with 7,337 servants. This number may be exaggerated; if you'll recall, Jeremiah indicated that the total number of people sent into exile totaled 4,600; it is hard to believe that there were nine times as many of them after just fifty or sixty years.

Rebuilding the Temple

After the Judeans returned and settled into their new living situation, the first thing of major significance to happen was the rebuilding of the Temple. It is telling that the returnees did not start by repairing the ruined walls of Jerusalem but by rebuilding the

sacred place of worship. The reason is clear: those in charge of the return were completely committed to "getting it right" this time and emphasizing the worship of Yahweh as the most important aspect of the life of the community.

The two leaders of the people were the high priest Jeshua and the new political leader, Zerubbabel, a grandson of King Jehoiachin. Their first act was not to reconstruct the building, but to build an altar on which they could make sacrifices—burnt offerings—to Yahweh (3:1–6). Of greatest importance was to begin again to observe the sacrifices prescribed in the Torah. The building itself had to wait.

The Temple itself began to be reconstructed the second year after the exiles had returned, so in 537 B.C.E. (3:8) under the leadership of Zerubbabel and Jeshua. We are told that when the foundations were laid, there were mixed reactions. Some of the people shouted for joy, but many of those who had seen firsthand the original Temple in all its Solomonic glory wept (3:12). This new Temple was clearly a paltry effort in comparison with what was once one of the splendid architectural achievements of the Levant. The building of the Temple proved to be an on-again, off-again affair. It was not completed for twenty-two years, 515 B.C.E. (6:15).

On a linguistic note, there is an odd shift of languages in the book of Ezra in the middle of the episode describing the rebuilding of the Temple and continuing on into the next section on the rededication to the Torah. Ezra 4:8–6:18 is written in

FIGURE 6.1. Picture of Ezra reading the Law, from a second-century B.C.E. synagogue discovered in the city of Dura-Europas.

Aramaic, rather than Hebrew. Aramaic was the official language of the Persian empire, and was eventually to become the language of Palestine (as the Romans were later to call the land area that we today think of as Israel and Palestine). It was the language of Jesus and his disciples, for example. It is similar to Hebrew in many ways, as they are both Semitic languages. The shift in language at this point may be explained by the fact that in this

section of Ezra there are several official documents—for example, a letter to the Persian King Artaxerxes—which would have originally been written in Aramaic.

Rededication to the Torah

There is a large time gap—over 50 years—between the end of Ezra 6 and the beginning of Ezra 7: chapter 6 ends in 515 B.C.E.; chapter 7 picks up at 458 B.C.E. A good portion of chapters 7–10 is written in the first person (starting in 7:28), and it is widely thought that at these points the author has included a memoir that was actually written by Ezra himself.

Ezra is introduced in 7:1, 6. He is said to have come from Babylonia under the reign of King Artaxerxes (ruled 465–424 B.C.E.). This shows that all of the Judeans did not return to the land when offered the chance by Cyrus. In fact, we know that a large number stayed where they were. For centuries there was a strong Jewish community in Babylon. Ezra is said to have been a "scribe skilled in the Law of Moses" and he was of the priestly line, a direct descendant of Aaron. Being a scribe meant that he was literate (unlike almost everyone else in that day and time); scribes in particular knew how to read and write the sacred traditions of Israel. He was, then, an expert in Torah. This emphasis on Ezra's knowledge of the Law of Moses is important: the returnees seem bound and determined to follow the Law, and their religious leader will be one who is completely committed to the Law, unlike the vast majority of the kings described in the Deuteronomistic History.

Ezra returns to the land with an imperial decree (7:21–26); the Persian king instructs him to appoint magistrates and judges for the people, who are to "know the laws of your God." Those who do not know them are to be taught them by Ezra. And the land is to be ruled strictly by this particular rule of law: "All who will not obey the law of your God and the law of the king, let judgment be strictly executed on them, whether for death or the banishment or for confiscation of their goods or for imprisonment" (7:26).

One problem in particular afflicts the community once the exiles have returned: the intermarriage of Judeans with non-Judeans in the land. As I pointed out earlier, this was a very real and dangerous matter for anyone wanting to keep the bloodlines pure: after the Assyrian destruction,

FIGURE 6.2. The famous Cyrus Cylinder, covered with cuneiform writing. It is about nine inches long. On it the Persian king indicates how he conquered Babylon with the help of the Babylonian god Marduk.

intermarriage more or less eliminated the existence of the ten northern tribes of Israel. In the south they took the matter with utmost seriousness, in ways that may seem harsh to modern readers. Ezra—writing now in the first person—indicates that some of his officials approached him to let him know that the Levites in particular have married women from among the other peoples settled in the area: Canaanites, Hittites, Perizzites, Jebusites, Ammonites, Moabites, Egyptians, and Amorites. The problem with intermarriage was quite clear and pressing: "Thus the holy seed has mixed itself with the peoples of the lands, and in this faithlessness the officials and leaders have led the way" (9:2).

Ezra is deeply distressed and requires a severe and drastic measure to circumvent the problem. Any Judean who has married a "foreign woman" is required to divorce his wife and send her away, along with her children (10:3,10–11). It may be that Ezra and those leaders who sided with him in this decision were concerned not only with bloodlines, but also with what they knew to be the history of their people. Remember what happened with Solomon and his wives and concubines, who, according to the Deuteronomistic Historian, turned him away from the exclusive worship of Yahweh to serve other gods.

Once this rather pressing matter has been cleared up, Ezra calls the people together in order to have them hear the Torah of God read aloud so that they can both know what it has to say and commit themselves publicly to keeping it. This episode appears out of order in the books of Ezra–Nehemiah, since it is found not in Ezra but in Nehemiah 8–9; but chronologically it must have happened after the incidents narrated in Ezra 10, and here the story is told in the third person (it is not part of Ezra's memoir).

And so the Law is read from early morning till midday, as the people listen. An interesting problem has arisen, however. Many of the people cannot understand the Law and need to have it explained to them (8:8–9). Some interpreters think this means that the people needed help understanding all the nuances of the Torah, since they had never heard these regulations before. More likely, though, there is the problem of language referred to earlier. The people in Judea at this point have probably adopted Aramaic as their language. The Torah, of course, is written in Hebrew. It may be that the people hearing the Law cannot understand it because it is written in a different language. Those who are helping them to understand, then, are not explaining the Law to them. They are translating the words into the peoples' native tongue.

This may be the beginning of the targums. A **targum** was eventually to become a standard feature of Jewish religion. It is a translation of the Hebrew text of scripture into Aramaic, originally delivered orally and eventually written down, so

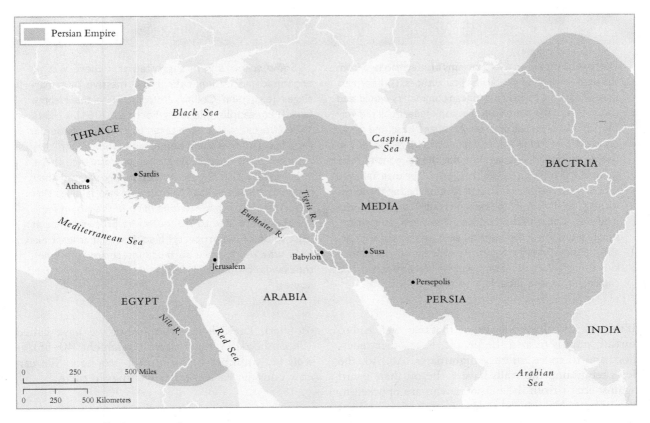

FIGURE 6.3. The Persian empire.

that those who did not know how to read the Hebrew could at least understand what the text said. There are surviving targums of every book of the Hebrew Bible except, interestingly, those three that already have portions of them written in Aramaic: Ezra, Nehemiah, and Daniel.

On the basis of this reading of the Torah, the people commit to keeping it. There is a day of national confession of sin (sins the people committed against God and his Law) and the leaders literally sign the covenant, agreeing to keep it down to its finest details.

The Reconstruction of the Walls

The final key event that took place after the return was the reconstruction of the destroyed walls of Jerusalem. For this series of episodes the key figure is no longer the scribe and priest Ezra, but the eventual governor of Judea, Nehemiah. Once again not only do these chapters portray him as the main character (Nehemiah 1–7; 11–13); they were actually written by him, in the first person, again as a

kind of memoir. They relate incidents that took place in 445 B.C.E.

The account begins with Nehemiah indicating that he was living in Susa, one of the main cities of Persia, when he heard from travelers come back from Judah that the walls of Jerusalem and its gates were still lying in rubble (1:3). He prays to God, reminding him that he had promised that if the people would repent he would relent and allow them to return to the land.

Nehemiah, as it turns out, is the cupbearer to the king of Persia, Artaxerxes. With easy access to the king, Nehemiah requests that he be allowed to return to his homeland (temporarily) in order to oversee the rebuilding of Jerusalem. The king grants his request, he returns to the land, is upset that the walls are in such a state, and begins the process of rebuilding.

As you would expect in any good narrative—even one written in the first person—problems arise. On one hand the neighboring peoples, especially the governor of Syria, are not pleased that Jerusalem is being rebuilt and think that this can only lead to trouble.

BOX 6.2 THE TEMPTATION TO INTERMARRY

We have already seen two problems of intermarriage from the point of view of various biblical authors: (1) intermarriage with those outside the Judean community would lead to the loss of the bloodlines that took Judeans all the way back to the patriarchs of Israel, Abraham, Isaac, and Jacob; (2) in the past (recall Solomon!) intermarriage had led the people of Israel and Judah to adopt the religions of their spouses and to begin to worship gods other than Yahweh.

But why was intermarriage so enticing for those returning to Judea from exile in Babylon? Were the Jebusites, Canaanites, Amorites, Perizzites, and so on, simply more attractive human beings and so more desirable partners? Were they more exotic and so much more interesting? Were there simply more of them, making the choice of a spouse easier? Or something else?

Some scholars have suggested that there was an economic motivation behind the massive intermarriages (e.g., John Collins, *Introduction to the Hebrew Bible* [Minneapolis: Augsburg Fortress, 2004], p. 434). When the exiles had been taken to Babylon, of course, they had to leave their homes and land. When they returned, other people had taken up residence there. Is it possible that the returnees simply wanted their property back, and that by marrying into families that now possessed what had long been in their own families they were able to reacquire the property—or at least some of the property? If so, it would at least explain why there were so *many* intermarriages when thousands of Judeans returned to their ancestral homes.

If the city is fortified once more, that may well lead to further actions to arm the people, to another rebellion, and to more military nightmares. And so, the Jews rebuilding the walls have to be on their guard against attack from the outsiders who are opposed to the effort. Nehemiah indicates that the laborers worked in shifts, part of the day building walls and part of the day posted as armed guards. The ones bringing the stones for construction carried their load in one hand and a weapon in another (4:16–17).

There were also internal problems. In order to participate in this massive effort, people have had to stop their farming, to mortgage their property, to borrow money just to survive. This work is not paying them anything, and they are impoverishing themselves to do it. Nehemiah intervenes and sees that they can continue the work without having to ruin their lives in the effort (ch. 5).

At the end, the wall is completed in 52 days (6:15). The walls are dedicated to God, the people reconfirm their commitment to God, and Nehemiah becomes the governor of the province for twelve years.

EXILIC AND POST-EXILIC PROPHETS

During this period of the Babylonian exile and return, a number of Hebrew prophets produced their work. Among them was one of the major

prophets, Ezekiel, and the author we have called "Second Isaiah" (the writer of Isaiah chs. 40–55), as well as a number of the minor prophets. We can now consider each of their writings in turn.

Ezekiel

We have already looked at two of the major prophets: Isaiah of Jerusalem, from the eighth century B.C.E., and Jeremiah from the sixth. Both were located in Judea, both were predicting that God would destroy the people by the onslaught of a foreign power. Ezekiel was Jeremiah's younger contemporary and, like him, he too was a priest originally from the southern kingdom. But he was one of the first taken into captivity to Babylon in the first exile of 597 B.C.E., possibly because he was from an aristocratic family. He, unlike the others, was actually writing from Babylon. His prophetic ministry began in 593 B.C.E. according to the dating he himself provides in 1:2 (the fifth year of the exile of King Jehoiachin), seven years before the final destruction of Jerusalem by Nebuchadnezzar in 586 B.C.E. He continued his prophecies until 571 B.C.E., fifteen years after the destruction and the final captivity.

And so Ezekiel is a highly unusual transitional figure, delivering his prophecies both before and after the fall of Judah. As one might guess, before the final destruction his predictions are dire, as he can see the writing on the wall: Babylon will

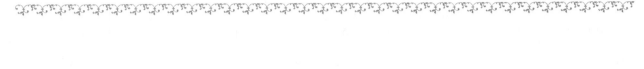

At a Glance: Ezra and Nehemiah

The books of Ezra and Nehemiah were written by a single author and together narrate the events that transpired as the Judeans in exile in Babylon were allowed to return home by King Cyrus of Persia, after he defeated the Babylonians in 539 B.C.E. Together the books record the arrival of the first wave of returnees and the rebuilding of the Temple under the leadership of the governor Zerubbabel and the high priest Jeshua. It is completed in 515 B.C.E.

Later, Ezra, a scribed trained in the traditions of the Torah, asserts his authority and urges the people to commit themselves to the laws of Moses. One major problem that he faces is the intermarriage of Judeans with foreigners; his solution is to require divorces on a massive scale. Later still, Nehemiah arrives in Jerusalem and organizes the rebuilding of the walls of the city, which were completed in 445 B.C.E.

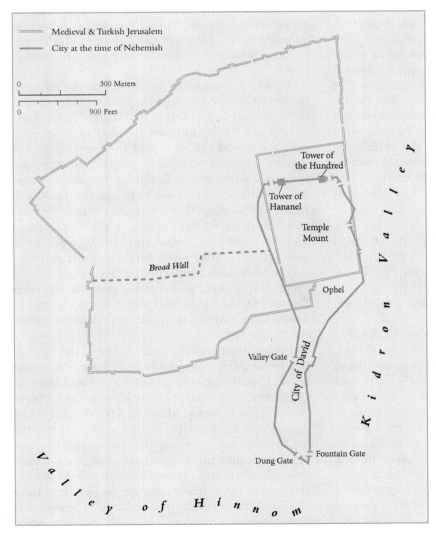

FIGURE 6.4. Jerusalem and its walls at the time of Nehemiah (in contrast to its size in the Middle Ages).

destroy his country. But afterward his proclamations take on a cast of hope as he believes that God will restore his people: after their suffering they can anticipate a revival and a bright future.

STRUCTURE OF THE BOOK   Unlike the other prophets we have examined so far, whose proclamations were largely delivered in poetic lines (we will be studying Hebrew poetry in the next chapter), Ezekiel is written almost entirely in prose. But graphic prose it is. It begins with an awe-inducing, brain-melting, almost impossible to understand let alone explain, vision of the Almighty himself and his heavenly attendants (ch. 1). Here the prophet sees God on his throne, surrounded by angelic beings of very odd description. The prophet struggles for words to make sense of this sight that is virtually unlike anything that anyone ever sees or has seen. The words come, but they are themselves awkward and clumsy in their descriptions—not because the writer is unskilled, but because the sight itself is virtually beyond description. Among other things the passage—the opening portion of the book—is meant to convey the idea that God is totally Other, unlike what we experience in our everyday lives, exalted, glorious, far beyond what we can imagine, awe-inspiring, the Almighty. Ezekiel's reaction is the only proper one: he falls on his face in either terror or worship or both.

After this opening vision, the book divides itself rather neatly into clear-cut sections:

- The Coming Destruction of Judah and Jerusalem (chs. 2–24)
- Prophecies Against the Nations (chs. 25–32)
- The Coming Restoration (chs. 33–39)
- The New Temple and New Jerusalem (chs. 40–48)

THE CALL OF THE PROPHET (2:3–3:3)
After Ezekiel sees the vision of God on his throne, while still flat on his face, he hears a voice—from God—telling him to stand and listen. God tells him that he is sending him to "a nation of rebels who have rebelled against me" (2:3). This, of course, is Judah. The voice indicates that the mission may bear no fruit (one remembers the call of Isaiah in Isaiah 6, where God was even more direct: no one would accept the prophet's message). But at least, the voice indicates, if a prophet makes a proclamation against the people they will have no excuse for failing to listen.

And then in a highly symbolic act, God is said to give Ezekiel a scroll, with writing on front and back, filled with "words of lamentation and mourning and woe" (2:10). Ezekiel is instructed to eat the scroll, and in his mouth "it was sweet as honey." The point of this rather bizarre episode is that Ezekiel has internalized the word of God that has been given to him to proclaim. It may be a bitter message, but since it comes from the Almighty it is sweet to the taste of the prophet. He now is prepared to deliver his prophetic renunciation of the people of Judah.

THE MESSAGE OF CONDEMNATION   Ezekiel's message—like that of the prophets before him—is one of condemnation and coming destruction. He is concerned about a range of transgressions against God, but the majority of them are related to the serious cultic violations of the people: their practices of worship are abhorrent to God. That this should be an overriding concern of a priest only makes sense.

Ezekiel is particularly incensed that the religious leaders of the people back in Jerusalem have "defiled" the sanctuary; that is, the Temple (5:11). They have done this by introducing idols of other gods into the sacred precincts and by engaging in the worship of foreign deities. In chapter 8 the prophet is given a vision of the Temple in Jerusalem. There he sees all sorts of idols (8:11) and the leaders of Judah sponsoring their worship (8:11). He sees women "weeping for Tammuz." This was a ritual undertaken by pagan followers of the Mesopotamian god Tammuz, who was a **fertility god;** that is, a divine being associated with the crops who, like the crops, was thought to die every year; his followers "weep" for him out of sadness over his annual death. God vows to slaughter the idolaters among the people (9:4–6).

Ezekiel then sees the inner court of the Temple and twenty-five men worshiping the sun as it rises in the East. And the problems are not just idolatry. Other transgressions are ethical in nature: "Have you seen this O mortal [this is what God calls Ezekiel throughout this book]? Is it not bad enough that the house of Judah commits the abominations done here? Must they fill the land with violence and provoke my anger still further?" (8:17). All the leaders and people have grown corrupt, as indicated most clearly in chapter 22. The princes of the people have destroyed human lives and greedily stolen what is not theirs (22:25); the priests have perverted God's teachings and profaned his holy things (in the Temple; 22:26); the officials have shed blood for their own gain (22:27); the prophets have uttered false visions and lies to cover over the truth (22:28); the people have committed extortion and robbery and have oppressed the poor and the needy (22:29). It is, all told, a hopeless situation.

In a highly graphic image reminiscent of what we saw in the book of Hosea, God likens Judah to a flagrant whore. He raised Judah when she was young, bathed her, clothed her, adorned her to make her beautiful (16:9–13). But then she used her beauty to attract other lovers and prostituted herself to them. These "others," of course, are gods other than Yahweh. Judah started to follow the gods of Egypt, Assyria, and Babylon (16:15–29). And in fact she was worse than a whore because she did it all for free. Because of all this, her lovers will turn on her and shame her, destroy her, stone her, cut her to pieces, and burn her houses (16:35–41). It will be an ugly end to a life of shame.

GOD'S RESPONSE Ezekiel's view of God's impending response, then, is very much like that of his prophetic predecessors. There will be a massive destruction of the land and its people. Like other prophets, Ezekiel is told to "act out" his proclamation through prophetic object lessons. And so, in chapter 4, he is to take a brick, paint an image of Jerusalem on it, and set up a siege wall against it with a ramp and army camps and battering rams. Then he is to lie on his left side for 390 days, and his right side for 40 days. All of this is to show that Jerusalem will be laid under siege and destroyed. The punishment of the northern country of Israel will last 390 years (this, of course, is not accurate, as the north never was restored) and of Judah 40 years (that number too is not representative of what happened).

In chapter 5 Ezekiel is told to shave his head and beard, and to divide the hair into three parts. One third he is to burn, another third to strike with the sword, and the final third to scatter to the winds with only a small number set aside in reserve. So too with the people of Jerusalem: a third will die of famine, a third will be slaughtered, and a third will be scattered among the nations.

Moreover, since the sanctuary has been defiled, God will remove himself from it—and so from his people. In chapter 10 Ezekiel has a vision that almost (but not quite) matches the breathtaking vision of chapter 1, with which it is closely connected. In this one the heavenly attendants are the cherubim who are seated on the ark of the covenant; they are here portrayed as real, winged, creatures, who rise up above the Temple and carry the glory of God away from it. This is a powerful message. The God of Israel is not restricted to a certain place. He may choose to dwell in Jerusalem, but if he decides to remove himself he can do so by abandoning Jerusalem and his people, and in a spectacular way. This idea that God—and the worship of God—need not be restricted to Jerusalem was to become a very important idea in Judaism, since most Jews, starting with the Babylonian exile, have not lived in close proximity to the sacred place in Jerusalem. But for Judaism, as it was later to develop, God was not just a national god of one location; he was the God over all who could be worshiped wherever his faithful people lived and met in community.

One other important aspect of Ezekiel's message: more than other writers we have considered, in his proclamation sin and judgment are not—are emphatically not—only communal in nature. They are also, and principally, individual. In chapter 18 Ezekiel quotes the ancient proverb: "The parents have eaten sour grapes, and the children's teeth are set on edge." This proverb was meant to say that the sins of the parents would be visited on their children, that future generations would need to pay the penalty for the transgressions of those who came before them. We find that teaching already in the Decalogue, where we are told that God is "a jealous God, punishing children for the iniquity of parents, to the third and fourth generation of those who reject me" (Exodus 20:5). Not for Ezekiel, however. Now the sins that a person commits are his or her own and must be paid for individually, not by later generations: "it is only the person who sins that shall die" (18:4). And so, a righteous person who turns to iniquity will have to die for it; a wicked person who turns to do what is right will be saved (18:26–28).

PROPHECIES OF RESTORATION Because Ezekiel was making his proclamations not only before the ultimate destruction of Jerusalem in 586 B.C.E., but also for another fifteen years afterward, it is no surprise to see that many of his prophecies are about the hopes of restoration for a people that has been punished for its sins. Even among the oracles delivered early in the book, there is the claim that after punishment the people of Judah will be restored to the land of Israel. The land at that point will be cleansed of all its abominations. And the people will be themselves created anew by God himself: "I will give them one heart, and put a new spirit within them; I will remove the heart of stone from their flesh and given them a heart of flesh, so that they may follow my statutes and keep my ordinances and obey them" (11.:17–20; reiterated in 36:22–28).

In particular, Ezekiel prophesies that a king like David will rule the people once more; the land will experience a utopian-like existence, with no wild animals to fear, abundant rain, rich crops, and no terrors from any enemies. And then "They shall know that I, the LORD their God, am with them, and that they, the house of Israel, are my people" (14:23–30).

It is this promise that the nation will be brought back to new life that makes sense of the most famous passage in all of Ezekiel, the vision of the Valley of Dry Bones (37:1–14). The prophet is led out in a vision to see a valley filled with very dry bones. And God asks him "Mortal, can these bones live?" Ezekiel admits that he has no way of knowing, and God instructs him to prophesy to the bones, telling them to come to life and to grow sinews, flesh, and skin, and to receive again the breath of life and to live. Ezekiel does so, and it happens. The bones rattle, come together, and grow sinews, flesh, and skin—and then have the breath of life put into them.

It is an amazing sight. Readers have often taken it to mean that at the end of time there would be a resurrection of the dead. Those who had died and decayed, so only their skeletons remained, would be brought back together at the resurrection to enjoy eternal life. But that is clearly not what Ezekiel means in his own context—as the author himself indicates. For God tells him "Mortal, these bones are the whole house of Israel" (37:11). The nation is dead, as lifeless as a valley full of bones. But God will restore the people to life and breathe his spirit into them, and they will live anew as a nation devoted to God and guided by his spirit.

This newly restored nation will be given a new Temple and a new Jerusalem in which to dwell. In a very detailed set of instructions (a lengthy stretch of chapters that only an avid architect could love), we are told the character, size, dimensions, and features of these renewed places (chs. 40–48).

SECOND ISAIAH

From our earlier discussions of the book of Isaiah, you will recall that scholars for over a century have realized that there are actually three different authors represented here, whose work was all spliced together at a later time. Isaiah of Jerusalem, from the eighth century B.C.E., is responsible for most of what are now chapters 1–39. The portion of the book we will consider now is called "Second Isaiah" (chs. 40–55). We do not know who the actual author was, or even his name. But his points of view and religious outlook are similar in many ways to those of Isaiah himself, once you account for the very different circumstances within which he is writing. Whereas Isaiah of Jerusalem was writing before the destruction of the north by the Assyrians, in a context when the Assyrian armies were threatening his home country of Judah as well, Second Isaiah is writing after the destruction of both countries—the north in 722 B.C.E. by Assyria and the south in 586 B.C.E. by Babylonia.

We are not sure when exactly this anonymous writer produced his oracles, but he is normally dated some years after the exile began and certainly before it came to a decisive end with the decree of Cyrus that allowed the exiles to return to the land to rebuild the Temple and to reconstruct the city of Jerusalem itself. A fair guess would be to say that he is writing in 550 B.C.E. or so, early in the reign of Cyrus but before his troops had conquered Babylonia. In this context, as we have already seen, the prophet's message is not one of judgment, in contrast to that of his predecessor. There was no longer time or need of that, as the nation had already been destroyed. His message instead was of consolation and hope. The people now had suffered for their sins and God was willing to start with them anew, restoring them to their land and reestablishing them as the chastened people of God.

The Overarching Message of Second Isaiah

Reading Second Isaiah carefully shows very clearly that we are now dealing with a prophet in a completely different situation from those of his predecessors who were predicting a coming judgment of the people. For this writer, Israel has already been punished for its sins: the destruction is past. "Who gave up Jacob to the spoiler and Israel to the robbers? Was it not the LORD, against whom we have sinned? . . . So he poured upon him the heat of his anger and the fury of war" (42:24–25). And now that the nation has been punished, God will use his "anointed one"—none other than the Persian king Cyrus—in order to bring salvation and restoration.

> Thus says the LORD, your Redeemer, who formed you in the womb. . . . who says of Jerusalem, "It shall be inhabited," and of the cities of Judah, "They shall be rebuilt, and I will raise up their ruins . . . who says of Cyrus, "He is my shepherd, and he shall carry out all my purpose. . . . Thus says the LORD to his anointed, whose right hand I have grasped to subdue nations before him and strip kings of their robes." (44:24–45:1)

This was indeed a radical and new message. As we have seen, the promise of a coming messiah was rooted in traditions that go all the way back to the united monarchy, when God promised David that he would always have a descendant who would serve as king, sitting on the throne of Israel (2 Samuel 7:12–16). The king, of course, was known as "the anointed one," meaning that he was the one specially favored by God who would mediate and implement God's will on earth. The term "anointed one" is a literal translation of the term "*mashiah*," translated into English as "messiah."

Later Jews came to think of a future messiah, a son of David who would restore Israel to its rightful place as a sovereign state committed to serving God. But here in Second Isaiah it is a pagan monarch, Cyrus of Persia, who is called God's anointed one, his messiah. Second Isaiah, of course, does not mean that Cyrus is a descendant of David of Israel. But he is the one through whom God will accomplish his plan on earth; he is the one God has chosen to bring salvation to his people. He may be a pagan, and the king of a foreign country that was to dominate Israel, but he would be the one through whom God would work to achieve his purposes. Once again we see the prophetic emphasis that God is not simply a local God of Judah; he is the God of all nations and can use other nations both for judgment against his people and in order to bring them salvation.

Second Isaiah was obviously writing at a time when the Persians were on the rise, and he anticipated that they would eventually overthrow the Babylonians. And he was right about that. Some ten or fifteen years after he delivered this message (depending on when it is to be dated) Cyrus and his armies did overthrow the Babylonians in battle and established themselves as a world empire that controlled the Fertile Crescent, including the land of Judah. Second Isaiah, writing some years before this happened, thought that some such thing would take place. He is quite clear that he thinks Babylonia, the enemy of Judah whom God used in order to punish his people, will be destroyed:

> Sit in silence, and go into darkness, daughter Chaldea! For you shall no more be called the mistress of kingdoms. I was angry with my people, I profaned my heritage; I gave them into your hand, you showed them no mercy, on the aged you made your yoke exceedingly heavy. You said, "I shall be mistress forever." So that you did not lay these things to heart . . . But evil shall come upon you, which you cannot charm away; disaster shall fall upon you which you will not be able to ward off; and ruin shall come on you suddenly, of which you know nothing. (47:5–11)

Or, as he says later about the enemies of Judah (also called "Jacob"): "I will make your oppressors eat their own flesh, and they shall be drunk with their own blood as with wine. Then all flesh shall know that I am the LORD your Savior, and your Redeemer, the Mighty One of Jacob" (49:26).

The people of Judah can now rejoice, because God is once more their loving parent:

> Sing for joy, O heavens, and exult O earth; break forth, O mountains, into singing! For the LORD has comforted his people, and will have compassion on his suffering ones. But Zion [another name for Jerusalem] said, "The LORD has forsaken me, my Lord has forgotten me." Can a woman forget her nursing child, or show no compassion for the child of her womb? Even these may forget, yet I will not forget you. See, I have inscribed you on the palms of my hands; your walls are continually before me. (49:13–16)

And so, for Second Isaiah, there will be a glorious return from exile. It will be like that first time God brought his people to the Promised Land from Egypt; only now their way will be smooth and

FIGURE 6.5. A relief showing the enthroned king of Persia, Darius.

easy: "A voice cries out, 'In the wilderness prepare the way of the LORD, make straight in the desert a highway for our God. Every valley shall be lifted up, and every mountain and hill be made low; the uneven ground shall become level, and the rough places a plain" (40:3–4). This new exodus will be even better than the first one. Yahweh reminds his people that he is their Creator and King, and that he is the one "who makes a way in the sea, a path in the mighty waters"; he is the one who destroys "chariot and horse, army and warrior" (43:16–17). But the people are not to think about what happened long ago, at the Exodus; they are to look ahead to the new thing that God will do, which will be even more glorious. He will "make a way in the wilderness and rivers in the desert" (43:19). Even more than that, the deliverance from captivity can be seen as a new Creation. Just as, in a sense, the people of Israel came into being when God brought them out of Egypt and made his covenant with them, so too this new Israel will come into being when they experience the new exodus (See Box 6.3): "So the ransomed of the LORD shall return, and come to Zion with singing; everlasting joy shall be upon their heads, they shall obtain joy and gladness, and sorrow and sighing shall flee away" (51:11).

Since this new exodus is like a new creation, Second Isaiah does not hesitate in considering the land to which they will return a new Garden of Eden: "For the Lord . . . will make her wilderness like Eden, her desert like the garden of the LORD; joy and gladness will be found in her, thanksgiving and the voice of song" (51:3; see also 52:12–13).

Two Key Themes

In addition to the striking imagery of the new exodus, there are two other themes of Second Isaiah's moving proclamation that deserve to be highlighted: his stress on monotheism (Yahweh alone is God) and the conception of Israel as the "suffering servant of the LORD."

MONOTHEISM Second Isaiah is the first author we have encountered who can rightly be considered a monotheist. Other prophets and historians were quite insistent that Yahweh was to be the only God that the people of Israel worship; but the problem, for them, was precisely that there *were* other gods demanding worship. Second Isaiah has gone a step farther. These other gods are in fact not gods at all. Yahweh alone is God. (See Box 6.4, on henotheism.) This is a point repeated throughout the book:

Thus says the LORD, the King of Israel, and his Redeemer, the LORD of hosts: I am the first and I am the last; besides me there is no god (44:6); I am the LORD, and there is no other; besides me there is no god (45:5); There is no other god besides me, a righteous God and a Savior; there is no one besides me (45:21; see also 46:9).

For the author of Second Isaiah, not only will the glorious return from exile be like a new Exodus, it can even be likened to a "new Creation." Here the author is depending on ancient imagery that borrowed ideas of creation from other ancient Near Eastern myths. In these myths we are told that the creation of the world happened when a great warrior god did battle with a sea monster; after defeating this creature, he split its carcass in half to create the heavens and the earth—a tale followed to some extent in the creation epic we considered in chapter 2, *Enuma Elish*.

Scholars have long thought that the priestly account of Genesis is itself ultimately based on some such myth, when the "body" of water is divided into two parts (waters above and waters below, separated by the "firmament"), as the body of the sea monster was in the pagan versions. It has been noted that the word for the "deep" in Genesis 1:2 (*tehom*) is etymologically related to the name of the great divine opponent of the creator God Marduk, *Tiamat*.

The myths of creation that may have influenced Genesis are almost certainly alluded to by the author of Second Isaiah:

Awake, awake, put on strength, O arm of the LORD! Awake, as in days of old, the generations of long ago! Was it not you who cut Rahab in pieces, who pierced the dragon? Was it not you who dried up the sea, the waters of the deep? (Isaiah 51:9–10)

Here Rahab, conquered and cut up by God, is obviously not the prostitute of Jericho. (The words are spelled differently in Hebrew.) This is the name of the dragon, the sea monster that God conquered to create the world. But in ancient Israelite thinking it was also the exodus event—where God again "conquered the sea." This too could be considered a "creation," in this case the creation of his people Israel. And so sometimes the traditions of Creation and Exodus were intermingled, as here in Isaiah, as the author continues:

Was it not you who dried up the sea, the waters of the great deep; who made the depths of the sea a way for the redeemed to cross over? (Isaiah 51:10)

And, most significant for this author, what God did before (twice: creation and exodus) he is now about to do again, bringing the people back to the Promised Land as in a new exodus, and making them anew as in a new creation:

So the ransomed of the LORD shall return, and come to Zion with singing; everlasting joy shall be upon their heads; they shall obtain joy and gladness, and sorrow and sighing shall flee away. (Isaiah 51:11)

Because Second Isaiah sees the God of Israel as the one and only God, he is able to mock the gods of other peoples as worthless idols that people themselves make but that have no real existence. A workman is hired to make an idol (40:18–20); the person who wants it orders special wood so it won't rot away (as if God could rot away!) and then tries to get a special artisan to make it so it won't fall over. That's what the gods of other peoples are like. Or later, in an extended mockery (44:9–18), he indicates that a carpenter cuts down some trees; some of the wood he uses to warm himself and to make bread, and then some of it he makes into a god:

Half of it he burns in the fire; over this half he roasts meat, eats it and is satisfied. He also warms himself and says, "Ah, I am warm, I can feel the fire!" The rest of it he makes into a god, his idol, bows down to it and worships it; he prays to it and says, "Save me, for you are my god!" (44:16–17)

The author considers such worshipers of other gods to be ignorant, deluded, and stupid (44:18–20). Yahweh is not only the God of Israel. He is the only God there is.

THE SUFFERING SERVANT   No passage of Second Isaiah has intrigued readers and interpreters—especially among Christians—more than the four passages that are dedicated to describing a figure known as the "Suffering Servant." Some commentators have called these passages "songs," or "songs of the suffering servant." The passages are Isaiah 42:1–4; 49:1–6;

BOX 6.4 THE RISE OF MONOTHEISM

It is sometimes thought that ancient Israel was always strictly monotheistic, believing that there is only one God. But as we have seen repeatedly, that simply is not true. For one thing, over vast stretches of history many Israelites were in fact polytheistic, worshipping numerous gods—Asherahs, Baals, and a variety of non-Israelite pagan deities. More than that, many scholars have been convinced that at an early point in the history of Israel Yahweh was understood to have a female consort, who was enthroned with him (for this debate among scholars, see for example: http://members.bib-arch.org/publication.asp?PubID=BSBA&Volume=34&Issue=2&ArticleID=11).

In any event, it is clear that the historians and prophets whose works made it into the Hebrew Bible were quite insistent that the people of Israel *should* not worship other gods. That position both suggests that these other gods were, in fact, worshiped in ancient Israel and, just as significantly, that the authors who discourage their worship acknowledged their existence. Sometimes that acknowledgment is fairly explicit, as in the Decalogue: "You shall have no other gods before me."

The view that there are other gods, but that they are not to be worshiped—that there is only one God who is to be worshiped—is called "**henotheism**." It appears to have been the view of most of the biblical authors. It is not until we come to Second Isaiah that we begin to see the development of **monotheism**, the belief that there is only one God.

But if there is only one God, what is it that the pagans worship? Within the Judeo-Christian tradition there were two views that developed about that. One is the view found already in Second Isaiah, that the gods simply do not exist but are "made" as idols out of wood or metal by humans. The other view developed later, that these other gods did exist but were not true gods: instead, they were demons. This latter view is suggested in parts of the New Testament and became a standard critique of pagan religions by Christians in the second and third centuries C.E.

50:4–11; and 52:13–53:12. Scholars debate whether these passages were composed at the same time as the rest of the book or whether, instead, they existed independently of the book—possibly composed earlier by the author himself?—and were then incorporated into the book in four places.

In these passages, the Servant of Yahweh is said to have suffered horribly for the sake of others; but God will vindicate him. He, in fact, is the delight of Yahweh and will be used by him to accomplish his will on earth: "I have put my spirit upon him; he will bring forth justice to the nations . . . He will not grow faint or be crushed until he has established justice in the earth" (42:1, 6).

The author believes that this unnamed servant "shall prosper; he shall be exalted and lifted up" (52:13). But the most important, impressive, and well-known comments about the servant involve his horrible sufferings for the sake of others. These comments have been highly important since the times of the New Testament because Christian readers have widely thought that Isaiah was describing the crucifixion of Jesus for the sins of the world.

He was despised and rejected by others; a man of suffering and acquainted with infirmity; and as one from whom others hide their faces he was despised and we held him of no account. Surely he has borne our infirmities and carried our diseases; yet we accounted him stricken, struck down by God, and afflicted. But he was wounded for our transgressions, crushed for our iniquities; upon him was the punishment that made us whole, and by his bruises we are healed. All we like sheep have gone astray; we have all turned to our own way, and the LORD has laid on him the iniquity of us all. (53:3–6)

The author goes on to say that the servant was silent before his oppressors, that he was cut off from the land of the living, that he made his tomb with the rich, and that it was "the will of the LORD to crush him with pain." Doesn't this sound exactly like Jesus? Isn't this a prophecy about what would happen to the messiah?

In response to that common Christian interpretation, several points are important to make:

1. It is to be remembered that the prophets of the Hebrew Bible were not predicting things that were to happen hundreds of years in advance; they were speaking to their own contexts and delivering a message for their own people to hear, about their own immediate futures.

2. In this case, the author is not predicting that someone will suffer in the future for other people's sins at all. Many readers fail to consider the verb tenses in these passages. They do not indicate that someone *will* come along at a later time and suffer in the future. They are talking about *past* suffering. The Servant has *already* suffered—although he "will be" vindicated. And so this not about a future suffering messiah.

3. In fact, it is not about the messiah at all. This is a point frequently overlooked in discussions of the passage. If you will look, you will notice that the term "messiah" never occurs in the passage. This is not predicting what the messiah will be.

4. If the passage is not referring to the messiah, and is not referring to someone in the future who is going to suffer—whom is it talking about? Here there really should be very little ambiguity. As I mentioned, this particular passage (Isaiah 53) is one of four servant songs of Second Isaiah. And so the question is, whom does Second Isaiah himself indicate that the servant is? A careful reading of the passages makes the identification quite clear: "But now hear, O Jacob my servant, Israel whom I have chosen" (44:1); "Remember these things, O Jacob, and Israel, for you are my servant" (44:21); "And he said to me, 'You are my servant, Israel, in whom I will be glorified'" (49:3).

The book of Second Isaiah itself indicates who the Servant of the Lord is. It is Israel, God's people. In Isaiah 53, when the author describes the servant's *past* sufferings, he is talking about the sufferings they have experienced by being destroyed and exiled by the Babylonians. This is a suffering that has come about because of sins. But the suffering will be vindicated because God will now restore Israel and bring them back to the land and enter into a new relationship with them.

It may be fairly objected that the Servant is said to suffer for "our" sins, not "his" sins. Scholars have resolved that problem in a number of ways. It may be that the author is thinking that the portion of the people taken into exile have suffered for the sins of those in the land, some of them suffering for the sins of all. Those who have been taken into captivity have suffered displacement, loss, and exile for the sake of the sins of the nation. But now the servant—Israel—will be exalted and restored to a close relationship with God, and will be used by him to bring about justice throughout the earth.

There may be problems with this interpretation—as there always are with every interpretation—but the facts remain that the suffering servant is never described as the messiah, his suffering is portrayed as past instead of future, and he is explicitly identified on several occasions as "Israel." Later readers who have taken the passage as a reference to the messiah, then, have seen Jesus as one who "fills out" (or "fulfills") its original meaning—giving it a new meaning that it did not originally have.

Now that we have considered Ezekiel and Second Isaiah at some length, we can look more briefly at the writings of the other prophets from the post-exilic period.

JOEL

It is hard to estimate the date of the book of Joel. The author identifies himself as "Joel son of Pethuel" but says nothing else about himself and does not indicate when he was writing. The book is typically dated to the fifth or fourth century B.C.E. In any event, the purpose of his writing is clear. The land has been devastated by an invasion of locusts, and the author sees this as a harbinger of worse things to come, when God enters into judgment with his people, unless they repent and return to his ways.

The plague of locusts is described in graphic terms:

> What the cutting locust left, the swarming locust has eaten. What the swarming locust left, the hopping locust has eaten, and that the hopping locust left, the destroying locust has eaten. . . . It has laid waste my vines and splintered my fig trees; it has stripped off their bark

BOX 6.5 ISRAEL AS A LIGHT TO THE NATIONS

In the first servant song of Second Isaiah, Israel is said to be a "light of the nations":

I am the LORD. I have called you in righteousness, I have taken you by the hand and kept you; I have given you as a covenant to the people, a light to the nations, to open the eyes that are blind, to bring out the prisoners from the dungeon, from the prison those who sit in darkness. (42:1–8)

Here Israel is not thought of as the people of God who are to keep the treasures of his light to themselves; the enlightenment they enjoy is to be spread abroad as well. This "universalistic" strain—that God's calling of Israel was to have universal effect—is not found in all authors of the Hebrew Bible, but it is certainly in the

traditions of Second and Third Isaiah. The latter speaks about "foreigners who join themselves to the LORD, to minister to him, to love the name of the LORD, and to be his servants" (Isaiah 56:6). It is because of these people—pagan converts to be followers of Yahweh—that the Temple is not simply a place for the Judeans to worship: "for my house shall be called a house of prayer for all peoples" (Isaiah 56:7).

The universalistic impulse of Second and Third Isaiah was picked up by the early Christians such as the apostle Paul, who believed that it was precisely through Jesus that the gentiles—the non-Jews, the pagans—could be become part of the people of God. For these Christians, the covenant was not simply with the physical descendants of Abraham but with all people who would choose to worship the God of the Jews. For the Christians, this could be done only by accepting God's messiah Jesus.

and thrown it down; their branches have turned white. (1:4, 7)

The invasion reminds the author of an invading army, and drives him to urge his people to repent in view of the coming judgment of God:

Sanctify a fast, call a solemn assembly. Gather the elders and all the inhabitants of the land to the house of the LORD your God, and cry out to the LORD. Alas for the day! For the day of the LORD is near, and as destruction from the Almighty it comes. (1:14–15)

As we have seen in other contexts, the Day of the LORD is not, for the prophets, a good and happy day, but one in which God comes to wreak havoc and destruction among his people. For this author it is "a day of darkness and gloom, a day of clouds and thick darkness!" (2:2). All of this, of course, sounds like yet another invasion of locusts which darken the sky by their sheer multitude. It may be that a past invasion is seen to be sign of things to come— yet more locusts!—if the people don't repent.

And that is what the prophet urges them to do: fast, weep, mourn, and rend their hearts, as they "return to the LORD, your God" (2:12–13). For, the prophet declares, God is "gracious and merciful,

slow to anger, and abounding in steadfast love, and relents from punishing." The second half of the book becomes far more positive. God is said to have "pity on his people," and to be about to send them all those things that they very much needed but the locusts deprived them of: "grain, wine, and oil" (2:19). Their enemies are removed from them, and they and their land are restored. Moreover, the enemies of the people will be gathered together and judged and overthrown, but the people of Judah will emerge triumphant and glorious (ch. 3).

OBADIAH

Obadiah, just twenty-one verses long, is the shortest book in the Hebrew Bible. Unlike most of the other prophets, Obadiah does not deliver his proclamation against Israel or Judah but against Judah's neighbor Edom, for not helping Judah when it was attacked and destroyed. The author does not tell us when he was writing, but since the book presupposes that Judah has been overthrown, and since it appears that this is still a "fresh wound," it makes sense to think that it was composed soon after the Babylonian exile had begun—so possibly in the mid-sixth century B.C.E.

Edom is roundly charged for not assisting Judah in its time of need during the Babylonian invasion:

> On the day that you stood aside, on the day that strangers carried off his wealth, and foreigners entered his gates and cast lots for Jerusalem, you too were like one of them. But you should not have gloated over your brother on the day of his misfortune, you should not have rejoiced over the people of Judah on the day of his ruin. (vv. 11–12)

Because Edom behaved badly, it will itself receive a similar treatment: "For the day of the LORD is near against all the nations. As you have done, it shall be done to you; your deeds shall return on your own head" (v. 15). No one in Edom will survive (v. 18). But the Israelites will be restored to their land and their "kingdom shall be the LORD's."

Here we do not have the same kind of "schadenfreude" that we find in the far more vindictive book of Nahum, but it is vindictive enough. Edom is condemned for the way it has treated Judah, and with its condemnation will come total destruction.

HAGGAI

The short two-chapter book or Haggai is unusual among the prophets (though see also Ezekiel) in being written entirely in prose. It is also unusual in being so exact as to the time when it was written; on four occasions the author indicates precisely when his revelation from God came. Thus, for example, in the book's opening verse:

> In the second year of King Darius, in the sixth month, on the first day of the month, the word of the LORD came by the prophet Haggai to Zerubbabel son of Shealtiel, governor of Judah, and to Joshua son of Jehozadak, the high priest.

FIGURE 6.6. A relief carved into a cliff face in Persia, discovered in 1835, showing the Persian king Darius (the largest figure) facing the enemies he has defeated; over them is a symbol of the god Ahura Mazda, blessing the king.

This then is sometime in mid-August, 520 B.C.E., during the reign of Darius, king of Persia. By naming Zerubbabel and Joshua—two of the key figures of Ezra (where Joshua is called Jeshua)—the author situates himself even more firmly in context. We do not know who he was, but he was prophesying during the return to rebuild Jerusalem and the Temple.

In fact, the book is principally about the rebuilding of the Temple. If you'll recall our discussion earlier in the chapter, according to the book of Ezra the construction of the Temple was an on-again/off-again affair, taking some twenty-two years (537–516 B.C.E.). Haggai's prophecy comes during one of the slow times when no progress was being made. The book is designed to urge the leaders to get on with the work and to complete the job.

The book notes that there were some people arguing that it was not yet time "to rebuild the LORD's house." But Haggai is not satisfied with that view. The people have built their *own* houses, after all: "Is it a time for you yourselves to live in your paneled houses, while this house lies in ruins?" (1:4). As was the case with the pre-exilic prophets, Haggai has no qualms about claiming that God brings hardship on those who disobey his will. In this case, it comes in the form of a divinely inspired drought:

Because my house lies in ruins while all of you hurry off to your own houses, therefore the heavens above you have withheld the dew and the earth has withheld its produce. And I have called for a drought on the land and the hills, on the grain, the new wine, the oil, on what the soil produces, on human beings and animals, and on all their labors (1:9–11).

Zerubbabel and Joshua get the message, and they put the people back to work. In the next oracle God promises that the former splendor of the house from the time of the monarchy will be restored.

The book ends with a word of comfort spoken directly to Zerubbabel, the governor of Judah. God will destroy kingdoms and nations, but he will exalt Zerubbabel, making him like his own signet ring. In antiquity, an official's signet ring was used to place his stamp on a document; the stamp carried, then, his own authority. If someone else carried the official's ring, he had that authority himself. Zerubbabel will be like God's signet ring, carrying

God's authority: "for I have chosen you, says the LORD of hosts" (2:23).

ZECHARIAH

Just as the book of Isaiah is actually the work of three different authors, whose writings were spliced together and put on the same scroll, so too the book of Zechariah does not appear to be the work of a single writer. Scholars have long considered Zechariah 1–8 to be by one author (called First Zechariah) and 9–14 by a different one, living later (Second Zechariah).

First Zechariah

Like Haggai, with which it is closely associated, the author of First Zechariah gives us a precise date for when he began his prophecy: the second year of King Darius of Persia, in the eighth month—that is, in October or November 520 B.C.E. It too is written in prose.

The book consists of eight symbolic visions that predict that Jerusalem will be rebuilt and will be glorious. To take the first vision as an example: the author sees at night a man riding a red horse, and notices among a group of trees a number of horses. He asks an angel, who happens to be standing by to take his question, what these horses are (and presumably the riders who are on them). The angel tells him that they are the ones who patrol the earth, apparently as God's overseers, to know what is happening in the world. The horsemen come up to the angel and report that they have patrolled the earth and all is at peace. The angel responds by asking God himself how long he will withhold his mercy from Jerusalem, with which he has been angry "these seventy years" (the chronology doesn't work, since Jerusalem was not destroyed until 586 B.C.E.; "seventy" may simply be a round number meaning "for all these years"). God replies that he is about to act on Jerusalem's behalf, and the Temple in Jerusalem will soon be rebuilt. When that happens, "My cities shall again overflow with prosperity; the LORD will again comfort Zion and again choose Jerusalem" (1:17).

And so this again is a prophet of the return, prophesying in the context of the events narrated in Ezra and Nehemiah. Rather than condemning the leaders for not building the Temple (contrast Haggai), this prophet is in favor of what is happening and issues words of hope that all will be well with Jerusalem since God is on its side. It is a place to which all the Judean inhabitants of Babylon should come (2:6–7), the place where once more God will dwell: "Thus says the LORD: I will return to Zion, and will dwell in the midst of Jerusalem; Jerusalem shall be called the faithful city."

There are two—somewhat conflicting—passages that allude to a Davidic messiah in this new Jerusalem that will be holy to God. In the first (3:6–10), God tells the high priest Joshua (called Jeshua elsewhere, as we have seen) that a Davidic figure is soon to come: "I am going to bring my servant the Branch." From the pen of this prophet "the Branch" appears to be an allusion to a tradition—evidently widely known by this time—found in the writings of Isaiah of Jerusalem, which we discussed at an earlier stage (see also Jeremiah 23 and 33): "A shoot shall come out from the stump of Jesse, and a branch shall grow out of his roots. The spirit of the LORD shall rest on him, the spirit of wisdom and understanding . . . His delight shall be in the fear of the LORD" (Isaiah 11:1). In its context in Isaiah, this is a prediction that a future king from the line of David (the "stump of Jesse"; Jesse was David's

father) would come and rule the people Israel. Here in Zechariah that prophecy is reaffirmed to Joshua and his fellow priests. We are not told who the "branch" is, but most interpreters understand it to be a reference to Joshua's colleague Zerubbabel, the governor of Judah, who was from the Davidic line (grandson of King Jehoiachin).

The second reference to the Branch (6:11–13) is somewhat more confusing, because there we are told that Joshua himself is "a man whose name is Branch; for he shall branch out in his place, and he shall build the Temple of the Lord" (6:11–13). What adds to the confusion (is Joshua the Branch now, instead of Zerubbabel?) is that elsewhere in this book it is Zerubbabel who is said to be the one who will build the Temple (4:9). Interpreters have suggested a number of ways to resolve this problem. Possibly the prophet sees these two leaders of the returned people to be working so closely together, side by side, that it is not possible to differentiate the political leader (the governor) from the religious leader (the high priest).

Second Zechariah
Second Zechariah appears to have been written somewhat later, possibly in the fifth century B.C.E.

This text is obscure in many places and notoriously difficult to interpret. Still, certain features are clear. The prophet—whoever he was—pronounces judgment on the enemies of Israel and salvation for the people of both Judah and Israel: "I will strengthen the house of Judah, and I will save the house of Joseph. I will bring them back because I have compassion on them, and they shall be as though I had not rejected them" (10:6).

At that time, the land will be purified, and there will be no more idol worship of false prophets (13:2–6). Moreover, the enemies of Jerusalem will be overcome: "And on that day I will seek to destroy all the nations that come against Jerusalem" (12:9).

THIRD ISAIAH

We have seen that the unknown author of Second Isaiah (Isaiah 40–55) delivered a joyful message of consolation to the Judeans living in exile. The equally unknown author of Third Isaiah (Isaiah 56–66) has numerous similarities in writing style and themes to Second Isaiah, but presents a different message delivered in a different context. When this author was writing, the Judeans had already returned to the land and had started rebuilding the Temple. But things were not nearly as bright and hopeful as imagined by his predecessor, the author of Second Isaiah. Quite the contrary: life was harsh, the leaders of the people were corrupt, and the people were not the stalwart devotees of Yahweh that Second Isaiah had thought they would be. On the whole, the return was turning out to be seriously disappointing.

It is clear that the return to the land had already begun, as intimated for example in 56:8: "Thus says the Lord GOD, who gathers the outcasts of Israel, I will gather others to them besides those already gathered." Since some are "already gathered" that means that at least the first group of returnees had arrived. And they had settled in, as the author indicates that the Temple was in the process of being rebuilt (66:1). It appears, then, that his proclamation is almost exactly contemporaneous with that of Haggai and First Zechariah—writing sometime around 520 or 515 B.C.E. (so maybe thirty or forty years after Second Isaiah).

The author considers the leaders of the people (could this include Jeshua and Zerubbabel?) to be ignorant, ineffectual, lazy, and hungry for power:

Israel's sentinels are blind, they are all without knowledge; they are all silent dogs that cannot bark; dreaming, lying down, loving to slumber. The dogs have a mighty appetite; they never have enough. The shepherds also have no understanding; they have all turned to their own way, to their own gain, one and all. (56:10–11)

So too the people are full of iniquities; their "hands are defiled with blood," they "constantly tell lies," their "feet run to evil" and they "rush to shed innocent blood." "The way of peace they do not know and there is no justice in their paths" (59:1–8). This is not the happy community that Second Isaiah envisioned. Even more amazing—given everything Judah had been through—some members in the community are still participating in the worship of pagan idols (57:1–13).

But Third Isaiah is not all gloom and doom. He, like his predecessor, saw hope. If people will turn back to the Lord and do as he wants, "Then your light shall break forth like the dawn, and your healing shall spring up quickly. . . . Then you shall call, and the LORD will answer" (58:8–9). If they begin to act ethically, feeding the hungry and caring for the afflicted, then God will be their guide and the city will be rebuilt to be glorious once more (58:10–12). Zion itself will be exalted, so much so that strangers from other lands will flock to it, and "you shall enjoy the wealth of the nations" (61:6).

In possibly the most famous—and one of the brightest—predictions of this prophet, the end will turn out so much better than the present. The people will finally return to the Lord, after being judged harshly for their sins as a "rebellious people" who break the Torah and worship other gods (65:1–15). The result will be like an entire world created anew into a utopian kingdom:

For I am about to create new heavens and a new earth; the former things shall not be remembered or come to mind. But be glad and rejoice forever in what I am creating; for I am about to create Jerusalem as a joy, and its people as a delight. (65:17–18)

At that time there will be no more infant mortality; people will live in peace and prosperity; all people will be blessed: and "the wolf and the lamb shall feed together, the lion shall eat straw like the ox; but the serpent—its food shall be dust!" (65:20–25).

MALACHI

The final post-exilic prophet to consider happens also to be the final book of "the Twelve" and the last book in the English Bible. Like several of the other prophets we have considered, Malachi can be firmly situated in the time of Ezra–Nehemiah. But the book was clearly written sometime after Haggai and Zechariah, which were anticipating the completion of the Temple. Now, in this prophet, the Temple is up and running—and in his judgment, it is not running at all well. The priests have corrupted the Temple and the sacrificial worship of God is riddled with heinous problems. In light of this situation, the book is typically dated to sometime in the mid-fifth century.

Malachi has harsh words to say against the Jewish priests serving in the Temple, who "despise" the name of the Lord (1:6). This they do by not offering the proper sacrifices to God. In the Torah, animal sacrifices were to be without blemish and spotless. But the animals the priests are now offering are blind, lame, and sick (1:8). And so God responds, "I have no pleasure in you, says the LORD of hosts, and I will not accept an offering from your hands" (1:10).

And it is not just the priests who are a problem: "Judah has been faithless and abomination has been committed in Israel and in Jerusalem; for Judah has profaned the sanctuary of the LORD, which he loves, and has married the daughter of a foreign God" (2:11). It is difficult to know whether Malachi is referring to the problem that so obsessed Ezra—people of Judah intermarrying with those outside the community (women who worshiped "a foreign God")—or if he is speaking metaphorically, like Hosea, of those who have begun to worship pagan deities.

There are also enormous problems outside the sanctuary, which seems to be the author's principal concern: Jews are committing adultery, swearing falsely, oppressing the poor, the widow, and the orphan (3:5).

Malachi predicts that these various problems of the people will be resolved by God, who will be "sending my messenger to prepare the way before me, who will suddenly come to his Temple." This messenger's coming will not be a pleasant occasion for those who are not doing God's will; he will refine and purify the priests "until they present offerings to the LORD in righteousness." Then, and only then, will the sacrifices offered in the Temple "be pleasing to the LORD as in the days of old" (3:1–4).

But before that happens, there will be a violent destruction of those who are aligned against God: "See that day is coming, burning like an oven, when all the arrogant and all evildoers will be stubble; the day that comes shall burn them up" (4:1). The righteous, on the other hand, will exult in that day (4:2–3).

Many interpreters have seen this coming "messenger" as a key to this book, so much so that he may have given the book its title. The term "Malachi" may not be a personal name. In Hebrew it means "my messenger."

In any event the author goes on to indicate who that messenger will be: "Lo, I will send you the prophet Elijah before that great and terrible day of the LORD comes. He will turn the hearts of parents to their children and the hearts of children to their parents, so that I will not come and strike the land with a curse." This is a verse that looks backward to an earlier tradition that we have already examined, and forward to a tradition later developed in a distinctive way by the first Christians. The backward look is to the stories of Elijah, who according to 2 Kings did not die but ascended to heaven in a chariot of fire. He is to return, still with fire, in judgment on those who do not observe the sacrificial cult as Moses prescribed in the Torah. The forward look, as the Christians saw it, is to what happens in the Christian Gospels, which begin with the ministry of John the Baptist, who is identified in the first book of the New Testament as none other than Elijah (see Matthew 11:13: 17:9–13). This may well be why the Christian Old Testament ends with the book of Malachi. The New Testament then picks up exactly where the Old Testament leaves off, with the coming of Elijah in preparation for the coming of the Lord—who for the Christians is not Yahweh, but his son Jesus.

At a Glance: The Exilic and Post-Exilic Prophets

The exilic and post-exilic prophets include Ezekiel (who began prophesying from exile, but before the final destruction of Jerusalem in 586 B.C.E.), 2 Isaiah (the great prophet of consolation to those in exile), Joel, Obadiah, Haggai, Zechariah, 3 Isaiah, and Malachi. These various prophets can be dated to the sixth and fifth centuries B.C.E. (possibly the fourth in the case of Joel).

As was the case with their pre-exilic predecessors, these prophets believed they had a revelation from God to deliver to his people in light of their current circumstances. This often included a message of judgment when the people

were (still) not behaving in ways that God wanted, either in their lives together in community or in their cultic practices. Some of the prophets (2 Isaiah) expected that the return to the land would be a glorious time in the people's history; others of them living after the return (Haggai, Malachi, 3 Isaiah) found a different reality: the return was not so glorious at all. But most of these prophets still proclaimed a message of hope that if the people of Judea would be faithful to God, he would be faithful to them and bring in an age of peace and prosperity.

THE LATER HISTORY OF JUDEA

I will conclude this chapter by giving in very brief outline a sketch of the history presupposed in still later books of the Hebrew Bible (Daniel, not Malachi, was the last to be written).

In the Persian period, the land of Judah came to be a province of Persia called Judea. This will be its name in the time of the New Testament. So too, as we have seen, inhabitants of this land, and descendants of former inhabitants who maintained their ancestral religious and cultural traditions, were called Judeans, or Jews.

The Persian empire was to last for about two hundred years. In the mid- to late-fourth century, Greece, to the west, rose to prominence, especially under the leadership of Alexander of Macedonia, otherwise known to history as **Alexander the Great**. We will learn more about Alexander in chapter 9 as, somewhat ironically, his conquests proved to be more important for early Christianity than they were for the Hebrew Bible. Here suffice it to say that Alexander and his armies went on a massive campaign to the east, conquering Egypt and the Levant and eventually the entire Persian empire, by 330 C.E. Eventually they got as far east as the eastern edge of modern-day India, before turning back.

Alexander was himself, culturally, Greek (although he was from Macedonia). He actually had the great Greek philosopher Aristotle (disciple of Plato, disciple of Socrates) as his private tutor when

he was young. And so, he considered Greek culture to be superior to all others. One of his goals was not simply to establish a worldwide empire, but also to make that empire Greek. The spread of Greek culture was a process that is known as **Hellenization**, a term based on the Greek word for Greece, Hellas. Unfortunately Alexander died at the very young age of 33, while still on his military campaign, in 323 B.C.E.

Alexander's empire was distributed among his generals. The part of the world we are interested in—the land of Judea—at first came under the control of the Egyptians, ruled by a family known as the **Ptolemies**. But there was a constant struggle with the Syrians, ruled by a Greek military family known as the **Seleucids**. The Seleucids wrenched Judea away from Ptolemaic control in 198 B.C.E.

A few decades after that things became complicated in Judea. Throughout the Persian period, the province of Judea was more or less left to its own devices. There was a local government headed by a Judean governor appointed by the Persian king, and there were heavy tax revenues to be paid to the Persians. The high priest was in charge, ultimately, of the Temple and the important aspects of the religion. Judeans were allowed to live and worship as they saw fit. Under the Seleucids, that began to change. The Seleucids were particularly interested in bringing cultural unity to their empire, and they saw the process of Hellenization as a way to achieve that goal. Throughout the Seleucid empire the elite

The Return to the Land under Persia: 538 B.C.E.
Rebuilding of Jerusalem and the Temple: 520–430 B.C.E.
Conquests of Alexander the Great: 332 B.C.E.
Judea ruled by Egypt: 300–198 B.C.E.

Judea ruled by Syria: 198–142 B.C.E.
The Maccabean Revolt: 167–142 B.C.E.
The Maccabean Rule: 142–63 B.C.E.
Conquest of Palestine by Romans: 63 B.C.E.

members of society were encouraged to speak Greek and to adopt Greek dress and customs, as well as Greek religion. Greek institutions such as the gymnasium—where men and boys would exercise in the nude (the Greek word for naked is *gymne*), and which became cultural centers—were built in major cities throughout the empire. It came to be thought that if you were modern and cosmopolitan, you would adopt Greek ways.

Many indigenous peoples did not appreciate this intrusion of a foreign culture and customs, but others saw it as a good thing. Nowhere in the Seleucid empire were the tensions between the conservatives who wanted to keep the old ways and the progressives who wanted to change to the new more evident than in Judea, where the entire religion and cultural life was centered on the ancient traditions that were distinctive to Judaism and that made Jews Jewish. Many of the elite Jews, however, even in Jerusalem, were in favor of change and the adaptation of Greek culture. Conflict was sure to arise, and it did so in a big way.

In 175 B.C.E. a new king assumed the throne of the Seleucid empire, called **Antiochus IV Epiphanes**. He was destined to become one of the bad guys of Jewish history (right down there with King Nebuchadnezzar of Babylon). Antiochus wanted to extend his empire all the way to Egypt. Wars cost money, and Antiochus needed some. Among other things he accepted a large bribe from a Judean aristocrat named Jason in exchange for making him, Jason, the high priest. This did not sit well with other Judeans. And things got worse. More than his predecessors, Antiochus wanted to Hellenize the Judeans. He had a gymnasium built in Jerusalem not far from the Temple. Many of the elite welcomed the change with its movement to make Jerusalem more cosmopolitan. But then Antiochus went too far, in the opinion of a number of Judeans. In 167 B.C.E. he placed a statue of a pagan deity, identified with the Greek god Zeus, in the

Temple itself. He required Jews to sacrifice to the pagan gods. And he made it illegal for Jews to circumcise their baby boys and to maintain their Jewish identity.

A revolt broke out, started by a family of Jewish priests headed by a man named Mattathias and his five sons. The leadership of this revolt was soon taken over by his son **Judas**, whose nickname was "**Maccabeus**" (a word that means something like "hammer"; he was a tough guy). The family came to be known as the "Maccabeans" and the revolt was called the **Maccabean Revolt**. The family is also sometimes called the **Hasmoneans** after the name of a distant ancestor.

The revolt began as a small guerrilla skirmish in 167 B.C.E.; soon much of the country was in armed rebellion against its Syrian overlords. In less than twenty-five years, the Maccabeans had successfully driven the Syrian army out of the land and assumed full and total control of its governance, creating the first sovereign Jewish state in over four centuries (since the tragic events of 586 B.C.E.). They rededicated the Temple (this was one of their first acts, in 164 B.C.E., commemorated still in the Hanukkah celebration) and appointed their own high priest.

Ever since the time of King David—and starting again with the return from exile under Cyrus—the high priest, the highest official in the religion as centered in the Temple, came from one particular family of priests descended from a man of David's time named Zadok. To the disappointment and chagrin of many Jews, the Maccabeans did not appoint a Zadokite to be priest, but a member from their own priestly family. This was to cause all sorts of resentment and inner turmoil in Jewish circles in the years that followed.

The Hasmoneans ruled the land of Judea as an autonomous state for some eighty years, until 63 B.C.E. when the Roman general Pompey conquered it. The Romans will still be in charge of it when we

FIGURE 6.7.   Silver coin from Antioch with a portrait of Antiochus Epiphanes and the inscription "King Antiochus, a god made manifest".

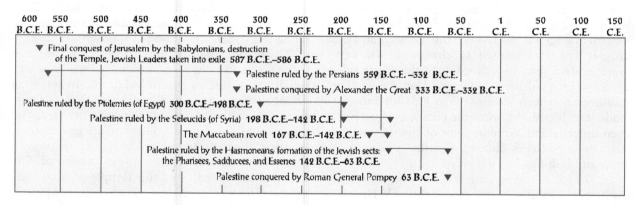

FIGURE 6.8.   Timeline of key events in Palestine from the Babylonian exile to the Conquest of the Romans.

move up to the times of the New Testament with the birth of Jesus, born during the reign of the first Roman Emperor, Caesar Augustus.

The period of the Hebrew Bible ends before this, however. The last book of the Jewish Scriptures to be written, which we will examine in chapter 8, was almost certainly the book of Daniel, written during the days when Antiochus Epiphanes was king of Syria and causing deep anger, frustration, and consternation among the Jews who rejected any efforts to be Hellenized and who wanted to remain faithful to their ancestral traditions.

Take a Stand

1. A friend who is also taking this class tells you that in her opinion, the prophecies of 2 Isaiah about the glorious return from exile were way off base: the realities did not at all meet up with the expectations. Do you agree? Sketch out a response to her based on the books of Ezra and Nehemiah.

2. Now deal with the same issue as above but base your sketch instead on some of the post-exilic prophets.

3. You are talking to your roommate about the Bible and he tells you that as far as he can see, all of the prophets are dealing with the same problems and are delivering the same message. You think this view is a bit simplistic. Pick two of the post-exilic prophets and discuss how different their contexts and messages are.

Key Terms

Alexander the Great, 162   **Hellenization**, 162   **Maccabean Revolt**, 163   **Seleucids**, 162

Antiochus Epiphanes, 163   **Judas Maccabeus**, 163   **Ptolemies**, 162   **Targum**, 145

Hasmoneans, 163

Suggestions for Further Reading

NB: For this and all chapters, see the relevant articles (e.g., "Nehemiah," "2 Isaiah") in the works cited in the Suggestions for Further Reading in chapter 1. For the books of the prophets, see the Suggestions for Further Reading for chapter 5. In addition, see:

Berquist, Jon L. *Judaism in Persia's Shadow: A Social and Historical Approach*. Minneapolis: Fortress Press, 1995. A historical study of the Persian empire, especially as it affected the Jews and their land.

De Silva, David. *Introducing the Apocrypha: Message, Context, and Significance*. Grand Rapids: Baker, 2002. This is mainly a discussion of the various books of the Apocrypha (see chapter 9), but it includes a useful historical sketch of the time period, including the Maccabean Revolt.

Friedman, Richard Elliott. *Who Wrote the Bible?* New York: HarperCollins, 1987. Explores the role played by the scribe Ezra in creating the final form of the Pentateuch.

Harrington, Daniel. *The Maccabean Revolt: Anatomy of a Biblical Revolution*. Wilmington, Del.: Glazier, 1988. A detailed study of the accounts of the revolt in 1 and 2 Maccabees.

7

The Poets and Storytellers
of Ancient Israel

WHAT TO EXPECT

In this chapter we move beyond the biblical books of history and prophecy in the Hebrew Bible to look at Hebrew poetry and storytelling. Even though large portions of the prophetic books are also in poetry, it is in the book of Psalms that we have the most striking instances of the genre. This is a book filled with deep emotional responses of Israelites to God. Equally striking, in their way, are the Lamentations on the destruction of Jerusalem and the erotic love poems of the Song of Songs.

The Hebrew Bible also contains a number of intriguing fictional accounts: Ruth, about a Moabite woman who boldly uses her wits and sexual prowess to preserve herself and her family from desolation; Esther, about a Jewish queen who saves the Jewish people from annihilation; Jonah, about a reluctant prophet swallowed by a great fish; and Daniel, about a wise young man with amazing adventures in exile in Babylon. We end this chapter by considering the rewriting of portions of the Deuteronomistic History in the books of 1 and 2 Chronicles.

In this chapter we will consider two different genres of literature: Hebrew poetry and the short story, both of which play a significant role among the books of the Hebrew Bible.

A number of the writings that we have already considered were composed in whole, or in part, as poetry rather than prose—for example, most of the prophets. You can tell in your English Bible when a translator wants you to recognize that a passage is poetry, since the lines are indented and not justified on the right hand margin. To see what I mean, simply look at any page of the book of Psalms and then any page of a historical book (say 1 Kings) and you'll see the difference.

We have not yet, however, talked about the nature of Hebrew poetry—a matter of some importance, because poetry in Hebrew works very differently

from the way it works in English. We will begin this chapter by considering the nature of Hebrew poetry, and then continue by looking at some of the major poetic books of the Hebrew Bible: the Psalms, the book of Lamentations, and the Song of Songs.

THE NATURE OF HEBREW POETRY

It is not difficult to understand how Hebrew poetry works but it is important to realize, off the bat, that it does not work at all like English poetry. There are, of course, many kinds of poetry in English. We have epic poems, lyric poems, sonnets, limericks, free verse, and that favorite of middle school teachers everywhere, the haiku. But there are certain things that can be said about the formal characteristics of English poetry in general. Unlike prose, poetry (with the exception of free verse) tends to use carefully compact construction characterized by distinct rhythms, often with accents on predetermined syllables and sometimes with rhyming schemes. The language is usually dense, and poetry relies heavily on metaphor and simile.

Hebrew poetry is also dense, and loaded with metaphor and simile, but the formal characteristics are completely different from English poetry. Hebrew poetry does have tighter construction than prose, but it is not based on rhyme or rhythms. It is based instead on conceptual parallels between corresponding lines. In Hebrew poetry, if—as is often the case—you have two lines of a verse, the first line will make a statement, and the second line will either repeat it using different words (that's the most common scheme), state the flip side of the coin, or build on the original idea by expanding it. What "rhymes" here are not the words but the concepts.

It will be easiest to explain how it works by giving some examples. We can classify Hebrew poetic lines in four types:

1. *Synonymous parallelism.* This is when the second line of a verse simply restates what the first line said, but does so in different words. Consider these examples from the second Psalm. This poem begins by lamenting the fact that the enemies of God's people have lined up to attack the chosen one, the king of Israel.

Why do the nations conspire
And the peoples plot in vain? (Psalms 2:2)

The second line simply repeats—and expands a bit—on the first (the nations = the peoples; conspire = plot in vain). Or take the fourth verse, God's reaction:

He who sits in the heavens laughs;
The LORD has them in derision. (Psalms 2:4)

There is the same pattern here; each part of the first line has a corresponding part in the second, stated in different words. As I indicated, you will find this pattern literally thousands of times throughout the Psalms and other Hebrew poetry—just open up any page at random and you'll see it.

2. *Antithetical Parallelism.* In this case, the second line of the verse states the *opposite* of what is in the first line—not in order to contradict it, but in order to show the flip side of the same coin. This kind of parallelism is not nearly as common as synonymous (except in a book like Proverbs), but it happens widely. Consider this instance from Psalm 1.

For the LORD watches over the way of the
  righteous,
But the way of the wicked will perish.
  (Psalms 1:6)

3. *Constructive Parallelism.* This kind of parallelism happens less commonly still; it is when the second line develops further the statement of the first line so that together they present a complete thought. And so, staying with Psalm 1:

They are like trees planted by streams of water,
Which yield their fruit in its season.
  (Psalms 1:3)

Or, in the next verse of the Psalm,

They wicked are not so,
But are like chaff that the wind drives away.
  (Psalms 1:4)

4. *Climactic Parallelism.* Sometimes this construction of a complete thought happens through the repetition of the key word(s) of the first line; this is a more rare form of parallelism but can be seen, for example, here and there in the Psalms. And so, from Psalm 29:

Ascribe to the LORD, O heavenly beings,
Ascribe to the LORD glory and strength.
  (Psalms 29:1)

Or from Psalm 92,

For your enemies, O LORD,
For your enemies shall perish. (Psalms 92:9)

A poem in Hebrew will make use of these different kinds of parallelism, and you can find more than one, sometimes all of them, within a single poem. There are numerous instances, as well, when the author will give just one line of text, or three. In the latter case, each of the three lines stand in one or another of these relations to the others. When you are reading Hebrew poetry you need to be alert to these different options, to prevent yourself from reading the wrong idea into what the poem is saying; for example, by thinking that the two lines of a synonymous parallel are making two *different* statements. At every point you should ask yourself what kind of parallelism is being used, and that will help you understand the poem.

As also mentioned, Hebrew poetry is very strong in imagery—especially metaphors. As with all figurative language, these metaphors are not to be taken literally or you destroy the point. They are used to help you understand more deeply the characteristics of the phenomenon or person being described. And so, for example, God is portrayed as a shepherd, or as a big bird; his people are sheep or chicks; sometimes a person is in danger of drowning in his sorrows or descending to the depths of Sheol. An overly literalistic reading of these images would lead to disastrous interpretive results.

Although poetry is widespread throughout the Hebrew Bible—including not only most of the prophets we have already considered, but also the books of Wisdom that we will explore in chapter 8—the best known book of poetry in the Bible is the book of Psalms.

THE BOOK OF PSALMS

Psalms has always been, and continues to be, one of the favorite books of the Bible—if not *the* favorite book—among the Bible's avid readers. It is a book that has provided comfort, hope, and consolation; it is a book that allows the reader to vent his or her frustration, bitterness, and anger; it is a book that complains and grumbles to God and that praises and thanks God. It is a book of many parts and many emotions, one of the great collections of poetry in the history of civilization.

Overview of the Psalms

The word **"psalm"** comes from the Greek verb *psallo*, which originally meant to pluck the string of

an instrument or to play a stringed instrument; eventually it came to mean to sing with accompaniment. The Psalms in the Hebrew Bible are not provided with any musical notation, but they were probably meant to be sung. The Hebrew title for the book is TEHILLIM, which means "praises." As we will see, this title is not altogether apt, as so many of the psalms are not praises at all; many of them express bitter complaints, laments, anger, and even an eagerness for violent revenge.

All of the Psalms, however, can be seen as poetic responses to and interactions with God. In this, the book of Psalms differs from almost all the other books of the Hebrew Bible. As we have seen, much of the Bible is about God's actions among humans, human missteps with respect to God, God's often violent response to those missteps, and human reactions to God's response. Either explicitly or implicitly, the historical books of the Bible and the prophets are about action. The Psalms, on the other hand, are not about action; they are about emotion. These various psalms are very human responses to life and to God and can be seen, ultimately, as a set of poetic prayers to God.

It is very difficult to assign a date to most of the Psalms. As we will see in a moment, a number of them are provided with "ascriptions," in which an editor has indicated whom the author was and, sometimes, in what circumstances he composed the psalm. But these are later additions to the text and cannot be trusted to give us real dates, for reasons we will see. On occasion a psalm will mention a historical event—for example, the destruction of the walls of Jerusalem—and in those cases we can say with fair confidence something about when it was written (if the walls were destroyed, the poem was composed sometime after 586 B.C.E.). Scholars have long debated the matter, but a general consensus is that the collection of Psalms as we now have it dates to the post-exilic period, possibly around the fourth century B.C.E. Individual psalms, obviously, could date earlier: as we will see, a number of psalms were written during the time of the kings.

The various psalms were written by different authors in different situations and they embody a remarkably wide-ranging set of emotions and responses, usually directed to God:

- *Praise.* The author praises God for who he is and what he is done.

- *Thankfulness.* The author thanks God for his mighty works or for a specific benefit that he has bestowed on the psalmist.
- *Anger.* The author vents his anger either against his enemies or against God himself for what has happened to him.
- *Bitterness.* The author expresses bitterness at the miserable life that he is being forced to lead.
- *Complaint.* The author complains to God that he is not being treated fairly or justly, by others or by God himself.
- *Vengefulness.* The author lets it all go and expresses a deep desire to have revenge on his enemies, often in violent and graphic language.
- *Hopefulness.* The author expresses hope that even though things are rotten now, God will intervene and make life good once again.
- *Vindication.* The author expresses a wish that God will make right what is wrong, and vindicate the righteousness of the one who is suffering unjustly.
- *Celebration.* The author rejoices in the good things that God has brought his way, often after a dark period in his life.

Obviously some of these occasions and emotions overlap with one another, and it often happens that more than one of them will be found in a single psalm.

Contents and Structure of the Book of Psalms

The book of Psalms—sometimes called the Psalter—is the longest book of the Bible. Altogether it contains 150 separate psalms. These are individual poems of different types (as we will see). Each psalm is a self-contained unit given without historical or literary context, a freestanding poem. In most instances there are no connections between one psalm and the next; they just occur, one after the other. In other instances there are smaller collections of psalms on the same topic.

ASCRIPTIONS It is sometimes thought—wrongly—that King David was the author of the entire Psalter. Even the book of Psalms itself shows that this is not correct: a large number of the psalms are ascribed to people other than David. Altogether about two-thirds of the Psalms have an ascription. Of these, seventy-three Psalms are ascribed to

David. But some of these could not possibly have been written by him, since they allude to events that happened after his time. And so, for example, the most famous psalm of them all, Psalm 23 (which begins: "The LORD is my shepherd, I shall not want"), has an ascription, "A Psalm of David." But at the end of the Psalm the author—clearly not David—speaks about dwelling "in the house of the LORD my whole life long." The "house of the LORD" in the Hebrew Bible refers to the Temple in Jerusalem. But the Temple, as we have seen, was not built until after David's day by his son Solomon. Similarly, Psalm 68 is said in the ascription to be one of David's Psalms, but it is even more explicit: "Because of your Temple at Jerusalem kings bear gifts to you" (Psalms 68:29).

One of the more famous ascriptions comes with Psalm 51, a powerful and moving psalm that begs God for forgiveness for sin that the author has committed:

> Have mercy on me, O God, according to
>   your steadfast love. . . .
> Wash me thoroughly from my iniquity,
> And cleanse me from my sin
> For I know my transgressions,
> And my sin is ever before me. . . .
> Against you, you alone, have I sinned
> And done what is evil in your sight.
> Purge me with hyssop, and I shall be clean;
> Wash me and I shall be whiter than snow.
>   (Psalms 51:1, 2–4, 7)

The ascription of this beautiful prayer of contrition is longer and more detailed than most: "To the leader. A Psalm of David, when the prophet Nathan came to him, after he had gone in to Bathsheba." This recalls one of the memorable stories from 2 Samuel as the background for such an abject appeal for forgiveness. Certain parts of the psalm may not seem to fit that particular situation very well: how is it against God, and God "alone" that David sinned? How about Uriah, whom David had murdered to cover up his own flagrant act of adultery with Uriah's wife? Didn't he sin against him as well? In any event, the psalm cannot have really been written by David in remorse concerning that incident with the woman next door. At the end of the psalm the psalmist asks God to "Do good to Zion in your good pleasure; rebuild the walls of Jerusalem" (51:18). This psalm was written after the

FIGURE 7.1. A sculpture of musicians found in the city of Ashdod; it was made in the early tenth century B.C.E., when Israelite authors were already producing "psalms." The middle figure is playing a stringed instrument (the word "psalm" comes from a term that means to pluck a musical string).

destruction of Jerusalem, some 500 years after David and Bathsheba were dead and gone.

Other psalms are attributed to Asaph (12 psalms), the sons of Korah (11), Solomon (2), Moses (1); Heman (1), and Ethan (1). Asaph, Heman, and Ethan were known to be three chief singers in the tabernacle during the reign of David (1 Chronicles 6).

DIVISIONS OF THE BOOK Whoever served as the final editor of the book of Psalms divided it up into five books, each of which ends with a **doxology**. A doxology is literally a "word of praise," and is either an entire poem or just a couple of lines that extends a blessing to Yahweh, the God of Israel. There does not appear to be any compelling logic for why the editor ended each book where he did; he possibly wanted to have five major collections of psalms to correspond to the five books of the Law of Moses. The arrangement then is as follows:

- Book 1: Psalms 1–41; the doxology is given in 41:13—it is not to be understood as a part of Psalm 41 but is the conclusion of the book; in this case the doxology is short and sweet:

    Blessed be the LORD, the God of Israel,
    from everlasting to everlasting.
    Amen and Amen.

- Book 2: Psalms 42–72; the doxology is 72:18–19.
- Book 3: Psalms 73–89; the doxology is 89:51.
- Book 4: Psalms 90–106; the doxology is 106:48.
- Book 5: Psalms 107–150; the doxology is the whole of Psalm 150, an entire psalm dedicated to praise to Yahweh so as to close out not just book 5 but the entire collection:

    Praise the LORD!
    Praise God in his sanctuary
    Praise him in his mighty firmament . . .
    Let everything that breathes praise the
        LORD!
    Praise the LORD! (Psalms 150:1, 6)

Major Kinds of Psalms

Not only is there a wide range of emotion expressed in the various psalms (sometimes several within the same psalm), there are different kinds of psalms written to achieve different purposes. We looked briefly at Psalm 51, a prayer of forgiveness in which the author confesses his sins to God, expresses his deep remorse for what he has done, and begs God to forgive him and restore him into a right standing. That could be seen as one kind of psalm. Among the other major types of psalms we can consider the following.

- *Hymns.* Hymns are songs of praise, often pure, unabashed, gushing praise for Yahweh, or an exhortation to praise Yahweh because of the good things he has done. Good examples are Psalm 136, or Psalm 100:

    Make a joyful noise to the LORD, all the
        earth
    Worship the LORD with gladness;
    Come into his presence with singing.
    Know that the LORD is God
    It is he that has made us, and we are his;
    We are his people, and the sheep of his
        pasture. . . .
    For the LORD is good
    his steadfast love endures forever,
    And his faithfulness to all generations.
        (Psalms 100:1–3, 5)

- *Thanksgiving.* Closely related to hymns are Psalms of thanksgiving (these categories can be seen as rough guides; there can be considerable overlap with some of them). These are expressions of thanks to God for specific things he has done. Good examples are Psalm 118 and Psalm 92:

> It is good to give thanks to the LORD,
> To sing praises to your name, O Most
>   High;
> To declare your steadfast love in the
>   morning,
> And your faithfulness by night . . .
> For you, O LORD, have made me glad by
>   your work;
> At the works of your hands I sing for
>   joy. . . .
> You have exalted my horn like that of the
>   wild ox;
> You have poured over me fresh oil.
> My eyes have seen the downfall of my
>   enemies;
> My ears have heard the doom of my evil
>   assailants. (Psalms 92:1–2, 5, 10–11)

- *Enthronement.* These are psalms that praise God specifically for being the King, the ruler over all. Good examples are Psalms 93 and 47:

> Clap your hands, all you peoples;
> Shout to God with loud songs of joy.
> For the LORD, the Most High, is
>   awesome,
> a great king over all the earth.
> He subdued peoples under us,
> and nations under our feet. . . .
> Sing praises to God, sing praises;
> Sing praises to our King, sing praises.
> For God is the king of all the earth;
> Sing praises with a psalm. (Psalms 47:1–3,
>   6–7)

- *Laments.* Laments are psalms that complain to God about suffering and that appeal to him for help; they often end with an assurance that he will intervene on behalf of the one suffering. Some of these laments are individual (a single person is in pain); others are communal (the entire community is suffering). Laments are a very popular type of psalm—possibly because religious people often turn to God especially when things are going badly. Altogether they make up sixty of the psalms in the entire Psalter.

Good examples are Psalms 6 and 22. Note here the intense imagery that the author employs (not to be taken literally!).

> My God, my God, why have you forsaken
>   me?
> Why are you so far from helping me,
> From the words of my groaning?
> O my God, I cry by day, but you do not
>   answer;
> And by night, but find no rest.
> Yet you are holy,
> Enthroned on the praises of Israel.
> In you our ancestors trusted;
> They trusted, and you delivered them. . . .
> But I am a worm, and not human;
> Scorned by others, and despised by the
>   people.
> All who see me mock at me;
> They make mouths at me, they shake their
>   heads;
> I am poured out like water,
> And all my bones are out of joint;
> My heart is like wax;
> It is melted within my breast . . .
> For dogs are all around me,
> A company of evildoers encircles me.
> My hands and feet have shriveled;
> I can count all my bones. . . .
> But you, O LORD, do not be far away!
> O my help, come quickly to my aid!
> Deliver my soul from the sword,
> My life from the power of the dog!
> Save me from the mouth of the lion!
>   (Psalms 22:1–3, 6–7; 14, 16–17, 19–21)

- *Royal.* A royal psalm is sung not in praise of God as king, but in praise of his anointed one, the king of Israel. Good examples are Psalms 2 and 45 (the former possibly composed for a coronation ceremony; the latter possibly for a royal wedding):

> My heart overflows with a goodly theme;
> I address my verses to the king;
> My tongue is like the pen of a ready scribe.
> You are the most handsome of men;
> Grace is poured upon your lips;
> Therefore God has blessed you forever
> Gird your sword on your thigh, O mighty
>   one,

in your glory and majesty . . .
Your royal scepter is a scepter of equity,
you love righteousness and hate wickedness.
Therefore God, your God, has anointed
   you
with the oil of gladness beyond your companions. . . . (Psalms 45:1–3, 6–7).

• *Wisdom.* We will be examining the wisdom traditions of ancient Israel in chapter 8. The wisdom
psalms stand in those traditions and represent
wise reflections on the nature of the world and
on how one should act. Good examples are
Psalms 37 and 73:

Do not fret because of the wicked,
Do not be envious of wrongdoers,
For they will soon fade like the grass
And wither like the green herb. . . .
Better is a little that the righteous person has
Than the abundance of many wicked.
For the arms of the wicked shall be broken,

But the LORD upholds the righteous . . .
I have been young, and now am old,
Yet I have not seen the righteous forsaken
or their children begging for bread.
They are ever giving liberally and lending,
And their children become a blessing.
   (Psalms 37:1–2, 16–17, 25–26)

• *Torah.* The Torah Psalms offer praise for the Law
of God as the greatest good. Good examples are
Psalm 119 (the longest chapter of the entire Bible)
and 1:

Happy are those who do not follow the
   advice of the wicked,
Or take the path that sinners tread,
Or sit in the seat of scoffers;
But their delight is in the law [Torah] of the
   Lord,
And on his law they meditate day and night
They are like trees planted by streams of
   water,

BOX 7.1 A PRAYER FOR VIOLENT REVENGE

The Psalms are filled with emotion and passion as the
authors exalt in the grandeur and greatness of God,
complain bitterly about the fate they have experienced,
and pour out their hearts in thanksgiving and in utterly
desperate prayers of hope. Sometimes the emotions
are as raw as freshly skinned meat. Nowhere is that
seen more clearly than in Psalm 137.

The setting of the psalm is clear from the outset, in
an opening verse that evokes the heart-wrenching sadness of the author's plight:

By the rivers of Babylon—
There we sat down and there we wept
When we remembered Zion.

The author is in exile from his beloved land, forced
to dwell among the hated Babylonians who taunt him
mercilessly, asking him to sing a song of his homeland for
which he passionately longs:

If I forget you, O Jeruslaem,
Let my right hand wither!
Let my tongue cling to the roof of my mouth,

If I do not remember you,
If I do not set Jerusalem
Above my highest joy.

Anyone who reads to this point of the psalm is completely on the side of the author, despairing of his plight
in a foreign land among those he disdains. But then he
goes a step further, and lets his full emotions out of
the bag as he passionately imagines the violent revenge
he would love to inflict on his enemies, one of the rawest
and most horrifying images of the entire book:

O daughter of Babylon, you devastator!
Happy shall they be who pay you back what you
   have done to us.
Happy shall they be who take your little ones
And dash them against the rock!

The Psalms are not meant to teach readers how to
behave; they are meant to be outlets for the authors'
deep emotions. And there are few outlets more revealing than the closing of this particular psalm.

Which yield their fruit in its season
And their leaves do not wither.
In all that they do, they prosper. (Psalms
    1:1–3)

In sum, a great number of the Psalms are among the favorite reading of Bible readers today, and always have been. Psalm 1, and its claim that blessings follow upon those who remain attuned to the Torah that God has given; Psalm 23, and its calm assurance that God is a shepherd who will guide his follower through life, even during the darkest of times; Psalm 51, and its expression of heartfelt contrition before God and plea that God will hear and offer his forgiveness; Psalm 89, and its appeal to God to remember the promises that he himself has made; and Psalm 137, possibly the most surprising of all, in which the author expresses bitter grief over being forced into exile and gives vent to a violent vindictiveness against the enemies who have overcome the people of Israel. (See Box 7.1.)

⸙ THE BOOK OF LAMENTATIONS

The second book of poetry that we may consider is the book of Lamentations. Traditionally it was thought that this book was written by the prophet Jeremiah (which is why, in English Bibles, it is included among the prophets). This identification made a good deal of sense. If you recall, in the book of Jeremiah there are six passages that have been identified as "laments," in which the prophet complains about his life, his situation, and the reception of his message, pleading with God to intervene on his behalf. The book of Lamentations is itself a series of laments, and it clearly dates from approximately the same time that Jeremiah was writing, in the mid-sixth century B.C.E. But there is a major difference between these laments and those of Jeremiah. In these it is not the prophet's personal circumstances that are the cause of complaint; it is instead the fate of the people. These poems were written after the fall of Jerusalem by someone who is emotionally devastated by what has happened. The great and beautiful city has been destroyed, and the author expresses his deep agony over the situation and prays that God will do something to punish those who have done this foul deed. At the same time, he acknowledges—in good prophetic

fashion—that it was because of Jerusalem's own failings that this horrible event has occurred. And he occasionally turns from confessing the community's sins that led to destruction and speaks of his own, personal failing. Modern scholars typically think that the author was someone other than Jeremiah. As with most of the Hebrew Bible, the book is anonymous and we cannot know who actually wrote it.

The book of Lamentations is five chapters in length, and if you look closely you will notice that each chapter is exactly twenty-two verses long, except chapter 4, which is sixty-six verses (22 times 3). There is a reason for this. There are twenty-two letters in the Hebrew alphabet. And these poems are based on **acrostics** (all but chapter 5). An acrostic poem is one in which the first letters of the first words of each verse together spell a word or are significant for some other reason. An alphabetic acrostic is one in which the first letter of each verse is the next letter of the alphabet (in Hebrew: Aleph, Beth, Gimel, etc., all the way to the last letter, Tav). In setting up the laments for the fall of Jerusalem as a series of acrostic poems, the author is saying something about the totality of the destruction: this is a disaster from A to Z (well, Aleph to Tav).

The third chapter is the one with 66 verses; in this case every set of three verses begins with the same letter of the alphabet. The fifth chapter is not an acrostic but does have 22 verses, keeping roughly within the theme. It is possible that the five chapters actually come from five different authors, and that a later editor chose to put them together into one longer book. We will be considering them, however, for the sake of convenience, as the work of a single author.

The sadness that emanates from these laments is felt already at the very beginning:

How lonely sits the city that once was full of
    people!
How like a widow she has become, she that
    was great among the nations!
She that was a princess among the provinces
    has become a vassal.
She weeps bitterly in the night, with tears on
    her cheeks
Among all her lovers she has no one to
    comfort her;
All her friends have dealt treacherously with
    her,
They have become her enemies.

Judah has gone into exile with suffering and
hard servitude;
She lives now among the nations, and finds
no resting place;
Her pursuers have all overtaken her in the
midst of her distress.
The roads to Zion mourn, for no one comes
to the festivals;
All her gates are desolate, her priests groan
Her young girls grieve, and her lot is bitter.
(Lamentations 1:1–4)

The author is not upset because he thinks that the
suffering that his people are enduring is undeserved.
On the contrary, he indicates that "the LORD has
made her suffer for the multitude of her transgressions" (1:5). There is no doubt in his mind that the
destruction was brought about by God: "The Lord
has become like an enemy; he has destroyed Israel.
He has destroyed all its palaces, laid in ruins its strongholds" (2:5). He himself may be living sometime after
the exile began: "Our ancestors sinned; they are no
more, and we bear their iniquities" (5:7). But the suffering is intense, as spelled out in occasionally graphic
terms: the people left in Judah are constantly under
threat by the sword; they are scorched with famine;
women are being raped; the leaders are being subject
to torture; young men are working as slaves; and
Mount Zion is virtually abandoned (5:9–18).

The author—or authors—ends each poem with
a prayer for vindication or a plea for help. And so,
from the first poem:

All my enemies heard of my trouble;
They are glad that you have done it.
Bring on them the day you have announced,
And let them be as I am.
Let all their evil doing come before you, and
deal with them
as you have dealt with me because of all my
transgressions;
for my groans are many and my heart is faint.
(1:21–22)

Or in even more vindictive terms, the end of the
third poem:

Give them anguish of heart;
Your curse be on them!
Pursue them in anger and destroy them
From under the LORD's heavens. (3:65–66)

THE SONG OF SONGS

It is hard to imagine a larger contrast between the
powerful, bitter, and angst-ridden poems that make
up the book of Lamentations and the collections of
beautiful, erotic, and touching love poems found in
the Song of Songs. This is its name in the Hebrew
Bible, and it means something like "The Best of
Songs." In English it is often called "The Song of
Solomon" because of the opening line: "The Song
of Songs, which is Solomon's." But that tradition of
its authorship is almost certainly not correct. The
book, as we will see, was written many centuries
after Solomon died in the tenth century B.C.E.; and
when Solomon is mentioned in these poems—as he
is on a couple of occasions—he is clearly someone
other than the author (see 8:11–12).

The book consists of a series of love poems—
actual love poems, involving a man and a woman—
some of them, as we will see, highly eroticized.
More than one reader has wondered how a book like
this ever came to be included in Scripture. It is not
clear how many poems have been strung together to
make up the book: some scholars count six, others
eleven, others thirty. What is less disputed is the fact
that we are dealing with a number of compositions
on the same theme, edited together in what is surely
one of the most unusual books of the Bible.

It is always difficult to date love poetry. At one
point in the book a Persian word appears (the
word for "garden"), which makes most interpreters
conclude that the book in the form it has come
down to us is post-exilic, possibly from the fourth
century B.C.E.

The poems consist of the thoughts and words of
various characters, in particular a gorgeous man
and a gorgeous woman, who are passionately in
love with each other. Occasionally the voices of
others are heard as well, such as the woman's female
companions. You can get a good sense for the erotic
passion of the book by the opening lines, put on the
lips of the female lover:

Let him kiss me with the kisses of his mouth!
For your love is better than wine
Your anointing oils are fragrant.
Your name is perfume poured out;
Therefore the maidens love you. (1:2–3)

The male lover later responds in kind:

FIGURE 7.2. The Song of Songs as found in an Italian manuscript of the fifteenth century.

Ah, you are beautiful, my love;
Ah, you are beautiful;
Your eyes are doves.
Ah, you are beautiful, my beloved,
Truly lovely. (1:15–16)

As the poems progress, it is clear that these two lovers in the throes of passion are not married to one another. At one point, for example, she is desperate to have him and has to go out on the streets to find him (3:1–4). When she finds him, she does not bring him back into a house they share together but takes him to bed in her mother's house:

Scarcely had I passed them,
When I found him whom my soul loves.
I held him, and would not let him go
until I brought him into my mother's house,
and into the chamber of her that conceived
   me.
I adjure you, O daughters of Jerusalem,

by the gazelles or the wild does;
Do not stir up or awaken love
until it is ready. (3:4–5)

The descriptions by one lover of the stunning assets of the other are rich in metaphor. The man speaks of his lovers' eyes as doves, her hair as a flock of goats, her teeth as a flock of shorn ewes come up from washing, her lips as a crimson thread, her cheeks as halves of a pomegranate, her breasts as two fawns. "You are altogether beautiful, my love; there is no flaw in you" (4:1–7). She speaks of him as radiant, his head is like gold, his eyes like doves, his cheeks like beds of spices, his lips like lilies, his body like ivory, his legs like alabaster, his speech as most sweet. For her "he is altogether desirable" (5:10–16).

There are passages in the Song of Songs that are even more erotic—quite explicit really—which unfortunately never make it into English with the kind of graphic character they have when you read them in the original Hebrew. (See Box 7.2.)

Many ancient readers—both Jewish and Christian—had trouble with this kind of passionate love poetry in the Bible. How could such raw eroticism be in Scripture? And so there developed traditions of interpretation that allegorized the book—that is, that claimed that what *seem* to be poems of passion between a man and a woman are actually allegories (that is, symbolic representations) for something else.

In some Jewish circles, it came to be thought that the book was not about human lovers but

At a Glance: Hebrew Poetry

Hebrew poetry is different from English in not using rhymes of sound, but "rhymes" of thought in parallel lines; in a two-line verse, the second line will repeat the first in different words, contrast with it, or build it to a fuller thought or climax. The book of Psalms is the best known instance of Hebrew poetry, 150 separate compositions in which a wide range of authors express their deep emotions to God: anger, bitterness, anxiety, lament, joy, thankfulness, heartfelt praise. The book of Lamentations consists of five alphabetical acrostic poems that deeply mourn the fate of Judah now that it is suffering in exile in Babylon. The Song of Songs is a poetic expression of the passion of a man and a woman, in which they describe their love and their desire in unbridled terms.

BOX 7.2 EROTICISM IN THE SONG OF SONGS

The full eroticism of the Song of Songs does not come across in most English translations. The following is a more literal translation of one of the key passages, provided by Hebrew Bible specialist Michael Coogan (adapting a translation of C. E. Walsh):[1]

I slept, but my heart was awake.
Listen, my lover is knocking.

"Open to me, my sister, my love,
My dove, my perfect one,
For my head is wet with dew . . . ."
My lover thrust his hand into the hole,
and my insides yearned for him,
I arose to open to my lover,
And my hands dripped with myrrh,
My fingers with liquid myrrh,
Upon the handles of the lock.
I opened to my lover,
But he was gone. (5:2–6)

[1] Michael Coogan, *The Old Testament: A Historical and Literary Introduction to the Hebrew Scriptures* (New York: Oxford University Press, 2006), p. 496; based on C. E. Walsh, *Exquisite Desire*, pp. 111–12.

about God's love for Israel. He was passionate for his people and loved them as deeply as ever a man loved a woman. Christian interpreters—many of whom would be even more scandalized by the graphic descriptions of the book than were their Jewish counterparts—took their lead from this Jewish allegorical interpretation and Christianized it, maintaining that the book is really about Christ's love for his church.

Both sets of interpretation have the virtue of being able to explain how something so highly charged and seemingly secular as this group of love poems could be considered part of the sacred text. The difficulty with both interpretations, however, is that they have wrenched the book out of its original context and ascribed some kind of other meaning to it, one that is more comfortable to this or that interpreter. The book, in fact, really does present a set of love poems, which celebrate sexual intensity and the erotic love that a woman and a man can have for one another when they are caught up in the throes of passion.

STORYTELLERS IN ANCIENT ISRAEL

Now that we have discussed some of the poetic books of the Hebrew Bible, we can turn to a different genre: the short story. We have, of course, seen lots and lots of stories already in the Pentateuch, in the Deuteronomistic History, and in Ezra and Nehemiah. It is difficult to differentiate those stories from the ones we will now consider, except to say that these here are told not in the context of a much longer narrative (as was the case, for example, with the tales of Abraham, Joseph, and Moses) but as freestanding compositions that begin and end within themselves. The closest analogy we have to the four books we will consider first— Ruth, Esther, Jonah, and Daniel chapters 1–6— would be a modern short story where there is a main character, a plot, and a resolution. After considering these four examples, we will consider one much longer narrative, found in the books of 1 and 2 Chronicles, an imaginative retelling of the history of the monarchy based on, but differing at key points from, that found in the Deuteronomistic History.

RUTH

One of the real gems among the books of the Hebrew Bible is the four-chapter book of Ruth, the tale of a Moabite woman married to and then widowed by an Israelite man, who then uses her wits, determination, and sexuality to ward off desolation. In the English Bible, the book appears in the middle of the Deuteronomistic History, even though it was originally not a part of it, because the opening verse indicates that its action took place "In the days when the judges ruled" (1:1). But it was written sometime after the Deuteronomistic History was produced; several words used in this gripping narrative are borrowings from Aramaic, and so the book appears to have been written in the postexilic period, possibly in the fifth or fourth century B.C.E. As with the other books we are considering in this chapter (apart from Jonah) it is found in the Hebrew Bible among the Kethuvim.

Among the distinctive features of this account is the fact that the main character is a woman—an unusual phenomenon in the Hebrew Bible, and striking for any reader who has read through the stories of Genesis, Exodus, Joshua, Samuel, and Kings (where the lead characters are almost—though not entirely—always men). Even more, this woman is not even an Israelite. She is from Moab, and for much of the Bible that was not good news. According to the Torah, the Moabites were not allowed to enter the "assembly of the Lord" even up to the tenth generation (Deuteronomy 23:3). In other words, even if a Moabite wanted to join up with the people of Israel (e.g., by converting to worship Yahweh and follow his Torah), he or she was not allowed to join in worship with the Israelites. And you may remember the attitude of Moses toward the idolatrous Moabites in Numbers 25:1–5.

The story of Ruth presents a Moabite in a different light. Ruth is a woman from Moab who enters into the land of Israel, converts to worship the God of Israel, is highly rewarded for her courageous (if slightly scandalous, by some modern standards) action, and in fact is destined to become the great-grandmother of one of the greatest Israelites of all, King David. In case we have not yet noticed it, this would be a good time: the Hebrew Bible is an extremely diverse collection of books with a wide range of perspectives on a large number of topics!

Overview of the Narrative

Because of a famine in the land of Israel, an Israelite man and his wife—named Naomi—along with their two sons migrate to Moab. The man dies, and then the two sons marry Moabite women, one of whom is Ruth. Both husbands die and that leaves the three women alone, with no male protection, in a world where it was very hard indeed to make a living if you were a woman. The story will be all about how they survive. Or at least how two of them do.

Naomi tells her widowed daughters-in-law to return to their parents' homes where they can be fed and protected by their families and can possibly remarry; she herself will be returning to Israel in hopes of finding a way of surviving there. The one daughter-in-law does as she is told, but Ruth refuses to do so with probably the most memorable statement of the narrative: "Do not press me to leave you or to turn back from following you! Where you go, I will go; where you lodge, I will lodge; your people shall be my people and your God my God" (1:16).

This moving statement of absolute devotion has its effect. Naomi and Ruth travel together, back to Naomi's home town of Bethlehem. But they need to find a way to survive. There was a tradition in ancient Israel (allegedly; whether it was actually observed historically or not is another question) that farmers were not to harvest all of the crops in their fields but were to leave some for the poor to collect for food (see Leviticus 19:9; 23:22; Deuteronomy 24:19). Naomi sends Ruth into the fields of a man named Boaz, who is a distant relative on her late

husband's side, where she gleans some of the crops. As fate (and good storytelling) would have it, Boaz notices Ruth and takes a shine to her, telling her how she can glean the most produce. When she returns home with her gleanings, she talks with Naomi and tells her how she has fared. Naomi then hatches an idea to make life much better for the two of them.

That night there is to be a kind of gathering at Boaz's threshing floor where they will be winnowing some of the barley, and then eating and drinking. Naomi advises Ruth to wait until Boaz has eaten and drunk (or rather, gotten drunk) and has gone down to sleep, and to go up to him and "uncover his feet." This is a euphemism in Hebrew, where "feet" refers to the genitals. It means that she is to initiate a sexual encounter with him. (See Box 7.3.)

Ruth does as she is instructed, the sexual encounter takes place, and Boaz decides he wants to marry her. The final chapter of the book describes the action that he undertakes to make it happen. This final episode relates to a procedure known as "levirate marriage"—similar to, but not identical with, the one mapped out in the Torah (Deuteronomy 25:5–10). In the legislation of Moses, if a man was married and he happened to die without producing an heir, his own brother was to marry the widow and any heir that was born would then carry on the name of the dead brother. That way his name would not die out from among the people. This is not exactly what happens in the book of Ruth, but the story depends on a similar line of thinking: Boaz is related to Ruth through Naomi's dead husband. But he is not the closest relative. And

---

BOX 7.3 RUTH'S SEDUCTION OF BOAZ

Different cultures, using their different languages, use different euphemisms for sexual organs. In older English literature, for example, a man's penis is sometimes referred to as his "member." Hebrew had its own euphemism for genitals. They were called "feet." You can see this in the Hebrew Bible. In Isaiah 6, for example, the prophet has a vision of the Seraphim next to the throne of God, who have six wings: with two they covered their eyes, with two they covered their "feet," and with two they flew. It makes sense that they would have wings to fly with, and that they would cover their

eyes in the presence of the one who is holy and who is not to be stared upon. But why cover their feet? They are covering their genitals, out of humility, in the presence of the divine.

When Ruth comes up to Boaz while he is asleep in the dark on the threshing floor, and "uncovers his feet," she is not exposing his toes. She is making a sexual advance. And she is fully welcomed; they spend the night together and then she sneaks off before it becomes light so that no one will know. Ruth was bold and daring and willing to take a risk. And it paid off in a very big way.

the closest relative is the one who is by law to have the first opportunity to marry her. Only if he refuses can the option move on to someone else.

And so Boaz meets the unnamed closer relative and offers the option of marriage to him. That one turns it down. This allows Boaz then to proceed with his plan. As he announces to the elders of the people "I have . . . acquired Ruth the Moabite, the wife of Mahlon, to be my wife, to maintain the dead man's name on his inheritance, in order that the name of the dead may not be cut off from his kindred and from the gate of his native place" (Ruth 4:10).

They marry, and Ruth conceives and bears a son, an heir. They name him Obed. He eventually was the father of Jesse, who was the father of David. Ruth, the forsaken woman of Moab, is then in the ancestral line of King David. Everyone interested in the monarchial line of ancient Israel can be happy indeed to know that the little incident that took place one dark night on the threshing floor in Bethlehem turned out so well.

Overarching Points of the Narrative

As with all short stories the book of Ruth is meant to provide an entertaining narrative, and it certainly does that. But it also is trying to make a number of points for its readers. The reader is most forcefully struck with the importance of family relations and personal devotion and commitment played out in the various scenes of the story: Ruth's commitment to Naomi; Naomi's concern for Ruth; Boaz's love for Ruth. This is a story about the power of personal relations and how interpersonal bonds can bring unity and hope out of desolation and potential despair.

In terms of ancient Israelite religion, this is a text that runs counter to the idea that only those who are related by blood to the descendants of Jacob (Israel) can be members of the covenant that God made with his people. Even converts who are committed to following the ways of God can enjoy the blessings of the covenant. Historically, it has sometimes been thought that the story is meant to oppose those who rejected any possibility of intermarriage between Judeans and foreigners (cf. the book of Ezra, written at about the same time). Here an intermarriage works very well indeed—in fact, it produces the line of Judeans leading up to the greatest king in the nation's history.

But above all this is an entertaining story of an enterprising and committed woman who uses her intelligence and sexuality to bring about her deliverance from destitution and her elevation, even, to a secure, respected, and prosperous life.

ESTHER

The book of Esther is another short story with a woman as the main character, and it too is about an intermarriage of a Jew and a non-Jew. But in this case it is Esther who is the Jew; her husband is a pagan figure of rather grand importance. He is, in fact, the King of Persia.

This book is one of a collection from the Hebrew Bible known as the "Five Scrolls." (See Box 7.4; all

---

BOX 7.4 THE FIVE SCROLLS

Ruth is one of the five books of the Hebrew Bible known in Jewish tradition as the **Megillot**, or "the five scrolls." In the order of their appearance in the Jewish Scriptures, these five are Song of Songs, Ruth, Lamentations, Ecclesiastes, and Esther. They are grouped together in the tradition because each of them is a short book that was read during special festivals during the Jewish calendar:

- Song of Songs during the Passover feast;

- Ruth during the Feast of Weeks;
- Lamentations on the ninth day of the month of Ab, which commemorated the destruction of the Jerusalem Temple;
- Ecclesiastes at the Feast of Tabernacles (called Sukkoth); and
- Esther at Purim (for reasons we will see later in this chapter).

FIGURE 7.3. A fresco depicting a scene from the book of Esther. She is on the far right; on the horse is her uncle Mordecai, who is approaching King Ahasuerus, who is sitting on the throne. The fresco was discovered in a synagogue in the city of Dura-Europas in northern Syria, and comes from the third century.

of these, obviously, are in the Kethuvim.) As with the other short stories, the book of Esther is difficult to date, but as its action takes place during the period of the Persian empire it is certainly post-exilic, probably from the fourth century B.C.E. It tells the story of a Jewish queen who saves the entire Jewish people from destruction. As such, it provides us with the first recorded attempt of a foreign power to destroy the Jewish people in an act of genocide. In this case we are dealing with a fiction. With later stories we will not be so fortunate, as they often involve real historical events.

There is almost nothing to suggest that Esther is describing an actual set of historical events. Among other things, the main characters—King Ahasuerus, Queen Esther, her cousin Mordecai, and the arch-villain Haman—are absent from any historical record. And there are gross historical inaccuracies (apart from making someone named Ahasuerus the King of Persia; it is often thought that the reference is to King Xerxes, ruler from 486–465 B.C.E.; the two names appear to be related etymologically); the

good Jew Mordecai is said to have been exiled from Judea to Babylon, but the action of the plot in which he figures appears to be set a century later.

The story of Esther is longer and the plot more involved than the simple tale of Ruth. It starts with King Ahasuerus, who is snubbed at a banquet by his queen, Vashti, and who decides to put her aside. A search is made throughout the empire for the most gorgeous female specimens (as they appear to be considered on this royal meat market), who are, in a sense, allowed to try out to be queen. As fate would have it, one of those chosen is the young Jewish woman Esther, cousin of Mordecai who raised her from childhood. Among all those brought into Ahasuerus's harem, it is Esther who pleases him most. She becomes queen.

Then begins the key subplot. A Persian official named Haman is elevated in the bureaucracy of the king, and relishes the attention he receives from all his underlings. Mordecai, who hangs around the palace gates, refuses to bow down before Haman and this makes the Persian official very mad indeed.

In order to strike a blow to Mordecai's impudence, Haman plots "to destroy all the Jews, the people of Mordecai, throughout the whole kingdom of Ahasuerus." Haman's people cast a "pur"—that is a "lot" (kind of like rolling dice)—to determine when the foul deed will be done. They settle on a date, and Haman convinces the King that the Jews are a disobedient people who need to be obliterated in toto. In his ignorance of the real situation, Ahasuerus agrees and letters are sent throughout the provinces "to destroy, to kill, and to annihilate all Jews, young and old, women and children" on the appointed date. The king, obviously, does not realize that his queen is a Jew. Just as obviously, she does not do anything—such as keep kosher or observe the Sabbath—to make him suspect. In other words, she is not following the Torah or doing anything different from any other women in the palace (except, presumably, sleeping with the king more regularly).

Mordecai impresses upon Esther the need to intervene with the king, since not only their people but they themselves will be targeted in the slaughter. Through a series of episodes Esther uses her charm, good looks, and talents to make the king open to granting her requests. When it comes out that she herself is a Jew and that Haman is a rotten fellow indeed, Ahasuerus has the bad guy hanged (on the gallows that Haman had built for his Jewish enemy, Mordecai) and rescinds the orders to have the Jews killed. In fact, more than that, Ahasuerus authorizes the Jews to attack and kill all of their enemies. And they do so.

From that day on, we are told, the Jews celebrated this great deliverance of the people from destruction in the annual festival of "Purim," thus called because of the "pur" (the lot) that was cast to determine the time of their annihilation—which, thanks to the interventions of Esther, never took place.

Purim is still celebrated by Jews today, even though, as I pointed out, the entire story of the book of Esther is a fiction, not a historical narrative. Obviously the annual celebration has taken on new and far more poignant meaning in our post-holocaust world. (As an example, see Elie Wiesel's book, *The Trial of God*.) It is commonly thought that Purim did not originally derive from this historical event of the attempted extermination of Jews by the King of Persia (since that is a fiction), but that the story of the attempted extermination of the Jews was invented as a way of explaining where the joyous festival itself came from. It is important to note that within the story, Ahasuerus agrees to have the Jews exterminated *not* because he considered them an inferior or dangerous race (as in modern forms of anti-Semitism, including those of Nazi propaganda), but because they were thought, as a people, to be disobedient to the king's laws. There is a big difference. If you break laws, you can be reformed and start keeping the law. If you're an inferior human being because of your race, there's not a sweet thing you can do about it.

One of the most startling features of the book of Esther is that even though it is about the protection and salvation of the Jewish people from certain destruction, there is almost nothing Jewish about the story per se. By that I mean that unlike all the other narratives we have considered (think of the stories of Abraham, Joseph, Moses, Ezra, even Ruth), there is no reference to the Jewish Ancestors, to Moses, to the Torah, to the covenant, or to Jerusalem in this book. Even more, God is never mentioned. Not once! This has startled not a few readers.

At the same time, the narrative can easily be read as providentially, divinely driven. Without God being mentioned, one can easily think of God as working behind the scenes, through human action, to protect and deliver his people. In this case he does so through a woman's bold and daring use of her good looks, sexuality, and influence.

JONAH

Of the various short stories found in the Hebrew Bible, Jonah is no doubt the best known of all. As it happens, the book is not located among the Writings, as are the other short stories we are considering. Jonah is one of the Minor Prophets, included among "the Twelve" in the Hebrew Bible. To some extent that makes sense, since the book is about Jonah making predictions of a coming destruction brought by God against a sinful people—a motif that we saw repeatedly in the other prophets. Moreover, the main character, "Jonah son of Amittai" (1:1) is named as a prophet in 2 Kings 14:25, where he is reported as having pronounced to King Jeroboam II that his kingdom would be largely extended. But the book of Jonah is not itself a book of prophecy. It is a short story about a prophet—one who was reluctant to do God's bidding, was punished for it, learned from the error of his ways, went on to make the proclamation that God demanded him to make, and then was bitterly disappointed when his preaching was effective. Jonah is the only prophet we know of who complained to God when people actually did what he told them to do: repented and turned to God. But his chagrin is understandable: he was told to preach to the city of Nineveh, capital of the hated Assyrians, and since they repented God decided not to destroy them. Nothing could be worse from the point of view of a hard-core advocate of Israel. It is not known when this story was produced, but it is probably post-exilic.

The four-chapter book of Jonah is straightforward and simple in plot. God tells Jonah to go preach to the people of Nineveh, and Jonah decides instead to head the opposite direction to Tarshish—possibly a city in Spain, about as far from Assyria as one could get without falling off the face of the earth. God is not one to have his will thwarted, however, and he raises up a storm at sea that scares the daylights out of the sailors manning the ship. When they discover that Jonah is at fault, they do as he tells them and toss him overboard. And that is when, obviously, he is swallowed by the big fish (which, for what it's worth, is not called a whale).

The prayer that Jonah prays in the belly of the fish, over the course of his three nights and days, is in fact a psalm, and it appears to many interpreters to have been written independently of the story for another occasion and inserted here, where a prayer to God was needed and this poem was ready to hand. The author who interpolated the psalm clearly saw enough similarities between the psalmist's prayer and the situation that Jonah had found himself in, especially in the psalm's opening lines:

> I called to the LORD out of my distress
> And he answered me;
> Out of the belly of Sheol I cried,
> And you heard my voice.
> You cast me into the deep,
> Into the heart of the seas,
> And the flood surrounded me;
> All your waves and your billows passed over
>   me. (Jonah 2:2–3)

It should be remembered, however, that Hebrew poetry is highly metaphorical and its symbolic language should not be taken literally. When this author speaks of being overwhelmed by the sea, he is speaking of how inundated he is in his troubles. He is no more literally in the ocean than he is literally in Sheol. Nor, as he says later, is he literally at "the roots of the mountains" or in the "land" or in "the Pit." These are all metaphors for just how bad it has gotten for him. Evidence that this is not a prayer originally composed for Jonah is that his own particular predicament is not mentioned. There is

BOX 7.5 JONAH IN LATER INTERPRETATION

Few people can read the book of Jonah without having some kind of mental image of the great fish spewing Jonah up on shore. This in fact became a standard image in early religious art, especially early Christian art, where it is one of the most common images found in the earliest Christian paintings. That is not because Christians were interested in the book of Jonah in its own historical context. On the contrary, it was because Christians thought that Jonah prefigured Jesus himself. Just as Jonah was in the belly of the great fish for three days and nights, to all intents and purposes dead to the world before being "brought back to life," so too was Jesus buried in the ground for three days and nights before reappearing alive to the world.

This comparison of Jesus and Jonah was not the creation of Christian artists starting in the second or third century, however; it is firmly rooted in the Gospels of the New Testament, where Jesus himself is said to have proclaimed the "sign of the prophet Jonah" would be the only sign given to those who refused to believe in Jesus—"for just as Jonah was in the belly of the sea monster for three days and three nights, so will the Son of Man be in the heart of the earth for three days and three nights" (Matthew 12:40).

FIGURE 7.4. Graphic picture of Jonah being thrown overboard and swallowed by a great fish (or sea monster?), from a mosaic in Aquileia in southern Italy.

no word here about being stuck in the belly of a fish. What the original author of this psalm is most concerned about is being able again to see God's holy Temple (2:4), a matter of no concern to the Jonah of this story. Probably, then, the author came upon this psalm, thought it was usable for his task, and inserted it into what is now chapter 2 of his story. In the context of the narrative, the prayer has its effect (even though it is not a prayer); God gives orders to the fish and it spews Jonah up on the dry land.

From there, to make a short story shorter, Jonah is told again to go preach the coming destruction to the people of Nineveh; he does so; they heed his call and repent of their sins; God then relents and no calamity is forthcoming. And Jonah (ch. 4) is really upset. God has a lesson to teach Jonah, though, and brings a bit of suffering on him (his shade bush is killed by an act of God) to convince him that it is only right that if Jonah is concerned for his paltry little discomfort, God can be concerned about a great city with so many people in it.

There are numerous lessons that an ancient reader might take away from this terrific little story. Here again we have a prophetic emphasis that God is not the God only of Israel but of all nations, and that he has power over all, even over that mighty world empire, Assyria. Moreover, God is portrayed as a God of mercy who really prefers not to enter into judgment but to extend his mercy to all who repent, even if they are the worst of enemies. This message no doubt rankled not only Jonah but his Judean hearers, who knew full well that Israel and Judah were destroyed and who believed that it was by an act of God, who was angry with his people of for sinning and *not* repenting. This account also shows—better than those of the real historic prophets, since here we are dealing with fiction—that the prophetic word can be powerful indeed. Jonah needs only say the word, and the entire city of Nineveh repents and turns to Yahweh. But most of all the story shows that no matter what, God's will cannot be thwarted. When he wants the people of Nineveh to hear his message, they will hear it, even if Jonah does his level best to keep it from happening. God is in control of all things, and his purposes will be achieved.

DANIEL 1–6

The book of Daniel is counted among the Major Prophets of the English Bible, but in the Hebrew Bible it is not one of the prophets at all; it is included in the Writings. This is almost certainly because it was the last book of the Hebrew Bible to be written (as we will see later), and when it came to be placed in circulation and more widely known, the collection of Latter Prophets was already considered to be a closed canon, containing, like the Former Prophets, four scrolls: Isaiah, Jeremiah, Ezekiel, and The Twelve.

In some respects it makes sense that Daniel is included as a book among the prophets in English Bibles, both because the main character is portrayed making prophetic utterances and because he has visions of prophetic importance. But in another sense this book is very different from the other prophets of the Jewish Scriptures. Daniel is not a historical figure who makes real-time proclamations to the people of Israel in light of their dire situation and almost certain coming destruction. The first six chapters of the book are a collection of short stories of a wise young man Daniel, taken to Babylon after the destruction of Jerusalem. The final six chapters contain a number of apocalyptic visions that Daniel allegedly had. There are good reasons for thinking that these two portions of the book originated separately from one another as different traditions associated with this person Daniel, and that they were put together only after both had been in circulation

for a time. One of the most obvious reasons for thinking so is that they are in fact of different genres of literature.

I will reserve discussion of the second half of this book for chapter 8, where I deal with the rise of apocalyptic thought within ancient Israel. Within Daniel 7–12 we find the first full-fledged instances of Jewish "apocalypses," a genre I will define at the appropriate time. For now we will focus on Daniel 1–6, the short stories associated with this famous, though fictional, character and several of his close friends in their lives together in a foreign land. These stories are obviously post-exilic, as they are all about life in exile. They are probably to be dated to the fourth or third century B.C.E. One of the peculiarities of the book is that, as happened with the book of Ezra, the language shifts partway through. Daniel 2:4b–7:28 is not in Hebrew but in Aramaic.

The Stories of Daniel 1–6

The opening chapters of Daniel tell many of the most popular stories still taught to children today, including the Three Youths in the Fiery Furnace and Daniel in the Lion's Den. The context for these and the other stories is set at the outset of the narrative, where we have a two-verse summary of the first wave of captives brought back to Babylon by King Nebuchadnezzar in 597 B.C.E. during the reign of King Jehoiakim of Judah (incorrectly dated by Daniel 1:1 to the third year of his reign; that is, 606 B.C.E.). Several of the most promising Israelite youth of royal blood are brought to be servants in the king's palace, and that is the setting for the stories that follow in next six chapters:

- The faithfulness of Daniel and his friends to the Torah (ch. 1). Daniel and his three friends, renamed Shadrach, Meshach, and Abednego (Daniel himself is renamed Belteshazzar, but I'll continue to call him Daniel) refuse to be defiled by the king's food and drink—apparently so as to keep kosher—and are allowed to experiment with a vegetarian diet. Not only do they not suffer from it, they thrive. They become the most prominent among the captives in the palace.
- Nebuchadnezzar's Dream (ch. 2). King Nebuchadnezzar has a bizarre dream, and when his own wise men cannot tell him what it is (a somewhat unreasonable demand, not only to explain what

FIGURE 7.5. Reconstruction of one of the gates of ancient Babylon discovered in the nineteenth century, called the Ishtar Gate, revealing the magnificence of the city; on the brick gate are images of dragons, bulls, and other creatures.

a dream means, but to say what it *was*), Daniel is brought in and tells the King both the dream and its interpretation. Kingdom of Babylonia will be succeeded by several others, after which God will bring in a kingdom that will never be destroyed. The King is amazed and rewards Daniel profusely.

- The Three Youths in the Fiery Furnace (ch. 3). Nebuchadnezzar builds a statue, and everyone is to bow down to worship it. Shadrach, Meshach, and Abednego refuse to do so and have to pay the prescribed price: they are thrown into an enormous and very hot fiery furnace. But they are protected by God, who sends his angel to allow them to escape unscathed, and the King is convinced that their God is truly God.

- Nebuchadnezzar's Second Dream (ch. 4). The King has another dream, and once again Daniel is brought in to interpret it. This one is about the King's own fate: although he is mighty, he will be humbled by God and driven out into the wilderness to live like an animal for seven years. This comes to pass, after which the king returns to power and devotes himself to the worship of the God of Daniel.

- The Hand Writing on the Wall (ch. 5). A new king of Babylon, Belshazzar, son of Nebuchadnezzar, throws a feast and a very strange event occurs: a hand appears and writes on the palace wall a brief but impenetrable message. Daniel is brought in and interprets the "writing on the wall": Belshazzar's kingdom is soon to end. That night Babylonia is overthrown by Darius, king of the Medes.

- Daniel in the Lion's Den (ch. 6). King Darius signs a law that anyone who prays to any god but himself will be cast into a den of lions. Daniel disregards the law, is captured by his enemies, and the king is forced to follow through, reluctantly, with the sentence. But miracle of miracles, Daniel is saved by God. Darius, in great relief, has Daniel's enemies thrown in, along with their wives and children, and they are torn to shreds. Darius issues an edict that everyone is to worship the God of Daniel.

There is no mistaking the fictional character of all these stories. Apart from their thoroughly miraculous character, they are filled with historical mistakes. Among the major problems: it is quite clear that the real king Nebuchadnezzar was never removed from his throne for seven years while he wandered around the wilderness living like an animal; he certainly never began to worship the God of Israel. There never was a son of Nebuchadnezzar named Belshazzar who ruled as the king of Babylonia. And the Babylonians were not conquered by a person named Darius, king of the Medes, but by Cyrus, King of Persia.

While it is easy for scholars to poke holes in the historicity of these accounts, their historical character is not really the point. They are stories—fictions created both for entertainment and in order to convey some lessons that the storytellers who told them wanted to teach. In a time when many former Judeans were living in exile—whether in Babylon or wherever else they may have escaped to after the destruction of their country—it was important to realize that they could still remain faithful to the God of their homeland. As I have mentioned before, this is something that made Jews distinctive in the ancient world. Most people, when they were transplanted to a new location, eventually adopted the cultural practices and religions of their new environs. Many Jews apparently did so as well (just as today there are Jews who have converted to the dominant religions where they live, or, say, in Europe and the United States, have become completely secular like so many other people). But others decided to remain faithful to the God of their homeland, even though they no longer lived there, and maintained their Judean

identity outside of Judea. This is what led to world-wide Judaism.

The stories of Daniel are, in part, meant to show that staying true to the traditions of the homeland was both desirable and possible. God was powerful not only in the land he had promised the ancestors. He was powerful throughout the world, and would reward those who kept the covenant even in difficult and trying circumstances. This was especially true when Judeans were located to other places, where it must have been difficult indeed to continue observing the Sabbath, keep Jewish festivals, follow the rules of kosher foods, and maintain other customs. The stories of Daniel show that they should nonetheless do so, and that doing so they would thrive. For God is not the God of Judea only; he is sovereign over all peoples and all lands, and is superior to the gods of all other peoples, even those of the great empires of the world.

1 AND 2 CHRONICLES

The books of 1 and 2 Chronicles are different from the short stories we have considered in this chapter. For one thing these books are not short, and their intent is not to tell fictional accounts about Jews and their adventures. The ostensible purpose of the books is to tell the history of Israel, and in fact to provide an alternative account of much of this history to that found in the Deuteronomistic History, on which these two books are based and which they very closely resemble. But in another sense the author of the work—the Chronicler, as he is called—provides an imaginative retelling of the story of the monarchy, and so I include it here as another instance of how stories in ancient Israel were sometimes told and retold.

As was the case with the books of 1 and 2 Samuel on one hand, and 1 and 2 Kings on the other, the two books of 1 and 2 Chronicles were originally a single book. They cover the same history as can now be found in 2 Samuel, 1 Kings, and 2 Kings, all of which served as the author's primary sources. Often his account is word-for-word the same as these books from the Deuteronomistic History. But there are key differences as well, that both reveal the author's creative impulses and that show what his distinctive emphases are.

For many years it was thought that the author of Chronicles also wrote the books of Ezra and Nehemiah. There are indeed significant parallels among these books. Today it is more commonly thought that despite their similarities, the differences are sufficient to indicate that the Chronicler was in fact a different author.

He was obviously writing later than the Deuteronomistic Historian, since he utilized that work as a source. It is difficult to say, however, just how much later. He does mention Cyrus, the king of Persia, at the very end of his account (2 Chronicles 36:22–23), repeating part of the decree that is found in Ezra 1:1–3 that allowed the Judeans to return home. This provides a nice bridge to Ezra itself, which is, of course, the next book in the English Bible. But it also indicates that the Chronicler was writing after the destruction of the Babylonian Empire in 539 B.C.E., and probably considerably later than the first wave of returnees came back to the land. In the genealogy that the author gives of King David (more than any other author of Scripture, the Chronicler *loves* genealogies), he traces the Davidic line seven generations after Zerubbabel, the governor of Judea mentioned in the book of Ezra (1 Chronicles 3). This must at least take us into the middle or end of the fifth century. Moreover, the Temple cult is central to his understanding, so it seems likely that the Temple itself must have been up and running. All told, it appears that he was writing at the end of the fifth or beginning of the fourth century B.C.E.

In the English Bible, 1 and 2 Chronicles are counted among the historical books, after the Deuteronomistic History but before Ezra and Nehemiah. It is striking that in the Hebrew Bible they are not found among the Former Prophets but in the Writings. In fact, they occur as the final books of the Hebrew canon. This too suggests that they were written at a fairly late date.

The structure of the two books is straightforward.

- *The Genealogy of Israel*: from Adam to the Exile (1 Chronicles 1–9). I mentioned that the Chronicler loves genealogies, and here is the proof. This section is nine solid chapters of father–son relationships from the first human being to the Babylonian exile. That's one amazing genealogy. This is one of the most obviously distinctive features of Chronicles in relationship to the

Deuteronomistic History, which is prefaced with accounts of conquest and the period of judges, not with an extended genealogy.
- *The Reign of David* (1 Chronicles 10–29)
- *The Reign of Solomon* (2 Chronicles 1–9)
- *The Reign of the Judean Kings* (2 Chronicles 10–36)

One of the ways that 1 and 2 Chronicles has been studied by critical scholars over the years is by comparing its stories with those of 2 Samuel and 1 and 2 Kings, on which the Chronicler depended for most of his information. It is possible to see what the Chronicler has omitted from the stories he inherited, what he has added to them, and what he has altered. These changes can give a good indication of what this author wanted to emphasize (and deemphasize) in particular.

His omissions are particularly striking in the stories about David and Solomon. Reading the Deuteronomistic History, it was quite easy to discern not only the strengths and virtues of these two kings but also their problems, weaknesses, and missteps (some of them horrible missteps). It is striking that many of the negative stories about these two and their reigns cannot be found in the work of the Chronicler. Specifically, he has omitted, among other things, the following:

- David's civil war with Saul
- His adultery with Bathsheba
- His arrangement to have Bathsheba's husband Uriah killed
- The rape of Tamar by Amnon
- The rebellion and palace coup of Absalom
- The murderous instructions David gave from his deathbed to his successor Solomon
- Solomon's enslavement of Israelites for his construction projects
- Solomon's foreign wives and their bad effect on him
- Virtually everything about the kings of Israel (the north)

It is fairly simple to draw some general conclusions from the Chronicler's decision not to retell all these stories in particular. He is principally interested in Judah, not Israel, and he has a particular fondness for its two greatest kings, David and Solomon. They are in fact his heroes, and many of their negative characteristics and actions are simply deleted from the stories retold about them.

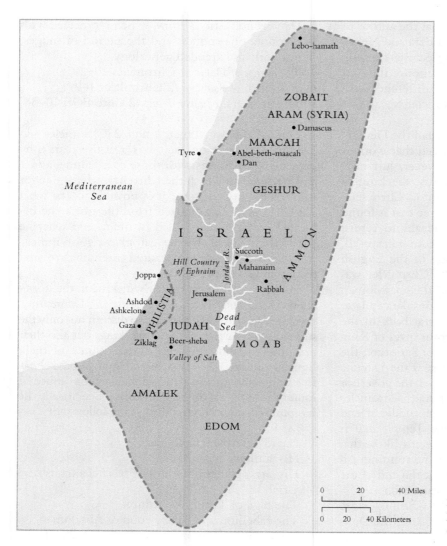

FIGURE 7.6. The kingdom of David as it is described in 1 Chronicles.

The Chronicler has also added some materials—in addition to the nine chapters of genealogy—to his account. Sometimes these come in large chunks, as in the extended information that he gives about the Levites in 1 Chronicles 22–29. This and the heightened emphasis on the Temple cult suggests that the Chronicler was particularly interested in the cultic life of Judea and the proper worship of God. It may be that in his own post-exilic community the refocus on proper cultic practices was seen to be particularly important.

At other times the additions come in small but instructive pieces. As an example: the author of 2 Kings looked upon King Manasseh of Judah as one of the worst monarchs ever to sit on a throne. He reversed the reforms of Hezekiah, rebuilt the shrines to pagan deities, erected altars for Baal, put up altars to other gods in the Temple itself, made his own son a human sacrifice, practiced soothsaying and augury, and, in short, in the somewhat understated opinion of the Deuteronomistic Historian, "Did much evil in the sight of the LORD" (2 Kings 21:2–6). The Chronicler agrees in his account that Manasseh did these wicked things. But in this case God judged him directly; he doesn't die without having to pay a price for what he does, as in 2 Kings. The LORD allows the king of Assyria to take him captive; and oddly enough (for some unexplained reason) he takes him into exile in Babylon.

But what is more striking, while in captivity Manasseh repents, prays to God for forgiveness, and

God restores him, sending him back to Jerusalem to be king once more. This appears to be designed to explain why, after all the evil Manasseh did, he was not ultimately punished by God, and why there was a delay in divine vengeance on Judah. There had been repentance and forgiveness.

There are other places where the Chronicler has simply altered a tradition that he inherited from the Deuteronomistic History. The most famous instance occurs in 1 Chronicles 21:1, when David makes a census of the people of Israel. God is deeply displeased with David for doing this and punishes him heavily for it. Apparently God wanted David to trust in divine power for deliverance from his foreign enemies, not in the size of the army he could field. What is striking is that the same story can be found in 2 Samuel 24, but there it is specifically the Lord himself who incites David to make the census—and then punishes him for doing so! And so, in the case of 2 Samuel, God takes out his wrath against Israel by forcing David to do something that was against the divine will. All of that appears to have been too theologically messy and convoluted for the Chronicler (why would God force you to do something he didn't want you to do?). And so he changed the account. According to 1 Chronicles 21:1 it was Satan who motivated David to take the census.

We are not told who Satan is in this passage. You will have noticed that Satan is remarkably absent throughout almost the entire Hebrew Bible. But we will see him again in our discussion in chapter 8.

The term "Satan" is a translation of the Hebrew SATAN, which literally means "adversary." In the book of Job he is the angelic being who stands in an adversarial relationship with the people of God (see also Zechariah 3). He appears to be understood in a similar light here. It was an evil, or at least an adversarial, power that drove David to do what he did, not the Lord God himself.

We can draw several overarching conclusions about what the Chronicler has achieved in this re-writing of the history of the monarchy. He is principally interested in the "glory days" of Judah. The northern kingdom of Israel scarcely figures at all in his account; not even its destruction by the Assyrians is mentioned. In particular the author wants to tell the story of the two great kings of all Israel, David and Solomon, in glowing terms, as he presents them without their character flaws and heinous acts (adultery, murder, despotism, and so on). In part, David and Solomon are celebrated for their roles in making sure that the Temple and its cult could come into being, and the cultic life of Judah is especially emphasized. Like his predecessor the Deuteronomistic Historian, the Chronicler saw that it was apostasy from the proper worship of Yahweh that led to the downfall of the nation. More than the Deuteronomist, however, he stressed the importance of personal sin and personal suffering, where the wrath of God falls not only on the nation as a whole but also on individuals within it.

At a Glance: Hebrew Storytelling

Although stories are told throughout the historical books of the Hebrew Bible—the Pentateuch, the Deuteronomistic History, Ezra–Nehemiah—there are several books that present self-contained stories of a highly fictionalized nature. Ruth tells the tale of a widowed Moabite woman who boldly uses her wits and sexual attractions to preserve her Judean mother-in-law and herself from desolation. Esther relates the story of the Jewish queen of Persia who uses her wiles and her great influence to prevent the annihilation of the Jewish people. Jonah is the story of a reluctant prophet of God who is punished for

disobedience by being swallowed by a great fish, only to be regurgitated and then to engage in a successful preaching mission—much to his own chagrin. Chapters 1–6 of Daniel relate the adventures of the young and talented Judean exile Daniel in the courts of Babylon, along with his three Judean friends who remain faithful to the God of Israel in very trying circumstances. 1 and 2 Chronicles represent a retelling of the story of the Judean monarchy that celebrates the great qualities of its kings—especially David and Solomon—while downplaying many of their shortcomings.

Take a Stand

1. You have a roommate who insists that the Bible's major concern is to convey *facts*—facts about God, about human sin, about salvation. As you have read through the poetry of the Hebrew Bible you have become convinced that the "facts" are not always the point, and that there is a lot more going on in the Bible than, for example, teachings about doctrine. Try to convince your roommate.

2. Your friend from high school has read some of the poetry and short stories discussed in this chapter and tells you that some parts of the canon are not clearly "religious" in any traditional sense. Do you agree or not? Explain your views.

3. Choose either Ruth, Esther, or Jonah and, in writing, discuss the features of the text that make some scholars argue that it is a work of fiction rather than a historical narrative. Next, explore the question of whether it is possible for fiction to convey important religious ideas, or whether it is only history that is important to religion, based on your understanding of the text you selected.

Key Terms

Doxology, 170   **Megillot**, 179   **Psalm**, 168

Suggestions for Further Reading

NB: For this and all chapters, see the relevant articles (e.g., "Psalms," "Esther") in the works cited in the Suggestions for Further Reading in chapter 1.

Alter, Robert. *The Art of Biblical Poetry*, 2nd ed. New York: Basic, 2001. A study of the literary features of the poetry of the Bible by an important modern literary critic.

deClaissé-Walford, Nancy. *Introduction to the Psalms: A Song from Ancient Israel*. St. Louis: Chalice, 2004. A thorough and detailed examination of the Psalms, written from a Christian perspective.

Levine, H. J. *Sing unto God a New Song: A Contemporary Reading of the Psalms*. Bloomington: Indiana University Press, 1995. A discussion of the Psalms from a modern, Jewish perspective.

Walsh, Carey Ellen. *Exquisite Desire: Religion, the Erotic, and the Song of Songs*. Minneapolis: Fortress Press, 2000. A refreshing and entertaining look at the Song of Songs, emphasizing its erotic character.

Wills, Lawrence M. *The Jewish Novel in the Ancient World*. Ithaca: Cornell University Press, 1995. A study of ancient Jewish fiction, including the stories of Daniel and Esther, and several deuterocanonical books.

8

Wisdom and Apocalyptic Literature

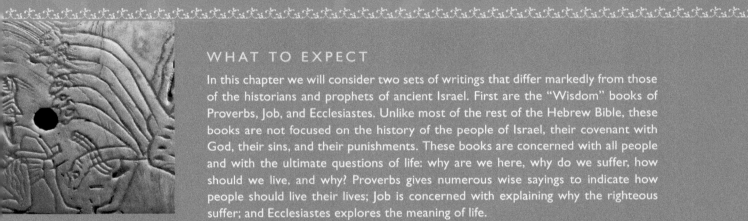

WHAT TO EXPECT

In this chapter we will consider two sets of writings that differ markedly from those of the historians and prophets of ancient Israel. First are the "Wisdom" books of Proverbs, Job, and Ecclesiastes. Unlike most of the rest of the Hebrew Bible, these books are not focused on the history of the people of Israel, their covenant with God, their sins, and their punishments. These books are concerned with all people and with the ultimate questions of life: why are we here, why do we suffer, how should we live, and why? Proverbs gives numerous wise sayings to indicate how people should live their lives; Job is concerned with explaining why the righteous suffer; and Ecclesiastes explores the meaning of life.

Next is the apocalyptic tradition that developed out of prophecy but differed from it in stressing that the people of God suffer not because God is punishing them for their wicked deeds but because there are forces of evil in the world aligned against God who are wreaking havoc here on earth. But God will very soon intervene to destroy these enemies and bring in a good kingdom. This view is first set forth in its fullest form in the visions of Daniel 7–12.

The historical books and the prophets of the Hebrew Bible share among themselves many of the same perspectives about God, history, the covenant, what it means to be Israel, and how God reacts to those who do not obey his expressed will. But as we have already seen, the Hebrew Bible is an incredibly diverse book with a wide range of perspectives and understandings about these and very many other matters. This diversity comes to particularly clear expression in the two types of writings we will consider in this chapter: books of wisdom and apocalypses. In their own ways—differently from one another—these types of writing present perspectives that can be seen as biblical alternatives to the dominant paradigm found throughout the Torah and the Prophets, both Former and Latter. We begin by considering the books categorized as "Wisdom": Proverbs, Job, and Ecclesiastes.

INTRODUCTION TO THE WISDOM LITERATURE

At the outset I should provide a working definition of the books known collectively as "Wisdom." These are books that focus on understanding the world and on how best to live in it, based on an intelligent assessment of life rather than on divine revelation to Israel.

To understand the foci of these books, it might be useful to summarize some of the distinctive features of the historical and prophetic literature of the Hebrew Bible. These features, in broad terms, apply to books as wide-ranging as Exodus, Joshua, 2 Samuel, Amos, and Ezekiel—in fact, to just about all of the books we have considered so far (even, to a limited extent, the poetry and most of the short stories). These are some of the major concerns of all that literature:

- God's actions, both in the world generally and among his own people in particular
- The history of Israel as the people of God
- The covenant or covenants God has made with his people
- The Torah, or direction/instruction he has given them (through Moses)
- Divine revelation, where God reveals himself directly to chosen humans
- National concerns; that is, an intense interest in the people of Israel specifically
- Communal orientation: the ultimate concerns are for the whole people of Israel, even if individuals are also important within that collective

We will see that the books of Proverbs, Job, and Ecclesiastes are very different from one another; but one thing that binds them together is that they lack almost completely these various concerns of the historical and prophetic writings. These books simply are not interested in God's historical acts (with the Israelite ancestors, at the Exodus, with the judges and kings, etc.), the history of the people of Israel, the covenant God has made with them, the Torah—and all the rest. These books have a different orientation and focus that include the following (these are broad generalizations, but they should serve to give the idea of how this literature differs from the other):

- Universal needs, desires, and lives, rather than national ones. Here the nation of Israel, its history, its governance, its accomplishments, its missteps, and its punishments are not in view; the concern instead is with what it means to be human and with people in general, not just with the people of Israel.
- Observation rather than revelation. The writer closely observes the world to see how it works,

and he does not acquire his understanding from a divine revelation that has been given.
- Individual rather than communal focus. The Wisdom literature focuses on the individual person, rather than his or her community. How can you, as an individual, understand the meaning of life or how to live it?
- Multicultural rather than Israelite. Wisdom traditions can be found in many cultures, both ancient and modern—and in many instances these traditions are very similar to one another, cross-culturally; there is nothing specifically Israelite at the heart and core of the Wisdom traditions of the Hebrew Bible (apart from the fact that even these books acknowledge the lordship of Yahweh; but there is little in them about Israel per se).

Of the Wisdom books found in the Hebrew Bible, one, the book of Proverbs, may be considered a representative of what we might call "positive wisdom." This is the more typical form of wisdom both within Judaism and cross-culturally. Positive wisdom attempts to describe the general orderliness of the world and to explain how people should live in accordance with it. Job and Ecclesiastes have a contrary emphasis and can be labeled "skeptical wisdom." These are writings that lament the world's lack of order, or the impossibility of understanding the world, and they try to explain how best to cope with life in light of this impossibility.

PROVERBS

We start by considering the one example of positive wisdom in the Hebrew Bible, the book of Proverbs. Proverbs contains a large number of "wise sayings" meant to express an understanding of the world gained by experience and maturity; implied throughout is a not-so-subtle claim that if people live the right way, life will be very good, happy, and prosperous.

General Character and Assumptions of Proverbial Sayings

By definition, a **proverb** (whether in the book of Proverbs or anywhere else) is a pithy and profound saying that encapsulates a distinctive understanding of the world and/or how best to live in it. We all are familiar with numerous proverbs from our own world: "A penny saved is a penny earned"; "a bird in the hand is worth two in the bush"; "a stitch in time saves nine."

There is a range of assumptions lying behind most proverbs. For one thing, there is a better way to live. It is better to be wise than foolish, better to be rich than poor, better to be respected than despised, better to be happy than miserable, better to be righteous than wicked. Moreover, proverbs typically embody a simple view of causes and effects. Proverbs tend to assume that the world works in a certain way, and that it is best to know what that is in order to lead happy, prosperous, and successful lives and to avoid failure, poverty, and despair.

All of this is not to say that God is left completely out of the equation in the book of Proverbs. This particular collection of wise teachings is, after all, part of the Bible, and God is indeed present in it, if only, in most cases, as a rather remote presence. Early on the book stresses that "The fear of the LORD is the beginning of knowledge" (1:7). And so these pearls of wisdom are understood to be set out within a context of commitment to the ways of Yahweh.

Because proverbs, by their very nature, tend to be universal statements about how the world works, there are very few datable observations in them. How can we possibly know when sayings such as the following were composed?

> Whoever diligently seeks good seeks favor
> But evil comes to the one who searches for it.
> Those who trust in their riches will wither,
> But the righteous will flourish like green
>   leaves. . . .
> If the righteous are repaid on earth,
> How much more the wicked and the sinner!
>   (11:27–28, 31)

These could have been composed at just about any period of history. There are, however, a number of proverbs that refer to kings—and presumably the author has in mind the kings of Israel and/or Judah. This would indicate that they, at least, derive from no earlier than monarchial times.

It is true that some of the Proverbs are attributed to specific authors and that we should, then, be able to provide a rough date for their composition based on these attributions. Sometimes King Solomon is said to be the author of this book—as 1:1 itself states

"The proverbs of Solomon son of David, king of Israel" (see also 10:1 and 25:1). Solomon as a great composer of wise proverbs goes back to the statement in 1 Kings 4:29–34, where the Deuteronomistic Historian, in his paean to Solomon's great wisdom, indicates that "he composed three thousand proverbs, and his songs numbered a thousand and five." Scholars today tend to think that it was precisely this tradition of Solomon as "the wisest man who ever lived" that led to the attribution of the book of Proverbs to him, even though much if not all of the book must date to a much later time in the history of Israel. In any event, it is worth noting that there are other attributions in the book as well: some of the book is attributed to "the Wise" (22:17; 24:23), and to Agur son of Jakeh (30:1), and to a King Lemuel (31:1). We have no idea who these other people were. And we have no idea who actually did compose the sundry proverbs found throughout the book.

Divisions of the Book and Its Poetic Character

The book of Proverbs divides itself into three distinct units:

1. *Several Wisdom Poems and Two Women* (chs. 1–9)
   • The book begins by calling on its readers to pursue wisdom and to follow the author's sage advice. Typical of its admonitions are the following:

   > Listen, children, to a father's instruction
   > And be attentive, that you may gain
   >   insight.
   > For I give you good precepts:
   > Do not forsake my teaching. . . .
   > Get wisdom; get insight: do not forget
   >   nor turn away
   >   from the words of my mouth.
   > Do not forsake her, and she will keep
   >   you;
   > Love her, and she will guide you.
   > Prize her highly, and she will exalt you;
   > She will honor you if you embrace her.
   >   (4:1–2, 5–6, 8)

   • Included in these opening poems are accounts of a "Strange Woman" and "Woman Wisdom"

- The passage about the Strange Woman (7:1–27) describes a young man who does not follow the path of wisdom but is sexually seduced by a Strange Woman; the reader is warned not to "turn aside to her ways" for "numerous are her victims" and "Her house is the way to Sheol, going down to the chambers of death."

- Historically far more significant has been the poem devoted to Woman Wisdom (8:1–36) (See Box 8.2.) Here wisdom is personified as an actual being, a woman created by God at the very "beginning of his work," who was with God before the creation of the heavens and the earth, and in fact was his daily companion as he created the universe. To know Wisdom, therefore, is to know the one that has always been in the presence of God and, by implication, was instrumental in forming the world to become what it is. And so,

Whoever finds me finds life
   And obtains favor from the LORD;
But those who miss me injure themselves;
   All who hate me love death. (8:35–36)

2. *Pithy Proverbs* (chs. 10–30). The bulk of the book consists then of one wise saying after the other; these are for the most part randomly collected and presented, with no context or organizational scheme. In a sense, they do not need a context since they are meant to be universally valid.

3. *Concluding Poems involving Two Women* (ch. 31). The book ends with the advice given by the mother of King Lemuel and with an acrostic poem that celebrates the ideal, good wife.

As we can see in the various proverbs already quoted, the sayings in all three major sections of the book are presented in poetic lines, and the various forms of parallelism discussed earlier are present here as well. There are numerous instances of synonymous parallelism:

Therefore walk in the way of the good
   And keep to the paths of the just.
For the upright will abide in the land
   And the innocent will remain in it. (2:20–21)

But more often than in the book of Psalms there are abundant instances of antithetical parallelism, as these proverbs often contrast the good and the wicked, the wise and the foolish, the rich and the poor, and so on:

The LORD's curse is on the house of the
      wicked,
   But he blesses the abode of the righteous.
Toward the scorners he is scornful,

BOX 8.1   BEATING YOUR CHILDREN: PROVERBS FROM ANOTHER LAND

In liberal child-rearing circles in our day and age, "spanking" a child is very much looked down upon and even condemned. Not so in many ancient societies. As a demonstration that ancient "Wisdom" differed very much, in places, from modern, and yet was at times remarkably consistent from one ancient culture to the next, consider the following passages taken from the book of Proverbs in the Hebrew Bible and the Assyrian text, "The Words of Ahiqar" from the eighth or seventh century B.C.E.:

PROVERBS

Do not withhold discipline from a young man; if you beat him with the rod, he will not die.

You should beat him with the rod, and you will save his life from Sheol (Proverbs 23:13–14)

THE WORDS OF AHIQAR[1]

Spare not your son from the rod;
Otherwise can you save him
   From wickedness?
If I beat you, my son,
you will not die;
But if I leave you alone,
you will not live (Ahiqar 81–82)

---

1   Taken from Michael Coogan, *Introduction to the Old Testament,* p. 471

But to the humble he shows favor.
The wise will inherit honor,
But stubborn fools, disgrace. (3:33–35)

Kinds of Proverbs

It is very difficult to delineate the different kinds of proverbs, but there are some differences among them and they can be broken down into these various types with the proviso that these are somewhat overlapping categories that are closely related to one another. It is impossible to draw hard and distinct lines between them.

1. *Observations.* Some proverbs simply make declarative statements about what life is like, based on the author's mature experience. For example:

   A wise child makes a glad father,
   But a foolish child is a mother's grief. (10:1)
   A fool takes no pleasure in understanding
   But only in expressing personal opinion. (18:3)
   House and wealth are inherited from parents,
   But a prudent wife is from the LORD. (19:14)

2. *Observation by analogy.* Sometimes these declarative statements take the form of a simile or analogy, of one thing to another:

   Like a gold ring in a pig's snout
   Is a beautiful woman without good sense. (11:22)
   Like a dog that returns to its vomit
   Is a fool who reverts to his folly. (26:11)
   A continual dripping on a rainy day
   And a contentious wife are alike. (27:15)

3. *Observation based on cause and effect.* Sometimes the observations imply a direct cause-and-effect relationship between a certain kind of action or characteristic and the result, good or bad:

   The righteous are delivered from trouble
   And the wicked get into it instead. (11:8)
   Whoever is steadfast in righteousness will live,
   But whoever pursues evil will die. (11:19)
   The hand of the diligent will rule,
   While the lazy will be put to forced labor. (12:24)

4. *Religious observations.* Some of these proverbs indicate that the cause-and-effect relationship is actually determined by the Lord himself; others simply urge a right standing with God.

   The LORD does not let the righteous go hungry,
   But he thwarts the craving of the wicked. (10:3)
   The good obtain favor from the LORD,
   But those who devise evil he condemns. (12:2)
   Those who mock the poor insult their Maker;
   Those who are glad at calamity will not go unpunished. (17:5)

5. *Normative observations.* Other proverbs are somewhat more direct in giving advice about how to live, either by implication or explicitly.

   When words are many, transgression is not lacking,
   But the prudent are restrained in speech. (10:19)
   Those who are kind reward themselves,
   But the cruel do themselves harm. (11:17)
   A generous person will be enriched
   And one who gives water will get water. (11:25)

All in all, these proverbs are meant to present wise observations on how the world works and sage advice about how best to live one's life in it. They tend to be unnuanced and clear-cut: do this and that will happen to you; live this way and this is what you can expect. They are based on years of experience and wisdom.

And yet, one can easily see that life is not always that simple or cut and dried. That was obvious, at least, to the authors who produced the books we are calling "skeptical wisdom," as we now will see.

JOB

The view of "positive wisdom," such as that found in Proverbs, is that if a person lives the right way and does the right things, she or he will succeed in life and be happy and prosperous. In some instances this appears to be imagined simply as "the way the world works." In other instances, the world appears to work that way because that is how God has set it up.

BOX 8.2 WOMAN WISDOM AS GOD'S CONSORT?

We have seen that in ancient Israel Yahweh was sometimes thought to have a divine consort, his "Asherah" (see p. 154). This was never accepted by the strict henotheists who wrote the historical and prophetic books of the Hebrew Bible; but in Proverbs, a book of Wisdom, there is a passage that some interpreters have thought represents a kind of modified or "tamed" view of Yahweh and his divine female companion from eternity past. Here she is not Asherah, but Wisdom herself, shown to be speaking in Proverbs 8:

The LORD created me at the beginning [or "as the beginning"] of his work,
   the first of his acts of long ago
Ages ago I was set up,
   at the first, before the beginning of the earth. . . .
When he established the heavens, I was there. . . .
When he made firm the skies above,
   when he established the fountains of the deep. . . .
Then I was beside him, like a master worker;

And I was daily his delight,
   rejoicing before him always,
Rejoicing in his inhabited world
   and delighting in the human race.

Later Christians would take the feminine companion of God at creation, "Wisdom" (Greek "Sophia"—a feminine noun, and sometimes regarded as a feminine deity) and transform her into the masculine "Word" (Greek: "Logos"—a masculine noun) and claim that this one in the beginning, who was with God, and was the one through whom God created all things, was in fact Christ before he became an incarnate human (see John 1:1–4). The difficulty for both Jews and Christians involved understanding how this other being (Sophia/Logos) could be divine, if in fact there is only one God. For the Christians, it is this puzzle that eventually led to the development of the doctrine of the Trinity: that even though God is manifest in three persons (Father, Son, and Holy Spirit—not one person, but three), there is still only one God (not three). This doctrine would not begin to be formulated clearly, however, until at least a century after the writing of the New Testament.

This is very similar to the view that the prophetic literature assumes on the national scale. When the nation of Israel does what God wants it to do, it thrives—politically, economically, militarily, and in every other way; but when it strays from the ways of God, judgment is sure to come and in very nasty ways: drought, famine, disease, war, political collapse, military disaster, and complete destruction. The solution is obviously never to stray from the path God has laid out, and life will be very good indeed.

The problem that some thinkers in ancient Israel had with both positive wisdom and the assumptions underlying classical prophecy is that the world simply does not seem to work the way it is supposed to. We will later see that Jewish apocalypticism arose in response to the prophetic optimism that following the ways of Yahweh would lead to peace and prosperity (apocalypticists realized that, in fact, that was not true). With the book of Job we see an attempt to counter these views as well. On an individual level, the bland and sanguine affirmations of proverbial wisdom simply do not stack up well against reality as

it is experienced in this world. It is certainly not the case that those who are righteous are the ones who have all the wealth and happiness. Quite the opposite: sometimes it is precisely the righteous who suffer, and suffer very badly indeed. In its reflections on this issue, Job provides us with arguably the most profound attempt to grapple with the problem of suffering from all of antiquity.

The "problem of suffering" is a perennial problem, especially for those who believe that there is a good and powerful God who is in control of this world. If he is, why is it that the righteous suffer? One can understand why sinners suffer: God must be punishing them. But if God is in control, and he is able to accomplish whatever he desires, and he desires only what is good for his people—why do his people suffer, especially when they do what he has asked them to do? This is a problem that has numerous solutions to it—some of which are probably occurring to you right now, as you think the answer is all too obvious. But to deep thinkers the answer has never been obvious, and the obvious answers are probably not the right answers.

The Enigma of Job

One of the difficulties that most readers have with Job—possibly without realizing that they are having the problem—is that they do not realize that this book is not simply the work of one author with one consistent view of how to explain the problem of suffering, specifically the suffering of the righteous. The book in fact has two separate parts to it, and scholars have long recognized that these two parts almost certainly come from two different authors writing at two different times. And, most important, these two authors had two different views of how to deal with the problem of suffering. When someone later combined their two writings into one larger piece, it created all sorts of havoc for interpreters, since the beginning and ending of Job (both of these are from one author) support a different view of suffering from that of the middle (which is from the other author).

On one level it is obvious that the beginning and end of the book (chs. 1–2; 42:7–17), on one hand, and the extensive middle on the other (3:1–42:6), are quite different from one another. Just look. The book begins and ends in a prose narrative about the righteous man Job who is compelled to undergo unspeakable suffering; the middle is in poetry and deals with conversations that Job has with four of his "friends" (whose reactions to Job seem anything but friendly).

There are very good reasons for thinking not only that there are two different genres of literature represented in these sections (a short story at the beginning, a poetic set of dialogues taking up the middle, and then a resumption of the short story at the end), but that these sections actually come from two different authors. Among other things, the names used to describe the deity are different between these parts: the personal name Yahweh occurs in the narrative prose; the names preferred in the poetry are God (*El* and *Eloah*) and Almighty (*Shaddai*). That is not a problem in itself, of course; but if you have two different genres of literature and two sets of names of God, you may be dealing with two different authors.

That is confirmed by the contrasts in the substance of what the two parts say. The parts are very different on two substantial issues. First is the portrayal of Job himself. In the story (at the beginning and end), Job bears with his suffering silently and patiently. He refuses to raise his voice or complain about his lot, but accepts it as coming to him from God for reasons he cannot understand. That portrayal of Job bears almost no relationship to the Job of the poetry. Here Job is anything *but* patient and silent. On the contrary, he is thoroughly impatient and demanding, loudly complaining about his unjust and unfair suffering, claiming that he has no right to have to suffer in this way, and demanding that God appear to him so that he can mount a self-defense in the face of the Almighty.

Second, the views of suffering—as we will see in greater detail in a moment—are also very much different from one another depending on whether you are reading the short story or the poetic dialogue. The short story is unambiguous about why Job is suffering: God is putting him to the test to see if he will remain faithful even when things go badly for him (through the machinations of the Satan figure). But that is not the view found in the poetic section, where Satan is not mentioned, a test is not referred to, and the need to remain faithful in the midst of pain and misery is not in view. In the poetry we learn that there is in fact no way we can understand why there is suffering, and that it is an affront to God even to pursue the question. Suffering is a big mystery. And God can do anything he wants. He is not to be challenged.

These are two different views of both Job and of how to deal with the question of suffering. The reason for the differences is that these two parts of Job come from two different authors, with two different perspectives. Someone later combined the two, leading to all sorts of confusion among readers who do not realize they are seeing two different perspectives. Here we will deal with each part, beginning with the author of the short story that begins and ends the book.

The Prose Narrative

The book begins by describing Job, who is not, as it turns out, an Israelite. He comes from the land of Uz, which appears to be a fictional place. Job nonetheless worships Yahweh and is unusually righteous and upright. As a result God has rewarded him handsomely. He has a large family—seven sons and three daughters—and an unbelievable number of sheep, camels, oxen, donkeys, and servants. He is so righteous that he not only makes sure that he himself never sins, but he regularly offers burnt sacrifices to God on behalf of his children in case any of them has sinned.

One day the "sons of God" come up to God in heaven, including one called Satan. The term "Satan," as I've mentioned in chapter 7, means "the accuser" or "the adversary." Here he is not portrayed as in modern popular imagination as the devil who is the head of demons and is destined for (or is now ruling in) hell; here he is one of the members of God's divine council. But he is the one who stands in an accusatory or adversarial relationship with humans. And especially Job.

God brags on Job's blamelessness and righteousness, and Satan replies that just about *anyone* would be that righteous if he could get so many goods out of the deal. God does not think so: he claims that Job is righteous because that is the right thing to be. Satan argues that if God were to make him suffer, Job would turn on him. And so God tells Satan to take away everything Job has, but not to hurt him physically. This is almost like a supernatural bet, to see if Satan can get Job to turn on God.

And he does his level best. Job has all of his goods plundered—all those oxen, donkeys, sheep, and camels. All of his servants are put to the sword. And all ten of his children are killed in a violent storm. Does Job, then, blame God? He obviously could do so, since God is the one, after all, who told Satan to do all this. But no, Job suffers in humility and submission: "the LORD gave, and the LORD has taken away; blessed be the name of the LORD" (1:20).

In the next scene the sons of God (= angelic beings), including Satan, appear before God once more, and God again boasts of Job's integrity. Satan argues that it is because he has not had to feel the suffering in his own body; if Job were afflicted physically, he would curse God. Once again God tells Satan to afflict Job, but to spare his life. And Satan inflicts "loathsome sores on Job from the sole of his foot to the crown of his head." Job scrapes the pus off his skin with a piece of pottery, and his wife tells him to "curse God and die." But he refuses: "Shall we receive the good at the hand of God, and not receive the bad?" (2:10). He is willing to suffer if it is God's will, and he will not question why God is doing this to him, or complain.

Three friends then come to Job: Eliphaz, Bildad, and Zophar. They can barely recognize him. They weep aloud and go into mourning, sitting with Job for seven days and nights, not saying a word but simply sharing his suffering with him. And that's where the story breaks off, before we launch into

FIGURE 8.1. Job being tormented by Satan, from a thirteenth-century stained glass window in Strasbourg, France.

the poetic dialogues of Job and his "friends" that take up most of the next thirty-nine chapters, written by a different author.

It is only in chapter 42 that the story resumes. Something has obviously fallen out of the text when the action picks up, because the Lord is angry with something the three friends have said, and tells Job to perform a sacrifice and pray for them. Afterward, since Job has passed the test and not questioned or cursed God, he is highly rewarded. In fact, he gets twice as much as he had before: sheep, camels, oxen, and donkeys. And he gets seven new sons and three new daughters. (See Box 8.3.) He goes on to live a long life, and he dies a happy man.

The view of suffering set forth in this story is rather simple. Sometimes suffering comes as a test from God to see if a person will remain faithful, even when things are going bad—or even very, very bad. Satan should not be seen here as an evil being who is the cause of all misfortune. He is one of the sons of God, a member of God's divine

BOX 8.3 DOES GOD MAKE IT ALL UP TO JOB?

For many readers the ending of Job makes a lot of sense—except one altogether important part. After Job has passed the "test" and remained faithful to God despite his enormous sufferings, according to the short story, God rewards him, giving him back twice the possessions that he had lost—twice as many sheep, donkey, and oxen. And he replaces his seven sons and three daughters with seven other sons and three other daughters.

But wait a second! It makes sense that you can replace livestock—even double your holdings. But can you replace *children*? If you lose a child, is it all made better by having another one? Does this mean that God can allow Satan to murder ten children, and make it up to Job later simply by replacing them later ("Don't worry: it was just a test!")? For many readers this is one of the most disturbing ideas in the entire Hebrew Bible.

council, who afflicts Job only because God tells him to do so. He is doing God's work, and there is one purpose behind it, and it is not to make Job miserable just for the sake of it. It is to see whether Job's faithfulness to God is driven by a desire for a good life and many possessions, or whether it is disinterested, a faithfulness that will stay strong even when put to a severe test. Suffering sometimes comes from God, this story is trying to teach, simply in order to see if we will remain faithful. And if we do, we will be rewarded even more.

It's a nice story, even if it does not ring true with how the world appears actually to work. But more important, the lesson it teaches about suffering is quite different from the lesson conveyed by the poetic dialogues in the middle of the book by a different author.

The Poetic Dialogues

Since the same characters appear in the poetic section of the book as in the prose narrative, either the author of the poetry was familiar with the story in a written form or there were various accounts of Job and his friends floating around in oral circulation in ancient Israel. Along with Bildad, Zophar, and Eliphaz, a fourth friend comes to be introduced as well into the poetic section, a man named Elihu.

I have a called this large middle section a "poetic dialogue." That is because, obviously, it is set in poetry and because it involves a discussion between Job and his friends, whose friendly advice is actually filled with animosity and condemnation. The dialogue involves a series of complaints by Job (who never complained in the prose narrative; in fact, the point of the narrative is that he never complains),

each one followed by a response by one of the friends. Job complains that he does not deserve what he is getting, and the first friend responds by telling him that he in fact probably does deserve it; Job complains again, the second friend responds similarly; Job complains again, the third friend responds. Then that sequence is repeated two more times, so that the chapters present a series of three different rounds of complaints and responses. The third round, unfortunately, got muddled a bit as scribes copied this long book over the centuries. In the third round of complaints and responses, Bildad's speech is only five verses long and Zophar's speech is missing altogether; and, most remarkably, Job himself starts arguing precisely *for* the position that in the rest of the book he has been arguing *against*. It appears that (by scribal error) Job has been given Zophar's speech, and a few other things got messed up in the process.

After these rounds of complaints and responses, we have the new friend Elihu introduced, who launches into a speech embracing the same themes and sentiments as the three friends, but for six entire chapters (chs. 32–37). It is widely thought that this section was inserted into the poetic dialogue by a by yet another author, who felt that the friends had not cinched their points well enough and decided to have a go at it himself, at length.

In the course of his own complaints and self-defenses, Job has declared that he wants an audience with God in person so that he can defend himself and show that his suffering is not deserved or fair. At the end of the dialogue, when all the speeches have been made, God shows up, in a big way, as the overwhelming Almighty Lord of All that he is, and lectures Job (chs. 38–41). Job then gives a weak and humbled response (42:1–6), and the poetic section then ends.

JOB AND HIS FRIENDS IN DIALOGUE

We can get a sense of all the back and forth, and a good idea of what the various adversaries think—Job on the one side, his friends on the other—by looking at the first round of complaints and responses. Job begins by cursing his life and wishing he had never been born:

> After this Job opened his mouth and cursed
>   the day of his birth. Job said:
> Let the day perish in which I was born
>   And the night that said,
>   A man-child is conceived. . . .
> Why did I not die at birth,
>   Come forth from the womb and expire?
> Why were there knees to receive me
> Or breasts for me to suck? (3:1–3, 11–12)

Eliphaz is the first to respond. He does not do so kindly but suggests that Job is not innocent and that his suffering in fact is deserved:

> Think now, who that was innocent ever
>   perished?
> Or where were the upright cut off?
>   As I have seen, those who plow iniquity
>   And sow trouble reap the same
> By the breath of God they perish
>   And by the blast of his anger they are
>   consumed. (4:3–5, 7–9)

Eliphaz goes on like this for two chapters. He tells Job to repent and God will restore him. But Job doesn't want to hear it. If he has done something wrong, he deserves to know what it is; in his view he is suffering even though he is upright. And God will not leave him in peace, but is constantly at him, forcing him to suffer:

> Then Job answered. . . .
> Teach me, and I will be silent,
>   Make me understand how I have gone
>   wrong.
> How forceful are honest words!
>   But your reproof, what does it reprove?. . .
> But now, be pleased to look at me;
>   For I will not lie to your face. . . .
> Is there any wrong on my tongue?
>   Cannot my taste discern calamity?
> When I say, say "My bed will comfort me,
>   My couch will ease my complaint,"

> Then you scare me with dreams
>   And terrify me with visions
> So that I would choose strangling
>   And death rather than this body. . . .
> Will you not look away from me for a while,
>   Let me alone until I swallow my spittle?
>   (6:24–25, 28–30; 7:13–15, 19)

Bildad then tries to have a go at Job, attacking him (the one suffering!) for his empty words, and insisting that if Job is suffering, it is because it is what he has deserved:

> How long will you say these things,
>   And the words of your mouth be a great
>   wind?
> Does God pervert justice?
>   Or does the Almighty pervert the right?
> If your children sinned against him,
>   He delivered them into the power of their
>   transgression (8:1–3).

A nice thing to say to someone who has just lost ten children in a tragic accident. Bildad goes on to tell Job to repent and things will be right with him. Job responds (chs. 9–10) by declaring that he knows he is innocent (9:15), but that he is simply too weak as a mortal to be able to contend with God, who would not listen to him even if he had the chance: "For he crushes me with a tempest, and multiplies my wounds without cause." If God were to appear to him, Job would be forced by his almighty presence to declare himself guilty even though he knows full well that he is innocent and blameless (9:16–20).

It is then Zophar's turn, and now he is getting angry, repeating the other friend's charges and laying it on thicker still: "Know then that God exacts of you less than your guilt deserves" (11:6). And on he goes. . . .

Zophar's speech ends the first round. Two more are to follow, with more of the same. Job is innocent and knows it; his friends assume that he cannot be and tell him so, urging him to repent. But Job has nothing to repent of. He really is innocent, and really does not deserve this suffering.

SOME OF THE KEY STATEMENTS OF THE DIALOGUE

There are a number of striking comments throughout these speeches. For one thing, Job does not take the view that his suffering will ultimately be vindicated, that all will be made right in the end, in the afterlife. According to this book there is no afterlife: death is the end of the story.

> As waters fail from a lake
>   And a river wastes away and dries up
> So mortals lie down and do not rise again;
>   Until the heavens are no more, they will
>   not awake
>   Or be roused out of their sleep. (14:11–12)

At times God's attacks on Job are portrayed in extremely violent and graphic terms.

> I was at ease, and he broke me in two;
>   He seized me by the neck and dashed me
>   to pieces;
> He set me up as his target;
>   His archers surround me.
> He slashes open my kidneys, and shows no
>   mercy;
>   He pours out my gall on the ground.
> He bursts upon me again and again;
>   He rushes at me like a warrior. (16:12–14)

Throughout it all, Job maintains his own integrity and refuses to confess to sins that he has not committed. His friends are wrong to say that he is suffering as he deserves. He in fact really is innocent:

> Far be it from me to say that you are right;
> Until I die I will not put away my integrity
>   from me.
> I hold fast my righteousness, and will not let
>   it go;
> My heart does not reproach me for any of my
>   days. (27:5–6)

Finally (this is before the insertion of the long speech by Elihu), Job resorts to appealing to God to appear to him so that he can plead his case to him in person:

> O that I had one to hear me!
> (Here is my signature! Let the Almighty
>   answer me!)
> O that I had the indictment written by my
>   adversary!
> Surely I would carry it on my shoulder;
> I would bind it on me like a crown;
> I would give him an account of all my steps;
> Like a prince I would approach him. (31:35–37)

As the saying goes, be careful what you ask for. God does appear to Job. But he doesn't give him a chance to answer or defend himself. Instead he appears in his Almighty Power and overwhelms Job with his Divine Majesty, choosing to reveal himself to Job out of a mighty whirlwind, upbraiding Job for all that he has said and for challenging God, who can do, and does do, whatever he chooses, since he alone is the Almighty:

> Then the LORD answered Job out of the
>   whirlwind:
> Who is this that darkens counsel by words
>   without knowledge?
> Gird up your loins like a man,
>   I will question you, and you shall declare to me.
> Where were you when I laid the foundation
>   of the earth?
>   Tell me if you have understanding?
> Who determined its measurements— Surely
>   you know!
>   Or who stretched the line upon it?. . .
> Have you entered into the springs of the sea,
>   or walked in the recesses of the deep?
> Have the gates of death been revealed to you,
>   or have you seen the gates of the darkness?
> Do you know the ordinance of the heavens?
>   Can you establish their rule on the earth?
> Can you lift up your voice to the clouds,
>   So that a flood of waters may cover you?
>   (38:2–5, 16–17, 34)

Job responds to this impressive show of divine power—God alone is Almighty, and Job is nothing in comparison—in humility: "See I am of small account, what shall I answer you? I lay my hand on my mouth" (40:3). But that is not good enough for God. He has another go at Job, again from the whirlwind:

> Gird up your loins like a man;
>   I will question you, and you declare to me.
> Will you even put me in the wrong?
>   Will you condemn me that you may be
>   justified?
> Have you an arm like God,
>   And can you thunder with a voice like
>   his? (40:7–9)

This goes on for another two chapters after which Job, overwhelmed, cowered, and unable to utter a word in his own defense, simply says,

I know that you can do all things
  And that no purpose of yours can be
    thwarted . . .
I had heard of you by the hearing of the ear,
  But now my eye sees you;
Therefore I despise myself,
  And repent in dust and ashes. (42:2, 5–6)

And that is where the poetic section ends.

Over the years scholars have proposed a wide range of options for interpreting this closing back-and-forth between God from the whirlwind and Job cowing down in awe before him. This interpretive decision is important, for in some sense the entire meaning of the poetic dialogue hinges on how we understand its climactic ending. One thing that is clear to all interpreters: the view of traditional wisdom is wrong; it is not the case that only the wicked suffer and the righteous prosper. Job really was innocent, and yet he suffered. But why? The answer depends on how we understand God's awesome appearance at the end and Job's response. Among some of the leading options of interpretation are the following.

- Job finally gets what he wants (in a good way): an encounter with God. This interpretation is true to a point, but the problem with it is that Job does not *actually* get what he wants, which is a chance to plead his case before God. God never gives him the chance, since he doesn't even let him talk and he certainly does not care to hear what Job might have to say.
- Job realizes his guilt before God after all, once God appears to him. The problem with this perspective is that Job does not seem to realize that he is guilty, just that he is a mere mortal. Job never admits to doing anything wrong—since in fact he hasn't done anything wrong—but only of having thought that he could make his case before God.
- Job comes to see that he has to put his individual problems in a global perspective, that compared with the massive issues facing all of creation his worries are of little moment. The problem with this point of view is that it assumes that it is in fact acceptable for Job to suffer, since he is just a tiny part of the huge created order. But this is not at all what God says, and it seems to run counter to the point of the whole book.

- Job comes to recognize that God has too much on his hands, with an entire universe to manage, to worry about his own individual suffering. The difficulty with this interpretation is that it is not true to the rest of the book, either. The problem has not been that God has been absent from Job's life, tending to the rest of the world; he has been far too present in Job's life—he won't leave him alone and punishes him even though he is innocent, having done nothing wrong.
- What is the solution to the poetic dialogue then? The key to the solution may be that Job desperately craves an answer to the question of why he is suffering, and yet God never gives him an answer. Read through God's two speeches. He never *does* explain why all this has happened to Job. He does not say that Job has simply gotten what he deserved (as the friends kept insisting), or that it has been a test of his faith (as in the prose narrative), or that it is all Satan's fault, or anything else. He gives no answer. Instead he informs Job that he, God, is the Almighty who cannot be questioned by mere mortals, and that the very quest for an answer, the search for truth and understanding, is an affront to him and his divine prerogatives. God is not to be questioned, and reasons are not to be sought. Anyone who dares to challenge God will be withered on the spot, squashed into the dirt by God's overpowering presence, forced to "repent" of even wanting to know the answer in the first place. The answer to suffering is that there is no answer and we should not expect to find one. To do so is an affront to God.

In the end, we are left with a view of suffering that other authors of the Bible would obviously object to (including the author of the prose narrative that begins and ends the book). Is it true that God can torture, maim, and murder with impunity because he is God? For no discernible reasons? And that if God does it, it is right? Does ultimate might make ultimate right? And are we, as mortals with intelligence and a sense of right and wrong, not allowed even to try to understand, even to ask why?

As with other books of skeptical wisdom, the book of Job leaves its readers with more questions than answers.

ECCLESIASTES

The book of Ecclesiastes is another example of skeptical wisdom, but it is a very different kind of book from Job. Here the dominant question is not about why the innocent suffer, or even about suffering at all, per se; it is about how to make sense of this world. We have seen that the writers of Proverbs—not to mention the historians, prophets, and poets we have read—seemed to understand the world. It made sense to them; there was a coherence to it, a logic to it, a divine purpose behind it all. But other people have never felt that way. For them, it is hard to understand why the world is the way it is, why things happen the way they do, why we should strive to be good—or even strive to be rich, or intelligent, or influential. What is the meaning of life? Why are we here? What will happen to us when we are gone? For anyone who refuses to settle for easy answers to these questions, the book of Ecclesiastes is a treasure trove. Here is an author who admits that he doesn't know the answers—although he very much wants to ask the questions. And in the end he decides that even if ultimate meaning is beyond our grasp, we should enjoy our lives as much as we can, for as long as we can. Because we won't live long; and once we die, we will not live again.

Like the book of Proverbs, the author of this book was allegedly Solomon. Unlike Proverbs, however, in this case the author goes out of his way to convince his readers that he really is Solomon. Ironically, he does so without ever calling himself by name. But he does indicate that he was the "son of David" and that he was the "king in Jerusalem" (1:1). Moreover, he portrays himself as exceedingly wise and fantastically wealthy. So he clearly is claiming to be Solomon. There is no way he actually was Solomon, however. The book appears to be dependent on philosophical traditions that we know about from around Hellenistic times (that is, when Greece was on the rise), and in its vocabulary are words that derive from Persian or Aramaic. So it was probably written in the fourth or third century B.C.E., at least 600 years after Solomon had been laid in his royal grave.

The name the author gives himself in Hebrew is Qoheleth (1:1). Unfortunately, it is not clear what the term means. It is sometimes translated as "teacher" or "preacher." It may mean, instead, something like "assembler"—that is, one who assembles wisdom.

Qoheleth wastes no time in communicating the thrust of his overall message to his reader, but gets right to it in 1:2:

> Vanity of vanities, says the Teacher (i.e., Qoheleth),
> Vanity of vanities! All is vanity.

The word translated "vanity" is the Hebrew word *hevel*. It is a little hard to translate into English. It refers to something that is transient, temporary, here just briefly before disappearing, of no lasting importance. It is the mist that floats just above the ground for a short while early in the morning and then is gone. Life is like that. It, and everything in it, is here briefly and then, before you know it, has vanished. And so the author rightly asks, "What do people gain from all the toil at which they toil under the sun?" (1:3). What is the point of working hard and earning good money? You die, and your money will no longer do you any good. Moreover, all knowledge of what you have accomplished will pass away. It is all *hevel*.

The world goes on and on and on, and nothing changes. There is nothing new. Everything comes, and goes, and comes back again (1:4–11). And so what, really, is the point of it all? Qoheleth very much wants to know: "I . . . applied my mind to seek and to search out by wisdom all that is done under heaven; it is an unhappy business that God has given to human beings to be busy with. I saw all the deeds that are done under the sun; and see, all is vanity and a chasing after the wind" (1:12–14).

For a while Qoheleth thought that the meaning in life could be learned by acquiring great wisdom. But then he realized that "this also is but a chasing after the wind"; in other words, a futile endeavor. Indeed, "in much wisdom is much vexation, and those who increase knowledge increase sorrow" (1:18). And so he wondered if the purpose of life lay in abundant pleasure. He built great works, houses, vineyards, gardens, and parks to enjoy. He gave himself every pleasure that money can buy. But at the end of it all, he realized that pleasure too "was vanity and a chasing after wind" (2:11).

The ultimate problem is that no matter how much wisdom you gain, or how many possessions

BOX 8.4 THE AFTERLIFE IN THE BIBLE

Many readers of the Bible are surprised to learn that the ideas of the afterlife in the Hebrew Bible are not closely related to what most people think today. The idea that after you die, your soul goes either to heaven or hell (or even purgatory), is not an idea rooted in the Jewish Scriptures. The few passages that refer to an afterlife in the Hebrew Bible assume that after death, a person goes to "Sheol." That is not the Hebrew equivalent of "hell"—a place of punishment for the wicked. It is the place where everyone goes, good or evil. It is sometimes spoken of as a place of rest (remember how Samuel was not pleased at having his rest disturbed in I Samuel 28); but as a rule it is not thought of as a pleasant place (think of all the horrors associated with going to Sheol in the book of Psalms). It is a shadowy kind of netherworld that everyone goes to when they die, like it or not.

Other authors of the Hebrew Bible deny that there is any afterlife at all, and indicate instead that death is the end of the story (see Job 14:11–12; Ecclesiastes 9:3–6).

As we will see, in the New Testament the dominant view is the idea of the future resurrection of the body, where people are brought back into rejuvenated bodies to have an eternal existence here on earth. (See Box 12.4.) This is based on the Jewish apocalyptic view we will discuss later in the chapter. Here too, souls do not die and go to one place or other for eternity. (See Box 8.5.) This latter idea was a later development, made by Christian theologians after the Bible had been written (although of course, as good theologians they argued that their views were based on the Bible).

you accumulate, or how many pleasures you enjoy—in the end you die, and then you are no different from a miserable, impoverished fool: "the same fate befalls all . . . for there is no enduring remembrance of the wise or of fools, seeing that in the days to come all will have been long forgotten" (2:14, 16).

Moreover, Qoheleth finds no comfort in the traditional teachings of positive wisdom. In no small measure this is because in his experience, they simply are not true: "In my vain life I have seen everything; there are righteous people who perish in their righteousness, and there are wicked people who prolong their life in their evildoing" (7:15; see also 8:14); "Again I saw that under the sun the race is not to the swift, nor the battle to the strong, nor bread to the wise, nor riches to the intelligent, nor favor to the skillful; but time and chance happen to them all" (9:11–12).

And one should not think that it will all make sense in the by-and-by. For in fact we have no assurance of an afterlife in which all the wrongs of this world will be made right, with the righteous receiving their reward and the wicked their punishment: "Who knows whether the human spirit goes upward and the spirit of animals goes downward to the earth?" (3:21); or, as he states more fully later:

This is an evil in all that happens under the sun, that the same fate comes to everyone . . .

But whoever is joined with all the living has hope, for a living dog is better than a dead lion. The living know that they will die, but the dead know nothing; they have no more reward, and even the memory of them is lost. Their love and their hate and their envy have already perished; never again will they have any share in all that happens under the sun. (9:3–6)

What then is the solution to how we should live our lives? Shouldn't we just die and get it over with? Not for this author. On the contrary, since the ultimate meaning of life is elusive, and since death will end it all, there is only one ultimate answer. We should live life to the fullest, as long as we can:

There is nothing better for mortals than to eat and drink, and find enjoyment in their toil (2:24); This is what I have seen to be good: it is fitting to eat and drink and find enjoyment in all the toil with which one toils under the sun the few days of the life God gives us; for this is our lot (5:18); So I commend enjoyment, for there is nothing better for people under the sun than to eat, and drink, and enjoy themselves, for this will go with them in their toil through the days of life that God gives them under the sun. (8:15)

FIGURE 8.2. Repository of bones piled up in a tomb cut out of rock, from the ninth to the seventh centuries B.C.E. Such a sight would no doubt have confirmed to the author of Ecclesiastes that this life is fleeting and we should enjoy it while we can.

This is not a counsel of despair. It is a full and satisfying way to live life when the ultimate meaning of why we are here cannot be answered. But readers of Ecclesiastes have not always been satisfied with this message, considering it a bit too dismal and too far removed from the traditional religious views espoused in the rest of the Hebrew Bible. And so it is no surprise to see that some readers in the ancient world actually decided to alter what the author of this book had to say, by adding some verses that brought the book better into line with more typical ways of religious thinking (just as editors altered the book of Amos, or the prophecies of Isaiah, or the story of Job, etc.). In this case, a later editor added some words to bring God—rather than the fleeting pleasures of the good life—more into prominence, at the very end of the book:

The end of the matter; all has been heard. Fear God, and keep his commandments; for that is the whole duty of everyone. For God will bring every deed into judgment, including every secret thing, whether good or evil. (13:13–15)

This concluding message seems to run counter to the entire tenor of the rest of the book. By putting it at the very end, the editor provided a means for interpreting everything that went before it, which now is read in light of the fact that there is a judgment day coming. But that is not the view of Qoheleth himself. In his view we die and that is the end of the story. That is not a message that needs to lead to utter despair, however, for we are now alive and we should celebrate life and all the little pleasures that it brings, enjoying it to the fullest. Our life will not last forever. In fact, it won't last long. And it is all we have: there is no reward in the afterlife. So we should revel in our existence as much as we can, for as long as we can.

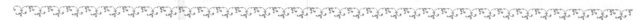

At a Glance: Wisdom Books

The books of Wisdom are not concerned with the history of Israel, the covenant God has made with his people, the sins they have committed, or the punishments they have suffered. These books are meant to have universal, not just national, Israelite, appeal, and they deal with the Big Questions of life: why we are here, why we suffer, how we are to live, and where we are to find meaning.

Proverbs is a book of "positive" wisdom, filled with wise sayings intending to direct the reader to live in the right way so as to be happy and prosperous. Job is a book of "skeptical" wisdom that calls into question the easy solution that says it is only the wicked who suffer. It is made up of two different books that have been spliced together: one says suffering can be a test from God to see if you will remain faithful in the midst of terrible misfortune, the other says suffering is a mystery and cannot be understood. A person does not have the right even to question God about it. The book of Ecclesiastes is also a book of skeptical wisdom; it maintains that life is short and fleeting, that ultimate meaning is hard to find, and so one should enjoy life as much as possible, for as long as possible.

APOCALYPTIC LITERATURE

Just as the Wisdom literature we have examined can be seen to run counter, in many ways, to the views assumed and set forth in the historical and prophetic books, so too with the Jewish traditions that scholars have called "apocalyptic." But apocalyptic literature is very different from what we find in the books of Wisdom, and is more properly to be understood as a development out of the prophetic tradition itself. These were developments that altered in significant ways the perspectives that the apocalyptic authors inherited from their forebears. In fact, apocalyptic literature can be seen as a reaction against the prophetic tradition that we have seen in book after book of the Major and Minor Prophets. As it turns out, the one place where the apocalyptic tradition is most clearly found is in one of the Major Prophets, the book of Daniel, the last book of the Hebrew Bible to be completed although some of its short stories may have been composed earlier. We have already considered the collection of these in Daniel 1–6. The rest of the book (chapters 7–12) contains a series of visions allegedly given to Daniel. These visions are prophetic to the extent that they are anticipating what is about to happen in the future; but they are very different from the prophetic perspectives otherwise found throughout the Hebrew Bible. To explain these differences I need to provide some background on the rise of Jewish apocalypticism.

The Rise of Jewish Apocalypticism

I can begin by giving a brief working definition of **apocalypticism**, to be supplemented by a fuller explanation of the phenomenon later. The term apocalypticism is based on the Greek word *apocalypsis*, which means an "uncovering," an "unveiling," or a "revelation." Jewish "apocalypticists" believed that God had revealed to them the heavenly secrets that could make sense of earthly realities. The short version is this: apocalypticists believed that God had shown them that there were forces of evil in control of this world, but that God was soon to intervene in history to overthrow these wicked powers and everyone who was aligned with them before bringing in a good utopian kingdom here on earth.

To make sense of this perspective—before fleshing it out more fully—it will help to provide a bit of historical information.

THE PROPHETIC PERSPECTIVE   We have seen that the classical prophets of the Hebrew Bible differed from one another in a number of ways—in the historical contexts that they addressed, in their manner of addressing them, and in the specifics of their messages. But there are certain common features that tie all the prophets together, especially with respect to their understanding of God, his reaction to Israel's failure to do his will, and the coming disasters that will occur as a result. If you were to ask a prophet like Amos, Isaiah, or Jeremiah why it is the people of God suffer, they would have a clear and ready answer. They suffer because God is punishing them for their sins. For Amos, that is why there have been droughts, famines, epidemics, and military defeats: God has been trying to get the people to recognize the error of their ways and to turn back to him. If they will do so, their suffering will end. But if they refuse, then even more massive destruction is coming. The prophets indicated that the military and political nightmares brought by the Assyrians and Babylonians were not the natural workings of history or the result of aggressive foreign policies as more powerful nations overran those that were weaker. They were the acts of God, punishing his people for their sins and unfaithfulness. If the people will repent, however, and turn back to him, he will relent, restore them into a good standing with himself, and the good times will return.

HISTORICAL CHALLENGES TO THE VIEW
In some ways the skeptical wisdom of a book like Job (in the poetic dialogues) is a reaction to this general view, that if you do what is wrong you will suffer but if you do what is right you will prosper. Job is concerned, however, about the individual sufferer as a person, not with the nation of Israel as a whole—the way, say, Amos, Isaiah, and Jeremiah are. So what happens when the entire nation does turn back to God, when it stops worshipping idols, when it works to relieve the suffering of the poor, the oppressed, and the helpless? What happens when the nation does what God instructs it to do—and it *still* suffers? In fact, suffers even more than it did when it was in defiant disobedience to God? What happens to the prophetic view then, when, based on historical reality, it appears not, in fact, to be right?

This was a question that Jewish thinkers no doubt pondered long and hard as the economic, political, and military success or failure of the nation appeared to bear no relationship at all to the question of its faithfulness to God and the Torah he had given. Matters especially came to a head during the Hellenistic period, specifically in the years leading up to the Maccabean Revolt as I sketched them back in chapter 6. If you'll recall, under Syrian rule, with the Seleucid King Antiochus IV, more commonly known as Antiochus Epiphanes, things got very bad indeed for those in Israel who wanted to remain faithful to God. Antiochus had a statue of Zeus placed in the Temple of Jerusalem, forced Jews to sacrifice to pagan idols, and made it illegal to circumcise Jewish boys or keep other aspects of the Law.

This was obviously a period of intense suffering for those wanting to keep their ancestral traditions as passed down from Moses to their own day. But how could one explain the suffering? The prophetic solution simply was not satisfying to many Jewish thinkers. The people of God were not suffering because they were worshiping idols, failing to keep the traditional rituals of Judaism, or oppressing the poor. They were suffering for just the opposite reason: because they were refusing to worship idols and were trying to keep the cultic and ethical laws of the Torah. There must be some other explanation.

And so Jewish thinkers came up with another explanation. It was not that God was punishing them. It was that there were other supernatural powers, opposed to God, who were punishing them. God was not at fault; his enemies were. For some reason, God had relinquished control of this world to evil forces who were determined to make life a living hell for God's people, and who were using the ruling authorities (such as Antiochus Epiphanes) to make it happen. That's why the Jews are suffering. But, according to this point of view, God had set a limit to the amount of time these forces of evil could exercise their power. And that time was almost up. God, very soon, was going to intervene in this awful state of affairs, reassert his sovereignty over the world and his people, destroy the forces of evil and the governments that they were using, and bring in a kingdom of God: one that he himself would run, through his own human intermediaries. God had "revealed" this to these Jewish prophets, the "apocalypticists" (as modern scholars call them).

This apocalyptic view contrasts with the prophetic view up and down the line. God is not making people suffer; the forces aligned against God are. The people are not suffering for doing wrong; they are suffering for doing right. The suffering will not end when the people repent; it will end when God destroys his enemies. (See Box 8.6.) This, in a nutshell, is the apocalyptic view. I can now spell out the various tenets of this world view in greater detail.

The Tenets of Jewish Apocalypticism
There are four major tenets held by ancient Jewish apocalypticists.

I. DUALISM.

Apocalypticists were dualists in the sense that they believed there were two fundamental forces in the world, the forces of good and the forces of evil. God, of course, was ultimately the power over all that was good. But according to apocalypticists, God had a personal, supernatural enemy, the devil. This is the period when Jews started thinking that the "Satan" figure, who showed up only a couple of times in the Hebrew Bible before, was in fact an evil power that was aligned against God and was his long-term opponent. Just as God had powers that did his bidding, so too did the devil. God had his angels, the devil had his demons. And there was more. There were other cosmic powers in the world. For example, there is the power of righteousness and the power of sin. There is the power of life and the power of death. In Jewish apocalyptic thinking, sin was not simply an act of disobedience against God. It was an actual demonic power in the world that was trying to ensnare people and force them to act in ways contrary to God's will. Death was not simply what happened to a person when the body ceased to function. It was an evil power that was trying to capture people; and when it succeeded, it annihilated them. The history of earth is the history of the battle between these forces of good and evil.

This cosmic dualism worked itself out in a kind of historical dualism as well. There are two ages of this world—the current age that we live in now, and the age to come. This age is the one that is controlled by the forces of evil. But in the age to come there will be no more evil. When God destroys all of his enemies, we will enter into this new age: one in which God will rule supreme, when there will be no more suffering, sin, or death. It will be a kingdom that will be ruled by God—the perfect age of peace, joy, and love.

2. PESSIMISM.

Jewish apocalypticists were not optimistic about the possibilities of life in this world. We live now in the evil age controlled by the devil and his minions. And there is nothing that we can do to improve our lot. We simply are not powerful enough. We are subject to the forces of evil, and they are gaining more and more power. We will not be able to make things better by any human effort. Things are only going to get worse and worse, until, at the end of this age, literally all hell breaks out. And when that happens, finally, God will intervene.

3. VINDICATION.

God will eventually reassert himself on this world and make right all that is wrong. He created this world and he is going to redeem it. He will vindicate his name and his people by destroying the forces that are aligned against him, the powers of evil such as the devil, the demons, sin, and death, in a cataclysmic act of judgment. Some apocalypticists believed that God would do this by sending a cosmic judge from heaven who would bring judgment upon the earth and personally overthrow all of God's enemies. And this included not only the supernatural powers at work in this world, it included everyone who has sided with them. All evil rulers, and in fact all evil people, will be destroyed at the coming judgment.

Moreover, this day of judgment would involve not only people living at the time. It would include both the living and the dead. It was the Jewish apocalypticists who developed the idea that at the end of the age there would be a resurrection of the dead, in which all people who have ever lived would return to their bodies and be brought back to life specifically in order to face judgment. Those who had sided with God and suffered as a result would be given an eternal reward; those who had sided with the powers of evil and become rich and influential as a result would be taken into eternal punishment. No one should think, then, that they can side with the wicked powers in charge of this world, prosper as a result, and then die and get away with it. No one can get away with it. God is going to raise everybody from the dead, and there is not a sweet thing anyone can do to stop him.

As you can see, this apocalyptic way of thinking was a kind of Jewish theodicy, an explanation for why there is so much suffering in the world if there is a good and powerful God in charge of it. For some mysterious reason God has relinquished control of this age to the powers that create such misery and suffering. But in the end, God will prevail and good will win out. In this way of thinking, evil does not have the last word; God has the last word. And death is not the end of the story. After death comes new life—and eternal reward for those who have remained faithful and suffered as a result. But when will this climactic moment in history happen,

BOX 8.5 RESURRECTION VERSUS RESUSCITATION

The idea of "resurrection" is an apocalyptic idea that did not exist before apocalypticists began to develop their thoughts in the years before the Maccabean Revolt. The driving force behind the idea was one of theodicy. The resurrection of the dead could make sense of all the pain and misery in the world, happening in particular among God's chosen people. This suffering was temporary. But God would reward his people by raising them from the dead and giving them eternal peace and joy. The wicked, on the other hand, would be raised bodily and face eternal torment.

You do not get that idea of a resurrection before Daniel (see Daniel 12:1–3). When people are raised from the dead earlier in the Hebrew Bible—for example, through the miracles of Elijah and Elisha in 1 and 2 Kings—it is assumed that they will die again. In other words, they have been resuscitated. But their bodies have not been transformed into an immortal substance, one that can live forever.

The idea of resurrection eventually became a common view in Judaism, and is at the very center of thought among the writers of the New Testament, who were themselves apocalypticists. When the early Christians said that Jesus was raised from the dead, they did not mean he had been resuscitated. They meant he had been resurrected—given an immortal body, never more to die. In fact, one can argue that without having an apocalyptic point of view, the early followers of Jesus would not have called his coming back to life a "resurrection," since apart from an apocalyptic perspective there was no such thing as resurrection.

this cataclysmic destruction of the forces of evil, this final resurrection of the dead?

4. IMMINENCE. Jewish apocalypticists maintained that they were already living at the end of the age. Things had gotten as bad as they could possibly get. The forces of evil were running rampant and there was no restraining them. But God had had enough. And he was soon to intervene in his mighty act of judgment. This would happen very soon. It was right around the corner. People who were suffering for the sake of righteousness should hang on and keep true to their faith. They will not suffer much longer. God, or his cosmic judge, sent from heaven, is soon to appear, and people will be rewarded for being faithful up to the very end. They just need to hold on for a little while. This is what God had revealed.

Apocalypse as a Literary Genre

At about the time of the Seleucid domination of Judea in the days of Antiochus Epiphanes there started to appear Jewish writings that presupposed, embraced, and set forth these kinds of apocalyptic views. In particular, it is at this time that Jewish "apocalypses" started to be written. The term **apocalypse** refers to a literary genre (just as there are epic poems, and short stories, and novels, all of them genres—so too there are apocalypses). There is a difference between the apocalyptic world view ("apocalypticism") and the literary genre that, better than any other, expresses it ("apocalypse"). That is to say, a Jew could be an apocalypticist and never write a book that we would call an apocalypse (although anyone who wrote an apocalypse would be an apocalypticist)—just as there are plenty of Marxists who have never written a *Communist Manifesto*.

We are especially interested in the apocalypse genre, however, because the final chapters of Daniel are the earliest surviving representative of the genre. There were other Jewish apocalypses written after the time of Daniel that did not make it into the Scriptures; and it became a popular genre among later Christians as well—as seen in the final book of the New Testament, the book of Revelation, also known as the Apocalypse of John.

Just like every other genre of literature, apocalypses share numerous stylistic features with one another that make them distinctive. The following are among the features that you will typically find in a Jewish apocalypse.

- *Prose Narrative Revelations.* Apocalypses are prose compositions in which a divine revelation is described—a secret "unveiling" of the heavenly truths that can make sense of earthly realities, especially those that make sense of the misery and suffering that people are experiencing on earth.

- *Pseudonymous Seers.* These revelations are given by God to a visionary, or a "seer" (or prophet). Invariably these seers, who describe what they have been shown by God, do so pseudonymously—that is, they write in the name of some other person, claiming to be someone else. In almost every case the name that the real author chooses is a famous person, a well-known figure from the religious past; for example, Abraham, Enoch, or even Adam. (We will see in a moment why authors chose to hide their identities behind the name of a famous religious figure of antiquity.)

- *Bizarre Visions.* These revelations are never given in straightforward fashion. Instead they involve very bizarre and confusing visions, filled with great and perplexing symbolism. Invariably these bizarre visions are so impenetrable that the seer himself cannot make sense of them.

- *Angelic Interpreters.* It is for that reason that there is always an angelic being on hand to explain what the vision means, both to the seer and, of course, to his reading public.

- *The Two Types of Visions.* There are two types of visions that seers typically have. Some involve a heavenly journey in which the seer is given a guided, though confusing, tour of heaven, to see the realities there that can make sense of what is happening down here. In other instances the seer is shown a vision that explains the future course of history. It may not be obvious that the series of symbolic visions that he sees (for example, a succession of wild and grotesque beasts, appearing one after the other) are in fact related to the future course of events on earth; but the angelic interpretation always makes this clear. There are some visions that represent a combination of these two types: a heavenly journey that reveals the future course of history (such as in the book of Revelation).

- *Triumphalist Movement.* These visions are always triumphalistic in nature. By that I mean that in the end, despite all the craziness that transpires before we get there, God triumphs over all. These visions invariably go from the very bad to the very good, and in that order.

- *The Function of the Pseudonymous Authorship.* There are two reasons that apocalypticists typically chose to write their visions in the name of a famous person of the distant past. On one hand, they chose the names of religious authorities who were thought to be especially close to God. Who better to be shown the future course of history or the secrets of heaven than Moses, Abraham, or Enoch, who were particularly attuned to God's revelations? On the other hand, there is a more specific explanation—at least in the cases of apocalypses that provide sketches of historical events leading up to the end. Suppose an author is living at a certain point of time when things have gotten very bad, and he is convinced that he is living in the last days. He wants to predict what is soon to happen in the very near future. By writing in the name of someone who lived long ago he is able to make predictions not only about what is going to happen soon, but also about what is to happen in the future of the person allegedly making the prediction. That is, if someone in the first century B.C.E. claims that he is Moses, living 1200 years earlier, he can have Moses predict a series of events to transpire down to his (the real author's) own day. And lo and behold, everything that Moses indicated was going to happen, did in fact happen! (Of course it did: the author is describing what *did* happen by having Moses predict that it *would* happen.) That makes the author's own predictions about what is about to transpire soon in his own future all the more believable to his readers, who think that "Moses" was right about everything *up to* their own day; so surely he is right about what will transpire next. This fiction of authorship, in other words, was a way of providing assurance to an author's readers that the end really was near and that he was fully authorized in his predictions, given by God himself through an angelic interpreter. Ultimately, these books are meant to provide hope and assurance to their readers: all will be made right in the end, which will be here very soon.

Daniel as an Apocalypse

As I indicated, Daniel provides the earliest full-blown apocalypse that we have. There are other passages in the Hebrew Bible that scholars have suggested embody clear—or reasonably clear—apocalyptic perspectives. In every case, these are passages that appear to have been added at a later time to a writing that was already in existence. This is the case, for example, with Isaiah 24–27, known as the "little apocalypse" of Isaiah, not written by Isaiah of Jerusalem in the eighth century B.C.E., but later interpolated into his work; so too Second Zechariah (chs. 9–14) contains apocalyptic elements.

But it is with Daniel 1–7 that we first see the genre come to full expression. Scholars have long recognized that, unlike the earlier stories of chapters 1–6, the visions recorded in these chapters were composed in the days of Antiochus Epiphanes, around 167 B.C.E. The two portions of the book were probably combined at a later time because of some of their thematic similarities, as we will see in a moment.

There are four visions altogether, and when you read them you will see that they are bizarre indeed (and probably hard to understand). Here I will not provide an interpretation of all four but will simply take the first one and explain it, showing how understanding the vision as an apocalypse can help unpack its message. As is true of the writings of the classical prophets, the writings of the apocalypticists (both Jewish and Christian) were not designed to predict what was going to happen hundreds or thousands of years after they lived. These authors too were writing for their own time, and their message was meant to provide hope for people in their own day.

The first thing to note is that all the features of the apocalypse genre that I have just set forth can be seen here. The vision of Daniel 7 has a divine origin and is interpreted by an angel. It is filled with bizarre images and symbols. Daniel describes a dream (a night vision) in which he sees four wild beasts coming up out of the sea, one in the shape of a lion with eagles' wings; another a bear lifted up on one side with tusks in its teeth; a third a leopard with the wings of a bird and four heads; and a fourth that he calls "terrifying and dreadful" (as opposed to the others?), a devouring beast with iron teeth and ten horns, causing destruction right and left, and then a little horn. This little horn has human eyes and a mouth that speaks arrogantly. What in the world? Less hard to understand is the next part of the vision, of the "Ancient of Days" (that is, God) sitting on his throne with thousands and thousands worshiping him before the books of judgment opened up. The beasts then have their power taken away, and Daniel sees "one like a son of man" (translated in the New Revised Standard Version as "one like a human being") coming on the clouds of heaven; and to him is "given dominion and glory and kingship, that all peoples, nations, and languages, should serve him. His dominion is an everlasting dominion that shall not pass away" (7:14).

All in all, it is a bizarre vision, and Daniel has an appropriate response: a splitting headache. He, like his readers, cannot make heads or tails of what he has seen, but fortunately—as always happens in these apocalypses—there is an angelic being nearby to give him the interpretation. Daniel is told that the four beasts each represent a king, or kingdom, which will succeed each other and create considerable havoc on earth. The fourth will be more terrible than the others. The ten horns represent a series of kings of this final kingdom, and the final little horn will be a most horrible ruler who will "speak words

FIGURE 8.3. The battle of a god and a seven-headed dragon, from the middle of the third millennium B.C.E. In the apocalyptic visions of the book of Daniel there are also bizarre creatures who are opposed by God; these images may well have been drawn from popular mythologies of the day.

BOX 8.6 PROPHETS AND APOCALYPTICISTS ON SUFFERING

One of the ways you can see the stark differences between a prophetic and an apocalyptic point of view (remembering that they have a lot in common as well) is by considering what each perspective says about why the people of God suffer. If you were to compare Amos 3–5 with Daniel 7, for example, you might come up with the following set of contrasting answers to several key questions.

1. Who is causing the people of God to suffer? Amos: God, who is punishing them for their sin; Daniel: the evil beasts opposed to God, who are afflicting God's people.
2. Who is at fault for their suffering? Amos: the people themselves; Daniel: the powers aligned against God.

3. So are those who are suffering themselves to blame? Amos: absolutely yes; Daniel: absolutely not.
4. When will the suffering end? Amos: when the people repent of their sins and return to God; Daniel: when God destroys the wild "beasts" afflicting his people.
5. How will it end? Amos: God will forgive the people, welcome them back, and restore them; Daniel: God will bring a cosmic destruction of the forces of evil and give his saints dominion over the earth.
6. What has to happen first? Amos: the people must be punished for their sins; Daniel: very little! The people need simply to hold on to their faith.

against the Most High, will wear out the holy ones of the Most High, and shall attempt to change the sacred seasons and the law" (7:25). But his time will soon be up, and his dominion over the earth will be taken away and "given to the people of the holy ones of the Most High; their kingdom shall be an everlasting kingdom, and all dominions shall serve and obey them" (7:27).

And that is the end of the vision. However one interprets it, this is the type of apocalypse that gives a "historical sequence" of events (rather than a vision of the heavenly realm); it has a clear triumphalist movement, because in the end the terrible beasts are destroyed in judgment and the saints rule forever; and the pseudonymous authorship "works" both by having an authority figure of the past, the famous wise man Daniel, see these things, and by having him be able to make predictions that in fact were post-dictions—"prophecies after the fact," if you will.

That becomes clear once you realize what Daniel is "predicting." Remember: Daniel is allegedly living in the sixth century B.C.E. during the Babylonian exile. He sees four kingdoms succeed one another (just as in Nebuchadnezzar's dream, in the short story of Daniel chapter 2). Interpreters have had little difficulty understanding what this is all about. The first beast is Babylon, of "Daniel's" own day; the next is Media (which, according to this book, conquered the Babylonians); the next is Persia; and the

next is Greece and its Hellenizing policies. The ten horns represent the kings of the Hellenistic Seleucid dynasty, and—this is key—the little horn that appears at the end that makes life miserable for the saints and attempts to "change the sacred seasons and the law" is none other than Antiochus Epiphanes.

All of that Daniel "predicts." But of course the author is simply recounting what he knows to have happened. And what happens next? The dominion over the earth is given not to another grotesque beast but to "one like a son of man"—in other words, to a humane ruler/kingdom (in contrast to the awful animals who had been ruling until now). And who is that one? The interpretation tells us. It is the "people of the holy ones of the Most High" (v. 27, see v. 18). That is, it is the saints—the people of God, the nation of Israel. They will become the new kingdom on earth, through whom God will rule. This is a triumphal ending indeed. Very soon that wretched opponent of God, Antiochus Epiphanes, will be destroyed along with his kingdom. And Israel will inherit the earth.

That never happened, of course—which is why later interpreters were compelled to come up with alternative interpretations, as is still happening today. It is important to remember, however, that this author was not predicting the distant future but his own future. He was writing to the people of his own day, the Jews who were experiencing persecution and severe suffering under the reign of a much-hated foreign tyrant. "Daniel" wants to assure his readers that their pain and misery will not last long. He wants to provide them a message of hope. The powers of evil are out in full force, but God will soon intervene and overthrow them in a cataclysmic act of judgment. And when he does, he will reward his faithful by giving them dominion over all the earth. In the meantime, all they have to do is to remain faithful and to wait.

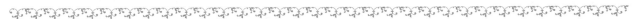

At a Glance: Apocalyptic Literature

Jewish apocalypticism is a world view that first emerged in the years leading up to the Maccabean Revolt among Jewish thinkers who were dissatisfied with the prophetic view that the people of God suffer because God is punishing them. In the apocalyptic view, the pain and misery in the world are instead caused by God's enemies who are aligned against his people; suffering may be intense now, but God will soon intervene to overthrow the forces of evil and bring his people into a good kingdom.

As a way of expressing this view, a new literary genre developed in ancient Judea: the apocalypse. Apocalypses were prose narratives written pseudonymously by authors who describe revelatory visions that they were allegedly given; these visions contained extensive bizarre imagery that was typically explained by an angelic interpreter. Sometimes these visions involved journeys to the heavenly realms; sometimes they involved views of what was to happen in the future. In both cases, the visions end hopefully with the triumph of God.

The book of Daniel is the first full-fledged apocalypse to be written, during the reign of Antiochus Epiphanes. It contains four visions altogether, the first of which portrays four wild beasts succeeding one another in control of the earth; these represent four kingdoms that are to arise before God intervenes in judgment to destroy them and give the kingdom to his saints.

Take a Stand

1. You are talking to your best friend about religion, and she tells you that she thinks the Bible is right: if you love God and do what he wants, your life will be good and you will be happy; but if you sin, you will be punished and your life will be miserable. Explain how you either agree or disagree with her on both points—whether that is the consistent teaching of the Bible, and whether you think it is true.

2. You are to participate in a class debate on the following resolution: *Resolved: The book of Job satisfactorily explains why there is suffering.* Take either side of the resolution, and argue your case.

3. You are on semester break during the holidays, and your best friend convinces you to go with him to the local Christian Bible Bookstore. While you're there you see several shelves of books on "prophecy," all of them using the book of Daniel (as well as other passages) to argue for what is going to happen sometime in the near future as the prophecies come to be fulfilled. From your class you have learned an alternative view about the apocalyptic literature: that it is *not* talking about what is to happen in our own future but is speaking to people of its own day. Explain the alternative view at length to your friend. Which view do you think is better, and why?

Key Terms

Apocalypse, 209   **Apocalypticism**, 206   **Proverb**, 192

Suggestions for Further Reading

NB: For this and all chapters, see the relevant articles (e.g., "Proverbs," "Apocalypse") in the works cited in the Suggestions for Further Reading in chapter 1.

Clifford, Richard J. *The Wisdom Literature*. Nashville: Abingdon, 1988. A good, readable introduction to the Wisdom literature of ancient Judaism.

Collins, John. *The Apocalyptic Imagination: An Introduction to the Matrix of Christianity*. New York: Crossroad, 1984. A good introduction to apocalypticism as it developed in the time immediately before the birth of Christianity.

Collins, John J., Stephen Stein, and Bernard McGinn. *The Encyclopedia of Apocalypticism. Vol. 1, The Origins of Apocalypticism in Judaism and Christianity*. New York: Continuum, 1998. An authoritative encyclopedia that deals with all aspects of ancient apocalyptic thought and apocalypses.

Crenshaw, James L. *Old Testament Wisdom: An Introduction*. 2nd ed. Louisville: Westminster John Knox, 1998. A thorough, insightful, and highly useful introduction to the Wisdom books of the Hebrew Bible and Apocrypha.

Ehrman, Bart D. *God's Problem: How the Bible Fails to Answer our Most Important Question—Why We Suffer*. San Francisco: HarperOne, 2008. An accessible discussion of different views of suffering in the Bible, including those of Job and Ecclesiastes.

Macleish, Archibald. *J.B. A Play in Verse*. Boston: Houghton Mifflin, 1958. An unusual suggestion for reading, but this is a terrific adaptation of the book of Job, a must-read for anyone interested in the deep issues dealt with in the book.

9

The World of Jesus and His Followers

WHAT TO EXPECT

As we move into our study of the New Testament, it is important to remember that we cannot understand any ancient writing without putting it in its proper historical context. In this chapter we consider various aspects of the context of the New Testament: the conquests of Alexander the Great; the political and cultural history of the Roman empire; and, especially, the world of early Judaism. In particular we will be interested in what Judaism was like in Palestine in the days of Jesus, and consider the four major sects of Jews: the Pharisees, Sadducees, Essenes, and the "fourth philosophy."

The second half of the chapter will consider a range of Jewish writings from roughly the period between the Hebrew Bible and the New Testament. These dozen or so books are not included in the Jewish canon of Scripture or in the Protestant version of the Old Testament, but they are considered deuterocanonical in the Roman Catholic and Orthodox traditions.

Throughout our study so far we have seen why it is important to know the context of a biblical writing if we want to interpret it correctly. You cannot understand what Isaiah meant when he said that "a young woman has conceived and will bear a son, and you will call his name Immanuel," without knowing that he spoke these words in the context of the Syro-Ephraimitic war against Judah. You can't understand the bizarre visions of the book of Daniel—for example, the fourth, terrible, beast with a little horn with human eyes and a mouth that speaks arrogantly—without realizing that he was writing in a time of severe persecution and suffering during the reign of Antiochus Epiphanes of Syria. The same is true of all the prophets and historical books. Knowing the context of a writing is fundamental for understanding what an author meant.

This is no less true for the New Testament than for the Tanakh. Here too we have to place the writings of the biblical authors in their appropriate context if we want to make sense of what they mean. Probably most readers of the Bible do not realize this. That would be one reason there are so many different interpretations of the Bible by people who consider themselves "experts" (just turn on the TV any Sunday morning and you'll see what I mean). Readers of the Bible who are not trained in history tend not to think in terms of historical context, and so simply read the words of these ancient authors as if they were writing in twenty-first-century America. But these authors were not American, and they were not writing in modern times. They lived in a different part of the world, in a different culture, with different customs, and different assumptions about the world and life in it. If you pretend that they were writing in our own context, instead of theirs, you take their words out of context. And anytime you take an author's words out of context, you change their meaning.

It is quite simple to show the importance of context for interpreting the writings of the New Testament. I can do so by giving a simple illustration, about a remarkable man who lived nearly 2000 years ago in a remote part of the Roman Empire.

ONE REMARKABLE LIFE

From the beginning his mother knew that he would be no ordinary person. Prior to his birth, a heavenly figure appeared to her announcing that her son would not be a mere mortal but would be divine. The boy was already recognized as a spiritual authority in his youth; his discussions with recognized experts showed his superior knowledge of all things religious. As an adult he left home to engage in an itinerant preaching ministry. He went from village to town with his message of good news, proclaiming that people should forgo their concerns for the material things of this life, such as how they should dress and what they should eat. They should instead be concerned with their eternal souls.

He gathered around himself a number of disciples who were amazed by his teaching and his flawless character. They became convinced that he was no ordinary man, but was the Son of God. Their faith received striking confirmation in the miraculous things that he did. He could reportedly predict the future, heal the sick, cast out demons, and raise the dead. Not everyone proved friendly, however. At the end of his life, his enemies trumped up charges against him and he was placed on trial before Roman authorities for crimes against the state.

Even after he departed this realm, however, he did not forsake his devoted followers. Some claimed that he had ascended bodily into heaven; others said that he had appeared to them, alive, afterward, that they had talked with him and touched him and had become convinced that he could not be bound by death. A number of his followers spread the good news about this man, recounting what they had seen him say and do. Eventually some of these accounts came to be written down in books that circulated throughout the empire.

But I doubt that you have ever read them. In fact, I suspect you have never heard the name of this miracle-working "Son of God." The man I have been referring to is the great neo-Pythagorean teacher and pagan holy man of the first century C.E., **Apollonius of Tyana**, a worshiper of the Roman gods, whose life and teachings are still available for us in the writings of his later (third-century) follower Philostratus in his book, *The Life of Apollonius.*

Apollonius lived at about the time of Jesus. Even though they never met, the reports about their lives were in many ways similar. At a later time, Jesus' followers argued that Jesus was the miracle-working Son of God and that Apollonius was an impostor, a magician, and a fraud. Perhaps not surprisingly, Apollonius's followers made just the opposite claim, asserting that he was the miracle-working Son of God and that Jesus was a fraud.

What is remarkable is that these were not the only two persons in the Greco-Roman world who were thought to have been supernaturally endowed as teachers and miracle workers. In fact, from the tantalizing but fragmentary records that have survived, we know of numerous other persons also said to have performed miracles, to have calmed the storm and multiplied loaves, to have told the future and healed the sick, to have cast out demons and raised the dead, to have been supernaturally born and taken up into heaven at the end of their lives. Even though Jesus may be the only miracle-working Son of God that we know about in our world, he was one of many talked about in the first century.

Clearly, then, if we want to study the stories about Jesus—and about his followers—we need to situate them in their own historical context, in the world of the first century C.E. The stories about Jesus were told among people who could make sense of them, and the sense they made of them related to their own world, which knew of divine beings who were also human. The environment in which Jesus was born and in which Christianity emerged is known as the **Greco-Roman world**.

THE GRECO-ROMAN WORLD

The "Greco-Roman world" is a term that historians use to describe the lands surrounding the Mediterranean from the time of Alexander the Great through the first three centuries or so of the Roman Empire, roughly 300 B.C.E. to 300 C.E.

Alexander the Great

I have already spoken briefly about Alexander in chapter 6. It could easily be argued that Alexander was the most significant world conqueror in the history of Western civilization. Born in 356 B.C.E., he succeeded to the throne of Macedonia as a twenty-year-old when his father, King Philip II, was assassinated. Alexander was single-minded in his desire to conquer the lands of the eastern Mediterranean. A brilliant military strategist, he quickly and boldly—some would say ruthlessly—over ran Greece to the south and drove his armies along the coastal regions of Asia Minor (modern-day Turkey) to the east, into the Levant, and then down to Egypt. He finally marched into the heart of the Persian Empire, overthrowing the Persian monarch Darius and extending his territories as far away as modern-day India.

In chapter 6 I pointed out that Alexander received a Greek education, tutored by none other than the great philosopher Aristotle, and that he considered Greek culture superior to all others. One of the reasons his conquest of so many lands around the Mediterranean mattered, historically, is that he dreamed not only of having all these regions under his control but also of introducing to them the ways of the Greeks, so as to provide a kind of cultural unity throughout his empire. As a conqueror he promoted the use of the Greek language among the aristocrats throughout his domain—wherever they happened to live—and built Greek-style cities, with gymnasiums, theaters, and public baths, to serve as administrative and commercial centers. Moreover, he encouraged the adoption of Greek culture and religion throughout his cities, especially among the upper classes. This is the process of Hellenization that I mentioned earlier.

Before he could achieve his dream of cultural unity, Alexander died an untimely death at the age of thirty-three (323 B.C.E.). As we have seen, his kingdom came to be divided up among his generals so that, for example, Egypt was ruled by the Ptolemies and Syria by the Seleucids, with Palestine (as the land of Israel eventually came to be called) in between ruled first by one and then the other. All that changed in time, with the conquests of Rome and the coming of the **Roman Empire**.

The Roman Empire

It is important for the study of the New Testament to have at least a rudimentary understanding of the rise of the Roman Empire, since Jesus himself was born during the reign of the first Roman emperor and was executed during the reign of the second, and since the early Christians then spread their religion throughout major urban areas of the empire.

The traditional date for the founding of Rome is 753 B.C.E. It began as a small farming village, which grew over time into a city spread over a large area that covered the "seven hills of Rome." For nearly 250 years Rome was ruled by local kings, whose abuses led to their ouster in 509 B.C.E. For nearly half a millennium thereafter Rome was a "republic"—meaning that it was governed by a group of aristocrats who made up the Roman Senate; these were the wealthiest and most influential members of the highest class in Rome.

As it refined its political and legislative systems, Rome also grew strong militarily. Eventually it conquered and colonized the Italian peninsula and sought control of the entire Mediterranean. Its chief rival was Carthage in North Africa, with which it fought three fierce wars known as the Punic Wars (264–241 B.C.E., 218–202 B.C.E., and 149–146 B.C.E.). Rome emerged the victor and began to expand its power yet further.

The late republic period saw an increasing number of internal struggles for power in Rome, many of them violent, as prominent generals and politicians attempted to seize control of the government. After Julius Caesar pronounced himself dictator, he was assassinated in 44 B.C.E. The republic (ruled by the Senate) was not transformed into an empire (ruled by an emperor) until Caesar's great-nephew and adopted son, **Octavian**, a wealthy aristocrat and Rome's most successful general, brought an end to the bloody civil wars that had wracked the city. Octavian assumed full control in the year 27 B.C.E. Soon he assumed the name **Caesar Augustus** (roughly meaning "the most revered emperor") and he wielded virtually supreme power over the state, even though the Senate continued to administer the massive Roman bureaucracy, which included the governance of provinces that eventually stretched from Spain to Syria. These provinces were conquered lands that were ultimately ruled by the Romans and that were forced to pay tax revenues to the Roman state.

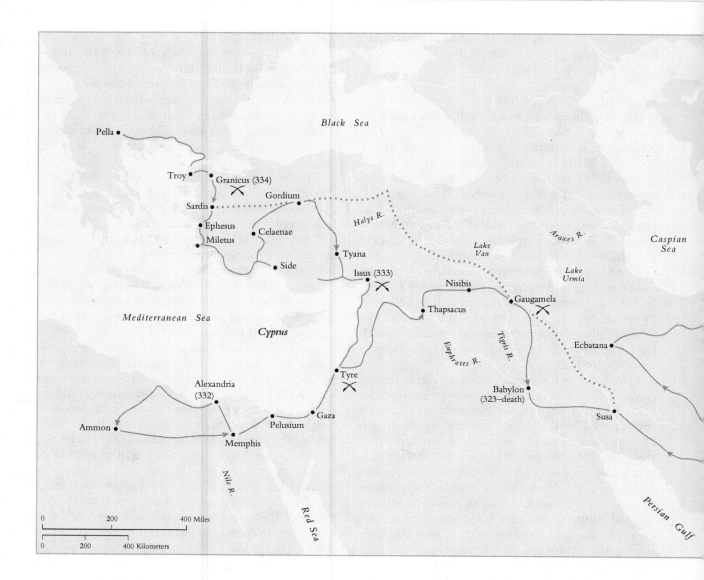

After the death of Caesar Augustus in 14 C.E. came a number of successors who were of varying temperaments and abilities. For the period of the New Testament, these emperors were the following:

- Tiberius (14–37 C.E.)
- Caligula (37–41 C.E.)
- Claudius (41–54 C.E.)
- Nero (54–68 C.E.)
- Four different emperors in the tumultuous year of 68–69 C.E., including, finally, Vespasian (69–79 C.E.)
- Titus (79–81 C.E.)
- Domitian (81–96 C.E.)
- Nerva (96–98 C.E.)
- Trajan (98–117 C.E.)

The Significance of the Pax Romana

For understanding early Christianity and the writings of the New Testament, this Roman environment is obviously of supreme importance. This was a time when the Roman Empire dominated the world of the Mediterranean from Palestine to Spain, from northern Africa to what was later called Europe. The empire was a massive area, and with the end of the civil wars under Octavian there emerged a time of relative peace and security—no major internal disruptions and relatively secure borders on the frontiers. This is the period known as the **Pax Romana** (literally: The Roman Peace), which lasted for two hundred years.

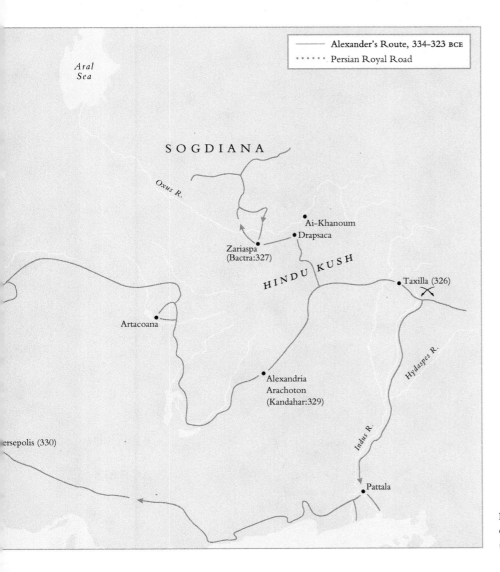

FIGURE 9.1. The journeys of Alexander the Great (334–323 B.C.E.).

In some ways, the cultural unity that Alexander had wanted for his own empire came to be a reality under Roman rule. Even though the native tongue of Rome was Latin, throughout the Roman Empire the common language spoken by the cultured elite was Greek. This meant that if you wanted to travel from one place to another, you could do so easily because there were no real language barriers. That ended up being highly significant for the spread of Christianity after the death of Jesus, as we will see. Missionaries, such as the apostle Paul, could speak Greek in any city in the empire and be understood without an interpreter.

Moreover, travel itself was possible. The Romans prided themselves in ridding the seas of pirates (they were not 100% successful, of course) and the roads of bandits. They built enormous road systems throughout their empire to make the movement of troops easier, and anyone could walk on the Roman roads. These were brilliantly constructed: you can still see them in parts of Europe today, 2000 years later. There was also a common Roman coinage used throughout the empire, so no one had to worry about problems with currency exchange.

There were, of course, differences in culture in different parts of the empire. But in major urban areas there was also a good deal in common from one location to the next—many of the same civic institutions and governing principles, many of the same cultural and religious facilities (gymnasiums,

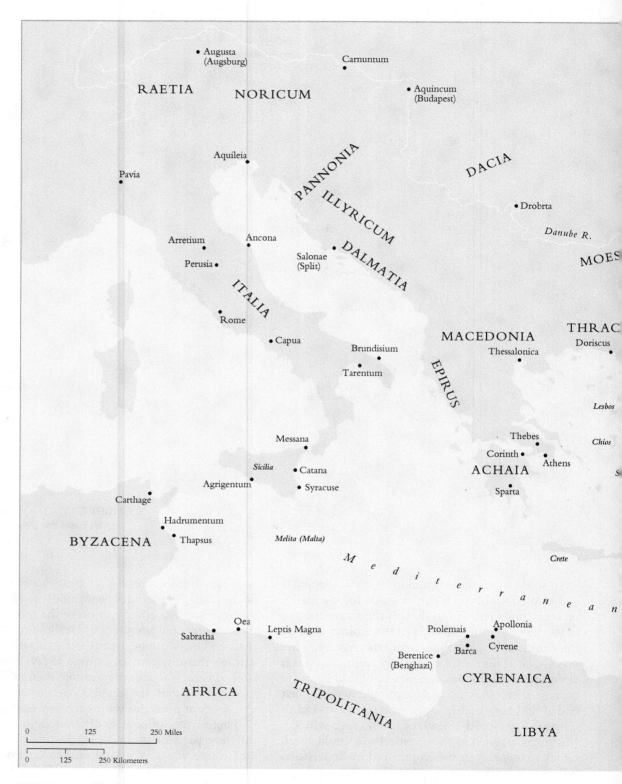

FIGURE 9.2.   The Roman Empire: central and eastern provinces.

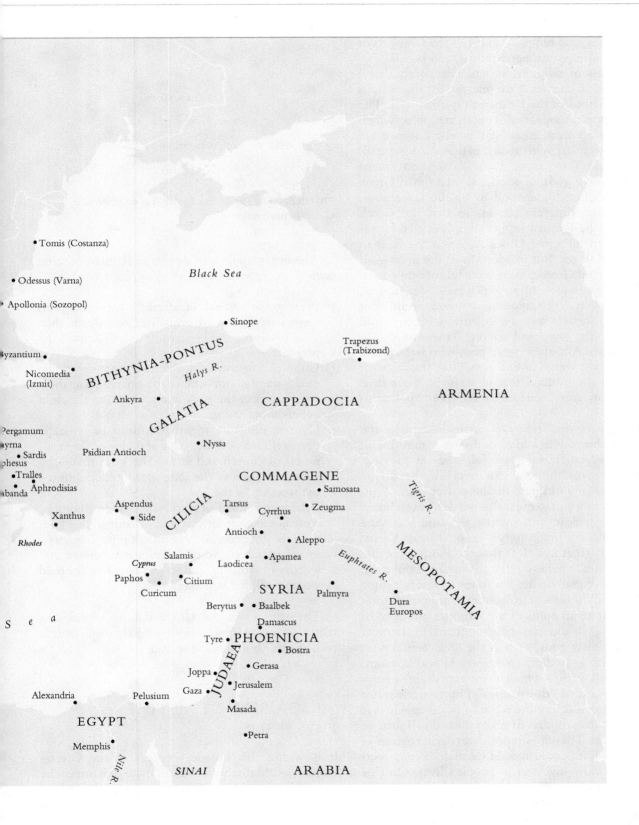

Tomis (Costanza)

Black Sea

Odessus (Varna)

Apollonia (Sozopol)

Sinope

Trapezus
(Trabizond)

Byzantium

BITHYNIA-PONTUS

Nicomedia
(Izmit)

Halys R.

ARMENIA

Ankyra

GALATIA

CAPPADOCIA

Pergamum

Smyrna

Sardis

Psidian Antioch

Nyssa

Ephesus

Tralles

COMMAGENE

Aphrodisias

Samosata

Labanda

Tigris R.

Aspendus

CILICIA

Tarsus

Cyrrhus

Zeugma

Xanthus

Side

Antioch

Aleppo

MESOPOTAMIA

Rhodes

Salamis

Apamea

Cyprus

Laodicea

Euphrates R.

Paphos

Citium

Curicum

SYRIA

Palmyra

Dura
Europos

Berytus

Baalbek

S   e   a

Damascus

Tyre

PHOENICIA

JUDAEA

Bostra

Gerasa

Joppa

Jerusalem

Gaza

Alexandria

Pelusium

Masada

EGYPT

Petra

Memphis

Nile R.

SINAI

ARABIA

public baths, and temples), many of the same sets of cultural assumptions, perspectives, and beliefs.

In terms of religious beliefs, the points that I made back in chapter 2 are relevant for the various pagan religions of the Roman Empire as well. The most important aspect of Roman religions, which sets them off from most of the religions you are probably familiar with today, is that these were all polytheistic. There were lots of gods. The Romans had their own gods, of course, similar to the Greek gods and often understood to be the same gods, going under different names, so that the Greek Zeus was the Roman Jupiter, the Greek Hera was the Roman Juno, the Greek Ares was the Roman Mars, and so on. But in addition to the great gods of Rome (and Greece) there were lots of other gods: different gods for different places—cities, towns, homes, forests, rivers, mountains—and for different functions, such as war, agriculture, weather, child birth, health, love, and so on. There were also family gods. And there were gods who were partly human: these were "divine men," like the emperor (who was so powerful that he must be more than mortal) or great spiritual men like Apollonius of Tyana.

It appears that many Romans imagined the world of the gods as a kind of divine pyramid with the fewest, but most powerful, gods at the top. Some Romans thought that over all the divine beings was one ultimate divine power (e.g., Zeus, or Jupiter, or a god so great that we don't even know his name); below him on the pyramid were the great gods of mythology—Juno, Mars, Venus, Diana, etc. (It is not clear that the Romans or the Greeks actually believed that the myths about these gods were literally true; the more educated people understood these to be great stories, but not historically accurate accounts of the activities of the gods. But these gods did exist.) Below them on the next tier were lesser gods, such as the local deities who were in charge of daily affairs—rain, health, crops, and so forth. Included in this tier were divine beings sometimes called "**daimonia.**" This term does not refer to "demons" in the sense of fallen angels that inhabit peoples' bodies to make them do all sorts of nasty things. They are simply lower divine beings—some of whom could indeed be malevolent—who are more daily involved in people's lives. On this tier also would be divine humans, who were so far superior to the rest of us that they must be partially divine. Below all these beings were humans.

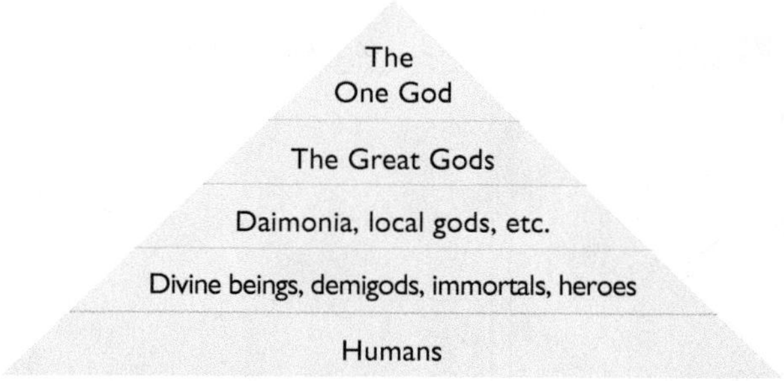

FIGURE 9.3. The Divine Pyramid as understood in Greco-Roman religion.

The other important aspects of Roman religion correspond to what I discussed in chapter 2:

- Present life instead of afterlife: these religions were less concerned with life after death than with receiving the benefits of divine help in the present.
- Cultic acts instead of doctrine: these religions focused on the importance of offering sacrifices and prayers to the gods, not on holding the right beliefs about them.
- Church and state together instead of separate: these religions did not have any idea of the separation of church and state. The gods made the state great, and so the state sponsored and urged the worship of the gods.
- Tolerance instead of intolerance: these religions were not exclusivistic; if you worshiped one god, nothing stopped you from worshiping another—or lots of others. All of the gods were divine and worthy of worship, and so you could and should worship all that you wanted.

This, then, was the Greco-Roman world into which Christianity was born, and through which, after the death of Jesus, it spread.

JUDAISM IN THE TIME OF JESUS

It is within this broader context of the Greco-Roman world that we need to situate Judaism in the days of Jesus and his followers. It is very difficult to establish demographic figures for the ancient world, but it is usually thought that in the first century C.E.

BOX 9.1 DIVINE RULERS AS SAVIOR GODS

The Roman emperor was often paid homage as a divine being, the "Savior" of the human race. Consider the following inscription set up in honor of Gaius Julius Caesar Germanicus, otherwise known to history as the emperor Caligula, by the city council of Ephesus in Asia Minor, around 38 C.E.:

> The council and the people [of the Ephesians and other Greek] cities, which dwell in Asia and

the nations [acknowledge] Gaius Julius, the son of Gaius Caesar, as High Priest and Absolute Ruler . . . the God Visible who is born of [the Gods] Ares and Aphrodite, the shared Savior of human life.

If Christians called Jesus the Son of God and Savior—who might his competition have been?

---

the Roman Empire comprised something like 60 million inhabitants. Of this total, it is usually thought that Jews made up something like 7 percent—so that there may have been some four million or so Jews living in the empire.

Life in the Diaspora

The vast majority of these Jews would not have been living in Palestine. This is one aspect of ancient Judaism that made it so very different from what we know about the nation of Israel for most of the periods covered in the Hebrew Bible; in those earlier times, being an Israelite meant, naturally, living in Israel or Judah. We have seen that the Assyrians destroyed the northern kingdom of Israel in 722 B.C.E., and the peoples living there were dispersed to other lands or intermarried with foreigners who were brought in from the outside. Eventually all the Israelite bloodlines were lost, and the ten tribes that originally inhabited this region permanently disappeared. When the Babylonians attacked Judah in the sixth century B.C.E., many Judeans escaped to places such as Egypt; many others, after the conquest, were taken back to Babylonia. When the Babylonians were defeated by the Persians, and the Persian monarch Cyrus allowed the Judeans in exile to return to their homeland, many of them decided to remain in Babylon instead.

These communities in Egypt and Babylon grew and grew over the years. Other Jews traveled to other parts of the world, put down roots, and so established Jewish communities in cities all around the Mediterranean. This dispersion of Jews throughout other lands, outside of Palestine, is called the **Diaspora**. As I indicated, there were far more Jews living in the Diaspora than in Palestine

in the days of Jesus, with large Jewish communities being found in such places as Rome, Alexandria in Egypt, Antioch in Syria, urban areas of Greece and Asia Minor, and—well, and in most major cities of the Roman Empire.

What makes the Jewish Diaspora so significant is that many of the Jews who settled in these other lands continued to retain their native customs and religion. That made Jews completely different from nearly everyone else in the ancient world who relocated from their homelands. Almost everyone else simply began to adopt the customs and religions of the new places where they now lived. But Jews were known to retain their own customs, beliefs, and practices as Jews, such as worshiping only the one God of Israel, keeping the Sabbath, observing Jewish festivals, circumcising their boys, and following kosher food laws. This made Jews not only unlike others who had resettled in new places but also unlike the local people in whatever place they lived. Jews were a people apart, a different "race" from others. That, in fact, is why they were called Jews—or (as the ancient Greek word can also be translated) Judeans. They adhered to the ways of Judea even though they didn't live in Judea.

Naturally, Jews living outside of Palestine wanted to come together as communities to participate in worship together. According to the laws of the Torah—especially, as we have seen, in the book of Deuteronomy—there was only one place on earth where sacrifices could be made to God, in the Temple in Jerusalem. Most Jews in the Diaspora could never afford the time or expense of making a trip to Jerusalem, although those who were wealthier saw it as a mark of pride to be able to travel there at some time in their lives, often during one of the major annual festivals such as the Passover feast.

During the Passover, pilgrims (the ones who could afford it) came to Jerusalem from around the world to commemorate the exodus event from centuries earlier by participating in the sacrifice of the Passover lambs in the Temple and holding the special Passover meal with all the symbolic foods that were customary for the occasion.

But what were Jews to do who could never make it to Jerusalem for such a festive event? And what were even the wealthy Jews, who could afford an annual trip, to do for their more regular weekly worship needs? By the time of the New Testament, another institution had developed within Judaism that allowed for the regular worship of God, although not through sacrifices. This was the Jewish **synagogue**.

The term "synagogue" is Greek for "gathering together." A synagogue was a gathering of Jews, weekly, to participate in the worship of God; eventually the term came to refer to the building where Jews would meet for their worship. We do not know when Jews started forming synagogues, although it may well have been as early as the first dispersion of Judeans from their homeland during the Babylonian exile. During a synagogue service—since sacrifices were not allowed outside the Temple—Jews would focus on discussing the sacred traditions of the Torah, which would be read and commented on in a sermon by a synagogue leader, and by saying prayers to the God of Israel. The Scriptures could then be discussed and reflected on. The synagogue services took place on Sabbath, the seventh day of the week.

As we will see in a moment, there were lots of differences among Jewish groups at this time—not every Jew believed or thought the same things. But there were also some very basic commonalities that appear to have been true of most Jews in most places, whether in Jerusalem, Alexandria, Antioch, Ephesus, Rome, or anywhere else in the empire. This made it easy on Jews who were wealthy enough to afford to travel. Virtually any city they came to would have a synagogue, and it was possible to make connections in the synagogue and to be with like-minded people who held the same religious beliefs and observed similar patterns of worship. Jews traveling in the Roman Empire had a natural "home" in almost any major city they visited.

Among the aspects of Judaism shared by almost all Jews throughout the empire were the tenets that I discussed in an earlier chapter. These included the belief in only one God (as opposed to the polytheistic pagans), who was understood to be the creator of heaven and earth, who chose Israel to be his people and made with them his covenant. Jews circumcised their boys to show that they belonged to the covenant and were, thus, God's elect people. Just as God had specially favored his people, he also provided them with a set of directions to follow in their relationships with one another and in their worship of him. The Law of Moses was part of the sacred tradition of Israel and was revered by Jews everywhere. Jews throughout the world—in the Diaspora and in Palestine—understood that the five books of the Torah were written by Moses and contained a divine revelation of what had happened in the past and what needed to happen in the present, as Jews determined to follow the instructions that God had delivered on Mount Sinai after the great event of the Exodus.

Jews, then, were distinctive in the empire for having a set of sacred books that guided their lives and worship. It may seem odd to us today, but no other ancient religion that we know of was rooted in sacred books; ancient religions in the Roman Empire did not have "scriptures." But Jews did. Different groups of Jews held different books as sacred, but all Jews accepted the Torah as given by God. At this time most Jews also considered the writings of the prophets to be authoritative revelations from God, and various Jewish groups considered yet other books—for example, Psalms, or the book of Daniel—to be authoritative as well. Judaism in this period is on the way to defining the Tanakh—the Torah, the Nevi'im, and the Kethuvim—which, in a slightly later period, was to become "the" Jewish Bible (as we will discuss in chapter 15).

Jewish Life in Palestine

Since Jesus was a Jew who was born and raised in Palestine, we need to understand what Jewish life was like specifically there, in the region that Jews continued to consider the "Promised Land." In chapter 6 I sketched the history of Israel up through the period of the Maccabean Revolt, when for the first time in over four centuries the people of Judah established themselves as an independent state under no foreign rule (after being overthrown and governed by the Babylonians, the Persians, the Greeks,

BOX 9.2 OTHER JEWISH MIRACLE-WORKING SONS OF GOD

Jesus was not the only one thought to be a miracle-working son of God, even within Judaism in his own day. His two most famous peers were probably **Honi the "circle-drawer"** and **Hanina ben Dosa**, both of whom are known through the writings of later Jewish rabbis. Honi was a Galilean teacher who died about one hundred years before Jesus. He was given his nickname because of a tradition that he prayed to God for much-needed rain and drew a circle around himself on the ground, declaring that he would not leave it until God granted his request. Luckily for him, God complied. Later sources indicate that Honi was a revered teacher and a miracle worker, who called himself the son of God. Like Jesus, he was martyred outside of the walls of Jerusalem around the time of Passover. To punish the Jews who had brought about his death, God sent a powerful wind storm that devastated their crops.

Hanina ben Dosa (= son of Dosa) was a rabbi in Galilee in the middle of the first century C.E. just after the time of Jesus. He was famous as a righteous and powerful worker of miracles, who (like Honi) could intervene with God to make the rain fall, who had the power to heal the sick, and who could confront demons and force them to do his bidding. Like Jesus, he was reputedly called the Son of God by a voice coming from the heavens.

Both of these miracle-working sons of God are portrayed somewhat differently from Jesus, of course. Most of their miracles, for example, were achieved through prayer rather than through their own power. But they are also different in significant ways from each other: Jesus and Hanina, for example, are both portrayed as exorcists whereas Honi is not. What is most interesting, however, is that anyone who called Jesus a miracle-working Jewish rabbi, the Son of God, would have been easily understood: other righteous Jews, both before Jesus and afterward, were portrayed similarly.

---

the Egyptians, and the Syrians). The independence achieved under the Maccabean rulers was to last just eighty years; in 63 B.C.E. the Roman troops under the great general Pompey entered Jerusalem and made all of Palestine subject to Roman rule. The land of Palestine was under Roman control during the days of Jesus and throughout the entire New Testament period.

POLITICAL LIFE IN PALESTINE Because of too many bad Hollywood movies about the Bible (and even some of the good ones), people today widely misunderstand Roman rule over the Jews in Palestine. You should not think that being subjugated to Rome meant that Jews were constantly confronted with Roman soldiers standing on every street corner making sure that the Jewish people understood that they were oppressed by a foreign power. Romans did not keep many troops in Palestine—there was no need for that. The Roman legions were stationed on the frontiers to protect against foreign invasion, and were brought into a region in the interior only if there was a military uprising that had to be put down. That did eventually happen in Palestine, about forty years after the days of Jesus. In 66 C.E. there was a violent surge in anti-Roman sentiment, a rebellion broke

out, Jews declared themselves in revolt, and the Romans sent in the troops from Syria, where they had been stationed on the border. They laid siege to Jerusalem and, after a painful three and a half years, they finally breached the city walls in 70 C.E. and ruthlessly murdered all the opposition and destroyed the Temple. This was one of the most horrific moments in Jewish history and is still commemorated by Jews today. The Temple has never been rebuilt.

In the days of Jesus, years earlier, there were occasional flare-ups and minor uprisings that the Romans easily took care of. But for the most part Romans were not actively involved in the affairs of Palestine. Someone like Jesus, who, as we will see, grew up in a rural area of the northern part of the land, probably never laid eyes on a Roman soldier during his daily life.

At this time Palestine (west of the Jordan river) was divided into three regions. Judea was in the south, and basically covered the same area as the nation of Judah from the time of the Hebrew Bible; its capital city was Jerusalem. North of Judea was the region of Samaria, which was inhabited by people who were considered (and somewhat despised) by many Jews to be a kind of "half-breed," born of the union of Jews and non-Jews (going all the way back to the Assyrian destruction of the eighth century). Further north was Galilee, a largely rural area (with just a couple of major cities) inhabited by Jews related by blood to those living in Judea. This is where Jesus came from; he was raised in the small and impoverished village of Nazareth.

There were two ways that Romans ruled the various lands that they conquered. In some instances they appointed a local aristocrat to be the king of a region, who was understood to be a kind of "client" of the Roman rulers. The client-king had the responsibility of raising the necessary taxes for the Romans; he also took care of all local governance. Government was conducted on the local level: the Romans did not impose Roman laws on everyone in the Roman Empire. The local laws and ways of governance were fine—so long as there were no rebellions and the tax revenues came in. When Jesus was born, the ruler of all Palestine was a client-king, Herod the Great. He was a local Jewish aristocrat (his enemies questioned whether he was actually of Jewish descent) who ruled ruthlessly as he saw necessary and did an excellent job, from the Romans' perspective, of keeping the peace and raising the taxes. Many Jews were not so pleased with his harsh policies.

The other way Romans ruled a conquered territory was by sending one of their own aristocrats in to serve as a governor. The imperial government back in Rome allowed Roman governors considerable license to do whatever they needed to do, given local conditions, to achieve both ends of their task (peace and taxes). Roman governors were virtually omnipotent in their provinces. They had the power of life and death. They were not, technically speaking, responsible to any local authorities—only to those back in Rome. They basically could do what they wanted and needed to do in order to keep everything running in good order. When Jesus was an adult, his home territory of Galilee was ruled by a client-king, Herod Antipas (the son of Herod the Great), but Judea was ruled by a Roman governor, Pontius Pilate. It is Pilate, as we will see, who exercised his authority and ordered Jesus' execution on charges of sedition against the state. That was the kind of thing Pilate did regularly, as part of his job.

THE CULTURE OF PALESTINE In both the north, Galilee, and the south, Judea, the common

History of Palestine	History of Christianity

63 B.C.E. Palestine conquered by Roman General Pompey

40–4 B.C.E. Herod made king of the Jews by the Romans

4–6 C.E. Judea ruled by Herod's son Archelaus

4 B.C.E.–30 C.E. Life of Jesus

4–39 C.E. Galilee ruled by Herod's son Antipas

6–41 C.E. Judea governed by Roman Prefects (Pontius Pilate, prefect in 26–36 C.E.)

27–30 C.E.? Public Ministry of Jesus

32–33 C.E.? Conversion of Paul

41–44 C.E. Agrippa 1, King over most of Palestine

34–64 C.E. Paul's missionary activities

44–66 C.E. Most of Palestine ruled by Roman procurators

49 C.E. 1 Thessalonians, Paul's earliest letter and the earliest surviving Christian Writing

66–70 C.E. First Jewish revolt

49–62 C.E. Paul's letters

FIGURE 9.4. Timeline of Palestine and Christianity from the conquest of Rome to the second Jewish Revolt.

language at this time was no longer Hebrew but Aramaic—a language, as we have seen, similar to Hebrew (comparable to the similarity of Portuguese and Spanish) but one used originally by the Persians when they controlled the land. In any event, Hebrew was no longer a spoken language. Everyone spoke Aramaic, and the upper-crust elite (e.g., people in the court of Herod) could speak Greek as

History of Palestine	History of Christianity
	64 C.E. Death of Paul and Peter
70 C.E. Destruction of Jerusalem/Temple	65–70 C.E. Gospel of Mark

80–85 C.E. Gospels of Matthew and Luke
80–110 C.E. Deutero-Pauline Epistles, Pastoral Epistles, General Epistles
90–95 C.E. Gospel of John
95–100 Book of Revelation

100–130 C.E. Rise of Gnosticism
ca. 120 C.E. 2 Peter

132–135 C.E. Second Jewish revolt (under Simon bar Kokhba)

well. Almost certainly Greek was not spoken by the lower classes. There is no good evidence to indicate, for example, that Jesus himself spoke anything except Aramaic.

The religion of Jews in Palestine was in many ways like that of Jews in the Diaspora. Even here (for example, in Galilee) there were synagogues—since it was not at all practicable for Jews to travel long distances, on foot, to attend the Temple whenever they wanted to worship. But the Temple was indeed a major feature of Palestinian Jewish life. The Temple had increased in size, magnificence, and importance from the days of its rebuilding in the fifth century B.C.E., when the Judeans returned from Babylon. King Herod the Great had been the last to make marked improvements, and it was by all accounts an amazing structure in Jesus' day (as we will see, Jesus probably saw it for the first time the last week of his life; he lived far north up in

Galilee and spent virtually his entire life there). The Temple complex encompassed an area roughly 500 yards by 325 yards, large enough to enclose twenty-five American football fields. From the outside, its stone walls rose 100 feet from the street—as high as a modern ten-story building. The gates to the Temple were so large that, according to one ancient source, they required 200 men to close them in the evening. From all of our ancient descriptions, the Temple appears to have been a fantastically beautiful set of buildings made with the best materials money could buy, including gold, which overlaid extensive portions of the structures.

As you might imagine, its construction was an immense feat. When all of its improvements were completed in 63 C.E., 18,000 local workers were reportedly left unemployed. It was destroyed, as I have mentioned, just seven years later during the Jewish uprising against the Romans.

The Temple functioned much as it did in the times of ancient Israel. This is where the sacrifices were made and where the priests officiated. Given the economic and religious centrality of the Temple, the chief priests were among the most powerful people in Judea. The high priest was the local ruler of the people and the main liaison with the Roman authorities.

The Formation of Jewish Sects

About a century and a half before Jesus, during the Maccabean period, different Jewish sects appeared, each of them emphasizing different aspects of the Jewish religion, often in opposition to one another. We know of these groups from the New Testament itself, which mentions three of them, and from the writings of the very important Jewish historian of the first century, **Josephus**. (See Box 9.3.) In one way or another, all of these sects are important for understanding the life of the historical Jesus and the early Christian Gospels. They are the **Pharisees**, the **Sadducees**, the **Essenes**, and the "**fourth philosophy**."

I should stress at the outset that most Jews in Palestine did not belong to any of these groups. We know this much from Josephus, who indicates that the largest sect, the Pharisees, claimed 6000 members and that the Essenes had 4000. The Sadducees probably had far fewer. (Remember, there were something like 4 million Jews in the world at the

BOX 9.3 FLAVIUS JOSEPHUS

Our best source of information about first-century Palestine is a person named Flavius Josephus (37–100 C.E.). Josephus is an unusually valuable historian: he actually lived in Palestine in the first century, knew most of its leading figures, and experienced firsthand not just its dominant culture but also its political and military crises.

Born to an aristocratic priestly family, as a relatively young man Josephus was appointed to head the Jewish troops in Galilee at the outset of the Jewish War against Rome (66 C.E.). As he later tells us in his autobiography, when his troops were surrounded by the Roman legions at the town of Jotaphatha, rather than surrender they agreed to a suicide pact. They were to draw lots to determine who would kill whom, with the final two then to commit suicide.

As it happened, one of the final two lots (by a trick or chance) fell to Josephus; but when all the others were dead, he convinced his surviving colleague they should turn themselves in to the Romans. Brought before the conquering general Vespasian, Josephus then had the good sense to utter a "prophecy" that he, Vespasian, would become the Roman emperor. As it turns out, the prophecy became a reality: Nero committed suicide and eventually Vespasian was declared emperor by his troops.

He never forgot that Josephus had predicted it. During the war Vespasian, and then his son and successor in the field, Titus, used Josephus as an interpreter, urging the Jews inside the walls of Jerusalem to surrender. They refused and were eventually destroyed in the onslaught of 70 C.E. when the walls of the city were breached, the Temple demolished, and the opposition slaughtered. Josephus was then taken back to Rome, set free, and appointed by Vespasian to be a kind of court historian.

Josephus adopted Vespasian's family name (Flavius), and spent the next twenty-five years or so writing books about the Jewish people, including a six-volume work on the Jewish Wars (which he obviously knew about firsthand) and a twenty-volume history of the Jewish people called the *Antiquities of the Jews* (from Adam and Eve up to his own time).

These works betray the clear slant of their author: Josephus, for example, wanted to show the Romans that Jews were loyal to the empire and to show the Jews that they could not resist the might of Rome. His political agenda notwithstanding, Josephus' books are extremely useful for historians wanting to know about the life, customs, society, leading figures, politics, and culture of first-century Palestine, written by competent scholar who was actually there at the time.

time.) What matters for our purposes, however, is not the size of these groups—for they were highly influential despite their small numbers—but the ways in which they understood what it meant to be Jewish, especially in light of the political crises they had to face.

PHARISEES   The Pharisees represent probably the best known and the least understood Jewish sect. Because of the way they are attacked in parts of the New Testament, especially in Matthew, Christians through the ages have wrongly considered the Pharisees' chief attribute to be hypocrisy. In fact, to become a Pharisee a Jew did not need to take a hypocritic oath.

The sect apparently began during the Maccabean period as a group of devout Jews intent above all else on keeping the entire will of God, as expressed in the Torah. The problem with many of the laws of Moses, however, is that they are ambiguous. For

example, the Ten Commandments require Jews to keep the Sabbath day holy; but nowhere does the Torah indicate precisely how this is to be done. Pharisees devised rules and regulations to assist them in keeping this and all the other laws of Moses. These rules eventually formed a body of tradition, which, to keep with our example, indicated what a person could and could not do on the Sabbath day in order to keep it holy and set apart from all other days. Thus, for example, when it was determined that a faithful Jew should not go on a long journey on the Sabbath, it had to be decided what a "long" journey was and consequently what distance a Jew could travel on this day without violating its holiness. Likewise, a worker who believed that he or she should not labor on the Sabbath had to know what constituted "work" and what therefore could and could not be done.

The rules and regulations that developed among the Pharisees came to have a status of their own and were known in some circles as the "oral" Law, which was set alongside the "written" Law of Moses. It appears that Pharisees generally believed that anyone who kept the oral Law would be almost certain to keep the written Law as a consequence. The intent was not to be legalistic but to be obedient to what God had commanded.

The Pharisees may have been a relatively closed society in Jesus' day to the extent that they stayed together as a group, eating meals and having fellowship only with one another; that is, with those who were like-minded in seeing the need to maintain a high level of obedience before God. They did not have close ties with those who were less stringent in maintaining purity before God and avoided, therefore, eating meals with common people.

It is important to recognize that the Pharisees were not the "power players" in Palestine in Jesus' day. That is to say, they appear to have had some popular appeal but no real political clout. In some ways they are best seen as a kind of separatist group. They wanted to maintain their own purity and did so in relative (not complete) isolation from other Jews. Many scholars think that the term "Pharisee" itself originally came from a Persian word that means "separated ones." Eventually, however, some decades after Jesus' execution, the Pharisees did become powerful in the political sense. This was after the Jewish War and the destruction of Jerusalem and the Temple in the year 70 C.E. With this calamity the other groups passed from the scene for a variety of reasons, and the descendants of the Pharisees were given more power by the Roman overlords. The oral tradition continued to grow and to be invested with greater authority. It was eventually written down around the year 200 C.E., and is today known as the **Mishnah**, the heart of the later Jewish sacred collection of texts, the **Talmud**.

SADDUCEES

It is difficult to reconstruct exactly what the Sadducees stood for because we do not have any literary works that clearly come from the pen of a Sadducee, in contrast to the Pharisees. The Pharisees are represented to some extent by the later traditions of the Talmud; by Josephus, who was a Pharisee; and by the one Pharisee who left us writings before the destruction of the Temple (after he had converted to be a follower of Jesus), the apostle Paul. To understand the Sadducees, however, we must turn to what is said about them in other sources such as Josephus and the New Testament.

During Jesus' day, the Sadducees were evidently the real power players in Palestine. They appear to have been, by and large, members of the Jewish aristocracy in Jerusalem who were closely connected with the Jewish priesthood in charge of the Temple. Most of the Sadducees were themselves priests (although not all priests were Sadducees). As members of the aristocracy, granted some limited power by their Roman overlords, Sadducees appear to have been conciliatory toward the civil authorities and cooperative with the Roman governor. The local Jewish council, called the **Sanhedrin**, which was called upon to decide local affairs, was evidently made up principally of Sadducees. With their close connection to the Temple, Sadducees emphasized the need for Jews to be properly involved in the cultic worship of God as prescribed in the Torah. Indeed, it appears that the Torah itself—that is, the five books of Moses—was the only authoritative text that the Sadducees accepted. In any event, we know that they did not accept the oral traditions formulated by the Pharisees. Less concerned with the regulation of daily affairs such as eating, travel, and work, the Sadducees focused their religious attention on the sacrifices in the Temple, and expended their political energy on working out their relations with Romans so that these sacrifices could continue.

ESSENES

The Essenes are the one Jewish sect not mentioned in the New Testament. Ironically, they are also the group about which we are best informed. This is because the famous Dead Sea Scrolls were produced by a group of Essenes who lived in a community east of Jerusalem in the wilderness area near the northwestern shore of the Dead Sea, in a place that is today called **Qumran**. Although the term "Essene" never occurs in the scrolls, we know from at least one ancient authority, the Roman writer Pliny the Elder, that a community of Essenes was located in this area; moreover, the social arrangements and theological views described in the Dead Sea Scrolls correspond to what we know about the Essenes from other accounts. Most scholars are reasonably certain, therefore, that the scrolls represent a library used by this set, or at least by the part of it living near Qumran.

The discovery of the Dead Sea Scrolls was completely serendipitous. In 1947 a shepherd boy, searching for a lost goat in the barren wilderness near the northwest shore of the Dead Sea, happened

FIGURE 9.5. Some of the caves in the wilderness west of the Dead Sea near the Qumran community, in which the Dead Sea Scrolls were found.

to toss a stone into a cave and heard it strike something. Entering the cave, he discovered an ancient earthenware jar that contained a number of old scrolls. The books were recovered by local Bedouin. When news of the discovery reached antiquities dealers, biblical scholars learned of the find and a search was conducted both to find more scrolls in the surrounding caves and to retrieve those that had already been found by the locals.

Some of the caves in the region yielded entire scrolls; others contained thousands of tiny scraps that are virtually impossible to piece back together, since so many of the pieces are missing. Imagine trying to do dozens of immense jigsaw puzzles, not knowing what the end products should look like, when most of the pieces are lost and those that remain are all mixed together. All in all, hundreds of documents are represented, many of them in fragments the size of postage stamps and others, perhaps a couple of dozen, in scrolls of sufficient length to give us a full idea of their contents.

Most of the scrolls are written in Hebrew, but some are in Aramaic (with yet smaller portions in Greek). Different kinds of literature are represented in these writings. They include at least partial copies of every book of the Jewish Bible, with the exception of the book of Esther, and some of them are fairly complete. These are extremely valuable because of their age; they are nearly a thousand years older than the oldest copies of the Hebrew Scripture that we previously had. We can therefore check to see whether Jewish scribes over the intervening centuries reliably copied their texts. The short

answer is that for the most part they did (but see chapter 15). There are also commentaries on some of the biblical books, written principally to show that the predictions of the ancient prophets had come to be fulfilled in the experiences of the Essene believers and in the history of their community. In addition, there are books that contain psalms and hymns composed by members of the community, prophecies that indicate future events that were believed to be ready to transpire in the author's own day, and rules for the members of the community to follow in their lives together.

Sifting through all these books, scholars have been able to reconstruct the lifestyles and beliefs of the Essenes in considerable detail. It appears that their community at Qumran was started during the early Maccabean period, perhaps around 150 B.C.E., by pious Jews who were convinced that the Hasmoneans had usurped their authority by appointing a high priest from the wrong priestly line (as we have seen, since the days of David the high priest had come from the family of a man named Zadok; when the Hasmoneans assumed control, they appointed one of their own to the office). Believing that the Jews of Jerusalem had gone astray, this group of Essenes chose to start their own community in which they could keep the Mosaic law rigorously and maintain their own ritual purity in the wilderness. They did so fully expecting the apocalypse of the end time to be imminent. They believed that when it came, there would be a final battle between the forces of good and evil, between the children of light and the children of darkness. The battle would

BOX 9.4 DIVINE REVELATION IN THE DEAD SEA SCROLLS

Two kinds of writing found among the Dead Sea Scrolls are of particular interest to historians of early Christianity. Both have to do with the Essenes' belief that God had revealed to members of the community the course of historical events.

The Biblical Commentaries. Like many other Jews, the Essenes believed that the prophets of Scripture had spoken about events that came to transpire in their own day, centuries later. In the words of the commentary on Habakkuk, "God told Habakkuk to write down that which would happen to the final generation, but He did not make known to him when time would come to an end." The Essenes had developed a particular method of interpretation to explain these secret revelations of God's divine purpose. Scholars have called this method of interpretation **"pesher,"** from the Hebrew word used in the Qumran commentaries to introduce the explanation of a prophetic statement. The commentaries typically cite a verse of Scripture and then give its "pesher," or interpretation. In every case the interpretation indicates how the prediction has come to fulfillment in the world of the Qumran community itself. For these

Essenes, the Hebrew Bible was not simply written for ancient readers: its real and ultimate meaning had to do with what was happening centuries later among the Essenes.

The War Scroll. This scroll details the final war between the forces of good and evil that will take place a the end of time. It sketches the course of the battles, gives regulations for the soldiers who fight, and describes the outcome that is assured by God as the "children of light" (the members of the Essene communities) overcome the "children of darkness" (the Romans, the apostate Jews, and everyone else). The war will take forty years, the first six of which involve overcoming the "Kittim" (the Romans), the rest being devoted to campaigns against the other nations.

This document, then, provides an apocalyptic vision of the final struggle between good and evil, between the forces of God and those of his enemies. While the War Scroll is unique among ancient Jewish literature in its graphic and detailed description of the future battle that will end the age, in general terms it related closely to apocalyptic texts written by other Jews in the period.

climax with the triumph of God and the entry of his children into the blessed kingdom. The Essenes, in other words, were Jewish apocalypticists.

Some of the scrolls indicate that the coming kingdom would be ruled by two messiahs, one a king and the other a priest. The priestly messiah would lead the faithful in their worship of God in a purified temple, where sacrifices would again be made in accordance with God's will. In the meantime, the true people of God needed to be removed from the impurities of this world, including the impurities prevalent in the Jewish Temple and among the rest of the Jewish people. These Essenes therefore started their own monastic-like community, with strict rules for admission and membership. A two-year initiation was required, after which, if approved, a member was to donate all of his possessions to the community fund and share the common meal with all the other members. Rigorous guidelines dictated what happened in the daily life of the community. Members had fixed hours for work and rest and for their meals, there were required times of fasting, and strict penalties were imposed for unseemly behavior such as

interrupting one another, talking at meals, and laughing at inappropriate times.

It appears that when the Jewish War broke out in 66 C.E., the Essenes at Qumran hid some of their sacred writings before joining in the struggle. It may well be that they saw this as the final battle, preliminary to the end of time when God would establish his kingdom and send its messiahs.

THE "FOURTH PHILOSOPHY" When Josephus writes about Judaism in his history of the Jewish people, he describes each of the sects we have discussed as a "philosophy," by which he means a group with a distinctive and rational outlook on the world. He never gives a name to the fourth sect that he discusses but simply calls it the "fourth philosophy." The tenets of this philosophy, however, are clear, and they were manifested in several different groups that we know about from various ancient sources. Each of these groups in its own way supported active resistance to Israel's foreign domination.

The view that characterized these sundry groups was that Israel had a right to its own land, a right that had been granted by God himself. Anyone who

At a Glance: The Context of Jesus and Early Christianity

The term "Greco-Roman World" refers to the lands surrounding the Mediterranean Sea from roughly 300 B.C.E. to 300 C.E. These lands were conquered by Alexander the Great, who wanted to spread Greek culture throughout this territory. Eventually the region came under the control of the Roman Empire. Jesus was born during the reign of the first Roman emperor, Caesar Augustus, at the beginning of a two hundred year period of relative peace known as the Pax Romana.

Palestine was ruled by the Romans either through a local aristocratic client-king or through a Roman governor. There were four major sects of Jews at the time, who exercised significant influence even though most Jews did not belong to any of them. The Pharisees developed oral traditions that were to be followed by those who were intent on keeping God's Law as carefully as possible. The Sadducees were the power players in Palestine, who stressed the importance of the Jewish priesthood and the worship of God in the Temple. The Essenes were a separatist group that strove to achieve its own purity by separating itself off from the polluting influences of the rest of the world. And the "fourth philosophy" urged armed rebellion against the foreign oppressors in order to win back the Promised Land for the people of Israel.

usurped that right, and anyone who backed the usurper, was to be opposed, by violent means if necessary. Among those who took this line in the middle of the first century were the **Sicarii**, a group whose name comes from the Latin word for "dagger." These "daggermen" planned and carried out assassinations and kidnappings of high-ranking Jewish officials who were thought to be in league with the Roman authorities. Another group that subscribed to this philosophy, somewhat later in the century, were the **Zealots**. These were Jews who were "zealous" for the Law and who urged armed rebellion to take back the land God had promised his people. More specifically, based on what we find in Josephus, Zealots were Galilean Jews who fled to Jerusalem during the Jewish revolt around 67 C.E., overthrew the priestly aristocracy in the city in a bloody coup, and urged the violent opposition to the Roman legions that ultimately led to the destruction of Jerusalem and the burning of the Temple in 70 C.E.

OTHER JEWISH LITERATURE OF THE PERIOD: THE DEUTEROCANONICAL OR APOCRYPHAL BOOKS

In addition to the Dead Sea Scrolls, there was other literature written by Jewish authors that cannot be found in the Hebrew Bible but that is of great importance for anyone interested in it. Of these other Jewish books, none is of greater historical significance than a collection of writings that can be found in some Christian versions of the Old Testament. These are the deuterocanonical writings, as they are called in the Roman Catholic and Eastern Orthodox traditions; Protestants typically designate them as the Apocrypha. The term "apocrypha" may not be altogether appropriate, as it is a word that means "hidden things"—or in this case, "hidden books." But there is nothing hidden about these books. They simply are books that are considered part of the canon by some Christian denominations, but not by Protestants and not by Jews. For Roman Catholic and Orthodox Christians they are in a kind of "second canon," hence the name deuterocanonical.

These books are important for understanding the Bible of the early Christians. Even though these books are not found in Hebrew manuscripts of the Bible, they were transmitted as part of the Bible in the ancient Greek translation known as the **Septuagint.** (See Box 9.5.) This was an important translation for Jews of the Diaspora, and eventually for Christians. As I have mentioned, most Jews by the time, say, of the Maccabean Revolt—or, later, of the days of Jesus—did not live in Palestine and so no longer had any facility in reading Hebrew. Most Jews, of course, could not read at all, since like most of the people living in the Roman Empire the vast majority of Jews—probably some 90 percent—were not literate. For most ancient people, to "read" a book meant hearing someone else read it aloud. The Scripture was "read" regularly in the synagogues, and people could hear it read and discuss its meaning. But virtually no one outside of Palestine could "read" it in Hebrew. The standard Bible for most Jews in the Diaspora was the Septuagint. This became the Bible for the Greek-speaking Christians at the very early stages of the Christian movement, as soon as missionaries spread the religion outside of Palestine. And the Septuagint included these dozen or so books that we are calling deuterocanonical, or apocryphal.

It was during the Protestant Reformation of the sixteenth century that Martin Luther and like-minded leaders of the Protestant movement declared that the only books of the Old Testament to be accepted as Scripture were those found in the Hebrew Bible—that is, the books regarded as canonical by Jews. Roman Catholics, on the other hand, declared that the writings of the Septuagint had always been part of the scriptures for Christians, and so should continue to be accepted as such. The Orthodox churches more or less sided with the Roman Catholics on this issue.

But there was not a unanimous view on the subject. There are ten books that are accepted as deuterocanonical in both the Roman Catholic and Orthodox traditions; four others are accepted by various Eastern Orthodox groups (for example, Greek orthodox and Russian orthodox churches), and a couple of others that are accepted as standing on the margins by one group or another.

All of these books were written by Jews and for Jews. Most of them were written after the final books of the Hebrew Bible and before the writings of the New Testament, so that roughly speaking they can be thought of as some of the "intertestamental" Jewish literature (i.e., written "between the testaments"). They represent some of the truly great and interesting writings of the time. Some of them are historical narratives, for example of the Maccabean period; others are historical fictions that teach religious lessons; others are expansions of books found in the Hebrew Bible; and others are books of Wisdom. Here we can consider briefly the ten books that lie at the heart of the "Apocrypha"—the books accepted by both Roman Catholic and Orthodox traditions as deuterocanonical.

Tobit

Tobit is a work of historical fiction—by which I mean it is a fictional tale set within a real historical context.

Originally the book was written in Aramaic, either in the late third century B.C.E. or the early second.

The narrative is set in the eighth century B.C.E. in the city of Nineveh, where the hero of the story, Tobit, has been exiled from his town in Galilee during the conquests of the Assyrian king Shalmaneser. In other words, the account is allegedly taking place after the destruction of the northern kingdom of Israel. The story involves two subplots that eventually come to be woven together. The first is about Tobit himself, who is very righteous and does great works of Jewish piety but runs into serious misfortune as he is blinded, in a rather unusual way, when bird droppings fall into his eyes. This makes his life miserable. The second is about his distant relative Sarah, living in Media, who has had the equally great misfortune of having had seven marriages, each of them ending on her wedding night when a demon killed her husband. The two plots are woven together through a journey of Tobit's son Tobias to Media to collect a fortune his father had left there. Accompanied by an angel, Tobias captures a large fish whose internal organs have magical powers: if burned they can drive away demons and they can be used to heal the blind.

By a fluke, Tobias meets Sarah; they fall in love, they marry, he uses his magical fish parts to drive away the demon intent on killing him on their wedding night, they return home with the treasure to Tobit, and the remaining fish parts are used to make his father see again. They then all live to a ripe old age and die happy. It's a great tale about the need to stay faithful in adverse circumstances and the power of God to turn truly lousy human experiences into good.

Judith

Judith is another work of historical fiction, in this case set during the reign of King Nebuchadnezzar "who ruled over the Assyrians" as we are told in the book's opening verse. This is not a great start for anyone who knows history, since Nebuchadnezzar was not the king of Assyria but of Babylon. This is historical fiction with a stress on the word "fiction." It was probably written in Hebrew originally, possibly during the Maccabean period when national hopes were on the rise and a story such as this would have resonated with its hearers.

The main character is one of the great heroes of Jewish tradition, Judith, who saves her nation from

BOX 9.5 SEPTUAGINT

Since the majority of Jews in the first century lived outside of Palestine, they no longer spoke Aramaic or read Hebrew but spoke the local language wherever they lived, with the more highly educated among them also speaking Greek—the lingua franca of the Roman world.

This posed a problem for reading the Jewish Scriptures, since they were written in Hebrew. And so, as one might expect, Greek-speaking Jews in the Diaspora prepared translations of Scripture: different translations at different times and places. The one translation we are best informed about, which became by far the most widely used, is called the Septuagint (often abbreviated as LXX). The name comes from the Latin term *septuaginta*, which means "seventy." This is a shorthand reference to the legend that the translation was made by seventy (or, as usually stated, seventy-two) Jewish translators.

The legend is best known from a fascinating document called the "Letter of Aristeas," allegedly written in the third century B.C.E. According to Aristeas, when the king of Egypt, Ptolemy II (285–247 B.C.E.) decided to expand his library to 500,000 volumes and wanted to include every important piece of literature in it, he conferred with his chief librarian Demetrius, who informed him that one major gap in his holdings was the sacred laws of the Jews. Ptolemy immediately sent a letter to the Jewish high priest in Jerusalem, requesting assistance in procuring a copy in translation.

In response, the high priest sent seventy-two translators, six from each of the twelve tribes of Israel, to Egypt. They were feasted (for seven days!) by their host, who questioned them about their religion and then secluded them to do their work of translation. Miraculously, they completed the work to perfection in exactly seventy-two days.

This entertaining account appears to refer only to the translation of the first five books of the Jewish Scriptures (the Pentateuch). But eventually, by the second century B.C.E., all the books were translated and they became the form of Scripture familiar to Jews throughout the Diaspora. The Septuagint became the Scriptures for the early Christians as well, who treated it as an authoritative text down to its very words. It is the Septuagint, not the Hebrew Scripture, that is quoted by the authors of the New Testament, most of whom did not know Hebrew but were thoroughly trained in Greek.

certain annihilation by a foreign power (think of the analogous situation under Antiochus Epiphanes). The first half of the book is a set-up: Nebuchadnezzar has gone on military conquest, requesting nations en route to provide their support, and Israel refuses to help. After his victory he turns to attack the recalcitrant nation by sending his general Holofernes and an enormous number of troops, who gather at a mountain pass in Israel near the village of Bethulia in preparation for destroying the Israelite resistance.

The second half of the book is about how Judith, an inhabitant of the village, intervenes in the affair. A widow who is both very beautiful and very pious, she is dismayed that the leaders of Bethulia refuse to trust God for their deliverance and so she takes matters into her own hands. Leaving the village, dressed in her most attractive clothes, she is taken into the Assyrian camp and welcomed by Holofernes, who eventually tries unsuccessfully to seduce her after a night of too much wine. As he lies sprawled out in a drunken torpor, Judith takes advantage of the situation; drawing his sword, she decapitates him, returns to her camp with the head, and the next day the Assyrians are thrown into confusion by the sudden death of their headless leader. A rout is on and Israel is saved.

Additions to Esther

The version of Esther in the Septuagint is markedly different from that in the Hebrew Bible: it includes six additions, which add another 105 verses to the story. These additions represent attempts to "fill in" the story in places where the Greek redactor felt that some more information would help round out what could otherwise be found in the tale. The additions not only explain parts of the plot that interested readers may have had questions about; they make the story far more religious. If you will recall, there is nothing about God—directly at least—in the Hebrew version of Esther; his name is never even mentioned. But in these additions God is all over the place, and it is clear that he is the one directing the action. The terms "God" and "Lord" now occur over fifty times in the book.

Probably these additions were made in the second century B.C.E. or even the first. These additions are as follows:

- A description of the dream of the Jewish hero Mordecai (it is a bizarre dream about two dragons, which will be interpreted in the final addition);
- The edict that Haman sent out, announcing the date when all Jews in the empire were to be attacked;
- Prayers by Mordecai and Esther;
- Esther's appearance, in gut-wrenching fear, before the king, who, luckily, welcomes her with open arms (this is a climactic moment in the narrative);
- The edict of Mordecai which serves to nullify the earlier edict of Haman;
- An interpretation of the opening dream of Mordecai.

The Wisdom of Solomon

The Wisdom of Solomon is a book of positive wisdom (recall Proverbs), which claims to be written by the great king of the United Monarchy. It fact it was written many centuries later, by a Jew in the Diaspora, possibly in the first century B.C.E. or the first century C.E.

The book celebrates Wisdom as the greatest gift to humans and insists that it involves proper fear and adoration of God, which will lead to eternal reward. Those who lead ungodly lives, on the other hand "will be punished as their reasoning deserves" (5:10). The exaltation of wisdom recalls Proverbs 8, where Wisdom appears as a female consort with God at the beginning of all things. Here too Wisdom is said to be "a breath of the power of God and a pure emanation of the glory of the Almighty . . . for she is a reflection of eternal light, a spotless mirror of the working of God" (7:25–26).

We have seen that the Wisdom literature of the Hebrew Bible differs from the writings of the prophets and historians because it shows no interest in the history of the nation of Israel or God's dealings with them, the covenant, the Law, the failures of the people, their punishments, and so forth. While that is true of Proverbs, Job, and Ecclesiastes, it is not true of the Wisdom of Solomon. Here, in fact, the interaction of Wisdom with the nation of Israel is laid out in powerful and graphic terms in a poetic retelling of God's interactions with his people in light of wisdom. In particular, chapters 11–19 reflect on the events of the Exodus tradition (Exodus 7–14), showing how God guided the history of his people in contrast to how he judged and punished his enemies, the Egyptians. This involves a series of seven contrasts. For example, God sent hail and lightning from heaven upon the Egyptians, but he rained manna from heaven upon his chosen people (16:15–29); and he plagued the Egyptians with darkness, but led the Israelites through the darkness with a pillar of fire (17:1–18:4).

Here, wisdom clearly involves knowing and following the ways of the God of Israel. The theological emphasis of the book is summed up at its very end: "For in everything, O Lord, you have exalted and glorified your people, and you have not neglected to help them at all times and in all places" (19:22).

Sirach

The book of Sirach was written by a person who names himself "Jesus son of Eleazar son of Sirach" (50:27). In Hebrew "son of Sirach" is "ben Sira," and that is what he is normally called in discussions of the book. In the Latin tradition the book is called Ecclesiasticus ("book involving the church"). The book was originally written in Hebrew, in Palestine, in 180 B.C.E.; it was translated into Greek (the translator himself tells us, in the book) by ben Sira's grandson, in Egypt in 117 B.C.E.

This book of Wisdom is similar in many ways to the book of Proverbs in the Hebrew Bible, in that it is a collection of wise sayings in poetry on a wide range of topics. Unlike Proverbs, Sirach—like the Wisdom of Solomon—is much more heavily invested in the history of the ancient Israelites and their relationship with God. Chapters 44–50 reflect on the "famous men, our ancestors in their generations"—that is the great heroes of the people: kings, wise men, musicians, and others. And so the author praises Enoch, Noah, Abraham, Isaac, Moses, Aaron, and so on.

The book celebrates Wisdom, again in exalted terms; Wisdom says of herself that "Before the ages,

The majority of the book consists of wise reflections and sage advice on many of the issues that people have to deal with in their daily lives: happiness, honor and shame, money, friendship, social relations (with a lot of things to say about women, some of them not very enlightened), and death. These wise sayings are ultimately, for this book, rooted in a recognition of the greatness of the God of Israel, the one who gave all wisdom: "All wisdom is from the Lord, and with him it remains forever. . . . There is but one who is wise, greatly to be feared, seated upon his throne—the Lord. It is he who created her; he saw her and took her measure; he poured her out upon all his works." (1:1, 8–9).

Baruch

The book of Baruch was allegedly written by a figure who appears in the book of Jeremiah as the prophet's personal secretary, Baruch the son of Neriah (see Jeremiah 32:12; 36:4). It was actually written some four hundred years later, probably in the second century B.C.E. or possibly the first, sometime after the Maccabean Revolt. It was originally composed in Hebrew.

The book claims to be written during the Babylonian exile and represents a reflection on the causes for this national disaster and a plea to God to intervene and show kindness once more to his afflicted people. The book is only six chapters in length, and begins by giving the (alleged) historical background to its writing; there follows an extensive confession to God that the destruction of Judah has occurred because of the sin of the people. God was just in sending such a horrendous punishment. But the author appeals to God for mercy and to restore his people to their proper place.

Most of the third chapter is a poem devoted to Wisdom, which the people of Israel abandoned when they departed from the ways of God. As in Sirach, Wisdom here is identified as "the book of the commandments of God, the law that endures forever" (4:1) This author takes a prophetic view of the Law: "all who hold her fast will live, and those who forsake her will die" (4:2).

The book ends with a poem meant to encourage the people who are suffering the calamity of exile. The nation has suffered for its sins, but God is soon to deliver them from their enemies and so they are to "take courage."

FIGURE 9.6. A fragment of the book of Sirach that was discovered at Masada; the fragment comes from a scroll and has portions of chapters 43 and 44.

in the beginning, he created me, and for all ages I shall not cease to be." But Wisdom does not belong to all people—she is a unique possession of Israel: "Thus in the beloved city he gave me a resting place, and in Jerusalem was my domain. I took root in an honored people, in the portion of the Lord, his heritage" (24:9, 11–12). In particular, Wisdom came to be manifest precisely in the Torah (24:23).

The Letter of Jeremiah

This is one of the shortest books of Apocrypha—it is only one chapter long, and in the Latin tradition of the Roman Catholic Church it is included as the final chapter of the book of Baruch. The book is allegedly written by the prophet Jeremiah, sent to the Judeans bound for Babylonian exile. In exile they will be among people who worship other gods through idols. This book is nothing but an attack on pagan idolatry.

The real historical context of the writing is a situation in which Jews around the world were surrounded by idol worship. It may have been produced in the aftermath of the Maccabean Revolt; it appears to have been composed in Hebrew or Aramaic.

Much of the book consists of a mockery of idols and those who make them. We are told that one idol "holds a scepter, like a district judge, but is unable to destroy anyone who offends it. Another has a dagger in its right hand, and an ax, but cannot defend itself from war and robbers" (6:14–15). In other words, idols are powerless not only to help their worshipers but even to help themselves. They are made by "carpenters and goldsmiths" and they can be put into any form that the artisan desires. "Those who make them will certainly not live very long themselves; how then can the things that are made by them be gods?" (6:45–47). "Like a scarecrow in a cucumber bed, which guards nothing, so are their gods of wood, overlaid with gold and silver" (6:70).

This kind of attack on idolatry makes a lot of sense to most readers today, as it did to Jews in antiquity. On the other hand, pagans who used idols in their worship would have been a bit baffled by it all, since as a rule they did not actually think the idols were gods. The idols were simply representations of gods and, sometimes thought, the physical means through which the transcendent gods worked their power. But to outsiders, such as Jews, the entire worship practices of pagans seemed foolish, and it was easy indeed to mock it by pointing out that idols are made out of wood that rots and metal that rusts, and so have no real existence or power.

The Additions to Daniel

We have seen that later redactors made several additions to the book of Esther in order to "fill out" the story in places. The same thing happens with the book of Daniel. These additions were probably composed independently of one another, as kinds of expansions on key points of the story. They were apparently written sometime after the Maccabean Revolt. There are three additions altogether:

- *The Prayer of Azariah and the Song of the Three Jews.* We have seen that Daniel 3 tells the story of the three Jewish youths who refuse to worship the statue of the king, and so are punished by being thrown into an enormous fiery furnace. They gloriously survive the ordeal—but what were they doing in there? This one chapter addition tells us: they were praying and praising God. Azariah is one of the three (in Daniel he is also known as Abednego); he prays to God a prayer of confession in which he acknowledges that the nation of Judah has been exiled for its sins, and he prays that God will deliver it from its woes. This is not a prayer related to the fact that he has just been thrown into a raging furnace, making it appear that it was a prayer that was composed independently of Daniel and added to the story only later (compare the prayer of Jonah in Jonah 2). In addition, the three youths all then break into a song of thanksgiving and praise to God as they are protected in the fiery furnace. This too is a psalm that was originally written independently of the story that has now been put on the lips of the devout youths.
- *Susanna.* This is a terrific short story of a woman who is falsely accused of sexual misconduct and condemned to be executed for it. But young Daniel intervenes in the proceedings and shows that the two men who have brought the accusation in fact are the ones who were ill-behaved (and sexually motivated) and that their accusations were false. She is vindicated, the men are executed, and Daniel is exalted.
- *Bel and the Dragon.* This is two brief stories attacking idolatry. In one, the idol Bel is shown by Daniel not to have any real existence but to be manipulated by its priests who are getting some very good meals out of the offerings allegedly being consumed by the god. The other is about a dragon that Daniel shows convincingly is not a divine being at all. This gets Daniel into trouble with his enemies, who have him thrown into a lions' den. As in the Hebrew Bible account, he is protected by God and they, his enemies, are eventually ripped to shreds by the lions as a reward for their efforts.

1 Maccabees

With the book of 1 **Maccabees** we move from the genres of fiction and wisdom to the genre of history. This is a historical narrative that details the events that led up to the Maccabean Revolt (chs. 1–2), and that transpired during the years of rebellion, for three generations of the family that led the uprising. It is our principal source of knowledge about the period, and so is of particular interest to historians of this crucial time in ancient Israel. It was originally written in Hebrew.

In chapter 6 I have already summarized the events that precipitated the revolt. The first two chapters of 1 Maccabees are particularly gripping in their portrayal of the Hellenizing policies of Antiochus Epiphanes, the escalation of tensions between Jews who welcomed the new cultural advances and those (including the author) who saw them as heinous attempts to destroy the Jewish faith and the Jewish people, and the heightened extreme measures taken by the monarch as he made it a crime against the state to retain Jewish practices and customs. But in his attempt to establish Hellenistic culture even in Judea—requiring sacrifice to idols and outlawing circumcision—Antiochus went a step too far. The family of Mattathias and his five sons started a local revolt in the town of Modein: Mattathias killed a Jew performing a pagan sacrifice, as well as the pagan official overseeing the act. Thus the uprising began.

Much of the confrontation with the Syrian oppressors was carried out as a kind of guerrilla warfare. It was Mattathias' son Judas (the *Maccabeus*—the "hammer") who took the lead. Chapters 3–9 describe the skirmishes, battles, and diplomatic efforts of Judas himself; chapters 9–16 describe those of his successors. It ends with the work of Judas' nephew John Hyrcanus, who became the high priest and ruler of the people from 134–104 B.C.E. The book was probably written soon after that.

2 Maccabees

The book known as 2 Maccabees is another account of the history of the Maccabean Revolt. Its author did not have 1 Maccabees as a source but was writing independently of it. His interest is principally with the events that transpired under the leadership of Judas Maccabeus, so that the book overlaps mainly with 1 Maccabees chapters 1–7. The author indicates that his work is in fact an abridgment of a much longer five-volume description of the revolt by someone named Jason of Cyrene. He has condensed Jason's work into a single volume. Unlike 1 Maccabees, this account was originally composed in Greek.

Whereas 1 Maccabees is a rather straightforward chronicle of what happened leading up to and during the revolt, 2 Maccabees takes a more impassioned and theological approach to the task. After a lengthy two-chapter introduction—which consists of two letters from Jews in Judea to those in Egypt, urging them to observe the celebration of Hannukah—the author devotes four chapters to describing the events leading up to the revolt and then chapters 8–15 to narrating key moments during the revolt itself.

Most famous—and justly so—are the stories told from the end of chapter 6 through chapter 7, of Jewish martyrs who refuse the demands of the tyrant Antiochus to eat pork and are willing to experience excruciating torture and death to remain faithful to the Law. The narrative is powerful and moving. First there is a 90-year-old Eleazar, who dies on the rack rather than violate the dictates of God's Law. Then there are seven brothers and their mother. The brothers are tortured one at a time in front of the others (the first has his tongue cut out and his hands and feet cut off and then, still living, he is fried in a large pan over a raging fire until dead). The others follow suit, one after the other. To escape, all they have to do is take a bite of pork. But they refuse—and the mother encourages them on. She too then is tortured and killed.

This is not simply a book designed to give a history lesson. It is meant to show what it means to stay true to the Law of God to the very end, no matter what. For this author, the Law is more important than life itself. And for these martyrs the reason is clear: there is to be a future resurrection of the dead, and if they are faithful now they will be rewarded then, Forever; whereas those who are not faithful will experience severe punishment in the life to come.

Other Deuterocanonical Books

As I mentioned, four other books are considered deuterocanonical in the Greek Orthodox and Russian Orthodox churches (but not the Roman Catholic). These are:

- 1 Esdras, a kind of rewriting of the history recounted in the books of 2 Chronicles, Ezra, and Nehemiah in the Hebrew Bible;

- The Prayer of Manasseh, a short one-chapter account of the prayer for forgiveness that the wicked king of Judah, Manasseh, allegedly made while captive in Babylon (see 2 Chronicles 33);
- Psalm 151, a short seven-verse Psalm celebrating David's life, told in the first person, which is the final Psalm of the Psalter in the Septuagint;
- 3 Maccabees, a book that is misnamed in that it is not a historical sketch of the Maccabean Revolt but a work of fiction dealing with the interaction of Jews in Egypt with the pagan king Ptolemy IV Philopator (221–204 B.C.E.).

These various books of the Apocrypha are a real treasure trove of ancient Jewish literature, of various genres, and various perspectives and emphases. Quite apart from the question of whether they should be considered scripture or not (in the Roman Catholic and Orthodox traditions, yes; in the Jewish and Protestant traditions, no), they are important literary and historical works that can help us round out our understanding of Judaism in that critical time in the centuries prior to the turn of the era, when Jesus of Nazareth came on the scene and a new religious movement within Judaism emerged, one that would become its own religion, Christianity.

PUTTING THE NEW TESTAMENT AND EARLY CHRISTIANITY ON THE MAP

Now that we have learned something about the political, cultural, religious, and literary world of Jesus and his followers, and before we start examining the books of the New Testament themselves, I would like to provide some basic information that will help us orient ourselves to the discussions of the chapters that follow. This will involve a very brief overview of some of the key names, events, and dates from the history of earliest Christianity, starting at the very beginning.

We will encounter a number of important figures in the pages of the New Testament, none, of course, more important than Jesus himself. As I have mentioned, Jesus came from the village of Nazareth in Galilee; according to two of the Gospels he was actually born elsewhere, in the town of Bethlehem in Judea, in the south. By a

quirk in how our calendars were established in the Middle Ages, Jesus is usually now thought to have been born around 4 B.C.E. (in the older designations of B.C./A.D., this creates a rather odd and anomalous situation: Jesus would have been born 4 B.C.—that is, four years Before Christ!). He spent most of his life in Galilee, including almost the entirety of his public ministry of preaching and doing good deeds. The last week of his life he went to Jerusalem to celebrate a Passover celebration, and because of his preaching was arrested by Jewish authorities and handed over to the Roman governor Pontius Pilate, who condemned him to crucifixion for crimes against the state: calling himself the Jewish king when only Rome could appoint a king. The date of Jesus' death is debated, but it is usually placed around 30 C.E. or so.

Jesus' birth, life, ministry, and death are all recorded in the four Gospels of the New Testament, which also narrate the events surrounding his resurrection. The book of Acts picks up the story at that point and narrates how the followers of Jesus spread the good news of his death and resurrection around the Roman Empire. The original followers are the twelve disciples that Jesus had during his ministry, with the exception of his betrayer Judas Iscariot, now dead. The early chapters of Acts are dominated by the activities of the apostle Peter (with some stories involving John, and fewer involving James). Also appearing on the scene is Jesus' own brother, also named James, who assumes a leadership role in Jerusalem among the believers in Jesus.

The book of Acts narrates the conversion of the most important figure of early Christianity, the apostle Paul, who starts off as a zealous Jew who persecutes the Christians for proclaiming a false message; but in a miraculous vision, Jesus appears to him and Paul converts to become the most important missionary figure in the book of Acts. Nearly two-thirds of this entire narrative contains stories of Paul's missionary work and other activities. In particular, Acts wants to stress that Paul preaches a message of salvation to gentiles—non-Jews. His gospel message is that these gentiles (former pagans) can become followers of Jesus without first becoming Jews. The gospel of Christ is not simply a form of Judaism; it is salvation for all people, Jew and gentile.

Paul eventually rouses the opposition of Jewish leaders and he is arrested for causing disturbances;

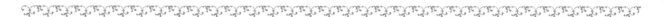

At a Glance: The Deuterocanonical Books/Apocrypha

There are ten Jewish writings from roughly the time after the Hebrew Bible and before the New Testament that are accepted by some Roman Catholics and Orthodox churches as deuterocanonical; they are not part of Jewish scripture and are considered Apocrypha by Protestants. They can be found in the Greek translation of the Bible, the Septuagint.

Tobit is a work of fiction that tells of the miraculous healing of the righteous man Tobit and the marriage of his son to a distant relative. Judith describes the deliverance of Israel through the bold actions of a great heroine of the faith. The Additions to Esther round out the story as found in the Hebrew Bible. The Wisdom of Solomon is a book of positive wisdom that celebrates God's wisdom as the greatest gift to humans. Sirach is a wisdom book that contains collections of wise sayings in poetry on numerous topics.

Baruch is a reflection on the cause of the disaster of the Babylonian exile. The Letter of Jeremiah is an attack on idols and those who worship them. The Additions to Daniel tell stories about the sixth-century Daniel and his companions. 1 and 2 Maccabees are both historical accounts of the events that transpired during the famous and important Maccabean Revolt, when Jews established themselves as a sovereign state in the Promised Land prior to its conquest by the Romans.

---

he travels to Rome to stand trial before the emperor, and the book ends with him in prison awaiting trial. It is usually thought that Paul was executed under the Roman emperor Nero in 64 C.E. If that date is right, then the book of Acts covers the first thirty years of the early church, from the resurrection of Jesus to the Roman imprisonment of Paul.

Paul is a central figure in the New Testament not only because of the book of Acts but also because of the thirteen Pauline letters—letters that Paul wrote, or allegedly wrote, to various churches and individuals during his Christian ministry. I say "allegedly" because, as we will see, scholars have long questioned whether all the letters that claim Paul as their author were actually written by him. It is generally thought that seven of these letters—called the undisputed Pauline epistles—certainly go back to Paul; but it appears that the other six are pseudepigraphic; that is, written by persons "falsely claiming" to be Paul, living at a later time.

The New Testament contains eight other letters that do not claim to be written by Paul. Most of these are also widely considered pseudepigraphic, not really written by the persons claimed as their authors. These include two letters allegedly written by Peter, one allegedly by Jesus' brother James, and another by his other brother Jude. The remaining four letters are all anonymous, but were accepted into the New Testament when church fathers became convinced that they were written by apostles: the book of Hebrews allegedly by Paul, and 1, 2, and 3 John by John the son of Zebedee.

The New Testament ends with the one apocalypse of the New Testament (cf. Daniel 7–12), the book of Revelation, written by a prophet named John (who does not indicate that he is John the son of Zebedee, Jesus' disciple). This book describes what will happen at the end of time when God destroys this evil world and all those who are opposed to him, and creates a new heavens and a new earth to be enjoyed eternally by the followers of Jesus.

In a nutshell this is the New Testament, the twenty-seven books that make up the Christian counterpart to the Old Testament. One of the hardest questions that teachers of the New Testament have to deal with is where to begin the study of it.

Many teachers prefer to start with the writings of Paul. This is because Paul's letters are the oldest books of the New Testament, the first ones to be written. Paul's letters are normally dated to the 50s C.E., some fifteen or twenty years before the first of our Gospels, Mark, which is usually thought to have been written around 65 or 70 C.E. Most readers of the New Testament do not realize, of course, that the first books printed in the New Testament (the Gospels) were not the earliest books to be written; it just seems more natural to think that the Gospels were produced first. But it is not so. Paul wrote years earlier. And so it does make sense, to many teachers, to begin with Paul as our earliest surviving Christian author.

The problem with beginning a study of the New Testament with Paul is that Paul bases his teachings on his understanding of Jesus—especially Jesus' death and resurrection (as we will see, Paul does not say much about Jesus' life *before* his death). And so it is hard to know what Paul is talking about, in many instances, without having some understanding about Jesus. But the primary sources we have for knowing about Jesus are the Gospels. And so, to understand Paul we need to know about Jesus and to understand about Jesus we need to know about the Gospels. That is why—ironically—a historical study of the New Testament often begins *not* with the books that were, historically, written first (Paul's letters) but with those that were written later (the Gospels).

And that is how we will begin our study. In the next chapter we will study the three earliest of our Gospels, Matthew, Mark, and Luke. The chapter after that will consider our last canonical Gospel, John, along with several later Gospels that did not make it into the New Testament (especially the Gospels of Peter, Thomas, and James); we will then, in the same chapter, consider what we can know about what Jesus really said and did and experienced, given the varying Gospel accounts of his life (which differ from one another in many significant ways). After that will be a chapter that discusses the life of Paul and the seven undisputed Pauline letters. That will be followed by a chapter dealing with later interpretations of Paul as seen in the book of Acts and in the six pseudonymous Pauline letters. Finally, we will then look at the other eight letters—the so-called "General Epistles"—and, as a climax to it all, the book of Revelation.

Take a Stand

1. Your roommate tells you that in his opinion, there is no reason to try to situate the New Testament in its historical context. Its meaning transcends all history, and it speaks to every context. Do you agree, either in part or completely? If so, explain why. If not, explain why knowing something about the Greco-Roman world (and Judaism as part of that world) is important for understanding the New Testament.

2. You are talking to a friend about religion, and she tells you she has always assumed that all Jews during the time of Jesus basically believed the same thing. Do you agree or not? If not, explain some of the differences among various Jewish perspectives.

3. Your best friend's father teaches Sunday School and has heard that you are taking a class on the Bible. He would like you to make a short presentation (15 minutes) on the Apocrypha to his class, since they are Protestants who know almost nothing about it. Make an outline of your presentation in which you explain the collection of books as a whole, and then take one of the books as an example to explain its contents in greater detail.

Key Terms

Apollonius of Tyana, 216

Caesar Augustus, 217

Daimonia, 222

Diaspora, 223

Essenes, 227

Fourth Philosophy, 227

Hanina ben Dosa, 225

Honi the "Circle-Drawer," 225

Josephus, 227

Maccabees, 238

Mishnah, 229

Octavian, 217

Pax Romana, 218

Pesher, 231

Pharisees, 227

Qumran, 229

Roman Empire, 217

Sadducees, 227

Sanhedrin, 229

Septuagint, 232

Sicarii, 232

Synagogue, 224

Talmud, 229

Zealots, 232

Suggestions for Further Reading

NB: For this and all chapters, see the relevant articles (e.g., "Alexander the Great," "Pharisees") in the works cited in the Suggestions for Further Reading in chapter 1.

Barrett, C. K., ed. *The New Testament Background: Selected Documents*, 2nd ed. New York: Harper & Row, 1989. A standard collection of Jewish and pagan texts relevant to the study of the New Testament.

Cohen, Shaye. *From the Maccabees to the Mishnah.* Philadelphia: Westminster Press, 1987. Perhaps the best place for beginning students to turn to for a clear overview of early Judaism.

De Silva, David. *Introducing the Apocrypha: Message, Context, and Significance.* Grand Rapids: Baker, 2002. A full and insightful discussion of all the deuterocanonical works examined in this chapter.

Rives, James. *Religion in the Roman Empire.* Maldon, Mass.: Blackwell, 2007. An authoritative but accessible overview of Roman religions, by one of the country's leading experts in the field.

Sanders, E. P. *Judaism Practice and Belief, 63 BCE–66 CE.* Philadelphia: Trinity Press International, 1992. A full, detailed, and authoritative account of what it meant to be a Jew immediately before and during the time of the New Testament.

10

The Synoptic Gospels: Matthew, Mark, and Luke

WHAT TO EXPECT

We begin our study of the New Testament by examining the three Synoptic Gospels: Matthew, Mark, and Luke. They are called "Synoptic" (from the Greek, meaning "seen together") because they tell so many of the same stories—often in the same sequence, sometimes in the same words—that they can be placed in parallel columns next to each other. Why do these three Gospels have so many similarities to one another, and yet are so different? That is called the Synoptic Problem. Scholars have long been convinced that these Gospels shared a number of sources, and have devised the "four-source hypothesis" in order to solve the problem.

Most of our attention in this chapter will be devoted to a careful examination of each of the Gospels and their presentation of Jesus. We will see that Mark portrays Jesus as a suffering messiah whom almost no one understood. Matthew emphasizes Jesus as a Jewish savior like Moses, who fulfilled the Jewish law and required his followers to do likewise. And Luke depicts Jesus as a great prophet who was rejected by his own people, so that the message of his salvation was to go to the gentiles.

We begin our study of the writings of the New Testament by considering the earliest of our surviving Gospels, Matthew, Mark, and Luke. The term "gospel" is based on an Old English term that means "good news." It is a fairly precise translation of the Greek term for these books, *euangelion* (the word from which we get "evangelist"—someone who "preaches the good news"). These three Gospels were originally written in Greek, as were all the books of the New Testament. They are often studied together because they are similar in so many ways. These three Gospels tell many of the same stories about Jesus, often in the same narrative sequence, and even in the same exact words. Since they are so similar to each other (while being different in key ways as well, as we will see), they are collectively called "the **Synoptic Gospels**," from the Greek word *synopsis* which means, literally, "seen together." You can put the stories of Matthew, Mark, and Luke in parallel columns next to each other on the same page, so that you can "see them together" to get a sense of their wide-ranging similarities and equally important differences. This will not be the case for the Gospel of John, which tells a very different set of stories about Jesus, in ways strikingly unlike the narratives of the first three Gospels.

THE STORYLINE OF THE SYNOPTIC GOSPELS

Looked at in broad terms, Matthew, Mark, and Luke share a similar story line. Matthew and Luke both begin with the story of Jesus' birth in Bethlehem, to a virgin named Mary. That story is not found in Mark. But in all three Gospels Jesus is raised in Nazareth, in Galilee, and he begins his public ministry as an adult by being baptized by John the Baptist, when the Holy Spirit comes down upon him. After that he goes into the wilderness for forty days to be tempted by the devil. When he returns from the wilderness, having successfully passed the test, he begins to make his public proclamation of the coming Kingdom of God, spending his entire time in the northern part of the land, Galilee.

Jesus' preaching attracts large crowds, and from this group of followers he chooses twelve to be his close disciples. Among the twelve, there is an inner circle of three: Peter, James, and John. Jesus' preaching is largely through parables and is principally about the new kingdom that God is very soon to bring to earth, in which the forces of evil will be destroyed and God will rule supreme. Jesus not only preaches, he also does spectacular miracles: casting out demons, healing the sick, miraculously feeding the hungry multitudes, controlling the natural elements, and even raising the dead. As his popularity increases, so too does opposition to him, especially among the Pharisees and the Jewish scribes (the experts trained in reading and writing the Torah). These do not believe that Jesus is empowered by God, and Jesus has a number of controversies with them.

Halfway through his ministry Jesus goes up to a mountain, taking with him Peter, James, and John, and there he is transfigured before them: he begins to radiate light and, to the astonishment of the disciples, suddenly Moses and Elijah appear beside him. After this great event Jesus begins to predict that it is his fate to go to Jerusalem to be rejected by the Jewish leaders, to be crucified, and then to be raised from the dead.

A large portion of the Gospels involves this final trip to Jerusalem. Jesus and his disciples go to the holy city to celebrate the annual Passover feast, and he is welcomed by the adoring crowds as the coming messiah as he rides into Jerusalem on a donkey. Once in the city, he goes to the Temple and disrupts the services there, overturning tables and driving out those selling sacrificial animals, declaring that the Jewish cult has become corrupt. His enemies among the Sadducees take notice and begin to plot his death. Jesus spends his last week in Jerusalem preaching his message of the coming kingdom to the gathering crowds.

Jesus celebrates the Passover meal with his disciples (the "Last Supper"), after which he is betrayed by one of the twelve, Judas Iscariot, and is arrested, tried by the Jewish Sanhedrin, and found guilty of blasphemy against God. The next morning they turn him over to the Roman governor Pontius Pilate, who finds him guilty of calling himself the king of the Jews. Pilate orders him to be crucified. Jesus is flogged and mocked, and then crucified along with two others. But that is not the end of the story. Jesus had predicted that he would be raised from the dead, and he is. On the third day after his execution, his women followers go to the tomb, find it empty, and learn that he has been raised. In two of the accounts, Jesus then appears to his disciples as the risen Lord and gives them his final instructions. And that is where the story ends.

THE SYNOPTIC PROBLEM

Scholars have long been intrigued by the question of why Matthew, Mark, and Luke are so similar in many ways but different in others. In particular, how can we explain the similarities? It cannot be an accident that they tell so many of the same stories, often in the same sequence and verbatim the same. You might imagine that different authors would choose to talk about *some* of the same things. But why would three independent writers happen to pick exactly the same stories to tell about Jesus' life, arrange them in the same order, and often tell them in exactly the same words? For most scholars—even some Christian scholars in antiquity—this can only be explained by assuming that someone is copying the account of someone else.

The problem of how to explain the similarities and differences among the Synoptic Gospels is called the **Synoptic Problem**. Specifically, the problem is this: how do we explain the literary relationships of Matthew, Mark, and Luke? Who is copying whom?

Just when scholars of the Old Testament were coming up with the Documentary Hypothesis to explain the sources behind the Pentateuch, New Testament scholars were devising hypotheses to explain the sources behind the Synoptics. The most popular hypothesis was developed in Germany and continues to be the view held by the vast majority of critical scholars today. It is sometimes called the **four-source hypothesis**.

The foundation for this hypothesis is that among the three Synoptic Gospels, Mark was the first to be written and was copied, in part, by both Matthew and Luke for many of their stories. This view is sometimes called **Markan Priority**: that is, Mark was prior to and used by the other two. There are numerous reasons for holding this view. Here are three of them:

Patterns of Agreement. If you lay out Matthew, Mark, and Luke in parallel columns and look at the word-for-word agreements in stories they all have, you will find that all three often have exactly the same words, that often all three have different words, that often Matthew and Mark have the same words when Luke reads differently, that often Mark and Luke have the same words when Matthew reads differently, but very rarely (and only in minor details) do Matthew and Luke have the same words when Mark reads differently. This makes sense only if Mark was the source for the other two: sometimes both of them copied him precisely, sometimes they both changed him but in different ways, sometimes Luke changed his wording but Matthew did not, and sometimes Matthew changed his wording but Luke did not. You would not get the same patterns of agreement if Matthew were the source for the other two, or if Luke were.

Sequence of Stories. As we will see, Matthew and Luke have a number of stories that are not found in Mark. What is striking is that if you look at the sequence of their stories (this story comes first, then this story, then that story), Matthew and Luke agree together in their sequence, for the most part, only when those stories come from Mark. This would make sense if they used Mark as a source: sometimes they both followed Mark's sequence, and sometimes one of them changed it. You won't get the same patterns of sequencing if Matthew or Luke were the source for the other two.

Characteristics of the Changes. Sometimes you will find an awkward verse in Mark—it may be worded in a confusing way or is in some way a bit odd. Often such verses are made clearer and less problematic in either Matthew or Luke. This suggests

that one or both of them have tried to improve their source (but they almost never do so in exactly the same way). This too suggests that Mark was the source for the others: it makes better sense that an editor will improve what his source has to say, rather than make it harder to understand (which would have to be the case if Mark were copying one of the others).

And so, on these grounds, scholars are widely agreed on Markan Priority (although this is not a unanimous view; then again, scarcely any view is unanimous among biblical scholars). So Mark was one of the sources for Matthew and Luke. The second prong of the four-source hypothesis is the view that Matthew and Luke both also used another source which no longer survives. This source is called "**Q**"—a designation taken from the German word *Quelle*, which means, sensibly enough, "source" (since Germans were the ones who came up with this idea).

The reason scholars think that there was once a source that we have called Q is because there are passages in Matthew and Luke that are not found in Mark. Most of these passages involve sayings of Jesus, such as the Lord's Prayer or the Beatitudes (there are only a couple of additional accounts of Jesus' deeds). Since Matthew and Luke could not have gotten these passages from Mark, where did they get them? There are reasons for thinking that Matthew did not get them from Luke, or Luke from Matthew. One reason involves an argument already mentioned for Markan Priority: sequences of narratives. These sayings almost always occur in different orders in Matthew and Luke, unlike the stories taken from Mark. So it looks like both of these Gospels had access to a document containing Jesus' sayings, and each author simply plugged the sayings into the sequence of events that he inherited from Mark as he thought appropriate.

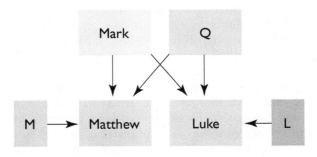

FIGURE 10.1. The four-source hypothesis.

BOX 10.1 THE CONTENTS OF Q

We cannot know the full contents of Q, but this has rarely stopped scholars from trying. One popular and widespread view, for example, is that Q did not contain a Passion narrative but consisted entirely of sayings of Jesus.

But the reality is that we cannot fully know what Q contained because the document has been lost. We have access to it only through the materials that Matthew and Luke both decided to include in their accounts, and it would be foolish to think that one or both of them included the entire document. Indeed, if only one of them included a passage from Q, then we would have no solid grounds for knowing that it came from Q rather than, say, M or L. It is entirely possible, for example, that Q had a Passion narrative, and that neither Matthew nor Luke chose to use it, or that only one of them chose not to do so (so that some of the verses of Matthew's or Luke's Passion narrative not found in Mark actually derive from Q). At the same time it is equally possible that Q was almost entirely sayings, without a Passion narrative. Regrettably, we will never know—unless, of course, Q itself should serendipitously turn up!

Among the materials that we *can* say were found in Q are some of the most memorable passages in the Gospels, including the following (for simplicity, verse references only from Luke are given):

- The preaching of John the Baptist (Luke 3:87–9, 16–17)
- The three temptations in the wilderness (Luke 4:1–13)
- The Beatitudes (Luke 6:20–23)
- The command to love your enemies (Luke 6:27–36)
- The command not to judge others (Luke 6:37–42)
- The healing of the centurion's slave (Luke 7:1–10)
- The question from John the Baptist in prison (Luke 7:18–35)
- The Lord's Prayer (Luke 11:2–4)
- The need for fearless confession in light of the coming judgment (Luke 12:2–12)
- The command not to worry about food and clothing (Luke 12:22–32)
- The parable of the unfaithful slave (Luke 12:39–48)
- Entering the kingdom through the narrow gate (Luke 13:23–30)
- The parable of the great wedding feast (Luke 14:15–24)

Q, then, is defined as the material found in Matthew and Luke that is not found in Mark. The Q material almost certainly comes from a lost Gospel, and it was almost certainly a text that was written in Greek.

Two of the sources of Matthew and Luke, then, are Mark and Q. But Matthew has a number of stories found only in Matthew, such as the visit of the wise men to see the infant Jesus. Where did he get these stories? Obviously not from Mark or Q. And so scholars posit another no-longer-existing source for Matthew, which they simply call M, for "Matthew's special source." In theory, **M** could have been one written source, several written sources, or a combination of written and oral sources.

So too, Luke has a number of stories not found in the other two Gospels, such as the parable of the Good Samaritan. These he must have gotten from somewhere (on the assumption that he did not simply make them up), and so scholars posit a special source for him as well, and call it **L**.

As a result, the four-source hypothesis maintains that the three Synoptic Gospels of Matthew, Mark, and Luke are ultimately based on four sources: Mark, Q, M, and L.

What About the Authors?

For many readers this view may sound a bit baffling. Weren't the Gospels written by the disciples of Jesus, and didn't they simply record what they saw happen? Scholars have long realized that this is probably not the case at all. We call the Gospels Matthew, Mark, Luke, and John since those are the traditional names associated with them. Two of these authors were allegedly Jesus' disciples: Matthew the tax collector and John the beloved disciple. Two others were companions of the apostles: Mark, the companion of Peter, and Luke, the companion of Paul. But when you read these Gospels carefully, you will notice that their authors never call themselves by these names (the titles indicating the names were added only later by subsequent editors), and they narrate all their stories in the third person (about what "they" were doing, not what "we" were).

Morever, it should not be overlooked that these Gospels are written in highly literate and rhetorically compelling Greek. The followers of Jesus—like Jesus himself—were lower-class peasants who spoke Aramaic. Even though there is some evidence that Jesus himself could read, nothing suggests that he could compose literature. And his followers were almost certainly uneducated (as Acts 4:13 explicitly says of Peter and John, for example). Learning to write (as in "compose a writing") took many years of training and almost never happened in a second language. Those who had the leisure and money for an education were always the very upper-crust elites, and Jesus' followers were not in that august group. These books, on the other hand, were written by later Christians from outside of Palestine, who were highly educated and whose native tongue was Greek, not Aramaic. They are anonymous—we don't know who the actual authors were. We continue to call them Matthew, Mark, Luke, and John simply because those are their traditional titles.

There is a fair unanimity about when these books were written. Jesus, as we have seen, probably died sometime around the year 30. Mark, the first Gospel, was written some 35–40 years later, around 65 or 70 C.E. (either right before or during the Jewish War against Rome); Matthew and Luke are both dated to about 10–15 years later than that, so around 80–85 C.E.; John is widely recognized as the latest of the Gospels, written, say, around 90–95 C.E.

THE GOSPELS AS BIOGRAPHIES

The Gospels represent a different genre of literature from anything that we found in the Tanakh. It is true that there are stories and legends of a number of great figures in the historical books—Abraham, Joseph, David, Solomon, and so on. But these stories are always embedded in larger narratives that have functions other than simply relating accounts of the lives of these great figures. The Gospels are all about Jesus, from beginning to end, and are organized chronologically to give an account of his life. No one should think that these accounts are simply meant to be factual itemizations of everything Jesus said and did. Whoever wrote these accounts decided which stories to tell and how to tell them, always with a view of achieving some greater literary purposes, as we will see. But all the Gospels, from beginning to end, are ultimately about Jesus' life and death. In terms of genre, then, unlike any of the writings of the Hebrew Bible, these books are best understood as ancient **biographies**.

When I say they are biographies, I need to emphasize that they are *ancient* biographies, not modern ones. We expect modern biographies to be filled with factually accurate information about the subject based on substantial research (interviews with family and friends, archival research, fact-checking, and the like). Ancient authors who wrote biographies did, of course, want to be accurate in what they said. But they did not have the same kinds of research tools available that we have today (no databases, for one thing). And ancient biographers had a different view of their task from that of modern biographers.

In our age we tend to think that as people grow up they are affected by a range of factors that influence who they are: they have formative experiences and important figures from their early life (parents, obviously; a beloved teacher) that shape the person they become. We today very much believe in character formation and personality development. But these are modern views. In the ancient world, people believed that a person's personality was implanted at the beginning and could be seen in the very earliest stages of his or her life. And so, in ancient biographies, there was no such thing as character development. People are who they are, and always have been.

Ancient biographers such as the Roman authors Plutarch and Suetonius told stories about their subjects that could best exemplify their characters and personality traits. Moreover, it was common in biographies to tell the very opening stories of the account in such a way as to reflect what the person's character was at the outset. As a rule these ancient biographies were less concerned with names and dates and more concerned with telling stories that reflected the real essence of the person.

We can expect to find the same things, then, in the Gospels of the New Testament. They will not be filled with names and dates, they will not portray formative influences, they will not indicate any character development. They will tell stories designed to show who Jesus really was, and they will begin their accounts with stories that will reflect his character at the very outset.

THE GOSPEL OF MARK

As we have seen, the Gospel of Mark was the first of our surviving Gospels to be written, probably in 65–70 C.E. some thirty-five or forty years after the death of Jesus. We have also seen that Mark was one of the sources used by Matthew and Luke. But what did Mark have as his own sources of information?

Mark's Sources of Information

Since the second Christian century it has sometimes been claimed that Mark was a companion of the disciple Simon Peter, who is regarded by all of the Gospels as the one who was closest to Jesus. There is nothing in Mark's Gospel to indicate that the author was Peter's companion, however. What is clear is that Mark, instead, was a highly educated Greek-speaking Christian who lived outside of Palestine. We do not know if he had written sources available to him for his telling of his stories about Jesus. What he almost certainly had available were oral traditions about Jesus' life and death.

As we will repeatedly see, after Jesus died around the year 30 C.E. his followers came to believe that God had raised him from the dead. In their opinion, he was the long-awaited messiah—the Son of David who was to be the ruler of all Israel. He was rejected in this role, however, by the Jewish leaders, and was crucified by the Romans. For Jesus' followers it was precisely his death and resurrection that fulfilled all the promises God had made to the people of Israel. The early Christians claimed that the salvation that Jesus brought was not deliverance from a foreign oppressor (the Empire of Rome) but deliverance from much mightier powers aligned against God, the powers of sin and death. These early Christians were apocalypticists (see the earlier discussion of the book of Daniel), and they believed that there were cosmic forces wreaking havoc among God's people. Jesus conquered these powers by his death and resurrection. In particular, the resurrection showed that he was more powerful even than death. Those who believed in him would be returned to a right standing before God and have eternal life.

The followers of Jesus who came to believe this soon after his crucifixion began telling stories about him in order to convert others to believe in him. Originally the stories were told to Jews in Jerusalem, and then missionaries went out to spread the news further abroad: Jesus was the messiah whose death and resurrection brought salvation to all who believed. Most of the people hearing this "good news" (= gospel) had never previously heard of Jesus. And so the Christian missionaries had to tell them stories about Jesus' life: what he taught while living, the miraculous deeds he performed, his death and spectacular resurrection. There was no other way to convert people to believe in him.

Soon, with missionaries such as the apostle Paul, these stories were being told to pagans to convert them to give up their worship of other gods, to accept the God of Israel as the only God, and to believe in Jesus his only son. As these gentiles converted, many of them spread the gospel among their families and friends. And when some of them converted they told the stories to their families and friends. Who told their families and friends. Who told their families and friends. And so it went, month after month, year after year, decade after decade.

And so, what were the sources of information for a Gospel writer like Mark? We don't know if he had predecessors who had written accounts before him. But he almost certainly acquired his stories about Jesus—his life, teachings, deeds, death, and resurrection—from the **oral tradition;** that is, from the stories about Jesus that had been told and retold and retold yet again for years and years throughout different regions of the Roman Empire.

You can imagine what might have happened to stories as they circulated in this way, by word of mouth, year after year, among people who had never known Jesus, did not know his language, Aramaic, did not know any of the disciples, or anyone who knew the disciples, had never been to Palestine, and who were telling the stories precisely in order to convert people to believe in Jesus. Stories change over time. So had the stories about Jesus. Mark inherited some of these stories and decided to put his own spin on them. But rather than doing it orally, he did it in writing. As a result, this was one of the most significant writings ever produced in the history of Western civilization—a Gospel that was the first (so far as we know) to be written about Jesus of Nazareth, a Gospel copied by two later authors in writings that came to form some of the most influential books of the Christian Bible.

How then did Mark tell his story? As was the case with the narratives of the Hebrew Bible, I will

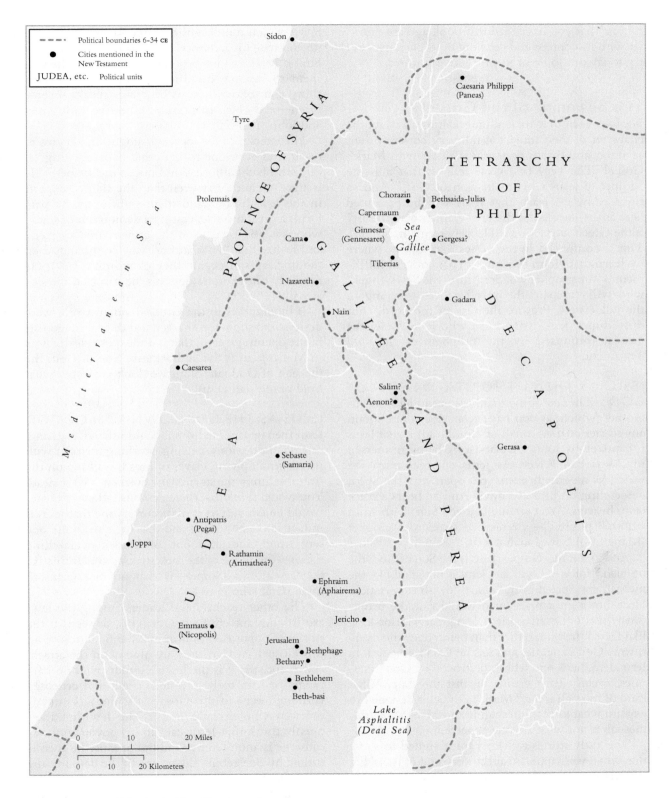

FIGURE 10.2. Palestine in New Testament times.

assume that you have read this book and are familiar with its content and the flow of its narrative, as I try to lay out some of its distinctive features.

The Beginning of the Gospel

We have seen that ancient biographies try to set the character of their subject at the very outset of their account, and that is certainly the case with Mark's Gospel. The very first verse tells us that it is the "gospel of Jesus Christ, the Son of God." And so right away, we learn that Jesus will be presented here as the messiah of the Jews (remember: "christ" is the Greek word for the Hebrew term "messiah"). This is confirmed in the verses that follow, where we learn that "John the Baptist" has come in fulfillment of the prophecy of Scripture, the "messenger" who will "prepare the way," a "voice crying in the wilderness, Prepare the way of the Lord." For this Gospel, Jesus is the Lord who is to come, the messiah promised by the prophets of the Old Testament.

JESUS AS THE AUTHORITATIVE SON OF GOD
The first thing that happens to Jesus in this Gospel (which, as you have seen, does not contain any stories of Jesus' birth or childhood) is that Jesus is baptized by John the Baptist by being immersed in the Jordan River. As Jesus emerges from the water, he sees the heavens split open with the Spirit descending on him as a dove. And he hears a voice from heaven, "You are my beloved Son, with you I am well pleased"—a reference again to a prophet (Mark 1:9–11; see Isaiah 42:7).

And so, for this Gospel, Jesus is the Son of God, the messiah. But as we will see, Jesus is not at all like the messiah anticipated in traditional Jewish expectation. He is not a great priest who would rule the people (since he is not even a priest) or a great warrior-king like David. Instead, rather than being one who overthrows God's enemies and sets up God's kingdom in Jerusalem, he is one who is destroyed by God's enemies, crucified for crimes against the state. What kind of messiah is *that?* Mark's Gospel is designed to explain what kind of messiah Jesus is. For Mark, this messiah is not what anyone expected.

The early stories of Mark are designed to show that whatever happened at the very end of Jesus' life (his mockery, suffering, and execution), he was indeed one endowed with God's power and special favor—as shown by his being "anointed" by the Spirit of God at his baptism. Immediately he begins to demonstrate his authority. He sees two men fishing—Simon Peter and his brother Andrew—and he tells them to become his disciples. They drop everything and follow him. When Jesus speaks, people listen—and obey. In similar fashion he calls James and John (1:16–20).

He enters into the local synagogue and begins to teach, and everyone realizes that he is teaching "as one who had authority, and not as the scribes." He is a greater authority even than the trained experts in the Jewish law. And then, right away, he performs a great miracle, casting a demon out of a man who was possessed. And the crowds are "amazed" and realize that "with authority he commands even the unclean spirits, and they obey him" (1:27). He not only can exorcise demons, he can heal the sick at will (1:29–31).

If biographies in the Greco-Roman world were designed to show the character of their protagonists in the opening scenes, that is done quite clearly here in Mark. Jesus is the authoritative Son of God, the messiah of God (although we don't yet know what kind of messiah he is).

JESUS AS THE UNKNOWN SON OF GOD
Jesus then engages in his public ministry of teaching, casting out demons, healing, working miracles with nature (multiplying loaves of bread, walking on the water, calming the storm), and even raising the dead. You would think that these demonstrations of power would be enough to convince everyone that Jesus is in fact someone special and that he is truly the one sent from God. But one of Mark's overarching theses—this is one of the most striking and distinctive features of this Gospel—is that no one seems to understand who Jesus is.

The other teachers and leaders among the Jews are in constant conflict with Jesus, as seen in the stories of opposition to him in 2:1–3:6. Throughout this Gospel, in fact, they are always on the attack, and eventually it is the Jewish leaders who will arrange for him to be arrested, tried, and crucified (although even in this Gospel it is the Roman authorities who execute Jesus). The Jewish leaders openly think that Jesus can do his powers not because he is anointed by God but because he is controlled by Beelzebub, the prince of the demons, the devil (3:22).

And they are not the only ones who do not understand: no one at all seems to "get" who Jesus

BOX 10.2 SON OF GOD/SON OF MAN

The way most people understand the terms **"Son of God"** and **"Son of Man"** today is probably at odds with how they would have been understood by many Jews in the first century. In our way of thinking, a "son of God" would be a god (or God) and a "son of man" would be a man. Thus, "Son of God" refers to Jesus' divinity and "Son of Man" to his humanity. But this is just the opposite of what the terms meant for many first-century Jews, for whom "son of god" commonly referred to a human (e.g., King Solomon; 2 Samuel 7:14) and "son of man" to someone divine (cf. Daniel 7:13–14).

In the New Testament Gospels, Jesus uses the term "son of man" in three different ways. On some occasions he uses it simply as a circumlocution for himself; that is, rather than referring directly to himself, Jesus sometimes speaks obliquely of the "son of man" (e.g., Matthew 8:20). In a related way, he sometimes uses it to speak of his impending suffering (Mark 8:31). Finally, he occasionally uses the term with reference to a cosmic figure who is coming to bring the judgment of God at the end of time (Mark 8:38), a judgment that Mark's Gospel expects to be imminent (9:1; 13:30). For Mark himself, of course, the passages that speak of the coming Son of Man refer to Jesus, the one who is returning soon as the judge of the earth. As we will see later, scholars debate which if any of these three uses of the term can be ascribed to the historical Jesus.

---

really is. Early on, his family tries to snatch him from the public eye because they think he has gone out of his mind (3:21). His townspeople from Nazareth take offense at his words and do not understand how he can have any authority since he is merely the carpenter from a local family (6:1–6). Yet more striking, his own disciples do not understand who he is, even though he has chosen them and given them private instruction (e.g., 4:10–20). When he does a great miracle they wonder, "Who then is this?" (4:41); and they are explicitly said not to perceive (6:51–52). Halfway through the Gospel Jesus expresses some exasperation with them: "Do you not yet understand?" (8:21).

At this halfway point it is interesting to ask: who *does* understand who Jesus is? Oddly enough, so far it is only the demons (3:11). Or rather, it is the demons and God, who calls Jesus his son at the baptism (1:11); Jesus, who hears God say it; Mark, who is writing about it; and you the reader, who is reading it. Other than that, for the first half of the Gospel, no one gets it.

THE ACKNOWLEDGED SON OF GOD

All of that changes at almost precisely the halfway point. A key and highly unusual healing story occurs in 8:22–26. A blind man is brought to Jesus to be healed, and Jesus spits in his eyes and asks if he can see. The man can partially see: people look like trees walking around. Jesus then lays his hands on his eyes and heals him completely. Here then is a blind man who only gradually comes to see. He is like the disciples.

In the very next story (8:27–30) Jesus asks the disciples if they know who he is. Peter gives what must seem like the right answer: "You are the Christ." So Peter gets it right, right? Wrong! Jesus goes on to explain that he, the Son of Man, must go to Jerusalem and be rejected, executed, and then raised from the dead. For Mark, this is the *kind* of messiah Jesus is— one who must suffer and die. And Peter's reaction is striking. He tells Jesus that that will never happen to him. In other words, Peter has come to understand that Jesus is the messiah but he does not know what kind of messiah he is. He is not a great warrior-king, as Jews such as Peter had anticipated. He is a messiah who must die for the sake of others. Peter only partially sees who Jesus is. He is like a blind man who only gradually gains his sight.

JESUS THE SUFFERING SON OF GOD

The suffering and death of Jesus are traditionally known as his "Passion," from the Greek word *pascho*, which means "to suffer." On three occasions, starting at this halfway point, Jesus predicts his Passion, and in each instance the disciples show they do not understand what he is talking about. Jesus responds to Peter's declaration that no such thing would happen by rebuking him and calling him "Satan" (8:32). He goes on to explain that following him will not lead to glory but to excruciating death: "Whoever would come after me must take up the cross and follow me" (8:34). In the next chapter Jesus makes another Passion prediction, and the disciples are said not to know what he means (9:30–31). In the next chapter Jesus makes his final prediction (10:33–34) and two of the disciples, James and John, show they have no clue what he is about: they ask him to be given seats of particular prominence when he comes into his glory (10:33–37). Jesus by this time is getting exasperated. He has told them repeatedly and they don't understand: he is not the glorious messiah they expect; he is the suffering messiah.

From this point on, the narrative of Mark marches inexorably toward the climax. Jesus' entire public ministry has taken ten chapters to relate; his final week on earth will take up the final six. Jesus enters into Jerusalem to the shouts of acclamation from the crowds (11:1–10); they too appear to expect a triumphant messiah. He enters the Temple and drives out those who are doing business there, incurring the wrath of the leaders in charge of the place (11:15–19). He teaches in the Temple and arouses yet more opposition as the crowds gather around him (11:28–13:36).

And then we come to the Passion narrative itself, the account of Jesus' suffering and death. He is anointed with oil by an unnamed woman, the only one who seems to understand his mission, as he indicates that she has anointed his body for burial (14:1–9). He holds his final meal with his disciples, a Passover feast, indicating that the broken bread represents his broken body and the cup of wine represents his shed blood. He goes out to the Garden of Gethsemane and prays for God to remove his fate from him, but to no avail (14:26–42). He is betrayed, as he had predicted would happen, by one of his own followers, Judas Iscariot. He is put on trial before the Jewish council, the Sanhedrin. The leader of the people, the high priest, demands Jesus to tell him if he is really the Son of God. Jesus replies that he is, and they find him guilty of blasphemy (14:61–62). He spends the night in jail, and the next morning the Jewish leaders hand him over to Pilate, who tries him on the charge of calling himself the King of the Jews. Pilate finds him guilty and orders his execution. Jesus is flogged and then crucified. He dies within six hours (15:1–39).

JESUS THE CRUCIFIED SON OF GOD

Mark's readers would have known full well what crucifixion entailed. Being nailed to a cross was the most horrific, shameful, torturous, prolonged, and humiliating form of execution used by the Romans. Crucifixions were done in public, in full view, as part of the shame and horror and as a disincentive for crime. They were reserved for the lowest of the low, slaves and anyone subversive of public order. Mark does not describe the procedure in gory detail, probably because he does not need to. Anyone reading this account in the ancient world knew what crucifixion was all about.

A person who was crucified was clearly not favored by God. Quite the opposite. Or so everyone

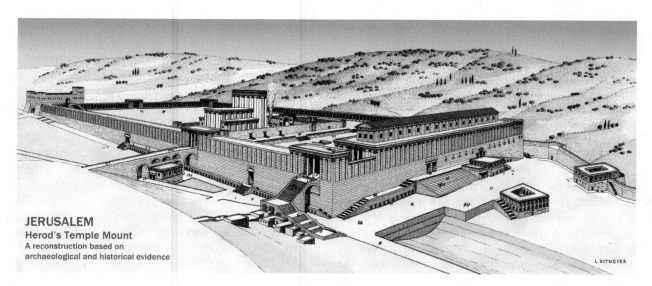

JERUSALEM
Herod's Temple Mount
A reconstruction based on
archaeological and historical evidence

L. RITMEYER

FIGURE 10.3.   A pictorial reconstruction of the Jewish Temple in Jerusalem in the days of Jesus.

thought. In Jesus' case, he dies with no one supporting him or his cause. He has been betrayed by one of his followers (Judas); denied three times by another (Peter); deserted by all the others. While being crucified he is mocked by the other criminals crucified beside him, by the Jewish leaders, and by those who are passing by. At the very end he feels abandoned even by God himself, as shown by his final words (the only words he speaks at the crucifixion): "My God, my God, why have you forsaken me?" (15:34) Is this a genuine question of Jesus? Does he really not understand why God has not come to his aid? This is a point on which interpreters differ. But one thing is certain: even if no one else in this narrative fully understands who Jesus is at his death, the reader knows.

This is because of what happens immediately after Jesus breathes his last. The curtain in the Temple rips in half, and the centurion, who has seen him die, declares, "Truly this man was the Son of God" (15:38–39). Both things are highly significant. As we saw earlier, the Holy of Holies in the Temple was the place where God himself was believed to dwell on earth. The Holy of Holies was separated from the rest of the Temple, and so from the rest of the world, by a thick curtain. Only once a year could someone go behind the curtain into the presence of God: the high priest on the Day of Atonement. But in Mark's Gospel, when Jesus dies the curtain is ripped in half. In other words, God is now accessible to all people—he has come forth from the Holy of Holies. No one any longer needs the Jewish high priest to perform a sacrifice for the atonement of sins. Jesus' death provides access to God for all people.

For all people—gentile as well as Jew. This is seen by the fact that it is the pagan centurion who observes Jesus' death and on that ground confesses him to be the Son of God. No one else in this Gospel has fully understood that it was precisely in his horrible and humiliating death that Jesus was the Son of God. Being God's Son did not mean ruling as a political authority over Israel, or conquering the Roman legions as a great warrior, or anything else Jews may have expected of a messiah. For Mark's Gospel, Jesus was the messiah precisely because he died as an atonement for sins. That, for Mark, is what the messiah was supposed to do. And his atonement is effective not only for Jews but also for gentiles—such as this centurion. But that is not the end of the story.

JESUS THE VINDICATED SON OF GOD

Jesus had predicted during his public ministry that he would be raised from the dead. And that, in

---

BOX 10.3 THE LAST TWELVE VERSES OF MARK

The Gospel of Mark is unique among the Gospels in ending abruptly: after his resurrection, Jesus is never said to appear to his disciples or to anyone else. Instead, when the women who visit the tomb on the third day find it empty and are told to inform the disciples that Jesus has been raised, they "fled from the tomb . . . and they did not say anything to anyone for they were afraid" (16:8).

The ending comes as a real surprise to many readers, who think that the women surely must have told *somebody*! After all, word of the resurrection did get out. And the three other Gospels go on to tell the stories of Jesus' appearances to his disciples after the resurrection. And how would Mark know that Jesus was raised if the women never told anyone?

Ancient Christian scribes who were making copies of the Gospel of Mark were also surprised by this abrupt ending, and so they did what scribes sometimes did: they changed the ending by adding some verses that made this Gospel more in line with their own beliefs and with the endings of other Gospels. The twelve new verses that were appended describe what, in the scribes' opinion, must have happened next: the women tell the disciples what they have seen and heard, then the disciples travel to Galilee and meet with Jesus, who gives them their final instructions before ascending to heaven.

This new ending does give a kind of closure to the account, but it is not original. It cannot be found in our oldest and best manuscripts of Mark, and its writing style and vocabulary are not consistent with the rest of the Gospel otherwise. It was added by scribes who simply did not want the book to end where it did. That is why most modern translations include the verses only in brackets with a footnote, telling their readers that the verses are a later addition. The Gospel originally ended with chapter 16, verse 8.

Mark, is just what happens. After he is dead, Jesus is buried by Joseph of Arimathea. On the third day afterward, several women go to his tomb in order to anoint his body with perfumes and spices to give him a proper burial. But he is not in the tomb. Instead they find a young man who tells the women that Jesus has been raised from the dead. They are to inform the disciples that Jesus will go before them and meet them back in their homeland, in Galilee. And then comes the most stunning verse of the entire Gospel: "And the women fled from the tomb . . . and they did not say anything to anyone, for they were afraid" (16:8). And that's where the Gospel ends. Jesus is raised from the dead, but the disciples never learn of it.

This is such a shocking ending that later scribes added twelve more verses in which the women do go tell the disciples, who do go to Galilee and do meet the resurrected Jesus. But these verses were not originally part of the Gospel. They were added by scribes who could not believe that the Gospel could end the way it does. (See Box 10.3)

But it does end that way. Jesus is definitely raised from the dead, showing that his death really was accepted by God as an atonement for sin. But just as the disciples never could understand Jesus while he was alive, so too they are not said to understand him even after his death. In fact, in this narrative they never learn that he has been raised from the dead as he himself predicted. But the reader learns about it and knows with some assurance, then, that Jesus really is the messiah that Mark has portrayed him to be. He is not a great warrior or a powerful king; he is not a mighty priest who rules the people of Israel. He is not what Jews familiar with the Scripture expected of a messiah. He is a suffering messiah, one whose goal in life was death—a horrible, excruciating death, a death that brought about salvation for the world of both Jew and gentile.

THE GOSPEL OF MATTHEW

The Gospel of Matthew was one of the favorite books among Christian readers in antiquity. In no small measure this was because it was widely thought to have been written by one of Jesus' own disciples, Matthew the tax collector, called to be Jesus' follower in Matthew 9:9–13. Scholars today widely discount this tradition, however. If you read

that passage yourself you can see one reason why: there is nothing in it to suggest that the writer is talking about himself (he narrates the "call of Matthew" in the third person, not as something that he himself experienced). Moreover, Matthew the tax collector in this passage is portrayed as a Palestinian Jew who was an adult in the 20s C.E.; whoever wrote the Gospel was a Greek-speaking Christian living at a much later time. It is usually thought, as we have seen, that this Gospel was written some fifty years or so after the death of Jesus, possibly sometime between 80 and 85 C.E. We have also seen that this author had several sources available to him: Mark, Q, and M (the last of which may have been a combination of written and oral sources).

The Beginning of Matthew

Since ancient biographies often set the tone of their narratives in their opening episodes, we do well to consider how Matthew begins. As with Mark, the first verse is important: "The book of the genealogy of Jesus Christ, the son of David, the son of Abraham." Right off the bat Matthew gives us a clear indication of how he is going to portray Jesus. He will emphasize that he is the Jewish messiah. The messiah, of course, was to be a descendant of David. And Matthew stresses that Jesus is that. And why does he mention that he is also the descendant of Abraham? Because Abraham was the father of the Jews. Mark as well, of course, portrayed Jesus as the Jewish messiah. But the Jewishness of Jesus will be an even more significant emphasis of Matthew, which is often thought of as the most "Jewish" of the four Gospels.

Immediately after this verse, Matthew (unlike Mark) launches into a genealogy of Jesus, starting with Abraham and tracing father–son relationships from there: Abraham, to Isaac, to Jacob, and all the way down to "Matthan, the father of Jacob . . . the father of Joseph, the husband of Mary, of whom Jesus was born, who is called the Christ" (1:15–16). And so the lineage of Jesus is traced from Abraham down to Joseph, Jesus' "father." But there is a problem at just that point, because Joseph in this account was not in fact Jesus' father. And why is that? It is because in this Gospel, Jesus' mother, Mary, is said to have been a virgin. There is nothing about that in Mark's Gospel. But in Matthew, Mary conceives her child by the Holy Spirit (1:18) not by having sexual intercourse with her husband Joseph. That raises all sorts of questions. For one thing, why does Matthew trace Jesus' bloodline back through Joseph, if in fact Jesus is not related to that bloodline through Joseph?

That question is not easy to answer, but one of the key points of the genealogy is certain: it is intended to show Jesus' close ties to the people of Israel all the way back to the father of the Jews, Abraham. This much is clear from the most interesting verse in the genealogy, the one at its end, which indicates that the genealogy of Jesus actually divides itself neatly into three sets of fourteen generations: "So all the generations from Abraham to David were fourteen generations; and from David to the Babylonian deportation fourteen generations; and from the Babylonian deportation to the Christ, fourteen generations" (1:17). That's amazing. Fourteen, fourteen, and fourteen. It is as if every fourteen generations something truly significant happens in Israel: the greatest king of Israel (David); the greatest disaster of Israel (Babylonian exile); and the greatest figure of Israel (the messiah).

Matthew no doubt wants to convey that as his lesson. For him, Jesus is in fact *destined* to be the messiah. But is the number fourteen itself significant for Matthew's genealogy? Readers have come up with two solutions to that question. On one hand, if "seven" is thought to be the "perfect" number in the Bible, fourteen is doubly perfect. And so this is the truly perfect genealogy. On the other hand, if you spell the name "David" in Hebrew and add up the numerical total of the letters—it adds up to fourteen! Jesus is the true descendant of David.

The problem with this fourteen-fourteen-fourteen sequence is the genealogy itself. If you compare the father-to-son names listed here with the genealogy of 1 Chronicles in the Hebrew Bible (Matthew's source of information for most of his genealogy), it is clear that Matthew has dropped out a few names. In Matthew 1:8, Joram is said to be the father of Uzziah (named in the Hebrew Bible also as Azariah); but in 1 Chronicles 3:10–12, he is Uzziah's great-great-grandfather. Why has Matthew left out these other names? Because if he had included them there would no longer be fourteen generations, and the genealogy would no longer seem perfect. You may also notice (by counting) that the last group of fourteen involves only thirteen generations. Matthew has produced this genealogy, then, not in order to give a historically accurate account of Jesus' ancestors (none

of these, technically, is his ancestor in any event since he was not related by blood to Joseph), but in order to emphasize something: Jesus' thorough Jewishness and his standing in line with the great king of the Jews and the father of the Jews.

The Birth of the Messiah

This stress on Jesus' Jewishness continues in Matthew chapters 1–2 with the account of Jesus' birth, which is never mentioned in Matthew's source, the Gospel of Mark. The account is intriguing for many reasons. For one thing, everything that happens is in fulfillment of the divine plan. It is the Holy Spirit, not Joseph, who has made Mary pregnant. This happens to fulfill the prediction of Scripture that "A virgin will conceive and bear a son" (quoting Isaiah 7:14; remember our discussion on p. 23–24). The birth takes place in Bethlehem, because that was predicted in Scripture (2:6). So was the family's flight to Egypt to escape the wrath of Herod (2:14). So was Herod's slaughter of the innocent children in Bethlehem (2:18). So was the family's decision to relocate in Nazareth (2:23).

This idea that everything about Jesus "fulfills" Scripture is found throughout Matthew's Gospel. On eleven occasions (including those just mentioned) Matthew states that something about Jesus was done in order to "fulfill what was spoken of by the prophet." In some instances it is easy to see what Matthew means: a prophet predicted something about the coming Savior (e.g., that he would be born in Bethlehem) and that's what happens with Jesus. At other times these **fulfillment citations**, as they are called, are a bit more complicated. These are instances in which something that Jesus does is not what a prophet predicted, but instead "fills full" the meaning of an event narrated in the Old Testament. For example, we are told that Joseph takes the family to Egypt to escape from Herod to fulfill what was written in Hosea 11:1: "Out of Egypt I have called my son." When you read Hosea itself, it is clear that it is not predicting something that will happen with the messiah; he is referring to the exodus event, when God brought his "son" Israel out of slavery. But for Matthew that event has been "fulfilled" by Jesus. That is, Jesus has "filled it full" of meaning because, just as God once saved his people from their slavery to a foreign power through Moses, now he has saved them in an even more important way, from their sins, through Jesus.

Understanding Matthew's fulfillment citations in this second way is useful for making sense of certain aspects of the opening chapters of this book. Think about the following events in rough outline and ask yourself how they may have resonated with a first-century Jew who was intimately familiar with the Jewish Scriptures. A male child is miraculously born to Jewish parents, but a fierce tyrant in the land is set to destroy him. The child is supernaturally protected from harm in Egypt. Then he leaves Egypt and is said to pass through the waters (of baptism). He goes into the wilderness to be tested for a long period. Afterward he goes up on a mountain and delivers God's Law to those who have been following him.

Sound familiar? If you have read the Jewish Scriptures as carefully as Matthew's readers had, it would. Matthew has shaped these opening stories of Jesus to show that Jesus' life is a fulfillment of the stories about Moses in Exodus 1–20: Herod is like the Egyptian pharaoh, the baptism is like the crossing of the Sea of Reeds, the forty days of temptation are like the forty years in the wilderness; the Sermon on the Mount is like the Law of Moses delivered on Mount Sinai.

These parallels cannot be found in Matthew's source, the Gospel of Mark, and they tell us something significant about Matthew's portrayal of Jesus. Certainly he agrees with Mark that Jesus is the suffering Son of God, the messiah. But here in Matthew, Jesus is also the new Moses come to set his people free from their bondage to sin (1:21) and to give them the new Law, his teachings, which are portrayed as the correct interpretation of the Law that Moses himself gave to the children of Israel.

Another story from Matthew's birth narrative is significant for understanding his overarching portrayal of Jesus. One of the most interesting tales of the New Testament—found only in Matthew—is the account of the wise men (sometimes called "magi") who come to worship Jesus after he was born (2:1–12). These wise men are coming from the east, following a star to the place where the King of the Jews was to be born. We are not told why anyone from another country would be interested in worshipping a Jewish king; but we are told that the star was leading them. It stops over Jerusalem, and the wise men go there to make some inquiries about the predicted place of the king's birth. Word gets around to Herod, who in fact *is* the king of the Jews. He calls in his Jewish scripture scholars, who tell him that the future king is to be born in Bethlehem. He informs the wise men and, lo and behold, the star reappears, leads them to Bethlehem, and stops over the house where the child is. The wise men enter in, worship the child, and then leave—going back a different direction, not wanting to inform Herod of the child's whereabouts since they learn in a dream that Herod is out to kill him, presumably because he sees him as future competition for his throne.

But what is this story all about? The answer lies in realizing who knows where the child is to be born, and who actually goes to worship him. It is the Jewish scholars who know the Scriptures and tell Herod that the child is to be born in Bethlehem. But, strikingly, they do not go to see him even though they know the scriptural predictions about him. Who does go? The gentiles who come from another land, who are *not* versed in the Scriptures. This story is meant to foreshadow what will happen subsequently. Jesus fulfills the Scriptures. He is nonetheless rejected by the leaders of his own people (the political authorities and scholars of scripture), who plot his death. There are others, however, who will come and worship him.

Jesus, Jews, and the Law of Moses

Matthew skips over all the intervening years between Jesus' infancy and his adulthood, as the next major event that happens is his appearance before John the Baptist. There are a couple of interesting differences between Mark's account of the baptism and Matthew's. For one thing, in Matthew the Pharisees and Sadducees—that is, the Jewish spiritual leaders—want to participate in John's baptism of repentance. But John turns them away, calling them a "brood of vipers" (3:7). Not a nice term for the religious elite! But John indicates that their lives are not holy and he will not baptize them until they begin to live the way God wants them to.

Another change is that John initially refuses to baptize Jesus as well, not because he is too sinful (as the Jewish leaders are) but because he is too perfect. When Jesus requests baptism, John tells him that it is he, Jesus, who should be baptizing him, John. But Jesus insists and John carries through with the act. In this Gospel there is no ambiguity about who is the greater of the two: it is Jesus, as John himself recognizes and as others appear to do as well. In this Gospel, when the voice comes from

BOX 10.4 THE GOLDEN RULE

The most familiar form of the golden rule is "Do unto others as you would have them do unto you." Many people think that Jesus was the first to propound this ethical principle, but in fact it was given in a variety of forms by moral philosophers from the ancient world. In most of these formulations it is expressed negatively (stating what should *not* be done) rather than positively.

The rule was found, for example, among the ancient Greeks many centuries before Jesus. One of the characters described by the Greek historian Herodotus (fifth century B.C.E.) said, "I will not myself do that which I consider to be blameworthy in my neighbor," and the Greek orator Isocrates (fourth century B.C.E.) said, "You should be such in your dealings with others as you expect me to be in my dealings with you." The saying was present in Eastern cultures as well, most famously on the lips of Confucius (sixth century B.C.E.): "Do not do to others what you would not want others to do to you."

Nearer to Jesus' time, the golden rule was endorsed (in various forms of wording) in a number of Jewish writings. For example, in the apocryphal book of Tobit we read, "And what you hate, do not do to anyone"; and in an ancient Jewish interpretation of the book of Leviticus we find, "Do not do to him (your neighbor) what you yourself hate."

Perhaps the best-known expression of the rule in Jewish circles, however, comes from the most revered rabbi of Jesus' day, the famous Rabbi Hillel. A pagan approached the rabbi and promised him that he would convert to Judaism if Hillel could recite the entire Torah to him while standing on one leg. Hillel's terse reply sounds remarkably like the statement of Jesus in Matthew 7:12: "What is hateful to you do not do to your neighbor; that is the whole Torah, while the rest is commentary. Go and learn it."

Jesus, in short, was not the only teacher of his day who taught the golden rule, or who thought that the essence of the Law of Moses could be summed up in the commandment to love.

heaven announcing that Jesus is the Son of God it does not come just to Jesus, as in Mark, but to anyone who will hear (rather than saying "You are my Son" it says "This is my Son," 3:17). That foreshadows another key difference from Mark. In this Gospel there is not a widespread ignorance about who Jesus really is. In this account people learn who Jesus is, know who he is, and confess who he is. Except the Jewish leaders, who are portrayed as recalcitrant and hardhearted.

The narrative flow of Matthew is much like that of Mark: Jesus is baptized, tempted in the wilderness, comes into Galilee and begins to preach about the Kingdom of God (called the Kingdom of Heaven here), calls the disciples, and engages in fantastic miracles. But one key difference is the emphasis on Jesus' teaching. Jesus teaches a lot more in Matthew than he does in Mark. In no small measure that is because, in addition to material from Mark, Matthew has incorporated the material he received from Q, the Synoptic source (*Quelle*) of sayings. It is interesting that Matthew has organized Jesus' extensive teachings into five collections of sayings, starting with the Sermon on the Mount in chapters 5–7 (the others: his instructions to the apostles in ch. 10; his parables of the kingdom in ch. 13; his other teachings on the kingdom and the church in ch. 18; and the "woes" against the scribes and Pharisees and his apocalyptic discourse describing the end of the age, in chs. 23–27). Some scholars have suggested that these five blocks of sayings have been created by Matthew in order once again to show Jesus as a new Moses, since the Law of Moses is found in five books, the Pentateuch.

In any event, no passage of Matthew is more important or better known than this first block of Jesus' teaching, the Sermon on the Mount. In some ways this sermon is all about life in the kingdom of heaven. Jesus begins by delivering the "**beatitudes**"—the "blessings" delivered to those who are experiencing hardship now but who will be rewarded in the future kingdom. Those who are poor in spirit, who hunger and thirst for righteousness, who mourn, who are persecuted, who are reviled, who make peace instead of war, who show mercy—these are the ones who will be blessed in the coming kingdom.

But how is one to inherit this coming kingdom? To many readers, Jesus' answer may come as a surprise. To inherit the kingdom one must keep the Law even better than the Jewish scribes and

Pharisees. This is the main point of a key passage, 5:17–20: Jesus states emphatically that he did not come to abolish the Law and the prophets (even though that's what many Christians have said over the years—possibly even in Matthew's day); he came to "fulfill" them. Nothing in the Jewish law can pass away until it is all fulfilled. Even more than that, the only ones who will be considered "great" in the coming kingdom of heaven are those who do all the commandments of the Law and teach others to do the same. In Matthew, Jesus is not opposed to the Law of Moses. He fulfills it himself in his birth, life, and death, and he requires his followers to fulfill it by keeping it even better than the leaders among the Jews.

Jesus goes on then to explain how one can "do the Law" better than the scribes and the Pharisees. This comes in the following passage, known as the "**antitheses**" (5:21–48). An antithesis is a contrary statement. In the six antitheses recorded in the Sermon on the Mount, Jesus states a Jewish law and then sets his interpretation of that law over and against it. In these antitheses Jesus does not contradict the Law. He does not say, for example, that the Law says "Do not murder, but I say to you, you should murder!" Quite the contrary, Jesus states the law and then indicates that it is not enough to keep its literal meaning; one needs to keep the very intention behind the law. The law not to murder is designed to promote peace and harmony in the community, and so Jesus' followers will not only not murder: they won't get angry with another. The law of adultery does not allow someone to steal the spouse of another; Jesus indicates that you shouldn't even desire to do so. The law that says "an eye for an eye and a tooth for a tooth" is meant to be a law of mercy: if someone knocks out your tooth, you are not to seek revenge by chopping off his head. The punishment is to fit the crime. But Jesus takes this law of mercy to an extreme: you should in fact turn the other cheek.

Far from absolving his followers from keeping the Law of Moses, Jesus requires them to follow it even more stringently than a literal reading would suggest. Many Christian readers of Matthew over the years have wondered if Jesus could be serious. Are you really not allowed to get angry, or to lust after an attractive person, or defend yourself? Some readers have suggested that Jesus wants to make the Law impossible to keep, so that people would realize that the Law cannot bring salvation. But there

is, in fact, nothing in the text to suggest either that Jesus is not serious or that he thinks keeping his interpretations are impossible. Matthew wants to stress the Law, not counter or dissolve it.

At the same time, Matthew is not simply giving a detailed list of do's and don'ts that need to be followed to enter the coming Kingdom. Another key passage for Matthew is 22:35–40, where a scripture scholar (a "lawyer"—meaning one skilled in the Jewish law) asks Jesus what the greatest commandment is. Jesus tells him that the most important commandment is found in Deuteronomy 6:5. You should love God with your entire being. And the second most important commandment is in Leviticus 19:18. You should love your neighbor as yourself. In sum, for Jesus, if you do these two things, you will indeed fulfill all that God requires, for, "On these two commandments hang all the Law and the prophets" (22:40).

Jesus, the Jewish Leaders, and the Jewish People

And so it is that Matthew very much appears to be a "Jewish" Gospel. In another sense, Jesus has long seemed to readers also to be "anti-Jewish." This anti-Jewishness represents an opposition to Judaism as it was being practiced in Matthew's own day, especially among the leaders of the Jews. As we have seen in the stories of the wise men and of Jesus' baptism, Matthew castigates the Jewish leaders as those who know, but do not do, the will of God. This castigation reaches a crescendo in chapters 21–23 (another passage not found in Mark). Jesus is opposed by the leaders in Jerusalem, and he lashes out in response. These Jewish leaders are like someone who says the right thing but refuses to do it (21:28–32); for that reason the most despised of sinners—tax collectors and prostitutes—will enter the kingdom of heaven ahead of them. He then tells parables against the Jewish leaders, indicating that God is going to visit judgment upon them and even destroy their city (21:33–44; 22:1–14).

The vitriolic attack on the Jewish leaders comes to its climax in chapter 23, which contains the "seven woes" against the scribes and Pharisees who are concerned only with praise and admiration, not with doing what is right; they are hypocrites, blind guides concerned with minutiae instead of what really matters, whitewashed tombs that are clean on the outside but full of rot and corruption

FIGURE 10.4. A miniature ivory panel that portrays of several scenes from Jesus' Passion in Matthew's Gospel: Pilate washing his hands, Jesus carrying his cross, Peter making his denials, and the rooster crowing.

within; they are a brood of vipers, murders of the righteous prophets of God, false leaders who shed innocent blood.

And it is not just the leaders who are condemned. In one of the most haunting scenes of the Gospel, when Jesus is put on trial, the Roman governor Pontius Pilate declares him innocent and calls for water to wash his hands of the whole proceeding against Jesus. Pilate tells the Jewish crowd that he is "innocent of this man's blood"; and then, we are told, the crowd (not just the leaders, but all the Jewish people assembled) cry out, "His blood be upon us and our children" (27:25). Here Matthew portrays the Jewish people as accepting the responsibility for Jesus' death, and passing on this responsibility to their descendants. This verse, of course, was used for hateful and heinous anti-Semitic purposes over the centuries as later Christians blamed later

Jews for the death of Jesus, as if they had anything to do with it.

Matthew ends, of course, with the trial, crucifixion, burial, and resurrection of Jesus. Unlike Mark, in this account Jesus actually appears to his disciples after his death and gives them his final words and commissions them to go forth and make disciples—not just of Jews but of "all nations"; that is, also the gentiles. For Matthew these future converts will be those who believe in Jesus and who will understand him as the Jewish messiah sent from the Jewish God to the Jewish people in fulfillment of the Jewish Law. Jesus, and the religion that he embraced and promoted, was Jewish to the core. Those who wish to follow Jesus cannot abandon the Law of Moses. They are to keep the Law of Moses—even better than the Jewish leaders. Those who do so "will be called great in the Kingdom of Heaven."

BOX 10.5 WAS MATTHEW A JEW?

Some scholars have come to doubt that the author of Matthew was a Jew, despite the heavy emphasis on Jesus' own Jewishness in this Gospel. One of the more intriguing pieces of evidence that is sometimes cited involves Matthew's interpretation of passages drawn from the Hebrew Bible, especially Zechariah 9:9, as quoted in Matthew 21:5: "Look your king is coming to you, humble, and mounted on a donkey, and on a colt, the foal of a donkey."

From our study of the Tanakh you will recognize the literary form of this passage. The author of Zechariah is writing in poetry and has used here "synonymous parallelism," where the second line of a couplet repeats the ideas of the first line using different words. Here the parallelism is between the "donkey" of the first line and the "colt, the foal of a donkey" in the second.

Matthew, however, appears to have misunderstood the parallelism, or at least to have understood it in a highly unusual way. For he seems to have thought that the prophet was speaking of two different animals,

one of them a donkey and other a colt. So, when Jesus prepares to ride into Jerusalem, his followers acquire *two* animals for him, which he straddles for the trip into town (21:5–7; contrast Mark 11:7). Some scholars have argued that no educated Jew would have made this kind of mistake about the Zechariah passage (none of the other Gospel writers, it might be pointed out, does so), so that this author could not have been Jewish.

Most other scholars, however, have not been convinced—in part because we know all sorts of educated authors from the ancient world, as well as the modern one, who seem to misread texts. This includes ancient Jewish interpreters of their own Hebrew Scriptures, some of whom produce interpretations that are no more bizarre than Matthew's interpretations of Zechariah (including some late rabbinic sources, which also indicate that Zechariah was referring to two animals). On these grounds, at least, the identity of Matthew as a Jew has to be left as an open question.

 THE GOSPEL OF LUKE

Since Luke has many of the same stories as Mark and Matthew, it will be similar to these other Gospels in a number of ways. It too will tell stories of Jesus' birth, baptism, temptation, teaching, miracles, trip to Jerusalem, death, and resurrection. But Luke puts his own spin on these stories—changing details here and there, adding stories not found in the other Gospels, emphasizing various points. His portrayal of Jesus, as a result, has a different focus. Whereas Mark stresses Jesus as the Son of God who had to suffer and die, and Matthew emphasizes that Jesus was the Jewish messiah rejected by the Jewish leaders, Luke will focus on Jesus as a Jewish prophet who made a proclamation to his own people, who rejected him, leading to the spread of the mission to the gentiles. It is important to note that unlike the other two Gospels, Luke wrote a second volume, the book of Acts. These two books were conceived as a unit: the first telling of the life and death of Jesus, the other telling of the spread of Christianity throughout the Roman Empire after his death. As we have already seen, the focus of Acts is the

mission to gentiles. The Gospel of Luke is a kind of preparation for that narrative. In it we see a Jesus who—like other Jewish prophets before him—is rejected by his own people. This is why the message is taken abroad.

Luke begins his Gospel with an important preface (1:1–4), four verses that his educated readers would have understood to be typical of works of ancient history. Historians in the ancient world typically began their accounts by describing the research they had done into their subject, the sources of information they had, and the care that they had taken to make sure their information was accurate. And this is exactly what Luke tells his readers as well. We today have a good sense of what some of these sources were that were available to Luke: the Gospel of Mark, Q, and the source, or collection of sources, we are calling L. It is interesting that Luke, in these opening verses, seems to imply that his predecessors who had written Gospels before him had not done a completely adequate job, so he wants to set the record straight. Does this suggest that Luke was not satisfied with Mark's account in particular?

In typical historian fashion, Luke dedicates his account to a patron; he calls him "most excellent

Theophilus." Some scholars have thought that the phrase "most excellent" indicates that this is some kind of high-ranking Roman official. If so, then possibly Luke is writing his Gospel in order to inform a person in power the true story of Jesus. This might make sense if, in Luke's day, Christians were experiencing persecution by Roman authorities. Throughout his Gospel—especially in the Passion narrative—Luke stresses that Jesus was no threat to the state and that he was innocent of all charges brought against him. So too in Acts, the Christians do nothing to deserve their persecution and prosecution. Maybe Luke wanted Theophilus, a Roman official, to know this. On the other hand, some scholars think that Theophilus is not the name of a real person but is a code name for "Christians." Literally the name means "beloved of God" (or "lover of God"). In that case Luke would be writing his fellow Christians in order to help set the record straight concerning who Jesus really was.

The Beginning of the Gospel

Luke probably did not have access to Matthew's Gospel, but he begins in a roughly similar way by telling the story of Jesus' birth and genealogy. There are very striking differences between these two versions of events. On the most obvious level, Luke does not tell of the visit of the wise men, the wrath of Herod, the flight to Egypt, or the slaughter of the boys in Bethlehem. His story does not, in fact, begin with the birth of Jesus but with the birth of Jesus' "forerunner" John the Baptist. In this account, John is born before Jesus and, as it turns out, they are relatives (their mothers are related; this is found only in Luke). The story of John's birth is designed in part to show that even though he came first, he was of secondary importance as the prophetic figure who was to "prepare the way" for Jesus himself.

Not only is John portrayed as a prophet in this account—as foreshadowed already here in his birth; so too is Jesus. Scholars have long noted that the birth narrative of Luke 1 appears to be closely modeled on the account of the birth of the prophet Samuel (1 Samuel 1–2). In both instances a devout Jewish woman miraculously conceives, to the joy and amazement of her family, and she responds in song, praising the God of Israel who exalts those who are humble and humbles those who are exalted (compare the song of Hanna in 1 Samuel 2:1–10

with the song of Mary in Luke 1:46–55). The astute reader will catch the resonances: Jesus is born like a great prophet.

Unlike Matthew's, in Luke's version of Jesus' birth Joseph and Mary are originally from Nazareth and have to make a trip to Bethlehem in order to register for a census during the reign of the Roman emperor Caesar Augustus. It just so happens that Mary goes into labor and gives birth while they are there (2:1–7). That is why, for Luke, Jesus was born in Bethlehem even though he was raised in Nazareth.

It is important to notice that there is a clear emphasis in the first two chapters of Luke on the Temple in Jerusalem. It is in the Temple that John's father Zechariah learns from an angel that he will have a son who will be the one go before the Lord "in the spirit and power of Elijah." If you'll remember from the last prophet of the Hebrew Bible, Malachi, Elijah was to come at the end of time. John is presented in the Gospels as an Elijah figure, in fulfillment of prophecy. The Temple is important in the accounts of Jesus' birth as well. After he is born, he is presented before God in the Temple (Bethlehem is near Jerusalem, so it was not difficult to go there). While there he is recognized as the one who had been promised, first by a righteous man Simeon and then by a prophetess Anna (2:22–38). The very next story takes place when Jesus is twelve years old—the one and only story in the entire New Testament about Jesus as a boy. His parents make a trip to Jerusalem for a festival, return home, and en route realize that they have forgotten to bring Jesus along. After a three-day search, his mother finds him in the Temple discussing matters of the Law with Jewish teachers (2:41–51).

These various themes will be played out throughout Luke's Gospel. John is the prophet from God who prepares the way for Jesus. Those who are most righteous in Israel recognize who Jesus is. The message comes to the heart of Jerusalem, the Temple. But, as we will see, not everyone accepts it. For that reason the message of Jesus moves out, away from the holy city Jerusalem, to the lands of the gentiles.

The idea that Jesus' message of salvation is for all people, Jew and gentile, may be suggested already in Luke's version of Jesus' genealogy. We have seen that Matthew's genealogy goes all the way back to Abraham, the father of the Jews, even though Jesus is not related by blood to this bloodline. Luke's genealogy has a similar problem, since here too Jesus'

BOX 10.6 THE VIRGINAL CONCEPTION IN MATTHEW AND LUKE

Both Matthew and Luke make it quite clear that Jesus' mother conceived as a virgin, but they appear to understand the significance of Jesus' virginal conception differently. In Matthew, Jesus' birth is said to fulfill the prediction of the Hebrew prophet Isaiah, who foretold that "a virgin shall conceive and bear a son" (1:23). Luke neither quotes this Isaiah passage nor indicates that Jesus' birth fulfills Scripture. What the event means for Luke is suggested in the story of the Annunciation (1:28–38, a passage found only in Luke), where the angel Gabriel assures Mary that her son "will be great, and will be called the son of the Most High, and the Lord God will give to him the throne of his ancestor David." Mary is disturbed by this pronouncement: how can she bear a son if she has never had sexual relations (1:34)? The angel's reply is striking: "The Holy spirit will

come upon you, and the power of the Most High will overshadow you; therefore the child to be born will be holy; he will be called son of God" (1:35).

Why, then, is Jesus conceived of a virgin in Luke? Evidently because Jesus really is God's son ("therefore . . . he will be called the Son of God"). In other words, his father is not a human but God himself.

As we will see later, Luke is generally thought to have been writing to a Christian community that was largely gentile. It may be that he has molded his portrayal of Jesus for these converts from other Greco-Roman religions. He presents the story of Jesus' birth in a way that would make sense to a pagan reader who was conversant with tales of other divine beings who walked the face of the earth, other heroes and demigods who were born of the union of a mortal with a god.

mother is a virgin who conceives by the Holy Spirit. Yet the genealogy is not hers but Joseph's, who only "supposedly" (Luke tells us) was the father of Jesus (3:23). But what is most striking is that Luke's genealogy—even though it too is of Joseph—is a different genealogy from Matthew's. Compare the two (Matthew 1:1–18; Luke 3:23–38) and you'll see. Luke's is set up differently in that it begins with Joseph and moves backward in time, whereas Matthew's starts at the beginning with Abraham and moves forward. But ask yourself: who is the father of Joseph, Jesus' "father"? Who is his grandfather? Great-grandfather? All the way from Joseph back to King David, the ancestors are different. Luke obviously has a different source for his genealogy than Matthew had.

An even more important difference is the end point. For Matthew, who wants to stress that Jesus is altogether Jewish, the line goes back to Abraham. But Luke's genealogy does not stop there. It goes all the way back to Adam. As in Adam and Eve! This is one amazing genealogy. But why would Luke want to trace Jesus' line all the way back to the first human being, from whom all humans spring? It appears to be because he wants to stress that Jesus is the savior not only of the Jews but of all people, Jew and gentile. And so the genealogy shows that he is related to all people, going all the way back to Adam.

The Beginning of Jesus' Ministry

I have indicated that ancient biographies stress their important points early on in their narratives. Like Matthew and Mark, Luke narrates Jesus' baptism and his temptation in the wilderness (somewhat oddly, he places the genealogy after the baptism rather than at his birth). What is striking is the very next story he tells, the first event to transpire in Jesus' public ministry. This story establishes in clear terms how Luke understands the meaning and significance of Jesus. You can tell that it is an important story for Luke because he has taken it from Mark, where it occurs roughly half way through his account of Jesus' life (Mark 6:1–6). But Luke has changed the order of events so that now this story is the very first thing that Jesus does in his public ministry. Moreover, he has added some important details to the story. This account sets the stage for everything else in the Gospel.

It is the story of Jesus being rejected by his own townspeople in Nazareth. As a visitor to the synagogue, in Luke, Jesus is given the opportunity to read and comment on the Scripture. He reads from the book of Isaiah, in which the prophet claims to be anointed with the Spirit of God in order to "proclaim the good news." After reading the passage, Jesus sits down and declares that the predictions of the prophet have now come to fulfillment—by implication, in him. The people in

FIGURE 10.5. Jesus' reception in the synagogue is a key story in Luke. Here are the remains of an ancient synagogue at Khirbat Shema, in Galilee, with an artist's cutaway drawing of what the synagogue would have looked like. This particular synagogue was first built about two centuries after the days of Jesus.

the synagogue can't believe what they're hearing. But Jesus launches into an extended sermon, not found in the other Gospels, in which he recounts two familiar stories from Scripture, one about the prophet Elijah sent to assist the widow of Zarephath during the drought he had caused, and the other about Elisha who healed none of the lepers of Israel, but only Naaman, the leper king of Syria (4:25–27). In both of these stories, from the books of Kings, God sent his prophet not to help his people the Israelites but to pronounce judgment against them for having turned against him. These prophets ministered to gentiles outside the people of God.

These are the stories that Jesus appeals to in order to explain how he is fulfilling the prophecies of Isaiah. He too is a prophet of God who—like Elijah and Elisha—will not receive a warm welcome among his own people in Israel. Because of this rejection, Jesus' message will go to the gentiles. As you might imagine, Jesus' sermon was not a smashing success. In fact, it very nearly was a smashing failure. The Jews in the synagogue rise up in anger and try to throw Jesus off a cliff. But he escapes, leaves town, and takes his message elsewhere (4:28–30).

For Luke, this opening scene shows what will happen throughout the Gospel. Jesus is a prophet who is opposed by his own people, who eventually will call for his death. As a prophet he knows this will happen. In fact, it has all been predicted in the Jewish Scriptures. By rejecting him, the Jewish

people will be rejecting the God he represents. And this will cause the message to go elsewhere, to the non-Jews, as narrated in the book of Acts.

Jesus the Prophet

For Luke, not only is Jesus born as a prophet (cf. Samuel) and not only does he begin his ministry as a prophet (cf. Elijah and Elisha), his life is portrayed very much like that of a prophet—one who (again like Elijah) makes a proclamation to his people and does great miracles through the power of God. His proclamation is in many ways similar to that of the great classical prophets of Scripture, such as Amos and Isaiah, urging proper ethical behavior among the people of God. Luke, more than any other Gospel, has a prophetic social agenda: Jesus here is particularly concerned with social justice and the treatment of the underprivileged, including women. Jesus' prophetic character is revealed by another key story, one found only in Luke among our Gospels, in which Jesus raises from the dead the only son of a widow from the town of Nain (7:11–17). The story is clearly reminiscent of a miracle by the prophet Elijah, who raises from the dead the only son of a widow from Zerephath (1 Kings 17:17–24). The similarity of the events is not lost on Jesus' companions. When they see what he has done they proclaim, "A great prophet has arisen among us" (7:16).

In addition, Luke stresses that Jesus must die like a prophet. We have seen that prophets in the Hebrew

Bible were not always the most popular of figures, but were often opposed (e.g., Elijah, Elisha) and sometimes violently (Jeremiah). In a passage that is found only in Luke, Jesus indicates why it is that he must make his fateful trip to Jerusalem:

Listen, I am casting out demons and performing cures today and tomorrow, and on the third day I finish my work. Yet today, tomorrow, and the next day I must be on my way, because it is impossible for a prophet to be killed outside of Jerusalem. Jerusalem, Jerusalem, the city that kills the prophets and stones those who are sent to it! (13:32–33)

For Luke, prophets are killed in Jerusalem, and that's why Jesus has to go there. And since he is a prophet, he knows what will happen to him when he arrives. He goes to his death knowing full well that the Scriptures predicted that the great prophet of God must die and, assured of his fate, he goes in fulfillment of God's will.

In describing Jesus' death, Luke has changed Mark's account in a couple of ways that may seem insignificant at first but that are actually of fundamental importance. If you'll recall, Mark portrays Jesus' death as a an atoning sacrifice for sins, as seen in the fact that immediately upon his death the curtain in the temple is ripped in half and the centurion, seeing Jesus die, declares that Jesus was the Son of God. Luke has altered the account. In his version the curtain does not rip in half after Jesus dies, but while he is still living on the cross, when the earth goes dark (23:45). Scholars have long debated the significance of this change, but probably for Luke the tearing of the curtain does not show that Jesus' death brings access to God (since it happens before his death) but that God has now entered into judgment with his people as symbolized by this destruction within the holy place of the Temple itself.

And now, rather than declaring that Jesus was the "Son of God," the centurion who sees him die declares that he was "innocent." Here the emphasis is not on the fact that his death showed that he was the suffering son of God; it is instead on the fact that Jesus did not deserve to die. He, like the prophets before him, was an innocent victim of the hateful actions of others.

What both of these changes suggest is that Luke does not share Mark's view that Jesus' death brought

about an atonement for sins. There is another indication that this is the case. Earlier, in Mark's Gospel, Jesus spoke of his coming death as bringing salvation: "The Son of Man came not to be served but to serve, and to give his life a ransom for many" (Mark 10:45). Here Jesus' death ransoms others who deserve to die—that is, it is a substitution for the death of others. It is striking indeed that Luke omits this verse. And why does he do so? This may sound odd, but it is because for him Jesus' death does not bring atonement for sin.

Then why does Jesus die? For Luke, Jesus dies because he is a righteous prophet who was rejected by his own people in a severe miscarriage of justice. And how does Jesus' death then lead to the salvation from sin? When you read volume two of this author's work, the book of Acts, you will find the answer quite clearly. When the apostles in Acts try to convert others to believe in Jesus, they proclaim that Jesus' innocent death shows how sinful people are. When people recognize their sinfulness they break down and confess to God, begging for his forgiveness. And then God forgives them. For Luke, Jesus' death is not an atonement for the sins of others; it is a death that leads people to ask for forgiveness.

Let me illustrate the difference. If you owe me a hundred dollars but cannot pay, there are a couple of ways we could deal with your dilemma. You could find someone else to pay your debt for you. That would be like atonement (Christ dies for the sake of others). As an alternative, you could ask me to forgive you the debt, so that no one needs to pay. If I agree, then that would be like forgiveness (Christ's death leads people to ask for forgiveness). Mark understands Jesus' death as atonement; Luke as an occasion to ask for forgiveness. It's a big difference.

One other emphasis of Luke is that everything that happens to Jesus—and later to the church, in the book of Acts—is according to the plan of God. God had planned all things from the beginning, as laid out in the Jewish Scriptures. And what happens is what was foreordained. Jesus as the great prophet knows all that. He knows what will result from his public ministry, he knows that he must die, and he knows that he will be raised from the dead. All this is according to the divine plan and, as the prophet sent from God, Jesus is the one who both fulfills the plan and proclaims it to others.

THE SYNOPTIC GOSPELS AND THE PROBLEM OF HISTORY

So far in our study of the Gospels we have been interested in seeing how each of the Gospels wants to portray Jesus. You may have noticed that we have *not* yet asked any questions about what Jesus really said and did. There is a difference between explaining how Matthew tells the story of the wise men who visited the infant Jesus and asking whether there really were wise men who visited the infant Jesus; there is a difference between saying that in the Gospel of Luke Jesus tells the parable of the Good Samaritan and saying that Jesus really did tell the parable of the Good Samaritan. At the end of the next chapter, after exploring some of the other Gospels, we will move to ask the historical questions: what can we know about what Jesus really said and did? But here at this point it would be useful to take a step back from our three Gospels and point out why they present problems for historians who want to know about such things.

As I indicated at the beginning, these are Gospels written 35–50 years after the events they describe, by people who were not there to see any of these things happen, who have simply heard stories about Jesus that had been in oral circulation for decades. That should make one wonder if they have written historically accurate accounts. The bigger problem is that different ones of these Gospels tell the same stories but do so differently. Some of the differences can easily be reconciled.

FIGURE 10.6. One of the earliest surviving portrayals of Jesus' crucifixion, from a miniature ivory panel of the fourth century.

But others are very difficult—or even impossible—to reconcile.

For example, we have seen that Matthew and Luke present different genealogies of Jesus. Readers over the years have tried to reconcile the differences—for example by claiming that Matthew gives us Joseph's genealogy and Luke gives us Mary's (which is why the father is different, the grandfather, the great grandfather, etc., all the way back to David). The problem is that both genealogies are explicit: they are of Joseph.

Or think about the birth narratives themselves. On one hand we get completely different stories in the two—in one we have the wise men, in the other the shepherds; in one we have the wrath of Herod and the flight to Egypt, in the other we have the journey to Bethlehem from Nazareth because of a census in the days of Caesar Augustus. Such differences can be reconciled simply by saying that Matthew reports part of the story and Luke another part. But there are other differences that are not so easy to reconcile.

For one thing: where were Joseph and Mary from originally? Everyone probably thinks the answer is Nazareth. But read Matthew carefully. There is nothing in Matthew to suggest that they traveled to Bethlehem from somewhere else. The wise men, who have been on the road a long time, find them in a house in Bethlehem. This is probably some months or even over a year after Jesus was born, since when Herod wants to kill the child he orders his troops to kill every boy two years and under. If Jesus had been born last week, there would be no need to kill the toddlers (note: Matthew says he gave the order "based on the time he had heard from the wise men"). The wise men took a long time to get there, and this appears to be where Joseph and Mary actually live. Proof is seen in the decision of Joseph, when coming back from their flight in Egypt, to resettle in Nazareth. His first inclination is to return to Judea, where Bethlehem is, but he can't do so because the ruler Archilaus is worse even than his father Herod. And so they have to move to a different region, Galilee, in the north. Their original home appears to be Bethlehem, for this account. But not for Luke.

Or consider one other problem. Luke indicates that Joseph and Mary stayed in Judea for just over a month, after Mary made the offering in the Temple for purification after giving birth. This was to be 32 days later according to the Torah (Leviticus 12). And then they returned home to Nazareth. But if that's true, how can Matthew be right that they fled to Egypt? If they are back in Nazareth then the visit of the wise men to Bethlehem does not make sense, and there is no time for the flight to Egypt.

Combine this with the fact that we know from history that there was, in fact, no worldwide census that everyone had to register for in the time of Caesar Augustus. And how could there have been? Joseph allegedly has to go to Bethlehem to register because he is a descendant of David. But David lived a thousand years earlier. Is everyone in the Roman Empire returning to the home of their ancestors from 1000 years earlier? Suppose the next Congress passes a tax law and we all have to register for it by going to our ancestral homes from a thousand years ago. Where would *you* go?

There is no record of any such worldwide census. It almost certainly never took place. Then why does Luke *say* it took place? Because he knows full well that Jesus came from Nazareth, but he had to be born in Bethlehem. Why? Because that's where the savior was supposed to come from. So too with Matthew: Jesus was raised in Nazareth but born in Bethlehem. Both Luke and Matthew solve the problem of how that could be, but they do so in different ways—in fact, in contradictory ways.

That means that these accounts are probably not giving us history as it actually happened. They are telling stories. These stories in some ways are like the legends we saw in the Hebrew Bible in Genesis, Exodus, Joshua, Judges, 1 Samuel, and so on. The Bible is not only a book that is rooted in history; and it is not only a book that can be examined critically in order to figure out what really happened in the past; it is also a literary work that is filled with stories, some of which never happened, at least as related, but that are meant to convey deep and important religious lessons.

At a Glance: The Synoptic Gospels

As a solution to the "Synoptic Problem," scholars widely accept the "four-source hypothesis." Mark was the first Gospel written ("Markan Priority") and was used for many of their stories by Matthew and Luke, who also used a special source, Q (from the German word *Quelle*), for much of their sayings material. In addition, Matthew had access to one or more special sources called M and Luke to one or more sources called L.

Mark's Gospel presents Jesus as a Jewish messiah that no one expected. Rather than being a great warrior or king, Jesus was a messiah who had to suffer, die, and be raised from the dead. During his lifetime, no one appeared to understand that this is who the messiah was supposed to be; but it was the death of Jesus that brought about salvation to the world. Matthew's Gospel agrees that Jesus was the suffering messiah but, more than its predecessor Mark, Matthew emphasizes the Jewishness of Jesus, who is the Jewish messiah sent from the Jewish God to the Jewish people in fulfillment of the Jewish law. For Matthew, following Jesus means following that law even better than the leaders among the Jews. Luke stresses that Jesus was a great prophet who had come to his people, and, like other prophets within the biblical tradition, Jesus was spurned and rejected. This all was according to divine plan, however, and as a result the message of salvation was to go forth to the non-Jews, the gentiles.

Take a Stand

1. A student in your class tells the instructor that she doesn't see what the "problem" is with the Synoptic Problem. In her opinion, three different authors might easily have written down the same stories about Jesus, sometimes in the same words, without anyone copying anyone else—especially if they were eyewitnesses. Do you agree or disagree? Give your reasons.

2. Suppose you are a first-century Jew, and a Christian who wants to convert you has given you the Gospel of Mark to read. And suppose you do not find its claims that Jesus is the messiah at all convincing. Explain why. (In your explanation, point out what the messiah is to be like in the Jewish tradition, and show how Jesus as portrayed in Mark is not like that.) Now suppose you are the Christian. Make a case to your Jewish friend that Mark's understanding of Jesus is in line with the expectations of the messiah from the Jewish Scriptures.

3. Choose the Gospel of either Matthew or Luke and argue, in writing, whether its presentation of Jesus can be understood without knowing anything about the Hebrew Bible. Is understanding the narratives of the Old Testament (e.g., about Moses, or Elijah, or the nation of Israel) fundamental for seeing how Jesus is portrayed in this Gospel? Support your points.

Key Terms

Beatitudes, 257

Biography (ancient), 247

Four-source hypothesis, 245

Fulfillment citations, 255

L, 246

M, 246

Markan Priority, 245

Q, 245

Son of God, 251

Son of Man, 251

Synoptic Gospels, 243

Synoptic Problem, 244

Suggestions for Further Reading

NB: For this and all chapters, see the relevant articles (e.g., "Matthew," "Synoptic Problem") in the works cited in the Suggestions for Further Reading in chapter 1.

Burridge, Richard. *What Are the Gospels? A comparison with Greco-Roman Biography*. 2nd ed. Grand Rapids: Eerdmans, 2004. A thorough study that emphatically argues that the Gospels are best understood as a kind of ancient biography.

Hooker, Morna. *The Message of Mark*. London: Epworth, 1983. A very nice overview of the most significant features of Mark's Gospel; ideal for beginning students.

Powell, Mark Allan. *What Are They Saying about Luke?* New York: Paulist Press, 1989. An excellent survey of modern scholarly views of Luke's Gospel, for beginning students.

Senior, Donald. *What Are They Saying about Matthew?* New York: Paulist Press, 1983. An overview of scholarly views of Matthew's Gospel, excellent for beginning students.

Stein, Robert. *The Synoptic Problem: An Introduction*. Grand Rapids: Baker Book House, 1987. A good book-length treatment of the range of issues involved in the Synoptic Problem.

The Gospel of John, Later Gospels, and the Historical Jesus

WHAT TO EXPECT

After the Synoptic Gospels comes the Gospel of John, arguably the favorite book of the Christian canon among avid readers of the New Testament. In this chapter we will see how John is so very different from the other three Gospels and consider what sources may have been at the author's disposal. In particular we will consider its unique portrayal of Jesus and ask why it is so different from what we find in the earlier Gospels.

John may be our latest canonical Gospel, but it was by no means the last Gospel to be written. We will consider four of the other later Gospels: one that preserves just sayings of Jesus, two that tell stories of his birth and adventures as a young boy, and one that gives an alternative account of his trial, death, and resurrection.

Finally we will turn from examining these literary portraits of Jesus to seeing what we can say about the historical figure himself, what he really said, did, and experienced. There we will see how to use the Gospels as historical sources, and we will learn what portrait of Jesus emerges when we do so as we examine what it means to call Jesus a Jewish apocalyptic prophet.

In this chapter we continue our study of the New Testament by considering the last of the canonical Gospels to be written, the Gospel of John; we will then see that the four Gospels of the Christian Bible are not the only ones that were produced: that there are, in fact, many later accounts of Jesus' words and deeds that did not make it into the New Testament. In the final half of the chapter we will consider how all of the available Gospels may assist us in knowing what Jesus really said, did, and experienced.

 ## THE GOSPEL OF JOHN

The Gospel of John has always been one of the most beloved books of the New Testament. It is here that Jesus makes some of his most familiar and yet extraordinary declarations about himself, where he says that he is "the bread of life," "the light of the world," "the way, the truth, and the life." This is the Gospel that identifies Jesus as the Word of God "through whom all things were made." It is here that he makes the astonishing claim that "before

Abraham was, I am," where he confesses that "I and the Father are one," and where he tells Nicodemus that "you must be born again." And it is in this Gospel that Jesus performs some of his most memorable acts: turning the water into wine, raising his friend Lazarus from the dead, and washing his disciples' feet. These sayings and deeds, and indeed many more, are found only in the fourth Gospel, making it a source of perpetual fascination for scholars of the Bible. The distinctive character of this Gospel can be seen just where we would expect it, given what we have come to learn about ancient biographies: at the very beginning.

The Prologue of John

This Gospel begins in a completely different way from the other three we have already examined, with a highly elevated and rhetorically powerful poem-like prologue that introduces us to the subject of the narrative. Here, however, the subject is not named as Jesus—until the end of the passage. Instead, the subject is identified as the mysterious "Word" of God:

> In the beginning was the Word, and the Word was with God, and the Word was God. He was in the beginning with God. All things came into being through him, and apart from him nothing came into being that came into being. In him was life, and the life was the light of humans. . . .

Anyone who reads this for the first time and who is knowledgeable about the Hebrew Bible immediately thinks back to the very beginning, Genesis 1, the creation of the world, where "all things" did indeed come into being. And how did they come into being? When God spoke his word: "Let there be light, and there was light." Here, in the prologue of John, the "word" is not simply something that God speaks to create all things; the word is a personified being, who exists alongside God, through whom all things were made. But since it is precisely the word that God speaks, it is also equal with God. His Word is who he is. And so the "Word was with God and the Word was God."

We are not told yet who, or what, this Word is, other than the fact that it was he who created the universe (v. 3), who provided life and light to all humans (vv. 4–5), and who entered into the world

that he made, only to be rejected by his own people (vv. 9–11). John the Baptist testified to this Word (vv. 6–8), but only a few people received it; those who did so became children of God, having received a gift far greater even than that bestowed by the servant of God, Moses himself (vv. 12–14; 16–18). It is not until the end of the prologue that we learn that this Word eventually became a human being, and that human was Jesus Christ (vv. 14, 17).

Scholars have long suggested that this prologue may be an ancient Christian hymn or poem that the author himself, or someone else, composed to worship Christ. In this poem Jesus is not merely a great human called by God to be his messiah, or the son of God like other sons of God. Jesus is the fleshly being that came into existence when the preexistent Word of God that created all things became a human. Christ is the Word of God made flesh.

This Gospel will not provide us with a biography of a mere mortal. Its subject is one who was with God in eternity past, who was himself divine, who created the universe, who was God's self-revelation (his "Word") to the world, who came to earth to bring light out of darkness and truth out of error. He is a divine being who became human to dwell here and reveal the truth about God. This Gospel will present a view of Jesus that is very different from those of the Synoptics and that is far and away the most exalted among our New Testament narratives.

John and the Synoptics

This elevated beginning leads us to consider the relationship of John with the Synoptic Gospels. Once the prologue ends, the Gospel in very, very rough outline seems like one of the other Gospels. Jesus is first associated with John the Baptist; he engages in a public ministry of teaching and doing miracles; he goes to Jerusalem the last week of his life, where he is betrayed, denied, tried, crucified, and raised from the dead. So there are indeed basic similarities of John with the others. But the differences are stark indeed.

Suppose you were simply to list the key events of the Synoptic Gospels. Two of them begin by having Jesus born of a virgin in Bethlehem. In all of them he begins his public ministry by being baptized, after which he is tempted by the devil for forty days. He comes from the wilderness and begins his ministry; the first miracle he does in our earliest

Gospel is an exorcism, and throughout these accounts he is shown casting out demons. In addition he preaches about the coming Kingdom of God, most commonly by telling parables. Half way through the Gospels he experiences his transfiguration, which leads then into the trip to Jerusalem. In the Passion narrative he celebrates a Passover meal with his disciples in which he institutes the Lord's supper ("this is my body," "this is the cup of the new covenant in my blood"). Afterward he goes to Gethsemane where he asks God to allow him not to experience his coming Passion. He is then arrested by the authorities and made to stand trial before the Jewish Sanhedrin, who find him guilty of blasphemy before handing him over to the Romans for trial and execution.

These stories make up the backbone of the Synoptic accounts of Jesus. What most casual readers of the New Testament have never realized is that none of them is in John. Reread the Gospel for yourself and see. There is no reference to his virginal conception or birth in Bethlehem; no narration of his baptism. He does not go into the wilderness to be tempted by the devil, he never casts out a demon, he does not preach about the coming kingdom, and he never tells a parable. He does not experience the transfiguration, he does not institute the Lord's supper, he does not pray in Gethsemane to escape his Passion, and he is not tried by the Sanhedrin and found guilty of blasphemy.

If John does not have these stories about Jesus, what does it have? The majority of John's stories are found only in John, nowhere else. To be sure, many of the same characters appear in this Gospel including Jesus, some of his family, the male disciples, several women followers, John the Baptist, Jewish leaders, and Pontius Pilate. And there are some stories in common, such as the feeding of the 5000, the walking on water, and many of the events of the Passion narrative. But most of the stories in John are only in John. Only here, for example, do we hear of some of Jesus' most impressive miracles: turning water into wine (ch. 2), healing the man born blind (ch. 9), or raising Lazarus from the dead (ch. 11). Only here to we get the long discourses of Jesus, including the dialogues with Nicodemus in chapter 3, with the Samaritan woman in chapter 4, with his Jewish opponents in chapters 5 and 8, and with his disciples in chapters 13–17 (Jesus himself talks for virtually the entirety of these five chapters).

The differences between John and the Synoptics are not merely in the different stories they tell. John is also different, in a stark way, in *how* he tells his stories and in what he emphasizes about Jesus. Suppose, for example, you were to consider what Jesus teaches about. You may have noticed that in the Synoptic Gospels Jesus talks a lot about God, about how to please and serve God, about how to act in relationship to God, and about the coming Kingdom of God. But he almost never speaks about himself, indicating who he is. Strikingly, in John, Jesus spends most of his lengthy discourses talking almost exclusively about himself. He indicates who he is, where he has come from, and why he is here. He is the one who has come from God; he will be returning to God; he is in fact equal with God. He has come so that people can be given life; anyone who believes in him will live for eternity; anyone who rejects him will be condemned. These are the messages that Jesus delivers over and over again in this Gospel. It is all about his identity. You find almost nothing like that in Matthew, Mark, or Luke.

Or take the deeds of Jesus. When you read through the Synoptic Gospels and see Jesus performing miracles—why does he do them? It appears to be because he is compassionate and wants to help people who are in need. And what happens when someone asks him to do a miracle in order to prove who he is? When that sort of thing happens in the Synoptics, Jesus turns cold and insistent: he decidedly will *not* do a miracle in order to prove his identity; he will not provide a "sign" to show who he is (see Matthew 11:38). It is interesting that in the Synoptic Gospels Jesus' amazing deeds are called "miracles." They are not "signs" to show that he is the Son of God.

And what about John's Gospel? Here, as it turns out, Jesus' amazing deeds are not called miracles. They are called signs! And Jesus does them precisely to prove who he is. In fact, for this Gospel if Jesus does not prove who he is by doing signs, no one will believe in him—as he explicitly states at one point in the Gospel (4:48). The signs of the fourth Gospel prove that what Jesus says about himself is true. And so he says that he is the "bread of heaven"—meaning that he is the one who can provide the heavenly sustenance for eternal life; and he proves it by multiplying the loaves of bread to feed the multitudes (ch. 6). He says that he is the "light of the world" and he proves it by healing a blind

BOX 11.1 THE JEWS IN THE FOURTH GOSPEL

You will notice in reading through the fourth Gospel that the phrase "the Jews" is almost always used as a negative term of abuse. The Jews are portrayed as the enemies of Jesus who are consequently opposed to God and aligned with the devil and the forces of evil (see especially 8:31–59). Vitriolic statements of this kind may sound anti-Semitic to our ears—as indeed they should. And it is true that hateful acts of violence have been perpetrated over the years by those who have taken such charges as divine sanctions for oppression and persecution.

Despite these harsh statements about Jews in the Gospel of John, however, even here Jesus and his followers are portrayed as Jews who subscribe to the authority of Moses and participate in the Jewish cult and the

Jewish festivals. If Jesus and his followers are Jews, how can all Jews be lumped together and branded as the enemies of God?

This tension between condemning Jews on one hand, and affirming Jesus' own Jewishness on the other, characterizes the fourth Gospel. Later in the chapter we will see that the Johannine community started out as a group of Jews who believed in Jesus as the messiah. Over time, their views of Jesus changed. And with them changed their views of those Jews who did *not* believe in Jesus. They came to be thought of as the enemy, rather than as the chosen people. Whether the Gospel of John should be seen as thoroughly anti-Jewish or not is a question scholars have long debated.

man, demonstrating that he can show people the light (ch. 9). He says that he is the "resurrection and the life" and that anyone who believes in him will never die, and he proves it by raising a man from the dead (ch. 11). Unlike the Synoptics, where it was unthinkable that Jesus would prove his identity through signs, in this Gospel Jesus does signs for one main reason: to prove his identity. In fact, the author tells us that this is the point of the entire account: "Jesus did many other signs in the presence of his disciples, but these are written so that you may believe that Jesus is the Christ, the son of God, and that by believing you might have life in his name" (20:30–31).

Whereas in the Synoptics Jesus did not talk about himself and refused to do signs to prove who he was, in John he spends almost the entire Gospel talking about himself and doing signs to prove that what he says about himself is true. This book is very different from the earlier Gospels.

The Sources of the Fourth Gospel

Given these stark differences, scholars have debated whether John had ever read the Synoptic Gospels. Different scholars have different opinions (as, of course, they do on just about everything), but the majority view seems to be that he had not. His stories come from other sources—certainly from oral traditions in circulation in his community, but

probably also from earlier, written accounts of the life of Jesus that no longer survive.

There are in fact three solid arguments for thinking that John utilized earlier written sources.

1. *Differences in Writing Style.* Different passages of the Gospel appear to be written in different writing styles (e.g., the Prologue). If you were to read a page from Mark Twain and then a page from Virginia Woolf, you would have no trouble realizing they came from different authors. Different styles in John suggest the same.

2. *Repetitions.* Sometimes the same story is told in John in different words. Most strikingly: Jesus' farewell address to his disciples in chapter 14 sounds very much like what he continues then to say in chapter 16—virtually the same topics, the same themes, and the same points. That would make sense if there were two sources that narrated the same speech and the author spliced them together in his account.

3. *Literary Seams.* There are some places where the author appears to have combined two different accounts written originally by two different authors and, as a result, created a discrepancy that is otherwise hard to explain. I'll give three examples:

   a. In 2:11 Jesus is said to perform his "first sign"; in 4:54 he is said to perform his "second sign." Fair enough. But in 2:23 it says that he

a  b

FIGURE 11.1. Two portrayals of Jesus as the Good Shepherd (see John 10): one from an ancient Christian sarcophagus, and the other from a fifth-century mosaic in Ravenna, Italy.

performed many other signs. How could he do many signs before performing his second sign?

b. In 5:1 Jesus goes to Jerusalem, does a miracle there, and spends the rest of the chapter talking about it. Then in 6:1 the author says that "Jesus went to the other side of the sea of Galilee." The other side? He wasn't on either side—he was way down south, in Jerusalem.

c. My favorite. At Jesus' last meal with the disciples, Peter asks him "Lord, where are you going?" (13:36); a few minutes/verses later Thomas says "Lord, we do not know where you are going" (14:5). Jesus then launches into a speech, in the middle of which he says, "I am going to him who sent me; yet none of you asks me, 'Where are you going?'" (!) (16:5)

All of these problems can be explained if the author utilized a variety of written sources that he combined together, adding his own touches either here and there or a whole lot throughout. Scholars have long thought that among John's sources were an account of Jesus' signs. He does seven of them here. Possibly this was a source that narrated seven (the perfect number) of signs, indicating which one was first, which second, and so on (which is why

the author got into trouble with 2:23 by saying that he did many other signs between the ones numbered one and two, creating an unintentional literary seam). This source may have ended with what is now 20:30–31, a statement that the signs have been told to convince people to believe that Jesus is the messiah.

In addition, the author may have had several sources containing the discourses of Jesus. This would be why chapter 14 and chapter 16 sound so much alike: same discourse, different accounts of it. And it would explain why Jesus complains about no one asking him "where are you going" when in fact two disciples have already done so (they did so in one source, his complaint is from another). There may also have been a written source that provided John with his account of the Passion.

The Varying Emphases of John

The idea that there were different sources behind the fourth Gospel makes sense of one other striking feature of this book. As you have read through the book carefully, you may have noticed that different stories told about Jesus in this Gospel do not all portray him in the same way. Some of them emphasize the points I have already made, that he is thought of as a preexistent being who is highly exalted and is in fact equal with God. You find passages like that not only in the Prologue, which we have examined, but elsewhere scattered throughout the Gospel. Jesus is regularly saying things about himself that get his Jewish opponents seriously riled—so seriously that they are convinced that he has committed blasphemy by claiming to be a divine being, and so try to stone him to death.

Exalted teachings of Jesus about himself include the various "I am" sayings. It is striking that Jesus says "I am" only two times in Mark and Luke, and five times in Matthew. That is because, as we have seen, he does spend much time talking about his identity in these Gospels. By contrast, he says "I am" forty-six times in John. Among his important self-identifications are the seven "I am" sayings in which he speaks of himself symbolically as the one who is uniquely important for eternal life ("I am the bread of life"; "I am the resurrection and the life"; "I am the way the truth and the life, no one comes to the Father but by me"; etc.). Even more important are the several places where Jesus simply says "I am"—as in John 8:58, where he tells his Jewish opponents that "before Abraham was, I am." Readers have long thought, probably rightly, that Jesus is referring to the episode involving Moses and the burning bush in Exodus 3, which we discussed in chapter 3. There God gives his personal name to Moses by saying "I am." If that is what Jesus is saying about himself, he is claiming to be God. Maybe not God the Father (since in this Gospel Jesus does pray to the Father, and he is clearly not talking to himself); but God in some sense, one who is equal with God. That is why elsewhere Jesus can say "I and the Father are one" (10:30). That is quite a statement to make about oneself. You won't find anything like it in the Synoptics.

But the striking thing is that there are other passages in John in which Jesus is not identified in such exalted, high terms. These other passages portray Jesus as a mere mortal, not as one equal with God. Take for example the early story in which Jesus first meets up with his future disciples, in 1:35–42. John the Baptist sees Jesus and calls him "the Lamb of God" (meaning that he is the one who will die to bring salvation; the Passover lamb, of course, was not divine). Two of his disciples follow after Jesus and address him as "Teacher" (nothing divine about that either). And, after talking with him, they go off and find Peter to tell him that they have now found the "messiah" (recall: the messiah is not God in ancient Judaism). Here Jesus is obviously called lots of things, but nothing approaching the exalted titles found in the Prologue and the "I am" sayings. Instead he is a teacher, the expected messiah, and a lamb who will be slaughtered.

Why is it that some passages portray Jesus in highly exalted terms, but other passages in terms much more familiar to, say, readers of the Synoptic Gospels? The traditional theological answer, of course, is that Jesus is both things at once, both God and man. And so some passages portray him as divine and others as human. But it is striking that none of these passages I have mentioned explicitly identify Jesus as both divine and human at one and the same time. Some passages portray him one way, and some in another.

Scholars have long wrestled with this situation, and one of the most common solutions to it suggests that the different views of Jesus ultimately come from different sources that the author used. These different sources were written at different times in the community. Over time the views about Jesus within the community changed, as the people in the community experienced hardships and struggles and developed their theological reflections on God and Christ. The sources that were written earlier in the history of the community had different theological assumptions and views of Jesus from the ones written later.

Look back at this story in 1:35–42 and you will notice something very interesting linguistically. On three occasions the story gives a key word in Aramaic, which the author translates for his readers into Greek. You can see this even if you are reading in English. In verse 38 the disciples call Jesus "rabbi," and the author tells you that this is the Aramaic word for "teacher." In verse 41 the disciple Andrew finds his brother Simon and tells him that he has found the "messiah," which the author tells you means "Christ." And in verse 42 Jesus meets Simon and tells him that he will call him "Cephas," which the author indicates is the word for "Peter."

Why the Aramaic words, and why the translations? It appears that this is a story that circulated very early in the history of the community to which the author of the fourth Gospel belonged. Scholars call it the **Johannine Community**. This community must have begun its life in Palestine, where

BOX 11.2 JOHN'S DE-APOCALYPTICIZED GOSPEL

The Synoptic Gospels are filled with apocalyptic pronouncements of Jesus (see, for example, Mark 13 and Matthew 24–25) and, as we will see at the end of this chapter, the historical Jesus himself was almost certainly an apocalyptic prophet. But when we come to the Gospel of John, the last of our Gospels, we find the apocalyptic message seriously toned down. For John, eternal life is not a future event. As the author puts it early on in the narrative, using the present tense: "Whoever believes in the Son has [present tense] eternal life" (3:36). Eternal life in this Gospel does not come at the end of time, when the Son of Man arrives on the clouds of heaven and brings in the kingdom. Eternal life is here and now, for all who believe in Jesus. That is why Jesus does not deliver an "apocalyptic discourse" in this Gospel (cf. Mark 13) or speak about the coming Son of Man or the imminent kingdom of God. The kingdom of God for this Gospel is entered by those who have faith in Jesus, in the present (see 3:3).

That a person's standing before God is determined not by the future resurrection, but by the present relationship with Jesus, is illustrated by John's account of the dialogue between Jesus and Martha in the story of Lazarus. Jesus informs Martha that her recently deceased brother will rise again (11:23). She thinks he is referring to the resurrection at the end of time (an apocalyptic notion) and agrees with him (11:24), but he corrects her. He is referring to possibilities in the present, not the future. "I am the resurrection and the life. Those who believe in me, even though they die, will live, and everyone who lives and believes in me will never die" (11:25–26).

We have seen that Jewish apocalypticists maintained a dualistic view of the world, in which this age belonged to the forces of evil whereas the age to come belonged to God. In John's Gospel this dualism does not have a temporal dimension (this age and the future age) but a spatial one (this world and the world that is above). Those who are from the world that is above belong to God, those from below belong to the devil. How does one belong to the world that is above? By believing in the one who has come from that world, Jesus (3:31). Thus, in this Gospel Jesus' proclamation is no longer an apocalyptic appeal to repent in the face of a coming judgment; it is an appeal to believe in the one sent from heaven so as to have eternal life in the here and now. John, in short, presents a de-apocalypticized version of Jesus' teaching. (For a remnant of the older apocalyptic view, found even here, see 5:28–29).

Aramaic was spoken. They told their stories in Aramaic (which was the native tongue of Jesus as well). Eventually, when these stories began to circulate outside of Palestine where, possibly, the community had moved, they were translated into Greek, and only the key words were left in Aramaic so that they would pack a real punch. These stories early in the community came to be written down in a source. The author of John used this source and, realizing that his Greek-speaking audience might not recognize the key Aramaic terms, he translated them into Greek.

This story about Jesus, then, would be one that was from a very early period of the community's history, and it portrays Jesus in very human terms—as a rabbi who was the long-awaited messiah, whose death brought about salvation. That sounds like the view of Mark. But other passages, such as the Prologue, are thoroughly Greek, highly poetic, and very exalted in their views. As are the "I am" sayings. These would have come from other sources later in the community. They portray Jesus as divine.

FIGURE 11.2. Portrayal of Jesus raising Lazarus while his sister Mary pleads for Jesus to help; from the lid of a small fifth-century silver ornamental box.

According to this theory, the Johannine community started out as a group of Jews in Palestine with a Synoptic-like understanding of who Jesus was as the Jewish messiah whose death brought salvation. For one reason or another they ended up

At a Glance: The Gospel of John

John is unique among the Gospels. Most of the stories about Jesus in this, the last canonical Gospel, are found only in this Gospel (outside the Passion narrative), just as most of the stories of the Synoptics are not found in John. Based on differences in writing style, repetitions, and "literary seams," scholars are confident that John must have had sources for his accounts other than the Synoptics. At the least this would include the "signs source," several discourse sources, and a Passion narrative.

Most impressive is John's overall portrayal of Jesus. Unlike the Synoptics, here Jesus' teachings are almost entirely about who he is, where he has come from, and how he can provide eternal life. Here his deeds are not miracles to help those in need so much as signs to show that what he says about himself is true. It appears that this new view of Jesus emerged over time as the Johannine community developed its understanding of Jesus so that he was not a mere mortal, but himself divine.

---

leaving Palestine and relocating. And the more they thought about Jesus and the amazing things that he did, and the incredible importance of both his life and his death, they began to think of him as more exalted than a mere human messiah. Over time they began to think of him as the Son of God in a more highly exalted sense. He was not simply one who proclaimed God's word. He *was* God's Word. And so he appeared on earth as one who was preexistent, who became incarnate, who came from above to lead others back to the realm whence he himself had come. He was in fact equal with God. And only those who believe in him could have eternal life. This is the end result of the thinking of the Johannine community, and the final view set forth in the finished edition of the fourth Gospel.

THE OTHER GOSPELS

Matthew, Mark, Luke, and John were not the only Gospels produced by the early Christians. They were simply the four that came to be included in the New Testament. Indeed, it is striking that the author of one of them, Luke, indicates that he had "many" predecessors in producing a narrative of the things Jesus said and did (1:1). It is unfortunate that apart from the Gospel of Mark, all of these earlier accounts have been lost (although we do know, at least, about Q; and we can say a few things about the sources we are calling M and L, as well as the signs source of the fourth Gospel, etc.).

In addition to these sources that lie behind the New Testament Gospels, we have over forty other Gospels that still survive today (either entirely or in fragments). The vast majority of these are of little value for anyone interested in knowing what Jesus really said and did. They tend to be highly legendary and they were produced in later times—the second, third, fourth century and beyond into the Middle Ages. The four canonical Gospels are also the four earliest that survive. Still, it is important to recognize the existence of these later Gospels because they show that Christians did not stop reflecting on the significance of Jesus or refrain from writing accounts of his life once the books of the New Testament were completed. Stories about him continued to be told, and changed, and invented for centuries. They continue to be invented even today, as you can see by watching any of the versions produced in Hollywood.

We will not be able to examine all of these non-canonical Gospels, but we can consider four of the most important ones. These Gospels are very different from one another (and from those of the New Testament): one is a "sayings Gospel," containing nothing but Jesus' teachings; two are "infancy Gospels," dealing with the background to Jesus' birth and with his young life; and one is a "Passion Gospel," an alternative account of his trial, death, and resurrection.

A Sayings Gospel

The Coptic Gospel of Thomas is without a doubt the most significant discovery of a new Gospel in

FIGURE 11.3. The Gnostic books (including the one containing the Gospel of Thomas) discovered in 1945 near Nag Hammadi, Egypt, and the place where they were found.

modern times. It was uncovered with a cache of other documents near the village of Nag Hammadi, Egypt, in 1945 (I will discuss this discovery later in this chapter). It is called the "Coptic" Gospel of Thomas because it is written in Coptic, the ancient Egyptian language (there is another Gospel of Thomas, as we will see, and it is important not to get the two confused). Originally this Gospel of Thomas was written in Greek; the surviving Coptic manuscript, then, represents a translation made at a later time.

The manuscript that was discovered, which contained other writings as well, was produced in the middle of the fourth century C.E., but there is clear evidence that the Gospel of Thomas was originally composed much earlier than that—probably in the early second century. This would put it within thirty or forty years of the Gospel of John. Some scholars date it even earlier, into the first century, the time of the New Testament Gospels, although that scholarly opinion is not the majority view.

I am calling this a "sayings Gospel" because it consists of nothing but sayings of Jesus—114 of them altogether. There is no narrative context for these sayings—that is, no stories of any kind (no miracles, no controversies, no death and resurrection)—just one saying after the other, usually introduced simply with the words "Jesus said," but sometimes involving a conversation where the disciples ask a question and Jesus responds. In terms of genre, the book looks a lot more like a book of Wisdom than a New Testament Gospel. It is a collection of wise teachings meant to bring enlightenment to the one who will understand.

Understanding is of primary importance for the author of the Gospel of Thomas. This is one of the most striking features of these sayings: the author begins by telling us the following: "These are the secret words which the living Jesus spoke, and Didymus Judas Thomas wrote them down. And he said 'The one who finds the meaning of these words will not taste death'" (saying 1). How significant is the interpretation of these sayings? It is of eternal significance: the way to have eternal life is to interpret them correctly. For this Gospel, it is not the death and resurrection of Jesus that bring salvation. It is the correct understanding of his secret teachings.

Who is this author? We don't know who actually wrote the book, but the author claims to be Didymus Judas Thomas. Didymus is a Greek word for twin; Thomas is the Aramaic word for twin. This is someone's twin, whose name is Judas or Jude. In the New Testament, Jesus has a brother named Jude (Mark 6:3). In parts of the ancient church it was believed that Jude was actually Jesus' twin brother; in fact, his identical twin. (See Box 11.3.) Who better to know the teachings of Jesus than his twin brother?

Many of the sayings of Jesus in this Gospel will sound familiar to anyone who knows the Synoptic Gospels. Here we read about the blind leading the blind; about "blessed are the poor"; about the parable of the mustard seed. More than half of the sayings in Thomas are found in the canonical Gospels. Other sayings sound vaguely familiar, but with a kind of twist: "Let him who seeks not cease seeking until he finds, and when he finds, he will be troubled, and when he is troubled, he will marvel, and he will rule over the All" (saying 2).

Yet other sayings don't sound at all like the New Testament: "On the day when you were one you became two. But when you have become two, what will you do?" (saying 11); "When you undress without being ashamed, and you take your clothes and put them under your feet as little children and tramp on them, then you shall see the Son of the Living One, and you shall not fear" (saying 47); "Whoever has come to understand the world has found only a corpse, and whoever has found a corpse is superior to the world" (saying 56); and the shortest saying in the Gospel: "Become passers-by" (saying 42).

The meanings of these sayings are in no way obvious: if they were, they would not be called secret! But when you look at all the sayings together, a certain sense does emerge from them. This Gospel portrays the world we live in as an inferior place, in fact, as a corpse. People should not be invested in life here. In fact, some people do not actually belong here. Their souls have come here from the heavenly realm and become entrapped in their material

---

BOX 11.3 THOMAS THE TWIN OF JESUS

Some of the Christians in Syria thought that Jesus' brother Judas (or Jude), mentioned in Mark 6:3, was actually his twin. Hence the name Judas Thomas, "Jude the Twin." This idea is puzzling for most modern readers. If these ancient Syrian Christians believed that Jesus was unique in being born of a virgin, how could they also think that he had a twin brother?

Unfortunately, none of the ancient Syrian texts that allude to this belief answers the question. But we may be able to gain some insight by considering other places in ancient literature in which twins are born, one the son of a mortal and the other the son of a god. The most famous account comes from Greek mythology in the tale of the birth of Heracles (Hercules) and his twin brother, the mortal Iphicles. The story was retold many times, perhaps most memorably in a humorous play titled *Amphitryon*, by the Roman playwright Plautus, in the second century B.C.E. I have summarized the plot in Box 2.3 (review the summary).

What I did not indicate at that point was that the main character, the woman Alcmene, was already pregnant by her husband, Amphytrion, before spending a long night in the embrace of the king of the gods, Zeus. As a result of this second encounter she becomes doubly pregnant. She eventually gives birth to two sons: Iphicles, the human son of Amphytrion, and Heracles, the divine son of Zeus. Did the ancient Syrian Christians know tales such as this and think that it might be possible for Jesus and Judas to be twins, born at the same time of the same mother, one being the son of God and the other the son of Joseph?

bodies. One needs to escape the prison of the body, stripping it off from the soul, in order to return to one's heavenly home. One can learn the means of doing so by understanding Jesus' secret teachings. Nothing else about Jesus matters—not his miracles, not his crucifixion, not his resurrection. He has come from a higher realm to communicate the secret knowledge that can lead to salvation from this corpse of a world and this prison of a body. For this author the kingdom of God is not a place that will be here on earth. It is a liberated existence that one enjoys by escaping the material world and the body that inhabits it. The followers of Jesus should not live for the pleasures of life, which only serve to tie them to the body; they should stress the inner being and seek for liberation by receiving the true knowledge of who they really are—souls from a higher realm—as communicated by Jesus' secret teachings.

Since the discovery of this Gospel, scholars have wondered whether any of its unusual teachings may go back to Jesus himself or whether, instead, they represent later reflections on the significance of Jesus by followers living in a later time and a different place. It is true that some of the sayings may be those of Jesus—at least some of the ones that sound like those in the Synoptics. But many of the other sayings appear to have been created by Christians who had an alternative understanding of the importance of Jesus—not as the crucified messiah but as the revealer of secret truths that can bring salvation.

Infancy Gospels

The Gospels of the New Testament present only a few accounts relating to Jesus as a young boy (e.g., the visit of the wise men and the flight to Egypt in Matthew; Jesus as a twelve-year-old in the Temple in Luke). Later Christians were curious about these early periods of Jesus' life and so told stories about them. The legendary character of these stories is easily detected.

One of the most important and influential accounts of Jesus' "infancy" is the Infancy Gospel of Thomas, which is not to be confused with the Coptic Gospel of Thomas. It is difficult to say when this Gospel was written, but it may have been at some point in the early second century. Lying behind its narrative is a question that intrigues some Christians even today: if Jesus was a miracle-working Son of God as an adult, what was he like as a kid? According to this account, he was more than a little mischievous.

When Jesus first appears in the text, he is making clay sparrows by a stream on the Sabbath. A Jewish man passing by sees what he has done, goes to tell his father Joseph, who comes and upbraids Jesus for violating the Law by not keeping the Sabbath day holy. Instead of apologizing, the child Jesus claps his hands and tells the sparrows to be gone. They come to life and fly off chirping, thereby destroying any evidence of wrongdoing.

One might have expected that with his supernatural powers, Jesus would have been a useful and entertaining playmate. As it turns out, however, the boy has a temper and is not to be crossed. When a child accidentally runs into him on the street, Jesus turns in anger and declares, "You'll go no further on your way." The child falls down dead. (Jesus later raises him from the dead, along with others that he has cursed on one occasion or another.) And Jesus' wrath is not reserved for children. When Joseph sends him to school to learn to read, Jesus refuses to recite the alphabet. His teacher pleads with him to cooperate. Jesus replies with a scornful challenge: "If you really are a teacher and know the letters well, tell me the power of Alpha and I'll tell you the power of Beta." More than a little perturbed, the teacher cuffs the boy on the head, the single largest mistake of an illustrious teaching career. Jesus withers him on the spot. Joseph is stricken with grief and gives an urgent order to his mother: "Do not let him go outside: anyone who makes him angry dies."

As time goes on, however, Jesus begins to use his powers for good. He saves his brother from a deadly snakebite, heals the sick, and proves remarkably handy around the house and carpenter shop: when Joseph the carpenter miscuts a board, Jesus is there to correct his mistake miraculously. The account concludes with Jesus as a twelve-year-old teaching in the Temple, surrounded by scribes and Pharisees who listen to him and bless Mary for the wonderful child she has brought into the world.

The blessing of Mary is a theme that gets played out in some of the other infancy Gospels as well, most famously in a book called "The Proto-Gospel of James." The book is called a "proto-Gospel" because it deals with events that happened prior to Jesus' birth, particularly involving the miraculous character of his mother Mary. Jesus obviously did not come into the world in a normal way, according to the Christians, since his mother was a virgin. But why was she, in particular, chosen to be the mother of the son of God? The accounts of this Gospel provide some pious reflections that give an answer: Mary herself was born miraculously and was set apart for the service of God at a young age.

The stories found in this account provided many of the legends about Mary and Joseph that became "common knowledge" throughout the Middle Ages. Mary's parents are said to have been a righteous and exceedingly wealthy Jew named Joachim and his faithful wife, Anna (so that Mary did not come from lower-class peasant stock, as the opponents of Christianity often alleged). Mary's birth is supernatural—much like the prophet Samuel in the Hebrew Bible and John the Baptist in the New Testament: her mother is older and barren, until God hears her prayers and gives her a child. Mary is raised in complete holiness: at the age of three she is given over to the Temple where she lives until she is twelve, cared for by the priests and fed daily by an angel of God. When she turns twelve, the priests cannot allow her to say any longer in the Temple (she has reached the age of menstruation and will compromise the purity of the sanctuary), and so they seek for someone suitable to be her adult guardian. All the single men of Israel are summoned, and one is miraculously chosen: an elderly widower, Joseph, who has grown sons from his previous marriage (so that Jesus' "brothers" were in fact his stepbrothers, not the children of Mary).

After Joseph takes Mary into his home he does not lay a finger on her; while he is away building houses, Mary conceives Jesus through the Holy Spirit. She is sixteen at the time. Everyone suspects that she has committed adultery, or that Joseph has been more to her than an adult guardian: but supernatural signs show that she is pure and that he didn't have anything to do with it.

Near the time of her giving birth, Joseph and Mary have to make a trip to Bethlehem to register for a census. But before they can reach the town, Mary goes into labor. Joseph finds a cave in the wilderness where she can give birth in private, and she does so—while Joseph, outside, observes time literally stand still as the Son of God comes into the world. Joseph procures the assistance of a Jewish midwife who comes to see the new mother. Another midwife, Salome, declares that she will not

FIGURE 11.4.   Image of Madonna and child, from ceiling fresco in Padua, Italy, by Giotto di Bondone, c. 1305.

believe Mary is a virgin until she has given her an internal postpartum inspection. To her shock and amazement, Mary is still "intact" even after giving birth. Here then Mary not only has a virginal conception, as in the New Testament, she remains a virgin even after giving birth.

All of these stories became part of the Christian lore surrounding Mary, the mother of Jesus, who came to be venerated in the church not only as the Blessed Virgin but also, eventually, as the "mother of God."

A Passion Gospel

We do not have many Gospels that contain only accounts of Jesus' passion, but one of the most interesting is also one of the earliest of our non-canonical Gospels, the Gospel of Peter. A book containing this intriguing account was discovered in 1886 in a cemetery in Akhmim, Egypt. The book itself is complete and contains portions of four different writings (so that it is a small anthology). Unfortunately, what came to be known as the Gospel of Peter begins in the middle of a sentence and ends in the middle of a sentence. In other words, this is not a complete copy. The portions that survive cover the trial of Jesus, his death, and his resurrection. Whether the entire Gospel contained more than that—whether it was a "complete" Gospel like those of the New Testament—is much debated. What is not debated is the authorship of this text. Its author directly claims to be Simon Peter, Jesus' disciple (unlike the New Testament Gospels: remember, these are all anonymous, only later attributed to their traditional authors). No one thinks Peter could have written it, though. The author is claiming to be someone other than who he really is. The account appears to have been composed sometime in the early second century.

The narrative begins in the middle of the scene in which Pilate is washing his hands at Jesus' trial, an episode found only in the Gospel of Matthew in the New Testament. It is striking that here in the Gospel of Peter we are explicitly told that "none of

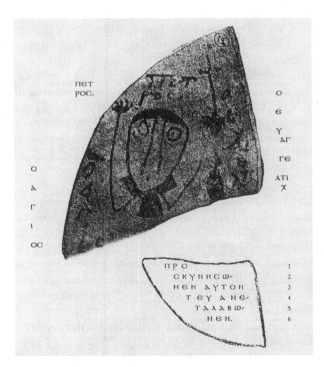

FIGURE 11.5. An ostracon (pottery shard) from the sixth or seventh century depicting the "evangelist Peter" and urging (on the back side) its readers to revere his Gospel.

the Jews washed his hands, neither did Herod nor any of his judges." This prefigures the emphasis we will see throughout this account. It is not the Roman governor Pilate who is responsible for Jesus' execution. It is the Jewish leaders. And in fact, the Jewish people themselves share the blame. This is a heavily anti-Jewish version of the story. Here it is the Jewish king Herod (not Pilate) who orders Jesus to be crucified.

The crucifixion scene itself differs in key ways from the New Testament accounts. In this version, while being crucified Jesus is completely silent "as if he felt no pain." Some scholars have wondered if this writer thought of Jesus as a purely divine being, and not fully human—one who did not feel any pain. Those crucified with him certainly could. One of them maligns the soldiers for what they were doing to Jesus, and the soldiers then decide not to break the man's legs so that his suffering would be prolonged (a crucified person died of suffocation when he could no longer hold up his body to provide space for his lungs to breathe; by breaking the legs the soldiers ended the torment faster, since then the person could no longer relieve the pressure on his chest cavity).

By far the most striking passage of the narrative, however, comes at the end. Here we have an actual account of Jesus' resurrection. It comes as a shock to many readers of the New Testament to learn that the canonical Gospels do not narrate Jesus' resurrection. They don't? No, they don't. In the New Testament Jesus is crucified and buried, and on the third day the women go to the tomb to find it empty. But there is no account of Jesus actually emerging from the tomb at the resurrection. But there is such an account here in the Gospel of Peter. And an amazing account it is.

A crowd has come in order to watch the tomb. During the night hours, they hear a great noise and see the heavens open up. Two men descend from there in great splendor and, as they descend, the stone before the tomb starts to roll away. They enter into the tomb. The guards go tell the centurion what is happening, and they see three men emerge from the tomb. Two of them are so tall that their heads reach up to the sky; the third, whom they are supporting, is taller still: his head reaches above the sky. And behind them, out of the tomb, there emerges the cross. A voice comes from heaven and asks, "Have you preached to those who are asleep?" And the cross replies, "Yes."

Here, then, is a giant Jesus and a walking-talking cross. It is hard to believe that this Gospel was lost for so many centuries.

The soldiers run and tell Pilate what has happened, and the Jewish leaders arrange for Pilate to keep the soldiers silent. The next day at dawn, not knowing what has happened, Mary Magdalene and several other women go to the tomb to provide an adequate burial for the body, but the tomb is empty except for a heavenly visitor who tells Mary that the Lord has risen and gone. The manuscript then begins to tell the next episode in the first-person (so this is Peter talking): "But I Simon Peter, and Andrew, my brother, took our nets and went to the sea; and with us was Levi, the son of Alphaeus, whom the Lord. . . ." (v. 60). And that's where the manuscript breaks off.

How we wish we knew what happened next! It appears that Jesus will show up and have a discussion with his disciples while they are fishing, as happens, for example, in John 21. But it is certainly frustrating not having the entire Gospel, beginning, middle, and end.

The Gnostic Gospels

As I mentioned earlier, the Coptic Gospel of Thomas was among a collection of writings discovered by accident (by several local peasants—not archaeologists) in 1945 near Nag Hammadi, Egypt. There were thirteen books altogether in the find and these books were all anthologies, containing fifty-two writings altogether. As a group they are often referred to as the **Nag Hammadi Library**.

This was one of the most significant archaeological discoveries of the twentieth century, in no small part because most (not all) of the writings appear to have been written by and for Christians who are known to scholars as Gnostics. The term **"Gnosticism"** refers to a group of religions that we know about principally from around the second Christian century and later. Scholars debate whether Gnosticism started out as a kind of Christianity, or if had an independent existence and then later came to be influenced by Christianity. For many of the Gnostic religions (there were lots of them, and they were all different from one another in key ways), Jesus was an important figure—in fact the key figure for salvation. But it was not because his death brought an atoning sacrifice for sins. It was because he brought the "knowledge" from above that can provide liberation to souls trapped in this material world in human bodies. The Greek word for knowledge is *"gnosis"*—and that is why these people are called Gnostics.

Many of the writings in the Nag Hammadi library either divulge the Gnostic myths that lie behind the complicated Gnostic systems, or at least presuppose these myths; a couple of these writings are actually called Gospels, because Jesus figures prominently in them. According to the Gnostic myths, there is not just one God but an entire panoply of gods. Some of the myths explain how these gods came into existence. Moreover, in these myths the material world we live in was not created by the one true God; it was the creation of lower, inferior, sometimes malevolent deities. The Jewish God is one of these—not the ultimate divine being, but an ignorant being who foolishly thinks he is the only God. The material world was created as a place of entrapment for sparks of the divine that actually come from the heavenly realm of the gods. Some of us have a spark trapped in these, our miserable bodies. The way to escape this entrapment is by learning the secret knowledge about who we really are, where we came from, how we got here, and how we can return.

Needless to say, these Gnostic Gospels—such as the Gospel of Philip, or the Gospel of Truth, or the Secret Teaching of John, or the Revelation of James—are intriguing and fascinating reading. They present and embody a very different form of Christianity from that presented in the New Testament, and show convincingly that early Christianity was not simply one thing, with one way of belief. It was lots of different things.

Going Behind the Gospels

But what was Christianity at the beginning? What was the "earliest" form of Christian belief? That question ties closely to our next area of discussion. We will see in the next chapter that Christianity is not simply the religion that Jesus himself taught. Rather, Christianity as it developed after Jesus' death is better understood as the religion that is *about* Jesus. But in order to understand how later Christians—including the Gospel writers but also, significantly, Paul and other apostles—understood the religion about Jesus (e.g., about his death and resurrection), it is important to understand the message that Jesus himself proclaimed in his life, deeds,

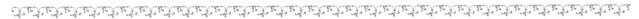

At a Glance: The Later Gospels

- The Gospel of Thomas is a collection of 114 sayings of Jesus, with no narrative context, discovered in 1945 with a group of other writings near Nag Hammadi, Egypt. Many of the sayings of this Gospel are like those in the Synoptics; others are very different indeed, portraying this world as a "corpse" and Jesus as a divine revealer whose secret teachings can lead one to escape the material trappings of this world and so have eternal life.
- The Infancy Gospel of Thomas (unrelated to the Gospel of Thomas) is an "infancy Gospel" that describes the adventures of Jesus between the ages of five and twelve. In this entertaining account Jesus is shown as a very powerful but highly mischievous boy who can wither those who irritate him or perform miracles on their behalf when he chooses to do so.
- The Proto-Gospel of James relates stories that happened "prior to" the Gospel accounts; the focus of attention is on Jesus' mother Mary, her miraculous birth, divine upbringing, relationship with Joseph, virginal conception, and virginal delivery of the Son of God.
- The Gospel of Peter is a fragmentary account of Jesus' trial, death, and resurrection, with many parallels to the New Testament versions but with a heightened stress on the culpability of the Jews in the death of Jesus and an elevated emphasis of the miraculous nature of his resurrection.

and words. And so that is our next order of business. Given all the Gospels—each of them with a different perspective on who Jesus was—what can we know about the life of the man Jesus himself?

THE HISTORICAL JESUS

As we have seen, it is one thing to know what various Gospels say about Jesus' words, deeds, and experiences, and another thing to know what actually happened in Jesus' life. All of the Gospels are different; each has its own slant on who Jesus was and what he said and did. One of the most interesting tasks of New Testament scholarship is to move behind what the written accounts say, to see what really happened.

Problems with our Sources

The only way we can know what a person from the past said and did (whether we are referring to Solomon, Julius Caesar, Jesus, Napoleon, or Abraham Lincoln) is by examining sources from the period that provide us with information. Most of our sources for the past are literary; that is, they are texts written by authors who refer to the person's words and deeds. But sources of this kind are not always reliable. Even eyewitness accounts are often contradictory, and contemporary observers not infrequently get the facts wrong. Moreover, for the distant past the great bulk of our sources do not derive from eyewitnesses but from later authors reporting the rumors and traditions they had heard.

Most historians would agree that for reconstructing a past event (or the life of a past person) the ideal situation would be to have sources that:

- are numerous, so that they can be compared to one another;
- derive from a time near the event itself, so that they are less likely to be have been based on hearsay;
- were produced independently of one another, so that their authors were not in collusion;
- do not contradict one another, so that one or more of them is not necessarily in error;
- are internally consistent, suggesting a basic concern for reliability; and
- are not biased toward the subject matter, so that their authors have not skewed their accounts to serve their own purposes.

With that in mind, what can we say about our sources of information for the historical Jesus? We can divide our consideration into two broad categories of sources: non-Christian (i.e., Jewish and pagan) and Christian.

NON-CHRISTIAN SOURCES The first thing to say about pagan (that is, non-Jewish, non-Christian) sources is that Jesus is never mentioned by any such source of his day—or, in fact, of the entire first Christian century. Period. We have lots of documents from this period from scholars of religion, philosophers, historians, scientists, poets, literary figures of all sorts. In no document of any kind does Jesus' name ever appear.

If we restrict ourselves to pagan sources from within a hundred years of Jesus' death (30 C.E.—130 C.E.), we do find a couple of references to him. The first is in a letter written in the year 112 C.E. by a Roman aristocrat named Pliny, governor of one of the provinces of Asia Minor (modern Turkey), who indicates that there were Christians in his region who worshiped Christ "as a god." That is all he says about Jesus—he gives no information about his life or death. The only other certain reference occurs a few years later in the writings of Tacitus, a Roman historian who, in his account of the city of Rome, discusses how in 64 C.E. the Roman emperor Nero used the Christians as scapegoats for the large fire in Rome that he himself may have ordered arsonists to start. Tacitus indicates that these Christians were followers of Christ, who was "executed at the hands of the procurator Pontius Pilate in the reign of Tiberius"(*Annals* 15:44). That is not much to go on, but at least it shows that something was known about Jesus among the literary elite of Rome in the early second century.

We do not fare much better with Jewish sources of the period (there are not as many Jewish writers as pagan, of course). But Jesus does appear to be mentioned twice in the writings of the Jewish historian Josephus, in the year 93 C.E., in his twenty-volume book *The Antiquities of the Jews* (See Box 11.4). In one reference Josephus simply mentions that Jesus was called the messiah and had a brother named James. The other reference is lengthier and indicates that Josephus knew that Jesus had the reputation for being a wise man, that he did remarkable deeds, that he had many followers, and that he was condemned to be crucified by Pilate at the instigation of the Jewish leaders. Here too this is not much for us to go on if we want to know what Jesus really said and did while living, and what led to his death. But at least it shows that the greatest historian among the Jews of the first century knew something about who Jesus was. The surprise for many readers is that Josephus and the pagan sources

don't say more. If Jesus really was able to heal the sick, cast out demons, control the forces of nature, and raise the dead—wouldn't he have been talked about more? One possible conclusion is that Jesus did indeed live and teach, but that the reports of his miracles were not widely known outside of his circle of followers. So what can we say about the sources that they themselves wrote?

CHRISTIAN SOURCES We have obviously not looked at all the Gospels ever written about Jesus, but we have looked at several of the earliest ones from outside the New Testament. Most readers will have no trouble recognizing that in almost every instance these other Gospels are presenting us not with historically reliable information about what Jesus really said and did, but with later legendary accounts. The historical Jesus did not zap his playmates and wither his teachers as a five-year-old; he did not emerge out of his tomb as tall as a mountain; he did not teach the Gnostic myths of the Nag Hammadi Library. The non-canonical Gospels are endlessly fascinating and truly important for understanding how Christianity developed in later centuries, but they are less useful for establishing what Jesus himself actually said and did.

There are, of course, twenty-three other books of the New Testament outside the four Gospels, and so one might hope that there would be stories in them about Jesus' life. But unfortunately, to the surprise of many readers, there is very little there indeed. Even the apostle Paul, our earliest author, says very little about what Jesus said and did between the time he was born and the time he died. It is easy enough to make a list of all the information that Paul provides simply by reading his letters carefully. For your list, you won't need more than a 3 × 5 card. (See Box 11.5.) The other New Testament writers tell us even less.

Whether we like it or not, if we want to know about the historical Jesus we are more or less restricted to considering the accounts of his life and death as found in the four Gospels of the New Testament. That is not because this historical quest is driven by religious motives or theological concerns, or because only Christians are interested in the question. It is because these are our earliest sources and they are the only ones that have a chance of providing us with any information at all that is not obviously late and legendary.

BOX 11.4 THE TESTIMONY OF FLAVIUS JOSEPHUS

Probably the most controversial passage in all of Josephus's writings is his description of Jesus in book 18 of *The Antiquities of the Jews.*

> At this time there appeared Jesus, a wise man, if indeed one should call him a man. For he was a doer of startling deeds, a teacher of people who receive the truth with pleasure. And he gained a following both among many Jews and among many of Greek origin. He was the Messiah. And when Pilate, because of an accusation made by the leading men among us, condemned him to the cross, those who had loved him previously did not cease to do so. For he appeared to them on the third day, living again, just as the divine prophets had spoken of these and countless other wondrous things about him. And up until this very day the tribe of Christians, named after him, has not died out. (*Antiquities* 18.3.3)

This testimony to Jesus has long puzzled scholars. Why would Josephus, a devout Jew who never became a Christian, profess faith in Jesus by suggesting that he was something more than a man, calling him the messiah (rather than merely saying that others *thought* he was), and claiming that he was raised from the dead in fulfillment of prophecy?

Many scholars have recognized that the problem may be solved by looking at how, and by whom, Josephus's writings were transmitted over the centuries. For in fact they were not preserved by Jews, many of whom considered him to be a traitor because of his conduct during and after the war with Rome (see Box 9.3). Rather, it was Christians who copied Josephus' writings through the ages. Is it possible that this reference to Jesus has been beefed up a bit by a Christian scribe who wanted to make Josephus appear more appreciative of the "true faith"?

If we take out the Christianized portions of the passage, what we are left with, according to one of the most convincing recent studies, is the following.

> At this time there appeared Jesus, a wise man. For he was a doer of startling deeds, a teacher of people who receive the truth with pleasure. And he gained a following both among many Jews and among many of Greek origin. And when Pilate, because of an accusation made by the leading men among us, condemned him to the cross, those who had loved him previously did not cease to do so. And up until this very day the tribe of Christians, named after him, has not died out.[1]

---

1   Translation taken from John Meier, *A Marginal Jew: Rethinking the Historical Jesus* (New York: Doubleday, 1991), p. 61.

But these Gospels too are problematic as historical sources. I am not saying that they are problematic as literary portrayals of Jesus or as documents of faith. I am now simply thinking of them as historical sources that can provide us with real information about what Jesus actually said and did. The Gospels are problematic in that way, for reasons we have already seen. They do not claim to be written by eyewitnesses and almost certainly were not written by eyewitnesses (even if they were, it would not necessarily mean they were accurate). They were written between 35–65 years after Jesus' death by people who did not know him, living in different countries and speaking a different language. These are not the kind of multiple, early, independent sources a historian might hope for. Remember: two of them (Matthew and Luke) used one of them (Mark) as their primary source. What is even more disturbing is that these Gospels are at variance in all sorts of ways, with large numbers of differences, discrepancies, and even contradictions between them.

One reason there are so many discrepancies is that these authors inherited their stories from the oral tradition. After Jesus died (and, in fact, before he died) people were telling stories about him. These stories circulated by word of mouth, year after year, decade after decade. We should not think that since the ancient world was primarily an oral culture rather than a written one (since most people were illiterate) that people back then took great pains never to change the stories they told (as some Christian apologists today sometimes claim). In fact, if anthropological studies of oral cultures have taught us anything it is that in such settings stories get changed all the time, as a storyteller will always adapt a story in light of the audience and the situation.

And it is perfectly clear that the stories about Jesus were being changed. Otherwise they would all be consistent with one another with no contradictions. But that is not at all the case. It is equally obvious that Christians were making up stories about Jesus. Whoever first told the tales of Jesus as the five-year old, friend-zapping, teacher-withering, mischievous son of God was making it up. And we don't need to wait until the later Gospels to see this kind of inventiveness taking place. Whoever came up with Luke's story of a worldwide census under Caesar Augustus was not basing it on historical fact. The story was made up.

The Gospels, in short, are our best sources of information about what Jesus really said and did; but they are, at the same time, highly problematic as historical sources. Historians who have wanted to reconstruct the life of the historical Jesus have therefore had to avoid two extremes in dealing with the Gospels. One extreme is to ignore the problems and pretend the Gospels are all perfectly accurate, historically trustworthy, biographies of Jesus. They

are not that. The other extreme is to throw up your hands in despair and declare that we can't know *anything* about the historical Jesus. That is not true either. These Gospels can be used as historical sources; but they need to be used carefully, following rigorous methodological principles. When these principles are followed it becomes clear that we can indeed say some things about what it is Jesus really said, did, and experienced. The following are among the criteria that historical scholars have applied to these sources in their quest for the historical Jesus.

Criterion One: Antiquity

Since stories change over time, and tend to get exaggerated, it is best to rely more heavily on sources that are closest in time to the events that they narrate. Gospels from the fourth century will, as a rule, be less likely to contain historically reliable information about Jesus than Gospels from the first century. More than that, we should give particular credence to the earliest of these canonical

Gospels—and their sources. John's Gospel is the latest of the four and, as we have seen, its portrayal of Jesus is highly theological and fully developed. As a rule, it will not contain as much historical information as the Synoptics (even if many readers prefer its theology to that of the Synoptics). Among the Synoptics, Mark is the earliest and so should be paid special attention. Q dates from about the same time as Mark, and so it too should figure highly in the historians' estimation.

Criterion Two: Independent Attestation

Any time you have two or more witnesses that corroborate one another's report of an event, without having collaborated with one another, then there is a decent chance that this version of the story is how it happened. If you have only one witness, that one may have made it up; or if you have two who talked together ahead of time, one of them may have given the idea to the other. What you want are multiple, independent witnesses.

We have that with the Gospels. Mark did not know Q; M did not know L; John did not know the Synoptics; and for that matter, the author of Thomas probably did not know any of the canonical Gospels. Paul didn't know any of the Gospels (since they hadn't been written yet) and so far as we can tell, the Gospel authors hadn't read Paul's writings. Anything found in several of these sources is independently attested. And so, for example, it is independently attested that Jesus came from Nazareth (Mark, L, John); that he was early on associated with John the Baptist (Mark, John, Q), that he told parables about the Kingdom of God (Mark, Q, M, L, Thomas), and that he was crucified by Pontius Pilate (all over the map). Just because these are multiply attested does not mean necessarily that they are historical, but the chances are greatly improved. I should stress: even if a saying or deed of Jesus appears in only one Gospel (for example, the parable of the Good Samaritan), that does not necessarily mean that it does not go back to Jesus. But you cannot show that it probably *did* go back to Jesus based on this **criterion of independent attestation**.

Criterion Three: Dissimilarity

We know that Christians were changing and even making up their stories about Jesus, probably from the beginning. Obviously they did so in order to make the stories say what they wanted them to say. What if we have traditions about Jesus that do *not* seem to reflect what the Christian storytellers would have wanted them to say? It would be hard to explain such traditions as being invented by Christians for their own purposes. And so why do such traditions exist? Most likely because they really happened. This is called the **criterion of dissimilarity**. If a tradition about a saying or deed of Jesus is dissimilar to what the Christians would have wanted to say about him, it is more likely to be authentic.

It is hard to think of any reason that a Christian would invent the idea that Jesus came from Nazareth, a little one-horse town that no one had ever heard of. If you wanted to invent a hometown for a messiah it would be Bethlehem, or Jerusalem, or—Rome. But not Nazareth. Why do the sources consistently indicate Jesus came from Nazareth? Probably because he really came from there. So too, it is hard to think of why Christians would invent the idea that Jesus was baptized by John, for two reasons. One is that it was widely understood in early Christianity that the person baptizing was spiritually superior to the one being baptized (the church member does not baptize her pastor). But who would want to claim that John was Jesus' superior? More than that, John was baptizing for the remission of sins. Who would have said that Jesus had sins that needed to be forgiven? If Christians would not make up such accounts, why then are there stories of his baptism? Because he was baptized by John at the beginning of his ministry.

A final example is one that might strike you as odd. Christians would almost certainly not have invented the idea that Jesus was crucified. But why not? Isn't that the whole point? Remember everything we have said and learned about the Jewish expectations of a future messiah. He would be a powerful warrior-king, or a great priestly leader of the people, or a cosmic judge of the earth. Whatever one Jew or another thought about the future messiah, it was that he would be a great and powerful leader of Israel. Who expected a messiah to be crucified? Precisely no one. If Christians who confessed Jesus to be messiah wanted to invent a story about his fate, they would have said he became the King in Jerusalem and now rules over the Romans. Why didn't they say that? Because everyone knew it wasn't true. He was destroyed by the Romans, executed in the most humiliating way possible. This is not what someone would make up about their messiah. So Jesus really was crucified.

Criterion Four: Contextual Credibility

The previous three criteria have all been "positive." They can be applied to all the traditions about Jesus in order to see what he really did say and do. They cannot be used to show what he did not say and do. This final criterion can be used in that way, however, and so is our only "negative" criterion. The criterion of **contextual credibility** is this: If there is a tradition about Jesus' words or deeds that cannot plausibly be fit into a first-century Palestinian Jewish context, then it cannot be accepted as historically accurate. As a simple example, in the Gnostic Gospels Jesus sometimes is portrayed as describing the Gnostic myths about how the realm of the gods came into existence and how humans came to be trapped in this material world. We have no indication that any such views were found among rural Palestinian Jews of the first century. Jesus almost certainly would never have taught such things.

But what did he teach? Since the early twentieth century, scholars in Europe and North America have overwhelmingly thought that Jesus is best understood as a Jewish apocalyptic prophet.

JESUS THE APOCALYPTIC PROPHET

You may want to reread our discussion about Jewish apocalypticism back in chapter 8, in connection with the book of Daniel. By way of quick review: apocalypticism emerged during the time of the Syrian king Antiochus Epiphanes, when Jews were persecuted for keeping their religious traditions. The prophets of the Hebrew Bible before this had insisted that the reason the people of God were suffering (from natural disaster, political upheaval, military defeat) was because they had disobeyed God and he was punishing them. Apocalypticists had to deal with the reality that Jews were trying to do what God had commanded them to do and were still suffering. In fact, they were suffering as a direct result of following the Law. They developed the idea that it was not God who was causing the

suffering, but the powers of evil that had been unleashed on the world, forces that were opposed to God and his people.

Apocalypticists developed a dualistic view of the world. There were forces of good and evil doing battle, and evil was in the ascendancy. The history of the world itself was thought of dualistically: there is the present age controlled by the forces of evil, and a future kingdom of God in which there will be no more evil at all but God will reign supreme. This age is filled with demons, disasters, wars, pain, misery, and suffering. But God was soon to intervene in this course of affairs to overthrow the powers of evil and bring in a good kingdom on earth. Some apocalypticists thought this kingdom would be brought by a messianic figure, sometimes called the Son of Man (from Daniel 7:13–14).

And when would this age end and the new one arrive? When would good finally triumph over evil? When would God's kingdom come to replace the evil kingdoms of earth? It was going to happen very soon. Any day now. "Truly I tell you, some of you standing here will not taste death before they see that the kingdom of God has come in power." These are the words of Jesus (Mark 9:1). Or as he says later, "Truly I tell you, this generation will not pass away before all these things take place" (Mark 13:30).

Jesus preached about a coming kingdom of God. But this was not a teaching of "heaven," the place your soul goes when it dies. This was a real kingdom, here on earth, to be brought by the Son of Man. This cosmic judge of the earth would enter into judgment with everything and everyone who was opposed to God. But those who adhered to Jesus' teachings and aligned themselves with God would be rewarded in the future kingdom. "Whoever is ashamed of me and of my words in this adulterous and sinful generation, of that one the Son of Man will be ashamed when he comes in the glory of his Father with the holy angels" (Mark 8:38).

Before laying out more fully the apocalyptic message and mission of the historical Jesus, I need to give the convincing reasons scholars have adduced for seeing him in this way, as an apocalyptic prophet.

Grounds for Seeing Jesus as an Apocalypticist

If you carefully sift through our earliest sources for knowing about Jesus, trying to understand which

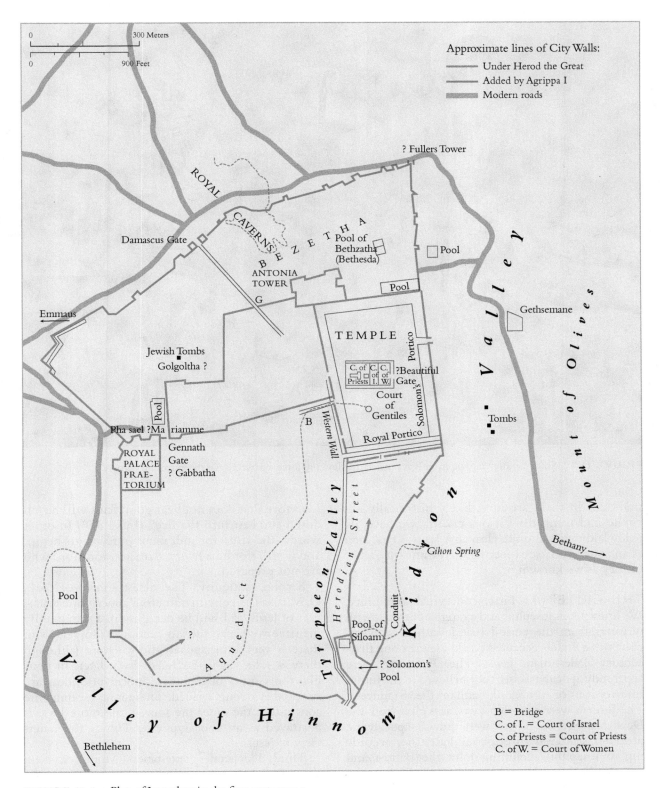

FIGURE 11.6. Plan of Jerusalem in the first century C.E.

FIGURE 11.7. Sixth-century mosaic from Ravenna, Italy, showing Jesus separating the sheep from the goats.

traditions in them are most likely historically accurate and using the various criteria we have already laid out, it is quite clear that Jesus is best seen as an apocalypticist expecting the imminent end of history as we know it.

THE CRITERIA First, contextual credibility. We know from Josephus and a range of other Jewish writings from the period that Jewish apocalypticism was a widely accepted world view among first-century Palestinian Jews. The Pharisees were apparently apocalypticists: they believed in the future resurrection of the dead, unlike the Sadducees. The Essenes were apocalypticists, as is clear from the Dead Sea Scrolls. There were Jewish apocalyptic prophets scattered throughout Palestine, according to Josephus, including John the Baptist and others like him. John himself, according to the Q source, proclaimed the following: "The ax is already laid at the root of the trees; every tree

therefore that does not bear good fruit will be cut down and cast into the fire" (Luke 3:9). In other words, the time for judgment is ready to begin, and it will not be a happy occasion for those who are not prepared.

Second, antiquity. The oldest sources—Mark, Q, M, and L—contain numerous apocalyptic teachings of Jesus (as I will be detailing in a minute). By the time we get to the last canonical Gospel, John, there is very little apocalyptic teaching (although there is some, as in 5:28–29). Even later, in texts like the Gospel of Thomas, apocalyptic ideas are attacked as wrong-headed. There is no escaping the conclusion: the older the source, the more Jesus is portrayed as an apocalypticist. This is the oldest view of Jesus.

Third, independent attestation. Moreover, these sources all portray Jesus in this way independently of one another. Mark did not know Q, Q did not know L, L did not know M, M did not know Mark, and so forth and so on. Apocalyptic traditions are found throughout these early sources, all of them independent.

Fourth, dissimilarity. There are a number of apocalyptic teachings on the lips of Jesus that pass the criterion of dissimilarity. For example, Mark 8:38, quoted above. The way individuals respond to Jesus is the way the Son of Man will respond to them. If you were to read that saying without believing, yourself, that Jesus is the Son of Man, or without knowing that he was commonly thought of as the Son of Man, there would be nothing in the saying to indicate that he was talking about himself. Just the opposite: he seems to be talking about someone else. Would Christians come up with a saying in which Jesus describes the Son of Man apparently as someone other than himself? It seems unlikely.

Or take Jesus' description of the Last Judgment in Matthew 25, when the Son of Man judges the "sheep" and the "goats." The sheep are people who are given an eternal reward of paradise because they did good deeds for the Son of Man when he was in need. They fed him, clothed him, visited him in prison, and so on. They object: they have never seen him before. The Son of Man replies that inasmuch as they did it to any of the needy, they did it to him. The goats, however, are sent to eternal punishment because they refused to do such good deeds for others in need, and so to the Son of Man, whom they too have never seen. This almost certainly is a story that reflects something Jesus himself taught. And why? Think for a second: what did early Christians think that a person needed to do to be given an eternal reward? Was it by doing good deeds? No, not at all! It was by believing in Jesus. As we will see, that is the dominant view of the apostle Paul and others like him. One cannot be "saved" by good deeds, only by faith in Christ. But in this story the people who are saved are not given an eternal reward because they have believed in Jesus. On the contrary, they not only have not believed in him, they know nothing about him. They are saved by doing good deeds. This is not a story later Christians would invent, because it presents a view of salvation different from that embraced by the early Christians. And so, it almost certainly goes back to Jesus. And it is a thoroughly apocalyptic story.

A final argument. Based on the criteria, as we have seen, we know with relative certainty how Jesus began his public ministry. It was by associating with John the Baptist and being baptized by him (it is contextually credible, independently attested, dissimilar, and ancient). Why did Jesus associate with John, instead of, say, with the Pharisees or the Sadducees or the Fourth Philosophy, or with anyone else? Obviously because he was drawn to John's message in particular. And John's message was thoroughly apocalyptic: the end was soon to be here, and people needed to prepare for it or they would be condemned. Not only do we know how Jesus began his ministry, we know what happened in the wake of his ministry after his death. Christian communities started to emerge and grow around the Mediterranean. And how should we characterize the beliefs of the earliest Christian communities? They were thoroughly apocalyptic. We will see this when we get to the apostle Paul, who, like Jesus, expected the end to come very soon with the coming of a cosmic judge to destroy the forces of evil. (In his case, he thought the judge was Jesus himself.) And so we know how Jesus' ministry began, and we know what happened in its wake. The beginning and end were both heavily apocalyptic. And what came between these apocalyptic bookends? The middle: Jesus' public ministry itself. The beginning and end are the key to the middle: if they are both apocalyptic, then the middle must have been as well. Jesus was almost certainly an apocalypticist.

THE APOCALYPTIC PROCLAMATION OF JESUS
What then can we say about the specifics of Jesus' proclamation? The first words recorded of Jesus occur in our earliest surviving Gospel, Mark, where Jesus begins to preach and does so with an apocalyptic message: "The time has been fulfilled, the Kingdom of God is at hand. Repent and believe the good news" (Mark 1:15). I think this summarizes all of Jesus' teaching. When he says the time has been fulfilled he means that there has been a certain amount of time allotted to this age. And it is almost over. The Kingdom of God is almost here—it is right at hand. This Kingdom, for Jesus, is not heavenly bliss for your soul: it is an actual kingdom here on earth, to be ruled by God through his messiah. Some people will be allowed to enter into the joys of that kingdom, others will be dismissed from it to face judgment. People need to believe this good news and get ready. For it is almost here.

BOX 11.6 O LITTLE TOWN OF NAZARETH

Little can be known about Jesus' early life, but one thing that can be said for certain is that he was raised in Nazareth, the home village of Joseph and Mary. This tradition is multiply attested (Mark 1:9; Matthew 1:23 [M]; Luke 4:16 [L]; John 1:45) and passes the criterion of dissimilarity with flying colors: Nazareth was a little one-horse town—not even that—with no claim to fame, unknown even to most people who lived in Palestine. Who would invent the story that the Savior of the world came from *there*? As Nathaniel asks in surprise in the fourth Gospel, "Can anything good come out of Nazareth?" (John 1:46).

Nazareth is never mentioned in the Hebrew Bible; Josephus, who was a general of the Jewish troops in that region (see Box 9.3), mentions forty-six other towns there but never Nazareth. And it is not named in the Jewish Mishnah, which was codified in Galilee.

Archaeologists have conducted excavations of Nazareth to help determine what it must have been like in Jesus' day. By all accounts, life was fairly grim. There is no evidence of any public building (synagogue, town building), of a paved street, of imported goods, of any luxury items of any kind. The hamlet appears to have depended almost entirely on local agriculture for survival. Estimates vary, but it appears that the habitable part of the village took up less than ten acres in Jesus' day. The best estimate at the population put it anywhere from two hundred to four hundred people total. The housing was primitive, hovels and peasant homes built over small caves, made of hewn field stones piled on one another, insulated with mud, clay, and dung mixed with straw, with roughly thatched roofs and dirt floors.

Jesus' youth, in short, was the impoverished life of a peasant in a remote agricultural area. Small wonder that the earliest Gospels indicate that as an adult he spent all his time preaching in small villages and rural areas, avoiding the big cities until he made his final and fatal trek to Jerusalem.

Throughout his teaching Jesus proclaims that this kingdom is soon to arrive; he describes what it will be like, and he urges people to be ready. This kingdom is to be brought by the cosmic judge that Jesus calls the Son of Man—a reference to the vision in Daniel 7. Jesus, however, does not think the Son of Man is the entire people of Israel (as the "one like a son of man" is interpreted in Daniel 7:13–14); instead, like other apocalyptic Jews of his time, Jesus thinks of the Son of Man as an actual figure, a cosmic judge to be sent from God on the clouds of heaven. Scholars have long debated the question of whether Jesus thought that he himself was the Son of Man. In my opinion the answer is no. When he talks about the future Son of Man as a coming judge, he almost always seems to be referring to someone other than himself. Those are the "Son of Man sayings" that almost certainly go back to Jesus, since Christians, as we have seen, would not have made them up. But what about all those sayings in the Gospels where Jesus talks about the Son of Man and it is clear that he *is* talking about himself ("The Son of Man must go to Jerusalem and be rejected . . . and killed")? Those are sayings that do *not* pass the criterion of dissimilarity (since later Christians thought of Jesus as the Son of Man),

and so we cannot know if Jesus ever said any of these things.

When the Son of Man comes, according to Jesus, there will be a massive judgment. It will be like a fisherman who makes a great catch. He hauls in his net and throws away the fish he does not want, keeping only the good ones: "So it will be at the end of this age; the angels will come and separate the evil from the righteous, and they will cast them into the fiery furnace" (Matthew 13:49). At this judgment there will be a complete reversal of fortune. Those who are in power now have been placed there by the dominant forces of this age, the powers of evil. Those who are suffering now are those who side with God. And that will be reversed in the coming Kingdom, where the "last will be first and the first last." That is why "everyone who humbles himself will be exalted and everyone who exalts himself will be humbled" (Q: see Matthew 23:12).

People then need to prepare for this coming kingdom. They do so by listening and following the teachings of Jesus as one who had the correct understanding of God's Torah, as found in the Scriptures. In particular, Jesus teaches that his followers need to trust God as a child trusts a parent. Things may be bad now, but you can trust God to

FIGURE 11.8. A portrayal of Jesus' triumphal entry, found on the famous sarcophagus of a Christian named Junius Bassus.

make everything right. And in preparation for that kingdom people need to devote themselves to one another in the present. That means following what God really wants, as he himself taught in the Torah. You should do unto others as you would have them do to you. You should love your neighbor as yourself. These are the central teachings of Scripture, for Jesus. It is commitment to and trust in God and love of one another that are required for those who want to inherit the kingdom.

Those who have begun to do so are already starting to see what the kingdom will be like. It will be a kingdom of peace, love, and justice. And so, those who work for peace, live for love, and strive for justice can begin now, already, to get a glimpse of what it will be like in a big way when the kingdom arrives. That's why the kingdom is like a tiny mustard seed that gets planted and then grows into an enormous shrub (Mark 4:30–32) It has a small beginning in the lives of Jesus' disciples; but when the Son of Man arrives in judgment, it will spread throughout the whole earth.

THE APOCALYPTIC DEATH OF JESUS

After his baptism by John, Jesus spent almost his entire public ministry in Galilee proclaiming this message. He gathered twelve disciples around himself (independently attested); this may have been an apocalyptic act, showing that the future people of God would be like the original people of God, the twelve tribes of Israel. Jesus went from village to town urging people to repent in preparation for what was soon to come with the arrival of the Son of Man. He enacted his message in many of the things he did. His opponents were angry that he spent so much time with the lowlifes, sinners such as the hated tax collectors, and the prostitutes. But he did so to make a point: the future kingdom was not going to come for the high and mighty. These would be judged severely for their acts of oppression and hatred. God sides with the sinner, the lowly, the oppressed, the despised. Jesus' actions matched his words. And his actions and words are eventually what got him into trouble precisely with those who were in power, whom he so deeply despised.

In the last week of his life, Jesus travelled to Jerusalem in order to participate in the annual Passover feast. In our earliest sources, it was his first time to the big city. What he saw did not please him. The Temple—with all its spectacular grandeur—struck him as inimical to the truth of God, who was not behind power and splendor; he was the God of the poor and oppressed. Jesus—according to multiply attested traditions—entered into the Temple and overturned the tables of those exchanging Roman currency for Temple currency (they did this so as not to allow idolatrous coinage, with pictures of the divine emperor, into the Temple) and driving out those selling sacrificial animals. For Jesus, evidently, this was all a racket, making a "business" out of what was supposed to be the pure worship of God.

More than that, Jesus predicted that when the end came—very soon—the Temple itself would be destroyed. That may have been the ultimate point behind his violent actions against the moneychangers and sellers of animals: he may have been enacting a parable, as the prophets Jeremiah and Ezekiel had done so many centuries earlier. In this case, by overturning the tables and causing a ruckus, he may have been declaring that this is what God would be doing in a big way very soon. God was not on the side of the religious authorities of the Jews. On the contrary, when the Son of Man arrived it was they who would face judgment.

Those who were in power took notice of what Jesus did and decided to keep a close eye on him. As we have seen, the Passover was the single most attended pilgrim festival in Jerusalem, and the size of

BOX 11.7 ANOTHER APOCALYPTIC JESUS

Jesus of Nazareth was not the only apocalyptic prophet who proclaimed the imminent judgment of God, which would befall not just the Jewish enemies (the Romans), but some of the Jews themselves. Josephus tells us about several other such prophets from around the time of Jesus (not to mention John the Baptist). Remarkably, one of these other figures was also named Jesus (which was not an unusual name at the time).

According to Josephus (*Jewish Wars*, Book 6), about thirty years after the death of Jesus of Nazareth there appeared in Jerusalem a man named **Jesus the son of Ananias**, who came to the holy city during an annual feast and began to proclaim aloud: "A voice from the east, a voice from the west, a voice from the four winds, a voice against Jerusalem and the holy house [i.e., the Temple] . . . a voice against the whole people." The local

authorities found this purveyor of doom a nuisance and had him beaten, but that did not stop him. He continued to proclaim loudly, in public, "Woe, woe to Jerusalem." The Roman procurator then had him arrested and flogged within an inch of his life. But, deciding that he was literally crazy, the procurator had him released.

For another seven years this Jesus continued to proclaim that the destruction of Jerusalem was coming, until the city was laid siege in the late 60s and he himself was killed by a stone catapulted over the walls by the Romans.

In any event, Jesus of Nazareth was not the only Jewish prophet to proclaim the coming destruction of the city, nor the only one to be opposed by the local Jewish leadership, nor the only one to be arrested and punished by the Roman governor. He was not even the only one like this to be named Jesus!

---

the city would swell many times over as Jews from around the world came to commemorate the exodus event. The Roman authorities took this weeklong celebration (which was connected with the Feast of Unleavened Bread) quite seriously: this was the time of year when the Roman governor, in this case Pontius Pilate, would come into Jerusalem to take up residence along with his troops. They were there to keep the peace. And they were not idiots. They realized that this annual celebration commemorated the time when, according to Jewish tradition, God had saved his people from their foreign oppressors. Many Jews were not celebrating the feast simply because of what God had done before, but because of what they expected him to do again: act once more to overthrow the enemy, in this case the Romans. The Roman authorities were intent on making sure no riots broke out; they were particularly assiduous in watching any potential troublemakers who could stir up the crowds—anyone, for example, who was preaching a message of the imminent destruction of the enemies of God.

That one of Jesus' own disciples, one of the twelve, decided to betray him for money is multiply attested and it passes the criterion of dissimilarity (this does not seem to be a tradition early Christians would have been proud of). It is hard to know why Judas did what he did. Maybe he expected Jesus to be a messiah figure who would destroy the Romans,

and was bitterly disappointed when he did not rouse the masses. Maybe he thought Jesus had gone too far in his opposition to the Jewish establishment. We will never know. But Judas decided to betray Jesus, and he told the authorities what they needed to know.

Jesus had a last meal with his disciples, where, according to our early reports, he indicated to them that he knew he did not have long. It did not take a crystal ball to realize what would happen during the Passover to someone urging people to prepare for the coming intervention of God when he would overthrow the evil kingdoms of the earth to bring in his own kingdom, centered in Jerusalem, ruled not by a foreign emperor but by a Jewish messiah. Jesus had been gathering the crowds, the time was tense, and the authorities were ready to quell any dangerous action.

Jesus went out to pray in a garden and it was there that Judas led the authorities to him. The Jewish leaders were intent not to have any riots break out, and Jesus had been gathering a following. Much better to have him taken out of the way than to stir up the masses and force the Romans to intervene, sword in hand. The Jewish Sanhedrin, however, had no authority to execute a troublemaker. Rome reserved that right to itself.

And so the Jewish authorities handed Jesus over to the Roman governor Pilate, and charged him

FIGURE 11.9. Jesus is said to have been buried by Joseph of Arimathea in a tomb hewn in the rock, with a stone that rolled before the door (see Matthew 26:60)—possibly much like this one. (Note the round rolling stone to the left of the entrance of the tomb.).

Jesus proclaimed would be ruled by a messianic figure. Jesus explicitly told his twelve disciples that they themselves would be "seated on twelve thrones ruling over the twelve tribes of Israel" in that kingdom (Q; see Matthew 19:28). Presumably the twelve would be ruling under the authority of the future messiah. But who would that be? Jesus was the one who chose the twelve. It was adherence to his words that could bring someone into the coming kingdom. Did Jesus teach the disciples, privately, that he was the one that would be the future messiah? That he would be the king of the coming kingdom?

If so, then everything falls into place. The reason Jesus was charged with calling himself king of the Jews is that he really did call himself that. But not publicly. How did the authorities learn? They bribed an insider for information. And Judas gave it to them. Judas told the authorities Jesus' private instructions, and it was all they needed. The Jewish authorities informed Pilate. Pilate put Jesus on trial asking if it were true that he saw himself as a king. Jesus could not very well deny it, since that is indeed how he saw himself. That was all Pilate needed to know.

The governor had the power of life and death. If he wanted, he could order a person executed on the spot. He did so with two other troublemakers that morning. And he did so with Jesus. The trial may have only taken a couple of minutes. He ordered this rabble-rouser, this troublemaker, this apocalyptic prophet, this self-proclaimed king to be crucified. His soldiers flogged Jesus, took him outside the city, and nailed him to the cross. He was dead within six hours.

with political insurgency. They did not tell Pilate that he was a blasphemer. Pilate would not have cared about that. They told him that he was calling himself the King of the Jews.

It is an intriguing charge because, as you will have noticed, Jesus actually never calls himself that in the Gospels. So why was he charged with it, and eventually executed on those grounds? I have repeatedly pointed out that the coming kingdom that

At a Glance: The Historical Jesus

The early Gospels are valuable not only because they give us literary portraits of Jesus, but also because they can be used as historical sources to reveal what Jesus himself actually said, did, and experienced. They need to be used critically, however, since they are not eyewitness accounts written by people who saw these things happen. Instead they were written decades later by unknown authors who reported the stories that they heard, which had been in oral circulation for many years. Scholars apply several major criteria to these sources to see what they can reveal about the historical man Jesus: antiquity, independent attestation, dissimilarity, and contextual credibility. When examined in light of these criteria, the Gospels show that the historical Jesus is best understood as an apocalyptic prophet who anticipated that God was very soon going to intervene in the course of historical events to overthrow the forces of evil and bring in a good kingdom here on earth, in which there would be no more pain, misery, or suffering.

Take a Stand

1. In your New Testament class you are required to participate in a debate on the following resolution: *Resolved: The view of Jesus in the Gospel of John differs completely from the view set forth in the Synoptics.* Take either side of the resolution and argue your case.

2. Your roommate tells you that she does not want to read any of the Gospels outside of the New Testament because she is sure they are not interesting. Explain, on the contrary, what's interesting about them.

3. A friend of yours who is a religious skeptic tells you that in his opinion the Gospels cannot provide us with any information at all about the historical Jesus. In his view, since they were written so long after the fact, by people who were not there to see any of these things happen and who contradict one another in many instances, the Gospels cannot provide us with any historical insights. Do you agree or not? Develop a lengthy argument, one way or the other.

Key Terms

Contextual Credibility
    (Criterion), 288
Dissimilarity
    (Criterion), 287

Gnosticism, 282
Independent
    Attestation
    (Criterion), 287

Jesus, son of Ananias,
    294
Johannine community,
    274

Nag Hammadi Library,
    282

Suggestions for Further Reading

NB: For this and all chapters, see the relevant articles (e.g., "Gospel of Thomas," "Jesus") in the works cited in the Suggestions for Further Reading in chapter 1.

Ehrman, Bart D. *Jesus the Apocalyptic Prophet of the New Millennium.* New York: Oxford University Press, 1999. A fuller treatment of the issues and views set forth in the present chapter about the historical Jesus, for popular audiences.

Ehrman, Bart D. *Lost Scriptures: Books that Did Not Make It into the New Testament.* New York: Oxford University Press, 2003. A collection of the early Christian writings that were excluded from the canon, including the various "lost" Gospels.

Foster, Paul, ed. *The Non-canonical Gospels.* London: T&T Clark, 2007. Clear and accessible essays describing some of the most important non-canonical Gospels, written for nonspecialists.

Kysar, Robert. *John the Maverick Gospel.* Atlanta: John Knox, 1976. All in all, probably the best introduction to the unique features of John's Gospel for beginning students.

Meier, John. *A Marginal Jew: Rethinking the Historical Jesus.* 4 vols. (so far!) New York: Doubleday, 1991, 1994, 2001, 2009. Written at an introductory level, but filled with erudite documentation in the endnotes, this is one of the finest treatments of the historical Jesus by a modern scholar.

Smith, D. Moody. *The Theology of John.* Cambridge: Cambridge University Press, 1994. A clearly written and incisive discussion of the major themes of the Fourth Gospel, for beginning students.

12

The Life and Letters of Paul

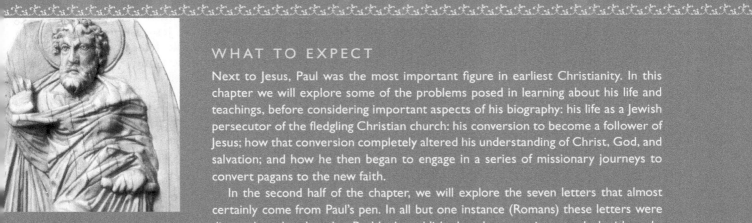

WHAT TO EXPECT

Next to Jesus, Paul was the most important figure in earliest Christianity. In this chapter we will explore some of the problems posed in learning about his life and teachings, before considering important aspects of his biography: his life as a Jewish persecutor of the fledgling Christian church: his conversion to become a follower of Jesus; how that conversion completely altered his understanding of Christ, God, and salvation; and how he then began to engage in a series of missionary journeys to convert pagans to the new faith.

In the second half of the chapter, we will explore the seven letters that almost certainly come from Paul's pen. In all but one instance (Romans) these letters were directed to churches that Paul had established, and were written to deal with problems that had arisen after he had left the community. For each of the letters we will establish the context and occasion of the writing, and then see how Paul addresses the situations that had caused him such concern. In so doing we will get a good sense of the major issues that Paul had to face as a missionary, teacher, pastor, and theologian.

We move now from the Gospels and the life of Jesus to the letters and life of the apostle Paul. It is safe to say that apart from Jesus, Paul was the most important figure in the history of early Christianity. This can be seen in three ways. First, with respect to the writings of the New Testament itself: there are twenty-seven books in the New Testament, and thirteen of them—nearly half—claim to be written by Paul. One other book (Hebrews) was accepted into the New Testament because church fathers believed (wrongly) that Paul wrote it. One other book, the book of Acts, is largely written *about* Paul. So all told, fifteen of the twenty-seven books are directly, in one way or another, connected with Paul.

Second: the rapid spread of Christianity throughout the Roman Empire. The followers of Jesus started out around 30 C.E. as a small group of Jews in Jerusalem (eleven men, a handful of women), who came to believe that Jesus had been raised from the dead. Within thirty years there were Christian communities scattered throughout the major urban areas of the Roman Empire, from Jerusalem to Antioch of Syria, to Ephesus in Asia Minor, to Rome—and to lots of places in between. Probably, by that time, the majority of followers of Jesus were gentiles, not Jews (if not a majority, at least a significant minority). And who is responsible for the spread of Christianity throughout the empire? Lots of people! But the one we are best informed about is Paul, who established churches throughout Asia Minor, Macedonia, and Achaia (modern Turkey and Greece). How successful would the Christian mission have been without Paul? It is impossible to say. But many historians have attributed the early success of the mission to his missionary efforts. In no small measure that is because he, more than anyone else of record, insisted that gentiles could be followers of Jesus without first becoming Jews. For men, that meant they did not have to be circumcised; and for men and women it meant not having to adopt foreign Jewish customs involving such things as kosher food laws and Sabbath observance.

Finally, there is the matter of theology. Paul was one of the very rare intellectuals in the earliest Christian church. He was highly educated and very smart. Some of his letters are dense and rich in their theological thought. In places they are not easy to grasp, even for highly educated scholars. He was the first brilliant Christian theologian; in many respects, the views of later theologians—from Augustine to Aquinas to Martin Luther and on to many others in between and before and after—were based on their reflections on the writings of Paul. In particular it is Paul, more than anyone else we know about from the early church, who helped to transform Christianity away from the religion proclaimed *by* Jesus to the religion *about* Jesus. Paul's form of the faith was one built completely on the significance of Jesus' death and resurrection for salvation. It was not built on the apocalyptic teachings of Jesus and Jesus' urgent insistence that his followers keep the demands of the Torah in preparation for the coming Son of Man. For Paul, a right standing before God did not come from keeping Torah at all. It came from believing in the death and resurrection of the Son of God.

FIGURE 12.1. Portrayal of one of Jesus' apostles preaching the Gospels, with scroll in hand, from a fifth-century ivory panel now in the Louvre (Paris).

PROBLEMS IN THE STUDY OF PAUL

In some ways it is easier to know the teachings Paul taught than to know the teachings of Jesus, since in Paul's case we actually have writings from his hand. So far as we know, Jesus never wrote anything. But Paul did, and we have some of his letters. There are nonetheless serious difficulties in knowing about Paul's life and teachings.

Pauline Pseudepigrapha

The word "**pseudepigrapha**" literally means "writings inscribed with a lie." It is an alternative term for the more common word "forgery" and refers to a writing that is produced by a person who is falsely claiming to be someone famous. If I were to write a book under a made up name, like Henry Dunkelmeier, that would be a pen name. But if I wrote a book claiming to be Stephen King or Barack Obama, that would be a forgery. I would be claiming to be a well-known person when, in fact, I was someone else.

This happens in the modern world on occasion, and it happened even more in the ancient world when it was somewhat more difficult to detect forgery (since most people couldn't even read, let alone read well enough to know they were being duped).

When forgery was detected in the ancient world, it was almost always condemned and objected to as lying, a form of literary deceit. But authors wrote forgeries anyway, and we have lots of examples among pagan, Jewish, and Christian writings. The people who produced these forgeries were not necessarily driven by wicked impulses. There are instances in which almost everyone would agree that it is appropriate to tell a lie. Some people in antiquity thought, as many think now, that if a greater good could be achieved by telling a lie, then that could justify the deceit.

Since the nineteenth century scholars have realized that some of the books in the New Testament that claim to be written by Paul were probably not written by Paul, but by people claiming to be Paul. New Testament scholars tend to call these books "pseudepigrapha" rather than forgeries, usually because they want to avoid the negative implications of the latter term. But whatever we call these books, they were probably written by authors who wanted their readers to *think* they were Paul, when they were in fact someone else. There are three groups of Pauline letters (also known as epistles): (a) the **Pastoral epistles** of 1 and 2 Timothy and Titus; most scholars are reasonably certain that Paul did not write these; (b) the **Deutero-Pauline epistles** of Ephesians, Colossians, and 2 Thessalonians; there are more debates about these three, but the majority of scholars still think Paul probably did not write them; and (c) the **Undisputed Pauline epistles**—that is, the remaining seven, which everyone more or less agrees Paul wrote: Romans, 1 and 2 Corinthians, Galatians, Philippians, 1 Thessalonians, and Philemon. (There are no other writings from Paul's hand apart from these seven—none outside the New Testament, for example.) In this chapter we will be dealing with these seven, since it does not make sense to use letters Paul did *not* write to discuss what he taught. The others we will consider in chapter 13. Part of our discussion there will involve exploring why scholars think Paul did not write these other books.

The Occasional Nature of the Letters

Even restricting ourselves to the seven undisputed Pauline epistles does not solve all of our problems in studying Paul. Another is that all the letters that Paul did write are "occasional." By that I do not mean that Paul occasionally wrote letters; instead I mean that Paul wrote letters only for certain

---

BOX 12.1 OTHER SOURCES FOR THE LIFE OF PAUL

Just as a number of legendary accounts of Jesus sprang up from the first century through the Middle Ages, so too a number of accounts of Paul and the other apostles appeared. One of the earliest and most interesting of these was called the *Acts of Paul and Thecla*, which is largely about a female convert of Paul, an aristocratic young woman who is drawn to his message—which is quite different from the one he proclaims in the New Testament, as we will see in Box 12.5.

As was the case with the apocryphal tales about Jesus, these stories about Paul are less important for what they tell us about the man himself than for what they reveal about Christianity in the years during which they were told. Something similar can be said of the interesting set of correspondence forged by a third-century Christian in the names of Paul and Seneca, the famous philosopher and mentor of the emperor Nero. Written some two hundred years after both parties were dead (both of them killed, according to tradition, by order of Nero), these fourteen letters were meant to show that Paul's significance as an author was recognized by one of the greatest philosophical minds of his day. In the second letter that "Seneca" addresses to Paul, he claims to be particularly impressed with Paul's writings and expresses his desire to make them known to the emperor himself:

I arranged some scrolls [of your letters] and have brought them into a definite order corresponding to their several divisions. Also I have decided to read them to the emperor. If only fate ordains it favourably that he show some interest, then perhaps you too will be present; otherwise I shall fix a day for you at another time when together we may examine this work. And if only it could be done safely, I would not read this writing to him before meeting you. You may then be certain that you are not being overlooked. Farewell, most beloved Paul.

occasions. Nearly all of these letters were written to churches that Paul had established earlier and that were having problems of one sort or another—false teachings in their midst, problems of immorality among their members, ethical or doctrinal questions or disputes. Paul wrote his letters to deal with these problems, as the occasion arose.

That makes interpreting these letters complicated, because we do not always know the occasion except as we can try to reconstruct it from the letter itself. And, as we have seen, if we don't know the context of a writing it is very difficult indeed to interpret it correctly. Moreover, since all of Paul's surviving writings are occasional, that means that there will be a lot of important things that really mattered to Paul that he never got around to mentioning in his letters since he had no occasion to do so. And so we cannot trust that by reading these letters we will know everything that was of supreme importance for Paul. There will be lots of important things he simply doesn't talk about.

The Problem of Acts

As I pointed out, the book of Acts—which is the second volume produced by the author of the Gospel of Luke—is largely about Paul, his conversion, his missionary activities, his arrest, his trials, and his self-defense. Traditionally if someone wanted to know about Paul's life, they would simply read the book of Acts, which tells story after story about Paul. Scholars have long recognized, however, that this is a problem. We have seen that the Gospel of Luke was probably written in 80–85 C.E. Acts was almost certainly written sometime after that. But Paul is thought to have died in the persecution of the emperor Nero against the Christians in 64 C.E. That means that Acts was written at least twenty years after Paul's death, and over 50 years after a number of the stories that it tells (since Paul would have converted sometime around 32 or 33 C.E.).

There are reasons for thinking that the author of Acts heard these stories about Paul from the oral traditions about him, just as he learned his stories about Jesus from other oral traditions. It has often been claimed that the author of Acts—we'll just call him Luke—was actually one of Paul's traveling companions for part of his missionary work. This is because on four occasions in the book of Acts the author begins to speak in the first person about what "we" were doing (instead of what "they" were

doing; the first time is in chapter 16). And so he seems to include himself among Paul's companions. More recent scholarship has called into question whether the author actually was one of Paul's companions, however. In no small measure that is because whenever you compare what Paul has to say about himself in the undisputed letters with what Acts has to say about him—what he taught his followers, what he preached to potential converts, where he went and when and with whom—in almost every instance there are discrepancies. Sometimes these are minor details, sometimes they are highly significant. We will examine some of these discrepancies in the next chapter. For now suffice it to say that if you want to know what Paul himself really taught and did, you have to use Acts gingerly, with a critical eye, hopefully finding corroboration of what Acts says with something that Paul himself says.

Why then did the author use the first person pronoun ("we") when he wasn't actually with Paul for his journeys? Probably for the same reason that other authors claimed to be Paul when they weren't (for example, the author of Ephesians or the author of 1 Timothy): because doing so helped authenticate his message as being one that actually was closely tied with Paul himself.

In what follows we will first look at what we can say about Paul's life—who he was, what he did, and what he experienced. Then, in the second half of this chapter, we will examine each of the seven letters that he almost certainly wrote.

A BRIEF BIOGRAPHY OF PAUL

By carefully reading the letters of Paul, and critically sifting what is said about him in the book of Acts, it is possible to say some things with confidence about his life and teaching.

Before His Conversion

Paul provides a couple of tantalizing backward glances to his life before he became a follower of Jesus (Philippians 3:4–7; Galatians 1:13–14); other information can be gleaned from the book of Acts (used carefully). What Paul emphasizes most emphatically is that before his conversion, he was a highly religious and zealous Jew who followed the traditions of the Pharisees. He does not tell us where he was born, raised, or educated. According to the book of Acts he came from Tarsus, a city of Cilicia; but Paul never says so, and there may have been reasons for Luke wanting to locate Paul there, since it was famous as a major center of learning. By placing Paul there he gives his hero solid academic credentials. Luke also indicates that Paul was educated in Jerusalem under the greatest rabbi of his day, Gamaliel, but again Paul says nothing of the sort. What is clear is that Paul was originally from the Diaspora. His native language was Greek, and there is no solid evidence to suggest that he could read, write, or speak Aramaic or Hebrew. He was obviously highly educated—it took many years of training to learn not only how to read but also to write, and he writes at a very high level of proficiency. We can deduce from this that he must have come from a relatively aristocratic family that could afford to send him to school for years. Probably fewer than 5 percent of the population of the empire was that lucky.

In any event, Paul was a highly educated and zealous Jew. He prided himself, he tells us, in following the traditions passed along by Pharisees. This would mean, among other things, that he was an expert in the Torah and fervently believed in keeping the Torah to the best of his abilities. That will be a significant point for what happens later, as we will see. Paul insists in Philippians that he not only tried to keep the Law, but that he did in fact keep it: "with respect to the righteousness found in the Law, I was blameless" (Philippians 3:6). This too is an important point, because many people today think that Paul was someone who very much wanted to keep the Law but was unable to, and that this was why he turned to Christ. But that is not what Paul himself says. He *was* in fact righteous as far as the Law was concerned. That does not mean, of course, that he never sinned. The Law itself has a way of dealing with people who sin. That, after all, is in part what the sacrifices are for, as prescribed by the Torah.

The other important point that Paul mentions about his life before becoming a follower of Jesus is that his religious zeal drove him to be a violent persecutor of the Christians. This is a point on which the book of Acts agrees. Unfortunately, Paul never explicitly indicates what it was about the Christians that made him want to persecute them. But there are some hints in his letters, and it is not too difficult to make some good inferences.

From the very beginning, of course, the Christians were saying that Jesus was the messiah. For reasons you can imagine, given what you know from the history of Israel, that claim sounded completely ludicrous to most Jews. The messiah was supposed to be the powerful leader of the people who overthrew the enemy and established Israel as a sovereign state in the land. But Jesus was just the *opposite* of that. Everyone knew that Jesus had been crucified. To call Jesus the messiah was a ridiculous idea for most Jews. It would be like calling someone sent to the electric chair for treason against the state the Lord of the universe. Nothing could be more absurd.

But for Paul the problem was even deeper than that, because of how Jesus was executed. He was nailed to a cross. The reason that was a particular problem is because of a passage in the Torah, Deuteronomy 21:23, which says "cursed is anyone who hangs on a tree." Paul, in his later life, quotes the verse in Galatians 3:13. Before he became a follower of Jesus, he took this verse very seriously to mean that anyone who was hanged on a tree—crucified— stood under God's curse. But Christians were saying that Jesus was God's chosen one, the one of God's special favor. They had gotten it precisely wrong. God had cursed Jesus, not showered favor on him. And so, calling Jesus God's messiah was not just ridiculous. It was blasphemous. And that may well be why Paul was so zealous in his opposition to this marginalized Jewish sect.

Paul's Conversion

But something happened to change Paul's mind. We only wish that Paul would have told us more— far more—about it. All he gives are a few hints, presumably because his original readers knew the entire story full well. According to the book of Acts, Paul was traveling to the city of Damascus to persecute the Christians there, and Jesus appeared to him in a blinding flash of light. Paul himself never speaks of being "blinded by the light" on the road to Damascus. What he says in his recollection of the event in Galatians 2:16 is that "God revealed his Son to me." This sounds more like a kind of mental realization, that Paul came to see things differently from before and suddenly realized that in fact Jesus was the Christ, the Son of God. But what brought about that realization? There is another hint in the letter of 1 Corinthians, where Paul states categorically that Jesus "appeared" to him after his resurrection (1 Corinthians 15:8). Paul claims to have seen Jesus alive, after his crucifixion.

We do not know the precise year that this happened. If Jesus died, say, in the year 30, then there would have had to be some time for the Christians to start converting people, to move outside of Jerusalem and Palestine, to establish churches wherever Paul was living at the time (Damascus?), and for Paul to have engaged in persecuting activities against the church. It is usually thought that all of that would have taken a couple of years or so; in that case Paul would have converted in, say, 32 or 33 C.E. It happened because he saw (or believed he saw, at least) Jesus alive, even though he had been

crucified two or three years before. This vision changed everything for Paul, or if not everything at least a whole lot.

What the Resurrection Confirmed for Paul

Since Paul was a Pharisee before he became a Christian, he already would have held to an apocalyptic view of the world. Specifically, Pharisees, like other apocalypticists, maintained that at the end of this evil age, when the day of judgment arrived, there would be a resurrection of the dead. Those who had sided with God would be rewarded;

FIGURE 12.2. For Paul, the crucifixion was of utmost importance. Here is one of the earliest visual representations of the crucifixion, from a cypress panel door in the church of Saint Sabina in Rome, nearly 350 years after Paul's day. Earlier Christians were reluctant to portray the crucifixion.

those who had opposed him would be punished. Now you need to ask yourself: if someone believes that the resurrection of the dead is to happen at the very end of this age, when history as we know it was to come to a crashing halt, what would that person think if they came to believe that someone had been resurrected? Their immediate thought would almost certainly be, "It has started!" That is, the resurrection of the dead has begun.

This was Paul's conclusion. Before believing in Jesus he thought that the resurrection was soon to come. When he came to believe that Jesus was raised, he concluded that the end was already here. He, then, was living at the end of time, in the last days. And so far as we can tell, this was a view that Paul held until the end of his life. Years later, when writing to the Corinthians, Paul speaks about Jesus as "the first fruits of the resurrection" (1 Corinthians 15:20). This is an agricultural image. When the farmer goes out to collect the harvest on the first day, they call it the "first fruits" and they have a party that night to celebrate the beginning of the harvest. And when does the farmer collect the rest of the harvest? The next day. He doesn't wait fifty years. If Jesus is the first fruits of the resurrection, it means that the resurrection has begun and all the others are soon to be raised along with Jesus.

And that is why Paul himself believed he would be alive when the end came. He—like Jesus—thought that it was very near. But unlike Jesus, who thought that it would be brought by the Son of Man, Paul thought it would be brought by Jesus. For Paul, Jesus was not simply resuscitated from the dead so that he would die again. He was given a resurrected, transformed, immortal, imperishable body, and then he was exalted up to heaven with God. But only for the time being. Soon he was to return from heaven, and when he did, everyone else would be raised, imperishable. This was to happen soon. And Paul would be living when it did. That is the clear implication of Paul's own words in 1 Thessalonians 4:13–18 and 1 Corinthians 15:51–57. He would be one of those who would still be alive when the end came.

What the Resurrection Changed for Paul

In many ways, what *changed* for Paul once he came to believe that Jesus had been raised from the dead

---

BOX 12.2 PAUL ON THE ROAD TO DAMASCUS

The book of Acts narrates the events of Paul's conversion on the road to Damascus on three separate occasions. The event itself is narrated in 9:1–19; Paul later recounts it to a hostile Jewish crowd after his arrest in 22:6–16; and then again to King Agrippa in 26:12–18. When you compare these accounts carefully, you will find a number of apparent discrepancies, including the following more obvious ones:

- When Jesus appears to Paul in chapter 9, Paul's companions "heard the voice but saw no one" (9:7). But when Paul recounts the tale in chapter 22, he claims that they "saw the light but did not hear the voice" (22:9).
- In chapter 9 Paul's companions are left standing while he is knocked to the ground by the vision (v. 7). But according to chapter 26 they all fall to the ground (26:12).
- In the first account Paul is instructed to go into Damascus to receive instruction from a disciple of

Jesus named Ananias. In the last account he is not sent to Ananias but is instructed by Jesus himself (26:16–18).

These may seem like minor details, but why are the accounts at odds with one another at all? Some scholars have proposed that there were different versions of the story and that Luke incorporated three of them. If this is right, then we are left with the problem of knowing which one is the most accurate. Others have suggested that Luke knew only one version of the story but modified it for each of the contexts in which it was retold: the hostile crowd in chapter 22 and the court trial in chapter 26. This view seems reasonable, but it also creates problems for the historian who wants to know what really happened. If we have grounds for thinking that Luke modified two of the accounts for literary reasons, why shouldn't we think that he (or his sources) modified all three?

was far more significant than what was confirmed for him.

PAUL'S VIEW OF JESUS   First and most obviously, Paul's view of Jesus himself radically changed. Before he experienced the resurrection, Paul thought that it was ludicrous to call a crucified man the messiah—and worse than that, it was blasphemous, since God himself had said that anyone who was hanged on a tree was cursed. But if God raised Jesus from the dead (and there was, of course, no *other* way for Jesus to get raised from the dead), that meant that Jesus did not stand under God's curse but under God's special blessing. That changed everything.

If Jesus was the man specially blessed by God, how can one explain the fact that he was crucified? For one thing, that does not seem like a particularly impressive way for God to show his favor to someone—having them subjected to an inhumanly painful and humiliating death. And for another thing, there was that verse in Deuteronomy that said that God cursed the one who hanged on a tree. How could one make sense of it all?

Paul appears to have done what any good, highly educated, devoted Jew would have done. He went to his Scriptures to try to figure it all out. Like some Christians before him, and like many others since, Paul began to notice that there were numerous passages in the Jewish Scriptures that speak of a righteous man suffering unjustly. And in some of these passages, such as the Servant Songs of Isaiah, this one who suffers unjustly does so for the sake of others. Moreover, after he suffers, God vindicates him. That, Paul decided, is what happened with Jesus. He suffered unjustly, not because of his own sin but for the sins of others. In a sense, Jesus was like one of the animal sacrifices in the Temple: it was a death that was the substitute for others. Jesus' death was a kind of atoning sacrifice. It was his death that brought about a restored relationship with God.

But what about that passage in Deuteronomy that indicated that God cursed anyone who hanged on a tree? Paul came to think that God cursed Jesus not because of anything he had done, but, on the contrary, so that Jesus could himself take the curse that was owed to others. Christ had to be crucified (it would not have worked if he were stoned or strangled) because he had to bear the curse that others deserved for their sins.

And so the death of Jesus did not nullify the claim that he was the messiah. He precisely was the messiah—and it was clear that he was, because of the way he died and the way that God then had raised him from the dead.

But Jesus' death was even more important than that. As an apocalypticist Paul believed that there were evil powers in the world, demonic forces that were wreaking havoc here on earth. Two of these chief powers (in addition, say, to the devil) were the powers of sin and death. Sin was not simply an act of disobedience for Paul, a mistake someone makes or a violation of the law. Sin was a cosmic force, a power that was trying to enslave people, and when it succeeded, it compelled them to act in ways contrary to God. Death for Paul was not simply what happened when the body stopped functioning. It too was a cosmic power, the greatest of the powers. For when it managed to take control of a person, it brought complete annihilation.

Paul came to believe that Jesus conquered the powers of sin and death. He "knew" that Jesus had conquered the power of death, because death could not hold him in its grip. Jesus overwhelmed death itself when he came back from the dead. And if he overcame death in his resurrection, he overcame sin in his death. His death conquered the power of sin. Christ, in short, was God's answer to the powers of evil in the world. It was through Christ's death and resurrection that a person could find atonement for sins and could also receive the power to overcome sin and death.

These would have been new, vibrant, powerful thoughts for Paul. But they created a problem as well. As a good, scripture-based, devoted Jew, committed to the ways of the Pharisees, Paul had always seen the Law as the greatest gift God had ever given his people, the chosen people, and as the very center of what it means to be obedient to God and a member of his covenantal community. If Christ's death and resurrection now appeared to be the means that God brought salvation to his people— what about the Law?

PAUL'S VIEW OF THE LAW   Paul's understanding of the Law in light of his faith in Christ is extremely complicated. Some scholars have wondered, given the variety of things Paul says about the Law in his letters, whether he ever managed to construct an entirely consistent view. At the very least it seems clear that Paul came to believe that a

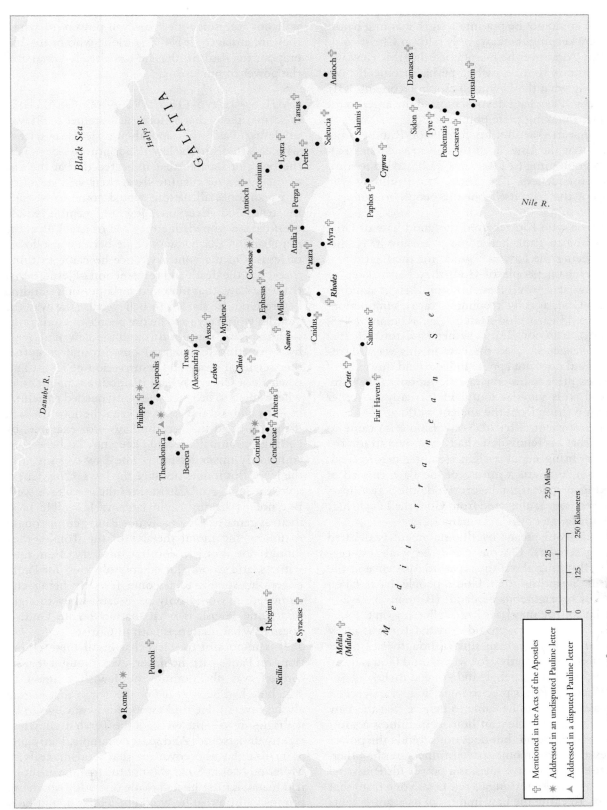

FIGURE 12.3. Places associated with Paul in the New Testament.

person could not be put into a right standing before God by keeping the Law; only faith in Christ could do this. Moreover he maintained that this view was not contrary to the Law but, perhaps ironically, was precisely what the Law itself taught (Romans 3:31). As we will see, Paul devotes most of the letter to the Romans making these points.

It appears that after his conversion Paul began to think that the Law, even though in itself an obviously good thing (see Romans 7:12) had led to some bad consequences. The problem for Paul, however, was not the Law itself but the people to whom it was given.

Those who had received the good Law of God, according to Paul, had come to misuse it. Rather than seeing the Law as a guide for their actions as the covenant people of God, they began keeping the Law as a way of establishing a right standing before God, as if by keeping its various injunctions they could earn God's favor (e.g., Romans 4:4–5; 10:2–4). It is not clear whether Paul thought that Jews *intentionally* used the Law in this way. Moreover, Paul does not appear to have held this view of the Law prior to his conversion, but only afterward. Indeed, this view is found in virtually no other Jewish writing from the ancient world.

In any event, after his conversion Paul came to think that his fellow Jews had attempted to use the Law to bring about a right standing before God. For him, this was a misuse of the Law. Instead of making people right before God, the Law shows that everyone is alienated from God; the Law brings a "knowledge of sin" (Romans 3:20).

What Paul means by this statement is debated among scholars. On one hand, he is almost certainly thinking about the repeated insistence in the Jewish Scriptures that God's people have fallen short of his righteous demands (Romans 3:10–20). In addition, he may have been reflecting on the sacrificial system that is provided by the Torah as a way of dealing with human sins (although Paul never mentions this directly), for why would God require sacrifices for sin if people didn't need them?

Whatever Paul's precise logic, it appears certain that as a Christian he came to believe that the Law points to the problem of human sinfulness against God, on one hand, but does not provide the power necessary to overcome that sinfulness on the other. Sin itself, as we have seen, is a power for Paul, and the Law can do nothing to release anyone from that power. Keeping the Law in most of its requirements

will not free someone from the powers to which they are enslaved. It is Christ alone who brings liberation, for Paul, in that he has already conquered the power of sin.

PAUL'S VIEWS OF JEWS AND GENTILES

It seems likely that before he became a follower of Jesus, Paul the apocalyptic Jew subscribed wholeheartedly to the Jewish Scriptures—especially the book of Isaiah—that indicated that at the end of the age, after turning from their vain devotion to pagan idols, all nations would come to worship the true God. Everyone, Jew and gentile, would eventually acknowledge the God of Israel. Paul did not abandon that view once he became a follower of Jesus. On the contrary, once he came to think that it was the death and resurrection of Jesus, rather than the Law, that mattered for a person's standing before God, he started to believe that the way the gentiles would come to be the people of God, along with the Jews, was not through the Law at all (e.g., by converting to Judaism) but through accepting the sacrificial death and resurrection of Jesus. This is why as a Christian Paul maintained that gentiles who wanted to be right with God needed to believe in Jesus and did not need to keep the Law. In fact, if they decided to keep the Law—for example, by getting circumcised and keeping kosher—they completely misunderstood. The Law was given to the Jews. But it does not save the Jews. Only Christ saves the Jews. And Christ saves the gentiles as well. But not by having them become Jews. He saves them as gentiles. Obviously (for Paul) gentiles ought to follow the moral dictates of the Torah—they should not murder, commit adultery, bear false witness, and so on. But equally obvious (for Paul), if gentiles sought to become Jews by being circumcised, it would only be because they thought that being Jewish is what matters before God. It doesn't. What matters is faith in Christ.

It is important to stress that in all these reflections on Paul's part, he never, ever, thought that he himself was abandoning the Jewish religion in which he had been raised or the Torah that he had always revered. He understood his new views to be the right views—the views of the Torah itself, when rightly understood. And so, for example, Paul came to realize that the covenant that God made with Moses on Mount Sinai was not the first covenant he had made. Earlier he had made one with Abraham, promising him that he would be a blessing not only for his descendants but for all nations (Genesis 12:3 "in you all the families of the earth will be blessed"). Abraham believed God's promise and was rewarded with a right standing before God (Genesis 15:6). All this happened *before* God indicated that the sign of the covenant would be circumcision (Genesis 17), and obviously hundreds of years before Moses arrived on the scene. The promises to Abraham are for all the nations, not just the Jews, and they are not tied to circumcision or the Law of Moses. They are fulfilled, according to Paul, in Christ, who brings salvation, apart from the Law, to all people, both Jew and gentile. And for Paul, that is the teaching precisely of the Law itself. When we speak of Paul "converting," then, we do not mean that he stopped being a Jew in order to be a Christian. He converted in the sense that he had been a persecutor of the Christian church and then became its greatest apostle; he converted from a hatred of Christ and the Christian mission to being an avid follower of Christ and a leader of the mission. But even after that change, he still considered himself a faithful Jew who understood his message to be the good news of how the promises given to the Jewish ancestors had now found their true fulfillment in Christ.

Paul's Work on the Mission Field

Paul's letters provide us with only scant and scattered information about what Paul did after he converted. The one thing we know for certain is that he devoted himself completely to spreading the Christian gospel. The only direct comments that

Paul makes about his life immediately after his conversion are found in Galatians chapters 1–2. Here Paul says quite emphatically that after he came to believe in Christ he did not—he decidedly did not!—go to Jerusalem to consult with the apostles of Jesus who were still located there. As we will see more fully later when we examine the letter to the Galatians itself, Paul wants to stress this point because he wants it to be quite clear that his gospel message did not come from any other human, not even the disciples of Jesus. He got his message directly from Jesus himself. And so, Paul maintained, no one should think that his distinctive proclamation is what he learned from others, or that he has altered the "original" teachings of the other apostles. He did not even speak with any of them. Paul's ultimate message was that gentiles can be saved by faith in Christ apart from keeping the requirements of the Jewish law. And he got this message from the source itself, when Jesus appeared to him.

Paul indicates that after he became a follower of Jesus he went to Arabia. He does not say why. He then returned to Damascus (which suggests that this is where he was living; possibly he was raised there?) for three years, and then—and only then—he went on a two-week trip to Jerusalem in order to confer with Peter and James, the brother of Jesus, who by this time was one of the leaders of the Jerusalem church. Paul does not indicate what the conference was about. Some readers have assumed that Paul wanted to learn more about the life of Jesus from the two people who would be best able to tell him—Jesus' closest disciple and his own

FIGURE 12.4. We sometimes forget that ancient travelers going on foot would often have had a rough go of it. These are the famous "Cilician Gates" in the Taurus mountains: the gorge—sixty feet across at its widest point—through which Paul would have had to pass in order to travel north from Tarsus into Asia Minor.

brother. But if that is the case, it is very strange that Paul in his letters gives very little indication that he knew much at all about the things Jesus said and did during his life. It may be that Paul knew more than he let on. Or it may be that his brief two weeks in Jerusalem with Peter and James were about something else. Possibly they were discussing not the past (the life of Jesus) but the future (how the mission was to be conducted).

In any event, Paul went from there into the regions of Syria and Cilicia, where he spent fourteen years there, presumably spreading the gospel. His mission was to convert gentiles. He considered himself the "apostle to the gentiles," just as others—chiefly Peter—were apostles "to the Jews." The big question that lots of the earliest Jewish followers of Jesus had, as I have intimated, was not whether gentiles could also become Christian. Everyone agreed that they could. The big question was whether gentiles could become Christians without first becoming Jews. Many, possibly most, of the earliest Christians thought that *of course*, necessarily, Jesus' followers must be Jewish (either born Jews or Jewish converts). For them, Jesus was the Jewish messiah sent from the Jewish God to the Jewish people in fulfillment of the Jewish law—and so anyone who wanted to be his follower naturally had first to become Jewish. That meant, obviously, abandoning the worship of pagan gods. But it also meant getting circumcised to join the people of the covenant (if they were men), observing the Sabbath, keeping Jewish festivals, following kosher food laws, and keeping all the other aspects of the Law of Moses. Paul, as we have seen, thought just the opposite.

After his fourteen years in Syria and Cilicia, establishing gentile churches, the matter came to a head and there was a conference in Jerusalem to settle the matter once and for all. The conference is a major topic of the book of Acts (ch. 15) and plays an important role in Paul's letter to the Galatians (ch. 2). These two accounts differ in some significant ways, but from Paul's version it is clear: he managed to convince the Jerusalem apostles that the gentile mission was both valid and divinely inspired, and that settled the matter. This gave Paul the license to continue his preaching activities, and at this point he appears to have headed farther to the west, going to major cities in Asia Minor, Macedonia, and Achaia.

Paul does not tell us how he actually went about converting gentiles and starting churches. It is relatively clear from his letters that he focused on major urban areas—Ephesus, Thessalonica, Philippi, Corinth, etc. This makes sense, since cities had the most dense populations, allowing him to reach more people at once. But how did he reach them? There is nothing to suggest that Paul held major evangelistic rallies like you find in modern times in such venues as the Billy Graham crusades. These require vast resources and the cooperation of local officials, and Paul had neither. You might think that Paul would go into a city and just start preaching on a street corner and hope to win converts. But Paul says nothing about that, either.

The book of Acts indicates that he started churches by first going to the local synagogue of whatever city he was in, making contacts there, and trying to convert Jews. In every instance, in Acts, Paul finds opposition among the Jews and so then he tries his luck with gentiles. The problem with this view of Paul's approach is that Paul himself is emphatic that he was not a missionary to Jews but to gentiles; and when you read letters such as 1 Thessalonians and 1 Corinthians, it is quite clear that his churches were in fact made up of gentiles who had converted from paganism, not Jews.

Some hints of how Paul proceeded can be found in a few passages of his own letters. In 1 Thessalonians Paul reminds his converts how he and his missionary companions worked among them "night and day so that we might not burden any of you while we proclaimed to you the gospel of God" (2:9). Recent scholarship has taken Paul seriously that he was literally "working" among his potential converts. In this view, Paul was a manual laborer of some sort. According to the book of Acts he worked with leather goods (18:3). Traditionally this verse has been interpreted to mean that he made tents, although the word used in Acts could refer to any range of occupations involving animal skins.

But in any event, it appears that Paul's mission was carried out as follows. Paul and his companions (he was with Timothy and Silvanus in Thessalonica, for example) would arrive in town and set up a small business, possibly some kind of Christian leather goods shop. People would come in for business and Paul would take the opportunity to engage them in conversation. Work places were more like that in the ancient world, where business could be conducted more leisurely and fewer people were having to punch a clock (actually, no one did). Most of Paul's customers would have been pagan, and Paul would have engaged them in serious conversation in order to convert them to give up their pagan religions and adopt his own—faith in the God of Israel and in Jesus his Son, who died for the sake of others and was raised from the dead.

One might imagine that Paul did not succeed with most of his conversation partners. But he succeeded with some, and these converts may have converted their families, who may have converted some of their neighbors, and so it went. Eventually there would be a small group of Christians in town (say a couple of dozen). They would meet together every Sunday morning (the day of the resurrection) in order to talk about their faith, to learn more from Paul, to read the Scriptures (the Old Testament—in the days before there was a New Testament), to hear them interpreted, to pray, to strategize how to convert more people into the group, and so on.

As soon as Paul was convinced that the group was strong enough to continue without him, he would pick up shop and move on to the next city to start again. The idea was to get cells of Christians started in all the major cities and to spread the religion through them. Paul was just one person, but with fervent converts in strategic locations the religion could begin to multiply.

Once Paul moved on, he would stay in communication with the church he had left behind. He would often receive word about the problems they were having: alternative teachings to those Paul had delivered, infighting among the church members, evidence of immoral activity, doctrinal or ethical dilemmas, and so on. When Paul heard of the problems he would write a letter to the congregation. And some of these are the letters that we have: letters written by Paul, back to the congregations that he had established, to deal with their problems (with one exception, as we will see: the letter to the Romans).

Paul obviously wrote far more letters than the seven that we now have in the New Testament. He actually refers to other letters in these, and one can imagine that he wrote dozens of them. But only seven, for one reason or another, survive. Would that more would turn up! In any event, these seven have long been treasured by Christians and provide a storehouse of information about the earliest

Christian communities in the 50s C.E. They are our oldest surviving Christian writings, written more than a decade before our first Gospel (Mark) and possibly forty years before the last canonical Gospel (John). As such they give us valuable insights into what was happening among the followers of Jesus in the years after his death, especially in the gentile mission field of Paul. These letters show that we are dealing with a vastly different phenomenon from the one we found in the life and teachings of Jesus. These letters are elegant testimony that the Christianity of Paul and his followers was far more the religion about Jesus the resurrected Lord than the religion of Jesus the Jewish apocalyptic prophet.

To understand each of these letters we need to reconstruct as best we can the occasion that led Paul to write it, and then see how he has responded to the occasion. There is no way to establish the occasion other than reading the letter itself and seeing what issues Paul is trying to address. We will try to place each of the letters in some kind of plausible context. It is very difficult to know the correct chronological sequence of the letters. This is an issue scholars have struggled with for centuries. Today there is a fair consensus that 1 Thessalonians is almost certainly the first of the letters to be written (which makes it the earliest Christian writing of any kind to survive from the ancient world), and Romans is almost certainly the last. And so we will begin with 1 Thessalonians, then look at the five intervening letters (in their canonical sequence, since it is hard to establish their chronological relationships), and end with the letter that is widely regarded as the most important of the lot, the letter to the Christians of Rome.

Each of these letters is structured like typical letters in Roman times: they begin by naming the sender and the addressees, followed by a prayer or blessing, and then, normally, an expression of thanksgiving to God for the congregation. This is followed by the body of the letter where the main business at hand is addressed. The letters end with closing admonitions and greetings to people in the congregation, some references to Paul's future travel plans, and a final blessing and farewell. For each of these letters I would suggest that you begin by reading it carefully, then read my brief analysis of it, and finally read it again with that analysis in mind. This will help you keep the distinctive messages of each letter in mind.

At a Glance: The Life of Paul

There are three major difficulties in reconstructing the life of Paul: a number of the writings in his name are pseudepigaphic; all of his authentic letters are occasional; and the accounts found in the book of Acts are not always reliable. A close reading of his letters reveals, however, important information about his life. Before becoming a follower of Jesus Paul was a zealous Jew who persecuted the early Christians. Because of a "revelation" that he said came from God—a vision of Jesus himself after his death—Paul came to believe that Jesus really was the messiah. This belief confirmed many of the apocalyptic views that Paul held before following Jesus, but it changed completely how he understood Jesus (he was the messiah), the Law (it had no role in making a person right with God), and Jews and gentiles (they were on equal footing before God). Armed with these new understandings, Paul went onto the mission field, traveling to major urban areas of the eastern Mediterranean in an effort to convert pagans to the new faith. His missionary modus operandi may have involved starting a Christian business in a new city and using the workplace as an opportunity to meet new people and converse with them, sharing with them his gospel message.

I THESSALONIANS

1 Thessalonians is usually dated to around 49 C.E., about sixteen or seventeen years after Paul's conversion and about twenty years after the death of Jesus. Christianity had already come a long way from the apocalyptic proclamation of Jesus in Galilee—a long way geographically and religiously.

Thessalonica was a major port city, the capital of the Roman province of Macedonia and one of the principal targets chosen by Paul for his mission in the region. Paul indicates in the letter that after establishing the church there, he and his companion Timothy headed to Athens, presumably to start a church there as well. He soon became anxious to learn how the Thessalonians were faring and sent Timothy back to them to find out. Timothy has now returned and brought a report (see 1 Thessalonians 3:1–6), and this letter is Paul's response.

For the most part the news was good. The church in Thessalonica continued to be strong and they were still deeply grateful for the work that Paul had done for them. But there were a couple of problems, one external and one internal. The external problem was that the community was beginning to experience persecution; the internal problem was that members of the congregation had become confused or had started to doubt some of Paul's basic teaching about when the end of the age was to arrive. 1 Thessalonians deals with these matters.

This is one of Paul's friendliest and most upbeat letters. It is remarkably personable, with professions of heartfelt gratitude and affection flowing from nearly every page, especially in the first three chapters. Paul is grateful for the congregation and their ongoing love and devotion.

On the problems they were facing, he first reminds them that he had told them in advance that they could expect to suffer. We are not sure why the congregation was being persecuted, but it may be that since it was made up of former pagans (see 1:9–10), other members of the larger community had become upset that these Christians were not participating in the pagan festivals in celebration of the pagan gods. The gods, as we have seen, could get angry if they were not worshiped, and from the pagan perspective, if any disasters occurred it surely would be the fault of those who did not participate in the community's worship. Paul tells the Thessalonians to hold fast and to remember that Jesus too had to suffer, as had the original Christian churches in Judea (2:14–16). In the face of opposition the Christians are to continue to lead upright, moral lives, and especially not to engage in sexual immorality (4:1–4); they are to live lives of love toward one another and to work to gain the respect of outsiders (4:9–12).

The big problem they faced, however, had to do with Paul's apocalyptic teaching. Paul had told them that the end of the age was imminent, that Jesus was to return from heaven very soon bringing the kingdom with him. But it had not happened. And now some members of the congregation had died. Those who were left wondered if these

BOX 12.3 CHRISTIANS MALIGNED AS PERVERTS AND CRIMINALS

There is no solid evidence to suggest that specific allegations of wrongdoing were being made against the church in Thessalonica at the time of Paul's writing that led to their persecution. But we do know that other secret societies were widely viewed with suspicion and that certain standard kinds of slander were leveled against them. The logic of these slanders is plain: if people meet together in secret or under the cloak of darkness, they must have something to hide.

It is possible that Paul was aware of such charges and wanted the Thessalonian Christians to go out of their way to avoid them. Such a concern would make sense of his injunctions to maintain pure sexual conduct and to keep a good reputation among outsiders.

You might be amazed at the kinds of accusations that were later leveled against the Christians that they were cannibals and perverts who killed babies and then ate them. Consider, for example, the comments of Fronto, the tutor of the emperor Marcus Aurelius and one of the most highly respected scholars of the mid-second century:

They [the Christians] recognized each other by secret marks and signs; hardly have they met when they love each other, throughout the world uniting in the practice of a veritable religion of lusts. Indiscriminately they call each other brother and sister, thus turning even ordinary fornication into incest. . . . It is also reported that they worship the genitals of their pontiff and priest, adoring, it appears, the sex of their "father.". . . The notoriety of the stories told of

the initiation of new recruits is matched by their ghastly horror. A young baby is covered over with flour, the object being to deceive the unwary. It is then served before the person to be admitted into their rites. The recruit is urged to inflict blows onto it—they appear to be harmless because of the covering of flour. Thus the baby is killed with wounds that remain unseen and concealed. It is the blood of this infant—I shudder to mention it—it is this blood that they lick with thirsty lips; these are the limbs they distribute eagerly; this is the victim by which they seal their covenant; it is by complicity in this crime that they are pledged to mutual silence; these are their rites, more foul than all sacrileges combined. . . . On a special day they gather for a feast with all their children, sisters, mothers—all sexes and all ages. There, flushed with the banquet after such feasting and drinking, they begin to burn with incestuous passions. They provoke a dog tied to the lampstand to leap and bound towards a scrap of food which they have tossed outside the reach of his chain. By this means the light is overturned and extinguished, and with it common knowledge of their actions; in the shameless dark with unspeakable lust they copulate in random unions, all equally guilty of incest. (Minucius Felix, *Octavius* 9:2–6)[1]

---

1   Translation of G. W. Clark, *The Octavius of Marcus Minucius Felix* (Mahwah, NJ; Newman, 1974).

unfortunates had lost out on their chance to inherit the coming kingdom. Paul's letter is, in large measure, a response to this problem.

The key passages are 4:13–18 and 5:1–11. First Paul assures his readers: those who have died have not lost out on their eternal reward. He explains this by laying out his scenario for what is to happen at the end of the age—still very soon. Jesus himself will descend from heaven, those of his followers who have died will rise from the dead and meet him in the air, and then all his living followers will join them in the air, to live together always. Paul seems to believe that he will be one of those still living at the time.

This scenario presupposes a kind of three-storied universe: God and Jesus are up above us, in heaven; we are here on earth; the dead are down below us. Jesus has ascended to heaven and he will come down; the dead will go up; and then we will go up. It is hard to know how Paul would have explained this cosmic event in a universe such as the one we know from astronomers today, where there simply is no up and down.

He goes on to say, then, that this end will come suddenly, when people least expect it—like a thief in the night. And so the Thessalonians need to remain ready, as it could happen at any time. The letter ends then with a set of exhortations and greetings.

FIGURE 12.5. A shoemaker and cord-maker at work, from an ancient sarcophagus. These were manual laborers like Paul, who according to Acts 18:3 was a leather-worker.

I CORINTHIANS

After Paul had established the church in Thessalonica he moved on and eventually came, with his companions, to Corinth. Corinth was a large and prosperous city south of Thessalonica in the Roman province of Achaia, of which it was the capital. It was a major center of trade and communication, and had a rather dicey reputation in antiquity as a playground that provided commercialized pleasures for the well-to-do. A comic poet of Greece invented the word "to Corinthianize," which meant to engage in promiscuous sexual activities. In any event, many people today know about the city only because of the letters Paul wrote to the Christians there, and these letters have done little to improve the city's dubious reputation.

Paul may have spent a good deal of time in Corinth; Acts states that he was there for a year and half, and it indicates that he did indeed engage in his leather goods business there (Acts 18:1–11). His converts were, again, almost entirely converted pagans. After the church was well enough established he went to other climes and ended up in the city of Ephesus, in Asia Minor. While there he received news of the Corinthian church from two sources, an oral report from "Chole's people" (1:11) and a letter that some of the members had written to him (see, e.g., 7:1). The people from Chloe may have been slaves of this wealthy woman, a member of the congregation, who were travelling to Ephesus on their mistress's business. In any event, the news Paul received from both sources was not good. This was a church in a boatload of trouble.

1 Corinthians deals with all of the problems of the church, one by one, as Paul had heard of them. It is not difficult to reconstruct the problems, in broad terms, from what Paul has to say in response to them. To begin with there were serious divisions

within the church, as different factions and cliques had formed, each of them claiming that their particular views were authorized by one Christian leader or another: Paul, Apollos (a charismatic Christian who followed Paul to Corinth and worked in the church), Cephas, and even Jesus himself. The leaders of these various factions all claimed that their verbal eloquence and physical power (ability to do miracles?) showed that they indeed represented the "true" understanding of the faith.

This problem was particularly grievous to Paul, and he deals with it in four whole chapters (chs. 1–4) not by saying that "his" faction was right, but by saying that *all* the factions were wrong. The gospel is not "proved" by eloquence, wisdom, and power. Just the opposite, the gospel is based on a view that is weak and foolish: salvation comes from a cruci-fied man, after all. Paul himself appears weak and foolish. Those who think that Christianity is all about superior wisdom and preternatural power have completely misunderstood. The church needs to get unified and to avoid all factions.

Paul also had to deal with immorality in the church. Some of the Christian men were evidently visiting prostitutes and bragging about it (ch. 6) and one man was actually sleeping with his stepmother (ch. 5). Paul does not explain directly what moti-vated these kinds of behavior, but he hints that the problem is that there are people in the Corinthian community who have taken the message of their salvation too far. These people appear to have thought that the salvation that Christ brought to them meant that they were already liberated from their bodies and that it was only their souls that ultimately mattered; it was the soul that would be saved but the body would perish. For them, this showed that with God the body is not what matters. And if the body doesn't matter, then it doesn't matter what you do with your body. And so, for them, what we might think of as sexual immorality is in fact a matter of indifference to God.

Paul is outraged by this view, and insists that the community continue to conform to standard views of moral life. The man living with his stepmother is to be excluded from the community, and the men visiting prostitutes need to realize what they are doing. When a man has sex with a woman he becomes "one" with her; but because Christians have been united with Christ, they are "one" with him. That means, by implication, that these men are making Christ "one" with a prostitute. And that can't be good. They need to cease and desist.

Other problems involved the congregation's life together. Some members of the community were suing others over some issue or another (Paul doesn't say what) in civil court (ch. 6). Some members were eating meat that had been sacrificed to pagan idols (chs. 6–8). These people maintained that idols don't really exist, since there is really only one God, and that it is therefore not a problem to eat the meat (which, presumably, was less expensive to buy since it had been used already). But they were offending others who thought that this was nothing other than idol worship.

There were also enormous problems in the wor-ship services—real chaos breaking out (chs. 12–14).

FIGURE 12.6. Paul evangelized the cities he visited by setting up a small business and discussing his Gospel with customers. Shown here are the remains of some of the street-front shops that can still be found in the ruins of Corinth.

From the letter we learn a good deal about how worship services worked in Paul's churches. Paul believed that when anyone converted to believe in Jesus and was baptized received the Holy Spirit, the Spirit then gave each person a "gift" to help the community of believers in one way or another—some had the gift of teaching, others of healing, others of speaking prophecies from God, others speaking such prophecies not in human languages but in angelic tongues, others of being able to interpret these foreign tongues, and so forth. Everyone had a gift, and all the gifts were to help the community in its life together. But the Corinthians had emphasized some gifts more than others—especially the more spectacular ones, such as speaking in tongues. As a result there was spiritual one-upmanship happening in the worship services, as one person tried to show he was more spiritual than another by speaking in tongues more loudly and frequently than the next person.

Paul is incensed by all this behavior and insists that the gifts are given not for self-aggrandizement but to strengthen the body of Christ. The gifts are to be exercised in love for others, not in order to advance oneself (ch. 13).

The major problem of the congregation is the one Paul deals with last. I have already alluded to it. Some of the Corinthians thought that salvation involved the spirit but not the body. They thought, in fact, that since they had become Christian and were related now to Christ, they too, like Christ, had conquered the powers of sin and death. And that meant they had already begun to enjoy a resurrected existence. They were already enjoying the full benefits of salvation.

Paul the good apocalypticist thought this view was completely wrong, and he spends all of chapter 15—the final substantial chapter of the body of the letter—dealing with it. Christians have *not* yet experienced the resurrection. When Jesus was raised, he was raised *in the body*. That means that the

---

BOX 12.4 POSSIBILITIES OF EXISTENCE IN THE AFTERLIFE

Some interpreters have thought that Paul and his Corinthian opponents disagreed about the resurrection because they had fundamentally different understandings about the nature of human existence, both now and in the afterlife. Perhaps it would be useful to reflect on different ways that one might conceive of life after death.

Annihilation. One possibility is that a person who dies ceases to exist. This appears to have been a popular notion in the Greco-Roman world, as evidenced by a number of inscriptions on tombstones that bemoan the brevity of life which ends in nonexistence. One of the most widely used Latin inscriptions was so popular that it was normally abbreviated (like our own R.I.P. for "Rest in Peace") as N.F.N.S.N.C.: "I was not, I am not, I care not."

Disembodied Existence. Another possibility is that life after death is life apart from the body. In some strands of Greek thought, influenced above all by Plato, the body itself was thought to be the bane of human existence because it brought pain, finitude, and death to the soul that lived within it. These people did not think of the soul as immaterial; it was thought to be a "substance," but a much more refined substance than

the clunker of a shell that we call the body. The catch Greek phrase sometimes used to express the notion that the coarse material of the body is the prison or tomb for the more refined substance of the soul was "sōma sēma," literally, "the body, a prison." For people who thought such things, the afterlife involved a liberation of the soul from its bodily entombment.

Bodily Resurrection. A third possibility is that the body is not inherently evil or problematic but has simply become subject to the ravages of evil and death. For many Jews, for example, the human body was created by God, as were all things, and so is inherently good. And what God has created he will also redeem. Thus, the body will not ultimately perish but will live on in the afterlife. How can this be, given the indisputable fact that bodies eventually decay and disappear? In this view, God will transform the physical body into a spiritual body that will never experience the ravages of evil and death, a glorified body that will never get sick and never die. As a Jewish apocalypticist Paul maintained this third view of the nature of human existence, whereas his opponents in Corinth, like many Christians after them down to our own day, appear to have subscribed to the second.

Christian resurrection also will be in the body. And that obviously has not yet happened (just look at your body!), but is yet to happen. It will happen when Jesus returns from heaven, and all those who believe in him will be materially transformed and given immortal, imperishable bodies. It is only then that the Christian can expect to experience the full benefits of salvation, and not before. Knowing this would go a long way to solving all of the Corinthians' problems. It would show them that the body matters, and that it matters what you do with your body, so that you must behave ethically; and it would show them that the body of Christ—which is the community of believers—needs to be tended to and cared for, and that everyone needs to work together for the common good as they await that future day when they, like Jesus, will be raised to a new existence, in their bodies, for life eternal.

2 CORINTHIANS

Paul's second letter to the Corinthians has long intrigued and perplexed scholars of the New Testament. In the first nine chapters Paul is filled with joy for the congregation. He indicates that for a while, their relationship had been tense: he had paid a second visit to them (presumably after writing 1 Corinthians) and someone had publicly insulted him, so that he left town in humiliation (see 2:1–11 and 7:5–12). He then wrote another, very harsh, letter to them, which was taken to them by his companion Titus. But Titus has now returned and brought good news: the letter, and Titus' own presence, have done the trick and the Corinthians are now back on Paul's side. Paul gushes his appreciation and bubbles over with joy for their renewed relationship with them, delighted that he can now cancel his next (third) visit to them since it is no longer necessary.

But then, all of a sudden, in chapter 10 things seem to be very different indeed. The final four chapters (10–13) are not joyful in the least. Paul is bitter and incensed that the Corinthians have questioned his authority and badmouthed his person (10:2, 10–11). He threatens to come to them a "third" time in judgment, and this time he will not be lenient. And he warns the congregation against newcomers who have come into their midst, whom

he sarcastically calls "superapostles" (11:5). They evidently have claimed they are superior to Paul, as shown by their greater rhetorical skills and personal power.

Based on the stark differences between the two parts of 2 Corinthians, scholars have long thought that we have here two separate letters that were later spliced together, and that what is now the second part of the letter was actually the earlier of the two to be written. The sequence of events may have been as follows:

1. Paul made his first missionary visit to Corinth and converted people there.
2. He heard of problems in the community and then wrote 1 Corinthians.
3. He then paid a second visit to the church and was publicly humiliated and left.
4. After he left, the superapostles arrived and maligned Paul and his message.
5. Paul wrote a "painful" letter to the church there. Part of this letter is now found in 2 Corinthians 10–13, where he threatens a third visit to them.
6. Titus took the letter to the Corinthians, and they realized the errors of their ways and returned to Paul's good graces; Titus brought the good news back to Paul.
7. Overflowing with joy, Paul wrote a letter of gratitude, in which he says he can now cancel the trip as it is no longer necessary; most of this letter is now found in 2 Corinthians 1–9.
8. At a later time someone (possibly in the Corinthian congregation) took the two letters and combined them into what is now 2 Corinthians.

Much of the letter as it has come down to us reminds the Corinthians of their past relationship with Paul and exhorts them to live a life fitting of the gospel. Paul's apocalyptic views are strongly in focus, especially in his attacks on the superapostles in the painful letter of chs. 10–13. These missionary figures have gotten matters precisely wrong. This evil age is not one in which the forces of evil have been overcome. That will happen only at the end. This is an age of weakness, pain, suffering, and oppression. This is why Paul boasts of how weak and powerless he himself is (see ch. 12): that is the sign of the true apostle. Jesus himself was crucified, and those who are his followers in this age can expect to suffer as well.

GALATIANS

Galatians is one of the deepest and most profound of Paul's letters, and arguably the most intense. Even though there are some extremely dense passages in the book—some of them almost impenetrable—the situation behind it is relatively simple to reconstruct. Paul had been traveling through the region of Galatia, which is in the central part of Asia Minor, and he had taken ill and was nursed back to health in one of the cities there (we never learn which one; the letter is addressed to Christians in the entire region, who appear to have been afflicted with the same problems). He managed to convert a number of former pagans during his convalescence and some churches had sprouted up as a result. After Paul left to engage in missionary activities elsewhere, other Christian missionaries arrived and proclaimed a different gospel message from the one first delivered to them by Paul. These missionaries—whom Paul considers to be false apostles—maintained that to belong to the people of God, the Christian converts had to become part of the Jewish covenant community. That meant keeping the Jewish law. In particular, the men had to be circumcised. This was what God himself had said to the father of the Jews, Abraham, when he first made his covenant with him (Genesis 17), and God had not changed his mind or altered the rules. It was not enough to believe in Christ: one had to keep the Law as well. If Paul said otherwise, it was because he had perverted the gospel message that he had received from Jesus' own disciples in Jerusalem. It was their gospel, not Paul's, that was to be followed. Paul was not authorized to preach what he did.

Paul found this message outrageous on every level, in no small measure because a number of the Galatians evidently considered it convincing. When Paul learned of this situation he fired off this letter in white-hot anger. This is the one letter that Paul that does not begin by thanking God for the congregation. In it Paul is at times sarcastic in his attack on his Christian enemies; at one point he indicates that he hopes that the knife slips when they themselves submit to circumcision, and that they castrate themselves (5:12).

For Paul, the idea that a gentile would have to be circumcised ran completely contrary to the truth of the gospel. Circumcision, for him, was not simply a rather unpleasant operation (or rather, an enormously unpleasant one) that was unnecessary for salvation. For him, any gentile who decided to get circumcised completely misunderstood the gospel, for his actions would suggest that Christ's death and resurrection were not sufficient for salvation. And for Paul that was a totally blasphemous idea.

Paul begins the letter by giving a rare autobiographical account of his life and background and conversion (chs. 1–2), principally to show that he received his gospel not—decidedly not—from the Jerusalem apostles, but from a revelation of Christ himself. To disagree with Paul, then, is to disagree with God. Moreover, the Jerusalem apostles themselves agreed with his views at the famous Jerusalem conference. If anyone thought differently later he was just being a hypocrite, as in the case of Cephas (2:11–14). The middle of the letter lays out in forceful terms Paul's insistence that the Law cannot contribute to a person's salvation, that no one can be made right with God by doing the works of the Law, but only by faith in Jesus—whether the person is Jewish or gentile. The final two chapters of the letter stress that even though salvation comes apart from the Law, that does not mean that Christians can engage in lawless behavior. On the contrary, Christians who are empowered by the Spirit are precisely the ones who can lead lives that are pleasing to God; no one else can, because all others are still living lives "in the flesh" rather than "in the Spirit."

More than any of Paul's letters, apart from Romans, it is here in Galatians that he develops his ideas on "justification by faith, apart from works of the Law." A person is justified—that is, put in a right standing with God—only through faith in Christ's death and resurrection. The Law has nothing to do with it. Why then did God give the Law? For Paul, the Law was given to provide instruction and guidance to the Jewish people and to keep them "in line" until the fulfillment of the promises to Abraham could come (see 3:19–29). This happened with the death of the messiah. All who believe in that death are the "children of Abraham," whether Jew or gentile (4:21–30).

PHILIPPIANS

Philippians is a relatively short and seemingly simple letter, but it too has proved complicated for modern scholars to assess. For one thing, as happened in

BOX 12.5 PAUL'S GOSPEL OF SEXUAL ABSTINENCE

Paul's gospel message was principally about how a person can be right with God through the death and resurrection of Jesus. Later Christians, however, came to think that other things were equally—or even more—important for salvation. In particular, some Christians in later years came to think that what really mattered for salvation was to live for the world above rather than for life here on earth. Some of the Christians insisted that this had been the apostle's teaching from the very beginning. According to these later Christians, the way to have eternal life was to deny the body its earthly pleasures, including, most of all, the pleasures of sex. We find this message placed on Paul's lips by an author living about a century or so after his death, in the book known as the *Acts of Paul and Thecla*. This is an account of Paul's missionary preaching in which he teaches that to be saved a person should abstain from sex. This teaching is put in the form of "Beatitudes" like those known from the Sermon on the Mount. As Paul is said to have preached:

Blessed are those who have kept the flesh
    chaste, for they will become a temple of God.

Blessed are those who are self-controlled, for
    God will speak to them;
Blessed are those who have renounced this
    world, for they will be pleasing to God;
Blessed are those who have wives as if they
    did not have them, for they will be the heirs
    of God; . . .
Blessed are those who have departed from the
    shell of this world because of the love of
    God, for they will judge angels and be
    blessed at the right hand of the Father; . . .
Blessed are the bodies of the virgins, for these
    will be pleasing to God and will not lose the
    reward for their chastity; for the word of the
    Father will be an accomplished act of salva-
    tion for them on the day of his Son, and they
    will receive an eternal rest.

Just imagine how different Christianity would be if everyone had become convinced that this in fact was the historical Paul's actual preaching.

---

2 Corinthians, the tone of the letter seems to shift drastically half way through (starting with 3:2), from a joyful and friendly letter to Paul's converts in the city of Philippi, in eastern Macedonia (northeast of Thessalonica), to a severe warning against false teachers whom Paul attacks and maligns. Some scholars have thought that, as with 2 Corinthians, we are dealing here with two letters that were only later spliced together.

Whether one letter or two, the various occasions for the letter are quite clear from what Paul has to say in it. Paul was writing the letter from prison (1:7). He does not say where he was in prison or what the charges against him were. The Philippians had learned of his needs and sent him a gift of money through one of their leading members, named Epaphroditus (4:14–20). Epaphroditus had reported the situation of the church to Paul. They were experiencing persecution, and there was some division in the church centered on two women, Euodia and Syntyche, who for some reason were at odds with one another (4:2). While with Paul, Epaphroditus had become ill, "near to death," and the Philippians had learned of it and become concerned (4:25–30). But Epaphroditus had recovered, and Paul was sending him back with this letter. The letter explains Paul's situation and thanks the church for their moral and material support. In the letter Paul also urges the congregation to strive for unity—especially with respect to the two feuding women. And he spends a good bit of time explaining that hardship such as both he and they are facing can lead to the success of the Gospel (e.g., 1:12–26).

In all these exhortations Paul is concerned that the Philippians manifest deep love for one another, caring more for others than for themselves. In that context, in 2:6–11 Paul recites a kind of hymn or poem that was composed either by himself or someone else about what Christ had done for the sake of others—leaving behind the glory that was his in order to become a human, and as a human to die on the cross. As a result of Christ's act of humility, in which he became a slave for the sake of others, God exalted him to a position even higher than he had before, so that now he is lord of all. Christians should follow Christ's example of self-denial and self-giving for the sake of others. By implication, if they do so they too will be exalted.

This, in Paul's view, is what Epaphroditus had done (his trip almost killed him), and what Paul himself was striving to do, to the point of being willing to be imprisoned for the sake of the gospel. And it was what all Christians should do, as they imitate their Lord whose kind and selfless acts brought salvation to the world.

PHILEMON

Paul's letter to Philemon is unique among the undisputed letters for several reasons. It is by far the shortest letter—long enough only to fill a single papyrus page. This, as it turns out, is about the normal length for a letter in the Greco-Roman world; Paul's other letters are monstrously large by comparison. Moreover, this is the only letter of Paul's written to an individual. The recipient is Philemon, one of Paul's converts who appears to be the head of a Christian community. Traditionally it has been thought that the church was located in the town of Colossae, but there is no way to know for sure.

Paul was writing from prison and for a specific purpose. Philemon owned a slave named Onesimus who had run off, possibly taking some of his master's money with him (v. 18). Onesimus had met up with Paul—either because he himself had been thrown in prison or because he had tracked Paul down. The latter seems more likely: the Roman Empire was an enormous place, and it seems improbable that the slave of Paul's convert would just happen to end up in the same jail cell. Moreover, it was a legally recognized practice in the Roman world for a slave who had incurred his master's wrath to appeal to a trusted friend of the master for intervention and protection. That appears to be what was happening here.

As it turns out, after meeting with Paul Onesimus had converted to become a Christian. Paul is writing Philemon to urge him to receive Onesimus back without punishing him, as a brother in the faith. If Onesimus owes Philemon anything (for example, by having stolen something), Paul himself will pay.

Some readers have thought that Paul was actually urging Philemon to set Onesimus free. But the letter says nothing about that, and that interpretation may be wishful thinking by more enlightened readers of the modern period who recognize the evils of slavery. Instead, Paul stresses that Onesimus has been "useful" to him (a play on words: the name Onesimus means "useful"). Moreover, he asks Philemon to "provide me with a benefit" (v. 20). This has led to some speculation: is Paul asking Philemon, who is deeply in his debt (as his convert), to present him with a gift in the person of Onesimus, the slave?

ROMANS

The letter to the Romans has been, historically, the most influential of Paul's writings. In no small measure that is because Paul uses this letter to wrestle with many of the key theological issues of his day. The book expresses some of the most fundamental aspects of Paul's understanding of the Gospel. It is because of its occasion and purpose that this letter, better than any other, reveals Paul's understanding of his message and mission.

The Occasion and Purpose of the Letter

Romans is the only Pauline letter that is not addressed to a church that Paul himself founded, written in order to deal with the problems it was experiencing. Paul makes it quite clear that he had never yet been to Rome, let alone started the church there (1:10–15). And yet a careful reading of the letter shows that in it Paul lays out the essential characteristics of his gospel message and the implications that he draws from it (as we will see). Why would he need to explain himself to a church he had neither founded nor visited? A clue may come at the end of the letter, where he indicates that he very much wants to come to Rome and to use the church there as a base of operation for a further mission to the west, as far as Spain (15:23–24). It appears that Paul would like the Christians in Rome to provide moral and financial support for this mission.

But throughout the letter Paul appears not only to explain his views about the gospel but also to defend them. That suggests that Paul's lengthy discourse (this is the longest of his letters) was written because the Romans had only a dim knowledge of who he was and what he stood for, or, even worse, that they had heard a good deal about him and were suspicious of him, his mission, and his message (see, e.g., 3:8; 6:1, 15; 7:1). If that is the case, Paul wrote the letter in order to give a full accounting of himself, to explain what he stood for, to explicate in the clearest terms he could the essence of his gospel message, and by so doing to assuage the fears of his readers—all in an effort to win the support of his mission to the west. That is why, of all Paul's letters, Romans provides us with the clearest exposition of his proclamation.

The Theme of the Letter

After the standard opening of the letter, where Paul names himself and his recipients and offers a prayer of thanksgiving for them, he states the theme of his writing:

> For I am not ashamed of the gospel; it is the power of God for salvation to everyone who has faith, to the Jew first and also to the Greek. For in it the righteousness of God is revealed through faith for faith; as it is written, "The one who is righteous will live by faith" (1:16–17).

This theme statement deserves a careful unpacking. First, Paul is not ashamed of the gospel. He rather is proud of what his gospel message is. And the reason: this gospel is God's powerful means of salvation; by implication, there is no other means. This salvation comes to those who have faith. The word "faith" is an English translation of the Greek word that in its verbal form means "to believe." Faith for Paul is not a matter of intellectual assent to a set of propositions about God, Christ, the resurrection, or anything else. Faith is a wholehearted conviction and commitment to something, a complete trust. Paul stresses in this letter that the salvation of God comes to those who believe in Christ—that is, to those who have full trust in his death and resurrection to bring about a right standing before God. This salvation comes to the Jew first, and then to the Greek (by which Paul means "to the gentile"). Jews were the first to receive this gospel, since Jesus was himself a Jew; but now it has equally gone to the gentiles. This gospel reveals God's righteousness. It is "right" for God to save both Jew and gentile, and by doing so he has not gone back on his promises

to his people the Jews. This is a major theme of Romans: God is still the God of the Jews. Jesus' death and resurrection are a fulfillment of the promises to the Jews; it is this work of Christ that God has used to bring salvation to both Jew and gentile. The Jewish Scriptures themselves proclaim this gospel. Here Paul quotes the Prophet Habakkuk about living by faith. For Paul, those who are made right with God through faith will find life, as the prophet himself foresaw.

Pauline Models for Salvation

Before sketching how Paul lays out his gospel message in Romans, it may be useful to consider in broader terms what Paul has to say about his gospel message. One of the difficulties with Paul's writings is that he conceptualizes the act of God's salvation in different ways, using different models for explaining how it is that the death and resurrection of Jesus can bring about salvation. Among the various models that Paul uses (these are not the only ones) are two that we can call the "**judicial model**" and the "**participationist model**." These models each have a different conceptual basis, but Paul does not see them as at odds with one another. They are simply different ways of trying to imagine, and explain, how the death and resurrection of Jesus "work" in order to bring salvation to people who are alienated from God.

THE JUDICIAL MODEL   There should be no difficulty understanding the judicial model, since it uses ideas and images that are familiar to us from our own experience. In this model God is imagined and portrayed as both a lawgiver and a judge. God has given people a law and, unfortunately, they have broken it. All of them have broken it. For this model, this is what is meant by "sin"—an act of disobedience to the law of God. And since God is a judge, he has found people guilty because of their sin and condemned them to pay a penalty. The penalty, in every case, is death. And so everyone is subject to the death penalty because everyone has sinned.

In this model, Christ dies in order to pay the penalty that everyone else owes. Imagine it in other terms: if the penalty for a crime were a fine, and the criminal could not pay the fine, in theory he could find someone to pay his fine for him and he would be set free. In this case the penalty owed is death, and Jesus willingly pays it for others. And

God accepts the payment. The proof that he accepts payment is that Jesus is raised from the dead; he is raised because the debt has been paid, and needs to be paid no more. Jesus' resurrection shows that the payment "worked." But it works only if those who actually owe the penalty accept payment. And that is what faith is—a trusting acceptance of Jesus' death as the payment of the penalty the person owes for sin. In this model, the Law cannot save a person. The Law is part of the problem: by breaking it, people have incurred a penalty. The solution can come only outside the Law, by Christ who paid the penalty that others owed, as received by faith.

THE PARTICIPATIONIST MODEL   The participationist model is very different indeed. Careful readers of Paul will have noted that "sin" for him is not only an act of disobedience; sometimes he refers to sin as a cosmic power in the world that is trying to enslave people and force them to do what it wants (see Romans 5–7). In this model sin is still the human problem, but not in the judicial sense that people have committed acts of disobedience; it is instead in the apocalyptic sense that sin has enslaved people and forced them into alienation from God. But if the problem is enslavement, the solution has to be liberation. And it is Jesus' death that brings the liberation.

In the participationist model Jesus took sin into himself and then died on the cross, in effect killing the power of sin. And the resurrection is again key—not because it shows that God accepted payment of the penalty (as in the judicial model), but because it shows that Christ conquered the power of death. And if he conquered the greatest power, death, then he must have conquered the other powers as well, including the power of sin.

That may explain how Jesus himself escaped the powers of sin and death—but how does it relate to humans? In this model, the salvation that Christ provides others is not received by faith (a trusting acceptance of the payment, as in the other model) but by baptism. Paul believed that when a person is baptized as a follower of Jesus, he or she is, in a mystical way, united with Christ in his death. Just as Christ went into the ground after his death, the person being baptized goes under the water. At that moment the person "participates" in the death of Christ by becoming (mystically) one with him (which is why I call this the participationist model). And since the person is united with Christ in his baptism, that means that the person has experienced, with Christ, liberation from the power of sin.

And so Christ sets people free from the powers that enslave the world when they are baptized into him. This view of things can be found especially in Romans 6, but it lies behind much of what Paul says in Romans 5–8.

The Two Models Compared

And so in both models the problem is "sin." But in one of them "sin" is an act of disobedience and in the other it is a cosmic power. In both, the solution to the problem is Jesus' death. But in one it is because that death paid the penalty that others owed,

FIGURE 12.7.   Baptism was an important Christian ritual for Paul's churches (see Romans 6:1–6) and it continued to be significant down through the centuries. Pictured here is the baptistery of the oldest surviving Christian church (in the city of Dura, Syria), from about two centuries after Paul.

BOX 12.6 OTHER MODELS OF SALVATION IN PAUL

In addition to the judicial and participationist models, Paul has other ways of conceptualizing God's act of salvation in Christ, even though he rarely explains how the analogies work in detail. Consider, for instance, the following:

- Sometimes Paul likens salvation to a reconciliation in which two people have had a falling out. A mediator (Christ), at a sacrifice to himself, intervenes and restores their relationship (e.g., see Romans 5:10 and 2 Corinthians 5:18–20).
- Paul often describes salvation as a redemption in which a person's life is "purchased" by God through the price of Christ's blood, much as a slave might be purchased by gold (Romans 3:24; 8:23). Never does he explain, however, from whom or what the person is being purchased (the cosmic forces? the devil? sin?).
- Paul sometimes portrays Chris's death as a sacrifice that, like the sacrifices of animals in the Jewish

Temple, was designed to bring atonement with God. This view embodies the ancient view that the blood of a sacrifice "covers over" the sins of the people: the technical term for this act of covering is "expiation" (Romans 5:25).
- At other times Paul compares salvation to a rescue from physical danger, in which a person is confronted with peril and certain death only to be saved by someone who heroically intervenes at the cost of his own life (see Romans 5:7–8).

These models are not mutually exclusive; sometimes Paul applies several of them even within the same passage. Consider for yourself the theologically packed statement of Romans 3:21–2, where Paul uses the judicial, participationist, redemptive, and sacrificial models at the same time.

and in the other it is because Jesus' death conquered the powers aligned against God. In both models the resurrection is absolutely fundamental. But in one it is because it shows that the penalty has been accepted as paid in full, and in the other it is because it demonstrates that the cosmic powers have been defeated. In both models the follower of Christ can have salvation because of Jesus' death and resurrection. But in one it is through a trusting acceptance of Christ's death and in the other it is by being baptized into his death.

Paul did not see these models in opposition; in fact, in his thinking, they wove themselves together in complicated ways. The reason everyone sins (= commits acts of disobedience) is because everyone is enslaved to sin (= a cosmic power); the reason everyone is enslaved to sin is because the first man, Adam, sinned (disobedience) and that brought sin (cosmic power) into the world. The person who has faith (trusting acceptance of the payment) will also be baptized (participating in the victory). And so on.

More than any other book, Romans presupposes these two models. When you read through the book again, pay special attention to what Paul has to say about "sin," and ask yourself, in every instance, what he appears to mean by it; and pay attention to what he says about the importance of

faith, baptism, atoning sacrifice, and the powers opposed to God.

The Flow of Paul's Argument

Finally I can give a very brief outline of how the argument of Romans works, from section to section.

The Human Dilemma: All are Condemned (1:18–3:20). Both gentile (1:18–32) and Jew (2:1–29) are alienated from God, because all have sinned (judicial notion: 3:1–8) and all are under the power of sin (participationist 3:9). This is the view of the Jewish Scriptures themselves (3:10–20).

The Divine Solution: Salvation through Christ's Death (3:21–31). Jesus' sacrifice, not the Jewish law, provides the solution, so that Jews and gentiles are on equal footing before God.

The Gospel Message is rooted in Scripture (4:1–25). Scripture itself shows that Abraham was justified by trust in God, rather than by following the Law.

Christ's Death and Resurrection Bring Freedom from the Powers Opposed to God (5:1–8:39). Believers are saved from God's coming wrath (5:1–11) and from the death brought in by Adam's sin (5:12–21); those united with Christ have overcome the power of death and sin (6:1–23), and so no longer have to be enslaved to sin (7:1–25); the human "flesh" which was enslaved to sin no longer needs to submit to this power (8:1–17). Eventually the powers will be destroyed altogether and salvation will finally come (8:18–39).

The Gospel Message is Consistent with God's Dealings with Israel and Represents a Fulfillment of His Promises (9:1–11:36). This is the key portion of the letter. The salvation that God has provided in Christ is not a violation of his promises to the Jews, but is consistent with the way he has always worked, since he has always chosen people on the basis of his own will, not on the basis of works. Jews are wrong to think the Law is a means of salvation. Many Jews have been faithless, but God is faithful and he will save all Jews; the salvation of the gentiles is intended to make Jews jealous so they will turn back to God, thus fulfilling the divine plan for his chosen people and the world.

The Law-free Gospel Does not Lead to Lawless Behavior (12:1–15:13). Believers in Christ are to live in self-sacrificing love for one another and to lead upright lives following the ethical demands of God.

Close of the Letter (15:14–16:27). Paul concludes by explaining why he wrote, discussing his travel plans, and sending greetings to a number of people in the congregation.

CONCLUSION

Romans is the last letter we have from Paul's hand, and it is impossible to know whether he ended up making Rome the base for his mission to Spain. According to the book of Acts he was arrested in Jerusalem before making his trip west, but ended up in Rome anyway as he was to stand trial there before the emperor. That seems a bit unlikely historically (the emperor was a rather busy fellow). But it may be true that Paul did end up in Rome. Later tradition indicates that he was martyred there in the year 64 C.E., during the persecution of Christians under the reign of Emperor Nero.

At a Glance: The Undisputed Letters of Paul

Nearly all of Paul's undisputed letters are written to churches he had established, to help them deal with problems that had arisen after he had left to start new communities of faith elsewhere. The following are the major occasions and themes for each of the letters:

- I Thessalonians is written principally to comfort the Christians in Thessalonica who were suffering and who misunderstood Paul's teaching about the imminent return of Jesus, who would soon come from heaven to raise the dead, and then the living, to eternal life.
- I Corinthians addresses a multitude of problems that had arisen in the church of Corinth involving dissension, immorality, and false teaching. Paul deals with each problem individually before addressing the overarching issue of the nature of the future bodily resurrection.
- 2 Corinthians appears to be two separate letters: one a letter of warning (chs. 10–13) in which Paul threatens to come to the community again in anger, and the other a later letter (chs. 1–9) of comfort written after the tensions he had had with the church had been resolved.

- Galatians is an angry letter written to oppose Christian missionaries who argued, with good success, that the gentile Christians in the region of Galatia had to be circumcised and keep other aspects of the Jewish law to be fully right with God.
- Philippians is a joyful letter written to the Christians of Philippi to thank them for their financial gift, to urge them to be unified, and to encourage them to react joyfully to their suffering.
- Philemon is the one letter of Paul's written to an individual. Paul urges Philemon to accept back without punishment his runaway slave Onesimus, who has now become a Christian.
- Romans is the only letter of Paul's not written to his own church and converts. In it Paul wants to explain in full his gospel message in an effort to convince the church in Rome to support him in his mission to the west. As such, this letter explains more fully than any other Paul's gospel of salvation through Christ—using both the judicial and participationist models—and the implications of that salvation for the relationship of Jews and gentiles.

Take a Stand

1. Your instructor has set up an informal debate in your class on the question of whether it is easier to know about the teachings of Paul or the teachings of Jesus. What do you think? Take either side of the issue and argue it thoroughly and carefully.

2. Your best friend tells you that in her Sunday School class, her teacher has argued that when Paul became a Christian he stopped being a Jew. Do you agree or not? Explain your reasons.

3. How does knowing the context of the Pauline letters help explain their message? Choose one of the undisputed Pauline letters and make your case.

Key Terms

Deutero-Pauline epistles, 299
Judicial Model, 319

Participationist Model, 319

Pastoral epistles, 299
Pseudepigrapha, 298

Undisputed Pauline epistles, 299

Suggestions for Further Reading

NB: For this and all chapters, see the relevant articles (e.g., "Genesis") in the works cited in the Suggestions for Further Reading in chapter 1.

Dunn, James D. *The Theology of Paul the Apostle*. Grand Rapids: Eerdmans, 1998. A clear and full overview of the major theological views of Paul, by a leading British New Testament scholar.

Fitzmyer, Joseph. I *Pauline Theology: A Brief Sketch*. 2nd ed. Englewood Cliffs, N.J.: Prentice Hall, 1989. An excellent overview of Paul's teachings by a prominent Roman Catholic scholar, for beginning students.

Keck, Leander. *Paul and His Letters*. Philadelphia: Fortress, 1979. An insightful overview of Paul's theology as expressed in his letters.

Roetzel, Calvin. *The Letters of Paul: Conversations in Context*. 3rd ed. Atlanta: John Knox, 1991. Perhaps the best introductory discussion of each of the Pauline epistles.

Wedderburn, A. J. M. *The Reasons for Romans*. Edinburgh: T&T Clark, 1988. The most complete book-length discussion of the reasons that Paul wrote his letter to the Romans.

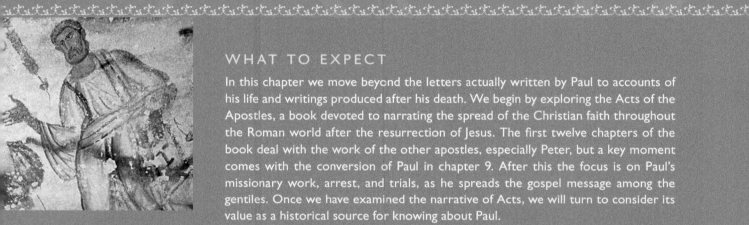

13

The Acts of the Apostles
and the Deutero-Pauline Epistles

WHAT TO EXPECT

In this chapter we move beyond the letters actually written by Paul to accounts of his life and writings produced after his death. We begin by exploring the Acts of the Apostles, a book devoted to narrating the spread of the Christian faith throughout the Roman world after the resurrection of Jesus. The first twelve chapters of the book deal with the work of the other apostles, especially Peter, but a key moment comes with the conversion of Paul in chapter 9. After this the focus is on Paul's missionary work, arrest, and trials, as he spreads the gospel message among the gentiles. Once we have examined the narrative of Acts, we will turn to consider its value as a historical source for knowing about Paul.

We will then move to the six Deutero-Pauline epistles, letters that claim to be written by Paul but that were almost certainly written by other authors simply *claiming* to be Paul. In each case we will consider the occasion and major themes of the letter, as well as the reasons scholars have invoked for thinking that Paul in fact did not write them.

Now that we have studied the life and teachings of the apostle Paul, we can move on to consider ways that Paul was understood and portrayed in later times, after his death. Our focus in this chapter will be on the Acts of the Apostles, in which Paul plays a central role, and the Deutero-Pauline epistles, the letters that have a secondary standing in the Pauline canon. The reason for this secondary standing is that these six books of Ephesians, Colossians, 2 Thessalonians, 1 and 2 Timothy, and Titus were probably not written by the apostle but by later authors claiming to be him. That is to say, they are all pseudepigraphic. Before exploring these later expressions of Pauline Christianity in some detail, it may be useful to say some general things

about how Paul was understood in his own time and later.

PAUL DURING AND AFTER THE NEW TESTAMENT

One could argue that Paul was even more important after his lifetime than during it. Many people think of Paul as the most significant figure in early Christianity outside of Jesus, and rightly so, for reasons we have seen. But there are some indications that at the time, in say, the 50s of the Common Era, Paul was not as central a figure as he became later. For one thing, it is worth noting that in just about all the churches Paul established he had opponents whose views differed radically from his and whom he saw as endangering his mission and message. These people must have been a threat. And there seems to have been so many of them! That would suggest that in his own day, Paul was one voice among many. His was the voice that won out, but that may not have been the obvious outcome at the time. Moreover, these opponents of Paul were not all advocating the same views. His opponents in Galatia, for example, maintained that true followers of Jesus needed to accept circumcision and keep the Jewish law. Paul replied, hot with anger. His opponents in Corinth, on the other hand, maintained that they were already leading a resurrected existence and were enjoying the full benefits of salvation. Paul thought this too was utterly wrong. It is interesting that some of the people in Corinth who bought into this "aberrant" message belonged to the faction that claimed Paul as their hero and leader (1 Corinthians 1:12).

And so there are two major points to make: in his own day, Paul was not universally regarded as the ultimate apostolic authority whose views alone could be accepted as true, and even those who did appeal to his authority advocated views, at times, that he found objectionable.

None of that changes, but rather it intensifies in the decades after Paul's death. By the second century there are some groups of Christians who consider Paul the archenemy. These are the spiritual descendants of Paul's opponents in Galatia, Jewish Christians who continue to think that to follow Jesus means adhering to the Jewish law. From this perspective Paul, who stressed justification by faith apart from the Law, got it precisely wrong. Other Christian groups revered Paul but despised each other—each group claiming that it had the "true" interpretation of Paul. And so, for example, some groups of Gnostics insisted that Paul advocated their point of view; other Christians from the "orthodox" tradition insisted that no, Paul supported *their* point of view. And so it went.

Each of these various groups produced writings that attested their various theological perspectives, produced by authors claiming to be Paul. And so, for example, we know of forgeries in Paul's name from the second century, such as 3 Corinthians—a book that vehemently attacks the Gnostic claim that believers need to escape their flesh in order to have salvation (see Box 13.3). We also have a letter that Paul allegedly sent to the church of Laodicea (see Colossians 4:17) and a set of fourteen letters that supposedly went back and forth between Paul and the greatest philosopher of his day, Seneca. All of these books were forged in the name of Paul; none of them appears to represent the views of the historical Paul.

We also have accounts of Paul's life from later sources, including one book from the second century that is called the "**Acts of Paul**." This narrative is filled with terrific, but highly legendary, accounts of Paul. In one of the most famous portions of the book, Paul converts a wealthy aristocratic woman named Thecla, who overhears a sermon that Paul delivers next door. But this sermon is unlike anything you will find from Paul's pen in the New Testament. In it Paul claims that the way to have eternal life is to practice sexual renunciation, even if you are married (see Box 12.5). Here it is not faith in the death and resurrection of Jesus that matters, but a person's ongoing virginity. Thecla finds this message compelling and converts to be a follower of Paul (and through him, of Jesus), much to the consternation of her family and, especially, her fiancé. She unceremoniously calls off the wedding so that she can lead a life of abstinence. This decision leads to a range of very interesting stories, as Thecla is denounced and condemned to death—on a couple of occasions—for violating all the acceptable norms of her society, only to be saved miraculously by divine interventions time and again.

In another story in the Acts of Paul, the apostle is traveling through the wilderness and meets up with a talking lion who asks to be baptized. Paul graciously complies. Much later, when Paul is condemned to execution, he is taken into the arena to fight the wild beasts. And who should appear by his side but his friend, the talking lion. They both miraculously escape and go their merry ways.

None of these stories (especially the lion!) has any historical basis. Still, they are valuable for showing how Paul came to be understood and portrayed in later times. But one does not need to wait until the second century to see Paul represented in ways that differ from his own self-presentation in the seven undisputed Pauline epistles. One can see this already in the writings of the New Testament, especially in the Acts of the Apostles and the Deutero-Pauline Epistles.

THE ACTS OF THE APOSTLES

We have already learned a few things about the book of Acts in some of our earlier discussions.

It is the one and only history of the earliest church in the New Testament, which narrates how Christianity spread throughout the Roman world through the missionary work of the apostles. A key figure here is Paul, who after his conversion becomes the central character of the book for about two-thirds of its narrative. The plot covers just over 30 years, from the resurrection of Jesus until the imprisonment of Paul in Rome prior to his death.

The book was written by the same author who produced the Gospel of Luke. It is dedicated to the same person, Theophilus; and at the beginning the author reminds his reader what the first volume contained (Acts 1:1–4). In some sense, then, we can consider Luke–Acts to be a two volume work. Somewhat unusually for the ancient world (or the modern one, for that matter), these two volumes are actually different genres of literature. But that is more or less because of the nature of the material. Luke (as I will continue to call him) really had little choice. The Gospel, of course, is about the birth, life, death, and resurrection of Jesus, and so was naturally written as a kind of religious biography— just as the other Gospels of the New Testament were. The book of Acts, however, is not about a single individual. Even though Paul figures prominently in it, he does not make an appearance until chapter 7. Acts is really about the spread of the Christian movement, from its inauspicious beginnings among a small group of Jesus' followers in Jerusalem, throughout the Roman Empire. It is more like a "history" of a people, such as you can find in other ancient historians; for example the history of the Jews in Josephus's 20-volume history, *The Antiquities of the Jews*.

A history of a people that is arranged in chronological sequence is called a **general history**, and that is the kind of book Acts is. We should not have the same expectations of ancient general histories as we do of historical books produced in our own day. Ancient historians did not have massive archives to turn to, or data retrieval systems; they often preferred oral traditions to written sources; and a lot of times they simply had to make things up for their narratives to hold together. That was especially the case with public speeches. Most general histories from antiquity contain numerous speeches by the main characters of the action; these speeches often take up something like a fourth of an entire book. That is the certainly the case with the book of Acts as well, where the apostles regularly deliver speeches to non-Christian crowds in order to convert them, to Christian communities to build them up, and to ruling authorities to defend their own actions. Ancient historians, such as the famous Greek **Thucydides**, were quite forthright that they had no real access to the speeches they narrated, as these were delivered years, decades, or even centuries earlier. No one took notes. And so Thucydides indicates that when he put a speech on the lips of one

---

BOX 13.1 LUKE'S ARTISTRY AS A STORY TELLER I

Readers of the New Testament have long noticed many clear similarities between what happens to Jesus in the Gospel of Luke and to Christian believers in the book of Acts. These parallels show that Luke was no mere chronicler of events, set on providing an objective account of the early years of the Christian movement. He compiled this history with a clear purpose, part of which was to show that the hand of God was behind the mission of the church as much as it was behind the mission of Jesus. Thus, for example, at the beginning of Jesus' ministry in Luke, he is baptized and receives the Holy Spirit; when new believers are baptized in the book of Acts, they also receive the Spirit. The Spirit empowers Jesus to do miracles and to preach in Luke; so too it empowers the apostles to do miracles and to preach in Acts. In Luke, Jesus heals the sick, casts out demons, and raises the dead; in Acts, the apostles heal the sick, cast out demons, and raise the dead. The Jewish authorities in Jerusalem confront Jesus in Luke; the same authorities confront the apostles in Acts. Jesus is imprisoned, condemned, and executed in Luke; some of his followers are imprisoned, condemned, and executed in Acts.

These parallels are not simply interesting coincidences. One author has produced both books, and he uses the parallel accounts to make a major point: the apostles continue to do Jesus' work and thereby prolong his mission through the power of the same Spirit. Thus they engage in similar activities, experience similar receptions, and suffer similar fates.

of his characters, he necessarily made it up himself and tried to come up with something that was both appropriate for the occasion and plausible for that particular character. Luke has done the same thing. Modern historians could never get away with that; but we are dealing with ancient literature here, not with books written last year.

The Beginning of the Narrative

Luke begins his narrative right where he left off in the Gospel of Luke, with the appearance of Jesus to his disciples after the resurrection. In Acts he indicates that Jesus spent forty days with them, presenting them with "many proofs" (1:3) that he was alive again (a rather odd statement: one wonders how many proofs would be necessary) and speaking to them about the kingdom of God. The disciples think that now Jesus has been raised, the end is surely about to come, and they ask him if now is the time. In response, Jesus delivers one of the key statements of the entire narrative:

> It is not for you to know the times or the seasons that the Father has set in his own authority. But you will receive power when the Holy Spirit comes upon you, and you will be my witnesses both in Jerusalem, and in all of Judea, and Samaria, even to the end of the earth. (1:7–8)

In some ways this can be considered a kind of programmatic statement for all that happens in the rest of Luke's narrative. In Acts 2, as we will see, the disciples receive the Holy Spirit on the Day of Pentecost. Just as Jesus was empowered by the Spirit at his baptism, so too are they. The Spirit-filled apostles begin to spread the gospel message of Jesus in Jerusalem. They then move outside of Jerusalem into the surrounding country of Judea and on to Samaria. Then, for the bulk of the book, they (or at least Paul and his companions) spread the gospel through gentile lands until it finally comes to Rome.

The spread of Christianity in this book will not only be geographical, but also ethnic. At the beginning it will be Jews who convert, in Jerusalem; in Acts 8 the "half-Jews" of Samaria receive the Spirit; and then starting in Acts 10 it is gentiles who come to faith. One of the major issues addressed by the book is the same one that Paul himself had to deal with years earlier in his letters: do these gentiles need to become Jews in order to be Christians? Acts has the same view as Paul: the answer is a resounding no.

Back to the beginning. After Jesus gives his final words to his disciples in Acts 1:8, he ascends to heaven in full sight of them all. Soon thereafter all the followers of Jesus gather together (now there are said to be 120 of them somehow), and Peter delivers his first speech to them. In it he describes how Judas Iscariot met his fate after betraying Jesus. It is an interesting account (1:18–19), in part because it seems to stand at odds with the only other discussion of Judas's death in Matthew 27:3–10 (read the two accounts and try to figure out the differences: ask yourself who bought the field Judas died on, why was it called the "field of blood," and how did he die?). Peter goes on to say that the apostles must choose another apostle to take Judas' place, since there need to be twelve of them. It is not completely clear why that is the case: as readers have frequently noted, most of the apostles play virtually no role in the rest of Acts, and the book never indicates why there must be twelve. But Peter sees this as a divine necessity, and he quotes two passages of Scripture to show that so it has been foreordained (1:20). This in itself is interesting. For Luke, who was the author both of this account and of this speech (remember: no one was taking notes. Luke was writing some fifty years later), the Scriptures not only predicted what would happen to Jesus (see Luke 24:27) but also what was to happen in the church. The early Christian community was actually predicted, for Luke, by the Old Testament prophets.

The Day of Pentecost

The next major event happens in Acts 2, on the Day of Pentecost. Pentecost was another annual Jewish feast, celebrated fifty days after Passover. In this account, the followers of Jesus are gathered together on the occasion and they suddenly hear a sound like a strong wind and see tongues like fire alighting on one another's heads. They begin to speak in foreign languages that none of them has previously learned. They are outdoors when this happens, and other "nonbelievers" (that is, Jews who were not Christian) who have come from different countries for the feast hear them and marvel because they are preaching the gospel to them in their own native tongues.

This narrative is clearly meant to show that the gospel will go to other lands and its spread will be empowered by the Holy Spirit that comes upon believers. In this instance the outsiders mock the Christians for being drunk, which gives Peter another occasion to stand up and give a speech. It is a very interesting speech, the first evangelistic message recorded from early Christianity. Peter declares that what has just happened is a fulfillment of prophecy (2:17; quoting Joel 2:28). And he quickly shifts to talk about Jesus, whom he describes as a mighty man who did amazing miracles, who was lawlessly executed by evil people but vindicated by God who raised him from the dead.

It is important at this point to recall what we found in the Gospel of Luke, that Jesus' death was not portrayed as an atoning sacrifice but as a reason to realize your guilt before God and to repent, so that God would forgive you (see p. 264). That is exactly what happens here. Peter never says that Jesus died for the sins of others. He says that these people (from around the world) are guilty for killing Jesus and so they should repent for the forgiveness of sins. And it works. Three thousand people convert right away and are baptized.

This is the beginning of an amazing ministry in Jerusalem by the apostles. Now that they have the Holy Spirit they can do miracles just as Jesus did. In the next chapter Peter and John heal a lame man, and the crowds are amazed. Peter takes the opportunity to preach another sermon about how Jesus was wrongfully killed but God raised him from the dead, just as the prophets predicted. And five thousand more people convert (Acts 4:1–5:4). We are obviously dealing with exaggerated numbers here. At this rate there won't be any non-Christians left in all of Jerusalem.

But at this point another of Luke's key themes comes into play. Peter and John are opposed by the Jewish leaders—just as Jesus had been before them. Throughout the narrative of Acts, God will work miracles through the apostles; the Jewish authorities will oppose them, the apostles will be persecuted and prosecuted, but God will nonetheless work through their preaching and save the masses.

The Conversion of Paul

There are a number of stories told in these opening chapters of Acts about the apostles and their work

FIGURE 13.1. Peter, Jesus, and Paul, the three most important characters of Luke–Acts, from a catacomb painting in Rome.

in Jerusalem. One of the overarching themes is that there is complete unity among all those who convert to the faith and, especially, among the apostles themselves. Outsiders may try to infiltrate the apostolic band; there may be persecution from the Jewish authorities; there may be weighty theological issues that have to be resolved; difficulties of one sort or another may arise. But since the apostles are guided by the Spirit there will be no dissension within their ranks and no trace of disunity. This portrayal of the absolute cohesion and unity of the early Christian community stands in some tension, obviously, with what we previously have seen from the writings of Paul.

In chapter 7 of Acts is the account of the first Christian martyr, Stephen, who is put on trial before the Jewish authorities and delivers a very long speech that shows that Jesus fulfilled the predictions of the Old Testament narratives. Highly aggravated by Stephen's claims, the Jewish crowd attacks him and stones him to death. And we are told that present at the stoning was "a young man named Saul." That is the Hebrew name of the person we have come to know so well by his Greek name, Paul.

The account goes on to describe Saul's persecution of the Christians (8:1–3). But then one of the key events of the book occurs. Saul, the great persecutor of the church, is traveling to the city of Damascus when Jesus appears to him in a blinding light. Saul realizes that Jesus is in fact raised from the dead, and he becomes a believer (ch. 9). He makes his way into Damascus, where he meets a Christian named Ananias who heals his blindness. Saul immediately begins a preaching ministry.

We have already seen from Paul's own letters that he considered himself the apostle to the gentiles, and one might well think that he was the one who came up with the idea that gentiles could follow Jesus without first becoming Jews. But this is not the view of the author of Acts. Acts goes out of its way to show that on this point there was complete unity in the apostolic community, in no small part because God revealed this truth first to Peter, not to Paul. In a highly significant narrative in chapters 10–11, Peter is shown in a dream from God that it is not important to keep the kosher food laws, and he is instructed to go to the city of Caesarea to speak with a Roman centurion Cornelius. Peter obeys, and addresses Cornelius and other gentiles gathered in his house. As he is speaking, the Holy Spirit comes upon them all and they are converted and baptized. Peter realizes that this means that gentiles can receive the Spirit just as Jews can, and that it is not necessary for them to adopt the ways of Judaism in order to believe and be baptized. He returns and reports his findings to the Jerusalem apostles (ch. 11).

BOX 13.2 LUKE'S ARTISTRY AS A STORY TELLER 2

Luke's literary artistry is not limited to creating parallels between the Gospel and Acts (see Box 13.1). Just as interesting are the parallels between the main characters in the narrative of Acts itself, particularly between Peter, the main character of chapters 1–12, and Paul, the main character of chapters 13–28.

Several examples of these parallels stand out. Both Peter and Paul preach sermons to Jewish crowds, and what they have to say is in many respects remarkably similar (e.g., see the speeches in chapters 3 and 13). Both perform amazing miracles: both, for example, cure the sick without having any direct contact with them. Thus Peter's shadow can bring healing (5:15), as can Paul's handkerchiefs (19:12). Both are violently opposed by leaders among the Jews but vindicated by God; they are imprisoned for their proclamation yet delivered from their chains by divine intervention (12:1–11; 16:19–34). Perhaps most important of all, both become absolutely convinced, on the grounds of divine revelation and the success of their proclamation, that God has decided to admit gentiles into the church without their first becoming Jews (chapters 10–11, 15). These parallels reinforce our earlier impression that throughout this narrative Luke is intent on showing that God is at work in the Christian mission. Those who are faithful to God give similar speeches with similar results; they perform similar miracles, receive similar revelations, and experience similar fates. Luke's artistry, then, serves a clear thematic purpose.

The Missionary Journeys of Paul

A key shift in the narrative occurs in Acts 13. Up to this point, Peter has obviously been the main character of the action. Some of the other apostles, such as John, appear on occasion, but for the most part this is an account of the activities of Peter. All of that changes with chapter 13. Paul and his companion Barnabas are commissioned to go forth and spread the gospel abroad. And they do so. From chapter 13 to chapter 20 Paul engages in his three missionary journeys to cities in Asia Minor, Macedonia, and Achaia—places mentioned as well in Paul's own letters. Unlike Paul's letters, in this account Paul invariably first goes to the local synagogue of whatever town he is in and preaches the gospel of Christ to the Jews there, in some places for weeks. But just as invariably he rouses opposition among the Jewish leaders, who drive him out of the synagogue and sometimes punish him more severely, for example by beatings. Once he is actually stoned, but rather than dying like any other normal human being he simply gets up afterward and continues to the next town to preach there (14:19–20). For the book of Acts, there is no stopping the Christian mission or its leading missionary Paul. The Spirit is in charge and the mission will go forward.

Paul's evangelistic sermons are very interesting, not least because they sound almost exactly like Peter's evangelistic sermons from the beginning of the book. Read Paul's speech in chapter 13 and compare it to Peter's in chapter 3. The words of the uneducated Galilean fisherman Peter could have been delivered by the Hellenistic intellectual Paul, and vice versa. And why is that? It is because neither one of these persons actually delivered these speeches. They were composed by Luke. It is especially striking that Paul's characteristic emphases from his own letters play almost no role in his sermons in Acts—for example, that Jesus' death was an atoning sacrifice and that his resurrection is the key to salvation.

After the first missionary journey of chapters 13–14 comes the famous Jerusalem conference of chapter 15, which we discussed when examining Paul's version in the book of Galatians. From Galatians we gain the impression that Paul had to engage in some serious arm-twisting in order to convince the Jerusalem apostles that the gospel could go to gentiles without requiring them to keep the Law. That is not at all the case according to the

account in Acts. There are some false brothers who hold to the scandalous idea that faith in Jesus requires circumcision and adherence to the Law. But none of the apostles buys it. Peter explains about his dream and the conversion of Cornelius. James speaks on behalf of the gentile mission. Paul and Barnabas have their chance to talk. And it is agreed all round, gentiles do not have to keep the Law except for some very basic requirements such as abstaining from food offered to idols and sexual misbehavior.

Paul returns to the mission field, and in the following chapters we have accounts of his missionary exploits and significant successes.

Paul's Arrest and Defenses

After Paul's third missionary journey he makes a fateful trip to Jerusalem (you will be noticing that there are numerous literary parallels between what happens in Luke and what happens in Acts; Jesus too made such a journey). While in Jerusalem he is encouraged by James to make a special sacrifice in the Temple to show that he has not abandoned the Law of Moses (ch. 21). This too is a key theme of Acts. Even though Paul believes in converting gentiles, he himself remains Jewish through and through. He never does anything in violation of the Jewish law. Gentiles do not have to keep it. But as a good Jew, Paul himself does keep it.

He nonetheless has opponents in Jerusalem, and they have him arrested. He is taken into Roman custody and allowed to make a defense to the Jewish crowds (ch. 22). He is then made to face trial before the Jewish Sanhedrin (ch. 23). When the Roman tribune learns of a plot to assassinate him, he has Paul removed to await trial (ch. 23), and there he makes his defense before the governor Felix. But Felix, hoping for a bribe, leaves him in prison for two more years. By the end of that time, Felix has been replaced as governor by a man named Festus; Paul is afraid that now he will not get a fair trial, and so he appeals, as is his right as a Roman citizen, to have his case heard by the Roman emperor (nothing in Paul's writings indicates he was a Roman citizen; and the idea that just anyone could get a hearing from the emperor is a bit bizarre). He is sent to Rome, experiences a shipwreck on the way (ch. 27), but finally arrives and the book ends with him preaching to anyone who would hear him in the Roman prison (ch. 28).

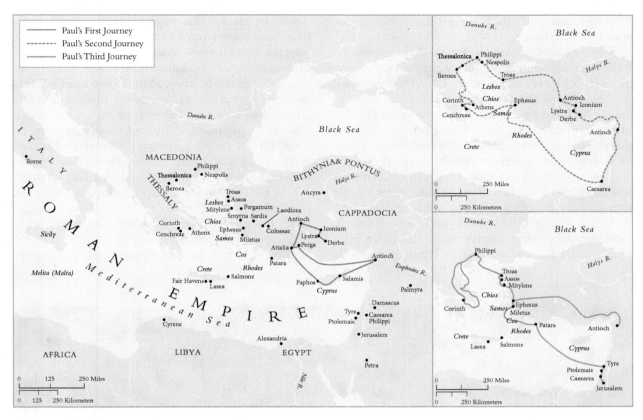

FIGURE 13.2. Paul's missionary journeys, according to the book of Acts.

Throughout these chapters Paul gives numerous defenses for himself and his behavior. In them he insists that he is a Jewish Christian who has done nothing at any time contrary to the Law of Moses. He claims that he is being opposed because he believes in Jesus and has taken his message to the gentiles. But his persecution is completely unfounded: neither his newfound faith nor his gentile mission compromises his Jewish religion. Quite the contrary, these represent fulfillments of Judaism.

Some people have argued that since the book of Acts ends with Paul in prison, it must have been written soon thereafter—say, in the year 63 or 64. Surely, this reasoning goes, Acts would report Paul's death if Luke knew about it. But in fact, that is not at all certain. For one thing, if the majority of scholars are right that the Gospel of Luke was written in 80–85 C.E., and that this book is a sequel to it, then obviously the author was writing a couple of decades after Paul's death. And one can think of very good reasons for Luke not mentioning his execution. In the book of Acts, Paul is a man who

cannot be stopped. This author may well have not wanted to report the event that showed that Paul actually could be stopped—and, in fact, was stopped decisively. And so, rather than record the fact that Paul was unceremoniously executed, Luke stops his narrative on a triumphal note. Paul may be in prison, but he is preaching there and still winning converts. The mission must go on.

The Historical Value of Acts

Now that we have considered the narrative and many of the themes of the book of Acts, we can turn back again to the question of its historical value. Does Luke give us an accurate account of what actually happened in the early years of the church, and in the life and teachings of Paul? Here I can restate the view I set out earlier: it appears that the book of Acts is about as accurate historically, with respect to Paul, as the Gospel of Luke is with respect to Jesus. It is reasonably accurate in many of its broad strokes, but the details are off, sometimes by a wide margin; and there are some major, important differences.

This is best shown by a detailed comparison of what Acts says about Paul with what Paul says about himself, wherever the two overlap. First consider the teaching of Paul. Here I will take just one example: both Acts and Paul lay out the apostle's view of pagan idolatry, yet they differ from one another sharply. In the book of Acts Paul preaches to a group of Greek philosophers in Athens (Acts 17:22–31), and he informs them that they are in error to worship idols. Their fault is understandable, though: they have been ignorant and have not realized that there is only one God. God is willing to overlook their ignorance and forgive them. Contrast that with what Paul himself says in Romans 1:18–32.

There he claims that pagans have always known that there is only one God, but they have willfully rejected that view—known to everyone—to make idols for themselves, knowing full well these were not really gods. For that reason God does *not* forgive them, but instead punishes them for acting contrary to what they knew to be true. Well, which is it? Were pagans ignorant and readily forgiven by God? Or did they act knowing full well what they were doing and so are subject to divine wrath? Some interpreters have claimed that the accounts can be reconciled: since Paul is talking to pagans in Acts he is less likely to say what he really thinks, in order to convert them. But that does not seem to make sense: Paul was never one to refuse to say what he thought, whatever the consequences. And it seems

FIGURE 13.3.   Reconstruction of central-city Rome, roughly as it would have looked in Paul's day.

unlikely that he would say just the opposite of what he thought to be true when trying to proclaim the truth. Acts appears to have altered what Paul really thought about the matter.

Acts and Paul contain discrepancies not only in Paul's preaching but also in the details of his life. This is seen time and again by comparing Paul's comments with the narrative of Acts. Sometimes the differences are matters of small details. For example, Paul himself indicates that when he went to Athens, Timothy was with him (1 Thessalonians 3:1–2); but Acts is quite emphatic that Paul went to Athens alone, without Timothy (Acts 17:4–5). It may seem like an insignificant point, but which one is right?

Sometimes the discrepancies are far more important. As we have seen, after Paul converts in Acts 9, the first thing he does after leaving Damascus is to make a beeline to Jerusalem to meet up with the other apostles (Acts 9:23–30). But Paul is quite emphatic in Galatians 1 that it absolutely did not happen that way: he did not go to Jerusalem for another three years, and then he did not associate with any of the apostles except Cephas and James. Paul swears this is true by taking an oath (1:17–20). This difference can hardly be reconciled, and it is important to both authors. Acts wants to stress that Paul and the apostles were and always had been on the same page, from the very beginning. And so Luke claims that they met up right after Paul's conversion. Paul, on the other hand, wants to stress that his gospel message is not a corruption of what he learned from the apostles: he never even met with them. Which view is historically right? In this case, Paul swears that he's telling the truth, and when he does that I tend to believe him. Luke, writing some fifty years after the event, just didn't know.

In other major ways Acts varies from Paul. As we have seen, Acts stresses that Paul never, ever did anything contrary to the Jewish law. That is the theme of most of the speeches he delivers when on trial, as in chapters 21–22 (and see 28:17). But Paul indicates in his own writings that he lived "like a gentile" when he was trying to convert gentiles (1 Corinthians 9:21); and the big argument that he had with Peter in Antioch was because Peter refused to do the same thing (Galatians 2:11–14). Again, which is it? Once more, I tend to trust Paul on the matter.

And so the book of Acts is our earliest account of the history of the primitive Christian community. But it is not an objective history that tells it like it really was. Luke has a number of points that he wants to make about the early church: it was God who revealed that gentiles could be saved without keeping the Law; there was complete harmony among the faithful Christians, no internal friction; in particular, Paul and Peter and all the others saw completely eye to eye on every matter, great and small; and most important of all, God was behind the mission from the beginning and nothing could stop it.

At a Glance: The Book of Acts

In terms of genre, Acts is best understood as a "general history" which narrates the history of a people through a chronological sequence of events, filled with speeches by its main characters. The book begins with the resurrection appearances and ascension of Jesus, and moves from the day of Pentecost to accounts of the dissemination of the Christian gospel through the Roman world. The narrative is concerned not only to show the geographical spread of the religion but also its ethnic spread as faith in Christ goes from Jews to Samaritans and then to gentiles, who are not required to become Jewish in order to be Christian.

The main figure for the final two-thirds of the book is Paul, the great apostle to the gentiles, who engages in three missionary journeys to pagan lands before being arrested by the authorities in Jerusalem and being forced to defend himself at trial on several occasions in the final portion of the narrative. The book closes with Paul in Rome, awaiting trial before the emperor, still preaching the gospel.

Although Acts is based on a number of sources, a careful comparison with the writings of Paul reveals numerous discrepancies. These suggest that the narrative is not to be taken as a historically accurate account of the life and teachings of Paul.

BOX 13.3 PAUL'S THIRD LETTER TO THE CORINTHIANS

We have already seen a sample of a Pauline pseude-pigraphon in the forged correspondence between the apostle and the Roman philosopher **Seneca** (see Box 12.1). Another example is the third letter that Paul allegedly wrote to the Christians of Corinth to oppose heretics who had arisen in their midst. As the following extract shows, the letter was in fact produced after Paul's death to attack views that proto-orthodox Christians of the mid-second century considered heretical, including the **docetic** view that Jesus did not have a real fleshly body and that his mother was not a virgin. Interestingly enough, these are issues that Paul himself never explicitly addresses in his authentic letters. Does the author of 3 Corinthians wish he had?

Paul, the prisoner of Jesus Christ, to the brethren in Corinth—greeting! Since I am in many

tribulations, I do not wonder that the teachings of the evil one are so quickly gaining ground. For my Lord Jesus Christ will quickly come, since he is rejected by those who falsify his words. For I delivered to you in the beginning what I received from the apostles who were before me that . . . God the almighty, who is righteous and would not repudiate his own creation, sent the Holy Spirit through fire into Mary the Galilean, who believed with all her heart, and she received the Holy Spirit in her womb that Jesus might enter into the world, in order that the evil one might be conquered through the same flesh by which he held sway, and convinced that he was not God. For by his own body, Jesus Christ saved all flesh. . . . (3 Corinthians 1:1–4, 12–14).

THE DEUTERO-PAULINE EPISTLES

The book of Acts is not the only writing of the New Testament in which Paul's teachings differ significantly from the historical, real Paul himself. We find the same phenomenon in the Deutero-Pauline epistles; that is, the six books that claim to be written by Paul but were probably written by other authors living in later times who merely claimed to be Paul. One might naturally ask why anyone would do so. The answers have seemed rather obvious to most scholars. For one thing, after Paul died there were members of his churches who were confronted with new situations that the apostle did not address in any of his surviving letters. If he were living today—what would he say? Some of these letters may have been written by authors who wanted to claim to be Paul so that they could have "Paul's" authoritative response to the situations in which they found themselves.

A related option is that there were people in Paul's churches who simply wanted their own voices to be heard, who wanted to assert some influence over the policies, practices, and beliefs of the church of their own day; but these people were complete "unknowns," people with no status or authority. What better way to have your views disseminated

and accepted as authoritative than to write them in the name of the apostle himself? By claiming to be Paul, these authors could yield great influence on the church of their day. And in many respects they were remarkably successful. These six letters, written by four different authors altogether (one writer produced three of them), were accepted by the early church as having really come from Paul's hand and were thus placed in the canon of sacred scripture. It was not until the nineteenth century that scholars began to realize that these books in fact were not written by Paul but by authors who were using his name for their own purposes.

We will want to consider the occasion of each of these letters, of course, as well as their overarching themes. But we will also need to consider the key critical question: what evidence exists that the letter was not in fact written by Paul? We will deal with these letters in the order in which they may have been written.

2 THESSALONIANS

A number of scholars have argued that 2 Thessalonians is not deutero-Pauline but was actually written by Paul. In part there are doubts over the authorship of the letter because in many respects it sounds so much like Paul otherwise—in particular it sounds very much like the Paul of 1 Thessalonians. But in the history of scholarship it has been precisely this relationship to 1 Thessalonians that has raised serious doubts over whether Paul could have written it. This may sound a bit ironic, but there is a certain force to the logic. None of Paul's other letters is so like any other as 2 Thessalonians is to 1 Thessalonians. The structures of the letters are very much alike—these are the only two letters in the Pauline corpus, for example, that contain two thanksgivings (not just one) to God for the recipients; the topics covered are virtually the same (no topic of 2 Thessalonians is not also covered in 1 Thessalonians); and most important there are entire lines of text that are exactly word-for-word the same. All of this may simply indicate that Paul wrote two similar letters to the Thessalonians. But later we will see reasons for thinking that in fact this second letter is not from Paul, but from someone who is trying to imitate Paul and who has done so with a copy of 1 Thessalonians in hand.

Like the first letter to the Thessalonians, this one is also said to be written by "Paul, Silvanus, and Timothy to the church of the Thessalonians" (1:1). Whoever the actual author of the letter was, its occasion is reasonably clear. It was written to a group of Christians who were undergoing intense suffering for their faith (1:4–6). We do not know how they were suffering—whether there was some kind of official governmental opposition to them, or hostility from the local population, or something else. We do know that the author wrote to assure his readers that if they remained faithful, they would be rewarded when Christ returned in judgment from heaven. When that happened, those who opposed the Christians and rejected their message would be punished with "eternal destruction." The saints, on the other hand, would enter into their glorious reward (1:7–12).

A second reason for the letter was that some members of the Christian community had come to believe that the end of time had already come upon them; that is, that the Day of Judgment was going to happen not in the indefinite future but right away (2:1–2). Some of those who thought this had their views confirmed by prophecies that were spoken by members of the congregation and, still more interesting, in a letter that was forged in the name of Paul (2:2). The author of 2 Thessalonians,

claiming to be the real Paul, warns his readers not to be deceived. Whatever an earlier forger may have asserted, the end had not yet come because there were certain events that had to transpire first (2:3).

The author describes these events in an interesting apocalyptic scenario. At present, he maintains, there is some kind of force that is restraining the final evil from yet appearing; but eventually that force will be withdrawn and an antichrist figure will be revealed on earth before Christ comes; this lawless person is ultimately "destined for destruction" (2:3). He will exalt himself, take a seat in the Temple in Jerusalem, and declare "himself to be God" (2:4). The author reminds his readers that he fully informed them of this scenario when he was first with them (2:5). Moreover, it has obviously not happened yet. And that means that the end is not coming right away. There is still some time, and they will know when the end is near: it is when these events take place.

From the final chapter of the book we learn that the problem in the congregation was not simply one of establishing the right timetable for upcoming events. Some members of this church were so persuaded that the end was absolutely imminent that they had quit their jobs and were simply waiting for it to happen (3:6–15). This was creating enormous problems because these people still had to live, obviously, in the meantime, and they were sponging off other members of the community in a case of apocalyptic freeloading. The author reminds his readers how he and his companions had lived among them, working for their own meals instead of relying on the support of others. That's what these people should do likewise.

As you can see, there are a number of Pauline themes in this short epistle: the necessity of suffering, the expectation of ultimate vindication, and the apocalyptic hope that stood at the core of Paul's gospel. These similarities include terms, phrases, and even sentences that are exactly like 1 Thessalonians. But do they indicate that Paul wrote the letter? The problem from the historian's point of view is that someone who had decided to imitate Paul would no doubt try to sound like Paul. If both Paul and an imitator of Paul could sound like Paul, how could we possibly know whether we are dealing with the apostle himself or with one his later followers trying to imitate him?

In fact there is a way to resolve this kind of historical whodunit, and it involves looking at the other side of the coin; that is, at the parts of the letter that do *not* sound like Paul and that in fact seem to be *contrary* to Paul. Such negative evidence is useful because we would expect an imitator to sound like Paul, but we would not expect Paul *not* to sound like Paul. It is the differences from Paul, therefore, that are most crucial for establishing whether Paul wrote this or any other disputed letter.

The most intriguing issue with respect to 2 Thessalonians is the one I have already delineated at length: the author writes to assure his readers that the end is not supposed to come right away. Other things must happen first. They should therefore hold on to their hopes and their jobs, for there is still some time left.

Does this sound like the same person who urged the readers of 1 Thessalonians to stay alert so as not to be taken by surprise when Jesus returns, since the end would come with no advance warning, "like a thief in the night" bringing "sudden destruction (1 Thessalonians 5:1–6)? According to 2 Thessalonians there will be plenty of advance warning. Whatever is restraining the man of lawlessness will be removed; then the antichrist figure will appear, exalt himself above all other objects of worship, establish his throne in the Jerusalem Temple, and declare himself to be God. Only then will Christ return. How is this like a thief in the night who comes when people least expect it?

It is particularly interesting that the author claims to have taught the Thessalonians these things while he was with them (2:5). If he had done so, it seems odd that he did not refer to any of his earlier teachings in the first letter, when the Thessalonians were concerned that some people had died before Jesus returned. The Thessalonians were much surprised by these deaths, since they thought Jesus was coming right away. If 2 Thessalonians is right that Paul had already told them the scenario that had to take place before the end, why didn't Paul remind them of that when they expressed surprise that people had died first? Even more, why were they surprised at all? If 2 Thessalonians 2:5 is right, then Paul never did tell them that it would all happen in the immediate future.

These problems make it very difficult to see how Paul could have written this second letter to the Thessalonians. This is someone trying to sound like Paul. It is interesting to see how he ends the letter: "I, Paul, write this greeting with my own hand.

This is the mark in every letter of mine; it is the way I write" (3:17). What this means is that the author is pretending to be Paul dictating the letter to a scribe, but signing the letter himself so that his readers could see his own handwriting and know the letter really came from Paul. That might make you think that yes, it really is Paul, but as it turns out this kind of "guarantee" of authenticity was one of the ploys commonly used by forgers to convince their readers that they were who they said they were. Another ploy is used in this letter, which I have already alluded to. This author, who is only claiming to be Paul, warns his readers against a letter that claims to be written by Paul but is not (2:2). This too is a trick forgers sometimes used. Why would a forger warn his readers against forgeries? Because then the readers do not suspect that he is doing what he is condemning. He has thus thrown the reader off the scent of his own deceit.

This author almost certainly was not Paul. Why does the letter sound so much like 1 Thessalonians, then? In fact these similarities themselves are another indication that Paul did not write the letter. In none of his other correspondence does he imitate his earlier letters (for example, by repeating the same sentences). You can consider his letters to the Corinthians, for example: they are nowhere near as close to each other in substance as the letters to the Thessalonians are. How would Paul, writing months after 1 Thessalonians, remember exactly what he said in that first letter so that he would repeat an entire sentence word for word the same? It stretches the imagination to think he could do that, and he never does it elsewhere in the undisputed letters. Even more to the point, this is exactly the sort of thing you would expect from an imitator of Paul who had the other letter in hand. He would use it to write his own letter, following its structure, covering the same topics, and sometimes even repeating the words—all to make it sound like Paul's letter.

But it was not Paul's. We don't know, obviously, who the actual author was. What we can say with some confidence is that it was written sometime after Paul by someone who was confronted with a new situation and who wanted to appeal to Paul's authority in trying to deal with it. There is no guarantee, of course, that if the letter is forged it was actually ever sent to Thessalonica; it may just as easily have been placed in circulation somewhere else. In any event, the people the author is addressing were so convinced that the end was coming right away that it was leading to problems. One can see why they might think the end was imminent, since that appears to be what Paul himself taught. But this author, also claiming to be Paul, wants to squelch that view. The end is not coming right away. There are things that have to happen first.

COLOSSIANS

Scholars also debate whether Paul himself wrote the letter to the Colossians, but as we will see there are good reasons for thinking that he did not. There is less debate about the reason the letter was written. The author claims to be Paul and to be in prison. While there he has heard news about the church in the town of Colossae in western Asia Minor. This is not a church that Paul established; it was started by his coworker Epaphras, a citizen of the place (1:3, 7–8; 4:3). The news that "Paul" has heard about the Colossians is mixed. On one hand he is pleased to learn that they have converted and committed themselves to Christ. On the other hand he has learned that they are afflicted with false teachers who are trying to convince them of a false religious view.

It is unfortunate that the author does not give us a full and clear description of what this false teaching was. He calls it a "philosophy and empty deceit" (2:8) but to understand what it was, for the most part we have to read very carefully what he says in order to oppose it and to reason back from there. He does indicate that his opponents engage in "self-abasement and the worship of angels" based on special visions they have received (2:18–19). They also insist on certain kind of ascetic activities, involving what can and cannot be touched and eaten (2:21–23). In addition, he counters their views by insisting that Christ, through his death, has erased the requirements of the Jewish law for believers. And so, at the very least, we can say that the opponents subscribed to mystical visionary experiences and the keeping of the Jewish law.

On this basis it appears that they were promoting some kind of Jewish mysticism, comparable to that we know of from other ancient texts, in which people were encouraged to experience ecstatic visions of heaven and thereby to be transported to the divine realm, where they would find themselves filled with the joy and power of divinity. People who advocated such views were often ascetic, urging one another not to indulge in the pleasures of the flesh, since salvation was to come to the spirit. One should not, then, be too closely tied to the body (which happens when you give in to bodily desires).

The author responds to this view very strongly by insisting that the believer does not need ecstatic visions to enjoy the benefits of salvation. Everything that is needed is already available through Christ. For Christ himself is the "image of the invisible God, the firstborn of all creation" (1:5). There is no need, therefore, to engage in the ecstatic worship of angels. These beings in fact are subservient to Christ and were actually created by him (1:16). Moreover it is Christ alone who is responsible for all the benefits that come to believers: he has reconciled everyone to God, and abolished all the "legal demands" of the Law. And so, no one should return to the Law (2:13–15).

The Colossians can already experience the full benefits of salvation and participate in the divine realm because they have been raised up to the heavenly places in Christ (3:1). That does not mean, of course, that they should neglect their physical existence in this world: they are still to live moral and upright lives and avoid the sins of the flesh.

Here again is a letter that looks similar in many ways to those that Paul actually wrote. The layout of the letter is similar, and the body of the letter sounds out a number of Pauline themes: the importance of suffering in the world, Jesus' death as a reconciliation, and the participation of believers in Jesus' death through baptism. There are nonetheless reasons for thinking that Paul did not write Colossians. One of the most compelling arguments is one that, unfortunately, you will not be able to evaluate without knowing the Greek language in which the letter was written. Experts in Greek style have examined the letter very carefully and compared it to the style of Paul's own writings. These investigations have revealed that time after time, in place after place, this letter is very different from Paul's. The problem is not that this letter uses a better or worse style than Paul. It is simply different (just as Jane Austen and James Joyce both wrote in perfectly acceptable styles, but you would never confuse the one for the other).

Other arguments are more easily explained just sticking with the English translation of the text.

BOX 13.4 THE RESURRECTION OF BELIEVERS IN COLOSSIANS

If Paul did write Colossians then his views about the time and significance of the resurrection of Christians changed, for here believers are said to already "have been raised with Christ" (3:1). Recall that 1 Corinthians was written in large measure against those who believed that Christians had already come to enjoy the blessings of the resurrected existence (see 1 Corinthians 15). The contrast in the verb tenses of Romans 6:4 and Colossians 2:12 (see italics) is also telling.

The question many interpreters have raised over the years is: which is it? Have Christians already been raised or not?

Romans 6:4	Colossians 2:12
For if we have been united with him in a death like his we *will* certainly *be united* with him in a resurrection like his. . . . But if we have died with Christ, we believe that we *will* also *be raised* with him.	When you were buried with him in baptism, you *were also raised* with him through faith in the power of God, who raised him from the dead.

The most important one may have occurred to you already. This author believes that Christians have participated with Christ not only in his death (at baptism), but also in his resurrection. In fact, he is quite emphatic on this point: believers have already been raised up with Christ "in the heavenly places" where they can enjoy the full benefits of salvation (2:12; 3:1). If this view sounds familiar, it should: it is the view that Paul himself argued against in 1 Corinthians. Throughout Paul's letters he is emphatic: believers have indeed died with Christ in their baptism; but they *will* be raised with him (see, for example Romans 6:4, and pay attention to the verb tenses: the death with Christ is past, the resurrection with Christ is future—this difference was a big deal for Paul; see Box 13.4). For Paul, the life of the Christian in this world was not one of unmitigated joy and ecstasy in experiencing the full benefits that were available in Christ. This world was still an evil place dominated by the forces of sin and death; those who sided with God would—and did—suffer in this world. That would all change when the end came and those who were in Christ would be raised from the dead. That, however, is a future physical event, not a past spiritual one.

For the author of Colossians, however, the spiritual resurrection had already occurred, just as it had for Paul's opponents in Corinth. It is, of course, possible that Paul changed his mind on the issue, although judging from the suffering he himself continually experienced—and that he thought he *ought* to experience as an apostle of Christ (see 2 Corinthians 11:16–30)—it is hard to think that he did. It is more plausible that Paul went to his grave believing, and consistently insisting, that Christians had not yet been raised up with Christ. And if that is so, it is hard to accept that he wrote the letter to the Colossians.

Once again we cannot know who *did* write the letter, although it was almost certainly a member of one of Paul's churches living at a later time, possibly toward the end of the first century. This author was encountering Christians who advocated some kind of mystical, ecstatic experience as a way of enjoying the full benefits of salvation, an experience that required strict ascetic behavior on the part of the participant. This author thought this was completely wrong: one does not need angels, visionary experiences, and rigorous lifestyles in order to enjoy all that is available in Christ, in whom dwells all the fullness of God's divinity. All one needs is Christ and the benefits he bestowed upon those who have been raised from the dead and exalted to the heavenly places.

EPHESIANS

There is less debate among critical scholars about the authorship of Ephesians than for the other two deutero-Pauline letters we have considered. As much "unlike" Paul as Colossians is, in terms of both style and substance, Ephesians is even more so. Unlike the other two letters, the ostensible occasion for this letter is a bit hard to discern. It seems to deal with a kind of general problem that could be found in a number of churches of the author's day, presumably near the end of the first century. There were tensions among Jews and gentiles in some of the churches, with the gentiles in particular being in the majority and looking down on their Jewish brothers and sisters. This author thinks this is an untenable situation, and he writes this letter in order to deal with it.

In particular this author wants to remind his gentile readers that even though they were formerly alienated from God, they have now been made one through the work of Jesus—one with the Jews through Jesus' work of reconciliation and one with God through his work of redemption (2:1–22). More specifically, Jesus' death has torn down the barrier that previously divided Jew from gentile: the Jewish Law (which is therefore no longer in force). As a result the two groups are now absolutely equal and can live in harmony with one another; moreover, Jesus has united both groups with God. Believers have not only died with Christ, they have been raised up with him to enjoy the benefits of a heavenly existence (2:1–10). This unity—of Jew and gentile, and of both with God—is what the author considers to be the "mystery" of the gospel that has now been revealed (3:1–13).

The second half of the letter contains exhortations for the readers to live in ways that show forth the unity that they have. It is to be evident in the life of the church (4:1–16), in the way Christians are distinct from others in society (4:17–5:20), and in the social relationships of Christians with one another—especially in their roles as wives and husbands, children and parents, slaves and masters (5:21–6:9). The book closes with an exhortation to continue the fight against the forces of the devil.

As was the case with Colossians—and even more so—experts in Greek writing style have shown that this letter is very different from those found among the undisputed Pauline epistles. The sentences here tend to be much longer and more complex than Paul's, and there are a large number of words that occur in this letter that do not make an appearance in Paul's writings otherwise. But even more convincing than arguments based on the Greek style are those involving the content of the letter. It would be useful for us to look at just one passage in particular which, on the surface, does indeed

look very much like the sort of thing that Paul might have wanted to say. But when you dig deeper into the passage it becomes clear that its views of things are very different from those of Paul, making it very difficult to imagine that Paul would have written it.

Ephesians 2:1–10 is the passage we will discuss. Read it carefully for yourself. Here the author recalls the conversion of the gentile readers from their earlier lives to the salvation they have experienced in Christ. There are a number of important Pauline themes here: a person's separation from God before being converted to Christ is spoken of as "death"; the devil is called "the ruler of the power of the air"; the grace of God is said to bring salvation through faith, not works; and the new existence a person now has should lead to a moral life. At first reading, this does sound like something Paul could have written.

But it is important to look closer. To begin with, there is a significant problem concerning the status of the believer. The description is strikingly similar to what we found in Colossians (the books are similar in numerous ways). Even though Paul's undisputed letters are quite emphatic that the resurrection of believers—even in a spiritual sense—has not yet happened, the author of Ephesians indicates that believers have been made alive with Christ and have been raised up with him and "seated . . . with him in the heavenly places in Christ Jesus" (2:6). The view of the Christian's exalted status is even more elevated here than in Colossians, since here the author is stressing that the believers have already experienced the same exalted state that Christ himself enjoys. In the first chapter of the book he claimed that at Christ's exaltation, God seated him "at his right hand in the heavenly places, far above all rule and authority and power and dominion, and above every name that is named" (1:20–21). That is quite an exaltation. And where are the Christian believers? They are seated up there with him. Can this be the same author who castigated the Corinthians for maintaining that they had already come to be exalted with Christ and were therefore already ruling with him?

Another difference from Paul's own letters is the way the author of Ephesians 2:1–10 conceptualizes the "works" that a person does in vain in order to achieve salvation. In Paul's own writings, gentiles are made right with God not by doing the "works of the Law" but by having faith in Christ's death.

And so, when Paul speaks about works he is referring to doing those parts of the Jewish Law that make Jews distinctive as the people of God: circumcising their boys, keeping kosher food laws, observing the Sabbath, and so on. That is Paul's principal concern: no one should think they need to do these Jewish "works" (and thus become Jewish) in order to be right with God. But when the author of Ephesians speaks of "works" that is not what he has in mind at all. He is speaking about "good deeds"—doing good things for other people. That is not what saves you. Paul may or may not have agreed (he probably would have agreed), but that simply is not the issue that he was dealing with or was concerned about. Paul's teachings about "works of the Law" have been transformed into a teaching about "doing good deeds."

Just as the notion of works appears to have lost its specifically Jewish content, so too has the author's former life in which he engaged in these works. As we saw in the brief biographical sketch in chapter 12, Paul himself spoke proudly of his former life as one in which he had kept the Jewish Law better than the zealous Pharisees who were his youthful companions. In his own words, "with respect to the righteousness found in the Law, I was found to be blameless" (Philippians 3:6). Paul's conversion was not away from a wild and promiscuous past to an upright and moral present. It was from one form of rigorous religiosity to another. What about the author of Ephesians? Here it is completely different. This author indicates that "all of us once lived among them [that is with the rank pagans] in the passions of our flesh, following the desires of flesh and senses (2:3)." He was as morally bad as the most licentious pagan on the planet. Is that Paul?

It is true that Paul himself occasionally speaks of having done the things that he knew he was not supposed to do (Romans 7), but in his undisputed letters the extent of his sins seems to involve such things as "coveting" (Romans 7:7–8), not the lascivious and dissolute lifestyle of the pagans that he sometimes maligned (see, e.g., Romans 1:18–32). In terms of his lifestyle, Paul lived "blamelessly." Not so the author of Ephesians.

And so Ephesians, like 2 Thessalonians and Colossians, appears not to have been written by Paul. Once again we do not know who the real author was, except to say that he was a member of one of Paul's churches, probably near the end of the first century, who wanted to address a new situation that had arisen. Tensions had erupted between gentiles and Jews in the churches that he knew, and he wrote to reaffirm what he saw to be the core of Paul's message: that Christ brought about a unification of Jew and gentile and a reconciliation of both with God. All members of the Christian church should respond to their new standing in Christ—as those already exalted with him and ruling with him in the heavenly places—by embracing and promoting the unity that was already theirs.

THE PASTORAL EPISTLES

We will be dealing with 1 and 2 Timothy and Titus as a group of three letters because it is widely thought, for very good reasons, that the three were written by a single author. The letters do not all have the same purpose, but they do cover many of the same topics, with two of them (1 Timothy and Titus) being very much alike. As a group they are traditionally called the "Pastoral epistles" because of their ostensible occasion: they are allegedly written by Paul to two of his subordinate coworkers: Timothy, who has been left behind in Ephesus to deal with the problems of the church there; and Titus, who has been left on the island of Crete for a similar reason. These letters are filled with pastoral advice to these "pastors" who need some assistance in handling the problems that have arisen among their flocks.

I have indicated that with the other deutero-Pauline letters there continues to be some debate among scholars concerning whether Paul could actually have written them. There is far less debate about the three Pastoral epistles. They are generally considered non-Pauline by critical scholars. In discussing the authorship of these letters we should constantly remember that we are not asking whether or not Christians in the early Christian centuries would have forged documents in Paul's name. We know for a fact that some did: 2 Thessalonians, for example, refers to a forged letter (so that either the author knows of a forgery in Paul's name, or he himself is writing one), and we have such forgeries as 3 Corinthians and Paul's letters back and forth with the philosopher Seneca. What we are asking, then, is not whether these letters *could* be forged in Paul's name (yes, they could), but whether they actually were. And here the answer appears to be a straightforward yes.

FIGURE 13.4.   Picture of a woman presiding at a *refrigerium*, a ritual meal held by families to commemorate the dead in early Christianity (in which the dead person was thought to be dining with the living on the commemoration of his or her death). The author of the Pastorals no doubt would have disapproved of a woman officiating at the meal.

Before discussing the issue of the authorship of these letters we should consider the occasion and overarching points of each of them.

1 Timothy

1 Timothy presupposes that Paul and Timothy had visited the city of Ephesus, and that Paul had decided to leave Timothy behind in order to bring false teachers under control (1:3–11), to bring order to the church (2:1–15), and to appoint moral and upright leaders who could keep things running smoothly (3:1–13). Much of the letter consists of instructions about how Christians should live and interact with one another; for instance, how they ought to pray; how they should behave toward the elderly, the widows, and their leaders; and what things they ought to avoid, such as pointlessly

ascetic lifestyles, material wealth, and heretics who corrupt the truth.

It is clear that the author is especially concerned about the false teaching that some members of the community were presenting, but it is less clear what exactly that teaching was. The author does indicate that some members of the congregations have become enthralled with "myths and endless genealogies." That has struck a resonant chord with scholars who know all about later forms of Christian Gnosticism, as we discussed in chapter 11. Recall that the Gnostics told myths about how the gods came into being in the divine realm; is this what the author is referring to? It is striking that at the end of the letter he tells his reader to "avoid the profane chatter and contradictions of what is falsely called knowledge" (6:20). The Greek word for "knowledge" is "*gnosis*,"—the word from which we get the term Gnosticism. Whether they are some very early form of Gnostic or not, these false teachers stress myths, genealogies, and *gnosis*—as the later Gnostics did. Moreover, they are particularly intrigued with the Jewish law, as the author attacks them for wanting to be (but obviously, in his opinion, not succeeding at being) "teachers of the Law" (1:7). Many Gnostic myths were detailed and mind-boggling expositions of the early chapters of Genesis—part, obviously of the Law. Finally we learn that these opponents were rigorously ascetic; they "forbid marriage and demand abstinence from food" (4:3). That too would fit with many forms of Gnosticism, as Gnostics believed that salvation came to the spirit when the spirit was liberated from the body, which meant that a person should not cave into bodily pleasures and desires. But there were lots of ascetic groups in early Christianity, so on balance it is not clear whether these opponents are some early form of Gnostic or not.

What is clear is that the author does not choose to attack the views of the opponents head on by arguing with them (contrast Paul's approach in his letters); he instead urges Timothy not to heed their words and to bring them into subjection (1:3). As we will see later, many of the instructions that the author gives to the leadership of the church may represent an attempt to get them organized in order to face these opponents with a unified front. He spells out, in particular, the qualifications of the bishops and deacons of these churches: they are to be men (only men!) who are morally upright and strong personalities who can serve as models to the community and command respect in the world outside the church.

The tight organization of the church is important also for the inner workings of the community. In particular the author is concerned about the role women should play in the congregation. In his view, they should not play much of a role at all. Not only are women not allowed to serve as leaders—whether as bishops (or "overseers") who had oversight of the spiritual well-being of the community, or as deacons (or "ministers") who may have tended to the community's physical needs. They are not allowed even to speak in church. Women are not to exercise any authority over a man. If they want to be saved, they should have babies (2:11–15). Not to belabor the obvious, but to many modern readers this has not seemed to presuppose a very enlightened view of the relationship of the genders. But this author is worried about the roles women were playing in the churches, especially the "widows" who appear to have been enrolled by the church and provided with some kind of material support in exchange for their pious deeds (5:4–16). This author evidently thinks that women in general and widows in particular have stirred up problems and are not to be trusted (5:11–13).

2 Timothy

The second Pastoral epistle presupposes a completely different situation. It too is written by "Paul"

BOX 13.5 CHURCH HIERARCHY IN IGNATIUS

The undisputed letters of Paul contain nothing like the structured hierarchy that begins to make itself evident in the works of later writers such as Ignatius of Antioch (early second century), who urges that the solitary bishop of the church should hold complete sway over his congregation and that the presbyters and deacons should also be given special places of authority (cf. the Pastorals). As Ignatius says to the Christians of Smyrna:

> Let all of you follow the bishop, as Jesus Christ follows the Father; and follow the presbytery as you would follow the Apostles. And respect the deacons as you respect the commandment of God. Let no one do anything that relates to

the church apart from the bishop. The only eucharist that is valid is the one performed by the bishop or by the person that he appoints. Wherever the bishop happens to be, consider this the entire congregation, just as where Jesus Christ is, there you will find the whole church. It is not fitting for anyone to perform a baptism or to celebrate the Lord's supper if the bishop is not present. But whatever the bishop should approve, this also is pleasing to God. . . . The one who honors the bishop has been honored by God; the one who does anything apart from the knowledge of the bishop serves the devil. (Ignatius Smyrneans 8–9) to Timothy (1:1). Now, however, Paul is said to be in prison in Rome and he is expecting to be executed soon after a second judicial hearing (1:16–17; 4:6–8, 17). Paul, in other words, is at the end of his life. In some ways this letter states his final wishes. He is writing Timothy not only to encourage him to continue his pastoral duties by uprooting the false teachers in his church (who represent a different false teaching from those of 1 Timothy), but also to join him as soon as possible, bringing with him some of his personal belongings (4:13, 21).

This letter is so personal that some readers have wondered how it could be forged. Why would a nonexistent author ask a nonexistent recipient to bring him his nonexistent cloak and papers? The reason is actually not that hard to understand, as scholars of ancient forgery have long recognized. By including all these personal references the author does indeed seem to be a real person writing to a real situation, so that it is a ploy to keep the reader off the track of what the author is really doing: pretending to be someone he in fact is not.

Part of that ploy gets played out in the author's casual references to Timothy himself. He is a young man subject to youthful passions (2:22). He is a third-generation Christian who was preceded in his faith by his mother Eunice and his grandmother Lois (1:5). He was trained in the Scriptures from the time he was a child and as an adult became Paul's missionary companion (3:1–11, 15). He was ordained to be a minister by the laying on of hands (1:6; 4:1–5).

One aspect of this description should strike readers as odd. How could Timothy still be a young man, if Paul is nearing the end of his life? We know from the book of Acts and from Paul's own letters that Timothy was a missionary companion of Paul from a time before he wrote the letters we now have, so presumably in the 40s and 50s C.E. He would have started with Paul on his travels only after he was already an adult. If the tradition is right that Paul was executed in Rome in the early to mid 60s C.E., how could Timothy still be thought of as "young" at the time? He would be middle aged—or older—at best. It is thus hard to situate this letter in a plausible chronology of Paul's life.

In any event, the letter is in part directed to "Timothy" in order to urge him to deal with the false teachers. These persons are seriously maligned by the author in a whole string of vicious name-calling (3:2–5) passages, but these kinds of comments

do not help us much if we want to know what it is they actually taught. On one point the author is crystal clear: two of these opponents have claimed that "the resurrection has already taken place" (2:17). This is a claim we have run across before in the Pauline letters. It appears to be the claim that was made by Paul's opponents in Corinth. And even more interesting, it is the claim that appears to be made by the authors of both Colossians and Ephesians. It should not seem odd that there could be Christians who took opposing views on important theological issues, all claiming support from the apostle Paul. We have seen already that in the city of Corinth there was a group who claimed to be "of Paul" (1 Corinthians 1:12), whom Paul strongly disagrees with, and into the second century there were various groups—for example Gnostics and the "orthodox" Christians who opposed them—who claimed Paul as their apostle and maintained that they were representing his views, even though the views they took were at odds with one another.

Titus

The book of Titus is far more like the first Pastoral epistle than the second. Indeed, the letter seems to be something like a *Reader's Digest* version of 1 Timothy, as it too gives a list of qualifications for church leaders and provides moral instructions for members of the congregation in their relations with one another.

The presupposed situation in this case is that "Paul" has left his trusted comrade Titus on the island of Crete as an apostolic representative to the church there (1:4–5). In particular, Titus is supposed to appoint elders, or bishops, in the churches of every town. Paul is writing to urge Titus to correct the false teachings, which sound very much like those also attacked in 1 Timothy. They involve "mythologies" that confuse the faithful (1:10–16) and "genealogies and quarrels about the Law" (3:9). Titus is told not to argue with these people. He is to warn them twice to change their views, and after that simply to ignore them.

A good portion of the letter contains the apostle's advice to different social groups within the congregation: older men, older women, younger women, younger men, and slaves (2:2–10). Toward the end the advice becomes more general in nature, involving basic admonitions to engage in moral behavior. The letter ends with the author's request that Titus join up with him in the city of Nicopolis, where he plans to spend the winter.

The Authorship of the Pastorals

Most scholars are reasonably convinced that all three Pastoral epistles were written by the same author. With 1 Timothy and Titus there can be little doubt. The writing style, subject matter, and specific content are altogether similar. 2 Timothy differs in key ways, but its vocabulary and writing style are closely aligned with the other two; to see for yourself, just compare the opening of 1 Timothy 1:2 with that of 2 Timothy 1:2. They are virtually word for word the same, and there is no other Pauline letter with this kind of opening.

As with the other deutero-Pauline letters, the decision of whether this author was Paul depends on matters of style and substance. In terms of style, these letters have long been recognized as strikingly different from the undisputed Pauline epistles. Some of the sophisticated studies of the letters, for example, have pointed out that apart from personal names, there are 858 different words used in the Pastoral epistles. Of these, 306 appear nowhere else in all of the other Pauline writings (including for this statistic even the other deutero-Paulines). This means that over a third of the vocabulary is otherwise not attested in Paul. And what is more interesting, over two-thirds of these non-Pauline words are used by Christian authors of the second century. Thus it appears that the vocabulary represented in these letters is more developed than what we find in the other letters attributed to Paul.

Yet more significant is the fact that some of the key words used in these letters are those used by Paul, but they mean something very different. As brief examples, Paul's word for "having a right standing before God" (literally, "righteousness") now means something else: "being a moral individual" (that is, an upstanding person; Titus 1:8); and the term "faith," which for Paul refers to a trusting acceptance of the death of Christ for salvation, now refers to the body of teaching that makes up the Christian religion (Titus 1:13).

Of course, this argument from vocabulary can never be decisive in itself. Everyone uses different words on different occasions, and Paul may have used words to mean different things at different times of his life. But these arguments from vocabulary can

be coupled with issues of substance to make the case against the Pauline authorship of these letters compelling.

We have begun to see some of these other arguments with 2 Timothy (written, of course, by the author of the other two: so if one of the letters can be shown to be a forgery, necessarily all three of them are). It is hard indeed to understand how Timothy could be a young man near the time of Paul's death in the early 60s. And with respect to the other two: if in fact some form of Gnostic thinking is under attack, that almost certainly would date the letters to well after Paul's day, when no such false teachings are at all in evidence. We do not get anything like full-blown Gnostic religions until the second century, but there may have been some early forms of such religions that were not fully formed by the end of the first century, which would be a plausible date for these letters.

An even more important indication that these letters cannot verifiably be situated into the time of Paul has to do with the central concerns of 1 Timothy and Titus, to establish the right kinds of bishops ("overseers") and deacons ("ministers") in the churches. To some extent, this concern to have proper leadership and established lines of authority relates to the major concerns of these letters to bring the false teachers under control and to bring order to the internal workings of the church. It is easier to control false teachings when someone is in charge who can exercise his authority in making sure that only the correct teachings are taught; and internal problems in the church (such as women speaking out when they should remain silent) are also easiest controlled when the lines of authority are neatly drawn.

But think about the church as we know it from Paul's own day. Among all the letters that certainly go back to Paul, the ones that give us the best information about how Paul's churches were organized are the letters to Corinth. As we saw, this was a very troubled church, with problems involving their weekly services of worship (improper observance of the communion meal, chaos breaking out with the excessive speaking in tongues), their internal lives together (factions forming around certain gifted teachers; some members taking others to civil court over disagreements); moral improprieties (men visiting prostitutes and one man sleeping with his stepmother); and false teaching (about the nature of the future resurrection of the dead). With all of these problems ravaging the church, you might well

FIGURE 13.5. Even though the author of the Pastoral epistles, and many of his male contemporaries, believed that women should not be involved with business outside the home, many women had to work in order to survive in the ancient Roman world, as seen in this funerary monument portraying two women working in a poultry/butcher shop.

wonder: why doesn't Paul write to the leaders of the church to tell them to get their people in order? Why doesn't he tell the bishops and the deacons to assert some control over the rampant behavioral problems and the false teachings? There is, in fact, a good and clear reason why Paul does not send a letter to the leaders of the church in Corinth. There were no leaders of the church in Corinth.

This becomes clear from the letter itself, which shows that rather than having a church hierarchy with leaders in official positions who could take charge of the congregation, Paul's churches were **charismatic communities**. The term *"charisma"* is the Greek word for "gift." It is clear from 1 Corinthians 12–14 that Paul's churches were not run by appointed leaders, but by everyone in the church participating together, contributing to the common good based on the "gifts" they had been given.

The way it worked was this. As we have seen, Paul believed that when a person was baptized, he or she received a gift from the Holy Spirit. There were all sorts of gifts that were given, but all of them were meant to help the church function and run smoothly in this short interim period between the beginning of the end of all things (with Jesus' resurrection) and the end of the end (with his return in glory). That time would not be long, and until the end of the end came the church had to function together. It did so based on the gifts that the Spirit gave to the individual members. And so, some members were given the gift of teaching, others the gift of healing, or of prophesying God's word, or of speaking God's words in unknown languages (the gift of tongues), or of being able to interpret these unknown languages (the interpretation of tongues). All of these gifts were vital; all were meant to contribute to the common good.

Paul's communities, in short, were charismatic communities in which there was no one leader in charge, no appointed officers who ran the show.

BOX 13.6 WOMEN IN THE CHURCHES OF PAUL

The Pastoral epistles appear to have a very different understanding of how women are to function in the Christian church than we find in the writings of Paul himself. No passage of the Pastorals is more striking in this regard than 1 Timothy 2:11–15. Here the unknown author, claiming to be Paul, indicates that women are to be silent, to be submissive to men, and to be sexually active with their spouses. If women want to enjoy the full benefits of salvation, they are to produce babies.

How different that is from the views found in Paul's own writings. Take just Romans chapter 16 as an example. Here, in his greetings to the church in Rome, Paul mentions a number of women and many of them obviously play roles of leadership. There is Phoebe, a deacon (or minister) in the church of Cenchreae and Paul's own patron, who has been entrusted by Paul with the task of carrying the letter to Rome (vv. 1–2). There is Prisca, who along with her husband Aquila, is largely responsible for the gentile mission and who supports a congregation in her home (vv. 3–4; notice that she is named ahead of her husband). There is Mary,

Paul's colleague who works among the Romans (v. 6). There are Tryphaena, Tryphosa, and Persis, women whom Paul calls his "co-workers" for the gospel (vv. 6, 12). And there are Julia and the mother of Rufus and the sister of Nereus, all of whom appear to have a high profile in this community (vv. 13, 15). Most impressive of all, there is Junia, a woman whom Paul names as "foremost among the apostles." Here is a woman who is not only an apostle, on a level with Paul, but a woman who is one of the *leading* apostles!

Clearly something happened in the churches of Paul after his own day to change the position and authority enjoyed by women. It is widely thought that eventually, as more men converted to this new faith, they took over and tried to silence the women who had played such a crucial role early on. It is this attempt to bring women under male control that is so evident in the Pastoral epistles, especially 1 Timothy 2, written by a latter follower of Paul who wanted to insist in Paul's name that women had to be silent and under the authority of the men. This, however, is not how it really was in Paul's own churches.

What do you suppose would happen over the long haul to communities like that, with no one person (or no small group of persons) calling the shots? What would typically happen would be what happened in Corinth: a good deal of chaos. And it does not take a degree in sociology to figure out how churches would eventually begin to deal with that chaos. They would get organized. People with leadership skills would take charge. Policies and procedures would be put in place in order to mold the community into an orderly and efficient body of believers.

That in fact is what happened after Paul's day. The end of the end never did come, and the church got organized. It developed church offices, with bishops, elders, and deacons having set responsibilities. These leaders had to meet certain qualifications to be selected. They were in charge of the internal workings of the church. And, as the

revered authorities who were in charge, they were the ones who could determine what was, and what was not, acceptable teaching. It is not hard to see where the Pastoral epistles fit on this trajectory from Paul's charismatic communities in the 50s C.E. and the more rigidly structured, hierarchically arranged churches of the second century. These books presuppose a situation that is much more like what we find in later times. They appear then to have been written after Paul's day.

Eventually the need to eliminate false teaching from the Christian communities led church leaders to appeal to greater authorities than themselves for the correct content of the faith. The early Christians, of course, utilized the Jewish Bible as their Scriptures. But as doctrinal and practical disputes arose, eventually Christians also needed uniquely Christian authorities. As we will see in chapter 15, this is what eventually led to the formation of the Christian canon of Scripture, a collection of writings that were seen to be authoritative for establishing what Christians should believe and how they should behave. The canon that formed was one that placed the teachings and life of Jesus at its center (in the Gospels) as well as the writings of the apostles (such as Paul).

It is interesting that we can see this movement to establishing specifically Christian writings as authoritative already here in the Pastoral epistles, showing once more that these books were written some decades after the life of Paul. In 1 Timothy 5:18 the author wants to insist that the leaders of the church deserve special honor (which may mean that they ought to be paid); he supports his point by quoting two passages from "Scripture." The first is from the Torah, Deuteronomy 25:4; but the second—also called Scripture—is a quotation of Jesus, very similar to what can be found in Matthew 10:10. This is an author who not only presupposes a much more advanced church structure than in Paul's day, with its appointed overseers, elders, and deacons, but also assumes that the words of Jesus found in a written text is a piece of Scripture of equal authority to the Torah itself.

There are other aspects of the Pastoral epistles that indicate that they come from a period after Paul had passed from the scene: their greater preoccupation with social arrangements in this world, and the Christians' respectability in the eyes of outsiders, than with the apocalypse that is soon to come; their insistence that leaders of the church be married rather than single and celibate (which was Paul's own preference for both himself and his converts); their assumption that Timothy is a third-generation Christian preceded in the faith by both his mother and grandmother; and their concern to silence women who, in the author's opinion, had gotten out of hand. This author is less concerned with the imminent end of the world than with the problems confronting a church that was to be here for the long haul. This was a church that needed to strengthen itself through tighter organization and to ward off false teachings that had proliferated with the passing of time.

At a Glance: The Deutero-Pauline Epistles

The deutero-Pauline epistles were written after the death of Paul by authors who wanted to claim his name and his authority in order to deal with problems confronting the church in their day.

- 2 Thessalonians is more like 1 Thessalonians than any two of Paul's genuine letters are to one another; but when the author makes his own theological points, these differ from Paul. The book was written to assure its readers that the end of all things with the return of Jesus was not to happen right away.
- Colossians differs from Paul in both writing style and theology—especially in its insistence that a spiritual resurrection has already happened. The author is writing to combat false teachers who subscribe to a kind of Jewish mystical thinking that undervalues the all-sufficiency of Christ.
- Ephesians differs even more from Paul in both style and theology. This author is concerned about the unity of Jew and gentile in the body of Christ and stresses that in Christ all are one with one another and one with God.
- The three Pastoral epistles of 1 and 2 Timothy and Titus were all written by the same author, who presupposes a church situation very different from that of the time of Paul. These three letters stress the importance of the local pastors in dealing with the problems in their community, especially those involving false teaching and church organization.

Take a Stand

1. Pick either side of the following resolution and argue your case in a class debate: *Resolved: The author of the book of Acts did not intend to present a historically accurate portrayal of Paul.*

2. You are telling a friend about your Bible class, and she is shocked to hear that scholars think that some of the letters ascribed to Paul in the New Testament were not actually written by him. In her opinion, an author who claimed to be someone other than who he really was would be lying, and there can be no lies in the Bible. These letters then *must* be written by Paul. How do you respond?

3. Compare 1 Corinthians and 1 Timothy. What does your comparison of these books tell us about the variety of theological points of view among Christians at the time of the New Testament?

Key Terms

Charismatic communities, 345   **Docetic**, 334   **Seneca**, 334
Thucydides, 326

Suggestions for Further Reading

NB: For this and all chapters, see the relevant articles (e.g., "Acts," "Ephesians") in the works cited in the Suggestions for Further Reading in chapter 1.

Beker, J. Christiaan. *The Heirs of Paul: Paul's Legacy in the New Testament and in the Church Today*. Philadelphia: Fortress, 1991. A clear assessment of the theology of the Deutero-Pauline and Pastoral epistles, especially in light of the views embodied in the undisputed Paulines.

Ehrman, Bart D. *Forged: Writing in the Name of God — Why the Biblical Authors are not Who We Think They Are*. San Francisco: HarperOne, 2010. An account of the phenomenon of literary forgery (pseudepigraphy) throughout the early Christian tradition, which asks how and why a Christian author would try to deceive his readers about his own identity; written for a popular audience.

Lincoln, Andrew and A. J. M. Wedderburn. *The Theology of the Later Pauline Letters*. Cambridge: Cambridge University Press, 1993. A clear overview of the major themes of Colossians and Ephesians.

Powell, Mark A. *What Are They Saying about Acts?* New York: Paulist Press, 1991. An overview of modern scholarship on the book of Acts, for beginning students.

Roetzel, Calvin. *The Letters of Paul: Conversations in Context*. 3rd ed. Atlanta: John Knox, 1991. Perhaps the best introductory discussion of each of the Pauline epistles, including the Deutero-Pauline and Pastoral letters.

Young, Frances. *The Theology of the Pastoral Epistles*. Cambridge: Cambridge University Press, 1994. A clear overview of the major themes of the Pastoral epistles.

14

The General Epistles and the Book of Revelation

ow that we have completed an examination of the various letters that claim to be written by Paul, we can move on to the final eight letters of the New Testament, which are usually called the "general epistles" or the "catholic epistles." The term "catholic" may be confusing in this context. It does not mean that these letters were written by or for Roman Catholics; the word instead comes from a Greek term that means "universal." These letters are called "universal" or "general" because they are understood to be written to Christians throughout the world to deal with more general problems, unlike Paul's letters that were addressed to specific communities (and one specific individual) to deal with specific problems. As we will see, this understanding of these letters is not particularly appropriate: some of them are indeed written to deal with specific problems of specific communities; and two of them, at least, are not actually epistles.

There are, nonetheless, broader issues raised by these various writings, and so in this chapter we will look not only at the message of each of these books but also at some of the general historical matters that they evoked. These broader considerations will occur in three excursuses: one on the relationship of Jews and Christians in the New Testament period and beyond; a second on the persecution of Christians in the Roman empire;

and a third on the relationship of "orthodoxy" and "heresy" in the early church.

We begin our examination with the so-called letter to the Hebrews. I say it is "so-called" because it is not a letter and it is not addressed to Jews.

THE LETTER TO THE HEBREWS

Although Hebrews is normally called an epistle, a quick reading will show that it does not have the form of one: there is no mention of the author's name or the names of his addressees, and there is no opening benediction or thanksgiving. In other words, it is lacking precisely the elements of letters that make them letters. When the author does describe his writing toward the end of the book, he calls it not a letter but a "word of exhortation" (13:22). That is a fair description of the book's contents, leading most scholars to think that it was originally a sermon delivered by a Christian preacher to his congregation.

If the book did indeed start out as a sermon, then its ending—which does sound like the way a letter would end—may have been added later, either by its author or by someone else who read the piece and then sent it on to another community. In this closing (13:20–25) the author—or the redactor—added a benediction, an exhortation, an indication of his travel plans, final greetings, and farewell. It is particularly intriguing that Timothy is mentioned in this final section. Does the author want his reader to infer that he is in fact Paul?

Author and Audience

The book does not claim to be written by Paul, but—like the New Testament Gospels—is anonymous. Modern scholars are convinced that Paul did not write it: the writing style is not Paul's and the major topics of discussion (for example, the Old Testament priesthood and the Jewish sacrificial system) are things that Paul scarcely mentions, let alone emphasizes. Moreover, the way this author understands such critical terms as "faith" (11:1) differs markedly from what you find in the writings of Paul. As a result, apart from knowing with reasonable certainty that Paul was not its author, we cannot say who wrote it.

We are in a better position to say something about the book's audience. The author presupposes that they are Christians who have undergone some serious persecutions for their faith, including imprisonment and the confiscation of property, even though none of them has been martyred (10:32–24; 12:4). From what the author tells them, it appears that they are not Jews but gentiles. For example, he reminds them of the instruction they received upon first coming to believe, including such matters as faith in God, belief in the resurrection of the dead, and eternal judgment (6:1–2). Surely Jews attracted to the Christian religion would already have known about such things. It seems more probable, then, that we are dealing with a group of gentile converts.

The reason they have traditionally been thought to be Jews—leading to the ancient title of the book "To the Hebrews"—is because the author works very hard to convince them that Jesus is superior to everything that Judaism has to offer. But he may be doing so not because he is concerned that they may return to their former religion but because he is trying to convince gentiles not to reject Jesus and become Jews. And that, in fact, is how the book is widely read by scholars today. This author wants to insist to his readers that if they were to abandon Jesus for Judaism—for example, to escape the kinds of persecution they were facing—it would be a serious mistake. It would mean preferring the "foreshadowing" of God's salvation to salvation itself, and to adopt the imperfect and flawed religion of the Jewish Scriptures rather than its perfect and complete fulfillment in Christ. For this author, Christ does indeed stand in continuity with the religion of the Jews as set forth in their sacred writings. But he is superior in every way to that religion, and those who reject the salvation that Christ alone can provide are in danger of falling under the wrath of God.

The Superiority of Christ

The superiority of Christ and the salvation he brings is the constant refrain sounded throughout this sermon, as the author enumerates instances of that superiority to all that can be found in the Jewish religion.

Christ is superior to the prophets (1:1–3). The Jewish prophets were God's spokespersons in former times, but now he has spoken through his own Son, who is the perfect image of God himself.

Christ is superior to the angels (1:4–11; 2:5–18). The angels of the Old Testament were God's special messengers; but Christ is actually his Son, exalted to a position of power next to God's heavenly throne. Angels were ministers for those destined for salvation, but Christ is the Son of God whose suffering actually brings that salvation.

Christ is superior to Moses (3:1–6). Moses was a servant in "God's house," but Jesus is the Son of the house.

Christ is superior to Joshua (4:1–11). Joshua gave the people of Israel peace (or "rest") after the Promised Land had been conquered; but as the Scriptures themselves indicate, the people of Israel could not fully enjoy that peace (or "enter into their rest") because they were disobedient. Christ brings a more perfect peace.

Christ is superior to the Jewish priesthood (4:14–5:10; 7:1–29). Like the Jewish high priests, Jesus was personally acquainted with human weaknesses that require a mediator before God; but unlike them, he was without sin and did not need to offer a sacrifice for himself before representing the people. He is superior to the priests descended from Levi (as all Jewish priests are) because he is the one promised in the Scriptures as the priest from the line of Melchizedek (Psalms 110:4), the mysterious figure whom Abraham, the ancestor of Levi, honored by paying one-tenth of his goods (Genesis 14:17–20). For this reason Levi himself, as represented by his ancestor, was inferior to and subservient to Melchizedek and the descendant from his line. If the Levitical priests had been able to make the people of God perfect, God would not have had to promise to send a priest from the line of Melchizedek into the world. Moreover, Christ is superior to these other priests because they are many, but he is one; and, unlike them, he needed to offer his sacrifice only once, not repeatedly.

Christ is a minister of a superior covenant (8:1–13). In the Scriptures, God promised to bring a new covenant (Jeremiah 31:31–34), thereby showing that the old covenant with the Jews was outmoded and imperfect. Christ is the minister of this new covenant.

Christ is minister in a superior tabernacle (9:1–28). The earthly tabernacle, where Jewish sacrifices were originally performed, was constructed according to a model that was in heaven. Unlike the Jewish priests, Christ did not minister in the earthly replica; he brought his sacrifice straight to heaven, to the real sanctuary, into the presence of God himself.

Christ makes a superior sacrifice (10:1–18). Christ's sacrifice was perfect, unlike those that had to be offered year after year by the Jewish priests. His death brought complete forgiveness of sins; there is therefore no longer any need for sacrifice.

The Goal of the Author's Exposition

It will be seen from all these comparisons that the author is not in the least bit opposed to the religion of the Old Testament. He quotes the Old Testament at length and believes that the religion found there was valid at its time. But it has been superseded by that which it was anticipating. The prophets predicted that something greater would come, and that was Christ. Moreover, the Old Testament religion was a kind of "foreshadowing" of what was yet to be. Christ is *like* the Old Testament religion in the sense that a building is like the architectural model for it. Once the building is complete, however, there is no longer any need for the model. Christ fulfills what was anticipated in the religion of the Jews of old, and it would be the height of foolishness to prefer the model to the reality.

Throughout the author's exposition of Christ's superiority, he makes exhortation after exhortation to his readers not to turn to Judaism in preference to the salvation brought by Christ. The first exhortation occurs in 2:1–4: if disobedience was punished in the Old Testament, what will happen to those who reject the ultimate salvation (provided by Christ)? Another occurs in 3:7–18: if disobedience to Moses (the servant of God) brought destruction, imagine what disobedience to Christ (the Son of God) will bring. More straightforward still is the exhortation in 6:1–6: there can be no hope for those who have "fallen away" after once "being enlightened"; that is, for those who leave the faith once having joined. They cannot then return to the faith because doing so would mean "crucifying the Son of God again." The warning of 10:26–29 is even more vivid:

> If we willfully persist in sin after having received the knowledge of the truth, there no longer remains a sacrifice for sins, but a fearful prospect of judgment, and a fury of fire that will consume the adversaries. . . . It is a fearful thing to fall into the hands of the living God.

After providing this exposition of Christ's superiority and making his exhortations to remain faithful to Christ, the author returns to the Jewish Scriptures to recount the deeds of all those there

EXCURSUS JEWS AND CHRISTIANS IN THE ANCIENT WORLD

The book of Hebrews is all about the relationship of those who have faith in Christ with Jews who do not follow Christ but adhere to a religion based on the Jewish Scriptures. This raises for us the broader question of how Christians generally related to Jews in the early church. We have already seen a range of perspectives among Jesus' followers on just this question. There were some early Christians who maintained that following Jesus meant keeping the customs and laws of Judaism. The logic of this position was clear and relatively straightforward: Jesus was the Jewish messiah sent from the Jewish God to the Jewish people in fulfillment of the Jewish Law, and therefore Christianity was a Jewish religion. To be a follower of Jesus meant to accept the Jewish God and to join the covenant that he had made with his people: by being circumcised, observing the Sabbath, keeping kosher food laws, and celebrating the Jewish festivals. This appears to have been the view adopted by Paul's Christian opponents in Galatia.

The opposite end of the spectrum from these "Jewish Christians" is not represented by Paul, or indeed by any of the authors of the New Testament. The extreme opposite view is one that says that Jesus was not the Jewish messiah, that he did not represent the Jewish God, and that the Jewish Scriptures were not provided by the true God. Even though we cannot find this extreme view embodied in any of the books of the New Testament, it is in evidence in later times, especially in the teachings of a second-century Christian named **Marcion**. Marcion claimed that his views were in fact those of Paul. Marcion pointed out that Paul differentiated between his gospel and the Jewish Law. For Marcion, this differentiation was to be seen as a precise and thorough one. The gospel was one thing, the law was another. The gospel was given by Jesus, the law was given by Moses. This law that Moses gave was indeed from God. But this could not have been the God of Jesus. The God of the law was harsh, cruel, and vindictive. He was certainly "just" in that he had given a law; moreover, since everyone had broken the law, it was "fair" for him to condemn everyone to death. But this is not like the God of Jesus, who was a God of love, mercy, and forgiveness. Marcion drew what seemed to him to be the ineluctable conclusion. There were two gods.

For Marcion, the God of the Old Testament created this world, called Israel to be his people, and gave them his law. Because everyone violated the law, he condemned them. The God of Jesus did not send his son into the world in fulfillment of the Jewish Scriptures. These belonged to the other God. Jesus came into the world to save people from the righteous judgment of the God of the Jews. As a result, the followers of Jesus were to reject everything that came from the Jewish God: his creation (it was not good), his law, and his scriptures.

And so there are two ends of the spectrum covering possible views of Judaism among second-century Christians. Some Christian groups continued to maintain their Jewish identity and insisted that to be a follower of Jesus, you had to convert to Judaism. These were groups of Jewish Christians, one of whom was called the **Ebionites**. Other groups rejected all things Jewish and insisted that Jesus had nothing to do with Judaism—so his followers should not, either. Chief among these groups were the **Marcionites**.

As happens with all spectrums, most Christians fell somewhere between these two extremes. We have already seen this with most of our New Testament authors. For example, the apostle Paul taught that Jesus was in fact the fulfillment of the Jewish Law, but he insisted

FIGURE 14.1. Coin of the emperor Vespasian, which commemorates the conquest of Judea by Titus with the inscription "Judea Taken Captive." The fall of Jerusalem was a significant event in the development of Jewish–Christian relations.

at the same time that gentiles who were not born under the Law should not—should decidedly not—be required to start following it, for example by being circumcised or keeping kosher. The book of Hebrews sees the Jewish Scriptures as having come from the one true God, but insists that the religion based on these Scriptures was a foreshadowing of something even better to come, which was brought by the Son of God who died as the perfect sacrifice for sins. Matthew, on the other hand, taught that while Jesus was the fulfillment of the Law, he himself kept the Law and insisted that his followers do likewise.

In addition to the question of how Christians understood their new religion in relationship to Judaism there is another matter of importance for understanding ancient Jewish–Christian relations: what did Christians, broadly speaking, think about their relationship to actual Jews who did not believe? This is a completely different issue and raises the question of how it is that Christianity eventually became an anti-Jewish religion. There can be no doubt that it eventually did so, even if there are debates among scholars about when and how thoroughly that happened. But the history of Christianity after the fourth century can largely be seen, in part at least, as a history of anti-Judaism, which eventually, in modern times, became a history of violent anti-Semitism. Already by the middle of the second century, as we will see in a moment, there were Christian leaders who were virulently anti-Jewish in their rhetoric. But why so? Jesus himself was Jewish, a Jewish teacher with Jewish disciples who learned from him his distinctive teaching of the Jewish Law. Christianity began as a sect within Judaism. How did it so quickly become an anti-Jewish religion?

They key to answering the question lies in understanding the radical nature of the claim made by the earliest Christians that the crucified Jesus was in fact the Jewish messiah. Even though it may seem odd to many Christians today, this claim struck most Jews as completely ludicrous (see our earlier discussion of Paul in chapter 12). The crucified Jesus was just the *opposite* of what Jews were expecting in a messiah—whether they were looking forward to a great warrior-king like David, or a cosmic judge of the earth sometimes called the Son of Man, or a great and powerful priest who would rule his people through his correct interpretation of the Jewish Law. For those Jews who expected the messiah (not all of them did, any more than all—or even most—Jews do today), he was to be a figure of grandeur and power who would overthrow the enemies of God and set up a kingdom here on earth. Jesus did not do that, and far from overthrowing the enemy he was unceremoniously destroyed by the enemy, tortured and publicly crucified. For most Jews, he was anything but the messiah.

But Christians insisted that he was the messiah, and that Jews had a wrong understanding of what the messiah would be. Christians, in effect, redefined the term messiah. Knowing that Jesus was crucified, and believing that he was the messiah, Christians devised the idea of the crucified messiah. To do so they read and reread their scriptures (the Jewish Bible) and found place after place that referred to a righteous one of God who suffered; sometimes this one was said to have suffered for the sake of others, and then to have been vindicated by God. Passages such as Isaiah 53 and Psalm 22 became important, and Christians claimed these Scriptures were referring to the messiah. Jews argued that they were not messianic in character—and could point out that in fact the term "messiah" never occurs in these passages. Christians were unpersuaded. God's righteous one must suffer; the messiah is God's righteous one, therefore the messiah must suffer. Jesus suffered, and he was the messiah.

This naturally led to a split between the few Jews who believed in Jesus and those many who did not. The split was made more radical and severe by the fact that the Christians insisted not only that Jesus was the messiah, but also that it was only by believing in his death and resurrection that a person could be among the people of God. Being born a Jew, being circumcised, keeping the Jewish Law—these things had nothing to do with it. Being a "true Jew" meant accepting the Jewish messiah. And people could accept Jesus as messiah whether or not they kept the Law.

This led to the ironic situation that Christians claimed to be true Jews—to be the heirs of the promises given to Abraham and the other Jewish ancestors, to be the ones who understood the true meaning of the Jewish Scriptures—without doing what the Scriptures indicated Jews had to do.

Why didn't Christians as a whole simply abandon the Jewish Scriptures and start their own religion, as teachers like Marcion urged them to do? One reason has to do with the broader understanding of religion in the ancient world. People in antiquity, as a rule, did not trust anything "new" or "recent" when it came to

(continued)

EXCURSUS JEWS AND CHRISTIANS IN THE ANCIENT WORLD *(continued)*

philosophy or religion. If it was new, it could not be true. If something was "true" it had to have deep roots in the past; it had to be accepted by the wise people of old, it had to have an established pedigree. One of the reasons Christians were persecuted, as we will see later in this chapter, is that they rejected the pagan religions but did not substitute for them anything from antiquity. The Christians worshiped a man who had been crucified just recently.

In order to claim antiquity for themselves—in part, in order to argue that they should not be persecuted as representing an anti-social, newfangled religion—they argued that their religion was in fact quite ancient. It was as old as the ancient Jewish prophets, as old as Moses. Moses lived 400 years before the Greek poet Homer; 800 years before Plato. And Moses predicted Jesus. Christians claimed the Jewish scriptures for themselves and insisted that these Scriptures did not belong, therefore, to the Jews. The Scriptures were a

Christian, not a Jewish, book. Jews also found this view to be ludicrous. Christians wanted to claim that the Scriptures were theirs, but they didn't even follow the laws set out in Scripture.

Tensions mounted over the years, as becomes more evident in the second and third centuries. Christian writers emerged who were violently anti-Jewish in their rhetoric—writers like **Justin Martyr** in the middle of the second century, who argued that God gave circumcision to the Jews so that governing authorities could easily see who had been "marked" as deserving to be persecuted; and writers like **Melito of Sardis** later in that century, who claimed that it was the Jews who were responsible for the death of Jesus and that since Jesus was God, the Jews were guilty for the murder of God (see Box 14.1). This is the first instance we have of Jews being charged with deicide.

It is easy to trace the later history of anti-Semitism to this kind of early Christian rhetoric against the

---

BOX 14.1 MELITO'S PASSOVER SERMON

Melito was a bishop of the city of Sardis in Asia Minor in the mid to late second century. Today he is best known for a sermon he wrote that lambastes the Jews for the role they played in the death of Jesus. In it we find the first instance of a Christian author claiming that since the Jews killed Jesus, and since Jesus was God, the Jews are guilty of deicide—the murder of God. This charge was used, of course, to justify all sorts of hateful acts of violence against Jews over the centuries. In part, the rhetorical eloquence with which the charge was sometimes leveled has contributed to the emotional reaction that it produced. Consider Melito's own gripping, if terrifying, rhetoric:

> This one was murdered. And where was he murdered? In the very center of Jerusalem! Why? Because he had healed their lame and had cleansed their lepers, and had guided their blind with light, and had raised up their dead. For this reason he suffered. . . . (ch. 72).
>
> Why, O Israel, did you do this strange injustice? You dishonored the one who had

honored you. You held in contempt the one who held you in esteem. You denied the one who publicly acknowledged you. You renounced the one who proclaimed you his own. You killed the one who made you to live. Why did you do this, O Israel? (ch. 73)

> It was necessary for him to suffer, yes, but not by you; it was necessary for him to be dishonored, but not by you; it was necessary for him to be judged, but not by you; it was necessary for him to be crucified, but not by you, not by your right hand, O Israel! (chs. 75–76)
>
> Therefore, hear and tremble because of him for whom the earth trembled. The one who hung the earth in space is himself hanged; the one who fixed the heavens in place, is himself impaled; the one who firmly fixed all things, is himself firmly fixed to the tree. The Lord is insulted, God has been murdered, the king of Israel has been destroyed, by the hand of Israel. . . . (chs. 95–96).

Jews. In the first and second centuries Jews vastly out-numbered Christians in the world. But in the fourth Christian century, after the emperor Constantine converted to become a Christian, the Christian church acquired real political power. And these later Christians took the violent rhetoric of their predecessors seriously, and acted on it. Jews became persona non grata in the Empire; synagogues were destroyed, property was confiscated, Jews were persecuted by mobs. And the ugly history of Christian violent anti-Judaism began in earnest.

who lived by "faith," acting on the assurance of what they had not yet experienced (ch. 11). Christ himself lived that way, and his followers need to emulate his example even if it requires suffering (ch. 12). The book ends with a series of exhortations to love one another, to refrain from sexual impropriety, to obey the community's leaders, and to abstain from false teachings, especially those that promote adherence to the laws of Judaism (ch. 13).

THE LETTER OF JAMES

The letter of James contains a large number of ethical admonitions to unnamed readers living outside of Palestine, who are called "the twelve tribes in the Diaspora." One might automatically think that the book is written by a Jew to (non-Christian) Jews, but it clearly is not that. The author indicates that he is a "slave of God and of the Lord Jesus Christ" (1:1). So he is a Christian and he is writing to Christians. And even though Jesus is not frequently named in the letter (in fact in just one other place, 2:1), the exhortations the author makes will sound familiar to anyone otherwise deeply familiar with the Christian tradition. A number of the moral instructions appear to reflect traditions of Jesus' own teaching (such as the Sermon on the Mount known from Matthew's Gospel). And so, for example, believers are not to swear oaths but to let their "yes be yes" and their "no be no" (5:12; cf. Matthew 5:33–37); loving one's neighbor is said to fulfill the Law (2:8; cf. Matthew 22:39–40); those who are rich are warned to fear the coming judgment (5:1–6; cf. Matthew 19:23–24).

At the same time, many of the book's ethical injunctions can be found in non-Christian Jewish writings and it is interesting that examples of good ethical behavior are drawn entirely from stories of the Hebrew Bible, not Christian traditions

(Abraham, 2:21; Rahab, 2:25; Job, 5:11; Elijah, 5:17). For these reasons, some scholars have argued that the book is best compared to a Jewish wisdom text—somewhat like Proverbs, but without as many one-liners—with only a thin Christian veneer. Some scholars think that the author took over a piece of Jewish writing and "Christianized" it by adding a couple of references to Jesus. More commonly it is thought that the author has simply strung together a number of important ethical admonitions that could otherwise be found in a variety of settings, such as Jewish wisdom literature and traditions of Jesus' own teaching, and applied them to the Christian communities he is addressing.

As we will see in a moment, the overarching emphasis of the book is that those who have faith (presumably in Jesus) need to manifest it in the way they live (1:22–27; 2:14–26). They are not only to talk as if they have faith; their faith needs to be seen in the way they behave, especially toward other people. Other recurring themes in the book include the importance of controlling one's "tongue" (that is, one's speech; 1:26; 3:1–12), the danger of wealth for those who believe (1:9–11; 4:13–17; 5:1–6), and the need to be patient in the midst of suffering (1:2–8, 12–16; 5:7–11). The author, however, is not concerned only with how people should behave as individuals; near the end of the book he turns to address the activities of the whole church as well, giving his readers advice about saying prayers, singing psalms, anointing the sick with oil, confessing sins, and restoring those who have strayed from the faith (5:13–16).

One of the big questions raised by the book concerns its author. He states that his name is "James," but he does not tell us which James he is. As you may have noticed, there are a lot of people named James in the New Testament: there is James the son of Zebedee, James the son of Alphaeus, James the father of Judas, and James the brother of Jesus. For most scholars, precisely the fact that the author does not tell us which James he is suggests that he expects his readers to know that he is a particularly famous James, who can get by simply by indicating his name (like someone claiming to be "Elvis"). This is especially the case since the author is not writing to a small compact community that could be expected to know who he is; he is writing to Christians spread throughout the world (throughout the entire Diaspora). And so he must be claiming to be the most famous James of all, "that" James, the brother of Jesus.

But the real author almost certainly could not have been the brother of Jesus. Among the compelling reasons for thinking so is that James, the brother of Jesus, could almost certainly not write.

There have been some very important studies of literacy done in recent years, which have shown beyond any doubt that the vast majority of people in the ancient world were illiterate—could not read or write. The most compelling analyses indicate that during the first century, in Roman Palestine, only something like 3 percent of the population could read. Those who could read would be able to read Hebrew (or possibly Aramaic); only a fraction of that number could read Greek. And few of those who could read would know how to write. Writing a composition—a letter, a poem, a story, a book—took many years of education. And that was almost always done in the native language (in this case Aramaic). In the ancient world, those who learned to write were only the upper crust, wealthy elite, who were almost always living in major urban areas.

The book of James is written in very good, rhetorically effective Greek. And who was James, the brother of Jesus? A lower-class peasant from a small hamlet in rural Galilee whose native tongue was Aramaic. If he knew any Greek at all, it was to make fumbling conversation. He would not have been sent away for years to school to learn the art of composition, let alone composition in a foreign language. This book is almost certainly pseudonymous, written by someone who was claiming to be James while knowing full well he was someone else.

But it makes sense that he claims to be James. Recall that in Galatians it was the "people from James" who caused the split between Peter and Paul in Antioch, when Peter decided no longer to take his meals with gentiles (because these people were so adamant about Jews keeping kosher). In early Christianity it was widely thought that just as Paul was the apostle who urged that gentiles could be

followers of Jesus without keeping the Law, it was James who insisted that keeping the Law was of utmost importance for all followers of Jesus.

Many readers have suspected that the book of James is in fact an attack on Paul's teaching of justification by faith apart from the works of the Law (as Paul argues in both Romans and Galatians, for example). It is striking that the book of James appears to take just the opposite point of view:

What does it profit, my brothers, if someone says he has faith but does not have works? Can his faith save him? . . . Do you want to be shown, you shallow person, that faith apart from works is barren? Was not Abraham our father justified by works . . . ? [he quotes then Genesis 15:6] you see that a person is justified by works, not by faith alone. (James 2:14–26)

Since Martin Luther and the Reformation in the sixteenth century, this passage has often been read as a direct assault on Paul's views. Paul says that faith justifies a person apart from works of the Law; James says works justifies a person, not faith alone. Paul says Abraham was justified by faith; James says he was justified by works. Paul quotes Genesis 15:6 to support his view, and so too does James. All this hardly seems to be an accident. James seems to be responding to Paul.

At the same time, when looked at closer, the book of James is not *exactly* responding to Paul. Paul in fact never says that "faith alone" saves. For him, someone who truly has faith will still necessarily live a good and morally upright life. Moreover when Paul speaks of "faith" he means, as we have seen, a trusting acceptance of the death of Jesus. James seems to mean, instead, the intellectual acceptance of a belief (like the demons, who believe that there is only one God; 2:19). Knowing the right things about God and Christ will not save a person, for James. Moreover when James speaks of works he is referring to good deeds, not to "works of the Jewish Law" as Paul is.

As a result, it may be that James is not directly attacking Paul but a later interpretation of Paul by some of Paul's followers. We saw in chapter 13 that the pseudonymous author of Ephesians took Paul's teaching of justification by faith apart from works to mean that it was not "good deeds" that would save a person but the grace of God alone, through faith in Christ (Ephesians 2:1–10). It may be that the pseudonymous author of James is responding to someone like that other pseudonymous author, so that the book of James is a forgery countering the view found in another forgery. In any event, the overarching teaching of this author is clear. For him, a person is not made right with God by thinking the right things or mouthing the right words. One has to put faith in action, because "faith without works is dead."

1 PETER

The book of 1 Peter is a letter written in the name of the apostle Peter to "the exiles of the Diaspora" in several of the provinces of Asia Minor: "Pontus, Galatia, Cappadocia, Asia, and Bythinia" (1:1). As with the book of James, these people in the Diaspora are not Jews; in this case it is crystal clear that the author is writing specifically to Christians, as the book is all about how to be a Christian in the world.

The author of this letter indicates that his recipients are "resident aliens." This term is sometimes used in ancient writings to refer to people who lived in a foreign country without being citizens or having the rights of citizens (more or less like people with "green cards," or even more, illegal aliens). Such people would feel alienated within their environment, and 1 Peter discusses what it means to be alienated from society at large and to suffer as a result. But it is probably best not to take 1 Peter to mean that the recipients of his letter were all, literally, (political) resident aliens: he is sending the letter to churches that cover a vast amount of territory, and there is no way that everyone in these churches had just one kind of citizenship classification or another. It is more likely, then, that he means the term in a figurative sense: the people receiving this letter are "aliens" wherever they live, because their true home is in heaven. For their temporary stay here on earth, they are foreigners—wherever they live.

The one thing we can say about these people who were leading an alienated existence in their lives is that they were suffering for it. And this author is writing his letter to help them deal with it. The word for "suffering" occurs more often in this short letter than in any other book of the New Testament, even more than in the much longer works of Luke and Acts combined, although those books too are concerned about Christians' suffering. Even when the author of 1 Peter is not talking directly about how to handle suffering, he appears to be speaking about it indirectly. Throughout the letter, for example, he urges his readers to live moral lives so that those on the outside can see that they are doing nothing wrong and causing nobody any harm. They are to be obedient slaves, submissive wives, and tender husbands, and they are to obey all governing authority and to be devoted subjects of the emperor. These are not simply pieces of moral advice; they are also guidelines for avoiding persecution from suspicious authorities and for putting to shame those who wrongfully cause abuse.

It is clear that the recipients are suffering persecution specifically for being Christian: they are not simply suffering because bad things have happened in their lives. Nonetheless, this author never suggests that they are experiencing some kind of "official" persecution by Roman officials. Instead he indicates that there is local opposition to their behavior. They used to behave like everyone else in their pagan environment, but now that they are Christian they have their own communities, lead their own lives, and follow a different set of moral principles. Their former families and friends are very upset about it and abuse them as a result (4:3–5). This author responds by telling his readers that they should not be surprised that they are suffering: their master, Christ himself, suffered (4:12–13). They should therefore follow his example and walk in his steps, not suffering for doing anything that is wrong (by breaking the law) but only for doing what is right. They are to live moral, upright lives, and if that leads to suffering, so be it (3:14–17; 4:14–15). If they do suffer because of their new Christian lives, however, they should always be prepared to "make a defense to anyone who demands from you an accounting for the hope that is in you." By doing so, Christians will put their enemies to shame (3:15–17). It is their moral behavior that will win over a skeptical world (3:1). When people look to see how upright their lives are, they will be put to shame for thinking them, the Christians, to be doing anything wrong (2:11).

Throughout his letter the author stresses that even though they are suffering, his Christian readers are the chosen people who have had a new birth and so are the true children of God (1:2–3, 14–19; 2:9). They are the ones in whom God himself lives, and so are special in the world (2:4–9). They should

EXCURSUS THE PERSECUTION OF THE EARLY CHRISTIANS

1 Peter obviously raises the question about Christians experiencing persecution. Many people have a false idea about the early persecutions of Christians—possibly because of too many bad Hollywood movies. Contrary to what is often thought, Christianity was not an illegal religion in the early centuries of its existence, and Christians did not have to go into hiding in the Roman catacombs to avoid the wrath of the emperors. Why then were the Christians persecuted and by whom? And when did official persecution, sponsored by Roman officials, begin?

The earliest Christians did indeed occasionally—not always—face animosity. We know this much from the writings of Paul, the book of Acts, and the letter of 1 Peter. In almost every instance, the opposition to Christians started at the grassroots level from their families, former friends, and communities. It was almost never started at the top, with Roman officials. Since the earliest Christians were Jewish, it makes sense that the opposition to them started out in Jewish communities in which Christians worshiped. If the case of the pre-Christian Paul is representative of why the earliest persecutions took place, it was precisely because of the Christian claim that a crucified man was the messiah. Most Jews simply wanted nothing to do with the Christians and their insistence that an executed criminal was the Lord of the universe. You too would probably not much appreciate someone coming into your community and declaring that a criminal sent to the electric chair a few years ago was the savior of the world, and that to have salvation you have to believe in him. At first you would probably ignore the person; if he were persistent you would make fun of him; if he kept pressing his point you might start getting really angry, and eventually trouble might break out. So too with the earliest Christians in their Jewish communities. Christians were seen as ridiculous, hard-headed, foolish, and, eventually, troublemakers.

Moreover, as we saw with 1 Peter, pagans who had converted to faith in Jesus gave up their former lives; when they did so, their erstwhile friends and companions found the change inexplicable and ridiculous. And there was an even bigger problem, eventually. We have seen in chapters 1 and 9 that pagan religions were focused on the idea that the gods did not demand much: they simply wanted to be worshiped, as they always had been. When they were ignored the gods could become

angry, and since they were so powerful, when that happened—look out! When disasters struck a community, it was frequently interpreted as a judgment of the gods for not being worshiped in a proper way. What do you suppose would happen in a community where a group of people steadfastly refused to worship the gods, and then disaster struck: an earthquake, a drought, a famine, an epidemic? Obviously, people reasoned, someone is at fault for the gods' anger. It must be the people who were refusing to worship the gods. That is, it was the Christians. They needed to conform to standard practice and revere the gods. If they refused, they needed to be forced to do so. And thus the persecutions of Christians, which were started in order to compel them to worship the gods that they considered to be dead idols or demonic forces. (Jews were not usually targeted for persecution because they, unlike the Christians, had a very ancient religion and so could claim an exemption.)

In addition to all this, Christians were considered dangerous to society because they worshiped in closed communities not open to the public. What did they have to keep secret? What exactly were they doing in there? Is it true that they were kissing one another as brothers and sisters? Were they committing incest? Is it true that they were eating the flesh and drinking the blood of the "son"? Were they killing babies and eating them? As crazy as it sounds, these were the charges that were brought against Christians over time. No wonder they did not have a good reputation with the public at large.

Persecutions of the Christians therefore happened on the local level at first. Contrary to what is sometimes thought, there was not a persecution of Christians throughout the entire Roman Empire, sponsored by Roman emperors, for many, many years. In fact it was not until the year 249 C.E., under the emperor Decius, that there was anything like an empire-wide persecution. Before then there were emperors who occasionally sponsored persecution in one place or another, but nothing on a massive scale.

During the period of our interest—the first and early second century—we know of only two emperors who were actively involved with any persecutions. The first was the emperor Nero in the year 64 C.E. The story is told by the Roman historian **Tacitus**, whose book *The Annals of Rome* describes events in the history of Rome up to his own day in 115 C.E. According to

FIGURE 14.2. Mosaic from a villa in North Africa, showing wild animals attacking a man. During the persecutions, Christians were sometimes martyred by wild beasts in the arena.

Tacitus, Nero had architectural plans for his capital city, Rome. But he could not very well implement these plans while the city was still standing. And so he ordered arsonists to burn a good bit of it down. They did so, and the people who were burned out of house and home were understandably distraught and came to think the emperor was responsible for what had happened. To take the blame off himself, Nero decided to pin the fault on a group of people who were widely known to be antisocial and hateful, and so he chose the Christians. He had the Christians in Rome rounded up, and he publicly subjected them to humiliating torture and death.

It is important to realize that in this first "official, imperial" persecution of Christians (a) there was no declaration that Christianity was illegal; (b) the persecution happened only in the city of Rome, not throughout the empire; and (c) the Christians were not

(continued)

EXCURSUS THE PERSECUTION OF THE EARLY CHRISTIANS *(continued)*

BOX 14.2 AN ALTERNATIVE VIEW OF CHRISTIAN MARTYRDOM

Most of the surviving Christian writings from antiquity take a positive view of Christian martyrdom, urging Christians to go willingly to their deaths for the faith and to endure all the tortures that humans can devise. By doing so, Christians would imitate the Passion of their Lord, Jesus.

But not everyone agreed. We know from the writings of several Christian authors, for example, that there were large-scale defections from the Christian ranks in times of persecution. Indeed, one of these authors, Tertullian, specifically attacks Christian groups for opposing martyrdom. These groups tried to persuade their fellow Christians not to be so foolish as to die for their faith. In their view, Christ died so that his followers would not have to do so. For them, anyone who embraced the need for martyrdom in effect denied that Jesus' death itself was sufficient for salvation (Tertullian, *Scorpion's Sting*, 1). It appears likely that such people urged Christians to perform the necessary sacrifices to the state gods without actually committing apostasy in their hearts, since God after all was concerned with the heart, not with such meaningless actions as tossing a handful of incense on a burning altar.

persecuted for calling themselves Christian but for committing arson. They were innocent, but that's not the point. The charge against them was not religious in nature.

The next imperially sponsored persecution that we know about occurred over fifty years later during the reign of the emperor Trajan. In chapter 11 I mentioned **Pliny**, a Roman governor of a province in Asia Minor, who was the first pagan to mention Jesus in any surviving source. The context in which he does so involves a problem that was occurring in his community. It was illegal there for groups of people to congregate together for social purposes, and Pliny discovered that Christians were violating this law by meeting together for their worship services. He found out what he could about the group and worked to disband it. More than that, he realized that the Christians were not worshiping the pagan gods—including the divine emperor himself. And so when Christians were brought to him he tried to force them to deny their faith in Christ and to perform a sacrifice to an image of the emperor. Those who refused to do so were executed. Those who did

what he asked (it simply involved tossing a handful of incense onto a fire on an altar) he let go.

This shows, among other things, that being a Christian was not exactly a crime. Crimes are punished after they are committed (e.g., murder or embezzlement), but these Christians who gave up their faith were not punished. And so it was a crime to *continue* being Christian, not to have been one before. Pliny wrote a letter about how he handled the problem, and the emperor Trajan wrote back approving his procedure. Christians had to be forced to accept the worship of the pagan gods. If they refused, they were to be dealt with severely.

Here again the persecution appears to have been driven by the pagan view that the gods could become very angry if not worshiped properly. Pagans had no problem with Christians believing in their own God, or even with them saying that Jesus was God. That was fine, so long as Christians also participated in the worship of the state gods. If they did not, that could lead to problems in the community as the gods became wrathful; and that, in turn, meant very bad news for the Christians themselves.

therefore not fear suffering. On the contrary, they should rejoice if they suffer for a good cause, and their suffering will result in salvation in the world to come (1:1–3, 9).

Who wrote these exhortations to Christians undergoing persecution? The book claims to be written by none other than Peter, the disciple of Jesus, one of Jesus' inner circle. But almost certainly it could not have been, for much the same reason that the book of James could not have been written by the brother of Jesus. What we know about Peter from the Gospels is that he was a lower-class,

Aramaic-speaking peasant, from the rural backwaters of Galilee, the small town of Capernaum. He was not a member of the upper classes; he was not one of the wealthy elite; he would not have gone to school for many years to learn to read and then many more years to write. If he could speak any Greek at all, it would have been for simple, broken conversation. He would not have been able to compose such a highly literary piece as the book of 1 Peter.

Some scholars have thought, then, that maybe Peter dictated the letter (to Silvanus? 5:12). But recent studies of ancient dictation practices, and of the use of secretaries by authors, have shown that we have very little evidence of anything like this happening—no evidence, in fact, of a secretary writing a letter in a different language for an "author," or composing such a complicated and rhetorically refined treatise as this for someone else named as the writer. What we have lots of evidence for in the ancient world is forgery—people writing works claiming to be someone famous so that readers would take their writing seriously. That appears to be what we have here: a book that claims to be written by Peter but that was actually written by someone else simply claiming to be Peter.

This would not be the only time it happened. As we will see, 2 Peter is also almost certainly pseudonymous. So too are a number of books from outside the New Testament: the Gospel of Peter, the letter of Peter to James, the letter of Peter to Philip, and the three Apocalypses allegedly written by Peter. Writing books claiming to be Peter was something of a cottage industry in early Christianity. In the book of 1 Peter we have possibly the first instance of it happening. In this case an author was dealing with a critical situation in which Christians were suffering for their faith. Claiming to be the great apostle, he wrote in order to encourage them in their suffering; to urge them to suffer only for doing what is right, not what is wrong; and to hold on to their hope, because if they remained faithful in their suffering they would be rewarded with a great salvation in the age to come.

2 PETER

There is less debate about the authorship of 2 Peter than for any of the other (possibly) pseudonymous

writings of the New Testament. It is almost universally recognized among critical scholars that whoever wrote the book, it was not Simon Peter. It is striking that, so far as we know, the letter was not known even to exist for a hundred years after it was most likely written; there is not a solitary reference to it until around 220 C.E., and it does not appear to have been widely circulated even after that. It was probably included in the canon simply because later church fathers assumed Peter must have written it.

That he did not do so is evident on numerous grounds. Not least is the fact, already mentioned, that Peter almost certainly could not write. In addition, it is widely recognized that this author has borrowed a large amount of his material (most of chapter 2) from the epistle of Jude—another book that is pseudonymous, as we will see. It seems unlikely that one of the leading apostles of the early church would have to rely on someone else's writing in order to know how to oppose false teachers, which is what this letter is all about.

Even though he was not Peter, he goes far out of his way to insist he is. This makes the letter different from 1 Peter—which was clearly not written by the same author, since the writing styles are so

FIGURE 14.3. Many Romans believed that the Roman gods were responsible for their military and political successes, as evident in this silver coin that shows a Roman goddess crowning the memorialized image of a soldier after a victory.

different. The book of 1 Peter does not try to "prove" it was written by Peter: it just claims to be. But the author of 2 Peter does try to prove it by insisting that he was personally present at the Mount of Transfiguration to behold Jesus' divine glory and hear the voice from heaven.

The author wants to insist that he is Peter so that he can have the authority he needs to dispute the ideas of the false teachers that he is writing this book to oppose. These others hold to "cleverly devised myths." We don't know what those myths are, or even who these people were—other than that "Peter" has some very nasty things to say about them. One of the most interesting things he says is that these opponents use the letters of Paul, but "twist" their meaning "as they do with the rest of the Scriptures" (3:16). This intriguing statement shows that the author was living at a time when Paul's letters were not only in circulation, they had been collected together and were already being considered to be equal to Scripture (i.e., the Old Testament). This too indicates that the book must have been written after Peter's day. The book is usually dated to the beginning of the second century, around 120 C.E., nearly sixty years after Peter would have been dead.

The author engages in a good deal of name-calling to oppose his (Christian) opponents, especially in chapter 2. Unfortunately, that kind of invective does not help us much if we want to know what the opponents actually taught. But at one point the false teaching becomes clear. These people appear to be "scoffers" who do not think that the end of the age is coming very soon (3:3–4). In other words, these teachers maintain that the apocalyptic end of the age is not imminent, and they are mocking Christians like this author for holding to such an untenable belief.

The author stresses that, contrary to these scoffers, the end is indeed soon to come. If it seems to be taking a long time, his readers need to remember that God has a different calendar from humans, since with God, "one day is like a thousand years and a thousand years are like one day" (3:8). This would mean, one might suppose, that if the end was still 6000 years away, it is still coming "soon."

BOX 14.3 PETER, THE SMOKED TUNA, AND THE FLYING HERETIC

Among the pseudepigrapha connected with the apostle Peter, none is more interesting than the apocryphal *Acts of Peter*, a document that details Peter's various confrontations with the heretical magician **Simon Magus** (cf. Acts 8:14–24). The narrative shows how Peter outperforms the magician by invoking the power of God. Consider the following entertaining account, in which Peter proves the divine authorization of his message by raising a dead tuna fish back to life.

But Peter turned round and saw a smoked tunny-fish hanging in a window; and he took it and said to the people, "If you now see this swimming in the water like a fish, will you be able to believe in him whom I preach?" And they all said with one accord, "Indeed, we will believe you!" Now there was a fish-pond nearby; so he said, "In thy name, Jesus Christ, in which they still fail to believe" [he said to the tunny] "in the presence of all these be alive and swim like a fish!" And he threw the tunny into the pond, and it came alive and began to swim. And the people saw the fish swimming; and he made it do so not merely for that hour, or it might have been called a delusion, but he made it go on swimming, so that it attracted crowds from all sides and showed that the tunny had become a live fish; so much so that some of the people threw in bread for it, and it ate it all up. And when they saw this, a great number followed him and believed in the Lord. (*Acts of Peter* 13)

In the ultimate showdown between the heretical sorcerer (Simon Magus) and the man of God (Peter), Simon the magician uses his powers to leap into the air and fly like a bird over the temples and hills of Rome. Not to be outdone, Peter calls upon God to smite Simon in midair; God complies, much to the magician's dismay and demise. Unprepared for a crash landing, he plunges to earth and breaks his leg in three places. Seeing what has happened, the crowds rush to stone him to death as an evildoer. And so the true apostle of God triumphs over his enemy, the preacher of heresy.

The author wants to stress that the end has been delayed to allow all people adequate time to repent and turn to the truth. But the Day of Judgment is nonetheless destined to come, and when it does it will appear "like a thief" (3:9). The certainty of this final day should drive people to live lives of holiness, as they wait for the final destruction of this world and the new age to come (3:11–12).

1, 2, AND 3 JOHN

The books called 1, 2, and 3 John are named this because early church fathers believed that they were written by the same person who produced the fourth Gospel, and they were convinced that this person was none other than John the son of Zebedee, the disciple of Jesus. John almost certainly did not write any of these books, since—like his fellow Aramaic-speaking, lower-class, fisherman Peter—he too would not have been able to write. And there are reasons for thinking that whoever wrote these books it was not the author of the Gospel of John, even though they share a number of themes and theological perspectives.

The books are typically called "letters," and that appears to be an appropriate designation for 2 and 3 John, which are only about a page each and are the shortest books of the New Testament. 2 John is written by someone who calls himself "the elder" to a mysterious person called "the elect lady." Later in the letter, the author stops speaking to the "lady" and speaks to a group of people ("you" plural, starting in verse 6). This shift has led most scholars to think that the "lady" is in fact a Christian community, the church that the author is addressing. 3 John is so much like 2 John that it appears to have the same author. The writing styles and many of the themes are the same, and again the author calls himself "the elder." In this instance, however, he addresses not an entire community but an individual named Gaius, lending his support to Gaius' side in a dispute that has arisen in the church.

The much longer book of 1 John does not appear to be a letter: the writing does not include the name of the author or his recipients, or anything else that makes letters appear to be letters. Instead, this book is an essay—or possibly an open letter?—that has been written to a community. It has numerous similarities to 2 and 3 John, and so was probably written by the same person. The historical circumstances behind the letters seem to indicate that he was living sometime later than the Gospel of John, and the writing style differs from that of the Gospel, so the author may have been a different writer living in the same community.

The historical situation that prompted these writings is suggested most clearly in a passage found in 1 John. According to 2:19, there has been a split in the community in which a group of people have left to start a community of their own:

> They went out from us, but they did not belong to us; for it they had belonged to us they would have remained with us. But by going out they made it plain that none of them belongs to us.

In reading these letters it is clear that the split has not been a happy one, and the issues involved theology. Those who have left the community are called "liars" and "antichrists" (literally: those opposed to Christ). The ones who have remained in the community, on the other hand, are those who "know the truth."

What is it, then, that the splinter group believes that has caused such a furor? At one point the author indicates that they have "denied that Jesus is the Christ." This may seem straightforward, but it cannot really mean that these people deny that Jesus is the Jewish messiah. They started out within the Christian community, and so were already Christians before splitting off. There is a hint as to what they believe later, in 4:2–3, where we are told that they refuse to confess that "Jesus Christ has come in the flesh." A similar statement is found in 2 John 7. This gives us the information that we need to know what was going on in the community.

Earlier in this chapter I mentioned the teachings of Marcion (see p. 352), who thought that Jesus did not come from the wrathful Jewish God who created this world but from another God who was superior to the Jewish creator. At the time I did not discuss what Marcion thought of Jesus himself. In Marcion's view, since Jesus did not belong to the creator he could not belong to the creation—which means that by the very nature of things, Jesus could not be a material being. He was a fully spiritual being, with no connection to this world of matter. But how could he "seem" to be a flesh-and-blood human then? According to Marcion, Jesus only *seemed* to be human. He did not really have a body. It was all an appearance.

Marcion was not the only one to have this point of view. Theologians call this understanding of Christ "docetism"—from the Greek word "to seem" or "to appear." There also were some Gnostics who thought that Jesus only "seemed" to have a real body. This view evidently had developed within this Johannine community as well. The splinter group that has left does not confess that Jesus Christ "has come in the flesh." That is, he did not have a real body. And *that* is the reason they deny that "Jesus is the Christ." Or to put it more accurately, they do not believe that the Christ is the (realhuman being) Jesus.

Why would someone come to believe this? It is related to the fact that over time, Christians developed views about Jesus in which he was not a purely human messiah but was in some sense God himself. We saw this movement when we examined the Gospel of John, and found that some stories presuppose a very human Jesus (e.g., John 1:35–42) and others presuppose a very divine Jesus (e.g., the Prologue: 1:1–18). It appears that as time went on in the Johannine community, some of the Christians developed their views even further. Not only was Jesus seen to be divine—God on earth. He was *really* God. And if he was really God, then he could not be a human. Why did he then "appear" to be a human? It is because it was all purely an appearance. This is a docetic view that developed within the Johannine community. These people were not Marcionites or Gnostics: they simply were another community that came to a similar view of Christ. The Johannine group that advocated the docetic view found the views of the rest of the community to be unacceptable, and so they left to start a community of their own (which may indeed later have developed into a Gnostic group). And the author of the Johannine epistles is opposing both them and their views, by insisting that Christ was indeed a real flesh-and-blood human being even if he was in some sense God.

That is why they author of 1 John begins his book the way he does, by stressing in his prologue that he himself was able to hear, see, and touch the "Word of Life" (i.e., Christ) that had appeared on earth. Christ was a real, physical being. If he was not, and did not really have flesh and blood, then he could not very well have shed his blood for the sake of others.

And this author stresses strongly that it is Jesus' blood that brings forgiveness of sins, since he made a real human sacrifice of himself (1:7; 2:2; 4:10).

For this author, the splinter group that has left not only has wrong views of Christ. They also engage in acts of immorality. The author claims that they do not practice God's commandments (2:4), that they do not love the members of the community as commanded (2:9–11; 4:20), and that they practice sin while claiming to have no contact with it (1:6–10). It is possible that the author understands the moral failures of the splinter group to be related to their theology. If they undervalue the fleshly existence of Jesus maybe they undervalue the importance of their own existence as well, so that they simply were no longer interested in keeping God's commandments and showing love to members of the community. This would explain why the author stresses in all his letters the need to continue to practice God's commandments and to love one another, unlike the hated docetists who have left the community.

JUDE

The short, one-chapter letter of Jude claims to be written by "Jude, the brother of James" (v. 1). Normally an author with a common name would identify himself in relationship to his father; by putting himself in relationship with his brother instead, this author is obviously claiming to have a very famous brother indeed. As we have seen, Jesus' brothers included both James and Jude (or Judas; Mark 6:3). James was the more famous, as the leader of the church in Jerusalem after Jesus' resurrection. The author of this short book is claiming to be his brother. By implication he is the brother of Jesus as well. As was the case with James, Peter, and John, however, there is almost no reason to think that the real, historical Jude would have been able to write, let alone write in highly literate Greek. He, like the others, would have been a lower-class, Aramaic-speaking, common laborer without an education—let alone an advanced education, let alone an advanced education in a second language in which he learned advanced skills of composition. This letter too, then, is almost certainly pseudepigraphic.

The book is concerned about false teachers who have invaded the Christian community (vv. 3–4).

EXCURSUS ORTHODOXY AND HERESY IN EARLIEST CHRISTIANITY

Several of the general epistles, as we have seen, are deeply concerned about "false teaching." This takes us to the question of the relationship of "orthodoxy" and "heresy" in early Christianity (I will define these two terms in a moment).

Christianity was highly unusual among the religions of the ancient world because it insisted that it mattered what you believed. As we have seen, in pagan religions "beliefs" played very little role at all: what mattered was how you worshiped the gods in the sacrifices and prayers you made. Not for Christians. There is only one God, Jesus is his Son, and he brought about the only way of salvation. If you don't believe the right things, you are condemned.

But different Christians and Christian groups advocated different forms of belief, as we have seen repeated. Paul's Christian opponents in Galatia maintained that you had to keep the Jewish Law to be a follower of Jesus, as did later Jewish Christian groups such as the Ebionites. These later groups were avidly monotheistic: there is only one God. And as a result, many of them insisted that Jesus himself could not be God. Otherwise there would be two gods, not one. Contrast that with the view of Marcion, who thought that in fact there were two gods and that Jesus was so much divine that he was not at all human. But which was it? Was Jesus a man but not God? Or was he God and not a man? Are there two gods or just one?

And then there were the Gnostics, who did not believe that there was just one or two gods, but many gods—and that this world was not the creation of the highest God but was a cosmic catastrophe created by lower, inferior divinities as a place of entrapment for sparks of the divine.

Why didn't these various groups simply read the New Testament to see that they were wrong? The answer should be obvious: there was no New Testament. The books that finally came to be embodied in the New Testament emerged out of these conflicts and came to be placed in a sacred canon by church fathers who were striving to combat each and every one of these other groups (as well as many more). These church fathers insisted that these groups all erred in one way or another. At the same time these other groups insisted that the church fathers were the ones who had gotten it all wrong, that their own views were

the ones taught by Jesus and his early followers. And they too had writings to prove it—Gospels, for example, that set forth their Gnostic, Marcionite, or Ebionite points of view, all of them claiming to be written by apostles.

How do we know that these other groups were wrong and that the church fathers were right? Ultimately, of course, that is a theological question about what is the right thing to believe. And I am not writing this book as a theologian trying to convince you about what you should believe. I am writing it, as I explained in chapter 1, to show how the books of the Bible can be understood literarily and historically. What, then, can we say about the *historical* relationship of these different perspectives on the Christian religion? This is usually discussed as the relationship between "orthodoxy" and "heresy" in the early church.

These terms themselves need to be explained. Technically speaking, "orthodoxy" is a word that means "correct belief" and "heresy" is a word that means "choice"—that is, the choice not to believe the right belief. The terms themselves pose problems for historians, since history has no way of demonstrating whether there is one God, two gods, or thirty-six gods. That is a decision for theologians, not historians. But historians *are* able to look at the history of Christianity and decide which Christian views were dominant where and when, and which views ended up "winning out" in the struggle among various groups. Scholars call the group that won the theological arguments "orthodox" not because this group was necessarily right, but because it won and decided for all time what Christians were to believe. The other groups that lost (Marcionites, Gnostics, Ebionites, etc.) are therefore called "heresies" not because they were wrong, but because they were declared wrong by the group that eventually won the majority of believers.

What is the historical relationship of orthodoxy and heresy? For most of Christian history the view of this relationship has been the one that was advocated most strongly by the first major historian of early Christianity, **Eusebius**, a fourth-century church father who wrote a ten-volume work called *The History of the Christian Church*. This work traced the history of Christianity from the time of Jesus down to Eusebius' own day at the beginning of the fourth century. In it he had to deal with many of the varieties of Christian belief that had

(continued)

been found in the Christian church over the years. His view of this variety is clear and straightforward. As a member of the "orthodox" church—that is, the side of things that ended up winning the debates—he maintained that the views of his group had *always* been the dominant and majority and correct view from the very beginning. Jesus preached an "orthodox" form of Christianity to his disciples; they taught their followers this orthodoxy, who passed it along to their successors, and so on—for 300 years. This "orthodox" view was that there was only one God; Jesus was his son, who was both fully human and fully divine; that the world was the true creation of the true God, that the Jewish Scriptures predicted the coming of Jesus into the world, and so on.

In Eusebius' view "heresies" sprouted up only when willful, mean-spirited, and demonically inspired people infiltrated the church and tried to corrupt its beliefs. That was true of the Jewish Christians, of Marcion, of different Gnostic leaders, and so on. But orthodoxy had been the original point of view and had always been the dominant point of view from the very beginning.

This "Eusebian" view was accepted for many centuries, since the groups that supported other perspectives were squashed by the winning group by the time the Roman Empire converted to Christianity. It just seemed right to people that their own theological beliefs had always been the majority and true beliefs of Christianity from the beginning. Most people still think that today.

But scholars are not so sure that this simple view of the relationship of orthodoxy and heresy is correct. In 1934 an important German scholar named Walter Bauer wrote a significant book called *Orthodoxy and Heresy in Earliest Christianity* in which he disputed Eusebius' point of view and argued something different. In Bauer's view, from as far back as we have historical sources, the *earliest* point of view in many parts of the Christian church was one that later came to be

declared a heresy. And so, for example, in parts of Syria and Asia Minor the original form of Christianity was Marcionite; in Egypt it was Gnostic; and so on. Eventually all these groups tried to gain more converts than the others and to squelch their opponents. It was the form of Christianity located in Rome that proved most successful in this attempt to establish itself as dominant. The "catholic" church (i.e., the one with universal appeal) was the result of these struggles, and it ended up being, in fact, the *Roman* Catholic church.

There has been a lot of scholarship on these questions over the past eighty years, and no one thinks that Bauer is completely right. In many of the details of his exposition, in fact, he appears to be wrong. But with new discoveries—such as the Nag Hammadi library mentioned in chapter 11—it appears that Bauer's basic instincts were right. Early Christianity was incredibly diverse; there were all sorts of views in very many places; all of these views claimed that they were right and that their views were propagated by both Jesus and his apostles; only one form ended up winning out; when it did so, it declared itself "orthodox" and insisted that all other views had been heresies from the beginning; and it then rewrote the history of the conflict to make it appear that its views had always been the majority views (in authors such as Eusebius).

More than the other groups, this orthodox group stressed the importance of a clerical hierarchy that could call the shots and tell people what to believe (as we saw with the Pastoral epistles). They insisted on a set creed to be recited in which their theological beliefs were embodied (for example, the two creeds still recited today by many Christians: the Apostles' Creed and the Nicene Creed). And they established a canon of scripture—a collection of books that claimed to have been written by the apostles and that supported and advanced the points of view that were considered orthodox (as we will see more fully in chapter 15).

The author claims that they have "denied" Christ, but it is hard to understand how that could be if they were part of the Christian church. It may be that, as was the case with the author of the Johannine epistles, this writer felt that anyone who believed something significantly different from what he himself believed was not a "true" Christian.

Most of his attack on these people involves accusing them of licentious and perverse lifestyles. They are "like irrational animals" (v. 10); they engage in "deeds of ungodliness" (v. 15), they are "grumblers and malcontents, they indulge their own lusts, and they are bombastic in speech" (v. 16). They are like the inhabitants of Sodom and

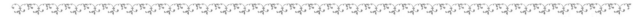

At a Glance: The General Epistles

Not all of the "general epistles" deal with broad, general concerns (as opposed to specific issues), and not all of them are "epistles." All of them are pseudepigraphic—either written by authors falsely claiming to be apostles or anonymous writings that tradition has (wrongly) assigned to apostles.

- Hebrews does not claim to be written by Paul, although it was accepted into the canon by church fathers who thought that it was. It is a sustained attempt to show that Jesus is superior to everything in Judaism; it is meant to prevent its readers from rejecting faith in Jesus so as to adopt the Jewish religion.
- 1 Peter is directed toward Christians who are suffering persecution for their faith and attempts to encourage

them to suffer only for doing what is right, as a witness to those who oppose them.
- 2 Peter is directed against teachers who are claiming that the end of the age is not soon to come.
- 1, 2, and 3 John are all written by the same anonymous author who is responding to a split in his church, in which some members have left to start their own community because of conflicts over the nature of Christ; those who have left insist that Christ was not a human but was completely divine.
- Jude is a vitriolic assault on false teachers, whose precise teaching is never described by the author.

Gomorrah, who "indulged in sexual immorality and pursued unnatural lust" (vv. 5–7). It is hard to know from this kind of attack what these people actually taught: the charges lack much substance. The opponents, thus, are "waterless clouds carried along by the winds; autumn trees without fruit, twice dead, uprooted; wild waves of the sea, casting up the foam of their own shame" (vv. 12–13).

In any event, the author feels that his community is in jeopardy from these "worldly people" (v. 19). And the false teachers need to realize what happens to those who oppose God and lead his people astray. They are in danger of facing God's judgment, in which they will serve "as an example by undergoing a punishment of eternal fire" (v. 7).

It is almost impossible to know when this author wrote his account; scholars tend to date it sometime toward the end of the first century.

THE APOCALYPSE OF JOHN

The New Testament ends with a book that can certainly be considered a fitting climax: the Apocalypse of John, also known as the book of Revelation. The author names himself as "John," but he gives no further indication who he is—no intimation of which "John" he might be. It was a common

name in the ancient world. The book was eventually included in the New Testament—after long and protracted debates by the church fathers—once it was widely believed that this John was none other than John the son of Zebedee, author of the fourth Gospel. As we have seen, this historical John—one of Jesus' disciples—almost certainly did not write the Gospel, and whoever did write it is not the same person as the one who authored the book of Revelation, as is obvious to anyone who compares the two writing styles of the books in Greek. Most likely, then, this author really was someone named John, but he is a John that is otherwise unknown.

By giving his real name, this author was highly unusual among those who wrote ancient Jewish and Christian apocalypses. As we saw in chapter 8, almost always such books were written pseudonymously by authors wanting to convince their readers that they were great religious figures from the distant past, who were worthy to receive a revelation straight from God and who could be trusted to reveal the heavenly secrets—often the future of the world—that could make sense of earthly realities, such as the terrible suffering being experienced by the people of God.

As we saw when considering the book of Daniel in that earlier chapter, apocalypses had a certain more or less set form. They were prose narratives that discussed secret revelations that were given to a prophet or seer; these revelations were invariably given by means of bizarre visions filled with symbolic images. Even the seer often could not understand what it all meant, but there was almost always an angelic being present who interpreted what it was the prophet had seen. In some instances these revelations involved a prediction of the future course of history; in other instances they involved a journey to the heavenly realm to see the realities that are merely being reflected here on earth. In either case, the revelations had a triumphalistic movement, from the horrible experiences of the present to the great fulfillment of all things at the end of time when God and his people would emerge triumphant.

The Content and Structure of the Book

The book of Revelation very much fits in with this pattern. The title comes from its opening words, "The revelation [or 'apocalypse'] of Jesus Christ, which God gave him to show his servants, what must soon take place" (1:1). This particular revelation combines the two forms that we have discussed: it is both a historical sketch of what is to take place and a heavenly vision.

The author's visions begin with an overpowering appearance of "one like a Son of Man" (1:12–20), who is, of course, Christ himself. Christ instructs John to "write what you have seen, what is, and what is to take place after this" (1:19). In other words, he is to (a) narrate the awesome vision of Christ that he has just had ("what you have seen"), (b) describe the present situation of the churches of his day ("what is"), and (c) record his vision of the end of time ("what is to take place after this"). The first task is accomplished in chapter 1. The second is undertaken in chapters 2–3, as Christ dictates brief letters to each of the seven churches of Asia Minor describing their situations and urging certain courses of action. These churches were experiencing difficulties: persecutions, false teachings, and apathy. Christ praises those who have done what is right, promising them a reward, but upbraids those who have fallen away, threatening them with judgment.

The third task is accomplished in chapters 4–22, which record John's heavenly vision of the future course of history down to the end of time. Briefly, the narrative unfolds as follows. The prophet is

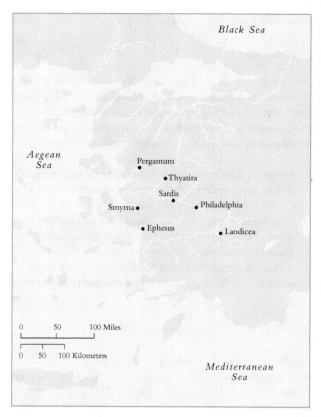

FIGURE 14.4.   The seven churches of Asia Minor addressed in Revelation 2–3.

taken up into heaven through a window in the sky. There he beholds the throne of God, who is eternally worshiped and praised by twenty-four human "elders" and four "living creatures" (angelic beings in the shapes of animals; chapter 4). In the hand of the figure on the throne is a scroll sealed with seven seals, which cannot be broken except by one who is found worthy. This scroll records the future of the earth, and the prophet weeps when he sees that no one has the authority to break its seals; however, one of the elders informs him that there is one who is worthy. He then sees next to the throne a "Lamb standing as if it had been slaughtered" (5:6). The Lamb, of course, is Christ.

The Lamb takes the scroll from the hand of God, amidst much praise and adoration from the twenty-four elders and the four living creatures, and he begins to break its seals (ch. 5). With each broken seal, a major catastrophe strikes the earth: war, famine, death. The sixth seal marks the climax, a disaster of cosmic proportions: the sun turns black,

BOX 14.4 THE BOOK OF REVELATION AS UNDERGROUND LITERATURE

Some readers of the book of Revelation have taken its mysterious symbols to suggest that it was "underground" literature. The symbolic language of the book, according to this interpretation, was used to keep the governing authorities from realizing that they themselves were under attack.

There may be an element of truth in this view, but one might wonder whether a Roman administrator was likely to sit down over the weekend to read a good Christian book. It seems more plausible that the principal function of the symbolism, whether in Revelation or in other apocalypses, lay elsewhere; namely, in the character of the material itself. Indeed, the heavenly secrets are by their very nature not straightforward or banal or subject to empirical demonstration; their mystery and splendor virtually require them to be conveyed in unearthly and bizarre symbols of the higher realities of heaven.

---

the moon turns red as blood, the stars fall from the sky, and the sky itself disappears. One might reasonably think that we have come to the end of all things, the destruction of the universe. But we are only in chapter 6.

The breaking of the seventh seal does not lead to a solitary disaster but to a period of silence that is followed by an entirely new set of seven more disasters. Seven angels appear, each with a trumpet. As each one blows his trumpet, further devastations strike the earth: natural disasters on the land and sea and in the sky, the appearance of dread beasts that torture and maim, widespread calamity, and unspeakable suffering (chs. 8–9). The seventh trumpet marks the beginning of the end (11:15), the coming of the antichrist and his false prophet on earth (chs. 12–13), and the appearance of seven more angels, each with a bowl filled with God's wrath. As the angels each pour out their bowls upon the earth, further destruction and agony ensue: loathsome diseases, widespread misery, and death (chs. 15–16).

The end comes with the destruction of the great "whore of Babylon," the city ultimately responsible for the persecution of the saints (ch. 17). The city is overthrown, to much weeping and wailing on earth but to much rejoicing in heaven (chs. 18–19). The defeat of the city is followed by a final cosmic battle in which Christ, with his heavenly armies, engages the forces of the antichrist aligned against him (19:11–21). Christ wins a resounding victory. The enemies of God are completely crushed, and the antichrist and his false prophet are thrown into a lake of burning sulfur to be tormented forever.

Satan himself is then imprisoned in a bottomless pit, while Christ and his saints rule on earth for a thousand years. Afterward, the Devil emerges for a brief time to lead some of the nations astray. Then comes a final judgment in which all persons are raised from the dead and rewarded for their deeds. Those who have sided with Christ are brought into the eternal kingdom; those who have aligned themselves with the Devil and his antichrist are taken away for eternal torment in the lake of fire. The Devil himself is thrown into the lake, as, finally, are Hades and Death itself (ch. 20).

The prophet then has a vision of the new heavens and the new earth that God creates for his people. A new Jerusalem descends from heaven, with gates made of pearl and streets paved with gold. This is a beautiful and utopian place where Christ reigns eternal, where this is no fear or darkness, no pain or suffering or evil or death, a place where the good and righteous will dwell forever (chs. 21–22). The prophet ends his book by emphasizing that his vision is true, and that it will come to fulfillment very soon.

Context and Meaning

As with all the apocalypses of the ancient world, it is important to situate the Revelation of John in some kind of historical context to make sense of its bizarre symbolism. There are hints scattered throughout the book that portions of it were written in the time of the emperor Nero (in the early 60s C.E.), although the final product is usually dated to the end of the first century, around the year 95 or so, during the reign of the emperor Domitian. It is clear from the letters written to the seven churches in chapters 2–3 that Christians were experiencing opposition to their faith and persecution. And there

BOX 14.5 AN ANCIENT COPYRIGHT CURSE

In the ancient world there was no such thing as copyright law and, as we will see later, scribes often changed the texts they were copying (by hand) in order to make them say what they wanted them to mean (see further chapter 15). How were authors supposed to protect their writing from being changed? The author of the book of Revelation tried one way, by uttering a dire curse on anyone who dared to modify his text:

> I testify to everyone who hears the words of the prophecy of this book: If anyone adds to them, God will add to him the plagues described in this book; and if any one removes any of the words of the book of this prophecy, God will remove his share from the tree of life and from the holy

city, as described in this book. (Revelation 22:18–19)

This is not a threat that the reader has to accept or believe everything written in this book of prophecy, as it is sometimes interpreted; it is in fact a typical threat to the *copyists* of the book that they are not to add or remove any of its words. Similar curses can be found throughout the range of early Christian writings. Unfortunately, they appear to have had little effect: scribes *still* changed the texts they copied, the threat of eternal torment notwithstanding! Even the book of Revelation has numerous differences among every surviving manuscript, so much so that there are places where it is very difficult, if not impossible, to determine what the author originally wrote.

is no doubt who is the great enemy of the church for this book: it is the Roman Empire. There are indications that some Christians have been martyred (6:5; recall the persecution in Rome under Nero). Like all apocalypses (and biblical prophecies, as we saw in our study of the Hebrew Bible), this book is not predicting what was to take place 2000 years after it was written. It was written in its own time and it had a message for its own day. The enemy is Rome, and God is going to destroy it.

This can be seen plainly in some of the more stark images of the book, which make very good sense if put in their own historical context. Read, for example, the description of the "Great Whore of Babylon" in chapter 17. She is seated on a beast full of blasphemous names; she is clothed in fine raiment and jewels, and holds in her hand a golden cup full of the "impurities of her fornication"; and she is said to be "drunk with the blood of the martyrs of Jesus." Who is this enemy of the Christians? We are told that the beast on which she sits is about to descend to the bottomless pit (v. 8); later in the book we learn that it is Satan who will go into the pit, so that this woman, whoever she is, is supported by the Devil. But who is the woman? The beast has seven heads, and we are told that these represent the seven mountains on which the woman is seated (v. 9). That is all we need to know. What city was built on seven hills? Rome. And so the

FIGURE 14.5. Coin minted in 71 C.E., showing the city of Rome seated on the seven hills (cf. Revelation 17:9).

angel explains at the very end, "The woman you saw is the great city that rules the kings of the earth." The enemy is Rome, called here "Babylon" because Rome, like ancient Babylon, destroyed Jerusalem and the Temple; she has committed fornication with the kingdoms of the earth because Rome has prostituted itself in its dealings with other nations.

Or take another image, an even more famous one. Earlier in the book we are given a description of another beast that has ten horns and many heads (ch. 13). One of its heads receives a mortal wound that is healed. The entire world follows the beast, which makes war on the saints and conquers them. It has power over all the nations of the earth and exploits them, demanding to be worshiped. The author then concludes his description by telling his readers who the beast is, by indicating that its "number" is 666.

Despite what you might read in popular books today that try to maintain that all of these predictions are still to come true, now, in the twenty-first century, it is important to locate this book and its images in its own time. By saying that the number of the beast is 666, the author is telling his reader that if you add up the letters in the beast's name, that will be the sum total. Ancient languages used their own alphabets for numerals (unlike English, where we use a Latin alphabet but Arabic numerals). And so, for example the first letter was worth one, the

---

BOX 14.6 FUTURISTIC INTERPRETATIONS OF THE BOOK OF REVELATION

One of the most popular ways to interpret the book of Revelation today is to read its symbolic visions as literal descriptions of what is going to transpire in our own day and age. But there are problems with this kind of approach. On one hand, we should be suspicious of interpretations that are blatantly narcissistic; this way of understanding the book maintains that the entire course of human history has now culminated with us! An even larger problem, however, is that this approach inevitably has to ignore certain features of the text in order to make its interpretations fit.

Consider, as just one example, an interpretation sometimes given of the "locusts" that emerge from the smoke of the bottomless pit in order to wreak havoc on earth in chapter 9. The seer describes the appearance of these dread creatures as follows:

> On their heads were what looked like crowns of gold; their faces were like human faces, their hair like women's hair, and their teeth like lions' teeth; they had scales like iron breastplates, and the noise of their wings was like the noise of many chariots with horses rushing into battle. They have tails like scorpions, with stingers, and in their tails is their power to harm people. . . . (Revelation 9:7–10)

According to one futuristic interpretation, these locusts are modern attack helicopters flying forth through the smoke of battle. The seer, living many centuries before the advent of modern warfare, had no way of knowing what these machines really were, and so he described them as best he could. They fly like locusts but are shaped like huge scorpions. The rotors on top

appear like crowns, they seem to have human faces as their pilots peer through their windshields, they are draped with camouflage that from a distance looks like hair, they have fierce teeth painted on their fronts, they are made of steel and so appear to have iron breastplates, the beating of the rotors sounds like chariots rushing to battle, and they have machine guns attached to their tails like scorpion's stingers.

What could be more plausible? The prophet has glimpsed into the future and seen what he could not understand. We, however, living in the age in which his predictions will come to pass, understand them full well.

The problem is that the interpretation simply doesn't work, because it overlooks some of the most important details of the passage. Consider, for example, what these locusts are actually said to do. The text is quite emphatic: they are not allowed to harm any grass or trees, but only people; moreover, and most significant, they are given the power to torture people for five months but not to kill them (9:4–5). Those who are attacked by the locusts will long to die but will not be able to do so (9:6). These locusts can't be modern instruments of war designed to destroy the enemy, because they are explicitly said to be unable to destroy *anything*.

The same problems occur with virtually every interpretation of the book that takes its visions as literal descriptions of events that will transpire in our own imminent future. These approaches simply cannot account for the details of the text, which is to say that they do not take the text itself seriously enough. It is more reasonable to interpret the text within its own historical context, not as a literal description of the future of the earth but as a metaphorical statement of the ultimate sovereignty of God over a world that is plagued by evil.

second two, the third three, and so on until you came to ten, then the next letter was twenty, then thirty, etc. Who then is this beast? Given the many similarities with the beast of chapter 17, we would not be too far afield to assume that it is another image of the Roman Empire. If so, the heads would be the rulers of the empire, some of whom demanded to be worshiped (as did some of the Roman emperors). There was a tradition in some Christian circles that Nero, the great enemy of the Christians, was to return from the dead and wreak havoc on earth. That would be like having a mortal wound and recovering. Could Nero have been the beast of Revelation 13?

That is almost certainly the case. If you spell the name "Caesar Nero" in Hebrew letters—they add up to 666. The author of Revelation is not referring to Hitler, Mussolini, Saddam Hussein, or the Pope, or anyone else in modern times. His enemy was

Rome and its Caesars. It was Rome that had dominated the other nations of earth, exploited their native populations, and oppressed the people of God; it was the Roman emperor who was worshiped as divine and who persecuted Christians and sometimes put them to death. This book is about how God was going to overthrow this emperor and his empire at the end of time, prior to rewarding his saints with the Kingdom in a new heavens and a new earth. The saints—those who followed the Lamb, Jesus Christ himself—needed to hold on for just a while longer. They may be suffering now, but God will soon intervene to overcome all the pain, misery, and chaos of this world. Christ is soon to return in judgment and when he does, all the forces of evil aligned against him, embodied more than anything else in the evil Roman Empire, will be destroyed. The faithful will be vindicated. And they will rule forever with their God and his Christ.

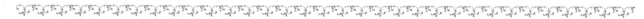

At a Glance: The Book of Revelation

The book of Revelation was written by a Christian prophet named John, who does not claim, however, to be the son of Zebedee, the disciple of Jesus. The author describes a heavenly vision that symbolically predicts events to transpire at the end of time, when God destroys this world in a series of cataclysmic acts of judgment before bringing in a new heavens and a new earth. The author understands this end-of-time scenario to be about to transpire soon.

The book is best understood in light of its genre. Like other apocalypses, it contains a prose narrative of visions

that are interpreted to the seer by an angelic companion; these visions are profoundly symbolic and highly repetitive, and they move toward a triumphalist climax in which good prevails over evil and God reasserts his sovereignty over the earth. In many instances the visions provide hints for their own interpretation, and when they are read in light of their historical context it is clear that the book sees the empire of Rome as the great enemy of God who is soon to be defeated in a cosmic act of judgment.

Take a Stand

1. Why have Jews and Christians had such a history of antagonism? Why, from the earliest of times, did Christians portray Jews as being opposed to God?

2. Why were the early Christians persecuted? Outline your answer in writing. On the surface this assignment may seem simple, but you will discover that it contains some complexities.

3. From this course, what have you learned of different views about being Christian in the earliest of times? Come up with five different views of Christianity that can be discerned from the writings of the New Testament (not necessarily five views represented by the authors of the New Testament; some of these Christian views may be ones that the authors *oppose*).

4. You are in a bookstore and notice a shelf full of books claiming that the prophecies in the book of Revelation are coming true in our own day and that the Anti-Christ—666—is soon to appear in our own day. What can you say either for or against this view? What's your opinion?

Key Terms

Ebionites, 352
Eusebius, 365
Justin Martyr, 355
Marcion/Marcionites, 352
Melito of Sardis, 354
Pliny, 360
Tacitus, 358

Suggestions for Further Reading

NB: For this and all chapters, see the relevant articles (e.g., "Jude," "Revelation") in the works cited in the Suggestions for Further Reading in chapter 1.

Chester, Andrew and Ralph Martin. *The Theology of the Letters of James, Peter, and Jude.* Cambridge: Cambridge University Press, 1994. A nice discussion of the social context and theological perspectives of these general epistles.

Lane Fox, Robin. *Pagans and Christians.* New York: Knopf, 1987. A long but fascinating and often brilliant discussion of the relationship of pagans and Christians during the first centuries of Christianity; for more advanced students.

Metzger, Bruce M. *Breaking the Code: Understanding the Book of Revelation.* Nashville: Abingdon, 2006. A simple-to-understand explanation of the symbols and images of the book of Revelation, for beginning students.

Ruether, Rosemary. *Faith and Fratricide: The Theological Roots of Anti-Semitism.* New York: Seabury, 1974. A classic study, compelling and controversial, that argues that Christian claims about Jesus in the early Christian writings, by their very nature, are necessarily anti-Jewish.

Wilken, Robert. *The Christians as the Romans Saw Them.* New Haven: Yale University Press, 1984. A popular study of the largely derogatory views of Christians held by several Roman authors; particularly suitable for beginning students.

15

Appendix: The Canon and Text of the Bible

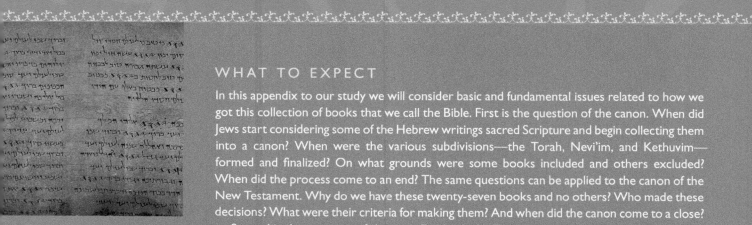

WHAT TO EXPECT

In this appendix to our study we will consider basic and fundamental issues related to how we got this collection of books that we call the Bible. First is the question of the canon. When did Jews start considering some of the Hebrew writings sacred Scripture and begin collecting them into a canon? When were the various subdivisions—the Torah, Nevi'im, and Kethuvim—formed and finalized? On what grounds were some books included and others excluded? When did the process come to an end? The same questions can be applied to the canon of the New Testament. Why do we have these twenty-seven books and no others? Who made these decisions? What were their criteria for making them? And when did the canon come to a close?

Second is the question of the text. For both the Tanakh and the New Testament, which handwritten copies (that is, manuscripts) still survive from the ancient world? How many manuscripts are there? What are their dates? How accurate are they? How many mistakes are in our manuscripts? And if our manuscripts are full of mistakes, can we know what the authors of the Bible originally wrote?

This appendix will deal with a set of fundamental problems that are not, frankly, on the radar screen of many readers of the Bible. The problems can all be summed up in one basic question: How did we get the Bible?

I am asking the question in two different ways, one related to the canon of the Bible—both Hebrew Bible and New Testament—and the other to the text. With respect to the canon: how did we get these books, and why do we have these books and not others? In the Hebrew Scriptures, in the English versions we read today, there are thirty-nine books (counted as twenty-four in the Jewish tradition). Why were these books chosen to be Scripture, and when in fact did that happen? The New

Testament makes up twenty-seven books. But who decided that it should be twenty-seven, and who got to choose which twenty-seven it would be? What about the other Gospels and epistles and apocalypses? Why were some of these not included? For both Testaments, who got to make these decisions? What were their grounds for making them? And when did the matter get resolved?

The question of how we got the Bible can also be asked with respect to the text of these books, both Hebrew Bible and New Testament. How have these books been handed down to us through the ages? The authors of the Bible did not publish their books electronically for the Kindle; they didn't have word processors or typewriters or even carbon paper.

So how did the books get passed down through the centuries?

The short answer is that they were copied by hand, year after year. We do not have the originals of any of the books of the Bible, but only handwritten copies from centuries later—in most cases, many centuries later. How can we be sure that we have the words that the authors originally wrote, and that our books of, say, Genesis, Isaiah, Psalms, Matthew, Romans, and Revelation correspond with the books as they were written so long ago?

These are obviously questions of fundamental importance. As the answers differ for the two testaments, I will deal with them separately. We begin by discussing the canons of the Hebrew Bible and the New Testament (note: I have already talked about issues involving the deuterocanonical/apocryphal books of the Christian Old Testament in chapter 9 and will not repeat that discussion here).

THE CANON OF THE HEBREW BIBLE

The term "canon" comes from the Greek word for "reed" or "rod." A canon was a straight edge that was used, for example, by a carpenter to make sure that an alignment was correct; but it could also be used as a measuring stick. Eventually the word "canon" came to be applied in other contexts, by analogy, to refer to a rule or standard by which something could be judged, and in that sense it came to be applied to a collection or list of books. In particular it referred to some kind of official or accepted or standard list of books seen to "fall in line." And so today we might speak of the canon of Shakespeare— which would be the plays and sonnets that he actually wrote—or the canon of Canadian literature (the books widely recognized as "great" literature of the country), or the canon of the Hebrew Bible.

The Older View of the Formation of the Canon

For many years there was a more or less standard, widely accepted view about when the canon of the Tanakh came to be formed. This view maintained that the Torah was finally accepted throughout Judaism as a canonical book (or five books, in one collection) by the year 400 B.C.E.; the Nevi'im (both

Former and Latter Prophets, were established in their final form by 200 B.C.E.; and the Kethuvim were finalized as a collection in 90 C.E. at the Council of Jamnia (about which I will say a few words below). According to this view, that was the same time and place that the Hebrew Bible was "closed"—that is, that the canon was completely set and no books, from then on, could be added in or taken out.

No one holds to this exact view today, but there are some things basically right about it. It is true that the canon did not come to be accepted all at once, in one fell swoop, but gradually over time as different sections of Hebrew Scripture came widely to be seen as fully authoritative at different periods in the history of ancient Israel. And the sequence is right: the first "sub-collection" to be formed and accepted was the Torah; then much later the Prophets, and then later still, and certainly last, the Writings. But the process was a bit messier than the older standard view allowed, and there is little evidence that the Council of Jamnia was where the final collection was ultimately authorized and made an "official" part of the Jewish religion.

Before laying out the more commonly accepted view today, I should say a few words about the Council of Jamnia. I have mentioned several times that the Roman armies suppressed the Jewish uprising of 66 C.E. by laying siege to Jerusalem and eventually destroying it, and its Temple, in 70 C.E. Obviously these horrible events had a cataclysmic effect on Judaism, which no longer had its religious center, a place for sacrifice, or a group of leaders (Sadducees) to look after its welfare. To help reconstruct Judaism and to move forward, there was a kind of council called in the Galilean city of Jamnia, where the leading Jewish teachers of the day—rabbis who were, in the main, related to the party of the Pharisees— came together to try to outline how the religion was to move ahead now that there was no active priesthood, no sacrificial system, no Temple.

Eventually Judaism was to shift away—of necessity—from an emphasis on Temple, cult, and sacrifice, to being very much a religion "of the book." The sacred traditions of Israel, especially as embodied in Scripture, were to become the focus of the religion as it emerged from the disaster of 70 C.E. That much is relatively certain. The older generation of scholars went further and argued that it was at this council that the canon was once and for all set. That, however, goes beyond the evidence. It now does not appear that the council of Jewish leaders at Jamnia established, fixed, and closed the canon of Scripture.

Contemporary Views of the Formation of the Canon

Today scholars tend to present a somewhat fuzzier picture of when and why the canon came to be formed, although there do seem to be some fixed points. It is widely held that the five books of the Torah were accepted by nearly all Jews as a set canon by the fifth century B.C.E., in the early post-exilic period. One piece of evidence comes from the Bible itself, in a post-exilic book, Ezra. The scribe Ezra himself is described as being "skilled in the Torah of Moses that the LORD the God of Israel had given" (Ezra 7:6). This suggests that it was widely known that there *was* a "Torah of Moses" and that the educated elite were sometimes being trained in understanding and interpreting it. The Torah is and always has been the same five books, and they have always been given in the same sequence (Genesis-Exodus-Leviticus-Numbers-Deuteronomy), since they trace a chronological tale. And so by the fifth century B.C.E., most Jews probably accepted the Torah as an authoritative group of texts connected principally with Moses.

The next sub-collection to be finalized was the Nevi'im, both Former Prophets (Joshua, Judges, Samuel, and Kings) and Latter Prophets (Isaiah, Jeremiah, Ezekiel, the Twelve), and this appears to have happened by the second century B.C.E. Evidence for this comes from a range of sources. The prologue to Sirach refers to "the Law and the Prophets and the others"; and books that were later to become the New Testament speak of the "Law and the Prophets" (e.g., Matthew 5:17; Luke 16:16). The reasons for thinking that the Nevi'im were finalized by the second century B.C.E., and not later, is that there are books of the Hebrew Bible that could have been included in this collection—given their subject matter—but in fact are not. Thus, for example, Daniel seems to be a prophetic book but it is not included in the "prophets." Why not? Probably because the canon of the prophets was fixed already by the time the book of Daniel appeared on the scene in the middle of the second century B.C.E.

Daniel was accepted as a Scriptural book eventually, of course. It just could not belong to a portion of the Bible that had already been "fixed." It and the other books were loosely connected with one another—unlike the Torah, the Former Prophets, and the Latter Prophets, which all cohere closely to one another in terms of subject matter. But even after the Law and the Prophets had been accepted as canonical texts, there were these other writings on the "margins"—the eleven books of the Kethuvim. That some of these were seen as authoritative by the second century B.C.E. is shown in the passage from Sirach quoted earlier, which speaks of "the others"

FIGURE 15.1.   The Psalm scroll discovered at Qumran, one of the Dead Sea Scrolls containing not only the Psalms of the Hebrew Bible but also several noncanonical psalms.

(or "the other books") without giving them a firm designation. So too, Luke 24:44 speaks of "the Law of Moses, the Prophets, and the Psalms"—a threefold categorization of the sacred Scriptures, the third part of which is identified by its longest and presumably most important book, the Psalms.

There were uncertainties about which books to include in this third group of Kethuvim. This is suggested, among other things, by the discovery of the Dead Sea Scrolls. Among the Dead Sea Scrolls were numerous copies of biblical books—some 200 of the scrolls contain books of the Bible (usually in fragmentary state). Every book that eventually came to be included in the Bible can be found among these scrolls—except for the book of Esther. Even though Esther is not found there, the scrolls contain numerous copies of a book known as "Jubilees" that some Jews considered to be a sacred text as well. Did the Jews at Qumran accept Jubilees as canonical, but not Esther? It is hard to say.

Other books of the Kethuvim were debated among Jews. The Song of Songs, for example, was a secular book celebrating the sexual love of an unmarried man and a woman. Was that really to be seen as part of canonical Scripture—even if Solomon did write it? Eventually Jews came to interpret the book in a different way, as we have seen, so that it no longer referred to human sexual love but to God's deep and profound love for Israel. There remains even today the question of whether the Song of Songs was eventually accepted as part of the canon *because* it was interpreted in this way (and so was relatively harmless as a love poem) or whether it was interpreted in this way because it was accepted as part of the sacred canon.

Most scholars agree that by the time of the destruction of the second Temple in 70 C.E. most Jews accepted the final three-part canon of the Torah, Nevi'im, and Kethuvim. From that time on, books could not be added and books could not be taken away. This was a twenty-four-book canon that came to be attested widely in Jewish writings of the time; eventually the canon was reconceptualized and renumbered so that it became the thirty-nine books of the Christian Old Testament. But they are the same books, all part of the canon of Scripture.

Grounds for Inclusion

It is very hard to know what criteria ancient Israelites used in order to decide which of their books should be accepted as parts of Scripture, in no small measure because we simply do not have any records of their discussions, debates, and disagreements (unlike for the New Testament). Some scholars have suggested that there were several criteria that were almost certainly applied by various Jewish leaders in making these decisions:

1. *Language.* Only books written in Hebrew (even if they had portions in Aramaic) could be accepted. None of the Jewish books written in Greek, for example, would be considered part of the sacred canon.
2. *Age.* Books had to have venerable authority. They could not be recent compositions. And so only books written before the fourth century B.C.E. could be accepted (books that were in fact written later—such as Daniel—were mistakenly taken to be older, as we have seen).
3. *Usage.* The books that became the canon were the ones most widely used in Jewish communities as authoritative tradition. In some ways the formation of the canon is a grassroots phenomenon: if books functioned as Scripture for a wide range of Jewish communities, they were eventually accepted as Scripture by the leaders who could make such decisions.

The Final Product of the Tanakh

The result of the Hebrew canon is what we have seen throughout our study. The Jewish Scriptures are a treasure trove of ancient Israelite writings. They were written at different times, by different authors, using different sources, embracing different points of view, advancing different understandings of major issues. They embrace different genres and they serve different functions. Together they may make up one thing—the Hebrew Bible—but in fact they are an entire array of things, the corpus of writings that cover the traditions, creations, thoughts, beliefs, and opinions of generations and centuries of ancient Israelite authors.

THE CANON OF THE NEW TESTAMENT

We are much better informed about the formation of the canon of the New Testament, in no small part because we have the writings of later church fathers who explicitly discuss the matter. We do not have nearly as much information as we would like—as is true for almost every set of historical events from the ancient world—but we have enough to give us a good idea of what motivated Christians to come up with a list of canonical books, what criteria they followed in deciding which books should be included, and how the process or canonization proceeded over the course of time.

Motivating Factors

In considering the formation of the Christian canon, the first and most obvious point to make is that Christians already had a body of Scriptures at the very outset: Jesus and his followers were, of course, Jews, and as Jews of the first century they accepted the Torah and the Prophets of the Hebrew Bible as their Scripture, along with some of the other books. But after the death of Jesus his followers came to adopt other written authorities as "Scripture" on a par with the books accepted by Jews as canonical. We can see this movement already within the pages of the New Testament. You may recall from chapter 13 that the pseudonymous author of 1 Timothy quotes two sayings as "Scripture"; one is a passage from the Torah, the other is a saying of Jesus (1 Timothy 5:18). By the time this author is writing, at the end of the first century, Jesus' words themselves are being taken as Scriptural authority. Eventually that will lead to the canonization of the teachings and life of Jesus as embodied in the Gospels. In addition, we saw in chapter 14 that the pseudonymous author of 2 Peter spoke of the letters of Paul and also included them among the Scriptures (2 Peter 3:16). Already by the early second century, then, we have Christians seeing writings about Jesus and writings by his apostles as scriptural texts. This is the beginning of the movement toward a Christian canon, which will consist of these two components: works relating to Jesus and writings by his apostles.

What was driving this movement toward establishing a canon? For one thing, the followers of Jesus were increasingly attempting to differentiate themselves from Jews, as we saw in chapter 14. If the Christians embraced a separate religion, they needed a separate group of authorities distinctive to themselves (while accepting, of course, the Jewish scriptures as well).

But there was an even more important factor motivating Christians to have written authorities for their views. As we have seen, Christians from the outset maintained that it was very important for members of the faith to believe the right things. Our earliest author, Paul, was insistent that his converts accepted his message and not the message of other apostles that he rejected; eventually there were many different interpretations of what it meant to be a follower of Jesus, not just the views of Paul and his sundry opponents. Over time different Christian groups developed distinctive views, with Jewish Christians saying one thing, Marcionites saying another, various groups of Gnostics saying other things, and—well—lots of groups saying lots of things about who God was (and how many gods there were!), what God's relation to the world was, who Jesus was, how salvation worked, and so on.

The striking thing is that all of the various Christian groups could back up their claims to represent the "true" interpretation of Christianity because all of them had books that were allegedly written by the apostles of Jesus themselves. And so there were Gospels of Matthew, and John, and Peter, and Thomas, and James, and Philip, and Mary and—and on and on, for a very long way. There were various accounts of the apostles' lives; there were letters allegedly written by Peter, Paul, James, and others; there were apocalypses allegedly written by John, Peter, Paul, Isaiah, and yet others.

Christians appealed to all of these books because they were living long after the days of Jesus and they needed to know which views were "true" and acceptable. It was the apostles who would know. And so, unknown authors wrote books *claiming* to be apostles in order to support their points of view.

The movement to define a canon was thus, in large part, a product of the conflicts between what we have been calling orthodoxy and heresy. These conflicts were waged in an effort to win converts to one point of view or another. The side that won these conflicts was the side that decided what Christian belief would be for all time to come. The winning side, for example, said there were not two or twelve or thirty-six gods, but only one God; that Jesus was not just a human or not just a divinity, but that he was both fully man and fully God at one and the same time; that the world was not a cosmic

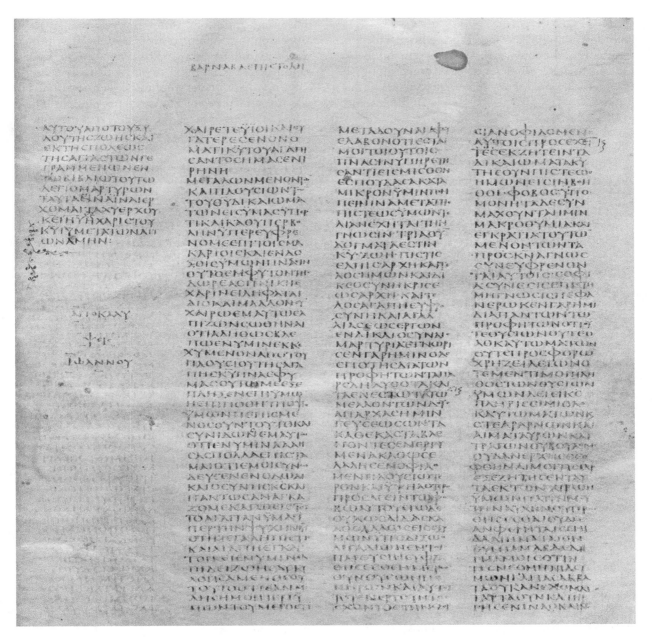

FIGURE 15.2. Codex Sinaiticus, the oldest surviving manuscript of the entire New Testament. This fourth-century manuscript includes *The Shepherd of Hermas* and the *Epistle of Barnabas* (the first page of which is pictured here), books that were considered part of the New Testament by some Christians for several centuries.

disaster but the good creation of the one true God. These became the standard views—so much so that they are the accepted views of virtually all Christians today.

The side that won these conflicts claimed they had always been the majority view within the religion. And they appealed to their own books to prove it, and rejected the books of the other groups. And so Matthew, Mark, Luke, and John were "in," and the Gospels of Peter, Thomas, James, and Mary were "out." It was all a matter of having written authorities to support your views.

The Criteria Used

The "orthodox" church fathers who decided on the shape and content of the canon applied several criteria to determine whether a book should be included or not. Four criteria were especially important.

1. *Antiquity*. A book had to go back to the very beginning of the Christian movement or it could not be accepted. If a really good and important book that was fully informed and "true" were written, say, last year, that would not be good enough for it be part of Scripture. The canon of Scripture contained books from the beginning of the Christian movement.

2. *Apostolicity*. Only books that were written by apostles could be accepted as part of the canon; this included the disciples of Jesus and their followers of the first generation. And so, for example, the writings of Paul were obviously acceptable; so too were the writings of the disciples Matthew, John, and Peter; and so too were the books of Mark, Peter's companion, and Luke, Paul's companion. If books were anonymous (such as the Gospels) they had to be attributed to apostles or they could not be considered canonical.

3. *Catholicity*. Only books that were universally used throughout the church could be accepted as part of the canon. (Recall: the term "catholic" means "universal.") Local favorites were not to be accepted by the church at large; a book had to be utilized by a broad range of churches throughout all of Christendom.

4. *Orthodoxy*. Most important of all, a book had to be "orthodox" in its perspectives and teachings if it were to be accepted as part of the canon of sacred Scripture. Any book that taught a "heretical" view could obviously not be from God or written by a true apostle. And so books had to be judged as presenting the "right teachings," or they had no chance at all of being included as canonical.

The Canonical Process

We have seen that there was a movement toward having distinctively Christian authorities already during the New Testament period itself and that early on, different Christian groups accepted and promoted different written texts as embodying those authorities. In almost every instance these texts were attributed to apostles. The first person who was actually known to have come up with a canon of Scripture, and to insist that these books and only these books were to be seen as canonical, was not a member of the orthodox church but, in fact, was a person who was later branded as one of the arch-heretics, Marcion.

In an earlier chapter I pointed out that Marcion accepted Paul as the apostle par excellence, and rejected all things Jewish as being not Christian. Marcion's views were very popular, and the Marcionite church spread far and wide in the late second century C.E. In about the middle of the century Marcion had relocated from his home in Sinope (northern Asia Minor) to Rome, the capital city of the empire and already home to one of the largest and most influential churches in the Christian world. Marcion spent some five years in Rome developing his theology and writing his books. No book was more important than a collection of sacred writings that he put together and then claimed was "the" Christian Bible.

Since, for Marcion, the Jewish God was not the true God, Marcion's Bible did not include any of the writings of the Old Testament. And since Paul was his hero, he included all of the writings of Paul that he knew—ten of them (all except the Pastoral epistles, which may not have been available to him). Throughout Paul's writings, of course, he refers to his "gospel," and so Marcion included a Gospel along with Paul's ten letters; this was a form of the Gospel of Luke. (Possibly because Luke was thought of as Paul's companion? Possibly because it was the Gospel Marcion grew up with?) That was the entirety of Marcion's canon of Scripture: eleven books altogether. He claimed that his view of the Christian faith was rooted in this canon and that it was authentic because these were the authoritative writings of the church.

Marcion's orthodox opponents had a different view of things, and it may have been Marcion himself who compelled other church leaders to argue for a different canon of Scripture. It was not long after Marcion that his opponents claimed that he had a skewed view of the Christian faith because he had eliminated from consideration books of Scripture that showed his views to be wrong. In the orthodox opinion, there was not just one Gospel (Luke); there were four, and Christians needed to heed what was said in all four to come away with a true understanding of the faith. Moreover, Paul was not the only "apostle" to be included in the canon: there were the writings of Peter, James, John, and Jude, as well.

Marcion may have provided the impetus for orthodox communities to decide on which books to be included, but there was not an immediate response that led to the finalization of the twenty-seven-book canon as we have it today. Quite the contrary, that did not happen for centuries. Still, by the end of the second century most of the orthodox churches agreed on the fourfold Gospel canon, the letters of Paul (including the Pastorals, which were seen as opposing Marcion), and the letters of 1 Peter and 1 John.

There continued to be debates for a long time over other books. Some church fathers wanted to include the Apocalypse of John, others wanted instead to include an apocalypse allegedly written by Peter, others wanted to include them both, and yet others wanted to include neither. Some church fathers thought Hebrews was written by Paul and so should be included; others thought it was not by Paul and should not be included. Some church fathers wanted to include a book called the Shepherd of Hermas; others wanted the letter allegedly written by Paul's companion Barnabas; others wanted a book known as 1 Clement. Some wanted the letters of 2 Peter, Jude, and James; others did not.

These debates went on for a very long time. The first time any church father of record indicated that there are twenty-seven books of the New Testament— and who named the twenty-seven books that we today have as the New Testament—was in the year 367 C.E., in the writings of an influential bishop of Alexandria, Egypt, **Athanasius**. In a letter sent to his churches, Athanasius specified that while other books (like the Shepherd) were worth reading, only the twenty-seven could be accepted as canonical.

It cannot be stressed enough that this letter was written nearly three hundred *years* after the individual books of the New Testament were first put into circulation. The New Testament did not drop from the sky a few weeks after Jesus died or after Paul finished writing his books. It was a matter of ongoing debate for decades and decades and, well, centuries. Even Athanasius's letter did not end the debates. It was not until the fifth century or so that most Christians agreed on the twenty-seven books that now are almost universally considered to be the canon of the New Testament.

THE TEXT OF THE HEBREW BIBLE

We have seen that the earliest writings of the Hebrew Bible were probably produced during the eighth century B.C.E. This is the date of the oldest prophets such as Amos and Isaiah of Jerusalem. When an ancient author produced a book, he obviously wrote it out by hand. And if anyone wanted a copy, he had to copy it by hand (or pay someone else to do it for him)—one page, one sentence, one word, one letter at a time. The term "manuscript" literally means "handwritten copy." The books of the Hebrew Bible were passed down in manuscript

At a Glance: The Canon of the Bible

The older view that the Tanakh was finalized by a Jewish council in the city of Jamnia is no longer held by scholars. But it is widely thought that the five books of the Torah were finalized as a group of Scriptural texts by the fifth century B.C.E.; the Nevi'im were finalized by the second century B.C.E., and the Kethuvim by about the time of the destruction of the Temple in 70 C.E. Important among the grounds for inclusion in the canon were the language, age, and widespread usage of the books.

The early Christians were motivated to collect a distinctive set of scriptures largely because of disputes over the right things to believe and practice in the religion. The Christians who engaged in debates over the canon stressed the need for books to be ancient, apostolic, catholic, and orthodox. Debates over which books to include lasted several centuries. The first to list our set of twenty-seven books was Athanasius, the bishop of Alexandria, Egypt, in 367 C.E.

form year after year, century after century. It was not until the invention of the printing press in the fifteenth century C.E. that things changed. Then it was possible to mass produce copies of books. And, more important, it was possible to make sure that every single copy of a book was exactly like every other copy, with no sentences, words, or even letters different from one copy to the next. That was not the case with manuscripts. Scribes who copied a text could change the text whenever they felt the need: maybe they thought the copy they were copying had a mistake in it and they wanted to correct it; maybe it didn't say exactly what they wanted it to say, and so they changed it. Moreover, scribes could simply make a mistake when they were not adequately trained to do the job of copying, or when they were inattentive or sleepy.

The Manuscripts

The first printed copy of the Hebrew Bible (that is, from a printing press) appeared in 1488. Before then, for over two millennia, the Bible had been produced and reproduced by hand in manuscript form. The printers of the fifteenth century and later, of course, had to decide what to print, and for that they had to use manuscripts that were available to them. If what they used were manuscripts with lots of mistakes in them, then necessarily the printed version of the Bible—now in many, multiple copies—would reproduce the mistakes made by the scribes who had, centuries earlier, copied the text by hand.

Today there are millions of printed copies of the Bible in Hebrew and in modern translations, all produced by modern means. But what manuscripts are these printings based on?

The oldest complete manuscript of the Hebrew Bible that we have, which is the basis for modern printings, is called the Codex Leningradensis (since it was located in Leningrad, Russia). It dates to about the year 1000 C.E. We do not have any complete manuscripts of the Bible before this. That means that the *oldest* complete manuscript is 1700 years after the earliest books of the Bible had been written, and 900 years after the canon was closed. A somewhat earlier Hebrew manuscript is named Codex Aleppo; it is not complete: about a quarter of it was lost in a fire in 1948. Earlier relatively complete manuscripts simply don't exist. The reason? It appears that in the Middle Ages, when Jewish scribes copied the Hebrew Bible, they destroyed the manuscripts they used to make

their copies once their own copies were complete. So the older copies they copied do not survive.

Our understanding of the text of the Hebrew Bible changed radically with the discovery of the Dead Sea Scrolls, as we will see. But not even among the Scrolls did we find complete manuscripts of the entire Bible. And so the key question: should we be concerned that the Jewish Scriptures/Old Testaments we read today are based on a manuscript that was copied from earlier manuscripts copied from earlier manuscripts—for many, many centuries? That the first surviving complete manuscript of the Hebrew Bible was made fully seventeen centuries after some of the books of Scripture were written?

The older view of scholars was that there is no reason to be concerned, because Jewish scribes from time immemorial followed very strict rules when copying their texts to make sure that they never changed a verse, or even a word, or even a letter. Jewish scribes were known to be highly scrupulous, so that the text known in the year 1000 C.E., it was believed, was the same as the text known in the year 1 C.E.

Scholars today are not quite as sanguine about the matter, for a variety of reasons. It is true that in the Middle ages Jewish scribes adopted a set of rules to ensure that they would not change the text. But when did those rules come to be put in place? They certainly were not in place in the years after Isaiah of Jerusalem produced his book, or even in the centuries immediately after that. So, what if the texts of the Hebrew Bible were changed—either a little bit or a lot—in the centuries *before* these rules came to be put in place? To deal with this question we need to consider a bit of background.

The Masoretic Text

The text of the Hebrew Bible that is read today, and that is at the basis of all modern translations, is called the **Masoretic Text**. It is called this because the Jewish scholars who devised the rules for copying scripture are known as the **Masoretes**. The term "masorete" comes from the Hebrew word *masorah*, which means "tradition." The Masoretes were the scholars who worked out ways to preserve the traditions of the Hebrew Bible. They were active between 500–1000 C.E.

To understand what the Masoretes accomplished, you need to remember that ancient written Hebrew was a language that used only consonants, not vowels. Any language that is written only in consonants is open, obviously, to serious problems of interpretation. Imagine if you were to write English that way. Apart from context, you would have no way of knowing whether the word "npt" was "inept" or "input" or whether "mnr" was "minor," "manor," "moaner," or "manure."

Over the centuries of their work, the Masoretes accomplished several gargantuan tasks. For one thing they standardized the entire consonantal text of the entire Hebrew Bible, so that there was an agreed upon text, with no variations. In addition, they devised a system of dots to be added to all the consonants in order to indicate the appropriate vowels, so that anyone reading the text would know which of the range of possible words was to be accepted as the "right" one. And they worked to make sure that no one would ever change the text again by implementing rules to be followed in the copying of the text.

All of this labor had a tremendous and long-lasting result. The Masoretes standardized the text. Moreover, scholars today are reasonably certain that when the Masoretes started their work, they were dealing with a consonantal text that was already well established, that changes had not been made—at least significant changes—for centuries, since at least the end of the first century C.E. And so we can, for the most part, rest assured that the Hebrew text we read now (if we read Hebrew!) is the same text that was in place 1900 years ago.

But what about before that?

The Dead Sea Scrolls

There are many reasons that the Dead Sea Scrolls have proved so important for scholars of ancient Judaism. One of these reasons has to do with the text of the Hebrew Bible. As I pointed out, over 200 of the scrolls contain texts of the Hebrew Bible. The most famous is a complete copy of the book of Isaiah. Most of the texts, however, are fragmentary—some of them are just scraps. Still, their importance cannot be undersold. Remember, the Masoretic text that printed Hebrew Bibles are based on is that found in Codex Leningradensis from 1000 C.E. The texts of the Hebrew Bible among the Dead Sea Scrolls are at least a thousand years *earlier* than that. By comparing the form of the text in the Scrolls with the manuscripts from around the year 1000, we can see how well the text had been copied over all those intervening centuries.

In the end there is some very good news and some not so good news. The good news is this: in many instances the Hebrew text found among the Scrolls is very, very similar to the consonantal text standardized later by the Masoretes. The copy of Isaiah is very much like the copy found in Codex Leningradensis.

The not so good news is that this is not the case with all of the books of the Hebrew Bible. Scholars had long noted, for example, that the Septuagint (Greek) text of the book of Jeremiah was about 15 percent shorter than the Masoretic Text (i.e., it had that many fewer verses/words), and scholars had suspected that it was because the Hebrew version of Jeremiah known to the ancient Greek translators was significantly different from the Masoretic Text. As it turns out, one of the scrolls discovered at Qumran has a Hebrew text of Jeremiah that is closer to that lying behind the Septuagint version than the Masoretic Text. Fifteen percent is a big difference. Other books of the Septuagint are also strikingly different from the Masoretic Text, for example, in the books of Samuel and Kings. It is possible that the Hebrew texts of all these books were in serious flux before the text came to be standardized by the end of the first century.

And what about the times before the scrolls from Qumran were produced? How much was the text in flux in the early centuries when it was copied by hand, time and again, among scribes who did not have and so could not follow the rules later laid down by the Masoretes? The reality is that we simply do not know how much the text got changed, in what places, and for what reasons in the early centuries of copying.

And so the short story is this. For many, many centuries the text of the Hebrew Bible has not changed in any significant way. But we cannot tell how it was altered between the time the books of the Bible were first produced and the time their texts came to be standardized near the end of the first century C.E.

THE TEXT OF THE NEW TESTAMENT

The problems presented by the manuscript tradition of the New Testament are very different from those of the Hebrew Bible. We have far, far more manuscripts of the New Testament, and these were not subjected to the kind of rigorous control that guided the medieval scribes of the Jewish Bible. As a result, there are far more variations among our manuscripts—a startling number—and some of these variations are highly significant.

The first printed edition of the Greek New Testament appeared in 1516. It was based on only a few manuscripts that were not of the highest quality. Even so, this edition—after a few later revisions—became the basis of many of the translations of the New Testament over the years, even after manuscripts were discovered that were older in date and better in quality. That is one reason why a translation such as the King James Version is less accurate than those made in more recent times: it is based on inferior manuscripts of the New Testament text.

The Manuscripts of the New Testament

Nowhere can the difference between the textual tradition of the Hebrew Bible and of the New Testament be seen more clearly than in the number of manuscripts scholars have available to them. There are over 5600 manuscripts of the Greek New Testament. Many of these are fragmentary (some are just tiny scraps), but many are complete copies of this or that book, or even of the entire New Testament. There are, in addition, many thousands of manuscripts of the New Testament as it was copied into Latin, and manuscripts in other languages such as Syriac, Coptic, Armenian, Georgian, Ethiopic, and a range of others.

These manuscripts range in date from the early second century down to, and past, the time of the invention of printing in the fifteenth century. Most of them are from the ninth century and later (so, some 800 years after the originals were produced). The oldest scrap we have is called P52. The "P" indicates that it is written on the ancient writing material called papyrus, and the "52" indicates that it was the fifty-second papyrus manuscript of the New Testament to be discovered and catalogued. It is a tiny fragment about the size of a credit card, with portions of John 18 (Jesus' trial before Pilate) written on the front and the back. Originally this would have been a complete manuscript of John; just this tiny scrap managed to survive, in a trash heap in Egypt. It is usually dated some time to the early second century. And so, whereas our oldest copy of the Hebrew Bible—prior to the discovery of the Dead Sea Scrolls—was some 1700 years removed from, say, the original writing of Amos or Isaiah, this, the oldest fragmentary copy of any of the books of the New Testament, is possibly just 30–50 years removed from the original of the Gospel of John. But it is only a tiny fragment.

And so the good news in dealing with the manuscripts of the New Testament is that we have an abundance of manuscripts, some of them strikingly early. The bad news is that most of the surviving manuscripts are not very early and, worse, these thousands of manuscripts contain many thousands

FIGURE 15.3. P52, a fragment of the Gospel of John (18:31–33, 37–38) discovered in a trash heap in the sands of Egypt. This credit card–sized scrap is the earliest surviving manuscript of the New Testament, dating from around 125–150 c.e. Both front and back are pictured here.

of differences among themselves. The differences in wording among manuscripts are called **variant readings**. There are a lot of them, and some of them matter.

The Variant Readings

There are so many variant readings among our New Testament manuscripts that despite advances in computer technology we have not been able to count them all. Scholars of the text have hazarded various guesses about how many variations there are: some think 200,000, some 300,000, some 400,000 or more. It is possibly easiest to put the matter in comparative terms. There are more variations in our manuscripts than there are words in the New Testament.

As frightening as that may sound, it must be tempered with a bit of perspective: the vast majority of these variations are insignificant, immaterial, and do not matter for a thing other than to show that scribes in antiquity could spell no better than college students can today (and the ancient scribes can be excused: they didn't have dictionaries, let alone spell-check). If the same word gets spelled six different ways in six different manuscripts, that counts as six variants. But if these spellings are simply just alternatives for the same Greek word, it obviously does not much matter how it is spelled. A lot of our differences are of this magnitude. A good proportion of the textual variations that we find cannot even be represented in English translation (that is, if you translate into English one variant or the other, it results in the same English translation). At the same time, there are a lot of other variations that do matter.

Scholars tend to differentiate between accidental and intentional variations. Accidental variations are ones that appear to have been made simply by mistake. Not only did scribes accidentally misspell words; sometimes they left out a word, or copied the same word twice; sometimes they left out an entire line, or an entire passage. That may seem strange, but it happened. Scribes were human and sometimes they were, frankly, a bit inept, careless, or just plain sleepy. And Christian scribes did not have rigorous rules for copying, as their Jewish counterparts did. Probably the majority of the variations in our manuscript are of this order. On the upside, it is relatively simple for scholars to detect mistakes that were made by accident.

The other kind of variation tends to be more interesting and to lead to more important results. This is when a scribe decided to change the text on purpose. Such intentional changes could be made for any number of reasons. Possibly the scribe was copying a familiar passage but the wording seemed wrong—it wasn't the way he remembered it. So he changed it to make it conform to how he already knew it. Or maybe the wording of the passage contained a problem, such as a grammatical error, or a geographical or historical faux pas. A scribe might try to "correct" the passage—even if the original text was, as a result, changed. There were times when a scribe simply did not like the way a passage was worded, as when it supported a point of view that he found problematic or just plain wrong. In that case he might change the text to make it say what he thought it was *supposed* to say. Nothing was stopping him.

The problem in all these cases of variation is that the next scribe who came along to copy the text—who used a manuscript with variations in it (and they all had variations)—would copy the changed text instead of the original text. And he would make mistakes of his own. And then the next scribe who used that manuscript would copy the mistakes of both of his predecessors, and add mistakes of his own. And so it would go. The only time a mistake would be eliminated was when a scribe recognized that his predecessor had not copied the text correctly and then tried to correct the mistake. But the problem is that there was no guarantee that he would correct the mistake correctly. If he corrected it incorrectly, then there would be three forms of the text: the original text, the mistake, and the mistaken correction of the mistake. The possibilities seem almost endless.

Significant Variations

Scholars have carefully combed through all of the oldest manuscripts of the New Testament and categorized and analyzed the significant variant readings. Even though most of them do not matter for much, some of them matter a lot. Here I can give a few examples.

As I pointed out in chapter 10, the Gospel of Mark ends with the women at the empty tomb being told to go tell the disciples that Jesus had been raised; they flee the tomb, however, and do not say anything to anyone about it. And that's the end of the Gospel. It's an amazing Gospel, but over the years readers have wondered if it could really end that way. Didn't the women tell the disciples? Didn't the disciples see Jesus after the resurrection? Didn't they come to believe he had been raised from the dead?

It isn't just modern readers who are puzzled by the ending. So too were ancient scribes, who added an ending of an additional twelve verses, where the disciples go to Galilee as directed and meet with Jesus to receive his final instructions. You will find this ending in most English translations in brackets, with a footnote from the translator indicating that it is not the original text.

An even more famous case is the story of Jesus and the woman taken in adultery in the Gospel of John. It is one of the best known stories of the Gospels (John 7:53–8:11). A woman has been caught committing adultery, and the Jewish leaders drag her before Jesus. They tell him what has happened and point out that the Law of Moses indicates that she is to be stoned to death. What does Jesus think they should do? These enemies of Jesus are setting a trap for him. If he tells them to stone her, he is violating his own teachings of love, mercy, and forgiveness; but if tells them to let her go, he is breaking the Law of Moses. And so he stoops down and begins to write on the ground and then looks up and says that the one who has never sinned should be the first to cast a stone at her. One by one, the accusers go away, ashamed of their own sins. Jesus then is left alone with the woman, whom he sends on her way with a warning not to sin again.

It is a terrific story, moving, powerful, and memorable. But unfortunately, it was not originally in the Gospel of John. Or in any other Gospel. It is a story that was added to the Gospel by later scribes. The reasons for thinking so include the fact that the story is not to be found in our earliest and best manuscripts.

There are other significant variant readings throughout the New Testament that involve very important matters, including such things as teachings on the Trinity, on whether Christ was really divine, on whether he was a real human, on whether his death was an atoning sacrifice, and so on. Scholars have to consider each of these problems one by one, both in order to see what the original text probably was and in order to understand why one scribe or another wanted to change it.

In the end, of course, we can never be 100 percent certain that we have the text as it was originally written by the authors of the New Testament—whether the anonymous authors of the Gospels, or Paul, or the pseudonymous authors of various other books. But scholars have worked assiduously on this problem for centuries and continue to work on it today. And every now and then new manuscripts turn up—sometimes very ancient manuscripts—that can help us know what the original text was. Still, there are hundreds passages in the New Testament for which scholars continue to debate about what the author originally wrote, and, at the end of the day, there are some passages where we may simply never know.

At a Glance: The Text of the Bible

Modern translations of the Hebrew Bible are largely based on a single manuscript called Codex Leningradensis, dating to the year 1000 C.E. The text of the Hebrew Bible was preserved and protected through the work of the Masoretes (500–1000 C.E.), who fixed the consonantal text and added to it vowel points for ease of reading and interpretation. The Dead Sea Scrolls show that many of the books of the Tanakh were copied carefully by scribes from the beginning of the common era; other books were changed to a greater extent, however, and it is impossible to know how much they were changed before the common era.

The Greek New Testament is contained in many more manuscripts—over 5600 Greek manuscripts of all or part of the New Testament altogether. These thousands of manuscripts contain hundreds of thousands of differences, or variant readings. Even though the vast majority of these variants are highly insignificant, some of them do matter a great deal for interpretation and meaning, and there are numerous places where scholars have not been able to agree as to what the original text actually said.

Key Terms

Athanasius, 381   **Masoretes**, 382   **Masoretic Text**, 382

Suggestions for Further Reading

NB: For this and all chapters, see the relevant articles (e.g., "Canon," "Text") in the works cited in the Suggestions for Further Reading in chapter 1.

Ehrman, Bart D. *Lost Christianities: The Battles for Scripture and the Faiths We Never Knew.* New York: Oxford University Press, 2003. An examination of the early conflicts among various Christian groups and the various "Scriptures" that they produced, with an eye to how we received the canon as we did.

Ehrman, Bart D. *Misquoting Jesus: The Story Behind Who Changed the Bible and Why.* San Francisco: HarperSanFrancisco, 2005. An account of the study of the manuscripts of the New Testament and of how they came to be changed over the centuries by scribes; written for a popular audience.

Gamble, Harry. *The New Testament Canon: Its Making and Meaning.* Philadelphia: Fortress, 1985. A clearly written and informative overview of the formation of the New Testament canon.

McDonald, Lee and James A. Sanders. *The Canon Debate.* Grand Rapids: Baker, 2001. An informed collection of essays dealing with a variety of issues related to the canon of both the Hebrew Bible and the New Testament.

Tov, Emmanuel. *Textual Criticism of the Hebrew Bible.* 2nd ed. Minneapolis: Fortress, 2002. A full and authoritative discussion of the text of the Hebrew Bible, for well advanced students.

Glossary

A

Alexander the Great: The great military leader of Macedonia (356–323 B.C.E.) whose armies conquered much of the eastern Mediterranean and who was responsible for the spread of Greek culture (Hellenism) throughout the lands he conquered.

anachronism: An event, institution, phenomenon, item, or anything else mentioned in a story that does not fit into the time period that the story presupposes.

ancestral history: A term used to describe Genesis 12–50, which tells the stories of the patriarchs and matriarchs of Israel, especially Abraham, Isaac, Jacob, and Joseph.

anthropomorphism: The explanation or interpretation of something that is not human (e.g., God, or a god, or an animal, or a plant) in terms that make it sound human.

ancient Near East: The region and the countries of antiquity that roughly correspond to what today we call the Middle East, including Egypt and the lands of Mesopotamia in the region of the Tigris and Euphrates rivers (especially Assyria and Babylonia).

Antiochus Epiphanes: Ruler of the Seleucid Empire, starting in 175 B.C.E., who attempted to Hellenize Jews in the Promised Land by force and made it illegal to follow the prescriptions of the Torah, leading to the Maccabean Revolt.

apocalypse: A literary genre in which an author, usually pseudonymous, reports symbolic dreams or visions given by or interpreted through an angelic mediator, which reveal the heavenly mysteries that can make sense of earthly realities.

apocalpyticism: A world view held by many ancient Jews and Christians that maintained that the present age is controlled by forces of evil but that these will be destroyed at the end of time when God intervenes in history to bring in his kingdom, an event thought to be imminent.

Apocrypha: A term that literally means "hidden things." When applied to the Bible, it refers to the books that are considered part of the canon of the Old Testament by Roman Catholic and Eastern Orthodox churches (who refer to these books as deuterocanonical—a "second canon"), but not by Protestant Christians and Jews.

apodictic laws: Laws that make a straightforward and absolute command, such as "You shall not murder" or "You shall not commit adultery." *See also* casuistic laws.

Apollonius of Tyana: A neo-Pythagorean teacher and pagan holy man of the first century C.E. who was thought by some to be a miracle-working son of God.

ark of the covenant: Elaborate wooden box that was believed by many to be the throne of God, seated between two angelic beings (cherubim) that covered the top; inside the box were the two tablets that contained the Decalogue. In later times it was believed that the ark had special sacred powers, for example, during times of war.

Asherah: A goddess worshiped in Canaan; sometimes the term is used to refer to the wooden pole taken to represent her.

Astarte: A goddess worshiped in Canaan; thought to be the consort of the storm god Baal.

Athanasius: An influential fourth-century church father and bishop of the large and important church in Alexandria, Egypt. Athanasius was the first church writer to list our twenty-seven New Testament books (and only these books) as forming the New Testament canon.

atonement: The restoration of a right relationship with a god after some kind of breach or transgression has occurred to make the god angry or distant.

B

Baal: A god worshiped in Canaan, thought to be the god of storms and of fertility.

Babylonian exile: A term that refers to both an event and a time period. The event was when the Babylonians, under their King Nebuchadnezzar, took the leaders of Judah into captivity in 586 B.C.E.; the time period is 586–539 B.C.E. (the latter date is when the Persians allowed the Judeans to return home).

beatitudes: A Latin word meaning, literally, "blessings," used as a technical term for the saying of Jesus that begins the Sermon on the Mount (e.g., "Blessed are the poor in spirit. . . ." Matthew 5:3–12).

biography (ancient): A literary genre consisting of a narrative of an individual's life, often within a chronological framework, employing numerous subgenres (such as sayings, speeches, anecdotes, and conflict stories) so as to reflect important aspects of his or her character; principally of instruction, exhortation, or propaganda.

C

Caesar Augustus. *See* Octavian.

canon: From the Greek word *kanon*, which means a ruler or a straight edge; the term came to designate any recognized collection of texts, such as the canon of the Hebrew Bible or the canon of the New Testament.

casuistic laws: Laws that indicate what is to be done if a certain course of action is taken (if this happens . . . then you are to do this).

charismatic communities: Communities of believers that were led not by appointed leaders but by the Spirit of God, which had bestowed a particular gift (Greek: *charisma*), useful for the functioning of the entire group, upon each member of the community. According to Paul (see 1 Corinthians 12–14), the gifts (*charismata*) included such abilities as teaching, preaching, healing, prophesying, speaking in tongues, interpretation of tongues, and so on.

Code of Hammurapi: A collection of laws attributed to Hammurapi, king of Babylonia in the early part of the eighteenth century B.C.E. Discovered on an eight-foot-high basalt stele in 1901, many of these 282 laws are similar to those found in the Torah.

contextual credibility (criterion): One of the criteria commonly used by scholars to establish historically reliable material; with respect to the historical Jesus, the criterion maintains that if a saying or deed of Jesus cannot be credibly fit into his own first-century Palestinian context, then it cannot be regarded as authentic.

conquest theory: The theory that Israel entered into the Promised Land more or less as described in the book of Joshua, through a massive conquest of the cities there. *See* immigration theory, peasant revolt, and gradual emergence.

cosmology: Any understanding of the world we live in, from the Greek word *cosmos*, meaning "world."

Covenant Code: The preexisting collection of laws, probably from E, found in Exodus 20:22–23:33; most of the laws are casuistic and are oriented to settled agricultural communities, involving such matters as slaves, violence, property rights, restitutions, and women.

covenantal lawsuit: A literary device found in some of the prophets in which God is portrayed as issuing a kind of legal indictment against his people for breaking their obligations under the covenant he had made with them.

cult: From a Latin phrase, *cultus deorum*, which literally means "care of the gods"; the term is used of any set of religious practices of worship. In pagan religions, these normally involved acts of sacrifice and prayer.

D

D: A designation for the third source of the Pentateuch (JEDP), called this because it the source is now found in the book of Deuteronomy; it was probably written in the seventh century B.C.E.

daimonia: Category of divine beings in the Greco-Roman world. Daimonia were widely thought to be less powerful than the gods but far more powerful than humans and capable of influencing human lives.

Day of Atonement: The day in the year when the high priest would enter into the Holy of Holies, into God's presence, and perform a sacrifice first for his own sins and then for the sins of the people.

Dead Sea Scrolls: Ancient Jewish writings discovered in several caves near the northwest edge of the Dead Sea, widely thought to have been produced by a group of apocalyptically minded Essenes who lived in a monastic-like community from Maccabean times through the Jewish War of 66–70 C.E. *See also* Essenes.

Decalogue: Literally the "ten words," a technical designation for the Ten Commandments.

Deuteronomic Code: Collection of Laws, from the D source, that make up Deuteronomy 12–26.

deuteronomistic history: Scholarly term for the books of Joshua, Judges, 1 and 2 Samuel, and 1 and 2 Kings (the Former Prophets in the Hebrew Bible), all written by the same author or authors, which record the history of ancient Israel between the entry in to the land and the exile in terms highly reminiscent of, and probably dependent on, the religious views set forth in the D source behind the book of Deuteronomy.

Deutero-Pauline epistles: The letters of Ephesians, Colossians, and 2 Thessalonians, which have a "secondary" (deutero-) standing in the Pauline corpus because scholars debate whether they were written by Paul. Sometimes the Pastoral epistles are included under this designation as well.

Diaspora: Greek for "dispersion," a term that refers to the dispersion of Jews away from Palestine into other parts of the Mediterranean, beginning with the Babylonian exile.

dissimilarity (criterion): One of the criteria commonly used by scholars to establish historically reliable material; the criterion maintains that if a saying or deed of Jesus does not coincide with (or works against) the agenda of the early Christians, it is more likely to be authentic.

docetic (view of Jesus): The view that Jesus was not a real human being but only appeared to be, from a Greek word meaning "to seem" or "to appear."

Documentary Hypothesis: The hypothesis, developed and popularized particularly by Julius Wellhausen, that the Pentateuch is made up of four separate sources (J, E, D, and P), each produced at a different time in the history of Israel and edited together only later into the five-book collection that we have today.

doxology: Literally "a word of praise." In the Psalms, either an entire poem or a poem of a few lines that extends a blessing to God.

E

E: The second of the Pentateuchal sources (JEDP) to be written, possibly in the ninth century B.C.E., and containing stories found in Genesis, Exodus, and Numbers; it is called E both because it uses the name Elohim for God and because it probably derived from the northern kingdom of the Israel, sometimes called Ephraim.

Ebionites: a group of second-century Christians who maintained their Jewish identity and insisted that followers of Jesus need to keep the Jewish law.

Enuma Elish: A Babylonian poem discovered on seven tablets, and published in 1876, that tell of the creation of the world by the Babylonian god Marduk, with many striking parallels to the account of creation in Genesis; the title comes from its opening words, "when above."

Essenes: An apocalyptic and ascetic Jewish sect started during the Maccabean period, members of which are generally thought to have produced the Dead Sea Scrolls.

Eusebius: Early-fourth-century church father known as the "Father of Church History," as his ten-volume book, *History of the Christian Church*, was the first to provide an extensive chronicle of Christianity's early years, from the days of Jesus down to Eusebius' own time (the early part of the reign of Constantine). Eusebius is the primary source of information for many of the events and writers of the first three centuries of the church.

Exile: *See* Babylonian exile.

F

Former Prophets: The first division of the Nevi'im, comprising the four books of Joshua, Judges, Samuel (counted as one book), and Kings (one book).

Four-Source Hypothesis: A solution to the "Synoptic Problem" which maintains that there are four sources that lie behind the Gospels of Matthew, Mark, and Luke: (1) Mark was the source for much of the narrative of Matthew and Luke; (2) Q was the source for the sayings found in Matthew and Luke but not in Mark; (3) M provided the material found only in Matthew's Gospel; and (4) L provided the material found only in Luke.

Fourth Philosophy: A group of Jews (or several groups) that Josephus mentions but leaves unnamed, characterized by their insistence on violent opposition to the foreign domination of the Promised Land. *See also* Sicarii, Zealots.

fulfillment citations: A literary device used by Matthew in which he states that something experienced or done by Jesus "fulfilled" what was spoken of by a Hebrew prophet in Scripture.

G

gentile: A non-Jew.

genre: A "genre" is a kind of literature with specific literary features; in the modern world, for example, there are short stories, novels, and limerick poems (each with their own distinctive features); in the ancient world there were myths, legends, biographies, epic poems, general histories, proverbs, and many other kinds of genres.

Gilgamesh epic: An ancient Mesopotamian epic poem about the life and adventures of a king named Gilgamesh, of particular interest to students of the Bible because of the tale in it told by Utnapishtim about the worldwide flood, with many parallels to the story of Noah and the ark in Genesis.

Gnosticism: A group of ancient religions, some of them closely related to Christianity, that maintained that elements of the divine had become entrapped in this evil world of matter and could be released only when they acquired the secret *gnosis* (Greek for "knowledge") of who they were and of how they could escape. Gnosis as generally thought to be brought by an emissary of the divine realm.

gradual emergence (theory): The theory that explains the presence of Israel in the Promised Land by means of a gradual emergence of a group of worshipers of Yahweh from among the indigenous people of Canaan, possibly with some having come from outside (maybe a group of slaves that escaped from Egypt).

H

Hanina ben Doa: A well-known Galilean rabbi of the first century, who was reputed to have done miracles comparable to those of Jesus.

Hasmoneans: An alternative name for the Maccabean family, from the name of a distant ancestor.

Hellenization: The policy of spreading Greek culture throughout conquered lands, from the Greek word for "Greece," *Hellas*.

herem: From a Hebrew word that means "devoted," used in reference to spoils of war (including people) who are God's alone and so are to be destroyed.

Holiness Code: The set of laws found in Leviticus 17–26, drawn from P, which emphasize the need for Israelites to be "holy" before God—that is, distinct and set apart from everyone else.

Holy of Holies: The sacred room in the Temple of Jerusalem where it was believed that God himself dwelled, seated on the ark of the covenant. Only the high priest could enter this room, and only once a year, on the Day of Atonement.

Honi the "circle-drawer": A first-century B.C.E. Galilean who was reputed to have done miracles and had experiences similar to those of Jesus.

I

immigration theory: The theory that Israel came to be in the Promised Land by immigration over time, as a group of people entered Canaan from the outside, settled in sparsely inhabited highlands, and infiltrated into the cities later, eventually taking control of them. *See* conquest theory, peasant revolt, and gradual emergence.

independent attestation (criterion): One of the criteria commonly used by scholars to establish historically reliable material; with respect to the historical Jesus, the criterion maintains that if a saying or deed of Jesus is attested independently by more than one source, it is more likely to be authentic.

J

J: The first of the Pentateuchal sources (JEDP) to be written, possibly around the time of Solomon in the tenth century B.C.E., and containing stories found in Genesis, Exodus, and Numbers; it is called J both because it uses the name Jahweh (German for Yahweh) and because it probably derived from the southern part of the land, Judah.

JEDP: The four sources that lie behind the Pentateuch, according to the Documentary Hypothesis.

Jesus, son of Ananias: A Palestinian Jew discussed by Josephus who, like Jesus of Nazareth, was an apocalyptic preacher of the coming end of the age; like Jesus he was arrested and prosecuted for his revolutionary proclamation, although he was not executed for his crimes. He was inadvertently killed during the siege of Jerusalem in the first Jewish Revolt of 66–70 C.E.

Jew: Originally from the word "Judean," which meant someone who lived in the Persian or Roman province of Judea (corresponding roughly to the southern nation of Judah in monastic times).

Johannine community: The community of Christians in which the Gospel of John and the Johannine epistles were written.

Josephus: Jewish historian of the first century C.E., appointed court historian by the Roman emperor Vespasian, whose works *The Jewish War* and *The Antiquities of the Jews* are principal sources of information about life in first-century Palestine.

Judas Maccabeus: The initial leader of the Maccabean uprising against the Syrians (under Antioches Epiphanes). Maccabeus was his nickname; it means "hammer." *See* Maccabean Revolt and Hasmoneans.

judicial model: One of the two principal ways that Paul understood or conceptualized the relationship between Christ's death and salvation. According to this model, salvation is comparable to a legal decision in which God, who is both lawmaker and judge, treats humans as "not guilty" for committing acts of transgression (sins) against his law—even though they *are* guilty—because Jesus' death has been accepted as payment. *See also* participationist model.

Justin Martyr: One of the earliest Christian "apologists" ("defenders" of the faith) and anti-Jewish author who lived in Rome in the mid-second century.

K

Kethuvim: "The Writings"—the eleven-book section of the Tanakh, the last to be recognized as Scripture by ancient Jews.

kosher food laws: Laws concerning what could and could not be eaten; in the Torah, for example, pork and shellfish are not allowed to be eaten by Israelites.

L

L: A document (or documents, written or oral) that no longer survives, but that evidently provided Luke with traditions that are not found in Matthew or Mark. *See also* Four-Source Hypothesis.

Latter Prophets: The second division of the Nevi'im, comprising the books of Isaiah, Jeremiah, Ezekiel, and "the twelve" (i.e., the twelve books called "minor prophets" in the English Bible).

legend: Fictional narratives about real or allegedly historical figures told in order to "entertain, to teach a moral, and/or to explain why things are as they are."

Levites: Descendants of Levi (the son of Jacob) who played a significant role in Israelite worship practices from early times, and eventually in the Temple in Jerusalem.

M

M: A document (or documents, written or oral) that no longer survives, but that evidently provided Matthew with traditions that are not found in Mark or Luke. *See also* Four-Source Hypothesis.

Maccabean Revolt: Indigenous uprising of Jews in the Promised Land against their Syrian overlords (under Antiochus Epiphanes), begun in 167 B.C.E. and leading to an independent sovereign state in the land until the Roman conquest. *See* Hasmoneans and Judas Maccabeus.

Maccabees: The family that started the Maccabean Revolt.

Major Prophets: The five larger writings of prophets in the English Bible: Isaiah, Jeremiah, Lamentations, Ezekiel, and Daniel.

manuscript: Any handwritten copy of an ancient text.

Marcion/Marcionites: Marcion was a second-century Christian scholar and evangelist, later labeled a heretic for his docetic Christology and his belief in two gods—the harsh legalistic God of the Jews and the merciful loving God of Jesus—views that he claimed to have found in the writings of Paul. His followers were called Marcionites.

Markan priority: The view that Mark was the first of the Synoptic Gospels to be written and was one of the sources used by Matthew and Luke.

Masoretes: Jewish scholars active between 500–1000 C.E. who worked to secure the text of the Hebrew Bible and to add a system of vowel pointing to it, assuring that the text would not be changed over the course of later copying.

Masoretic text: The Hebrew text of the Jewish Scriptures established by the Masoretes.

Megillot: The "five scrolls" of the Kethuvim, read during special festivals during the Jewish calendar: Song of Songs, Ruth, Lamentations, Ecclesiastes, and Esther.

Melito of Sardis: Second-century Christian leader from Asia Minor, whose eloquent Easter sermon on the story of Exodus casts vitriolic aspersions on the Jews.

messiah: From a Hebrew word that literally means "anointed one," translated into Greek as *christos,* from which derives our English word "Christ"—originally used to refer to the king of Israel who was anointed as part of his coronation ceremony. The term came to be used for a future deliverer of the people and was sometimes applied to a future warrior-king like David, or a cosmic redeemer from heaven, or an authoritative priest who would rule the people.

Minor Prophets: The twelve shorter prophets: Hosea, Joel, Amos, Obadiah, Jonah, Micah, Nahum, Habakkuk, Zephaniah, Haggai, Zechariah, and Malachi.

Mishnah: A collection of oral traditions passed on by generations of Jewish rabbis who saw themselves as the descendants of the Pharisees, finally put into writing around 200 C.E. *See also* Talmud.

myth: A story about God or the gods and their activities, which tries to make sense of the world and our place in it.

N

Nag Hammadi Library: Collection of books, principally Gnostic writings, discovered by accident near the village in Egypt named Nag Hammadi, in 1945.

Nazirite: An Israelite who took a vow to be specially dedicated to God by not touching a dead body, not consuming wine or strong drink or grape products, and not cutting one's hair (as, for example, Samson).

Nevi'im: Hebrew word for "prophets"; the second subdivision of the Tanakh, which includes both the Former and the Latter Prophets.

O

Octavian: The first Roman emperor 27 B.C.E.–14 C.E. Octavian was the great-nephew and adopted son of Julius Caesar, and a great general who brought unity to Rome after it had experienced prolonged and bloody civil wars. Early in his reign Octavian assumed the name "Caesar Augustus" which means something like "most revered emperor."

oral tradition: Any myth, legend, story, doctrine, idea, practice, or custom that has been handed down by word of mouth from one person to another.

P

P: The final source of the Pentateuch (JEDP), called this because it has principally priestly concerns; P material can be found in Genesis but especially in the legal sections of Exodus, Leviticus, and Numbers.

pagan: A reference to anyone who participated in any of the polytheistic religions of antiquity, an umbrella term for anyone not Jewish or Christian.

Pastoral epistles: New Testament letters that Paul allegedly wrote to two pastors, Timothy (1 and 2 Timothy) and Titus, concerning their pastoral duties.

participationist model: One of the two principal ways that Paul understood or conceptualized the relationship between Christ's death and salvation. This model understood sin to be a cosmic force that enslaved people; salvation (liberation from bondage) came by participating in Christ's death through baptism. *See also* judicial model.

Pax Romana: Literally "Roman Peace"; a term used to refer to a 200-year period starting with Octavian when the Roman Empire experienced relative peace and security.

peasant revolt (theory): The theory that explains the presence of Israel in the Promised Land by means of a revolt of the underprivileged and oppressed peoples in the land, sparked by a group of Israelites that escaped from Egypt.

Pentateuch: Literally, the "five scrolls" in Greek, a term used to designate the first five books of the Hebrew Bible, the Torah.

pesher: An ancient Jewish way of interpreting Scripture, used commonly in the commentaries from the Dead Sea Scrolls, in which a text was explained as having its fulfillment in persons or events of the present day.

Pharisees: A Jewish sect that may have originated during the Maccabean period, which emphasized strict adherence to the purity laws set forth in the Torah. *See also* Mishnah.

Pliny: Roman aristocrat who ruled the province of Bithynia-Pontus in the early second century C.E., and whose correspondence with the emperor Trajan contains the earliest reference to Christ in a pagan source.

pre-exilic prophet: A prophet making a proclamation prior to the Babylonian exile.

post-exilic prophet: A prophet making a proclamation after the Babylonian exile.

priests: Descendants from Aaron, brother of Moses and descendant of Levi, who officiated at the religious ceremonies of ancient Israel, either in the tabernacle or, in monarchial and later times, in the Temple in Jerusalem.

Priestly Code: A preexisting collection of laws from the P source found in Leviticus 1–16, chiefly concerned with priests and their activities (such as sacrifice) and concerns (such as ritual purity).

primeval history: A term used to describe Genesis 1–11, which narrates the events at the beginning of time; especially the stories of creation, garden of Eden, flood, and tower of Babel.

prophet: In ancient Israel, a prophet was a person who delivered God's message to his people; eventually the term came to refer to books that contained these messages (such as Isaiah or Amos); in Christian circles prophets were those who spoke God's message in the community's services of worship, possibly, on occasion, in a state of ecstasy.

proverb: A pithy and profound saying that encapsulates a distinctive understanding of the world and/or how best to live in it.

psalm: From the Greek verb *psallo*, which originally meant to pluck the string of an instrument, or to play a stringed instrument; eventually it came to mean to sing with accompaniment. A psalm is a poetic expression of emotions, reflections, or attitudes to God (such as anger, bitterness, joy, hope, thanksgiving, praise).

pseudepigrapha: Literally "writings inscribed with a lie," an alternative to the term "forgery"; both terms refer to writings that circulate under the name (usually a famous person) of someone who did not write them—either because the author lied about his identity or because the writing was falsely attributed to someone who did not write it.

Ptolemies: Greek rulers of Egypt after Alexander the Great.

Q

Q: The source used by both Matthew and Luke for the material that they share, principally sayings, that is not found in Mark; from the German word *Quelle*, "source." The document no longer exists but can be reconstructed (in part) on the basis of Matthew and Luke. *See also* Four-Source Hypothesis.

Qumran: Place near the northwest shore of the Dead Sea where the Dead Sea Scrolls were discovered in 1947, evidently home to the group of Essenes who had used the Scrolls as part of their library.

R

redactor: An editor; one who modifies a source or text that has been inherited.

Roman Empire: All of the lands conquered by Rome and ruled, ultimately, by the Roman emperor, starting with Caesar Augustus in 27 B.C.E.; prior to that, Rome was a republic ruled by the Senate.

S

Sabbath: The seventh day of the week, on which God is said to have rested after having created the heavens and the earth (Genesis 1:1–2:4); the day was set aside as a weekly day of rest in the Mosaic Law.

Sadducees: A Jewish party associated with the Temple cult and the Jewish priests who ran it, comprising principally the Jewish aristocracy in Judea. The party leader, the High Priest, served as the highest ranking local official and chief liaison with the Roman governor.

sacrifice: An offering, usually of an animal or other foodstuff, made to a deity.

Sanhedrin: The Jewish council, headed by the High Priest and appointed to run civil affairs in Jerusalem in the time of the New Testament.

seer: An alternative term for a prophet, called this because God had revealed to them a divine vision that they were then to articulate to the people.

Seleucids: Greek rulers of Syria after Alexander the Great.

Seneca: Probably the greatest Roman philosopher of the second half of the second century C.E. and tutor to the young Nero, later wrongly thought to have entered into a prolonged correspondence with the apostle Paul.

Septuagint: The translation of the Hebrew Scriptures into Greek, so named because of a tradition that seventy (Latin: *septuaginta*) Jewish scholars had produced it.

Shema: The words of Deuteronomy 6:4–5, which many Jews to this day continue to see as the cornerstone of the Jewish faith: "Hear, O Israel: The LORD is our God, the LORD alone. You shall love the LORD your God with all your heart, and with all your soul, and with all your might." The term "shema" is the Hebrew word that begins the verse: "Hear."

sheol: For much of the Hebrew Bible, the place to which souls go in the afterlife, a netherworld where people live forever in a kind of shadowy existence.

Sicarii: From a Latin term meaning "dagger," the term is used to designate a group of first-century Jews responsible for the assassination of Jewish aristocrats thought to have collaborated with the Romans. *See also* Fourth Philosophy.

Son of God: Any being—human or angelic—with a close relationship with God and who mediates God's will on earth; the term is especially used in the Tanakh in reference to the king of Israel.

Son of Man: A phrase used by Jesus in the Gospels to refer to a future cosmic judge of the earth who would destroy the forces of evil at the end of the age, based on an understanding of Daniel 7:13–14.

suzerainty treaty: A political treaty between an overlord, known as a "suzerain," and an underling or vessel; known from the people called the Hittites. The treaties consisted of six parts: identification of the parties; history of their relationship; stipulations placed on the vassal; provisions for deposit of the treaty; invocation of divine witnesses; indication of the blessings that would come to the vassal for keeping the stipulations and curses for failing to keep them.

synagogue: Jewish place of worship and prayer, from a Greek word that literally means "being brought together."

Synoptic Gospels: The Gospels of Matthew, Mark, and Luke, which narrate so many of the same stories that they can be placed side by side in parallel columns and so be "seen together" (the literal meaning of "synoptic").

Synoptic Problem: The problem of explaining the similarities and differences between the three Synoptic Gospels. *See also* Markan priority, Q.

T

tabernacle: The large tent that was used as the central sanctuary for the Israelites prior to the construction of the Temple by Solomon, believed by some to mirror the place where God dwelt in heaven. *See also* ark of the covenant.

Tacitus: Roman historian of the early second century C.E., whose multivolume work *The Annals of Rome* provides substantial information about Roman history from the beginning down to his own time.

Talmud: The great collection of ancient Jewish traditions that comprises the Mishnah and the later commentaries on the Mishnah, called the Gemarah. There are two collections of the Talmud: one made in Palestine during the early fifth century C.E., and the other in Babylon perhaps a century later. The Babylonian Talmud is generally considered the more authoritative.

Tanakh: Designation for the Hebrew Bible, taken from the opening initials of the three main divisions: Torah, Nevi'im, and Kethuvim (TNK).

targum: The paraphrastic translation of a Hebrew text of Scripture into Aramaic, originally delivered orally and eventually written down, so that Jews who no longer knew Hebrew could understand what the text said.

tetragrammaton: Literally "four letters," a reverential reference to the letters YHWH, which are taken to be the personal name of God in the Hebrew Bible (English: Yahweh), so holy that eventually Jews were not allowed to pronounce it.

theodicy: From two Greek words that mean "God's righteousness," a term that is used for any explanation of how

God can be "right" or "just" if there is so much suffering in the world.

Torah: A Hebrew word that means "guidance" or "direction" but that is usually translated as "law." As a technical term it designates either the Law of God given to Moses or the division of the Hebrew Bible that contains that Law (comprising the five books of Genesis, Exodus, Leviticus, Numbers, and Deuteronomy).

Thucydides: Famous historian of fifth-century B.C.E. Athens, best known for his account of the twenty-seven-year Peloponnesian War between Athens and Sparta. The account contains a number of speeches, which Thucydides frankly admitted to having composed himself as appropriate for the occasion (cf. the speeches in Acts in the New Testament).

U

undisputed Pauline epistles: The seven letters that scholars overwhelmingly judge to have actually been written by Paul: Romans, 1 and 2 Corinthians, Galatians, Philippians, 1 Thessalonians, and Philemon. *See also* Deutero-Pauline epistles and Pastoral epistles.

Y

Yahweh: The personal name of God in the Hebrew Bible, based on the consonants YHWH, the tetragrammaton (= the four letters), and thought by later Jews to be so holy that it was not to be pronounced.

Z

Zealots: A group of Galilean Jews who fled to Jerusalem during the uprising against Rome in 66–70 C.E., who overthrew the reigning aristocracy in the city and urged violent resistance to the bitter end. *See also* Fourth Philosophy.

Credits

CHAPTER 1

Figure 1-1   Photograph by Bruce and Kenneth Zuckerman, West Semitic Research, in collaboration with the Ancient Biblical Manuscript Center. Courtesy Russian National Library (Saltykov-Schedrin).
Figure 1-2   © Oxford University Press
Figure 1-3   © Oxford University Press
Figure 1-4   © Oxford University Press
Figure 1-5   Biblioteca Apostolica Vaticana
Figure 1-6   Department of Image Resources and Copyright Management of The Israel Museum, Jerusalem
Figure 1-7   en.wikipedia.org/wiki/File:P._Chester_Beatty_I,_folio_13-14,_recto.jpg
Figure 1-8   © British Library Board / Robana / Art Resource, NY

CHAPTER 2

Figure 2-1   The Pierpont Morgan Library / Art Resource, NY
Figure 2-2   © Oxford University Press
Figure 2-3   © Oxford University Press
Figure 2-4   Z. Radovan, Jerusalem
Figure 2-5   Ms 9/1695 f.11 Sacrifice of Isaac by Abraham, from the 'Psautier d'Ingeburg de Danemark', c.1210 (vellum), French School, (13th century) / Musee Conde, Chantilly, France / Giraudon / The Bridgeman Art Library
Figure 2-6   Joseph sold by his brothers, from a book of Bible Pictures, c.1250 (vellum), Brailes, William de (fl.c.1230) / Musee Marmottan Monet, Paris, France / Giraudon / The Bridgeman Art Library
Figure 2-7   © Oxford University Press
Figure 2-8   The British Museum

CHAPTER 3

Figure 3-1   © Oxford University Press
Figure 3-2   Jurgen Liepe
Figure 3-3   Or. 1404 f.5v The Ten Plagues of Egypt TtoB; the Plague of Locusts; the Plague of Darkness; Catalonia (Hebrew manuscript), . / British Library, London, UK / The Bridgeman Art Library
Figure 3-4   Z. Radovan, Jerusalem
Figure 3-5   © Oxford University Press
Figure 3-6   © Oxford University Press
Figure 3-7   The Granger Collection, New York

CHAPTER 4

Figure 4-1   © Oxford University Press
Figure 4-2   © Oxford University Press
Figure 4-3   Scala / Art Resource, NY
Figure 4-4   © Oxford University Press
Figure 4-5   © Oxford University Press
Figure 4-6   © Oxford University Press
Figure 4-7   Z. Radovan, Jerusalem
Figure 4-8   Erich Lessing / Art Resource, NY

CHAPTER 5

Figure 5-1   Z. Radovan
Figure 5-2   The British Museum
Figure 5-3   Erich Lessing / Art Resource, NY
Figure 5-4   © Oxford University Press
Figure 5-5   © Oxford University Press
Figure 5-6   David Harris

CHAPTER 6

Figure 6-1   Ezra reads the law (tempera on plaster), Jewish School, (2nd century) / Dura-Europos Synagogue, National Museum of Damascus, Syria / Photo © Zev Radovan / The Bridgeman Art Library
Figure 6-2   © The Trustees of the British Museum / Art Resource, NY
Figure 6-3   © Oxford University Press
Figure 6-4   © Oxford University Press
Figure 6-5   Z. Radovan, Jerusalem
Figure 6-6   The Granger Collection, New York
Figure 6-7   © The Trustees of the British Museum
Figure 6-8   © Oxford University Press

CHAPTER 7

Figure 7-1   Z. Radovan, Jerusalem
Figure 7-2   Fol.284r The Song of Songs, from the Borso d'Este Bible. Vol 1 (vellum), Italian School, (15th century) / Biblioteca Estense Universitaria, Modena, Italy / The Bridgeman Art Library
Figure 7-3   Z. Radovan, Jerusalem
Figure 7-4   user:YukioSanjo / Wikimedia Commons / Public Domain
Figure 7-5   Erich Lessing / Art Resource, NY
Figure 7-6   © Oxford University Press

CHAPTER 8

Figure 8-1   Erich Lessing / Art Resource, NY
Figure 8-2   Richard T. Nowitz
Figure 8-3   Courtesy of the Bible Lands Museum, Jerusalem

CHAPTER 9

Figure 9-1   © Oxford University Press
Figure 9-2   © Oxford University Press
Figure 9-3   © Oxford University Press
Figure 9-4   © Oxford University Press
Figure 9-5   Courtesy of Israel Antiquities Authority
Figure 9-6   Department of Image Resources and Copyright Management of The Israel Museum, Jerusalem

CHAPTER 10

Figure 10-1   © Oxford University Press
Figure 10-2   © Oxford University Press
Figure 10-3   Reconstruction by Dr. Leen Ritmeyer. © Ritmeyer Archaeological Design
Figure 10-4   © The Trustees of the British Museum / Art Resource, NY
Figure 10-5   Photo courtesy of Eric M. Meyers
Figure 10-6   © The Trustees of the British Museum

CHAPTER 11

Figure 11-1   Scala / Art Resource, NY
Figure 11-2   © RMN-Grand Palais / Art Resource, NY
Figure 11-3   Institute for Antiquity and Christianity, Claremont, CA
Figure 11-4   Alinari / Art Resource, NY
Figure 11-5   Kenneth Garrett/ National Geographic Image Collection
Figure 11-6   © Oxford University Press
Figure 11-7   Scala / Art Resource, NY
Figure 11-8   Scala / Art Resource, NY
Figure 11-9   Jurgen Zangenberg

Index